D1807769

Asia's Maritime
Bead Trade

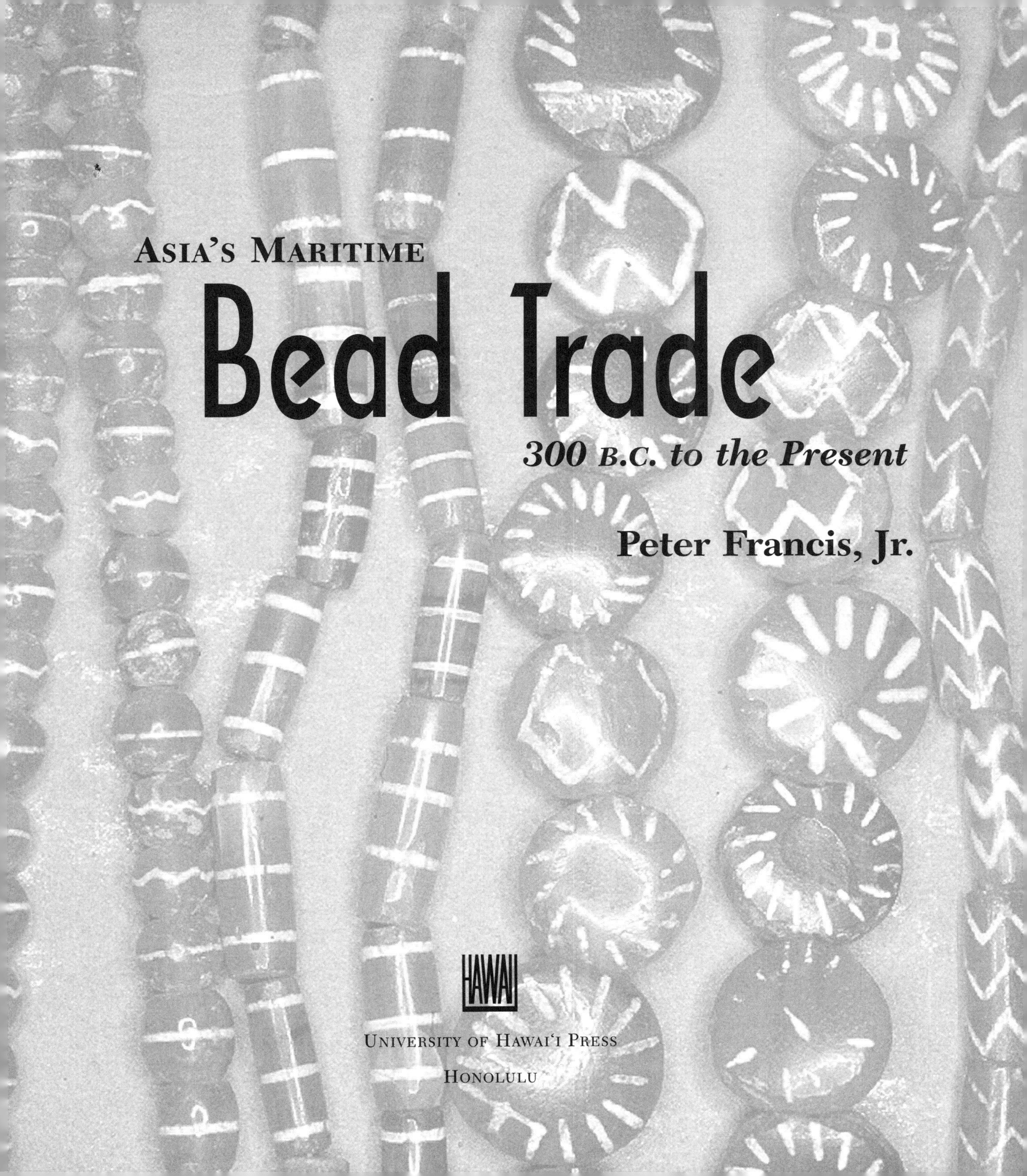

Asia's Maritime

Bead Trade

300 B.C. to the Present

Peter Francis, Jr.

University of Hawai'i Press
Honolulu

© 2002 University of Hawai'i Press
All rights reserved
Printed in the United States of America
07 06 05 04 03 02 6 5 4 3 2 1

Library of Congress
Cataloging-in-Publication Data

Francis, Peter.
Asia's maritime bead trade : 300 B.C. to the present / Peter Francis, Jr.
p. cm.
Includes bibliographical references and index.
ISBN 0-8248-2332-x (cloth : alk. paper)
1. Beads—Asia. 2. Beadwork—Asia.
3. Bead embroidery—Asia. I. Title

NK3650.F65 2002
338.4'767—dc21

2001027359

University of Hawai'i Press books are printed on acid-free paper and meet the guidelines for permanence and durability of the Council on Library Resources.

Designed by David Alcorn,
Alcorn Publication Design
Red bluff, California.

Printed by The Maple-Vail
Book Manufacturing Group

Contents

Black-and-white plates follow page   52

Color plates follow page   100

Preface

Trade or exchange is one of the more easily recognized past human behaviors. A critical segment of interchange has always been precious materials or gems, which have long been marks of beauty and status. The easiest way to retain and display a gem is to turn it into a bead. The simple bead was—and still is—held in reverence, but its potential for helping unravel the past has only begun to be tapped.

This book demonstrates the value of studying beads. It emphasizes: (1) A global perspective. Beads travel widely and have been preserved for centuries in both archaeological and living contexts. They can be understood only with an appreciation of their complete history. (2) An interdisciplinary approach. Some beads are most easily traced archaeologically, others historically, and still others ethnographically. In addition, many natural and material sciences can help us understand beads. The methodologies and data of different fields are applied in various sections of this book. (3) The scientific method. This involves the collecting and arranging of data, as well as formulating hypotheses and testing them to build an understanding leading to theory. (4) Original research. Although I acknowledge the work of others, my principal efforts have been to examine, explore, interview, and experiment. I have made a conscious effort to eliminate the hearsay and speculation that once characterized works on the production, use, and provenience of beads. (5) The human element. Beads are artifacts. They were made, traded, used, and ultimately disposed of by people. They have no purpose other than those assigned to them by humans.

This is by no means a definitive work. There are many gaps and no doubt errors of judgment and perception. Some gaps will be filled and some errors corrected quickly. Others will persist. This is but an opening of a debate to which more data, reasoned argument, and a desire to learn must be applied. Only then will the potential of bead studies be fully realized.

I am convinced that it is important to realize this potential—not because small, perforated objects are intrinsically consequential, but because they are artifacts. As such, they provide insights into the actions and even ideas of the people involved with them. These people are like us and unlike us, yet always a part of us. They, far more than their beads, are worthy of our respect and understanding.

The universality and complex history of beads attracted me while I was teaching English in Iran in the mid-1970s. This led me to an appreciation of archaeology, and I subsequently enrolled in the Department of Archaeology at Deccan College, Pune, India. By 1979, I was so engrossed in the subject that I founded the Center for Bead Research,[1] designed to collect and coordinate information on beads from all epochs and cultures.

In India, the archaeological site of Arikamēḍu in Pondicherry attracted my attention. Arikamēḍu is celebrated because it was the first site in South India identified as having trade connections with Rome. Its glass and stone bead industries intrigued me. My investigations into its ramifications expanded, ultimately growing into this book.

The first step beyond Arikamēḍu was the Indian Ocean Bead Trade Project with the support of John Carswell, the excavator of Mantai, Sri Lanka. Mantai's ceramic evidence attests to connections with lands both to the east and the west. The bead evidence confirmed this, and beads were made there as well. To better understand Mantai's trading patterns I focused next on western sites: Nishapur and Siraf (both in Iran), Fustat, Quseir al-Qadim and Berenike (Egypt), and Aqaba (Jordan). Carswell encouraged and often arranged for me to conduct this work.

Concurrently, Wilhelm Solheim urged me to expand my investigations into Southeast Asia. Solheim had long advocated a serious study of beads in East and Southeast Asia. Through his contacts, I extended my research and linked the data to my earlier work in Korea and China. Most recently, my research has expanded into Sri Lanka. The result is a database that covers most of the littoral of the Indian Ocean and Western Pacific, heavily drawn upon in this volume.

In a book as wide-ranging as this, several problems arise. The first is the transformation of other languages and scripts into English. Many foreign languages are dealt with in this text. Some present few problems; I generally follow the transliteration used in the source involved. Where alternate readings may be useful, I have cross-referenced them in the index. However, three complications remain.

One is the recasting of Indonesian place names into Bahasa Indonesia and new names used for various places. I have retained some of the older spellings (Java and Sumatra in place of Jawa and Sumatera), but have adopted some new names (Kalimantan and Sulawesi in place of Borneo and The Celebes).

In India, changing toponyms has become almost a sport. Because they are far more familiar, I have retained older names (Bombay, Madras, Baroda, Benaras) rather than use newer ones (Mumbai, Chennai, Vadodara, Varanasi), with the exception of Pune (old Poona).

As for Chinese, dynasties, personal names, and cities have been converted into *pinyin*. The geographic standard used here is the *Map of the People's Republic of China* (Cartographic Publishing House 1985). When possible, personal and dynastic names conform to *An Outline History of China* (Bai 1982).

The second issue involves some of the material I have chosen to include. Some readers may find details on particular issues tedious, such as "Roman" beads in Southeast Asia, "gold-glass" beadmaking in India, and the "Mutisalah problem" of Indonesia. These topics are complex, but integral to the story.

The last item could trouble professionals who read this book. I occasionally refer to beads I have seen that were not scientifically excavated. I have done so because there is no other data for them and they add information, however weak. This evidence is never preferred to archaeological testimony. Such beads are never ascribed to particular sites, only identified as being on the antiquities market in a particular country. Be assured, I stand with those who condemn illegal excavations as nothing but looting expeditions. When I first took a public stand on this in regard to bead collecting (Francis 1987a), it was not widely appreciated, but much of the bead-collecting community has since endorsed it.

Acknowledgments

A project of this magnitude is naturally dependent upon the cooperation, advice, encouragement, and assistance of a great many people. To all those who have contributed to this work, I offer my most sincere appreciation. Because of the large number of people involved, it is possible that I may omit someone from this section. It is done because of my own shortcomings, not from any lack of gratitude.

Those I want to thank the most are the people who encouraged me to undertake this project from the beginning or contributed to it on an extraordinary scale. They include Cyril Antony of the Pondicherry Museum, John Carswell, then with the Oriental Institute in Chicago, and Wilhelm Solheim of the University of Hawai'i. The late Elizabeth Harris was most generous in supplying information, samples, and stimulating ideas. I am very grateful to Ron Hancock of the University of Toronto for carrying out analyses of Indo-Pacific beads. Special thanks go to John Anthony, without whose wise and useful skills much of my investigations could not have been carried out.

Projects cost money, and there have been several institutions that have contributed funds used in this work. They include the Smithsonian Institution; the Asian Arts Council; the Hagop Kevorkian Fund; the Alden B. Dow Foundation; the Bead Museum; the Bead Study Trust (Margaret Guido Award); the Bead Society of Greater Washington; and the Bead Society (Los Angeles). Elizabeth Harris and Gabrielle Liese (on behalf of the Bead Museum) were also generous. The Northwest Bead Society, the Portland Bead Society, and the Bead Society of Greater Chicago also contributed discretionary grants, at least part of which were applied to this project; particular thanks go to them and to the Bead Society (Los Angeles), which helped fund illustrations in this volume.

I am especially grateful to people who donated graphics to this book. They include the illustrators Bo Breda, Lynda Dinneen, Cynthia M. Schave, and Jacqui Steinberg. Jyotsna Maurya also helped with some of the maps and diacritical marks.

Special thanks must be reserved for my patient editor, Pam Kelley, and for my equally patient and supportive parents, The Reverend Peter and Phyllis Francis. Although they mostly go unnamed, scores of librarians around the globe have my great gratitude, particularly Patty Perez, master of the Inter-Library Loan system at the Lake Placid Public Library.

The acknowledgments that follow are arranged geographically. Not all people are still at the institutions associated with them here. I have placed them where they were when they were kind enough to help me.

Australia: Robert Theunissen of the University of New England.

China: An Jaiyao of the Institute of Archaeology, Chinese Academy of Social Sciences; William Meacham of the University of Hong Kong; and interpreter and facilitator Shih Chiang.

Europe: Kishore Basa and Ian Glover of the Institute of Archaeology, University of London; Uta von Freeden of the Römisch-Germanische Kommission, Frankfurt am Main; Johan Callmer of Humboldt University, Berlin; Laure Dussubieux and Bernard Gratuze of the Institut de Recherches sur les Archéomatériaux, Orléans; Osmund Bopearachchi of Centre National de la Recherche Scientifique, Paris; Pierre-Yves Manguin; Paul Yule of the Institut für Ur- und Frühgeschichte, Heidelberg; Cordelia Rösch of the Mineralogisches Institut, Würzburg; Anne Hannibal and H. J. Weisshaar of Kommission für Allgemeine und Vergleichende Archäologie, Bonn; and Stefany Tomalin of London.

Ghana: James Anquandah of the University of Ghana, Legon.

India: Z. D. Ansari, G. L. Badam, S. B. Deo, Sunil Gupta, M. D. Kajale, Alok Kumar Kanungo, V. N. Misra, Pradeep Mohanty, Ravi Mohanty, M. L. K. Murthy, Malti Nagar, K. Paddayya, S. N. Rajguru, H. D. Sankalia, Satish Tyagi, and others at Deccan College, Pune; K. T. M. Hegde, R. N. Metha, and K. N. Momin of Maharaja Sayajirao University, Baroda; S. Nagarajan and K. Rajan of Tamil University, Thanjavur; C. Margabandhu, C. B. Mishra, and S. A. Sali with the Archaeological Survey of India; V. D. Misra of Allahabad University; V. V. Krishnasastry of the Department of Archaeology and Museums, Andrah Pradesh; K. V. Raman of the University of Madras; Vimala Begley of the Arikamēḍu Excavation; Giraud V. Foster of Johns Hopkins Hospital; Iravatham Mahadevan of the Indian Council of Historical Research; Natana Kasinathan and R. Nagaswamy of the Department of Archaeology, Tamil Nadu; Vishnu S. Wakankar of the University of Ujjain; and the following informants and facilitators: Habib Khan Abdulah and family, Jina Bhai, Mareya Dass, Antur Dipsingh, Shaikh Hussin Enayat, R. K. Gupta and family, Ashok Kumar, Raju Pillai, P. P. Rao, Mohsmedaiddik L. Shisger, Raja Ram Singh, Bukkar Bhai Balasingh Thakkur.

Indonesia: Hassan M. Ambary, Rokhus Due Awe, R. P. Soejono, Endang Sh. Soekatno, and others of the National Research Center of Archaeology in Jakarta; Suhardini Chalid and M. Wayono of the National Museum; Edi Sedyawati of the University of Indonesia; Muhammad Munir and Drs. Soetjipto of the National Museum of East Java; Bagus Arnawa and Prapto Saptono of the Trowulon Museum; Goenadi Nithaminoto of the National Research Center of Archaeology in Yogyakarta; Sumarah Adhyatman of the Adam Malik Museum; and other informants, including Redjeki Arafin, Darussalemsyah, E. Edwards McKinnon, Paiman, Ridwan, Sudarto, O. T. C. Sujoco, Darius Umbu, and Yunus.

Korea: Han Byong-Sam of the National Museum in Kyongju; Ji Gon-Gil of the National Museum in Seoul; Lee Kang-Seung of the National Museum in Puyo; Mr. Eun of the King Sejong University Museum; Sue J. Bae of the Royal Asiatic Society; In-sook Lee; and informants Park Che Chun, Kim Jae Eun, Park Bong Hee, and Chun Buyong Do; and interpreter and facilitator Bong Hyong-Jong.

Malaysia: Adi Haji Taha and Othman Yatim of the National Museum; Kamaruddin Zakaria of the Merbok Museum; Nik Hassan Shuhaimi of Universiti Kebangsaan Malaysia, Bangi; Latib B. Araffin of the Taiping Museum; Heidi Munan, Lucas Chin, and Edmund Kurui of the Sarawak Museum; and Sidi Munan and Raseh.

The Philippines: Artimeo Barbosa, Jesus Peralta, Wilfredo Ronquillo, Rey Santiago, and many other members of the National Museum staff; Pedro Besitan Jr. of the St. Louis University Museum, Bagio; Neves Valdes of the Bontoc Museum; and the following informants and facilitators: Adchongon, Henry Beyer, Joseph Blas, Columbus and Paulina Challipas, Fernande Fox, Daisy Giwao, Constance Gonzáles, Rosario D. Grinid, Helen Kimmayong, Lourdes M. Labrador, Angelita Legarda, Jose Lugay, Alex Ordillo, Joseph Tabayac, Cynthia Valdez, and F. William L. Villareal.

Singapore: Lee Chor Lin of the National Museum; John N. Miksic of the National University of Singapore; and Michael Flecker of Pacific Sea Resources.

Sri Lanka: Seneke Bandaranyake, Kanchana Dehigama, and the staff at the Postgraduate Institute of Archaeology, Colombo.

Taiwan: Jih-Chang Chester Hsieh of the Acadamia Sinica, Taipei, and the staff of the Taiwan Museum, Taipei.

Thailand: Pisit Charoenwongsa, Surapol Natapintu, and Amara and Tharapong Srisuchat of the Department of Archaeology, Fine Arts Department; Ptomrerk Ketudhat and Sumitr Pitiphat of Thamaset University; Richard W. Hughes and William Sersen of the Asian Institute of Gemological Studies; Natthapatra Chandavik and Chira Chongkol of the National Museum; and James and Virginia DiCrocco of the Siam Society.

United States: Bennet Bronson of the Field Museum, Chicago; Harold Conklin of Yale University; Steven Sidebotham of the University of Delaware; Don Whitcomb of the Oriental Institute, Chicago; David Whitehead of the Corning Museum of Glass; Mimi Swietochowski of the Metropolitan Museum of Art; Daniella and Ofer Bar-Yosef, K. C. Chang, and David Killick of Harvard University; Paul B. Titchenal of Jeffrey Pantaleo Consultants of Honolulu; Michael Aung Thwin of Northern Illinois University; John Gwinnett of the State University of New York, Stony Brook; and Lester Gorelick of Little Neck, New York.

Vietnam: Nguyen Thi Kim Dung of the Institute of Archaeology, Hanoi.

Part One: Introduction

1
The Scope of This Work

This book is not a global history of beads. It is limited to a logical unit of time and space, though the geographic and chronological parameters are wide. The maritime bead trade is of great antiquity, beginning before 2000 B.C. and enduring to the present day. This work covers more than two millennia, from the last few centuries B.C. until the present.

The Geographic Setting

The geographic foci of this trade are the Middle East (centered on the Persian Gulf and the Red Sea), South Asia, Southeast Asia, and East Asia. These represent the southern and eastern flank of Asia and adjacent islands. Some corroborating evidence is available from East and West Africa and some Pacific Islands.

The overland Silk Roads also linked much of this region, but they had severe limitations. They bypassed Southeast Asia and India, especially South India, the source of many of the world's greatest gems and outstanding glass beads. They were closed whenever China lacked the power to prevent central Asian nomads from attacking caravans. They were also arduous and dangerous.

The maritime routes were different. Although there is always the danger of pirates on the high seas, there are ways to avoid them. Sea travel is more often boring than oppressive. Ships can carry more than camels at a cheaper cost. India was at the very center of this trade, and Southeast Asia was a major participant.

Until the late centuries B.C., most small vessels "tracked" or followed the coasts, dropping anchor occasionally to conduct a little business and resupply food and water. The competence to sail directly across open seas was gained by different nations at different times, but the knowledge involved became widespread by the first century A.D.[1] Once open-sea navigation was adopted, sailors read their positions against the stars, calculated time more or less accurately, and traversed trackless saltwater from one port to another.

Maritime trade involved numerous complications ranging from the weather to food spoilage. Wherever routes led, there was the reality of culture shock. There were no people with tails, Amazons, or cannibals, but there was always the danger of unfriendly or hostile acts or partners who refused to trade (Ratnagar 1990). Even under the best conditions, different clothing, habits, religions, foods, and, above all, languages were inevitable. To interpret rationally the evidence preserved in trade artifacts such as beads, the operation of the trade routes must first be understood and important commercial sites identified.

For sailing ships, the prevailing winds are of the utmost importance. The Indian Ocean and South China Sea are dominated by the monsoon (from the Arabic meaning "season"), a weather system that blows winds in one general direction for a few months and then in the opposite direction for a few months, with periods of calm between. It owes its origin to the differences in sea and land temperatures at various times of the year.

In April, winds begin to blow in a northeastern direction (the southwest monsoon) over Sumatra and the Bay of Bengal, reaching mainland Southeast Asia by May. They increase until they are strongest and most continuous in July. They diminish over the next two months and by October the northeast monsoon (blowing southwesterly) develops over the northern part of the South China Sea. This system reaches its peak in January, then retreats until the cycle repeats the next year.[2]

Two geographical "choke points" along the Asian maritime route were of critical importance to traders. Their significance cannot be grasped simply by looking at a map.

One is the Palk Strait (Figure 1.1) that separates India from Sri Lanka (Ceylon). It is impossible to sail through it with an ocean-going ship because of Adam's Bridge,[3] a series of reefs and semisubmerged islands that only small vessels with shallow drafts can navigate.[4] Onesicritus, a naval commander under Alexander the Great, dimly perceived this. He said the voyage from India to Taprobane (Sri Lanka) was done in small vessels without keels or holds and prows at both ends (Hamilton and Falconer 1912, 3:81).

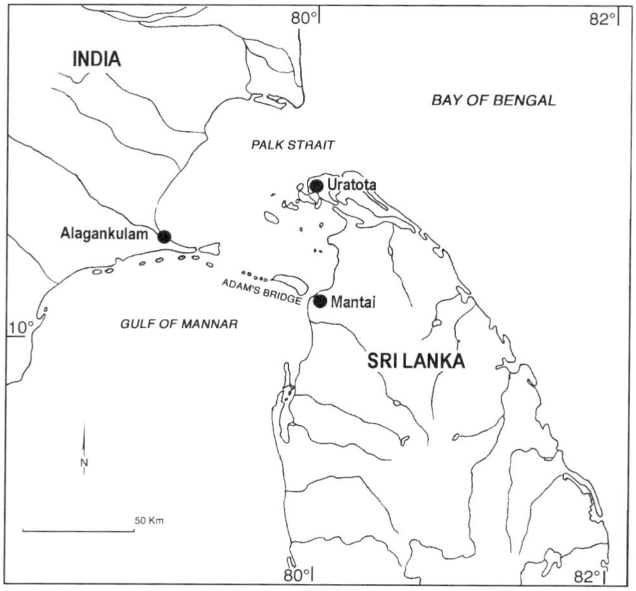

Figure 1.1. *Map of the Palk Strait between India and Sri Lanka. Only small ships with shallow drafts can navigate among the islands and submerged ridges popularly named "Adam's Bridge."*

One can sail around Sri Lanka, but this was not considered for a long time. Early Western geographers overestimated its size; it grew almost century by century. Despite the "more accurate information" available to Pliny in the first century A.D., the coast facing India was reckoned by him to be 10,000 *stadiorum* or 1,250 English miles (2,000 km) long (Rackham 1942, 404–405). The actual widest dimension of the island is 137.5 miles (ca. 220 km). In the next century, Ptolemy estimated the island to be fourteen times its true dimensions (Brown 1977, 77).

Indian informers enlarged the island into continental size (Brown 1977) and spread stories about the dangers of the seas around Sri Lanka (Siriweera 1990, 126), doubtless so that trade would pass through Indian rather than Sri Lankan hands. There were no known suitable ports along the southern Ceylonese coast for a long time. H. Hasan (1928, 77–86) maintained that the Persians learned to sail around Ceylon by the sixth or seventh century. Yet Nainar (1942, 72) called it "significant" that travel accounts of Istakhri (A.D. 950), Ibn Hauqal (975), and Maqdidi (985) all ended at Sarandib (Sri Lanka).

The other choke point is between the Andaman and the South China Seas. The water connection is the Malacca Strait, a long (ca. 800 km) passageway between Sumatra and the lower Malay Peninsula (Figure 1.2). It is somewhat out of the way, but its real impedimenta lie elsewhere. For one thing, the jagged Sumatran coast is dotted with mangrove swamps and river estuaries and there are numerous islands at the south end of the strait. Pirates favor both environments.[5] A determined political power with an effective navy can alleviate the hazard, but such a government did not always control the waterway.

More importantly, winds in the Malacca Strait are weak, and ships can take a month to sail through it. When the time needed to enter and leave the strait is added, the journey around the peninsula no longer seems ideal. The route on the other side of Sumatra and through the Sunda Strait between Sumatra and Java was little used because it was even longer and offered few profitable trading opportunities along the way.

The alternative is a land passage. The Malay Peninsula is quite narrow, only about 65 km wide at the Isthmus of Kra (Figure 1.2). If a ship were unloaded on one side, its goods could be carted across the isthmus and loaded onto another ship on the other side.

Overland routes were used in historic times (Gerini 1905) and may have been active much earlier. Bronson (1990; 1996, 194–196) minimized their importance, arguing that time was not a crucial consideration in the past and the savings of a few days or even weeks would not have repaid the expenses involved. Amara Srisuchat (1987) believed that many routes were used for extended periods.

Sailing to, through, and away from the Malacca Strait would have taken about six weeks. The overland route, though mountainous, can be crossed with elephants in an estimated four days (A. Srisuchat, 1990, personal communication). Unloading and loading would not have taken longer than it did at Panama before the canal was built, where ships unloaded in the morning, passengers and cargo took a four-hour train ride, and they were sailing on the other ocean that night (O. Lewis 1949, 188).

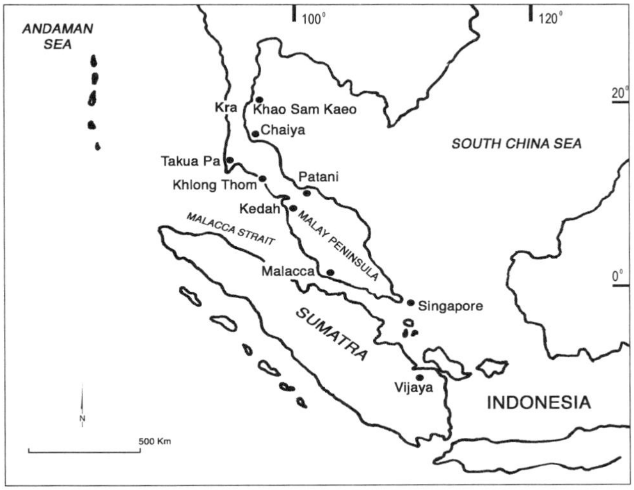

Figure 1.2. *Map of the Malay Peninsula and the Malacca Strait. Uncertain winds and the threat of piracy made the Malacca Strait less than an ideal passageway. The amount of commerce that passed through the alternate routes across the Malay Peninsula is still under dispute, but these itineraries were often more efficient than sailing through the strait.*

Four days on elephants and a half day at each port come to five days.

However, more is involved than the difference between five days and six weeks. By unloading exports and loading imports at the same dock at the right time, a return trip across the Bay of Bengal would take less than half a year. Going from India to the Malay Peninsula in July, a ship would wait a few months to return with the northeastern winds.

Alternately, if one started from India and went through the Malacca Strait, the southern end would be reached in August. Then there would be a four-month wait to catch the northeastern winds to reach China around February, another five months in China, perhaps as much as six months along the strait on the return, and two months sailing home. The whole trip would take two years.

Although we are more fastidious about time than the ancients, the difference between half a year and two years is substantial. Even sailors yearn for home. By trading at the Malay Peninsula rather than China, merchants would have realized a lower price, but their cash flow would have been constant, idle time would have been saved, and travel expenses lowered. For diplomats or other officials, the transpeninsular route would have been an overwhelming favorite.

It was physically possible to make a round trip entirely by sea from Egypt to China, but it took three years. People who undertook such long journeys usually had specific reasons to do so or a desire to travel far abroad. Arab and/or Persian merchants had colonies in China, but they were permanent emigrants and did not constantly travel back and forth.

Because of the circumstances outlined above, the maritime route was principally composed of three interconnected stages, rather than one long voyage (Figure 1.3). The Arabian Sea linked the West with India, the Bay of Bengal linked India with the Malay world, and the South China Sea linked the Malay lands with China. In the tenth century, Muslim traders learned to make a crossing in one season by leaving on just the right day, avoiding Sri Lanka, and refreshing at the Maldives. This southern route took them from Malaysia or Sumatra to the Red Sea, the Persian Gulf, or East Africa. However, this bypassed the riches of India.

On the tripartite route certain ports developed as centers of commercial exchange. On the western side of the Palk Strait was Mantai (Sri Lanka) and on the eastern Alagankulam[6] (Tamil Nadu, India) and Uratota[7] (modern Kayts) on the Jaffna Peninsula of Sri Lanka (Siriweera 1990, 129). On the western side of the Malay Peninsula were Khlong Thom (Thailand), Kedah (Malaysia), and for a short time Takua Pa (Thailand), and on the eastern side Khao Sam Kaeo, Patani, Laem Pho Chaiya, and Chaiya (Thailand). On the Malacca Strait route were Vijaya/Palembang (Sumatra), succeeded by Malacca (Malaysia), and in our day, Singapore. These are all essential sites in the Asian maritime trade.

One other specialized trading route may have operated independently of those just mentioned. The spices cinnamon and cassia[8] have long been known in the West. Classical writers often referred to their origin as from the south. Earlier writers usually cited Arabia as their source, and later ones talked about East Africa. Still others said they came from India. These spices do not grow in either Arabia or East Africa, but in Southeast Asia and China. Casson (1989, 122–124) was of the opinion that they were transshipped to India and then to East Africa in Indian or Arab ships.

Miller (1969), on the other hand, put forward a case for the spices to have been transported in Indonesian (Malay) rafts to Madagascar and the eastern coast of Africa. Whether all the details of Miller's hypothesis will prove true or not, the most compelling evidence he had (aside from the known early Malay settlement of Madagascar) is a passage from Pliny, who noted that the spice was bought from an intermediary, who in turn bought it from someone else:

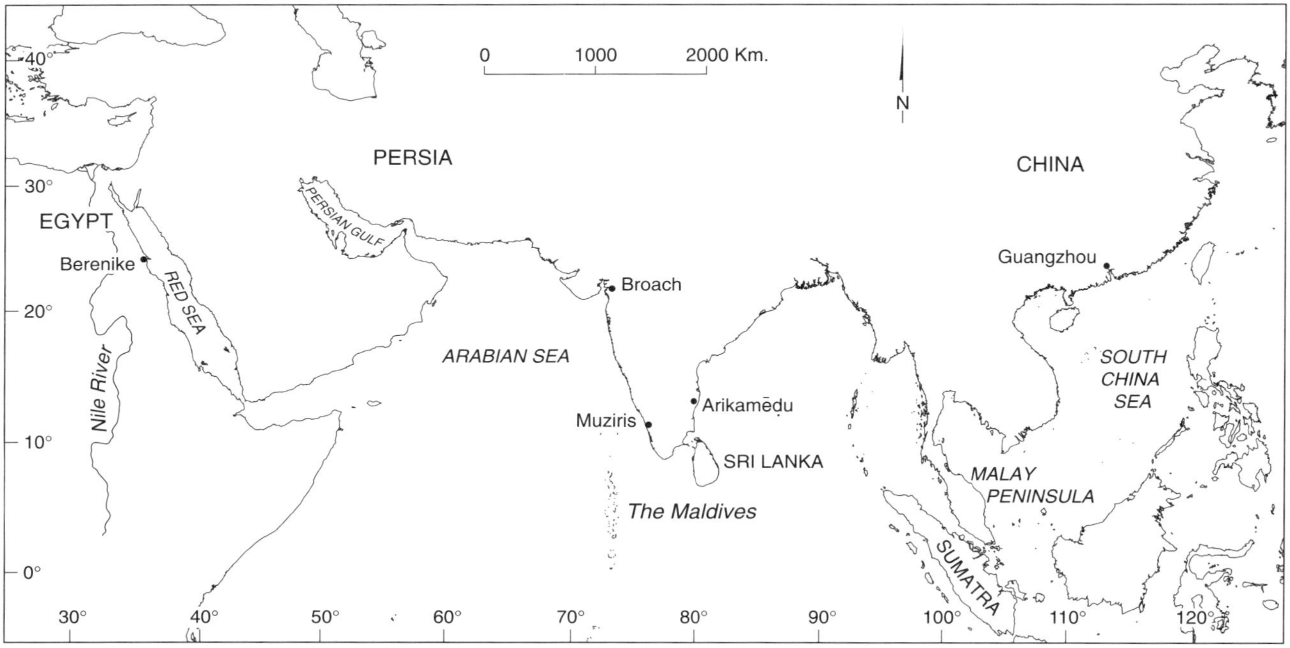

Figure 1.3. *Map of the Asian sea trade. This route was effectively divided into three stages: one from the Middle East to southern India, another from India to the Malay Peninsula, and the third from the Malay Peninsula to China. Dividing the trip into these stages allowed for quick returns after bartering for exotic goods brought to an intermediary port by others.*

> [They] bring It [cinnamon] over vast seas in rafts which have no rudders to steer them or oars to push or pull them or sails or other aids to navigation; but instead only the spirit of man and human courage. What is more, they put out to sea in winter, around the time of the winter solstice, when the east winds are blowing their hardest. These winds drive them on a straight course, and from gulf to gulf. Now cinnamon is the chief object of their journey, and they say that these merchant-sailors take almost five years before they return, and that many perish. In exchange they carry back with them glassware and bronze ware, clothing, brooches, armlets, and necklaces. And that trade depends chiefly on women's fidelity to fashion. (quoted in Miller 1969, 156)

Pliny did seem to be describing the Malay double-rigger canoe. If the so-called "Cinnamon Route" did operate, it was another maritime commercial route for beads to be traded from the West to island or mainland Southeast Asia, because Pliny specifically mentioned necklaces and "women's fidelity to fashion."

The Opening of the Maritime Bead Trade

One facet of early Asian maritime bead trade was the commerce in lapis lazuli, the paramount gem in ancient Mesopotamia (Oppenheim 1970, 10), from Badakhstan (northeastern Afghanistan). Many ancient texts refer to its functions (Rosen 1988, 25–34). It appears at Tepe Gawra, on the Tigris, about 4100 B.C.[9] and is relatively common by 3550 B.C. (Tobler 1950, 192–193; Herrmann 1968, 28–31). King Enmerkar of Uruk (ca. 2850 B.C.) petitioned the people of Aratta to send him the stone. His request tells us how it was transported:

> *Having loaded them on the crate-carrying donkeys,*
> *Having placed them on the sides of the transporting donkeys,*
> *The king, the lord of great wisdom,*
> *The lord of Erech, the lord of Kullab,*
> *Directed them on the road to Aratta*
> *To transport gold, silver (and) lapis lazuli . . . (Herrmann 1968, 38)*

However, by the Isin-Larsa period (ca. 2100 to 1900 B.C.) lapis lazuli was arriving by sea. Mesopotamian texts record that lapis lazuli, carnelian,[10] and ivory were brought by ship from Meluhha, the Harappān or Indus Valley civilization (Leemans 1960, 160–162). Harappā was the largest ancient civilization in area. Its northern outpost, Shortugai, controlled the source of lapis lazuli (Francfort and Pottier 1978). Harappā also spread south of the Narmadā River with its wealth in agates (see chap. 11).

An important player in the maritime trade was Oman. Tosi (1999) made the point that while other societies were building cities in the fourth century B.C., the Sea Arabs adapted to the sea, creating wealth by transferring resources between two centers. The presence of Harappān etched carnelians in North Grave A of Hili, Oman (ca. 2300 to 2100 B.C.), attests to an early maritime trade in beads (Cleuziou 1999).

The Old Testament[11] indicates Israeli trade in precious materials through Edom, at the head of the Gulf of Aqaba. Solomon (961–922 B.C.) used its harbor and its sailors:

> King Solomon built a fleet of ships at Ezion-geber, which is near Eloth on the shore of the Red Sea, in the land of Edom. And Hiram [of Tyre, in modern Lebanon] sent with the fleet his servants, seamen who were familiar with the sea, together with the servants of Solomon; and they went to Ophir, and brought from there gold . . . [and] a very great amount of almug wood and precious stones. . . . Once every three years the fleet of ships of Tarshish[12] used to come bringing gold, silver, ivory, apes, and peacocks. (1 Kings 9:26–28; 10:11, 22 [insertions mine])

An inscribed potsherd from Tell Qasileh (Buttrick 1962, 605–606) confirms Ophir as the source of at least some gold for Israel. The identification of Ophir[13] remains in dispute, but it must have been either India or some third country that traded with India.

Jehoshaphat (ruled 874–849 B.C.) also built ships of Tarshish to go to Ophir for gold, but they were wrecked at Ezion-geber (1 Kings 22:47). Ezekiel (ministered 593 to 571 B.C.) said that the merchants of Edom sold emeralds,[14] coral,[15] and agates to Israel (Ezekiel 27:16). The "precious stones of all kinds" (Ezekiel 27:22) from Sheba and Ra'ameh (the Arabian Peninsula) were probably ultimately from India.

India was self-sufficient in gemstones. The Vedas[16] mention only pearls, possibly from the Persian Gulf (Lad 1979, 196). However, Indian waters also yield pearls, and the *Atharva Veda* links them with the *śaṅkh,* the holy conch (*Xanthus pyrum* [Shende 1949, 367]). The *Mahābhārata*[17] mentions diamonds, emeralds, sapphires, sunstones, and moonstones (Lad 1979, 191). These are tentative identifications in late emendations, but all are local products. The gems most frequently mentioned in the epic—beryl, pearls, and coral—are the only ones that were worn on strings or gold chains (Lad 1979, 191). This suggests an early date for the exploitation of South Indian beryls (see chap. 12). However, coral[18] must be an import. It is found early in India: at Prakash, ca. 1700 to 1300 B.C. (Lad 1979, 197), and at Navdatoli, ca. 1600 to 1300 B.C. (Deo 1971, 359).

In sum, the western sector of the Asian maritime bead trade was opened before 2000 B.C. with the Harappāns bringing lapis lazuli and carnelian to Mesopotamia and the Sea Arabs trading between them. Coral was perhaps exported to India this early. Old Testament references suggest that ships sailed from the Gulf of Aqaba to India, perhaps Southwest India, beginning about 1000 B.C.

Despite the antiquity of this trade, only in the last few centuries B.C. did it link the whole area under study. Commerce increased dramatically in the third and second centuries B.C.[19] after the establishment of powerful empires around the Mediterranean and in Persia, India, and China. The Romans, Parthians, Maurya, and Han built vigorous, wealthy, and ambitious imperial units. Each produced surplus goods, and their leading citizens craved exotic imports to maintain their high status. With both surpluses and demand, trade expanded dramatically.

The Asian maritime trade has operated continuously since then, despite occasional changes among the major participants. Politics, economics, technology, and ecological adjustments affected the movement of goods and people as the trade waxed and waned.

Patterns in the bead trade along the Asian maritime routes never changed as abruptly as they did when Europeans arrived in Africa (Francis 1993a, 7–8) or the Americas,[20] where European trade beads became standard goods very quickly. In Asia, the process took much longer, and European beads (and European traders) did not become dominant until the late nineteenth century (see chap. 16).

The late phases of the Asian maritime bead trade are illuminated more through history and ethnography than archaeology. Beads are still critical cultural items, especially when used as heirlooms (see chap. 17). Some of these are Asian, a few over 1,000 years old, but others are more recent European imports (Francis 1989a, 2–18; 1992a, 3–12).

Merchants and Mariners

Who was involved in this trade? In one sense, everyone, because trade goods penetrated places as remote as the Forest Zone of West Africa and the uplands of Borneo. However, certain individuals specialized in commerce.

Mariners, with their navigational skills and knowledge of winds, ports, reefs, and storms, made the voyages physically possible. The business acumen of merchants generated the capital necessary for the trips. These groups were not necessarily mutually exclusive. Sailors often traded on their own account. Merchants were a mixed lot, some staying at home and others going abroad for years, though few became seamen. Contemporary accounts were written as navigational guides or to furnish cultural details to facilitate enterprise. Some governmental envoys, pilgrims, and curious tourists who participated in these journeys left us records.

Merchants and mariners came from a variety of backgrounds. Early in the trade, the Greeks and Egyptians were often referred to as "Romans," but only because they were subjects of the Roman Empire. The Romans learned much from the seafaring Arabs, including, it is said, how to sail to India on the trade winds. After the fall of the Empire, the Byzantines had a hard time competing with the Persians. Later, Muslims became the chief Western traders until outflanked by Europeans.

Indians, especially western Gujaratis, eastern Bengalis, and southern Tamils, participated. Sri Lankans were also very active, as befitting their island status. Malays (in the broadest sense including most indigenous peoples of Malaysia, Indonesia, the Philippines, and Taiwan) have long been great sailors. Their cousins populated the Pacific and at the beginning of the current era colonized Madagascar. In what is now Vietnam, the adventurous Sa Huynh culture was on the decline by the late centuries B.C., but was succeeded by Champa, which along with Funan, were the first states of Southeast Asia.

Although some southern Chinese engaged in seafaring and trade, most "Chinese" sailors and traders were not ethnic Han Chinese, because they long shunned this activity. China's heartland was in the north along the great rivers, and it was not until the eruption of central Asian Mongols that it was forced to become a serious sea power. China had relations with other maritime powers, but the active participants were mostly intermediaries, the Nan Yue at first, succeeded by Funan, and then Sumatran-based Srivijaya.

There are great gaps in our knowledge of the Asian maritime trade. Most work has concentrated on the Roman-Indian connection (see Begley and De Puma 1991), and less has been done on the other segments. Archaeology proceeds slowly and requires major commitments of funds, time, and energy.

There are few historic accounts of the trade. Some are records of those who sailed: Westerners such as the anonymous author of the *Periplus Maris Erythraei* (Casson 1989), Cosmas Indicopleustes (McCrindle 1897), and later Tomé Pires (Cortesão 1967); Arabs such as Ibn Battuta (Gibb 1929) and Sulaiman (Ferrand 1913; Tibbits 1979); and Chinese, including the pilgrim Yijing (Takakusu 1966) and records of the voyages of Zheng He by Ma Huan (Mills 1970). Some are compilations of other people's voyages, including those of Zhao Rugua (Hirth and Rockhill 1911) and Wang Dayuan (Rockhill 1915). From these and other sources, syntheses of regional trade have been compiled, as for the Romano-Indian trade (Warmington 1928, 1974), the Arab trade (Hourani 1951), the South China Sea (G. Wang 1958), Tang China (Schafer 1963), Sung China (Wheatley 1959), China-Africa (Duyvendak 1949), Malaysia (Wheatley 1961), Indonesia (van Leur 1955), Srivijaya (Wolters 1967, 1970), and Southeast Asia in general (Hall 1985).

Many nations and people were involved in this dynamic enterprise. The archaeological evidence is imperfect. Written records give only snapshotlike glimpses in time. These limitations constrict the data available for this study. This may be discouraging, but there is much room for optimism. The opening of bead research in this trade adds another tool to the kit of those interested in a fuller understanding of our shared history.

2

Beads, Bead Materials, and Beadmaking

Beads are small objects meant to serve as decorations, magical charms, counting and mnemonic devices, and status symbols. Nearly all beads and pendants (a subclass of beads) are strung through a hole piercing them or via a loop attached to them.

Beads are universal and one of the oldest forms of human expression. They can and have been made from virtually any solid material (Francis 1982a). They function in the economic, social, ideational, and aesthetic realms of culture. They encode human behaviors, including those difficult to assess archaeologically. The ancients held them in awe. They were magical as well as valuable. They incorporated powers and were both stores and evidence of wealth.

Beads are often dismissed as small, costly "luxury goods," of less value to society than mundane staples. However, nearly all goods involved in ancient long-distance trade were luxuries. Few were indispensable to the people importing them, and most had local substitutes. Frank (1990, 182–183, 235) argued that luxury items were crucial because they were integrated into social, economic, political, and ideological systems everywhere and their trade wove these systems together.

The beads considered in this book are made of glass, semiprecious stones, and some organically derived substances. In this chapter these materials are examined, as well as how they are made into beads and how the manufacturing techniques can aid in their identification. The description of beads and some of the vocabulary of bead research are also included.

Glass

All glass discussed in this book is a fabricated substance, technically a state of matter made by heating a metal or metalloid above its melting point and allowing it to cool below that point without crystallizing. Silica (Si) in the form of quartz sand (SiO_2) is the most common metalloid used in glass. Glass is amorphous, without a crystalline structure (Scholes and Greene 1975, 4; Francis 1998a).

Because the melting point of pure silica was too high for ancient furnaces to achieve, a flux, generally an alkali (usually soda [Na_2O] or potash [K_2O]) was (and still is) added to lower the melting point. Lime (CaO) or some other stabilizer must also be added.[1] The ancients may not have known this; the lime was nearly always present as an impurity[2] in the sand (Turner 1956a, 45T–46T). These ingredients are heated for several days (Plate 1), forming a dark, hard substance called "frit." Glassmakers break this up, add some scrap glass (cullet) and perhaps colorants, and then heat the mixture again. As if by magic, it melts and flows, and molten glass results.

When glass is first made, it is translucent green because of the universal impurity of iron in both the ferric and ferrous states. This color is called "bottle green," because cheap bottles are made from this untreated glass.

Many substances, chiefly metallic oxides, are added to impart various properties to glass. The most common additives are the colorants. With only iron or copper and the proper handling of the furnace (blowing air into it, muffling it, or leaving it open) nearly every color may be achieved. Special colorants, notably cobalt (Co) and manganese (Mn), have been used since antiquity. Even tiny amounts of cobalt yield a pleasing dark blue. Manganese in small quantity produces pink, which cancels out "bottle green" and clarifies the glass, earning it the name "glassmaker's soap."[3] Larger amounts produce violet. Antimony, tin, and arsenic were employed as opacifiers. Black glass is usually deep green or violet, made with large amounts of iron or manganese; an organic black glass also exists.[4] Many colorants have been experimented with in recent centuries as the science of chemistry has developed (see Weyl 1959).

The most important other additive to glass is lead. Lead is a glass former, and glass with 90 percent lead has been recorded.[5] Lead makes glass softer, easier to melt and cut, and more brilliant, especially when used with potash. Lead also aids in dissolving other metals added to color the glass.

The most ancient and universal way to make a glass bead is by "furnace-winding." A worker reaches into a furnace with an iron rod (a mandrel) and forms a peak of glass atop the batch held in a crucible. From the peak, he builds a bead on the mandrel by twisting it in the glass (Plate 2). He can decorate the bead with other colors or shape it with a paddle or other tool. After the bead has been worked, he gives it a final heating.[6] The bead can be knocked off the mandrel during a brief period when the iron cools and contracts faster than the glass. It is deposited into an annealing chamber, where it cools slowly (Color Plate 1).

Cold glass can be heated at a fire and dripped onto a wire or other mandrel in a process called "drip-winding" (Color Plate 2). In recent centuries, concentrated heat sources have been developed that allow workers to heat a glass rod (cane) and wind the soft glass around a wire; this is called "lamp-winding." Drip- and lamp-wound beads are not easily detached from the mandrel, so the mandrel is coated with a separator to help release the bead; the separator is often detectable (Color Plate 3).

The other major category of glass beads are "drawn," cut from tubes that have been pulled or drawn out from a hollow gather of glass and usually heated to round them off. The drawn beads of interest here are Indo-Pacific beads. The details of their manufacture are given in chapter 3.

There are several minor techniques used to make glass beads. "Segmented"[7] beads are made by constricting a heated tube to form bulges that are cut apart as single or multiple beads (Plate 3). The only archaeologically confirmed tools to make these are stone blocks with grooves in one face (Rodziewicz 1984, 241–243, pl. 72, nos. 359–367). "Folded" beads are made by heating one or two plaques of glass, bending them around a wire, and joining the edges (Plate 4). "Pierced" beads are made by piercing a heated plaque in the center and forming a bead (Plate 5). "Melded" beads include mosaic and other types made by joining several pieces of glass around a mandrel (Plate 6). These techniques are principally Middle Eastern and are discussed in chapters 9 and 10.

Glass bead manufacturing techniques produce distinct characteristics, providing clues to the origin of the beads. Most of these clues can be recognized by an informed examination of the bead. With practice, some colorants can be identified by sight. Fluorescence under ultraviolet light is a helpful tool. Lead glass can be detected by determining the specific gravity of the bead.[8] Chemical glass analysis can be very useful, but must be interpreted properly (Francis 1998a, b).

All wound glass beads have the fabric of the glass and any small bubbles (called "seed") oriented around the perforation (Plate 7). Furnace-wound beads generally have a thin layer of black iron oxide deposited by the mandrel in their perforations. Drip- and lamp-wound beads often have powdery deposits of the separator (notably kaolin).[9] All such deposits may be removed by friction in time.

In drawn beads, the glass is oriented along the perforation (Plate 8). These beads have no perforation deposits and are generally less decorative than wound beads. Segmented beads are hollow; folded and melded beads have seams.

Stone

"Stone" is an unscientific term denoting both rocks and minerals. Here it refers to minerals (except for the rock lapis lazuli), usually members of the quartz family. The origins of stone beads are often less easily identified than those of glass beads. There is not nearly as much work done on their sourcing by chemical composition, and their manufacturing processes tend to be conservative and less varied than those of glass.

Quartz (silicon dioxide) is an igneous mineral and the most widely used stone bead material. It is divided into four varieties, depending upon its crystalline structure.[10] Crystalline quartz (rock crystal, amethyst) cools slowly and has visible crystals. Faster cooling produces microcrystalline varieties, either fibrous (chalcedony, agate, carnelian) or granular (flint, jasper). Opal has a spherical crystal structure. It is friable and rarely used for beads, but opalized wood has a place in our story in the Burmese context.

The raw material for stone beads is found in different contexts. Indian carnelians are usually in secondary deposits along rivers (Plate 9). Chinese and Vietnamese jade is found as boulders in rivers and must be chipped or sliced on a wheel to reduce its size. Afghan lapis lazuli forms in veins and is removed by building a fire to heat the rock, then throwing cold water on it to shatter it.

Carnelian and agate (but not other stones) are first treated by applying heat to make them easier to chip, a trick known since Paleolithic times (Rowlett et al. 1974, 37). In India, they are covered with sawdust or rice husks either in a trough (Plate 10) or in overturned pots with holes punched in the base. The organic matter is then ignited.

The stone is next chipped into a crude shape known as a roughout. In western India, it is held against the tip of an iron stake driven into the ground and hit with a hammer of water buffalo horn mounted on a bamboo stick (Color Plate 4). Thinned quartz crystals with heavily battered tips are found in South India from the late centuries B.C. in beadmaking contexts (Plate 11). Whether they were the fixed point, the hammerhead, or a pecking device is not known.

The roughout is then ground into a blank. In modern India this is done against a wheel coated with emery held by lac and electrically turned (Plate 12). In the past, sandstone slabs were used for grinding (Plate 13). In South India, many beads were not ground but pecked (repeatedly hit) into shape, perhaps with quartz crystals or, as Leonard Gorelick (1986, personal communication) suggested, a diamond point.

The next step is to drill the bead. First, a worker makes a "dimple," a small depression to allow the drill to "bite." Today this is done with a large drill bit with a single diamond tip. In the past, chipping, pecking, sawing, and grinding were also employed.

A bow drill with a double-tipped diamond bit is still used in India to bore beads (Color Plate 5). The bow drill is a very old device, and the use of double-tipped diamond drill bits was introduced in the late centuries B.C. There were other ways to drill stone beads in earlier times, but this step has not altered during the period considered here.

Drilling is usually done from both sides. Otherwise, the distal end of the bead shatters before the drill

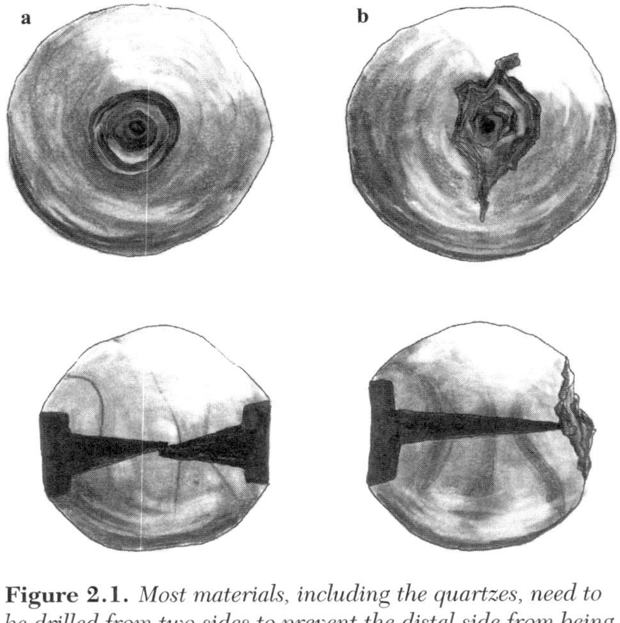

Figure 2.1. *Most materials, including the quartzes, need to be drilled from two sides to prevent the distal side from being split by the drill as it approaches the edge of the material. Beads drilled from only one side* (b) *have a distinctive cavity at one end. Sketch by Lynda Dinneen.*

emerges from it (Figure 2.1). Industries in which beads were drilled from only one side were usually less sophisticated than those that drilled from both sides.

Polishing is usually the last step in the process. Today Indians mechanically tumble beads. Historically, two men rolled a leather bag between them filled with beads, water, and agate dust (Summers 1851, 326; Campbell 1880, 202). This method was used for round beads; most faceted beads were polished by abrasion. Abrasion polishing used fine-grained sandstone (Plate 14) or teak or copper plates (Campbell 1880, 202). Bamboo (rich in siliceous nodules) is currently employed in Java (Color Plate 6) (Francis 1993b, 108). The order of perforating and polishing is reversed in some cases.

For carnelian and onyx, one more operation is carried out after polishing. Their colors must be altered because neither stone is ordinarily found in nature in the color for which it is known (Color Plate 7).

Western Indian carnelians are found in a bed of ferruginous silt and over time have absorbed iron from the sediment. When the beads are heated in a muffled furnace (Color Plate 8), the iron turns red and the carnelian color appears.[11]

Onyx[12] is made by soaking banded agate[13] in honey or sugar water for a few weeks over low heat. The porous layers absorb the sugar and when heated it caramelizes, making a brown (banded) onyx. If put into sulfuric acid it carbonizes, making a black (banded) agate. Brown onyx was known in Harappān times; black onyx makes its first appearance in the second half of the first millennium B.C.

Several of the processes just described obliterate traces of earlier manufacturing stages. It is rarely possible to tell whether a finished bead had been made from a pebble or cut from a large piece of stone. Nor can it be determined whether it had been ground or pecked into a blank. Only the last processes, polishing and drilling, can be discerned.

If a bead is tumble-polished, its surface will be smooth, including the interiors of indentations. The edges of facets will be rounded. If polishing is done by abrasion, the bead may still be shiny, but tiny abrasion marks are left on the surface and the interiors of indentations are not polished. Moreover, the edges of faceted beads are sharp rather than rounded.

Dimpling always precedes drilling. On tumble-polished beads, it is often easy to determine whether dimpling and drilling were done before polishing. If so, the dimple will be polished smooth. If not, the dimple will be rough.

Organic Materials

Many organically derived materials have been used for beads. This book covers only the four that were most important in the Asian maritime trade: amber, coral, ivory, and pearls. As with stones, these materials are often more difficult to source than many glass beads. In addition, some corrode relatively quickly,[14] especially pearls and amber.

The sources for amber and precious coral were limited in ancient times, aiding in the identification of their origin. Ivory and pearls are more widely distributed. The manufacturing of each material differed in the way it was carried out and by whom.

Pearls only need be drilled and this was often done near the area where they were fished. Ivory was frequently imported as tusks and cut in the region that imported it. Ivory beads were usually by-products of the making of larger objects. Coral and amber were exported both as finished products and as raw materials. Their manufacturing steps are similar to those of stones. Amber is the softest of these materials and the easiest to work.

Describing Beads

The classic bead description is the paper "Classification and Nomenclature of Beads and Pendants" read before the Society of Antiquarians by Horace C. Beck in 1926 (Beck 1928).[15] Ever since its publication, it has been the touchstone for describing and naming beads.[16] Beck (1928, 1) taught, "To describe a bead fully it is necessary to state its form, perforation, colour, material, and decoration." Building on this, van der Sleen (1973, 16)[17] added, "One of the first things to be known about a bead is how it has been manufactured, as this may be one of the first points to consider when we try to find out when it was made and used." This is particularly true with glass beads, which cannot be discussed properly without identifying their manufacturing process. To these lists, size should be added.

The following is a summary of the methods I use to catalog beads. It concentrates on the types encountered in this book.

1. Material. This identification should always be as precise as possible. "Glass" is sufficient for common soda-lime glass, but "lead glass" should always be recognized. For stones, the accepted mineralogical name is used and any alterations recorded. If the material is organic, it should be recorded as specifically as possible. For example, shell beads could be described as "cut from the columella of a large univalve"; "*Oliva* sp."; or "*Xanthus pyrum* var. *rapa*," depending upon how closely they can be identified.
2. Method of manufacture. This is critical for glass beads. Although often difficult to determine, it may also be important for beads of other materials.
3. Form. Beads are three-dimensional objects, though usually illustrated in two dimensions. Their shapes are described both ways. The starting point of the description is the perforation (the axis). Looking through it shows the cross section (perimeter). Looking at it lengthwise reveals the profile. Many common form names combine the two-dimensional section with the three-dimensional shape of the bead, as in square cylinder, octagonal barrel, or hexagonal bicone (two cones joined at the bases). When the cross section is round, it is usually not mentioned: cylinder, barrel, bicone. If the length and diameter of a bead are not roughly equal, it is described as "short" or "long."[18]

A bead with a round profile and cross section is a sphere. Very few beads are truly spherical, being somewhat flattened at the ends, and are called oblates, the most common bead shape. When the poles are flattened considerably, the bead is a suboblate.

Not all beads are geometric solids. Some represent plants, animals, or other objects and are described as such. There are also some common bead shapes, whose meanings are not immediately obvious (Figure 2.2): (1) collar: a bead with extra bits of material around both apertures; (2) melon: usually oblates with longitudinal gadroons or grooves, resembling a pumpkin. This is called *amalaka* in India, *nelli* in Sri Lanka, "tangerine" in Japan, and so forth; (3) tabular: a flat bead perforated through its longest axis, resembling a tabletop. They are described using the shape of their flat faces: round tabular, diamond tabular, and so forth.

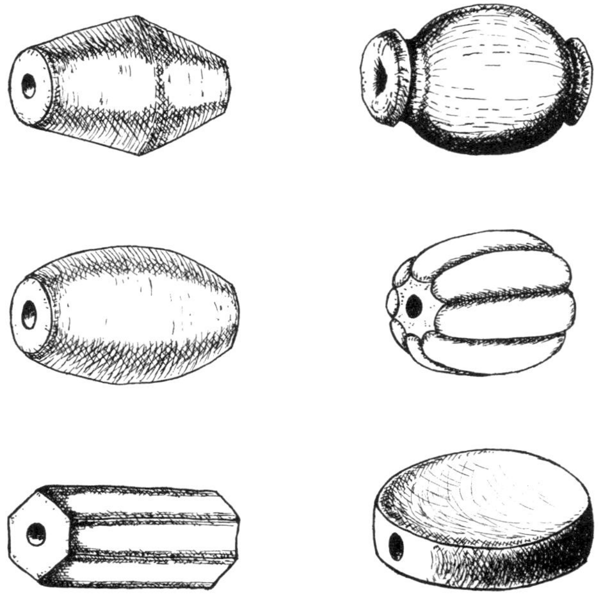

Figure 2.2. *Some bead forms discussed in the text.* Top row: *bicone and collar bead,* Middle row: *barrel and melon bead.* Bottom row: *hexagonal tube or prism and round tabular bead. Sketch by Cynthia Schave.*

4. Color. Bead colors are confusing, especially with glass. The human eye can distinguish over a million shades, and rarely do two people agree on what they see. Munsell color charts are ideal, but are expensive. Other charts do not have wide circulation. When in doubt, describe colors simply. "Light green" is better than "mint," "light blue" better than "sky blue," and "bright yellow" preferable to "lemon."
5. Diaphaneity. This describes whether a bead is opaque, translucent, or transparent. It is not recorded when this is obvious, such as with shell or carnelian. It is most important for glass beads, usually coupled with the color of the glass.
6. Size. The length of a bead is usually the length of the perforation, the diameter at right angles to this. Beads with odd shapes can be measured in various ways, with notes as to how the measurements were taken. It is usually sufficiently accurate to record sizes in tenths of millimeters.
7. Decoration. Beads can be coated, have decorations or other materials added to them, be incised, and so on. The decorative techniques of beads in the Asian maritime trade will be introduced as each is discussed in the text.
8. Perforation. This little hole is not simply a bit of nothing. It defines most beads. If it is off-center, the bead is a pendant. If it pierces the side of a long bead, it is a toggle.

   Beads with straight holes are probably glass; those with joints in the holes are drilled from both sides. Glass beads with conical holes are often furnace-wound, whereas holes with parallel sides may be drawn or lamp-wound. Perforation deposits offer other clues to manufacturing methods, as discussed earlier in this chapter.

   Drilled beads with eccentric (wobbly) holes were probably done with hand-held drills (see Gwinnett and Gorelick 1981). Those with hourglass or biconical perforations were drilled with stone tips or a stick and abrasives; double diamond tips leave straight channels, though they usually do not meet perfectly in the center, leaving a "joint" inside the perforation. This is just a sampling of what can be learned from examining perforations.

There has been debate over the utility of measuring the apertures of perforations. It is not always necessary, but should be recorded when it is likely to be important, for example with conical perforations. Measurements can help distinguish drills within tool assemblages (Francis 1988a).

This short summary of the categories and terms used to describe beads is by no means exhaustive. It is meant to acquaint the reader with the often-esoteric glossary of bead researchers to facilitate the reading of the text that follows.

Part Two: Indo-Pacific Beads

3

Introduction to Indo-Pacific Beads

Small, common things are often overlooked. This is true with beads generally and especially with the smallest and most ubiquitous of them. This section covers the most widespread trade bead of all times, quite possibly the most widespread trade item of any sort.

Their Background and Names

Indo-Pacific beads (Color Plate 9) are rarely more than 5 mm in diameter. In cross section they are usually round, but their profiles differ so much that they may be oblate, discoidal, tubular, or other shapes. They were made in a limited range of colors, with various hues: opaque reddish brown, orange, yellow, green, and black; semi translucent greens and blues; and translucent amber and violet. The glass is generally of indifferent quality, often containing many gas bubbles (seed) and refractory matter.

Horace Beck (1930a, 176–178) first reported on these beads when discussing material that Evans had excavated at Kuala Selinsing, Malaysia. Having a good grasp of bead distribution, he recognized them from other places including Pemba, Zanzibar, Rhodesia, South India, Sarawak, Java, the Philippines, and Korea. Later he reported on them from specific sites: Great Zimbabwe (Beck 1931), slab graves in Perak, Malaysia (Beck 1937a), "megalithic" graves in southern India (Beck 1930a), and Mapungubwe, Zimbabwe (Beck 1937b). He had little to say about them, except to note their similarity, their wide distribution, and that Kuala Selinsing was then the only known place of manufacture.

The first scholars to attempt global syntheses of beads also discussed them, but differed dramatically in their interpretations. W. G. N. van der Sleen (1956a; 1958, 208–212; 1973, 76–82)[1] coined the term "trade wind beads" for beads that had reached the East African coast by sea. His application of this evocative term was far too broad. It included glass beads made by both the drawing and winding techniques and even stone beads. In later papers he seems to have limited the term "trade wind beads" to the small drawn ones (van der Sleen 1966), though he was never explicit about this.

Alaistar Lamb (1965a, b) used the term *mutisalah* for opaque reddish brown (hereafter simply "red") beads he encountered in Southeast Asia. By doing so, he excluded beads that were precisely the same except for their colors. Unfortunately, he misunderstood the term as used in several eastern islands of Indonesia. *Mutisalah* ("false pearls") refers to heirloom beads in general. The red drawn bead is only one type of *mutisalah*, as discussed in chapter 17.

Lamb's use of *mutisalah* upset van der Sleen, who responded in a letter to the journal *Man* (van der Sleen 1966), in which Lamb had published. Van der Sleen said that small wound beads high in lead were the "true" *mutisalah*, whereas the beads Lamb described were drawn and lacked lead and were simply trade wind beads. Both had made the fundamental error of not grasping the complexity of heirloom bead traditions, but that was not to be understood for some time (Francis 1992a, 11–12; 1992b; see also chap. 17).

To anyone working with these beads, the controversy between the two leading researchers presented an enigma. Because van der Sleen died soon after the debate opened, Lamb's definition was adopted by some scholars. On the other hand, van der Sleen's *Handbook on Beads* in its several editions was long the standard text on the subject. Researchers in Africa adopted "trade wind beads" as a name for this group, but in Asia *mutisalah* was favored. The problem went beyond mere definition or nomenclature. Both scholars were acquainted enough with beads to distinguish wound ones from drawn ones. Moreover, each had their beads analyzed so that the presence or absence of lead was confirmed.

Even before understanding why there was disagreement over the nature of *mutisalah,* the sharp differences of opinion and the imprecise nature of the terminology lead me to reject both *mutisalah* and "trade wind beads" as names for the omnipresent drawn beads of whatever color. Hence, I coined "Indo-Pacific beads,"[2] initially to indicate their geographic distribution (Francis 1986a). Their distribution is even wider than the shores of these seas, but the term fits the location of their known manufacturers.

How Indo-Pacific Beads Are/Were Made

The spatial and temporal distribution of Indo-Pacific beads is one of the most important and extraordinary facts about them. They are found for a period of more than two thousand years in regions as far removed as Ghana and China, Mali and Bali, South Africa and South Korea. This remarkable dispersal leads one to wonder how they were produced, whether at one or more sites, and where.

At Papanaidupet (Chittor District, Andhra Pradesh, India) workers make small drawn beads principally for the Indian market. The unusual technique they use had never been recorded.[3] Beads and manufacturing wasters from the modern village precisely matched the forms of similar materials I collected from the surface of the archaeological site of Arikamēḍu in the Union Territory of Pondicherry, India. Not only were the beads comparable, but so were the waste products (Color Plate 10). There were several possible explanations for this resemblance. During the next few years, I tested these four hypotheses:

1. The similarity *was not* significant because the samples were *nonrepresentative.* The initial assemblages were small and may not have been true cross sections of the glass material at the two places.
2. The similarity *was not* significant because such glass wasters were common to *all* drawn glass beadmaking techniques. In this case they would result from both the unusual method used at Papanaidupet and from other means of drawing beads, which could have been employed at Arikamēḍu.
3. The similarity *was* significant and indicated that Papanaidupet was using the same drawing method as that used at Arikamēḍu. However, it *did not* indicate a connection between the two sites, because the technique had been independently invented twice.
4. The similarity *was* significant and *did* indicate that Papanaidupet was making beads the same way as it was being done at Arikamēḍu because the beadmakers of the two sites were linked genetically, culturally, or in some way historically.

Interviews with Tom André, Dudley Giberson, and Sara Young, contemporary American beadmakers using the drawing technique, confirmed that the wasters found in India were unique. Diagnostic wasters of most drawing operations are large, bulbous tube ends. These are absent from the Indo-Pacific material. Moreover, other drawing processes do not produce the typical small wasters of the Indo-Pacific material.

To test whether the original samples were representative required further trips to Pondicherry (where the Arikamēḍu material was housed) and Papanaidupet. In the summer of 1985, all the glass material from Arikamēḍu in the Pondicherry Museum, totaling some 25,000 pieces, was classified, counted, and weighed.[4] Subsequent trips to Papanaidupet documented the beadmaking process and clarified how each waste product was formed. The beadmakers confidently and correctly identified each stage of the process that produced a particular glass waster.

The outcome of this work verified that all the unique wasters made by the modern industry at Papanaidupet are duplicated in the Arikamēḍu material, and all wasters from Arikamēḍu are currently made by the bead makers of Papanaidupet. The one minor exception indicates a slightly different tool used at one stage at Arikamēḍu and is discussed later in this chapter.

The conclusion was inescapable. Arikamēḍu and Papanaidupet made/make beads the same way. The next question was why?

It was then universally assumed that Arikamēḍu had been abandoned in the second century A.D., following the work of Wheeler (Wheeler et al. 1946). No one at Papanaidupet knew anything about the history of the village or the beadmaking craft. The oldest man I was able to locate claimed to be eighty years old in 1985 and asserted that his father and grandfather had done the same work there. Thus, there was a gap of 1,600 or more years between the two sites.

The gap has now been filled. This is a critical part of the Indo-Pacific bead story and, indeed, the whole history of beads in the Asian maritime bead trade. It is the subject of the next chapter.

Making Indo-Pacific Beads

The following is an account of beadmaking at Papanaidupet, with notes on the few apparent differences in techniques used at Arikamēḍu. All steps in the beadmaking process are presented here, with particular attention to the wasters produced by each operation.

The first stage in making glass beads is to make glass. The glass used at Papanaidupet comes from two sources. Most is bought commercially from the factories of Firozabad, Uttar Pradesh, which has been the "glass capital of India" for decades. Firozabad provides colored ingots to most Indian glass bead- and bangle makers (Francis 1982b, 7–10). The Andhra Pradesh government attempted to set up a glass factory in Gudar (Gụdimallam) after Independence (Bhatnagar 1957, 130). Gudar is only 3 km from Papanaidupet, but it could not withstand Firozabad competition; glassmaking there failed. Since the mid-1980s, glass has been made at Papanaidupet with ingredients and workers imported from Firozabad. The new glass is of higher quality than that produced anciently at Arikamēḍu.

Glass is made at Papanaidupet in large clay crucibles fired in furnaces. Chemicals and the workers come from Firozabad, but the sand is from Gudar. A master takes some molten glass from a pot with a large scoop and pours it onto a flat stone where it cools into a large disk known as a "cake" (Plate 15). These are broken apart and

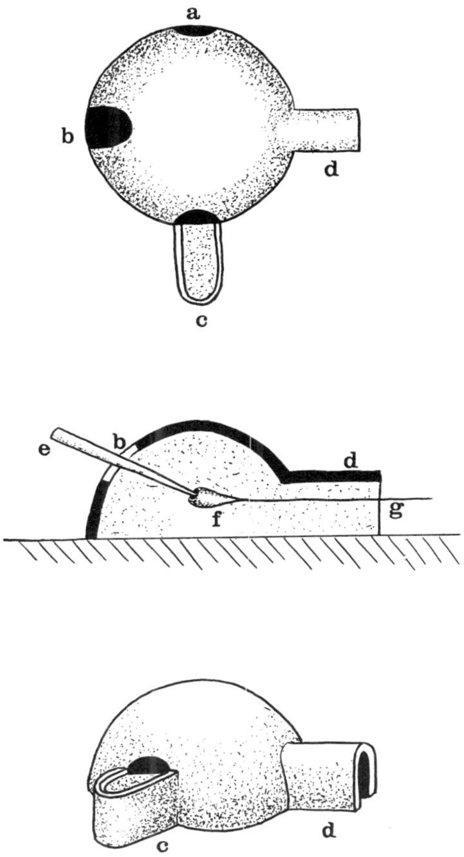

Figure 3.1. *Sketch of the tube-drawing furnace at Papanaidupet. The components are as follows:* a, *fuel port;* b, *high port for the* lada; c, *trough for melting glass;* d, *port for drawing tube;* e, *the* lada; f, *the cone of glass;* g, *the tube being drawn out.*

women remove as much of the refractory (nonmelting) matter as they can from the glass.

The broken chunks of glass go to another furnace elsewhere in the village where the tubes are drawn. This furnace superficially resembles traditional glass furnaces in Europe, the Middle East, and India. It is a low-domed affair made of stones covered with claylike mud, about 2 m high. It has separate ports for different functions. However, the Papanaidupet furnace differs from the usual design in several critical ways (Figure 3.1).

The Papanaidupet tube-drawing furnace has an opening on each of four sides. A low, partially subterranean, port is used to feed the wood fuel, in common with other traditional furnaces. The other three sides, however, have specialized ports not found on furnaces recorded anywhere else. On one side is a large, high port. Opposite it is a low port whose entrance is marked with a small tunnel, making the furnace look rather like an igloo. Opposite the fuel port is a small port opening onto a long, elevated trough or shelf. An additional unique feature is a short, low freestanding wall near the furnace.

The tools used for drawing tubes are unlike glassworking tools used elsewhere. The first ones to work the molten glass are called *gedda paru,* iron rods about a meter long set into longer wooden handles. *Gedda paru* is the Tamil term for the stick used to stir mud for building houses. The *gedda paru* in Papanaidupet stir molten glass. Two other tools are a long, tapered iron tube with the larger end about 10 cm wide, the *lada* or *ladha,* and the *cheatlek,* an iron rod with a bulbous end, a little longer than the *lada.* A long iron rod with a hook is used to draw the tube out initially (Plate 16).

The uniqueness of the furnace construction, the adjacent low wall, and the tools underscore the uniqueness of the method used for drawing tubes. It is tube drawing—rather than making glass or finishing tubes into beads—that is the crucial test for identifying Indo-Pacific beadmaking. This style of tube drawing is unparalleled and the wasters produced by it are characteristic.

To draw tubes, workers put 40 to 50 kg (88 to 110 pounds) of broken glass chunks onto the trough or shelf. A man feeds wood though the fuel port and lights the fire. Flames leap out through the port in front of the trough and slowly soften the glass. This part of the operation is overseen by one of the crew (Plate 17). The rest of the team of a dozen men go to sleep, because the fire is lit around 10:00 P.M. The duties of the wakeful man are to feed the fire and rouse the team around midnight when the glass is the proper consistency. The reason given for this schedule is that the heat of the furnace is unbearable during the day.[5]

Two men, often aided by others, pick up the softened glass on the ends of their *gedda paru,* each taking about half the glass. They place the glass into the high port and stir it continually until the chunks melt (Plate 18). At the end of this stage, a taffylike mass of glass is suspended between the two *gedda paru.*

Patches of glass left on the *gedda paru* eventually fall off or are knocked off. Thin, slightly curved "*gedda paru* flakes" have rough inside surfaces and shiny, smooth exteriors. They often end with a little "tail." They are diagnostic of this stage (Figure 3.2d).

The workers then transfer the glass to the thin end of the *lada.* Using the *lada* as a handle, they roll the glass along the top of the wall standing near the furnace.[6] This forms the glass into a cylinder and eventually a cone. Several men work this step because of the weight of the

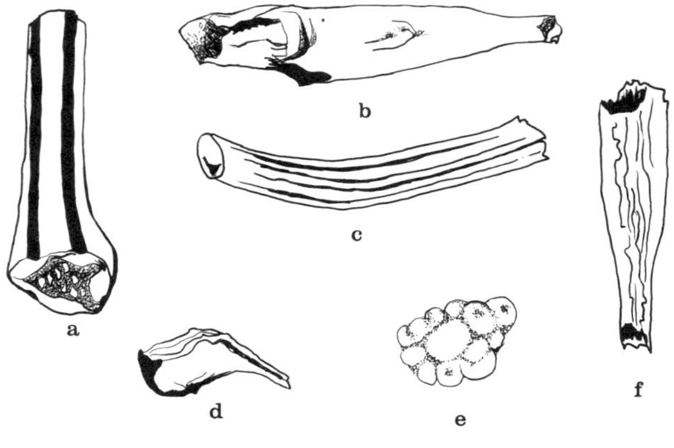

Figure 3.2. *Drawings of common wasters produced at Papanaidupet and Arikamēḍu;* a, *large knot in a tube;* b *and* c, *unperforated forms from the initial draw;* d, gedda paru *flake;* e, *clump of beads from reheating stage;* f, *thin-walled collapsed tube from the end of the draw. Sketch by Jacqui Steinberg.*

lada and glass. Two men hold the ends of a wooden log crosswise under the *lada* to help it roll along the wall (Plate 19).

After a satisfactory cone is formed, the men rest the *lada* on the wall and through its wide end insert the *cheatlek* rod (Plate 20). With the rod, they smash at the base of the glass cone until the rod pierces it[7] (Plate 21). The result is a perforated cone of glass.

The crew then takes the whole apparatus—the *lada* with the glass cone at one end and the *cheatlek* sticking out of the other—and inserts it into the high port. The cone is placed entirely within the furnace, with the *lada* and *cheatlek* projecting outside (see Figure 3.1).

Opposite the high port is the low port with the tunnel opening. One of two masters on the team inserts the long-handled iron hook through the tunnel into the heart of the furnace. He grabs at the open tip of the cone and pulls it toward himself. Once he has the tip of the cone, he walks backward about 5 m, drawing out the glass as he does so; he then drops the hook and grabs the glass tube. He continues to draw the tube out hand over hand, his palms protected only by a small wet square of jute packing. As he pulls, he breaks the tube into meter lengths on the backstroke of one hand (Plate 22). An assistant picks up the still-hot tubing and stacks it to one side.

It is usual for the master to make several attempts at securing the exact open tip of the glass cone. These trials result in short streams of glass that cannot be used and are flicked off the hook before making another try at drawing the tube. These diagnostic wasters are often twisted. Some are amorphous in shape. Some resemble small glass hooks; others recall sections of bangles. Nearly all lack central holes (Figure 3.2b, c).

The only glass wasters found at Arikamēḍu that are not duplicated in the Papanaidupet material are pieces crimped on one or both sides. A pincer device (rather than the hook) was apparently used for the initial draw from the cone. These pieces are only known from the Pondicherry Museum collections and cannot be assigned a firm date.

The drawing process elongates the perforated cone into a continuous tube whose diameter is determined by the rate of drawing. Thicker tubes are made when the master draws slowly, thinner ones when he draws faster. It takes about three hours to draw the whole cone into tubing. The work is exhausting, and two masters on each team relieve each other during the procedure.

It is interesting that the physical principle of this tube-drawing method is employed in modern machines used worldwide for beadmaking and other glass tubing. This is probably, but not certainly, coincidental. Edward Danner (1917) of the Libby Glass Company of Toledo, Ohio, invented the first successful tube-drawing machine, in which molten glass flows onto and over a tapered ceramic pipe through which a continuous stream of compressed air is blown. As the extruding glass emerges, the air preserves a hole along its length.

At Papanaidupet, the same thing happens. As the master draws the tube forward, air is removed and new air sucked in through the *lada*. The air expands in the heat of the furnace and continuously exits through the tube, keeping the aperture open.

At the end of the drawing process, the remnant of the cone comes off the tip of the *lada* and falls to the ground, collapsing upon itself. A distinctive "collapsed tube" results (Figure 3.2f). The end of this tube has a large diameter and very thin walls, producing a characteristic thin-walled "flare."

Drawing tubes is the basic operation for making drawn beads. The method detailed here is representative of Indo-Pacific beadmaking and unique to that industry. Glass wasters formed during this process mark centers of Indo-Pacific beadmaking.

Turning Tubes into Beads

Drawn tubes are not finished beads; they must be processed further. The Indo-Pacific system of making beads from tubes parallels the traditional European system[8] (Francis 1988b, 19–20; Karklins and Adams 1990). The waste products from the processing steps are indicative of beadmaking, but *not* diagnostic of Indo-Pacific beadmaking. Diagnostic wasters are only produced during tube drawing.

At Papanaidupet, men cut the tubes along the outside walls of their homes. Each man drives the flange of a flat iron blade into the ground in front of him. He holds a dozen or so tubes in one hand protruding over the blade edge. With the other hand, he brings a second blade down onto the fixed blade, chopping small segments from the tubes. These tend to scatter widely, so a sheet is affixed to the wall, helping to catch them (Plate 23).

This operation is identifiable by several wasters. Some short, cut segments "escape" and remain on the ground. Workers discard the ends of tubes when they are too short to hold comfortably while chopping. These tube ends are commonly 1.65 to 2.00 cm in length. They can be melted for a later glass batch, but some elude the recycling.

Evidence of human behavior is encoded into the beads at this stage. Depending upon the angle at which the worker lays the tubes on the blade, finished beads will have one or both ends slanting away from the 90° ideal.

One waste product is encountered at all stages of beadmaking. "Knots" are formed by refractory material that clog the tube, commonly inducing a swell in the side. These are useless to the industry. The tube makers remove large, obvious ones, the cutters smaller ones, and the bead stringers the smallest ones (Figure 3.2a).

Cut bead segments can be marketed as such, but are usually finished to remove the sharp edges resulting from the cutting.[9] To do this, a woman packs the segments into dung ash to prevent the beads from sticking together and the holes from collapsing. Her husband pours the mixture onto a large, flat, ceramic plate on the floor of a small, domed furnace with one port. He stirs the mixture with a large wooden paddle for twenty to thirty minutes (Plate 24). When the beads are rounded, they are placed in a large mortar in which the wife pounds the mixture with a large pestle to remove the ash from the beads.

Evidence for this stage is produced when the fire is too hot, the beads are left on too long, or insufficient ash is used. Two or more beads may melt together into a "clump" (Figure 3.2e). Overheated beads may also melt onto the ceramic plate.

Other operations follow. The beads may be shaken in a bag with rice husks to clean them further. If consistent diameters are desired, workers pour the beads through a series of sieves mounted on a wooden rack. The sieves are shaken so that progressively smaller beads fall through them.

In the end, the beads pass to women and girls, who dump them into flat winnowing baskets they hold in their laps. The women pass fifteen or so long, thin needles made from piano wire through the beads. After a few quick passes, several beads will be gathered on each needle and are slipped onto the thread strung through its eye (Plate 25). Strings are bunched into hanks of a pound (454 g) and sold in this condition. Those sold domestically are strung on cotton thread; stronger nylon thread is employed for export.

The stringers produce waste of their own: beads that cannot be strung. These include those with holes shut during the reheating process, beads with holes too small to string, and those with small knots. These knots, too tiny to have been detected during earlier stages, crowd the holes, forcing them into a crescentic shape.

Organization of the Papanaidupet Beadmakers

The beadmakers of Papanaidupet are organized in a near-feudal cottage industrial structure. The workers are paid by the piece and do not share in the profits. A few years ago, a cooperative was formed. Although its name is still written out in glass beads on a cement step of its former headquarters, it did not survive long.

The organization in the early 1980s (Francis 1984a) can furnish a theoretical model for the operation in earlier times. Something similar must have existed for the work to have been executed. Both the physically scattered nature of the labor and the hierarchical structure of the social order are typical of Indian village-based industries.

At the apex are four families. They make or buy the glass and store the beads in their *godowns* (warehouses). They own the glass throughout the process, pay for each step of its transformation, and market the finished beads. One family is not native, but came from Gujarat with enough capital to begin its own operation.

Next in status are some two dozen families who own tube-drawing furnaces on their property (Plate 26). The teams who do the drawing once paid daily rent to them. The payment fell to the master drawers and amounted to

10 percent of their wages (then about twice the Indian legal minimum daily wage). They viewed this as onerous and went on strike in February and March 1984 in protest. The issue was settled by having the merchants pay the rent. In 1984 an estimated 300 people were employed as tube drawers and at the thirty or so small reheating ("fire polishing") furnaces run by husband and wife teams.

Men, some of whom work at other facets of production, cut the tubes. Approximately 5,000 people were employed in tube cutting and bead stringing. Stringing is the largest single labor segment. It is spare-time work done by women and girls in Papanaidupet and neighboring villages. In the early 1980s, Papanaidupet had a population of about 15,000.[10]

Other Descriptions of Beadmaking at Papanaidupet

Papanaidupet beadmaking had never been adequately described before my investigations (Francis 1982b, 16–18). The only account commonly available was Dikshit's (1969), and it is secondhand. I have not located the work he cited, so I am not sure if Narayan Rao (1929) outlined the process correctly or was misinterpreted. Dikshit's description reads:

> Blocks of glass in viscous condition are taken to two stout iron bars [the *gedda paru*] and are heated over the furnaces. When sufficiently hot the viscous mass is transferred to an iron barrel with a bore of about ½ inch [the *lada,* which is much wider]. By centrifugal action the molten glass is allowed to settle on the sides of the barrel and then pushed out slightly by means of another rod [the *cheatlek*] in such a way that some portion of the mass in the barrel protrudes out. This is taken on two small thin rods [only one is used] and pulled out till the glass tube becomes as small as a needle. This is done continuously till the required quantity of glass is finished. (Dikshit 1969, 139; insertions mine)

Dikshit had no understanding of the process. He envisioned the glass coming *out from the interior* of the *lada.* He described the tools as being much smaller than they are in reality. It is unlikely that they have changed so radically in a few decades.

The other description of the Papanaidupet tube-drawing method is the careful observation of Stern (1987). However, her assertion that the knots produced by the process are the diagnostic wasters made by the system cannot be accepted (Francis 1990a).

Recording Indo-Pacific Beads

Any reader who has tried to classify Indo-Pacific or similar small drawn beads will appreciate how tedious it is to name all bead shapes. However, by recording diameter and length, whether the bead has been cut at an angle, and the "roundness" factor, it is possible to enter data in tabular form and later reconstruct the shape of a bead from it. A few words about this may be helpful.

Diameter and length are straightforward. If a bead was cut from the tube at an angle at one or both ends, this can be detected by looking at the bead while holding it in calipers to measure its length. Angled ends will

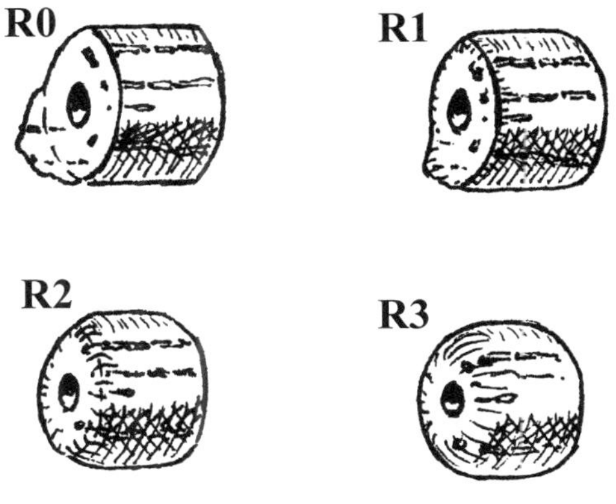

Figure 3.3. *Sketch of the "roundness" factor used to describe small drawn beads. A segment that has not been reheated and remains sharp is labeled R0. A bead with slight heating that barely changes its profile is labeled R1. More heating will bevel the edges of the bead, labeled R2. A bead heated enough to round off the profile is designated R3. Sketch by Cynthia Schave.*

form angles with the straight "jaws" of the calipers. This feature should be recorded as one angle, two converging angles, or two parallel angles.

The time and temperature of the final heating determine how round a bead becomes. A low temperature and a short period over the fire will just barely round off its edges. On the other hand, a high temperature and/or a lengthy time over the fire will result in a small oblate.

The degree of "roundness" (R) is difficult to quantify for small objects, so it is recorded in steps. Again, this feature is best seen when holding a bead in calipers to measure its length. The four steps are (fig. 3.3) as follows: R0, for beads that have not been reheated (usually unfinished segments); R1, for beads whose ends have only slightly run and maintain square profiles; R2, for beads heated enough to bevel the corners where the ends and sides meet; R3, for beads that have assumed a rounded profile.

Not only is it possible to reconstruct the shape of a bead from these data, but the information may provide clues to distinguish manufacturing sites or periods. The roundness factor has helped link beadmaking at Takua Pa, Thailand, with exporting at Laem Pho Chaiya, across the Kra Peninsula. Indo-Pacific beads at both sites have very high percentages of R1 type, indicating a short reheating time at Takua Pa. Relatively long beads (tubes) are a feature of production at Palembang and perhaps some other sites.

The significance of the Indo-Pacific beadmaking industry will become apparent in the following chapters. The beads became the most common type in the Asian maritime trade for nearly two millennia and assumed deep cultural meaning in several places. The beadmakers themselves must have moved to different locations to carry out their work. They also devised ways of transforming their basic semiproduct (the tubes) into other bead types.

4

Indo-Pacific BeadMaking Centers

The long period and wide geographic range in which Indo-Pacific beads are found, as well as their sheer numbers, suggest that more than one center may have produced them. The identification of Indo-Pacific beadmaking sites relies on recognizing the diagnostic wasters discussed in the last chapter. Some scholars assume that large numbers of beads alone indicate local beadmaking. Although the presence of many beads is significant, it does not by itself prove that beadmaking took place at a given site.

Several Indo-Pacific beadmaking sites have now been confirmed (Francis 1991a). They were originally identified based on the existence of manufacturing waste (Table 4.1), but have since been corroborated by analytical evidence (Appendix B). There may be others not yet verified.[1] When they are, they will add new data and perhaps change our perception of the nature of this industry. However, the picture outlined here would probably not be altered significantly.

Arikamēḍu

Arikamēḍu is a few miles south of the southeastern Indian city of Pondicherry, once the seat of French India and now the capital of a Union Territory. To date, it is the earliest known Indo-Pacific beadmaking site.

Arikamēḍu lies along the Ariyankuppam River (now a lagoon for much of the year), the northern branch of the Gingee (Color Plate 11). The site is located where the river takes a short northern bend before turning east again to discharge into the Bay of Bengal. This bend protects vessels that anchor in the lee of the land from any inclement turbulence in the bay. Fishing boats harbor here, and in the past oceangoing sailing ships did as well.

The name Arikamēḍu is the archaeological term for the site. It is derived from the Tamil, meaning "mound of Arukan," because a statuette of an avatar of Mahavir was found there (Cyril Antony 1992, personal communication). Mahadevan (1970) identified the place with ancient Virā or Vīrai, whose literary name can be reconstructed as **Vīrām-paṭṭiṇam* or **Vīrai-y-am-paṭṭiṇam*, the "port (paṭṭiṇam) of Vīrā or Vīrai." Vīrai was a city and is mentioned in the *Aka-nāṇūru*, a poem of the ancient Tamil-language *Sangam*[2] literature. The poem affirms that Vīrai had a harbor, was known for its salt pans, and belonged to the Vēḷir. In *Sangam* times the Vēḷir controlled what is now South Arcot District and Pondicherry. Vīrai was also home to two authors of *Sangam* poems, perhaps father and son. The name survives. Virampatnam (or Virampattinam) is the village adjoining the site of Arikamēḍu to this day.

Arikamēḍu-Virampatnam has long been identified with Podouké of *Periplus Maris Erythraei* Sea and Pôdouké Emporion of Ptolemy, based on its location. Mahadevan (1970) explained the Roman name as a corruption of the Tamil *potikai*, "a meeting place," either indoors or outdoors, associated with the Vēḷir dynasty at ancient Vīrai.[3]

Le Gentil visited the ruins in 1765. He observed Virampatnam villagers removing large, ancient bricks exposed along the riverbank (Le Gentil 1779, 100–113; Faucheux 1946, 1–2). In the 1930s, Jouveau-Dubreuil began collecting antiquities from the surface and buying them from local children. One find was an intaglio engraved with the portrait of a man. Jouveau-Dubreuil, a numismatist, identified it as young Augustus Caesar.

The Roman connection caused excitement. Jouveau-Dubreuil wrote a letter to the governor of Pondicherry proclaiming that here was "une veritable ville Romaine [a true Roman city]" and published a short note about it (Jouveau-Dubreuil 1940). In the early 1940s, the Service des Travaux Publics undertook haphazard excavations led by Father Faucheux and Raymond Surleau (Surleau 1943, 1946; Faucheux 1946; Pattabiramin 1946). Sample artifacts were sent to several Indian museums and the École Français de Extrême-Orient in Hanoi.

Some potsherds in the Madras Museum caught the eye of Sir R. E. M. Wheeler, then Director General of the Archaeological Survey of India. He identified some as

TABLE 4.1

Evidence for Indo-Pacific Beadmaking at Sites Identified in the Text

	Sites[a]									
Evidence	AR	KK	MT	OE	KT	KS	VJ	TP	SM	PN
Glassmaking										
Crucibles	x	x								x
Bottle-green chunks	x		x	x	x	x		x		x
Remelted glass	x		x		x	x		x		x
Glassworking										
Colored glass chunks	x	x	x	x	x	x	x		x	x
Drips and splatters	x		x	x	x		x		x	x
Lada tube drawing										
Gedda paru flakes	x									x
Twisted (etc.) tubes	x	x	x	x	x	x	x			x
Flares	x		x							x
Collapsed tubes	x									x
Beads from tubes:										
Knots in tubes	x		x		x	x		x	x	x
Cut segments	x	x	x	x	x	x	x	x	x	x
Tube ends	x		x	x	x					x
Bead clumps	x			x	x	x	x	x	x	x
Beads on ceramic tray	x				x					x
Discarded beads	x		x	x		x	x	x	x	x

[a] AR, Arikamēḍu; KK, Karaikadu; MT, Mantai; OE, Oc Eo; KT, Khlong Thom; KS, Kuala Selinsing; VJ, Vijaya; TP, Takua Pa; SM, Sungai Mas; PN, Papanaidupet.

Arretine ware, a luxury ceramic made in and around Arizzo, Italy, until about A.D. 50. Fragments of amphorae and other items from the Roman West were also found. Wheeler conducted excavations at Arikamēḍu in 1945 on more scientific lines than the French had earlier.[4] The campaign served as a "training school" for young Indian archaeologists, several of whom become leading scholars after Independence. The results were promptly published the following year (Wheeler et al. 1946).

Wheeler sought a common datum line to link the history of South India with the Roman West. He succeeded. However, his Eurocentric outlook caused him to interpret the site in a manner now recognized as erroneous. The most graphic account of his interpretation was offered in a popular work:

> This [ancient] village . . . doubtless consisted of simple fisher-folk, who caught the gullible fish[5] of the region from the shore or from small outriggers, gathered the fruits and juices of the palms, cultivated rice-patches, and lived in an unenterprising fashion just above subsistence level. To it suddenly, from unthought-of lands 5,000 miles away, came strange wines, table-wares far beyond the local skill, lamps of a strange sort, glass, cut gems.[6] Traders arrived across-country from the west coast to meet the large Indian east coast ships of which the *Periplus* tells us, laden with gemstones from Ceylon, pearls from Kolchoi (Colchi), or spices and silks from the Ganges. (Wheeler 1954, 147)

Presumably when the foreigners left, the bucolic scene resumed. The influence of Wheeler's work on South Indian archaeology cannot be overestimated. For a long time, it has been the touchstone for dating and cultural interpretations. However, many of his conclusions have been revised. Some are discussed in this chapter, and others will be dealt with in chapter 12.

The French archaeologist Jean-Marie Casal excavated in and around Arikamēḍu between 1947 and 1950 (Casal 1949; Casal and Casal 1956). His work was not as fully published as Wheeler's was, nor has it had the impact in India, not having been written in English. He made the important contribution of identifying an early "megalithic" component at the site and "megalithic" burials nearby.

Arikamēḍu was all but forgotten for several decades. In the early 1980s Vimala Begley (1983) began studying its ceramics and tentatively revised the chronology of the site. Simultaneously, I began studying its beads and cooperated with the Pondicherry Museum to arrange a display and publish a small guide to it (Francis 1987b). The Historical Society of Pondicherry published an article on Arikamēḍu beads (Francis 1984b) and held a mini-symposium with E. Marianne Stern and myself on Arikamēḍu glassmaking in 1985.

Begley secured permission to conduct further excavations there, jointly undertaken by the University of Pennsylvania and the University of Madras, with herself and K. V. Raman as directors, from 1989 to 1992. Steven Sidebotham of the University of Delaware, whose field is Roman Egypt and its eastern trade, was the trench supervisor.[7] As of this writing, the excavation report is being finalized, but a preliminary one is available (Begley 1993), and the first volume on the 1989–1992 seasons has been published (Begley 1996).

Arikamēḍu was settled a few centuries B.C. The original settlers used a distinctive black-and-red ware found in much of South India and usually called "megalithic." The term derives from the isolated secondary burials of certain people, occasionally marked with large stones. It is an inappropriate name, being derived from European parallels, and ridiculous when used in expressions such as "megalithic ware" or "megalithic beads." In a seminal work on the culture, Leshnik (1974) proposed using "Pandukal" (Tamil for "old stones"). This is not only a local term, but was also used by early European investigators of the culture.

The Pandukal people made stone beads at Arikamēḍu (see chap. 12). The method they used to make these beads is paralleled at other Pandukal sites. They are also the people who most logically provided the raw stone for the lapidaries.

The Pandukal relationship with the Indo-Pacific beadmakers is not understood. The Pandukal settlement was in the southern sector of the site, which yields the most evidence for glassmaking and tube drawing. Young Pandukal men are likely to have furnished at least the colorants for glassmaking along with the stones for lapidary work. Pandukal graves in the region include Indo-Pacific beads, as well as Pandukal stone beads. The Pandukal people brought ironworking to South India, and iron smithing and glassworking often parallel each other. On the negative side, there is no evidence for glassmaking or glassworking at other Pandukal sites.

By the end of the second century B.C., Arikamēḍu was receiving exotic goods brought in amphorae from the West, principally wine. The northern sector of Arikamēḍu was occupied then, and substantial brick structures, including one that Wheeler identified as a warehouse, were built. The northern sector is closer to the sea and at a lower elevation than the southern sector, and was ideal for a port. The ceramics of the northern sector differ from those of the southern sector, indicating different inhabitants. Several ceramics from the northern sector appear to have been large cooking pots and serving platters. They perhaps indicate the preparation and serving of meals for large groups, possibly sailors or traders.

The building of the northern sector marked the beginning of the urban phase at Arikamēḍu. This suggests an influx of outsiders or newcomers, whether North Indians, urbanized Tamils, Pandukal people, or (less likely) non-Indians.

Beadmaking, both in glass and stone, is in evidence from the earliest levels at the site. Unfortunately, the beginnings of Pandukal settlement and the urban phase cannot be dated because of natural and human factors that have prevented the excavations from reaching the lowest levels of occupation.

Arikamēḍu had contact with the Roman West. Items imported from Rome include pottery and glassware. Amphorae are found in large numbers, dating from the second century B.C. to the seventh or eighth century A.D. The luxury tableware once identified as Arretine is found there, exclusively among South Indian sites. Actually, none of it originated from Arizzo. This ceramic is now called *terra sigillata* and was made in a wider area for a longer period than was Arretine ware.

Perhaps the most significant discovery of the 1989–1992 excavations at Arikamēḍu was the evidence for occupation for a far longer time than had originally been assumed. Wheeler (et al. 1946, 24) placed the end of the site at about A.D. 200. Casal (1949, 31) agreed. Wheeler's team (1946, 91–93, 108) did find Chinese celadon from the Song-Yuan periods and Cōḷa coins of the eleventh century or so. However, these were dismissed as indicating despoiling for bricks, not occupation.[8] Chinese blue-and-white ware has also been found on the site.

The latest excavations have uncovered material that dates from the second century B.C. to the fifteenth century A.D. Seventeenth- to eighteenth-century artifacts have also been found, but they are related to the French mission built on one side of the site. Stray nineteenth- and twentieth-century artifacts have also been found on the surface.

Begley (1992, personal communication) once suggested that the site had been abandoned and reoccupied several times during its history, perhaps responding to circumstances arising from shifting sandbars at the mouth of the river. Although a site can be occupied serially in this way, it is not clear why glass and stone beadmakers would leave, only to return centuries later on several occasions. This is particularly true because there are no important raw materials (except for sand) at Arikamēḍu. This suggests that Arikamēḍu was continuously occupied from at least the second or third century B.C. to much more recent times. During this occupation, Indo-Pacific beads were being made there. The abandonment of Arikamēḍu is discussed later in this chapter.

Karaikadu

Karaikadu (also called Kudikadu and Nattamedu), is some 40 km south of Arikamēḍu and just south of Cuddalore. It is adjacent to a backwater lagoon of the Bay of Bengal that could have provided anchorage. Ceramics, both imported amphorae and "rouletted ware"[9] (long associated with Arikamēḍu), recall the Arikamēḍu assemblage. Beadmaking in glass and stone was also carried on there. K.V. Raman (1975, 1991) briefly excavated Karaikadu, tentatively dating it to the first century A.D.

Although Raman (1991, 129) considered Karaikadu as important as Arikamēḍu in "extent, location and cultural context," it was not occupied very long. It is unknown whether glass was made there or Indo-Pacific beads were just finished there. The chemical similarity between glass beads from Arikamēḍu and Karaikadu suggests the latter (see Appendix B). As a port, it does not compare with Arikamēḍu. It did not exist during what is called the "pre-urban" phase at Arikamēḍu; it was founded only after Arikamēḍu had established contact with Rome (S. Gupta 1995–1996, 56). Perhaps it was a "satellite town" for a century or so. Only more extensive excavation will clarify its historic position. However, because of the industrial building going on there now, that seems a remote possibility for the near future.

The Spread of Indo-Pacific Beadmaking: First Stage

In the early first millennium A.D., perhaps by the late first or early second century, Indo-Pacific beads were being made at four places other than Arikamēḍu and Karaikadu. These sites are now known as Mantai (Sri Lanka), Oc Eo (Vietnam), Khlong Thom or Khuan Lukpad (Thailand), and Kuala Selinsing (Malaysia) (Figure 4.1).

Mantai is in northwest Sri Lanka, controlling access to the Palk Strait from the west. In Singhalese it is called Mahātittha or "Great Port." It acted as the "western gate" to the Palk Strait and the port for Anurādhapura, the ancient capital, to which it was connected by river and road. It was occupied in the early centuries A.D., certainly by the second (Carswell 1983; Carswell and Prickett 1984; Dewaraja 1990a; Prickett-Fernando 1990; Silva and Bouzek 1990).

W. J. S. Boake first excavated Mantai in 1887. Six other excavations have been conducted since, the last and most extensive by Carswell, who began full-scale excavations in 1980. Work was interrupted by hostilities in the region. In 1986, he asked me to catalog the Mantai beads. It was soon evident that Mantai was not only an important hub of trade, but also a site of Indo-Pacific beadmaking. Although sporadic references to the Mantai port continued into the fifteenth century (Perera 1951, 112–113), the city was largely abandoned—or at least international trade had ceased—soon after the Cōḷa depredations at the end of the tenth century.[10] No imported ceramics later than the eleventh century have been found (Carswell 1983, 85; Carswell and Prickett 1984, 57–59).

Oc Eo is at the southern end of Vietnam. Its relics were recognized as early as the 1870s, but not systematically investigated until the 1942–1944 excavations by Louis Malleret. Those who believe it is too small to have been an important port (e.g., Hall 1982, 82 n. 5) have questioned his interpretation of the site. Work on Oc Eo and the surrounding area by the Vietnamese recommenced in 1982 (Le 1987). This has expanded the known size of the occupied area but raised questions about the role of the Oc Eo portion. Radiocarbon dating of recently uncovered sepulchers ran from 1,750 ± 50 B.P. (NC 82-BCX 2/1) to 1,470 ± 50 B.P. (NC 82-BCX b/A) or ca. A.D. 200 to 480.

Oc Eo was part of Funan.[11] Funan was the earliest organized state in Southeast Asia, first detailed by Pelliot (1903). Heavily Indianized, it was a key link in trade between India and China. For several centuries nearly all goods exchanged between these states passed through Funan. Funan was not simply a point of transfer. It also funneled the products of mainland Southeast Asia into this trading stream.

The precise role Oc Eo played is a matter of controversy. To Malleret it was the principal port, to others it was the capital city, and to Le it was chiefly a religious and burial center with a crafts quarter. It makes little difference to us, because it is clear that it was part of a large, diverse settlement where beadmaking was conducted. It was also at or near a major port that brought Oc Eo status goods from much of the known world.[12]

Oc Eo was an Indo-Pacific beadmaking site. Malleret (1962a, 243–271) reported the wasters he found in sufficient detail to mark the site as such, though he did not grasp the significance of what he had.[13] Glass analysis (Appendix B) confirms this.

The third site is in southwestern Thailand: Khlong

Thom, named after the *wat* ("temple") on whose grounds it is located. Locally it is called Khuan Lukpad (variously spelled) or "bead hill" because of the many beads looted there for the antiquities market. Looters have damaged the site heavily, and no full-scale excavation has ever been conducted there. Some artifacts are kept in a small museum at Wat Khlong Thom, though this collection contains items from other places as well.[14] The reports on the site and its beads (Rutnin and Ketudhat 1983; Veraprasert 1985; T. Srisuchat 1989; Bronson 1990) are based on limited or no excavations.

The glass wasters collected and excavated from Khlong Thom indicate that it was a site of Indo-Pacific beadmaking. Several glass analyses have been done for the site (Appendix B). The red glass generally resembles that of Arikamēḍu and Oc Eo, except that it often has a high alumina content. The one blue glass bead analyzed is quite different from blue glass at either of the other sites. Although the evidence for Khlong Thom beadmaking is still scanty, further scientific work there should clarify its role in Indo-Pacific beadmaking.

Khlong Thom has recently yielded early artifacts. These include first-to second-century glass mosaic beads with human faces (A. Srisuchat 1987), a touchstone with a Tamil inscription of the third century (A. Srisuchat 1996b, 250), and seals from the first to seventh centuries. The inscriptions on the seals include one in Brāhmī, a northern script used in South India, and six in the southern Pallava script (Veeraprajak 1985, 132–133). These finds indicate occupation during the first half of the first

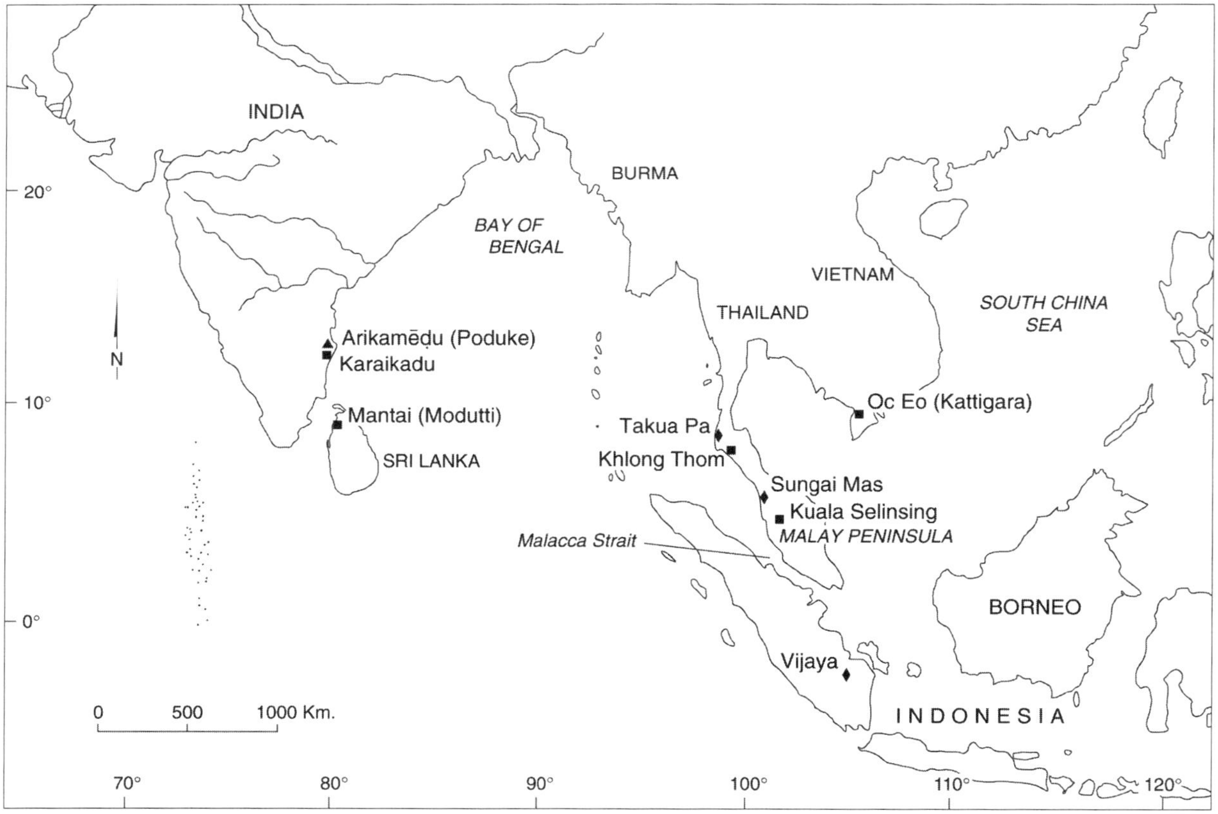

Figure 4.1. *Map of South and Southeast Asia showing the spread of Indo-Pacific beadmaking. The original site (Arikamēḍu) is marked with a triangle, early first millennium sites with squares, and later sites with diamonds.*

millennium A.D. Most recently, the occupation of Khlong Thom has been placed between the first and sixth centuries, divided into two periods (A. Srisuchat 1996b, 244–245).

Kuala Selinsing, Malaysia,[15] was mentioned in the last chapter as the first place where Evans (1928) and Beck (1930a) recognized Indo-Pacific beadmaking. Evans (1932, 88–90) originally dated the site from the sixth to the tenth or eleventh centuries. A few other excavations and explorations were carried out subsequently (see Nik Hassan 1991, 145–146). In 1963 Alastair and Venice Lamb along with B. A. V. Peacock[16] and Lord Medway made a number of visits to do some surface collecting. Among the finds was a gold-plated ear or nose ring similar to, but simpler than, one Evans had found earlier and was later lost. The India or Indianized decoration led Lamb (1964a, 167) to compare it with artifacts from Oc Eo.

Recent excavations at Kuala Selinsing (Pulau Kelumpang) by Nik Hassan Shuhaimi and Abdul Latib Ariffin began in 1988. Early results suggested dates from at least the second century B.C. to the tenth century A.D. (Nik Hassan 1991, 148); these have since been modified to the third century through the seventh or eighth centuries A.D. (Glover 1998, 30). The report of the finds of beryl, sodalite, moldavite, plasma, aventurine, cat's-eye, and jasper gems from this excavation (Tan and Samsudin 1990) has proven erroneous. One of these beads is carnelian and the others are glass.[17]

Malaysian archaeologists have assumed that Kuala Selinsing was not a trading port, but a center to gather jungle products and to make beads. However, a variety of recent finds, including ceramics similar to those at Oc Eo, a gold ring from India, a carnelian seal with a Sanskrit inscription from the fourth or fifth century, and glazed Chinese ceramics, suggests that it may have been a minor port of the Funanese state (Glover 1998, 30).

Correlations with Western Geographers

It is often difficult to correlate archaeological sites with names in historic records, though a few have been widely accepted. The complications are so notorious that some scholars have foregone any attempt to do so. However, this jeopardizes the potential value of combining historical and archaeological data into a picture of the past.

The correlations proposed here may not all be proven correct, but the exercise may stimulate thinking about these problems. Can the Indo-Pacific beadmaking sites of the early first millennium be identified with sites recorded contemporaneously in the West, in particular Ptolemy's *Geographia* (Stevenson 1991)?

It should be recognized that there are many problems working with *Geographia:* (1) Claudius Ptolemy was not a geographer but an astronomer and did not give us the sorts of details a geographer would, which in turn could help in identification. (2) He did not visit the places he listed, at least not in this region of the world. His information came from others, mostly sailors, and is at best secondhand. (3) His calculations of latitude and longitude, which look promising, were too far north by several degrees and too far west by even more. (4) The version that has been handed down to us had been edited, rearranged, and probably added to in Byzantine times and is not the original (Wheatley 1961, 138–139). Nonetheless, the exercise proved useful.

Virtually all writers on the subject have associated Arikamēḍu with Podouké of *Periplus* and Pôdouké of Ptolemy. The anonymous first-century mariner who wrote the *Periplus* did not travel beyond the Palk Strait but listed three ports from south to north on the east coast: Kamara, Podouké, and Sopatma. In the following century, Ptolemy's list of ports along this coast included Pôdouké Emporion.

A consensus already existed in the last century when McCrindle (1879, 143 n. 60) asserted that Podouké was Puduchchêri (more properly Putu-cēri), Tamil for "New Town," cognate with Pondicherry. Lassen and Yule equated it with Pulikat, near Madras, but Maliaphra of Ptolemy is more likely to have referred to the Madras (Mylapur) region (Raman 1991, 129–130). Most subsequent writers have used the "New Town" connection.

Mahadevan (1970) made a different case. He agreed that the *Periplus'* Kamara equals Ptolemy's Khabaris and Kāvēripaṭṭiṇam (Pūmpuhār), the great Cōḷa port. He equated the Periplus' Sopatma, not previously identified, with Ptolemy's Sobouras, and the Tamil Cō-paṭṭiṇam as modern Markanam. Arikamēḍu is some 100 km north of Kāvēripaṭṭiṇam and 35 km south of Cō-paṭṭiṇam, just where Podouké was supposed to be.

Ptolemy called Pôdouké an emporium. "Emporium" had a specific meaning for the Romans, ignored by those who argue that Roman subjects never lived at Arikamēḍu. Homer first used the word εμπορος *(emporos)* for a merchant who sailed on a ship belonging to someone else. By Roman times, it indicated a merchant who traded with countries beyond the Imperial frontiers. An "emporium" (εμποριον) could refer to any seaport, but was most often used to designate the area of a port in which the *emporos* resided. Within the Empire it was the merchant's residential quarter. Outside, it had the specific meaning of a group of Roman merchants living abroad (Huvelin 1904, 1733–1734; Peck 1962, 592).

Any doubt that once existed about Westerners living in Arikamēḍu can now be dispelled archaeologically. The fine Western tableware, *terra sigillata,* did not arrive in a single shipment as Stern (1991, 118) assumed, but is of sufficient variety to have been imported several times (Comfort 1991). Although Indians could have used it, it is unlikely that it would have been imported in the first place without a preexisting demand. Moreover, it is found in India only at Arikamēḍu. Just as telling is the importation of olive oil and *garum* (fish sauce), as evidenced by amphorae (Will 1991, 154). Some Indians would have welcomed wine, but olive oil and *garum* were foreign to their palates.

Three of the other five Indo-Pacific beadmaking sites of the early first millennium appear to have been emporia as well. Mantai has been widely identified as Ptolemy's Modutti on several grounds.[18] The archaeological evidence shows that Mantai was a central port for East-West trade,[19] and that suits Modutti as an emporium well.

As for Oc Eo, Malleret (1962a, 421–454) equated it with Ptolemy's Kattigara, and at least one writer perceived a consensus on this point (Chakravarti 1972, 110). The revisions of thought about the nature of Oc Eo do not substantially change this picture. The quantities of Western and Indian material recovered there indicate that if it was not the port proper, it was closely associated with it.

Khlong Thom is most likely Ptolemy's Takola. Ptolemy was not the only writer to mention this place; the port is also named in several ancient Asian documents and its identification has been a preoccupation of scholars for a century. Because of the similarity of names, Gerini (1909, 85–94) equated Takola with Takua Pa, in southwestern Thailand a little north of Phuket Island. However, Takua Pa (Khao Ko Kao) was only occupied during the ninth century (A. Srisuchat 1989; Bronson 1991) and could not have been Takola.

Braddell (1949) noted that Ptolemy's description would put Takola south of Phuket (Junk Ceylon) and suggested that it was somewhere near Trang. This argument quickly won over Nilakanta Sastri (1949, 25; 1978, 172–173). It has gained in currency and has been accepted by Wheatley (1961, 272) and several other scholars (see Braddell 1980, 40). The problem Braddell had with his own identification was that in the 1940s there was no archaeological site of the proper age with indication of foreign commerce in the area. However, Khlong Thom, though closer to Krabi than Trang, fits the description quite well, with Roman and Early Historic Indian artifacts, as noted earlier.

I shall not propose any correlations for Karaikadu or Kuala Selinsing. The former was apparently not occupied for very long and may not have been noticed by the Romans. If the latter were founded in the third century, it would be too late for Ptolemy to have included it. Its geographic situation makes it unlikely to have been a major port, nor have any Roman materials been located there yet.

Links Between the Early Indo-Pacific Beadmaking Sites

These contemporary Indo-Pacific beadmaking sites must have been in contact with each other. There is no problem assuming either a Karaikadu-Arikamēḍu link or contact between them and Mantai.

Commerce between India and Southeast Asia was well established. The historic development of Southeast

Asia owes a debt to India. This was once presumed to have taken the form of colonization by Indians and the building of "Greater India" (e.g., Majumdar 1944). This hypothesis is no longer considered valid. Rather, Indian ideas of religion and government, scripts and art styles, and other cultural elements were borrowed and transformed by the indigenous people (possibly first by the aristocracy). The "Indianization" of Southeast Asia was a reality, but does not indicate hegemony.

The Indo–Southeast Asian contact also led to the sharing of technological ideas and processes, including Indo-Pacific beadmaking. To envision Arikamēḍu beadmakers emigrating to nearby Karaikadu and Mantai requires no leap of imagination. However, we must consider why and how they went to the other places.

The other three sites were evidently incorporated into or at least aligned with the state of Funan. No matter how Oc Eo functioned, it must have been an industrial center close to a major port. Takola (Khlong Thom) was likely a part of Funan as well (Wheatley 1961, 14–25) and probably its major western port (Coedès 1968, 41). The evidence from Kuala Selinsing also suggests a Funanese connection (Glover 1998, 30).

Aside from archaeological finds, we know Funan only from scattered Chinese accounts. In the early third century a new king was chosen or ratified by popular acclaim, the renowned warrior Fan Shiman. He consolidated his hold over the Mekong Delta and then subjugated the Chams and other territories to the north. With a fleet of Malay sailors he expanded Funan farther by conquering "more than ten kingdoms," including Tunsun that "curves round and projects into the sea more than 1000 *li*." His conquests are said to have expanded his kingdom by 5,000 to 6,000 *li* (2,000 miles or 3,200 km). He laid plans to invade what is now Myanmar (Burma), but died before he could carry them out (Wheatley 1961, 14–15; Hall 1985, 63–65).

It is impossible to pinpoint the three kingdoms mentioned in the texts (see Wheatley 1961, 15–25), but the description of Tunsun curving around and projecting into the sea certainly fits the upper Malay Peninsula, and the entire peninsula may have been involved. Six thousand *li* would not be a bad estimate of the coastline from Oc Eo to Singapore. Whatever the extent of the annexed territory, it gave Funan the chance to trade not only with China but also India, as both coasts of the peninsula were acquired.

The Indian connection was important and grew over time. Before Funan annexed them, the peninsular chiefdoms already had strong connections with India, including Indians living in them. Sanskrit soon became a common language (at least of the court) in the older part of Funan. The first known Sanskrit inscription was written shortly after Fan Shiman's death, and Chinese envoys visiting in 240 found a Sanskrit vocabulary and Indian-derived technologies. In the fifth century, the new king chosen to rule Funan was the ruler of Panpan (apparently farther south than Tunsun), who "changed all the rules according to the custom of India" (Hall 1985, 67–69).

Indo-Pacific beadmaking may be viewed as part of this process, and the earlier "Indianization" of the peninsula may explain the distribution of beadmaking sites: one at or near the capital and the other two on the peninsula. The physical emigration of Indian beadmakers is the most likely explanation of the industry being there. Even someone familiar with working glass could not have easily copied the complex technology needed to make these beads. In addition, there is no indication of other glassmaking in Funan[20] (except perhaps the hexagonal bicones discussed in chapter 13).

Glassmakers and beadmakers move around. It is often said that this is because they have run out of raw materials, notably wood for their fires. A recent study of this phenomenon shows that other factors were more commonly at work (Francis 1994a). Beadmakers move primarily for political, social, and even personal reasons. However, such a radical overseas move from such motives does not seem likely. Khlong Thom, Sungai Mas, and Oc Eo are far from southeastern India. It would have required knowledge of far-off lands, money for transportation, and contacts to set up in a strange, new place.

Would the beadmakers have undertaken such a move themselves? Indian beadmakers are—and presumably were—of low status, neither well educated nor the masters of their own products. Beadmakers are low caste.[21] In British times, glass bead- and bangle makers in Tamil Nadu were the Valaiyal, a subdivision of the Kavarai. In other parts of Dravidia they were called Guzula, a subdivision of the Balija. The Kavarai and the Balija are equivalent and occupied low positions (Baines 1912, 97).[22] As seen in the last chapter, the beadmakers of modern Papanaidupet do not control the manufacturing or the commerce in beads.

The low status of beadmakers suggests that someone else with some degree of control over them decided to have them move and implemented it. One possibility is a government, but this assumes an official link between the sites, for which there is no other evidence. It is more likely that the link was unofficial or quasi-official and mercantile. This is hypothetical, but the picture becomes clearer in later history of the industry.

The Spread of Indo-Pacific Beadmaking: Second Stage

The crucial position of Funan in international trade as agent between China and the West (mostly India) came to an end during the seventh century A.D. The demise of the state was a long process during which Chenla (Cambodia) incursions weakened and eventually conquered the once-wealthy kingdom.

The role of Sino-Indian intermediary fell to a new state, Srivijaya. First recognized by Coedès (1918; 1968), Srivijaya was a polity with its capital at Palembang, Sumatra. It controlled Sumatra, the Malay Peninsula, and parts of Java. Its control of the Malacca Strait and much of the Malay Peninsula ensured its position in commerce (Figure 4.1).

Nearly everything about Srivijaya's history has been controversial. There is argument over whether it was a kingdom, an empire, a state, or a confederation. For years, these and other questions were the center of intense debate. Several conferences were held on Srivijaya, including four by SPAFA.[23] Chand (1987) wanted to place Srivijaya in Thailand. Others believed that Srivijaya never existed except in the imagination of Coedès.

However, the debate has turned in favor of those who champion Srivijaya based in Sumatra with Palembang as its capital. Historians, beginning with Wolters (1967; 1970), have shown that if Srivijaya did not exist, we would have had to invent it. Work by other historians (Y. Liu and Lapian 1991; Ikuta 1991) has confirmed Coedès' thesis.

Even more impressive is the archaeological evidence. Although Bronson and Wisseman (1976) found nothing to verify an ancient city at Palembang, more recent work has. The large-scale excavations under Pierre-Yves Manguin by Pusat Penelitian Arkeologi Nasional (National Center for Archaeological Research) have found unequivocal evidence of a major city. Artifacts include foundations of large buildings, inscriptions, ceramics dating from early in the Tang period (A.D. 618–906), and other impressive finds (Manguin 1987; 1992; 1993). In addition, two seaworthy wooden ships radiocarbon dated to the seventh century have been recovered (Ambary 1991).

The work has also located areas in which beadmaking and finishing were done. One is Kambang Unglen, where ceramics of the early Tang period and evidence for making Indo-Pacific and other beads is abundant.

Srivijaya filled the vacuum in commercial relations left by the fall of Funan. Indo-Pacific beadmakers also began working in Srivijaya, but exactly when is not now discernible. What mechanism was involved in their settling there remains to be learned.

Vijaya (used hereafter for the capital of Srivijaya, as it may have been called historically)[24] was not the only place within Srivijaya where Indo-Pacific and other beads were made. Two other sites, both in the lower Malay Peninsula, have been identified as sites of Indo-Pacific beadmaking: Sungai Mas in Malaysia and Takua Pa in Thailand (Figure 4.1).[25]

Sungai Mas ("Golden River") in Kedah is in the estuaries of the Muda and Merbok Rivers (Plate 27). Overlooking the area like a sentry on duty is Gunung Jerai (Kedah Peak). Up this mountain and in the surrounding lowlands are Hindu and Buddhist temples dating back to the fourth and fifth centuries. Inscriptions of similar dates have also been found. The area was first explored and recorded by James Low in the 1840s, but the wealth of remains was not recognized until a century later (Wales 1940). Many Malaysian and foreign scholars have studied it subsequently (see Chandran and Baharuddin 1980; Nik Hassan and Kamaruddin 1993).

The Muda-Merbok estuary is in constant flux. Its topography has changed several times since the first temples were built on Gunung Jerai and continues to change (Miksic 1977; J. Allen 1991). As geomorphic alteration occurred, including modifications of river drainages, major settlements shifted. Sungai Mas was the regional center in the tenth and eleventh centuries. Pengkalan Bujang, occupied from about the eleventh to fourteenth centuries, succeeded it.[26]

Takua Pa, in southwestern Thailand, was not ancient Takola, as discussed earlier in this chapter. The most recent excavations (A. Srisuchat 1989; Bronson 1990) show that Takua Pa was occupied only in the early ninth century A.D. Because of its short life span, it is noteworthy that it was an Indo-Pacific beadmaking site and made other glass beads as well (see chap. 10). The site is not at the village of Takua Pa proper, but on Khao Ko Kao (*kao* is "island" in Thai) in the wide Takua Pa River.

Takua Pa was only occupied in the ninth century. Beadmaking evidence disappeared at Sungai Mas by the end of the eleventh century. The end of production at Vijaya (Palembang) may have come when the capital was shifted to Jambi, which Wolters (1970, 90) puts between 1079 and 1082.

Glass for Indo-Pacific Beads

A question to consider is the origin of the glass for Indo-Pacific beads made at different centers. As discussed in the last chapter, beadmakers are not necessarily glassmakers. They may either make their own glass or use glass that has been made elsewhere. There are several possibilities of how glass came to be used for beadmaking at the Indo-Pacific sites. These include:

1. The glass was made outside Asia and imported as scrap glass or cakes. The Middle East or Mediterranean lands are thought to be the source of the glass itself. This is the position taken by Lamb (1965a) and Stern (1987, 1991), among others.
2. All the glass was made at one Indo-Pacific beadmaking site and sent to the other sites to be made into beads. The logical single source would be Arikamēḍu, the oldest and longest-lived of all these sites.
3. Glass was made at each Indo-Pacific beadmaking site independently. Similar recipes may or may not have been used.
4. Glass was made at regional centers for Indo-Pacific beadmaking sites at different times, for example at Arikamēḍu serving South Asia, Oc Eo serving Funan, and Vijaya serving Srivijayan sites.

One way to approach this question is to consider the analyses of glass pieces or beads from Indo-Pacific beadmaking sites to determine how similar or different they are. Several analyses from South and Southeast Asian sites have been published previously. In addition, a series of analyses done by Ron Hancock with the SLOWPOKE-2[27] nuclear reactor at the University of Toronto used samples I collected from Indo-Pacific beadmaking sites. The detailed results of these analyses are tabulated in Appendix B. Here only a summary of the more significant findings is presented.

1. The glass for Indo-Pacific beads is certainly not derived from Western glass, confirming my earlier conclusion (Francis 1988–1989, 5–11). Several differences exist between the glass of these two regions: (a) Red Indo-Pacific glass does not contain lead, a very rare occurrence for red glass in the West. (b) The non-red glass of Arikamēḍu is usually potash-based, a type of glass found in European glass only after about A.D. 1000. (c) Srivijayan and, to a lesser extent, Funanese glass is unusually high in aluminum, often more than 10 percent. Srivijayan glass is also generally very low in magnesium, lower even than the "low magnesium" glass of the West during the first century (Sayre and Smith 1967, 281–293).
2. There are considerable differences in the glasses of the different sites, though some

sites seem to have shared glass production or at least technology: (a) Arikamēḍu and Karaikadu, which were contemporary and are located very close to each other, used either the same glass or the same recipes and ingredients. Most remarkable was the use of potash and the special colorant for the dark blue glass, discussed in point 3 below. (b) Oc Eo and Khlong Thom, contemporary Funanese sites, also have similar glasses. The glass is probably soda-based, though potash measurements for Oc Eo are not available, and tends to be high in aluminum. (c) Kuala Selinsing, also in Funan, has distinct glass. It is very high in aluminum, very low in manganese, and the total amount of alkalies is often quite low. (d) The glasses of Vijaya, Sungai Mas, and Takua Pa look similar. It is quite possible that the glass for all three sites was made at the same place.

3. The translucent, dark blue glass beads at Arikamēḍu and Karaikadu have elevated amounts of manganese (about 1.5 percent) in a potassium glass, which, with small amounts of cobalt, yields the color. Some blue Indo-Pacific beads of Oc Eo may have followed the same formula (Malleret 1962a, table 7).[28] This is also seen at Khlong Thom and Takua Pa, though they are both soda glasses. This is an unusual, virtually unique, formula for dark blue glass.[29]

The colorant of this dark blue glass is of special interest. Cobalt is a very powerful colorant and only tiny amounts (0.025 percent) are needed to impart a deep blue to glass (Turner 1959, 273T–281T). It is unlikely that the cobalt was introduced as an ore, because cobalt ores are arsenic-rich (J. D. M. Smith 1942), and this is clearly not from an arsenic-cobalt ore. Moreover, cobalt ores are extremely rare in India and none is reported for the peninsula (Wadia 1990, 442). The high level of manganese is the key. India is a major manganese producer. There are several sources in the peninsula, and in the form of wad (bog manganese) it is available in the Vishakapatnam District of Andhra Pradesh (Wadia 1990, 104, 449–450), in the same region that probably yielded most semiprecious stones for the Arikamēḍu lapidaries. Cobalt is commonly found in wad and was probably introduced along with the manganese (Davison 1972, 343–345).

Wad containing cobalt and wad not containing cobalt were used for dark blue and violet glass, respectively. The people who supplied wad to the glassmakers most likely knew these properties through feedback from the glassmakers and identified regions in which the appropriate wad was found.

It may have been that Indian wad was exported to some Indo-Pacific beadmakers, because it might have been used for dark blue glass at Oc Eo, Khlong Thom, and Takua Pa. It was also used in dark blue beads from Gilimanuk and Sembiran (Ardika 1995), Bali. These beads were no doubt imports from Arikamēḍu.[30]

The Beadmakers

The beadmakers themselves were unlikely to have been anyone other than southern Indians, either Tamils or Pandukal people. They would not have taught the craft to anyone else under normal circumstances, because it was the basis of their livelihood. Nor is it an easily transferable technique. Indo-Pacific beadmaking was probably a well-guarded secret.

As discussed earlier in this chapter, the movement of these beadmakers suggests influence outside their immediate community. These migrations seem to have been well coordinated and were always associated with major cities (except perhaps Kuala Selinsing). The rulers of the places to which they migrated must have at least consented to the moves or even invited them.

Because of the low status of the beadmakers, they would have required a representative with connections to the governing authorities to speak for them. The common mechanisms for this in South India were organized groups of traders, generally called “guilds” in European languages, which were extremely powerful. In some cases they governed cities, issued money, and had their own armies or police forces. At least some guild members also enjoyed such vital privileges as riding in a palanquin, using the royal umbrella, and having a cloth to walk upon (Verma 1972, 80–81). Guilds were an important link in the economic well-being of Indian states.

Of the known South Indian guilds, two were celebrated for international trade, the *Ayyāvoḷe* and the Maṇikgrāman,[31] both variously spelled (Verma 1972, 79; Christie 1998, 2–3). The latter is associated with at least two Srivijayan Indo-Pacific beadmaking centers.

An inscription found near a group of sculptures, both of which apparently originated from Takua Pa, underlines the importance of the Maṇikgrāman. Nilakanta Sastri (1949, 28–29; 1978, 172–173) transcribed and translated it; it reads in part, "The tank built by Nangur-udaiyan (and) called Avani-naranam (is placed under) the protection of the Manikkiramam, the residents of the military camp. . . ."

Coedès gave a slightly different reading (Veeraprajak 1985, 133, 140), and Lamb (1964b, 80) mentioned some unidentified "imaginative speculation" in earlier translations. However, there is no dispute that the guards of the Maṇikgrāman provided security for the tank (a stone or brick structure designed to capture water during the rainy season and hold it for later use). Coedès dated the inscription to the seventh century (Veeraprajak 1985, 133), but Nilakanta Sastri and Lamb opted for the ninth, which we know now from excavations is correct. The tank itself was discovered recently (A. Srisuchat 1989, 36).

The Maṇikgrāman was apparently also prominent at Vijaya. There are several inscriptions uncovered from the excavations at Palembang that attest to this (J. G. de Casparis, 1991, personal communication).

Members of the Maṇikgrāman guild had wide contacts both within India and internationally and some are known to have lived abroad. It was a trading guild, without reference to the religion of its members (some of whom appear to have been Christians). It endowed a number of temples and collected customs duties. It also controlled five craft guilds and oil pressers (Appadorai 1936, 398–402; Verma 1972, 81; *Annual Report on Indian Epigraphy* 1986, 101–102). Beadmaking could have been one of the unidentified crafts.

The name Maṇikgrāman is highly suggestive. *Grāman* means "guild." *Maṇik* is derived from the Sanskrit *maṇikya*,[32] meaning "precious stone." It evolved into the Hindi *maṇi* and *maṇek*, meaning "bead"; the Tamil *maṇikam*, meaning "precious stone"; and the Malay and Indonesian *manik*, meaning "bead" (usually in the plural, *manik-manik*), and *manikam*, meaning "precious stone." The name Maṇikgrāman may not mean any more than "Diamond Matches," but the assumption that this guild dealt in beads as well as precious stones[33] is at least plausible.

The Maṇikgrāman was in an excellent position to be acquainted with Indo-Pacific beadmakers, coordinate their moves, and communicate between them and local rulers. They had the capital to finance moves, the contacts to make them feasible, and the opportunity to be in touch with rulers. They also had the marketing network to distribute the beads. This is a hypothesis, but it makes sense of the information available, some of which is otherwise difficult to explain. Who initiated these transplants and for what motives are important questions that cannot be solved with the current data.

It should also be noted that the Maṇikgrāman may not have existed in the early centuries B.C. The oldest inscription referring to the guild in India is from the late ninth century (Appadorai 1936, 390; Christie 1998, 2). The Takua Pa inscription may even be the oldest.

Although the foregoing is a more elaborately defined hypothesis than that proposed by Lamb (1965b, 95), it is not much different. He deserves credit for his prophetic words, "One is tempted to postulate, as with the stone beads, the existence of something like a nomadic bead making group, perhaps of Indian origin, which established itself at various South-east Asian centres where a bead demand existed."

The Later Years

Indo-Pacific beads ceased being made at Mantai in the tenth or eleventh century, with the virtual abandonment of the site. Southeast Asian production under Srivijaya stopped by A.D. 1100, as seen in the decline of the beadmaking centers and the concurrent drastic downturn in the Indo-Pacific bead trade, which is examined in the next chapter.

Yet, Indo-Pacific beads continued to be made. They were exported in quantity to Africa, and their continual production is evident in the preservation of the industry at modern Papanaidupet. The question is where the industry survived.

Carswell (1983, 85) thought that many citizens of Mantai might have gone to Nagapattinam when Mantai was abandoned. Nagapattinam was the leading port in Southeast India at the time and it had close connections with Srivijaya, as shown by inscriptions on the southern wall of the Rājarājaeśvara (or Bṛhad Īśvara) temple in Tanjore, sometimes called the "Leiden plates" (Nilakanta Sastri 1935, 224). J. Lavanha, writing in Mozambique about the importation of Indo-Pacific beads,[34] said in 1593, "[These beads] are made in India at Negapatam, whence they are brought to Mozambique and there they reach these negroes through the Portuguese who exchange them for ivory" (Theal 1898, 303).

However, there is no evidence for beadmaking, glassmaking, or glassworking at Nagapattinam. A thorough surface survey under my supervision in 1988 found Chinese and Islamic potsherds and a European clay pipe, but no indication of any sort of glassworking.

The recent excavations at Arikamēḍu indicate that it was occupied for a long time, with ceramics dating to at least the fifteenth century. By 1765, when Le Gentil described it as a ruin and a source of bricks for Virampatnam, it was certainly abandoned, but how long before that time cannot be surmised from his report.

In Papanaidupet, no oral tradition of its founding could be traced. The name means "Naidu's New Village" (Naidu is a common surname). No one in Papanaidupet had heard of "Old Naidupet."

The earliest historic reference to Papanaidupet is among letters written by Jesuits in southern India collected by Samuel Purchas: "Simon Sa writes from Meliapor [Madras], the twentieth of November, 1598, amongst many other things of Paparagiu, which in one house kept three hundred Brachmans [Brahmans] and gave hospitalitie to the Pilgrims which went to, or came from Tripiti, a famous Idoll three miles from Chandegrin. They purge their sinnes by washing their bodies and shaving their heads and beards" (Pimenta 1905, 219 [insertions mine]). Chandegrin is Chandragiri, then the seat of the Vijayanagar Empire. The "Idoll" three miles away is at the Tirumala Temple at Tirupati, a well-known pilgrimage destination, where one must still wash and shave the head to visit. Papanaidupet (Paparagiu) is a day's journey on foot from Tirupati, toward the mountain gap later exploited by the Renigunta railhead. Hence, the village was established by 1598.

In 1593, Lavanha said that Indo-Pacific beads were exported from Nagapattinam. A look at a map of South India at that time (Figure 4.2) shows that Indo-Pacific beadmakers would not have been in Papanaidupet then, because if they had been, their beads would not have been exported from Nagapattinam but from nearby São Tomé/Mylapur[35] (St. Thomas/Madras). São Tomé was then the richest settlement in Portuguese India (Danvers

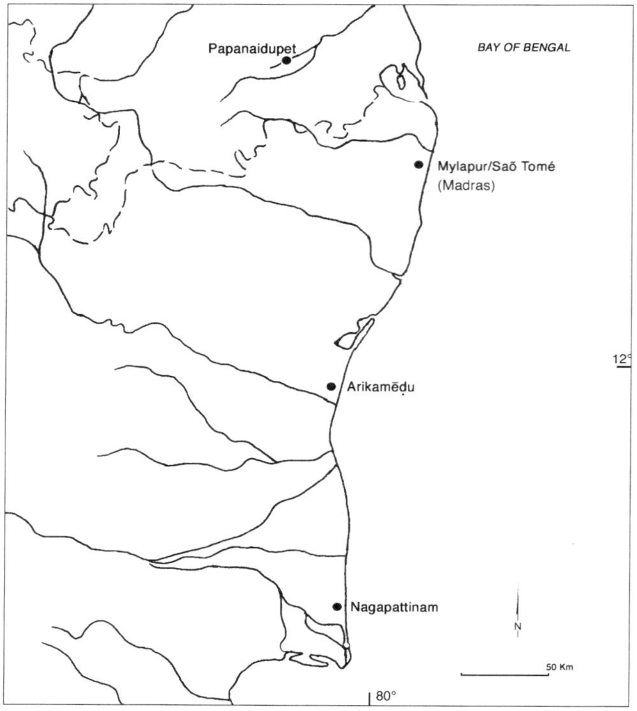

Figure 4.2. *Map of Southeast India showing the relative locations of Papanaidupet, Madras, Arikamēḍu, and Nagapattinam.*

1892, 39–40). Caesar Frederick (1905, 109) described its bustling port in 1567. Beads would certainly have been exported from there if they had been made at Papanaidupet.

Nagapattinam is considerably south of Madras, even south of Arikamēḍu. Because Nagapattinam exported the beads, but did not make them, they must have been made nearby. The best candidate[36] is Arikamēḍu.

This helps date the abandonment of Arikamēḍu, with a *terminus post quem* of 1593 (Lavanha's statement) and a *terminus ante quem* of 1734, when the French first recorded brick robbing (Faucheux 1946, 2). Arikamēḍu was most likely abandoned sometime in the seventeenth century, by which time we know Papanaidupet was established. A possible attraction may have been Papanaidupet's proximity (3 km away) to Gudar (Gụdimallam), whose good sand is still exploited for glass.

There are two possible linguistic connections between Arikamēḍu and the Papanaidupet region. One is at Gudimallam. This village is an old center with temple inscriptions dating back to at least the 1050s (Rangacharya 1985, 496). It was once called Vippirambedu (Rangacharya 1985, 496), but whether this can be linked to **Vīrai-y-am-paṭṭiṇam* or Virampatnam (*bedu* is "place" and *paṭṭiṇam* is "port" or "coastal city") remains to be learned.

The other connection comes from Le Gentil (1779, 111). In 1765, the local people told him that the Arikamēḍu ruins were the fort of a king or great man, one Vira-Raguen. The Vira part we know. If Raguen is cognate with "ragiu" of Simon Sa's Paparagiu (Papanaidupet) the population shift from Arikamēḍu—but not the beadmakers, at least not all of them—to Papanaidupet may have begun before 1598.

The Indo-Pacific bead industry produced one of the, if not the, most widespread and ubiquitous trade item of all time, surviving well over 2,000 years. Over the millennia, the beads were made in at least ten places now located in six modern nations: Arikamēḍu, Karaikadu, Mantai, Oc Eo, Khlong Thom, Kuala Selinsing, Vijaya, Takua Pa, Sungai Mas, and Papanaidupet, nearly all of which were important ports and nodes in international trade. The exceptions were Kuala Selinsing (which may not have been a port of much importance) and Papanaidupet. The precise status of Karaikadu is still unknown.

The study of these small beads may furnish clues to wider questions being asked by scholars about the past. They have the potential to generate hypotheses about the historical relations between people. The next chapter continues this theme with an overview of the trade in Indo-Pacific and related beads.

5

Indo-Pacific Bead By-Products and the Distribution of the Beads

Indo-Pacific beadmakers made not only the small beads described in the last two chapters, but others as well. The other bead types depended on the Indo-Pacific industry's ability to draw tubes. Thus, they are by-products or derived products of the main industry.

Indo-Pacific Bead By-Products

As with Indo-Pacific beads, these beads share a crucial trait: they were made from drawn glass tubes. However, with these beads the tubes were either specially prepared or finished differently than for Indo-Pacific beads. This chapter identifies these by-products of the industry,[1] with notes on their distribution.

Collar Beads

These beads have extra material surrounding both apertures, the so-called "collars" (Plate 28). Their bodies take different forms, but all have appendages at both ends.

The design is not exclusive to the Indo-Pacific bead industry. Faience and stone collar beads with gadrooned bodies were excavated at Ur from the third millennium B.C. (Woolley 1934, 366, fig. 21). One of faience was found at second millennium B.C. Mohenjo-Daro (Mackay 1938, pls. 136.58, 138.8). A few collar beads are said to be from the first millennium B.C. around the Mediterranean (Wheeler et al. 1946, 98). They are also known from North India. Taxila (Beck 1941), now in Pakistan, had several, of clay, shell, agate, garnet, and glass, ranging from the third century B.C. to the first century A.D.[2] The glass one, at least (Beck 1941, fig. IX.14), looks as though it came directly from Arikamēḍu. The shape was used for some gold-glass beads made in Egypt in the early centuries A.D. (Boon 1977, 194). They may well have been inspired from South Indian models.[3] Collars are employed on silver and other metal beads in a number of places. Some nineteenth- or twentieth-century Venetian lamp-wound beads were collared.

However, as a distinct style and specific bead type, collar beads are South Indian. Van der Sleen (1973, 74) asserted that they were never found outside India. This is not entirely correct, but they are far more common in South India than anywhere else. They can be made from any material, but faience, semiprecious stones (Francis 1986b; see also chap. 12), and glass were most widely employed.

Glass and stone collar beads were made in such numbers at Arikamēḍu that it must have been their principal place of manufacture. The evidence for local making is substantial and thus far only found there.[4] Stone collar beads are discussed in chapter 12, and glass ones here.

Wheeler et al. (1946, 96) devoted far more space to collar beads than any other beads in their Arikamēḍu report. They were divided into "grooved collars," simple tubes with grooves around both ends, and "lug collars," with flattened bodies and prominent collars on the ends. They concluded that the grooved collar beads predated the lug-collared ones. Dikshit (Sankalia and Dikshit 1952, 92–93) agreed, after examining collar beads from Arikamēḍu, Taxila, Koṇḍāpūr, and Brahmapuri. However, the recent Arikamēḍu excavation does not confirm this. Both types appear simultaneously in the earliest levels excavated.

Making grooved collar beads was a simple operation. A tube was reheated and a small tool, the edge of a paddle, or a wire formed a groove at the end and another one a centimeter or so along the length. The tube was then cooled and cut apart. The beads were afterward heated and tumbled in the same manner as Indo-Pacific beads.

The production of lug collar beads is not as easily envisioned, because the diameter of the bead is greater than that of the collars. Experiments suggest that a glass tube was heated and stretched out into a spindle shape. At either end of the spindle, where the tube's diameter was diminishing, the tube was grooved and the excess ends cut off. Then the bead was flattened into its final shape (Figure 5.1).

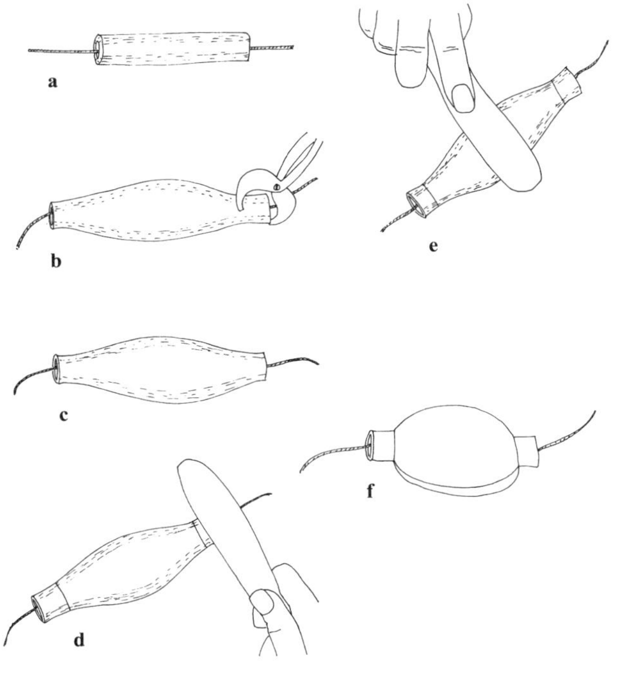

Figure 5.1. *Proposed method for making a lug collar bead. A section of a glass tube* (a) *is heated and stretched at both ends, perhaps with a pincer* (b). *This results in thinner ends* (c), *which are scored off from the body* (d). *The body is then flattened* (e) *and a lug collar bead* (f) *results. Sketch by Bo Breda.*

Collar beads are found at the other early first millennium Indo-Pacific beadmaking sites (except, to date, Karaikadu). They are so scarce at Mantai that they were probably imports. Collar beads like those at Arikamēḍu are also scarce at Oc Eo. However, Oc Eo has collar beads of larger diameter and somewhat different shape, being circular in outline. These might have been made there. Otherwise, there is no suggestion of manufacturing anywhere other than Arikamēḍu. Wherever the common small Arikamēḍu types are found, it is a strong indication of trade with that port.

Paddled Beads

Paddled beads were made from translucent green or blue green tubes. They were reheated and manipulated (probably with a flat metal paddle) into square, rectangular, and hexagonal tubes or small bicones. Evidence for their manufacture is abundant at Arikamēḍu, but absent elsewhere (Plate 29).

The hexagonal beads may have been imitation beryl crystals. Pliny (Eichholz 1962, 227) claimed that Indians had invented a way to stain quartz to imitate beryl, so highly esteemed in the early centuries of the Roman Empire. The only ancient sources for beryl were South India and Sri Lanka, and even the name is derived from Sanskrit (Warmington 1928, 250–251).

Trowbridge (1930, 81–83) questioned the feasibility of staining quartz crystal and suggested that Pliny was referring to glass imitations. The green staining of quartz is a doubtful operation (Kurt Nassau, 1996, personal communication). Some green quartz was found at Arikamēḍu. However, it is apparently the result of a botched operation to turn poorly colored amethyst into golden citrine.[5]

Hexagonal paddled glass tubes are not all that common at Arikamēḍu, nor are they particularly good beryl imitations. They would not have fooled Pliny, but may have been welcomed by Roman commoners as substitutes. Better lapidary-made imitations are known from

Ban Don Ta Phet, Thailand, and a few other places (Glover 1990b, 13–14; Basa et al. 1991, 371; Glover and Henderson 1995, 149).

Pinched Beads

This term describes beads that have been pinched from the ends of reheated tubes. No one knows what tool was used for this, but examination shows that the glass was manipulated at each end and pulled toward the apertures.[6] These beads are usually oblates or bicones. After a bead was shaped, it was reheated to smooth the ends (Plate 30).

Pinched beads are larger than Indo-Pacific beads, usually a centimeter or more in diameter, and this is precisely why they were pinched. It is not possible to make a large, round bead by cutting a segment of a tube and tumbling it. This works for small-diameter tubes, but once the diameter reaches a certain size (about a centimeter), tumbling only bevels the bead and does not make it round.[7]

There was obviously a market for beads in sizes larger than Indo-Pacific beads. Pinched beads satisfied the demand.

Only one pinched bead has been recorded from Arikamēḍu, and they were probably not made there. They are found at Kuala Selinsing, where they might have been made. At Sungai Mas there was a broken and unreheated example suggesting local manufacture. At Mantai and Oc Eo there were waste tubes of large diameters as well as finished beads. Both places quite likely produced them. They appear to have been principally products of Funanese beadmakers.

Square Drawn Tubes

The square cross section was evidentially achieved before the tube was drawn rather than being paddled into shape from rounded tubes. With the *lada* method, one would have to begin with a square cone of glass (Plate 31).

Square tubes are found at Mantai, Oc Eo, Khlong Thom, and other sites in mainland Southeast Asia, China, Korea, and Sarawak. Among Indo-Pacific beadmaking sites, they are in greatest numbers at Sungai Mas, Oc Eo, and Khlong Thom. Eight green ones were placed in the tomb of King Muryong of the Paekche Kingdom at Kongju, Korea. The king was buried in A.D. 526 (Francis 1985b, 12).

Striped Drawn Beads

Adding lines of color to the glass cone before drawing it out into a tube results in beads with longitudinal lines of contrasting color (Plate 32). Blue on white beads are the only ones of this type currently made at Papanaidupet.

Striped drawn beads are found in small numbers at many sites, including most Indo-Pacific beadmaking sites, but only two can be confirmed to have made them. At Mantai a tube end with stripes of several different colors on a black body was excavated from an area with other beadmaking waste. At Takua Pa, dark blue beads with six to ten thin white stripes were apparently locally made. Wasters from there included a small clump of such beads and a bead collapsed from reheating. One appears to have been pinched or segmented from a tube. This suggests that it was not cut as Indo-Pacific beads were, but was made as a segmented bead. (Other segmented beads were made at Takua Pa; see chap. 10.)

Distribution of Indo-Pacific and Related Beads

Indo-Pacific beads are so widely distributed in time and place that a complete inventory of them is probably beyond the capacity of any one person. The full extent of their distribution[8] will not be known until beads are more widely cataloged as they are excavated. They have great potential to enlighten us about trade patterns in the past. Some notes on their distribution are offered here to demonstrate the information their study can generate.

The Long Reach of Arikamēḍu

Indo-Pacific beads appear rather early on some Indonesian islands and elsewhere in Southeast Asia. Associated artifacts, including other beads, also suggest South Indian connections (Figure 5.2). This includes the luxury ceramic known as "rouletted ware," gold eye coverings in burials, the introduction of iron technology, and certain burial practices.

The "Buni Culture Complex," near Karawang, Java, is close to the spot where the oldest Sanskrit inscriptions on the island were found. It has never been properly excavated, but looters and farmers have recovered beads and other Indian-related objects, including "rouletted ware" (Walker and Santoso 1977, 39; Ardika et al. 1993) and gold eye covers (Bellwood 1985, 301).

At Gilimanuk, at the western end of Bali, R. P. Soejono excavated some eighty burials, containing beads, "rouletted ware," and a pair of gold eye covers (Bellwood 1985, 301). The original dating of the site was ca. 100 B.C. to A.D. 100. Nine radiocarbon dates (GrN-7125–7133) were later secured (Bronson and Glover 1984, 41), ranging from 195 B.C.–A.D. 65 to A.D. 240–450. The central average date is A.D. 111.[9]

At Sembiran, on the northern coast of Bali, Ardika (1995) found "rouletted ware" and other ceramics related to the Arikamēḍu corpus. Beads were found in conjunction with burials, including two carnelian and one gold bead. The site is dated from the last few centuries B.C. to the first few centuries A.D.

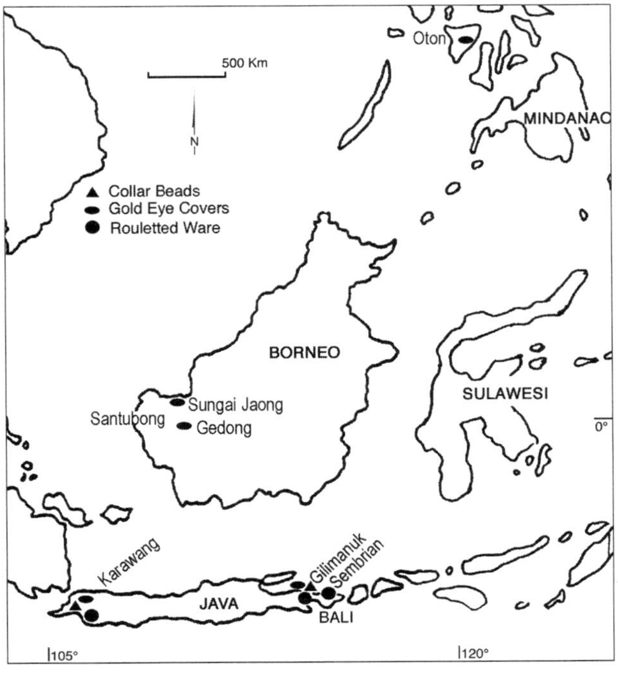

Figure 5.2. *Map of Southeast Asia showing occurrences of gold eye covers, "rouletted ware," and collar beads at sites with Indo-Pacific beads.*

"Rouletted ware," which is actually decorated by chattering rather than rouletting, has been studied intensively by Begley (1985; 1988; 1991a). This luxury ware was produced at or near Arikamēḍu, possibly in imitation of a Mediterranean style. It may have been made in other places as well, but the heart of production was in southeastern India. Begley (1996, 24–25) noted a few occurrences in Southeast Asia, but has been reluctant to draw conclusions about direct trade with Arikamēḍu without further evidence.

Gold eye covers discussed by O'Connor and Harrisson (1971, 76–77) were found in Bali, Sarawak, and the Philippines. They related the practice of using these burial goods to South India, particularly "megalithic" (Pandukal) burials (see Leshnik 1974, 189).

Ironworking at Santubong, Sarawak, was also related to South India by Harrisson and O'Connor (1969). The association of certain artifacts, early iron technology, and "megalithic" burials in western Indonesia led Bellwood (1985, 303) to note that evidence points to South Indian contact. However, he felt that the data were too diffuse to draw conclusions along these lines.

There is now more evidence for connections between these Indonesian sites and South India: beads. Indo-Pacific beads are common at these sites. Of the 6,000 beads from burials and occupation areas at Gilimanuk, over 3,700 were glass (Indraningsih 1985a, 4–5; 1985b, 137–140).[10] They look like a typical Arikamēḍu assemblage with no orange and a crumbly opaque green.[11] Hancock's analysis (Appendix B) showed the same potash-manganese-cobalt pattern in dark blue beads from Gilimanuk as at Arikamēḍu and Karaikadu. Dussubieux and Gratuze (2000) confirmed that two samples of blue glass beads were of potash glass with levels of manganese and cobalt similar to those of blue beads at Arikamēḍu.

The glass beads from Sembiran are also Indo-Pacific beads. The analysis done on them (Ardika 1995) showed them to be typical for Arikamēḍu beads, with a couple of exceptions.[12] Cobalt was not searched for, but the high manganese content of the blue bead (with potash as the alkali) suggests that wad was used to color it. The purple bead also has high manganese and potash content.

There are also collar beads at some of these Indonesian sites. A glass one of the "lug collar" type was found at Gilimanuk. Glass and stone ones have been found in the Buni area. Their shapes indicate that they were made at Arikamēḍu.

At Gilimanuk and the Buni Complex, Indo-Pacific and collar beads came from Arikamēḍu. The same appears to be true for the Indo-Pacific beads at Sembiran. The "rouletted ware" and other Arikamēḍu ceramics were also probably imported from there. The gold eye covers, "megalithic" burial practices, and the introduction of iron all have South Indian associations. This strengthens the case for early South Indian contact with Indonesia and strongly suggests that Arikamēḍu was a major port involved in this trade.

Arikamēḍu is also likely to be the source of beads in Japan at an early date. Dark translucent blue beads from Sasaka and Miyanomae from the Yayoi period (ca. 300 B.C. to A.D. 250) show the typical and virtually exclusive Arikamēḍu formula for blue glass, with potash the dominant alkali and a high concentration of manganese (S. Gupta 1999, 13).

It is clear from the foregoing that South India played a significant role in the connections between the Indian subcontinent and Southeast Asia at an early date. This should not, however, be construed to mean that only South India was involved in trade and other forms of communication with the region. As others have pointed out (e.g., De Casparis 1961), many parts of India, as well as Sri Lanka, have left their mark on the cultures of Southeast Asia.

Indo-Pacific Beads as Luxury Items?

Once Funan began making Indo-Pacific beads, its neighbors were potential customers. Hence, it is not surprising to find these beads in the region. They were common in the jar burials of northern Laos, in blue, yellow, green, black, and orange colors (Colani 1935, 26–32). The orange points away from Arikamēḍu[13] and toward Oc Eo, where this color was also common (Malleret 1962a, 263).

Colani, who did as admirable a job on the beads as was then possible, compared her finds with those from Kuala Selinsing (Colani 1935, 155–162) and Sumatra (Colani 1935, 218–223). She noted that Kuala Selinsing was considered a beadmaking site and thought the beads in Laos may have been from there.

Indo-Pacific beads are also common in the tombs of Han Chinese nobles, particularly those who lived in southern provinces. In Annam, Janse (1947, 51, pl. 75.1) found 5,000 blue and green Indo-Pacific beads in a single tomb and smaller numbers in other tombs. He asked Van Riet Lowe about them, who confirmed that similar beads were found in South Africa (Janse 1951, 167).

In Guangdong Province, China, Indo-Pacific beads are a conspicuous feature in many tombs of Han nobles. Strings without marked provenience are displayed in the Guangzhou (Canton) City Museum. They are principally blue and green: red was scarce. In the Guangdong Provincial Museum are four strands excavated from (presumably different) tombs at Zuben. Again, blue dominated, with a few opaque green, red, and yellow beads. One string of relatively large translucent blue beads in the Guangzhou City Museum is from the Western (Former) Han; the others are from the Eastern Han, A.D. 25–220.[14]

In Han period royal tombs of the Dian Kingdom in Yunnan, light and dark blue beads were found. Some were a little over a centimeter in diameter, and "Les autres perles sont extrêmement petites [The other beads are very small]" (Pirazzoli-t'Serstevens 1974, 257). This sounds like an all too typical description of Indo-Pacific beads, but without more information this is not verified.

The most spectacular Asian excavations of Indo-Pacific beads are in the royal tombs of the Paekche and Silla Kingdoms of Korea. In Kongju is the tomb of the Paekche King Muryong, whose reign began in 501. He died in 523 and was buried in 526. His queen died in 526 and was buried in 529. Their treasures included a dozen beads of hard stones, about the same number of amber beads, 123 beads of jet or some other coal, and more than 10,000 Indo-Pacific beads. In color they were translucent copper blue, dark blue, and violet and opaque yellow, green, and orange.

Kyongju was the capital of the Silla Kingdom. It was put on the world archaeological map after a policeman saw children picking up—what else?—small beads from a disturbed area. He alerted the authorities and the "Gold Crown Tomb"[15] was excavated. Along with the crowns, more than 20,000 Indo-Pacific beads, mostly blue, were uncovered.

Kyongju contains numerous royal tombs. All from the fourth century had been excavated by the end of 1984, along with some from the fifth and sixth. The director of the National Museum at Kyongju, Han Byong-Sam, has estimated that at least 100,000 beads had been uncovered (1984, personal communication). The bulk of them were Indo-Pacific beads, with shades of blue dominating. Beads in opaque yellow, green, black, and red were less numerous. Also common were larger blue pinched beads, likely from Oc Eo.

Indo-Pacific beads are also common items in Japanese tombs, during the Yayoi period (300 B.C. to A.D. 250) and even more so in the Kofun period (A.D. 250 to 600). In the Yayoi period they were concentrated in southern Honshu and western Kyushu and even more widely spread in the Kofun period. As mentioned earlier, Arikamēḍu is a likely source for the beads in the Yayoi period. In the third century soda-based glass became the principal bead material, perhaps indicating importation from Funanese sites (S. Gupta 1999). These beads were called "small beads" *(kodama)* and at least in the Kofun period, and perhaps earlier, were imbued with spiritual significance (D. Blair 1973, 45, 54).

The farther from the manufacturer one goes, the more a product is apt to be treated as a luxury item. Indo-Pacific beads, particularly blue beads, are found in early East Asian contexts buried with the wealthy and powerful (Figure 5.3). The masses of Indo-Pacific beads in the Paekche and Silla royal tombs suggest that a high social value was attached to them. There are also some literary hints that Indo-Pacific beads were viewed as luxuries by the Chinese court.

The *Wu Li (Calendar of the Wu)* covers the years A.D. 222 to 280, but was not published until the tenth century. Tributes sent from Funan and other countries in A.D. 225 included *liuli* (Pelliot 1903, 283). *Liuli* is glass, specifically opaque glass.[16] Opaque glass does not refer to glass vessels, because nearly all vessels then were translucent. It could, however, refer to beads. The only opaque glass made in Funan (if this was the source of the gift) was for Indo-Pacific beads.

The *Liang Zhou (History of Liang)* covers the period from 502 to 556 and was written by Yao Zulian (Yao Sseulien) in the first half of the seventh century. It recorded that in the year 519 King Rudravarman of Funan sent a tribute to the Liang emperor. Pelliot (1903, 270 and n. 3) was stuck on the meaning of the word modifying *zhu (tchou)*, suggesting everything from mica and nacre to glass or rock crystal lenses. I cannot comment on the modifier, but *zhu* means "beads" or "pearls" (and "pupil of the eye").

The ambiguities surrounding these Chinese sources aside, the archaeological record demonstrates that there was status attached to Indo-Pacific beads in the lands northeast of Funan, because they are buried with the

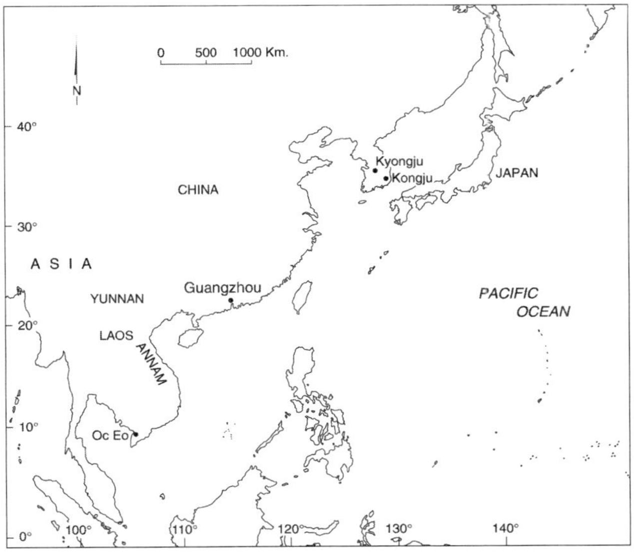

Figure 5.3. *Map of eastern Asia showing regions where Indo-Pacific beads were treated as luxury items, judging from their occurrences in high-status burials.*

nobility, royalty, and nouveau riche. It may be that at least some Funan production was meant for the luxury markets of China, Korea, and neighboring countries.

The End of Indo-Pacific Beadmaking in Southeast Asia

The collapse of the Srivijayan Indo-Pacific industry by the end of the eleventh century is evident in the abandonment of beadmaking sites within Srivijaya. All production had long stopped in Funan. Takua Pa was occupied only in the early ninth century. Production at Vijaya and Sungai Mas was over by A.D. 1100.

This is confirmed by evidence at importing sites. The best data we have is the type collection of the National Museum of the Philippines. It includes samples of each bead found at every excavated site in the country and is used as a registrar for all beads subsequently found. We can derive statistics about the Philippine bead trade, the one limiting factor being the yet imperfect chronology (Francis 1989c; see also Appendix A).

During the periods Fox dated to ca. 200 B.C. to A.D. 1200, Indo-Pacific beads account for 66.2 percent of all beads of all materials excavated at all sites in the Philippines.[17] However, in the subsequent period (ca. 1200 to 1450), they account for a mere 1.2 percent of all beads.

The same pattern is seen throughout Southeast Asia. In Sarawak, the ninth- and tenth-century sites of Kain Hitam and Sungai Jaong have predominantly Indo-Pacific beads. The twelfth- to thirteenth-century site of Bongkissam has only a few, and the thirteenth- to sixteenth-century sites of Gedong and Bukit Sandong have none.

In Indonesia, Indo-Pacific beads are at the Buni Complex, Gilimanuk, and Sembiran (Bali). Later, they dominate Srivijayan sites such as Vijaya, Air Sugian (South Sumatra), and Muara Jambi (Jambi) and megalithic sites including Pasemah, Sumatra (van Heekeren 1958, 41), and Matesih, Central Java (Ernawan 1987, 124).[18] After that, they are rare.

Their decline is typical at Banten, West Java. At the "prehistoric" settlement of Odel, Indo-Pacific beads were the only glass beads uncovered. From Banten Girang, whose florescence was the twelfth to thirteenth centuries (Edwards McKinnon 1991), few or no Indo-Pacific beads were found.[19] By the time the sultanate was established at Banten Lama by newcomers from Demak in 1527, Indo-Pacific beads were long gone.

Trade with the West

Westward, there was more territory for Indo-Pacific beads to conquer (Figure 5.4) Trade between India and the Roman West is well established (see Begley and De Puma 1991). The major Egyptian ports in Roman times were Leukos Limen (Quseir al-Qadim), excavated by the Oriental Institute of Chicago (Whitcomb and Johnson 1979; 1980; 1981; see also Sidebotham 1991, 22–35), and Berenike, excavated by the Delaware-Leiden Berenike Project team.

Quseir al-Qadim (Leukos Limen) had many Indian contacts. Teak, jute, and peppercorns were imported. Ceramics similar to Arikamēḍu local wares have been found with graffiti, one of which reads "Catan," a common South Indian name. Indo-Pacific beads were also imported; at least one was excavated from the Roman layers.[20]

Meyer (1992, 41, pl. 14.371) related a collar bead from there to two found in Nubia by Dunham and collar beads from India. If her X-ray side-view drawing is correct, the bead does not resemble Arikamēḍu collar beads. It appears to be wound, because the perforation is conical; she did not tell us how it was made. If it is wound, it has nothing to do with Indian collar beads.

Farther down the Red Sea coast at Berenike, Indo-Pacific beads account for only 4.1 percent (four examples) of the beads from Ptolemaic and Early Roman levels, but for 41.4 percent (369 examples) from the fourth to sixth centuries. They have not been chemically analyzed, but their colors[21] strongly suggest that the later ones came from Mantai (Francis 2001).

The Romans do not seem to have been especially interested in Indo-Pacific beads. As trade passed into Arab hands in the Islamic period, the same could be said of the Muslim world. Inland sites, such as Nishapur (Iran), Samad al Shan (Oman), and Fustat (Egypt), do not have Indo-Pacific beads.[22]

The situation is much different at Islamic port cities.

At Siraf, Iran, Indo-Pacific beads accounted for 39.7 percent of all glass beads and 18.3 percent of all beads. At Aqaba, Jordan, they made up 28.0 percent of the glass beads and 12.8 percent of all beads. They were also common in the Islamic strata at Quseir al-Qadim, though precise figures are not available.

Why is there a difference? Indo-Pacific beads were trade items for the Romans and Muslims. They are very common in East African sites.[23] If the reader needs reminding of their role in East Africa, recall that Beck first identified them as coming from Great Zimbabwe and Lavanha wrote of the Portuguese importing them to Mozambique in 1593.

Indo-Pacific beads were also traded to West Africa. The Muslims began trading with the Kingdom of Ghana[24] by the seventh or eighth century. Beads were staples. Yaqut (ca. 1124) described merchants from Sijilmasa, Morocco, going to Ghana, "Their wares are salt, bundles of pine wood . . . blue glass beads, bracelets of red copper, bangles and signet rings of copper, and *nothing else*" (Levtzion and Hopkins 1981, 169 [emphasis mine]).

This may not have been an exaggeration. Two centuries later, the intrepid Ibn Battuta wrote, "The traveler, in these countries has no need to burden himself with provisions for the mouth [food], or mets or ducats, nor of drachmas; one must carry with him a morsel of rock salt, ornaments or trinkets of glass, which they call nazhm [beads] . . . and a few aromatic substances" (Defrémery and Sanguinetti 1922, 393–394).[25]

Glass beads, especially blue ones, are common finds from looted West African sites once involved in the Arab-African trade.[26] Few have been scientifically excavated. From the descriptions[27] the following appear to have Indo-Pacific beads:

Kumbi Salah in modern Mali was likely the capital of the Kingdom of Ghana. A group of seven "minuscule"

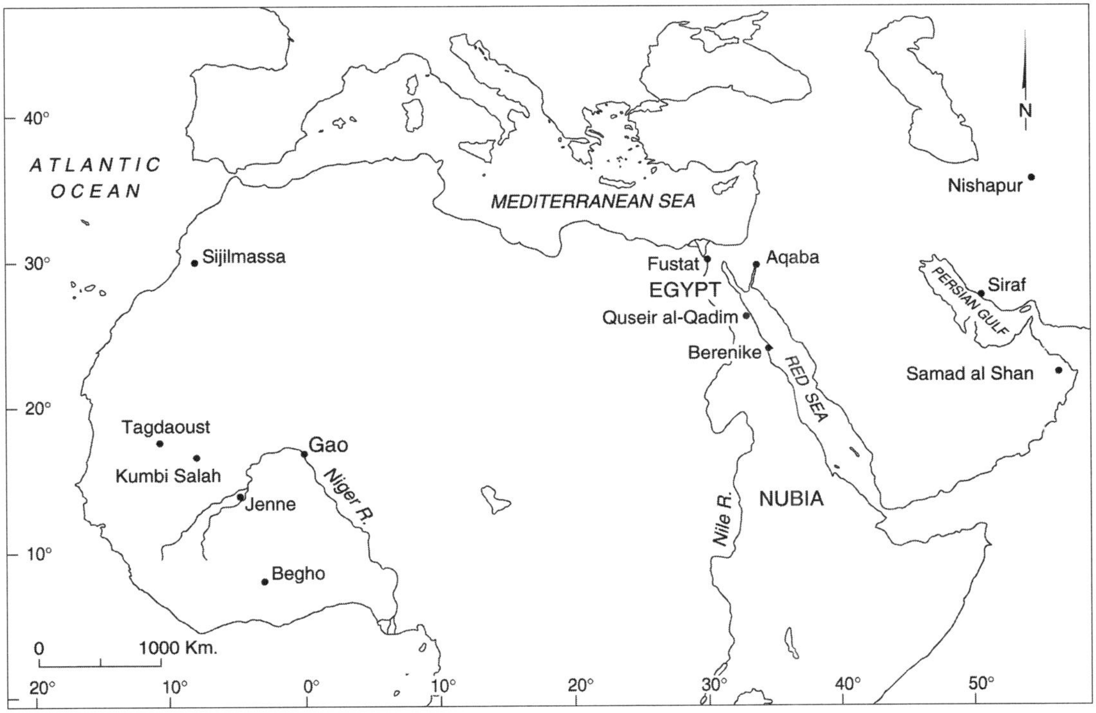

Figure 5.4. *Map of Africa and the Middle East showing areas that imported Indo-Pacific beads.*

drawn blue beads, 2 to 3 mm in diameter, was found (Thomassey and Mauny 1951, 459–460, fig. 11.10). Blue was by far the most common color there, as it was at Gao (Thomassey and Mauny 1951, 459). Blue beads and green beads with diameters from 3 to 13 mm found in the 1950 season (Thomassey and Mauny 1956, 137, figs. 14.20, 21, 23) probably also include Indo-Pacific beads.

Tegdaoust, in modern Mauritania, is probably ancient Aougaghost. It was described in the eighth century by al-Bakri (De Slane 1913, 317) as having "beautiful houses and solidly built edifices."[28] Although Vanacker's (1984, 33) otherwise excellent paper on the beads found there did not say if the small cylindrical and discoidal ones were drawn, I presume that they were. These two groups totaled 46.09 percent of the glass bead assemblage. The report did not indicate what colors they were, but overall, turquoise accounted for 11.9 percent of all beads. No other blues were reported. Some whites and blacks (30.32 percent of the total) might be corroded specimens.

Jenné (Djenné) or Jenné-jeno (Old Jenné) is in the Interior Niger Delta in modern Mali and has been a key trading station for millennia. Excavations found few beads, either because of ancient curating, digging at the wrong place (McIntosh and McIntosh 1984, 90), or the intense looting going on (McIntosh and McIntosh 1982, 418). The two earliest glass beads in sub-Saharan Africa were found there. Chemical analysis points to them being Indian, perhaps from Arikamēḍu (Brill 1995). One was in a level radiocarbon dated to 1790 ± 120 B.P. (McIntosh 1995, 421). Only fourteen glass beads were excavated. Four are Middle Eastern (a segmented bead, two melons, and an eye bead), one is perhaps Dutch, and seven are probably Indo-Pacific beads (McIntosh and McIntosh 1980, 164; McIntosh 1995, 247–252).

The farthest documented place to which Indo-Pacific beads traveled in Islamic times is the Forest Zone of West Africa. Begho, Ghana, is the only Ghanaian place name in Arab texts discussing the trans-Saharan trade (Posnansky 1971, 115–118). It was long connected with the trade to the north and was the earliest city in Ghana to receive Muslims. There are seven Indo-Pacific beads from the oldest quarter of the site, radiocarbon dated to the eleventh and twelfth centuries.[29] They are opaque red and yellow and translucent dark blue, blue green, and green.

How were Indo-Pacific beads taken to this then-remote corner of the world? They could have arrived via internal African routes from East Africa. However, it is more likely that they were brought from India, Sri Lanka, or Srivijaya to Red Sea ports (Quseir al-Qadim, Berenike, and Aqaba).[30] From Egypt they would have been transported across North Africa where they could be sent south, eventually all the way to the Forest Zone or even the coast. They were traded in the "Arab common market." As Posnansky (1973, 152) described it, "The Arab conquest of North Africa brought stability, an expansion of trade, and the creation of a huge common market and culture zone stretching right through to India. Demands were created for the products of West Africa, especially gold."

The preceding three chapters set the foundation for the Asian maritime bead trade because Indo-Pacific beads were the most prevalent items in that trade for two millennia. Small and unpretentious, they traveled great distances and played many roles.

Indo-Pacific beads have been largely overlooked, even though they were first recognized as a separate class of beads in the 1930s. Now that the outline of their astounding story is in place, more work should be done on them. What is required includes (1) proper reporting and cataloging of these beads whenever encountered; (2) recognition of associated beads and the trade patterns the group can illustrate; and (3) more chemical analyses to help determine origins and trade routes.

Some of this work is being done, but much more remains to be completed. The smallest beads may well require the most work to uncover their story. The rewards, however, are potentially very great.

Part Three: Chinese Glass Beads

Plate 1. *A furnace used for producing frit for glass-making in Purdalpur, India. The raw ingredient, the soil efflorescence* reh, *was heated for a couple of days to produce frit. The large hole in front is where the frit was removed.*

Plate 2. *Furnace-winding beads in Purdalpur, India. The young worker has several beads on his iron mandrel and is shaping the last one he wound with a small iron instrument. When done, the beads will be knocked off into a small pot in front of him similar to the one on the right.*

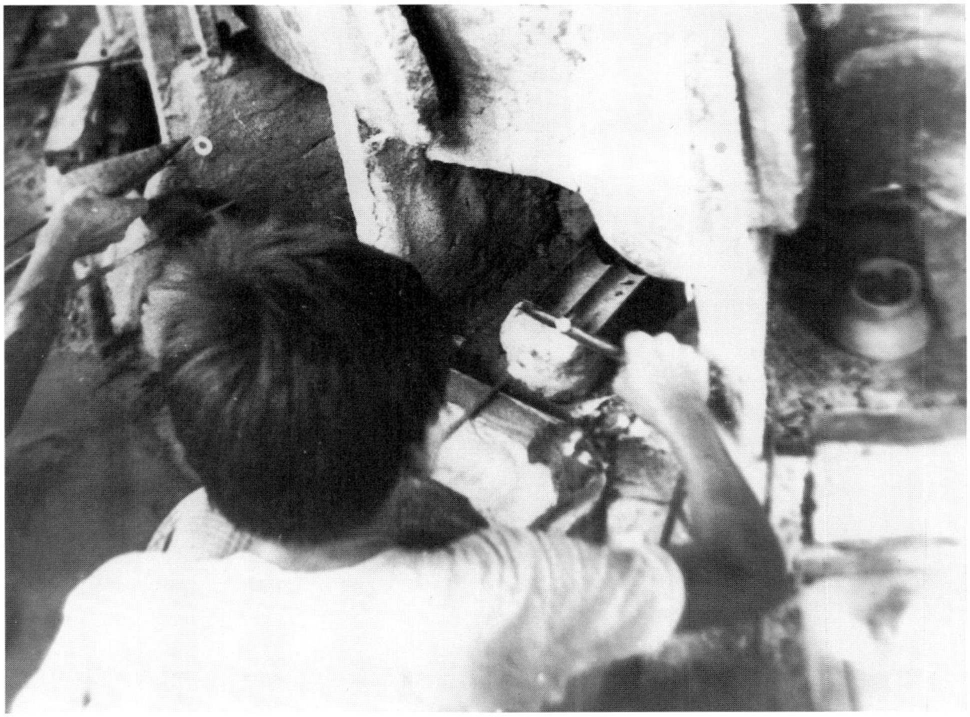

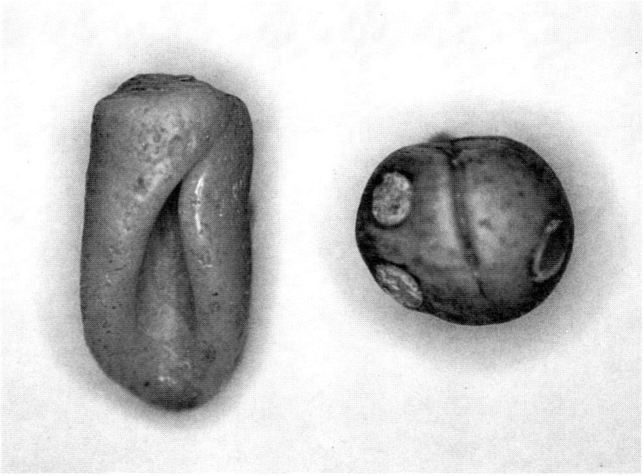

Plate 3 (Top left). *Segmented glass beads. These were a specialty of the Middle East for about 1,500 years, made by rolling a warm tube of glass over a stone mold or similar device to produce bulges along its length. These were then cut apart into single or multiple beads. Those pictured are from Fustat, Egypt. The longest bead is 15 mm long.*

Plate 4 (Bottom left). *Folded glass beads. These are single-strip folded beads. A heated plaque of glass was bent around a mandrel and the opposing ends fused, making a date-shaped bead on the left and a round bead on the right. The date bead is 20 mm long.*

Plate 5 (Top right). *Pierced glass beads. The bead on the left has a spiral decoration that could only be achieved by piercing. The one on the right shows the piercing action into the perforation. The left bead is 10 mm in diameter.*

Plate 6 (Bottom right). *Melded glass beads. These beads were produced by heating and fusing individual elements to build the body of the bead. The largest bead is 20 mm long.*

Plate 7. *Wound glass beads. The fabric of the glass and often the decorations of the beads encircle the perforation. These are from Pakistan. The largest bead is 19 mm in diameter.*

Plate 8. *Drawn glass beads. These beads were made from tubes drawn or pulled out of a gather of glass. The fabric of the glass parallels the perforation. Short segments of tubes are often reheated to produce "seed" beads. These are Venetian. The longest bead is 13 mm in diameter.*

Plate 9. *At the entrance of a carnelian and agate mine at Ratanpur, India, older members of the mining family sort stones for sale to Cambay dealers.*

Plate 10. *The initial heating of stones at Cambay to make them easier to chip is done either in overturned pots with holes punched in the bottom or in open troughs, as shown here.*

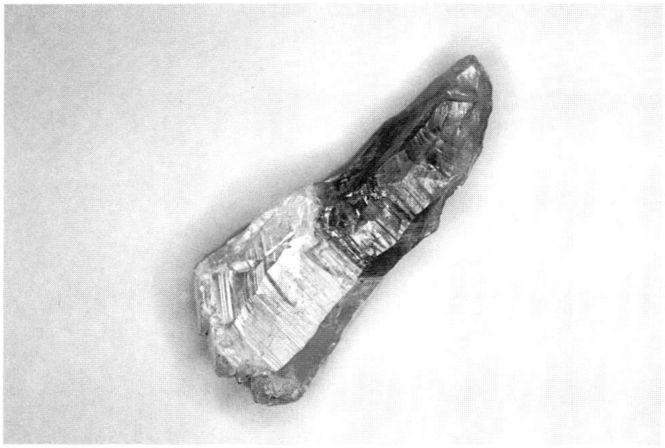

Plate 11. *Thinned quartz crystal, battered at the tip. This was found in an agate-working area in Kotalingala, India. Similar pieces have been found at Arikamēḍu. They were apparently used for chipping roughouts from stones, but whether as the fixed point or hammerhead is uncertain.*

Plate 12. *Grinding roughouts into blanks at Cambay. The process has been electrified for only a few decades.*

Plate 13. *Bead grinding stone of sandstone from Kotalingala, India.*

Plate 14. *Fine-grained sandstone blocks with facets. Surface finds at Kotalingala in an agate beadworking area, presumed to be polishers. The larger block is 34 mm in diameter.*

Plate 15. *A worker withdraws glass from a furnace in Papanaidupet in preparation for pouring a cake of glass on the small platform at the bottom of the picture. A cake is already cooling there.*

Plate 16. *Tools used for making tubes at Papanaidupet. The* gedda paru *are the first and fourth tools from the right. The fifth tool is the* lada. *Next to it is the curved piece of wood used to hold the* lada *while the glass cone is being shaped on the wall. It obscures all but one end of the thin* cheatlek. *The other tools are used to help stir the melting glass.*

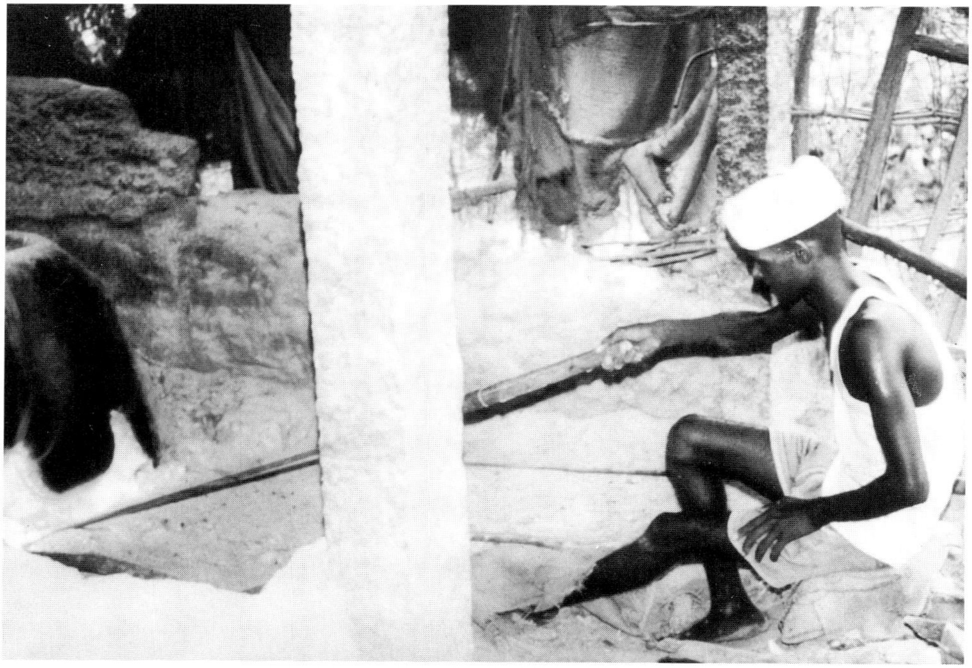

Plate 17. *A man tends the tube-drawing furnace at Papanaidupet by adding wood to the fire. Here he stokes the fire with a long iron rod.*

Plate 18. *The glass placed into the furnace and stirred by the* gedda paru. *A large ceramic bowl covering the opening is moved aside by the* gedda paru.

Plate 19. *Forming a cone of glass at Papanaidupet. The glass is on the* lada *and is being rolled along a short wall with the help of a piece of wood held under the* lada *by two workers on either side.*

Plate 20. *The glass cone (off to the left of the picture) is about to be pierced at Papanaidupet. The man on the left is holding the* lada *while the man on the right prepares to insert the* cheatlek, *held in his left hand.*

Plate 21. *Piercing the glass cone to make it hollow. The* cheatlek *is emerging from the tip of the cone.*

Plate 22. *Drawing of a continuous glass tube from the furnace. The master's hand is protected only by a small square of wet jute packing.*

Plate 23. *A worker in Papanaidupet cuts the tubes into short segments by laying the edges on a blade fixed in the ground and bringing a second blade down onto them.*

Plate 24. *A worker in Papanaidupet stirs cut segments of tubes in a small furnace with a long paddle. The segments, packed in ash, are on a ceramic plate above the fire. This operation rounds them off.*

Plate 25. *A woman of Papanaidupet strings beads by passing long, thin needles through loose beads held in a winnowing basket.*

Plate 26. *Exterior view of a tube-drawing furnace in Papanaidupet.*

Plate 27. *Topographic map of the Sungai Mas region Merbok Museum.*

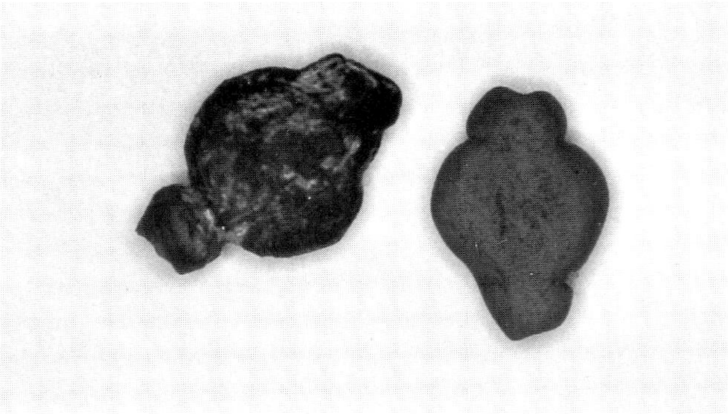

Plate 28 (Top left). *Two red glass collar beads from Arikamēḍu.*

Plate 29 (Top right). *A pierced bead from Arikamēḍu. The drawn solid cane was apparently reheated and pierced in a small clay mold. The cane is 16 mm long.*

Plate 30 (Right). *Pinched beads from Mantai.*

Plate 31. *Square drawn tube beads from Khlong Thom, Thailand. The longest bead is 16 mm long. Beads lent by Ian Glover.*

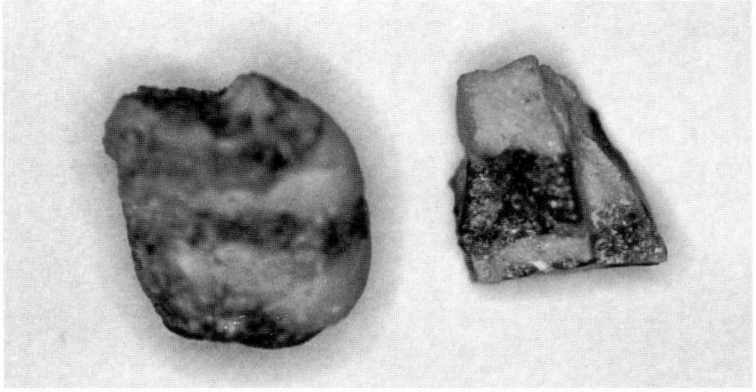

Plate 34. *Wasters of single-strip folded black and white striped beads from Kambang Unglen, Palembang (ancient Vijaya). The longest piece is 13 mm long.*

Plate 32 (Top left). *Striped drawn beads from Mantai.*

Plate 33 (Top right). *"Beads" recently made from the folded rims of ancient vessels. The "arrowhead pendant" is 29 mm long.*

Plate 35. *A section from a version of Ptolemy's map of India showing the region between Barygaza (modern Broach) and the Sardonyx Mountain. The Narmadā (Narmadus) flows past Barygaza, which is linked politically to Ozzene (modern Ujjain), though the latter is not actually on the Narmadā. The Sardonyx Mountain has been placed far inland, probably a result of Indian disinformation about the location of its gem sources.*

Plate 36. *The water tank atop Babā Ghor Hill in Ratanpur. This tank was associated with the Hindu temple that is now destroyed.*

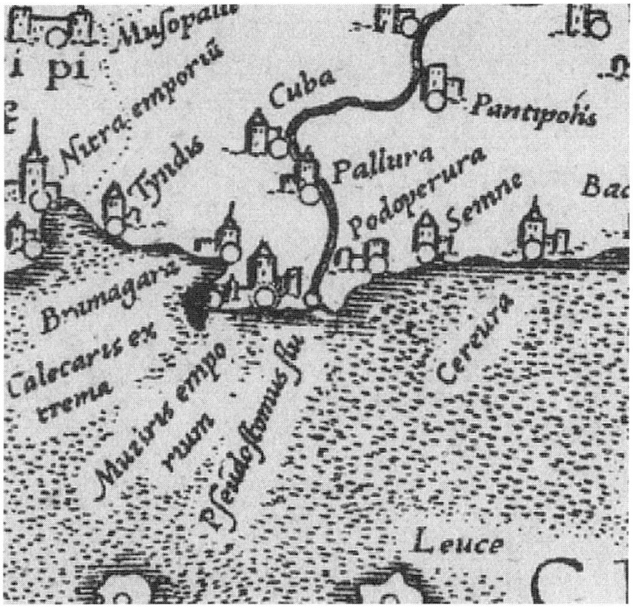

Plate 37. *Section of a reconstruction of Ptolemy's map of India with the important southwestern trading port of Muziris.*

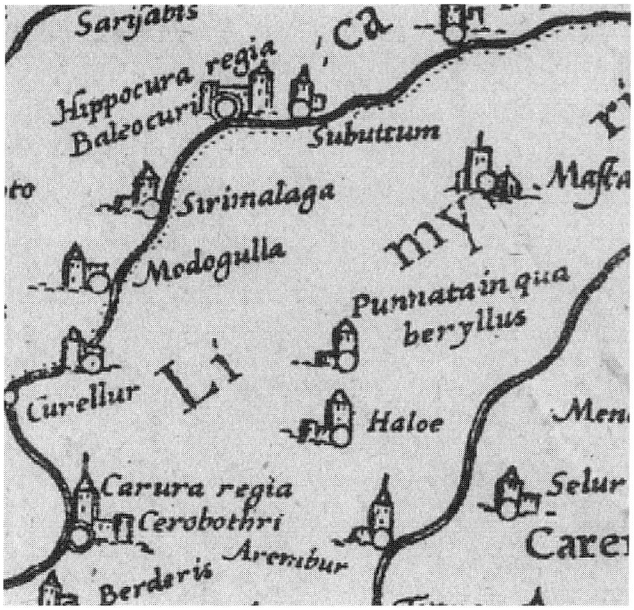

Plate 38. *Section of a reconstruction of Ptolemy's map of India showing Carura (Karur) and Punnata, the supposed source of beryl.*

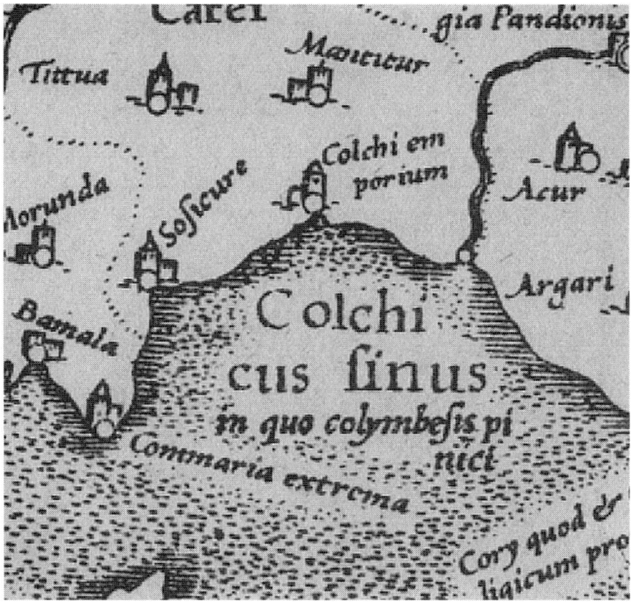

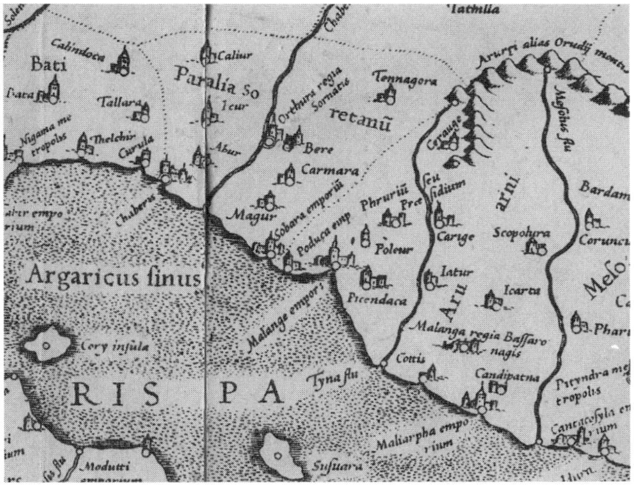

Plate 39 (Top left). *Section of a reconstruction of Ptolemy's map of India showing Colchi emporium and Bay.*

Plate 40 (Bottom left). *Section of a reconstruction of Ptolemy's map of India showing the three emporia known on the eastern coast, as well as Curula. Although the ports were known to Ptolemy, their interconnected nature was not understood.*

Plate 41 (Top). *Exterior and interior views of East Javanese mosaic beads.*

Plate 42 (Center). *East Javanese* pelangi *("rainbow") bead.*

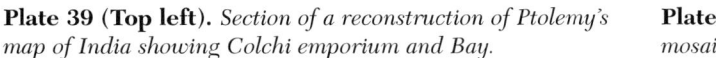

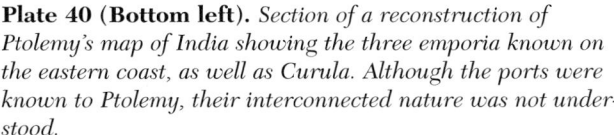

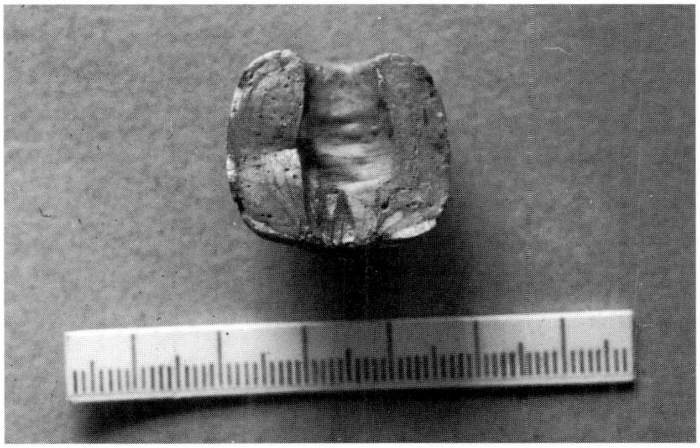

Plate 43 (Bottom). *Interior of an East Javanese white spotted bead. Notice the piece of white glass within the core and the unusual ridges along the perforation.*

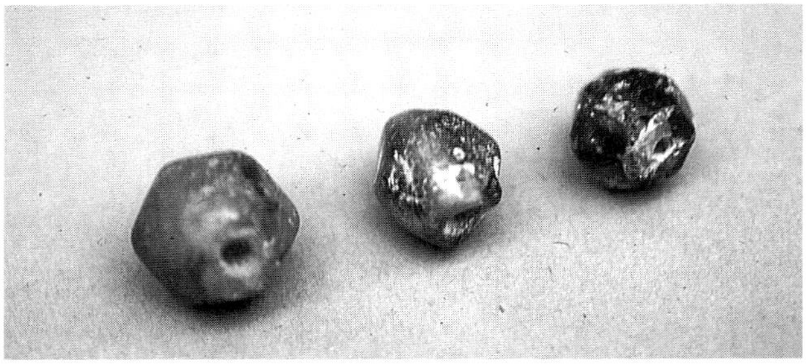

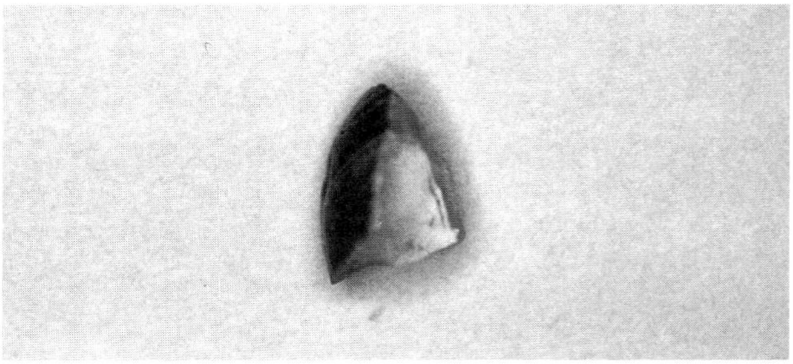

Plate 44 (Top left). *Overheated and collapsed white spotted bead from Jatiagung.*

Plate 45 (Bottom left). *Interior of East Javanese "big yellow" bead. The fragment is 30 mm wide.*

Plate 46 (Top). *Red disk beads, surface finds from Rajangana, Sri Lanka. The drilling of the hole is most easily seen on the broken specimen. The largest is 11 mm in diameter.*

Plate 47 (Center). *Wound and paddled hexagonal bicone beads from Uraiyur, the old Cōḷa capital. The largest bead is 6.8 mm in diameter.*

Plate 48 (Bottom). *Fragment of a siliceous (probably flint) bead found at Kambang Unglen, Palembang (Vijaya). Note that the exterior has been treated to sharpen the contrast between the bands of the stone, but the interior remains white. The fragment is 9 mm long.*

6
Glassmaking and Glass Beadmaking in China

There is something of a "problem" when it comes to an accounting of Chinese glass beads. The subject has long been ignored or even denied respectability. Sources of information are scarce and scattered. In this chapter what is known about Chinese glassmaking and glass bead production is highlighted. The trade in Chinese glass beads is discussed in the next chapter. In chapter 8 the identification of the beads involved in the trade is discussed. Somewhat ironically, though not uniquely,[1] a great deal of what is known about Chinese glass beads comes from information outside China proper.

Studying Chinese Glass Beads

The leading glass historians have been Europeans and Americans. Until recently, few of them believed that China was a glassmaking power, a glass beadmaking power, or much of a glass bead exporter. There were several reasons for that view, some legitimate and others not. Because this has been debated so long, we begin by considering what others have written about Chinese glass. The attitude toward Chinese glass and glass beads is an important factor in their study.

Westerners once conceived of the Chinese as rural and scientifically backward. The myth has been largely dispelled, much credit going to *Science and Civilisation in China,* edited and largely written by Joseph Needham.[2] China was often in the forefront of technological inventions and applications.

Chinese glassmaking was particularly disparaged. The few writers who suggested great antiquity for Chinese glass (e.g., Nesbitt 1879a, 134–135; 1879b, 651; Honey 1937, 211) were in the minority. Although Nesbitt (1879b, 651) conceded antiquity, he wrote, "The manufacture [of glass] has never greatly extended itself." Bushell (1914, 2:58, 60), a champion of Chinese art, remarked, "The Chinese themselves do not claim the invention of glass, and there is no reason to attribute any great antiquity to it . . ." and "The glass industry . . . has been carried out with indifferent success. . . ." Ayers (1965, 17) averred, "there is small sign of any sustained attempt on their [the Chinese] part to explore its [glass'] fuller potentialities: until more recent times, on the contrary, the dominant impression that emerges is one of rather localised activities, strictly limited in their scope and purpose."

Many Western scholars have assumed that the Chinese could not have invented glass on their own and it was introduced from abroad. Hurrians (Engle 1976, 1–38), Jews (Kurinsky 1991, 251–297), and Syrians or Indians (Hirth 1885, 232) have been suggested as the conveyers of glass technology. Hirth convinced many scholars that glassmaking was introduced to China only in the mid-fifth century A.D.

Glass historians often focus on vessels and other large objects. The Chinese did not make such things for a long time. Those who appreciate smaller objects, such as beads (R. K. Liu 1975a; b; 1995a, 52–71; b; Dohrenwend 1980–1981), have had more empathy toward Chinese glass.

Some scholars have perceived a ceramic/glass dichotomy. Nesbitt (1879b, 651) noted that China excelled in ceramics and Rome in glass, but not vice versa. Lamm (1939, 2593) formulated this into a general rule: cultures with thriving ceramic industries do not have similar glassmaking industries.

It has been argued correctly that the Chinese had adequate substitutes for the roles played by glass in the West. Oiled paper served for windows and porcelain for drinking and storage vessels. Jade and other precious stones were used for ornaments. Elaborate beads of the Late Zhou (the Warring States period, 473 to 256 B.C.) and the imperially dictated use of court beads during the Qing (1644 to 1911) were high points of Chinese glass bead history. The Chinese did not traditionally emphasize glass except as a substitute for jade and other stones.

In addition, Chinese scholars have not been interested in glass or glass beads until recently. Research in China remains extremely difficult for outsiders. Chinese glass beads were for a long time made principally for export and are not easily found in China.

As for beads, van der Sleen (1973, 99, 102) reported that Chinese museum officials told him that China never exported them. This was long considered the last word on the subject. No doubt that is what he was told. His mistake was to trust it uncritically.

A collation of historical records (Francis 1986c, 8–17; 1990c) formed (at least in my mind)[3] a picture, albeit sketchy, of continuous glassmaking and glass beadmaking in China. Yet, the old prejudices prevailed, whether from Eurocentrism, the bias for large museum-quality objects, or the slow rate of the diffusion of knowledge. The irony is that China was one of the great glass beadmaking and trading nations of the world.

The Early Ebb and Flow of Glassmaking in China

The Chinese were not the first to invent glass. Some scholars (Gan 1991) believe that it was developed there independently; others disagree. Glassmaking may have been an offshoot of metallurgy, ceramic or faience production, or a result of the Daoists' search for the elixir of life. The origin of Chinese glass is interesting, but it predates the scope of this study.

The earliest glass beads in China were not involved in the Asian maritime trade. Except for certain periods such as the Late Zhou we have rather little information about Chinese glass beads (or even Chinese glass) until the Song period beginning in A.D. 960. We shall first trace what is known about Chinese glass beads until the Song and thereafter consider centers where beadmaking certainly or likely was done.

Because most of the sources used in this chapter are dynastic histories, a few words about them will be instructive. China has long been a literate society. The mythical Yellow Emperor (Huang Di), said to have lived in the third millennium B.C., is credited both with the invention of writing and the founding of the first board of historiographers. Only the First Emperor (Shi Huang Di; ruled 221 to 210 B.C.) opposed historical writing, ordered his scholars not to study the past, and burned all nonessential books, including histories.

In time, it became habitual for succeeding dynasties to write the history of the preceding one. This was usually done officially, with the appointment of a historian or a group of them. These histories were sometimes revised, as with the *New History of the Tang* and *An Extension of the History of the Han Dynasty*. At other times, they were delayed, as with the histories of the Ten Kingdoms released during Tang times, of which I have more to say later. Although these histories were composed from extant records, they are of various quality because of the differences in care exercised and the problems raised from the long time intervals between some dynasties and the composition of their histories.

It should also be kept in mind that China has never been a monolith. It has fluctuated between periods of unity and disunity, with strong central powers alternating with small, often squabbling kingdoms. Glassmaking often flourished in one part of China while another region was unaware of it. The craft frequently spread during periods of disunity. As the center collapsed and smaller states were established, princes of each state would either have to import glass or initiate a local industry. The complex story that followed is summarized in Table 6.1.

The earliest glassy beads in China are technically faience, but glass was certainly being made well before the Han period (Gan 1991, 2). By the Late Zhou (fifth to third centuries B.C.) glassmaking was well established in China (Color Plate 12). The finds from the tombs of Loyang (W. C. White 1934) brought world attention to the spectacular nature of glass beads during the Late Zhou period.

The different types of glass beads in the Late Zhou (473 to 256 B.C.), as described by W. C. White (1934, 147–158), Seligman and Beck (1938), Liu (1975b, 1995b) and Dohrenwend (1980–1981), suggest that there was more than one beadmaking site at the time. The smaller eye beads of this group are spread from Xinjiang in the west, to Shandong in the east, to Henan in the north, and Guangdong in the south. They are concentrated in the old state of Zhu along the Yangtze River valley (Dohrenwend 1980–1981, 429), but where they were made is still unknown.

Glass beadmaking continued during the Han period, though it was generally on a less sophisticated scale than it had been earlier (Blair 1951a, 348–349; Dohrenwend 1980–1981, 433–435). This is not obvious from the written sources. The *Han Shu* (*History of the Han,* later known as *History of the Former Han*) by Ban Gu (Pan Ku) and his sister Ban Zhao (Pan Chao) has two references to glass. In both, the Emperor Wu Di (Liu Che [141 to 87 B.C.) is said to have imported it from Gandhara and countries of the *Nan Hai* or Southern Sea (Needham 1962, 105). Wu Di is also said to have had a glass factory (Missionnaires de Pékin 1777, 463), presumably in or near his capital of Xian. The missionaries who asserted this were quoting "les Annals des Han" (the Annals of the Han). This is presumably the *Han Shu* and was perhaps misread.

In the Three Kingdoms period (A.D. 220 to 280), the northern state of Wei, with its capital at Loyang, imported glass. The *Wei Lüe,* ca. A.D. 264, only mentions Western glass and its ten colors (Bushell 1914, 2: 59; Needham 1962, 107).

Writing about the Western Jin period (265 to 317) in the *Baopuzi*[4] *Neibian (On Immortals by Baopuzi),* the alchemist Ge Hong acknowledged that glass was not a

TABLE 6.1

Summary of Glass and Glass Beadmaking in China

Dynasty (Date)	Glass Products	Glassmaking Center(s)
Middle Zhou (771–474 B.C.)	Jadelike beads and small objects	Unknown
Late Zhou (475–256 B.C.)	Spectacular eye beads, composite beads, etc.	Zhu state?
Han (202 B.C.–A.D. 220)	Less elaborate eye beads, ear reels	Unknown
Three Kingdoms (220–280)	Unknown	Unknown
Jin (265–420)	Beads	South China
Northern Dynasties (336–588)	Windows, vessels	Pingcheng (near Datong)
Sui (589–617)	Celadonlike vessels	Unknown
Tang (618–906)	Vessels, ornaments, etc.	Unknown
Song (960–1279)	Coil, combed, ruby red, etc., beads	Guangzhou, Quanzhou, Suzhou
Yuan (1280–1368)	Beads	Guangzhou, Boshan
Ming (1368–1644)	Vessels, beads, snuff bottles	Boshan, Beijing
Qing (1644–1911)	Court chain beads, export beads, vessels, etc.	Boshan, Yanshen, Guangzhou

Chinese invention and that glass items were imported. However, he also remarked that glassmaking "is being commonly practiced" in southern provinces (Waley 1930–1932, 13; see also Brown and Rabiner 1987, 74).

The historiography of the following Southern and Northern Dynasties (A.D. 420 to 588 and 336 to 588, respectively) is quite complex. Li Shimin, the second Tang Emperor (626–649) ordered the writing of the histories of this period as well as a new history for the Jin, of which no less than eighteen already existed (Bai 1982, 218–219). The Southern and Northern Dynasties period was chaotic, with foreigners invading the north and Chinese surviving in the south. Four dynasties succeeded each other in the south, and in the north there were five dynasties, three of them ruling concurrently for some years.

The *Wei Shu (History of the Wei)*, written by Wei Shou in 554, covered the northern Wei dynasties. It said that during the reign of the first king of the North Wei (Dao Wu Di, reigned 346–409) a man from Dayueshi came to the capital (Pingcheng, Shanxi Province) and persuaded the emperor to let him make glass. He gathered the raw materials from nearby and made glass of five colors in the capital. He is said to have built a movable glass palace that could hold a hundred people. The glass was of a better quality than that imported from the West. After this exploit it was said that glass became much cheaper in China and ceased to be treasured (Harada 1962, 62).

The same story was told in the *Bei Shi (History of the Northern Kingdoms)* except that the king involved was the third Northern Wei king (Tai Wu Di, reigned 423–451). This story is more widely known (Hirth 1885, 230–231;[5] Needham 1962, 108). However, the *Bei Shi (Pei Shih)* is a less reliable source than the *Wei Shu*. It is a condensed version of separate histories of the Northern Dynasties done by Li Yanshou.

The homeland of the person said to have introduced glassmaking is under dispute. Harada (1962, 62) said that there was no state called Dayueshi, but it is usually taken to be somewhere near the border with India. There is archaeological evidence for glassworking in the north at this time. A stone coffin in Dingxian with Persian coins of the late fifth century contained typical Chinese objects in glass, such as a *bo* bowl and *ping* vessels, as well as some beads (Pinder-Wilson 1970, 67; L. Liu 1978, 308).

The *Nan Shi* (*History of the Southern Dynasties*, completed 659) relates that during the reign of Wen Di (Liu Yilong, 424 to 454) of Song, Westerners introduced glassmaking to his capital at Nanjing (Hirth 1885, 231–232). These were taken to be Syrians, but on what grounds is not clear.

In the following Sui dynasty (589–617) the biography of He Chou in the *Document of the Sui Dynasty* stated: "At the beginning of the first emperor's reign . . . glass manufacture had stopped for a long time. Craftsmen did not dare to disobey the emperor's orders. He Chou, a craftsman, adopted the method of making green china [celadon?] to make glass articles, and they were exactly like the real glass articles" (Huang 1991, 185).

It is in the Tang period (618–906) that we begin to have a sense of a more robust Chinese glassmaking industry. In the seventh century Yan Shigu, commenting on the *Han Shi*, affirmed that China was making glass in his day. Hirth and Rockhill (1911, 227–228 n) paraphrased him discussing glass *(liu-li)* saying, ". . . when making what was called *liu-li*, to use all (the ten kinds of coloured *liu-li* known in the West?) and to melt them down to a liquid state to which certain chemicals were added. The glass (thus manufactured) was, however, filled with air-holes (lit. hollow), and brittle, not the clear, true, genuine thing."

Hirth and Rockhill seem to have thought that this was a process involving the recycling of Western glass, though why all ten colors would be used in one operation is something of a mystery. Perhaps the phrase that gave them trouble referred to ingredients for making glass from raw ingredients. The term "hollow" could simply refer to hollow vessels, but their interpretations of the glass being bubbly makes sense of it being also brittle and cloudy.

Many Tang glass vessels have been identified (e.g., Pinder-Wilson 1970; Shi et al. 1987; Gan 1991, 3). However, few beads have been. Blair (1951a, 350) listed pendants, buttons, "small ornaments," parts of hairpins, and bangles as coming from the Tang period. It is also possible, but not yet verified, that some or all of the glass beads in the Shōsō-in in Nara, Japan, came from Tang China.

In sum, between the Late Zhou and the Tang glassmaking tended to wax and wane. Glassmakers are known to relocate. They are not peasants, and the raw materials for their craft (stone, clay, sand, and wood at the most elementary level) are widely available. They possess the one necessary scarce ingredient: knowledge. Knowledge is portable, and glassmakers around the world are notorious wanderers (Francis 1994a). Unified Chinese governments sought to control all aspects of life, including the location, output, and status of craft workers. In contrast, during periods of disunity glassmakers were encouraged to move, either driven away by human or natural disasters or enticed by newly elevated aristocracies.

Glassmaking, which had been lively in the Late Zhou period, was reported sporadically in subsequent periods. In some cases, outsiders were said to be responsible for its introduction; in other cases the Chinese themselves are said to have invented it. It seems likely that glassmaking never completely died out in China and that the official records simply did not record it. That the craft had to be brought anew to small, short-lived kingdoms during periods of turbulence is not surprising.

Song and Later Centers of Glassmaking in China

Latourette (1964, 497) observed that there is a tendency through Chinese history to concentrate industries in a few centralized places. Although that may describe some aspects of the ancient glass industry, it would be a mistake to take that idea too far. Chinese glass beadmaking seems to have been less centralized than that statement indicates (Figure 6.1).

Unfortunately, our knowledge of where Chinese glass was made is sketchy, even more so when it comes to beadmaking. Only one glass factory has been excavated

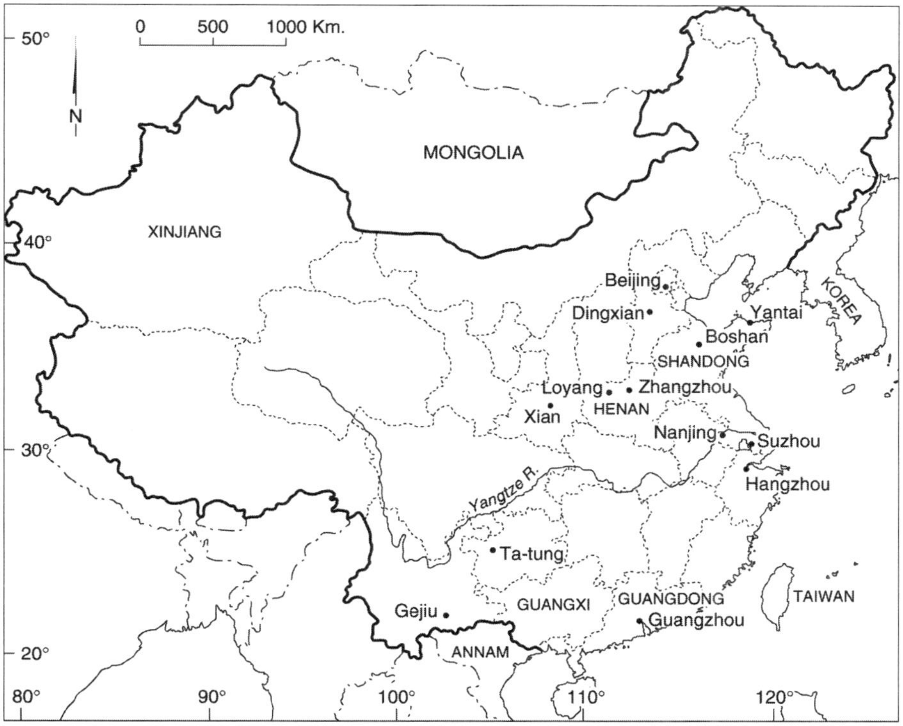

Figure 6.1. *Map of China showing regions where glass is known to have been made.*

in China, dating only to the fourteenth century at Boshan in Shandong (Brown and Rabiner 1987, 85 n. 10; Yi and Tu 1991). More interest by the Chinese archaeological community will help solve this problem, as it has for ceramic production.

For the Tang period (618–906) and especially the Song (960–1279) through the Qing (1644–1911) periods Dohrenwend (1980–1981, 440 [insertion mine]) remarked, "the harvest [of information on Chinese glass] is still very thin." That is no longer quite true. Chinese glass is being documented with increasing frequency. However, the centers of glassmaking and the history of glass beads still need to be sorted out.

Southern Centers

From the first millennium A.D., evidence points to glassmaking in the south. The non-Chinese Nan Yue lived in a region roughly south of the thirtieth parallel. During the first half of the first millennium, the area became sinicized. Chinese migrated from the north and the Nan Yue adapted Chinese culture.

Glassmaking in the south is first reported in a passage in *Strange Things of the South* by Wan Zhen around A.D. 300: "The basic substances of *liu-li* glass are minerals. In order to make vessels from them they must be worked by means of soda-ash . . . [which] is found on the shores of the southern seas [South China Sea]. . . . Without these ashes (the other minerals) will not dissolve" (Needham 1962, 107–108).

As noted earlier in this chapter, Ge Hong in the Western Jin (265 to 317) affirmed glassmaking in the south. He said, "The 'crystal' bowls from abroad are really made by compounding five sorts of ashes; and to-day this method is being commonly practiced in Chiao and Kuang" (Waley 1930–1932, 13; see also Needham 1962, 108). These regions refer to Guangdong, Guangxi, and adjoining parts of Vietnam as far south as Annam.

Guangzhou

Guangzhou (Canton), the principal city of the Nan Yue, was a glassmaking site, or associated with one, for a long time. There are references to glass being made in the city during the Song dynasty (Brown and Rabiner 1987, 74). It may also have been a place Wan Zhen and Ge Hong had in mind much earlier.

The Arab geographer al-Idrisi mentioned a glass center in southern China in 1154. Jaubert (1836, 100) translated the passage as: "Celle-ci est une ville célèbre . . . On y travaille le verre chinois." ("This is a celebrated city . . . They work Chinese glass.") Scholars have long worried that the city could not be identified with any known Chinese port (Nesbitt 1879a, 136; Jenyns 1982, 98). Nor can I do any better, though it is clear that it was near Guangzhou.[6] An elderly man interviewed by Chu and Chu (1973, 138) remembered his aunts making glass beads in his youth in some unidentified place near Guangzhou.

Glassworking is attested at Guangzhou from the late eighteenth century, but glassmaking was in doubt. Dr. Hugh Gillan, accompanying Lord Macartney in 1793–1794, observed at Guangzhou that the Chinese did not make glass themselves, but imported broken glass from Europe (Macartney 1963, 299). In early 1863, Guangzhou imported 3,063 kg of broken glass worth $US 177, not from Europe, but from elsewhere in China (Irish University Press Area Studies Series 1972, 300) and exported 58,213 kg of finished glass worth $39,490 (Irish University Press Area Studies Series 1972, 306). In the next decade Gray (1875, 236 n) said, "large quantities of glass were forwarded to China, from Australia," for working at Guangzhou.

S. Wells Williams was a careful observer of Chinese trade. His works indicate that glassmaking at Guangzhou became the norm during the nineteenth century. In the fifth edition of the *Chinese Commercial Guide*, published in 1863, he reported, "Fifty years ago, broken glassware was a considerable import at Canton, and a little is still brought, but the Chinese now make much of their own glassware" (S. W. Williams 1966, 91). By 1895 the situation had changed: "The manufacture of glass is carried on chiefly at Canton. . . . The importation of broken glass for remelting has entirely ceased . . . The furnaces are small, and from the ignorance on the part of the workmen, their products are not uniform." Among their products were "beautiful ornaments" (S. W. Williams 1885, 21).

Suzhou

Suzhou was another notable glassmaking center. It was famous for its glass lanterns (Gernet 1962, 188), including those of five colors. One type was known as a "Su-lantern" (Brown and Rabiner 1987, 75). At least during the Qing dynasty its glass was said to be inferior to that of Guangzhou (Brown and Rabiner 1987, 76).

An extraordinary object housed in the Suzhou Museum is an elaborately carved 1.22-m-high wooden reliquary pillar that may have held relics of Buddha. It was dedicated by Fan Yunsheng, a finance minister of the Northern Song, and encased in two wooden boxes in the third-story cellar of the pagoda at Ruiguangsi, Suzhou, in the year 1013. The pillar is decorated with some 40,000 pearls and 10,000 agate and glass beads. The wound glass beads dangling from the corners are in translucent blue, green, and red (*Beijing Review* 1980, 29; Yue and Liao 1985, 1813; personal observation, 1986). The pillar has been described, but its importance to the history of glass beadmaking has not been recognized. As will be seen in chapter 8, translucent red glass is an important Chinese contribution to the world glass story.

Quanzhou

The tentative identification of a third southern Chinese glass beadmaking center arises from the distribution of a certain type of bead, combed polychromes (see chap. 8). These beads are found in the heirloom beads of the Paiwan of Taiwan, the Kayan of Borneo, and the Toraja of Sulawesi. They have been excavated at Bubulungun and Luzon in the Philippines, Bongkissam and Bukit Sandong, Sarawak, and at Banten and Trowulan on Java. One has also been found at Fort Canning Hill, Singapore (Seidel 2000, 3).

All of these places are on the eastern route that connected China to Southeast Asia. The western route began at Guangzhou and continued south along mainland Southeast Asia and thence to the Indian Ocean or east to Java. The eastern route began at Quanzhou went across to Taiwan, then to Luzon and Mindoro and then either to Borneo or to Sulawesi (old Celebes) and Java (Ptak 1998).

The combed polychrome beads are not found on the western route (Singapore links the two routes). The beads of this type on the eastern route that can be dated cluster around the Yuan period, when this route was most heavily used (Ptak 1998, 12–13). Some, however, may be the result of trading during the Song period and others during the Ming period, officially or not. The distribution of these beads may well reflect their production at or near Quanzhou.[7] The use of combed decorations, unknown on other Chinese glass objects (R. K. Liu 1991, 62), might have been influenced by some members of the large Middle Eastern population that lived there (Ptak 1998, 8–9).[8] It is likely that the beads were made only for export.

The Rise of Boshan

In recent times, the best-known glassmaking region in China is not in the south but in the north. Beadmaking was conducted in a rough triangle bounded by Yantai, Beijing, and Zhangzhou, particularly on the Shandong Peninsula (Figure 6.1).

The concentration of glassmaking (and several other industries) in this region was due to the pressure put upon the Chinese population by what had been northern nomads, themselves being propelled southward by the ever spreading Mongols. Mountainous Shandong, rich in natural resources and accessible to most of the rest of China, was pressed into service by the rising demand for manufactured goods. The same circumstances turned China into a sea power and glass bead exporter. The situation is discussed in more detail in the next chapter dealing with trade in Chinese glass beads.

The only excavated glass factory in China is in Boshan (Boshanxian) in what is now the city of Zibo, Shandong. Twenty furnace pits were excavated. Judging from the ceramics and a coin, the archaeologists dated it to the fourteenth century, the early Ming period. The factory may have existed as early as the Yuan period (Yi and Tu 1991).

The first literary notice of glassmaking and beadmaking in Shandong is in *Diangong Kaiwu (The Creations of Nature and Man)* by Song Yingxing in 1637 (Sun and Sun 1966, 308–309), discussing the production of a false gem that the translators took to be lapis lazuli. However, translucent glass was being discussed: "[It] is similar to the Chinese quartz crystal and Cambodian quartz-prism in that all are lustrous and transparent. . . . It comes in many different colors. . . . All sorts of dyes and colors can be freely used to tint [it]" (Sun and Sun 1966, 308–309). The translators were evidentially reverting to the original etymology of *boluli* or more likely *boli,* derived from the Sanskrit *vaidūrya,* meaning "precious stone" of some sort (Yule and Burnell 1989, 88–89; Hirth and Rockhill 1911, 227; Needham 1962, 105–106).[9]

Another early center of glassmaking in Shandong was Yanshen (Yanshenzhen) in Qingzhoufu ("fu" is prefecture; Shandong was divided into ten). The records of one glassmaking family there, the Sun, date to the mid-eighteenth century, but glassmaking may be much older (Brown and Rabiner 1987, 73–74). It is certainly somewhat older. The Jesuit Father Du Halde in his *Description de la Chine* in 1735 noted glassmaking there: "The works of Liu-li, or Chinese glass, which is made at the great town of Yen-ching. This kind of glass is more fragile than that of Europe; it breaks when exposed to the hurts of the air" (Ayers 1965, 22).[10]

Nearly a century and a half later, Markham (1869–1870, 10–11) reported that beads, ornaments, and glass rods and bricks (canes and ingots) were produced at "Yenshing" and shipped all over the country. Hobson (1915, 200) wrote of a major pottery center: "Yen-shên Chên is quite close to Po-shan Hsein, and no doubt the industry at the two places is intimately connected."

However, it was Boshan that became the glassmaking center of China. Its production as described by Williamson in the 1870s has often been quoted:

> Long ago it was discovered that the rocks in the neighborhood of Poshanhsien [Boshanxian], when pulverized and fused with nitrate of potass [potash], formed glass; and for many years the natives have applied themselves to its manufacture. I found them making lanterns, beads, and ornaments in endless variety. They also run it into rods about thirty inches long, which they tie up in bundles and export to all parts of the country. The glass is extremely pure, they color it most beautifully, and have attained considerable dexterity in manipulation. . . . (Bushell 1914, 2: 61–62 [insertions mine])

One place where Boshan's canes were shipped was Beijing (Warren 1977, 101–103). This was done until recently (Blair 1951a, 368). Sprague and An (1990) reported that lead glass for beads was made in Beijing and that nonlead glass for beadmaking at Boshan was in decline since the observations reported in Kan and Liu (1984). E. T. Lewis (1994) documented a glass beadmaking factory recently set up in Gejiu, Yunnan (Figure 6.1). It once made its own glass, but now imports it (apparently from Boshan). The beadmakers were trained in Shandong.

There were other centers making beads and related glass products in China. Bangles, often technically allied to beads,[11] were reported being made at Jinanfu (probably Boshan) in Shandong and Dadongfu in Guizhou Province (Mesny 1899, 51–52). The *China Year Book* listed a glass factory making ornaments at Chefoo (modern Yantai) (Woodhead 1922, 773; 1927, 188). Our knowledge of this part of China's glassmaking history remains imperfect, but it is evident that despite the later domination of Boshan, it was only one of many Shandong glass ornament-making centers.

Foreign Influence and Observations

The earliest foreign visitors to China who left records were not very impressed with the glass they encountered. During the Ming period, the Jesuit missionary Matteo Ricci, who lived in China from 1583 to 1610, wrote in a letter, "At the present time they [the Chinese] are making glass, but very inferior to ours" (Ayers 1965, 21 [insertion mine]). In his diary[12] he wrote, "These people have also acquired the art of glass blowing, but their workmanship here falls far short of what we see at home" (Gallagher 1942, 22; 1953, 15).

During the Qing dynasty, a new impetus for glassmaking arose. Emperor Kang Xi (1662 to 1722) is said to have established twenty-seven imperial workshops in Beijing, at least some with the help of Jesuit missionaries. One, perhaps begun around 1680, was located on the palace grounds and was devoted to glass. It was possibly first under the direction of Ferdinand Verbiest (born Conrad von dem Voorst; 1623 to 1688) and more certainly later under Kilian Stumpf (Bell 1788, 42).[13]

The workshop attained a measure of success. In 1703 Kang Xi's favorite personal secretary, Gao Shiqi, called at the palace to bid farewell to the emperor upon his (Gao's) retirement. Because of his exemplary service he was granted an extraordinary tour of the palace, normally closed to mere mortals. The emperor then:

> [S]howed him new articles of glassware of excellent quality and artistic design. Then H. M said: "Although this glassware is only some sort of pottery, its success or failure on the market can affect politics. China can now produce a sort of glassware superior to the Western product." Then His Majesty bestowed upon His servant some twenty articles of glassware and a mirror-screen five *ch'ih* high [1.79 m; 5 feet, 10.5 inches] imported from Europe. (Fu 1966, 113 [insertion mine])

John Bell, who visited Beijing in 1720, reported on the workshop, having been left with the impression that the Chinese had never before known how to make glass:

> [W]e were conducted to the Emperor's glass-house, which his Imperial Majesty often visits with pleasure. It was erected by himself, and is the first manufactory of the kind that ever was in China. The person employed to superintend and carry on this design was Kilian Stumpff, a German father, lately deceased; a man in great favour with the Emperor, and well known in China for his ingenuity and literature. His Majesty is so fond of this glass-work, that he sent several of the most curious of its productions in a present to his Czarish Majesty [the Czar of Russia]. It is surprising that the Chinese, who have been constantly employed for so many ages in the manufacture of China-ware, should never have stumbled upon that of glass. (Bell 1788, 42–43 [insertion mine])

The workshop has been identified archaeologically. It had small furnaces until the mid-1700s, when a larger one was built (Yang 1985, 27–28). Beads are never mentioned among its products, which were a limited number of vessels meant only for royal use. However, the workshop is important in bead history because of the patronage of the emperor, which continued through the reign of Qian Long (1736 to 1796). The patronage extended to pottery glazes. Especially under Qian Long, glazes and glasses were given a new color repertoire.

In addition to more than thirteen decades of official patronage, the requirement that all officials and their immediate families wear beads naturally stimulated production (Color Plate 13). Chinese glass beads underwent significant changes not only in their colors, but also in improved quality and new uses (Francis 1990c, 125).

The most substantial intrusion of the Chinese glass industry was by the Japanese, apparently long before they invaded the Middle Kingdom. Forsyth (1912, 386) said: "Recently a large manufactory for the making of glass has been erected in Poshan. It is of foreign construction and under foreign management." The only foreign glass works in Boshan (Jinanfu) a decade later was the "Shantong Glass Factory" owned by Japanese (Woodhead 1922, 773). Woodhead (1922, 773–774) listed twenty glass factories of different sorts,[14] five of them owned by Japanese, another one scheduled to open, and two that could be for either glass or porcelain. Five years later he (Woodhead 1927, 187–189) listed thirty-two glass factories, one of them "Sino-British," five Japanese, and three Japanese-owned glass or porcelain factories. Two in Boshan (Jinanfu) were Japanese, though neither was then named "Shantong Glass Factory."

The Japanese at least contemplated setting up a glass industry in Manchuria. A report (East-Asiatic Economic Investigation Bureau 1931, 121) recorded, "Manchuria possesses favourable conditions for manufacturing glass, having an abundant supply of material of excellent quality, and a cheap fuel supply, and being favoured with advantageous climactic conditions." As might be expected, the report focused on modern glass works and their relationship with the Japanese. Beadmaking was not mentioned.

However, they may have known about Manchuria glass potential from another source. Batchelor (1892, 50) said that the Ainu women of northern Japan "are extremely fond of glass beads. Some of these beads are of Japanese make, others have come from China. The Ainu believe that the ancients got them from the *Rushikai*—that is, Russians and Manchurians." A detailed study on trade with the Ainu concluded that beads were made in Manchuria. "These beads were made in Manchuria and were known in China as *kitan* beads (from the land of the Khitan Tartar)" (Harrison 1954, 289). Whatever Manchurian glass bead industry there may have been is recorded late and entered the Asian maritime trade in only a marginal way.

Beginning in 1927 the Japanese selected five Korean youths to go to China, learn how to make glass beads, and return to their homeland to continue the craft (Francis 1985b, 31). After the Koreans returned home, they shipped their products to Japan, where they were repackaged, marked "Made in Japan," and sold to the world. This was still being done, though no longer for all beads produced, in the mid-1980s. There is little doubt that the Japanese did the same thing with Chinese production.[15]

Chinese Beadmaking Outside China

One other factor involving Chinese glass beadmakers must be considered: the presence of Chinese beadmakers outside China.[16] One such place was Banten in West Java.[17] The papers of John Saris (died 1646), a captain of the (British) East India Company, showed that there were Chinese making glass beads at the then thriving port in the early seventeenth century (Francis 1985c). Saris was a consummate observer. He lived in Banten for several years and on two occasions described the blue beads used in the Borneo trade, worth three shillings a hundred at Sukadana, Borneo. In a letter to the East India Company on 4 December 1608, he mentioned "blue glass beads which the Chinese make" (Danvers 1896, 22). In his diary he wrote about "All sorts of small Bugles, Bugles which are made in Bantam, of colour blue" (Saris 1905, 513).

There was also at least one Chinese beadmaker (likely working glass) in southern Borneo. George Cokayne, also of the East India Company, wrote to George Ball, head of the factory at Banten, on 15 June 1617: "Within this three or four days I shall see what profit will be found in the [Chinese] bead-maker. They say there is in his matters much profit. I believe I shall find in him as much as in the rest of his countrymen" (Foster 1901, 313). Cokayne's opinion of the Chinese was quite low, and he apparently did not get along with this one, either, because nothing more was recorded about the matter.

China is only now receiving the credit it deserves as a glass-making nation. Early Chinese beadmaking during the Late Zhou period is one of the artistic highlights of bead production anywhere in the world. The quality of beads declined during the Han, perhaps because of their availability from Western sources when the Silk Road opened. The Chinese continued to make beads for specific uses within their culture, especially imitation jade, for centuries. By Southern Song times, the export trade was an impetus for Chinese glass bead production. Chinese beads entered the world stage in a major way at that time, as discussed in the next chapter.

7

Export of Chinese Beads

China made glass and glass beads long before its products entered the Asian maritime trade. To see why this was the case, we need to look at the history of Chinese commercial relations.

Traditionally, China was a land-based society, centered in the north, along the Huanghe (Yellow River). This is the homeland of the "Han Chinese," the "Sons of Han." Theirs was an agrarian society and their principal foreign connections were with the peoples to the west. China's earliest opening to the wider world consisted of trade with the Roman West and the influx of India's Buddhism, both of which began in Han times (202 B.C. to A.D. 220).[1] Most of this commerce and religious exchange was done overland. Thus, it falls outside the focus of this work.

As for Chinese maritime trade, we must distinguish among four operations according to who was involved. They are (1) Chinese trade conducted by non-Han Chinese; (2) Chinese trade conducted by other Asians; (3) Chinese trade conducted by Westerners; and (4) Chinese trade conducted by the Han Chinese themselves.

Chinese Trade Conducted by Non-Han Chinese

The region south of the Yangtze River (Changjiang) was for a long time considered outside China proper (Figure 7.1). It was inhabited by people the Han Chinese called Nan Yue (Nan Yüeh) or "Southern People." Their life contrasted with that of the Chinese, because they ate rice rather than wheat and relied on seafood rather than land animals for protein. Sima Qian (Ssu-ma Ch'ien) described them in the *Records of the Historian* when discussing the early Han period in the age of Emperor Wu Di (141–87 B.C.):

> [The] region of Ch'u and Yüeh is broad and sparsely populated, and the people live on rice and fish soups. They burn off the fields and flood them to kill the weeds, and are able to gather all the fruit, berries, and univalve and bivalve shellfish they want without waiting for merchants to come around selling them. Since the land is so rich in edible products, there is no fear of famine, and therefore the people are content to live along from day to day; they do not lay away stores of goods and many of them are poor. As a result, in the region south of the Yangtze and Huai rivers no one ever freezes or starves to death, but on the other hand there are no very wealthy families. (Watson 1961, 490)

The people of this idyllic land did, in time, aspire to greater wealth, which they could obtain through trade. It is they who opened the "second Silk Route" via the South China Sea during Han times (G. Wang 1958, 6). It was they who carried on foreign maritime commerce as intermediaries between Southeast Asia and the northern Chinese court.

Beginning in the fourth century, ethnic Chinese started moving southward into this rich and warm land.

Concurrently, the Nan Yue began to be sinicized. Initially, there was a lack of general interest in overseas trade by the newly arrived Chinese. Guangzhou (Canton) and Hanoi developed as major, wealthy ports, trading silk from the north for luxury goods to sell to the north. Yet, they remained "frontier towns" in respect to China proper. The Nan Yue continued as the primary traders and mariners, and the Chinese became the port officials, often enriching themselves thereby (G. Wang 1958, 31–46).

This pattern persisted for centuries. Even in Tang times, most people of Guangdong were still Nan Yue. By the tenth century, acculturated Nan Yue and Chinese settlers who had come to love the sea dominated the maritime merchant class. This Chinese–Nan Yue fusion maintained the ancient sea trade patterns (G. Wang 1958, 115 n. 2). Even during periods of prohibition (1372 to 1567) they continued to trade, but as smugglers (Blusse and Zhuang 1991). They were also the major players in the lucrative Manila trade, where they met the Spanish galleons coming from Mexico (Cummins 1971, 305).

Chinese Trade Conducted by Other Asians

Chinese interest in maritime trade was awakened by internal events. In the turbulent period of the Southern and Northern Dynasties (A.D. 336 to 588), small king-

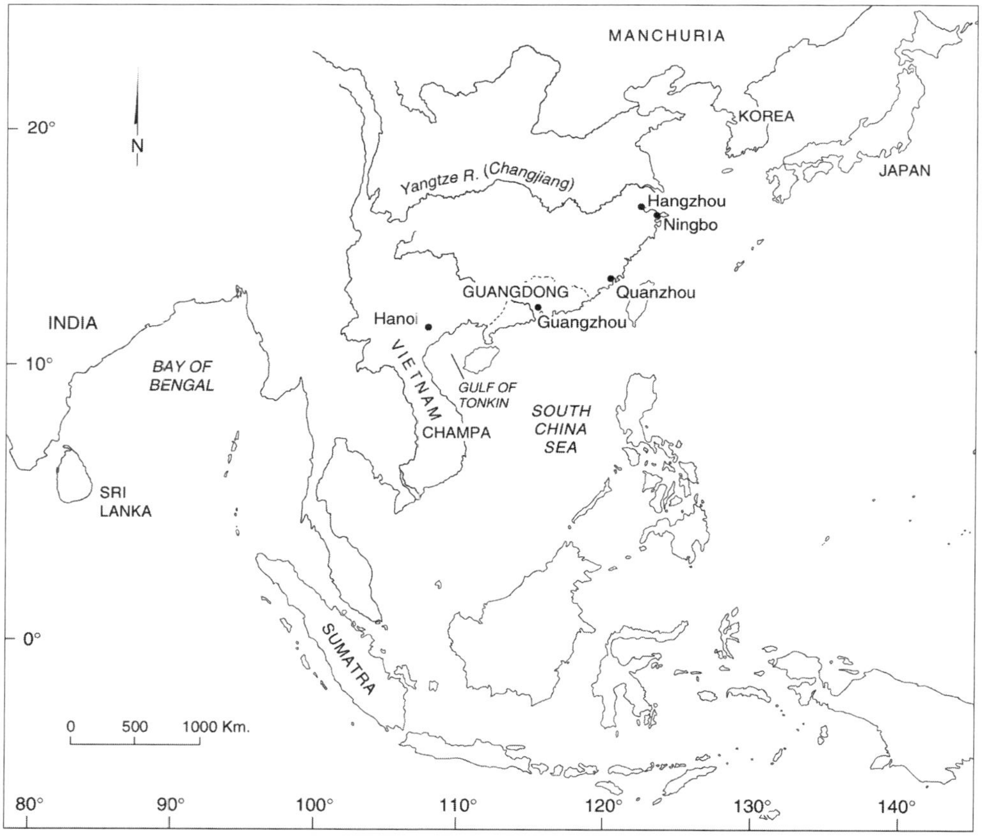

Figure 7.1. *Map of southern China showing areas controlled by the Nan Yue and settlements of the "New Chinese" in the region.*

doms fought and generally annoyed each other. In the process, the Southern dynasties were cut off from the old overland routes. It became necessary for them to trade by sea because there was an expanding demand for all the luxuries that had become requirements to the court. An oft-quoted passage from the *Liu Song Shu (History of the Liu Song)*, covering the years 420 to 478, explained this:

> When the Chin dynasty moved south it was separated from the Yellow River and Kansu by a great distance. The barbarians [? of northern China] obstructed the routes and the foreign regions were now as remote as Heaven. *Ta-ch'in* and India were far away in the vastnesses of the west. [Even] when the two Han dynasties had sent expeditions, these routes had been found to be particularly difficult and [some] merchandise, on which [China] depended, has come from Tongking; it had sailed on the waves of the sea, following the wind, and travelling from afar to [China]. [In between] there are also range upon range of mountains. There are numerous tribes with different and strange titles. Precious things come from the mountains and the sea by this way. There are articles such as rhinoceros' horn and kingfisher feathers and rarities such as serpent pearls and asbestos; there are thousands of varieties, all of which the rulers eagerly coveted. Therefore ships came in a continuous stream, and merchants and envoys jostled with each other. (Wolters 1967, 77)[2]

Wolters (1967, 285 n. 27) noted that this passage marks an important change in the Chinese conception of maritime trade. Furthermore, he pointed out that all this trade was directed one way, inward to China. Exports were merely commodities used to buy goods. The Chinese themselves did not go to sea. Nor could the Nan Yue handle all the increased trade. Their world, limited to the southern China coast and the Gulf of Tonkin, was too small to provide all the imported luxuries.

Other Southeast Asians became the chief traders. In the early centuries A.D. Funan and Sri Lanka filled this role. Sri Lanka had a long and close relationship with China due in no small measure to the island being the chief depository of Buddhist relics and learning (Werake 1990). The role of Funan was discussed in chapter 4. Both Funan and Sri Lanka eventually lost their position as major traders with China.

During much of the fourth and fifth centuries Funan struggled with Srivijaya to become the chief intermediaries between China and India (G. Wang 1958, 53–57). In time, Srivijaya triumphed (Wolters 1967). Funan, having been left out of the loop, became even more solidly "Indianized" (Hall 1982). Srivijaya remained the chief broker in this trade until the end of the eleventh century.

The island of Sri Lanka was a natural sea power with the largest ships at sea. In addition to early and good relations with China, it was a major trading partner with Persia. The Egyptian traveler Cosmas Indicopleustes in the first half of the sixth century noted Persian Christians (Nestorians) there, "and a Presbyter who is appointed from Persia, and a Deacon and a complete ecclesiastical ritual" (McCrindle 1897, 365). He described the trade of the island at a port (doubtless Mantai) in this way:

> The island being, as it is, in a central position, is much frequented by ships from all parts of India and from Persia and Ethiopia, and it likewise sends out many of its own. And from the remotest countries, I mean Tzinista [China] and other trading places, it receives silk, aloes, cloves, sandalwood and other products, and these again are passed on to marts on this side, such as Male [Malabar, southwest India], where pepper grows. And to Calliana [Kalyana, near Bombay] . . . And to Sindu [Sind, now in Pakistan] also . . . and to Persia and the Homerite country, and to Adulê [Adulis, Ethiopia]. And the island

> receives imports from all these marts which we have mentioned and passes them on to the remoter ports, while, at the same time, exporting its own produce in both directions. (McCrindle 1897, 365–366 [insertions mine])

However, once the "southern route" was established in the Early Islamic period, Sri Lanka was more often bypassed. As discussed in chapter 1, this route (going west) involved leaving a port in Malaysia or Aceh (northern Sumatra) at the right time of the year. Sailing directly west would take one to Somalia, enabling the ship to turn north for Persia, Oman, or Egypt or south for East Africa. The Maldives group is in the middle of this route and became a port of rest, refreshment, and reviving stores, particularly of water.

The period in which this route became dominant is still being debated. It is probably later than Gunawardana (1990, 32) suggested, with the sixth century as the high point for Sri Lankan commerce and a decline after that. Tampoe (1990, 87) put it in the eleventh and twelfth centuries. Naturally, it did not happen all at once. The decline of Mantai in the late tenth century resulting from the Cōḷa invasions may have been a determining factor in favoring the new route.

Funan, Sri Lanka, and Srivijaya were by no means the only ones involved in this trade. In the third century, the Chams and Indians were trading along with the Funanese and Ceylonese (G. Wang 1958, 44). When the Chinese themselves wanted to travel, as did Fa Xian (Fa-hsien) in the early fifth century, they went on ships owned and operated by non-Chinese (Giles 1923, 65–83). Kanshin (Kien-Tchen), a Chinese Buddhist at Guangzhou around A.D. 750, noted that the boats on the Pearl River were owned by Indian Brahmans, Persians,[3] and Malays among others "whose numbers are difficult to determine." He also noticed red, white, and other colored "barbarians" from Sri Lanka, the Arab lands, and "Kou-t'ang" (Goudang). The last-named place is unidentified, but its people were blond[4] (Takakusu 1929–1930: 446–447).

In northern waters, Koreans played the intermediary role. This was first conducted by the Paekche Kingdom (18 B.C. to A.D. 668), which brought Japan into the system (Best 1982). When Silla absorbed the Paekche Kingdom in 668, its mariners became the master seamen, followed by the Japanese and seafaring Manchurians (Schafer 1963, 11).

The only Chinese beads that can be identified as used in trade by one of these intermediaries are the most common type produced, the small, wound, monochrome coil beads, discussed in detail in the next chapter. They far outnumber Indo-Pacific beads at Barus, North Sumatra, Indonesia, on the northwestern coast where they are associated with Northern Song (960–1127) ceramics. Barus was the principal port for camphor, the finest of which grew in the Sumatran interior around Lake Toba. China used it heavily beginning in Tang times (618–906) (Schafer 1963, 166–168). The dynastic histories through the Ming did not mention any place on the western coast of Sumatra and discussed camphor as a tribute from Srivijaya (Groeneveldt 1876, 59–101).[5] Zhao Rugua during the Southern Song (1225) identified Barus and Borneo as sources of camphor, though most of his countrymen thought it came from Srivijaya (Hirth and Rockhill 1911, 193, 194 n. 1).

Chinese Trade Conducted by Westerners

Chinese trade conducted by West Asians and Indians opened in Han times (Yü 1967, 172–187). It was not until the seventh century that there is any clear evidence for Westerners making direct contact by sea with China (G. Wang 1958, 113–117). Throughout the Tang period (A.D. 618 to 906), foreign ships and sailors, rather than Chinese, took the initiative in commerce (Duyvendak 1949, 12–13).

The intrepid Yijing, who made two round-trip voyages from China, usually referred to the ships he took as "merchant ships." At the outset of his first voyage in 671, he wrote, "I came to the town of Kwang-tung [Canton], where I fixed the date of meeting with the owner of a Persian[6] ship to embark for the south" (Takakusu 1966, xxviii [insertion mine]).

Westerners, especially the Dashi[7] (Arabs), came to China and even established colonies of some size and prosperity. They married Chinese women and brought Islamic influence to the country. In parallel, some Chinese went west and introduced papermaking and other technologies (Zhang 1983, 92–98). Throughout, the transportation was done by Westerners coming to and going from China.

The Chinese were content to sit back, collect duty, and barter on home grounds. There was, however, a growing appreciation of the value of this trade, particularly in luxuries meant for the court or temples. A customs service was set up in Guangzhou (Canton), an old stronghold of the Nan Yue, by the eighth century. It was reorganized in 971 and declared a state monopoly a few years later. Late in the tenth century, a General Customs Office was set up at Hangzhou and at about the same time an inspector of customs was appointed for Hangzhou and Ningbo. Another was appointed for Quanzhou in 1087 (Figure 7.1).

This activity increased the luxury trade dramatically. In the years 1049 to 1053, 53,000 units (we do not know what a unit was) of ivory, rhinoceros horn, pearls, aromatics, and incense were imported by sea annually. By 1175 the amount had increased to 500,000 units (Duyvendak 1949, 16). Yet even at that late date, foreigners carried on most commerce. As Zhou Kufeï wrote in 1178:

> The coast departments and the prefectures of the empire now stretch from the north-east to the south-west as far as K'in-chóu [westernmost Guangdong], and their coast departments and prefectures (are visited) by trading ships. In its watchful kindness to the foreign Barbarians our Government has established at Ts'üan-chóu [Quanzhou] and Kuang-chóu [Guangzhou] Special Inspectorates of Shipping, and whenever any of the foreign traders have difficulties or wish to lay a complaint they must go to the Special Inspectorate. (Hirth and Rockhill 1911, 22–23 [insertions in brackets mine])

It is likely that Muslim traders, as well as traders from Srivijaya, took coil beads and Northern Song ceramics to Barus to exchange for camphor. Barus is recognized in the Arab literature as Fansur from the late eighth or early ninth century through the fifteenth. In those texts, it is exclusively associated with the camphor trade (Tibbetts 1979, 140–141).

Muslim trade with China continued until the Ming prohibitions. By the time those were lifted in 1567, Europeans had begun to be entrenched in most of Asia, outrunning and encircling their old religious and commercial rivals, the Arabs.

European global expansion took Chinese beads even farther afield. The Chinese took beads to Manila, the eastern terminus of the galleon trade for the Chinese. From there, the Spanish shipped some across the Pacific to Acapulco, Mexico (see chap. 16). They were then distributed at least to places in Nueva España (Francis 1994c) and La Florida (personal observation). The Russians, who were barred from using Chinese ports, bought beads along the Mongolian border and took them during their first expedition to Alaska under the Dane Vitus Bering. The beads they brought were in such demand that for many years thereafter Yankee skippers exchanged furs for them and other Chinese beads at Guangzhou and took them to Alaska. Native Americans traded the most favored beads as far south as the Columbia River (Francis 1994d).

Chinese Trade Conducted by the Han Chinese

During all this time, the negative evidence of Chinese involvement in the trade is significant. From the early fifth to late sixth centuries, G. Wang (1958, 58) noted, "The Chinese texts do not mention any Chinese ships carrying the trade." There were few Chinese abroad. The rare traveler who ventured abroad did so almost alone.

For the two years that Fa Xian was in Sri Lanka in the early fifth century he never encountered another Chinese, nor were there any others on the ship back home (Giles 1923, 65–83). The Chinese were also absent in Sri Lanka in the mid-sixth century. Cosmas Indicopleustes never wrote of Chinese ships, only Chinese goods (McCrindle 1897, 365–366)

The Chinese ignorance of foreign lands along the

sea route is evident in the itinerary from China to the Persian Gulf written by Jia Dan as late as 785 to 805 (Hirth and Rockhill 1911, 9–14). It is almost entirely secondhand and demonstrates that the Chinese themselves did not sail this route.

However, things change. Apart from the growing profitability of foreign trade, there were increasing threats to the Chinese heartland from the north and west. The states of Liao, Xia, and Jin in turn waxed in power on the northern borders of the Song Kingdom. The Song tried appeasement and bribes to bring the rivals into their camp, but to no avail. Eventually the Jin seized the initiative and in 1125 took the Liao Emperor prisoner. Two years later they captured the Song Emperor and his son at the fall of Kaifeng in 1127. Gao Zong, the brother of the Emperor of the (Northern) Song, assumed the throne as Emperor of the (Southern) Song. The old capital was gone, and a new one was established in Hangzhou.

Hangzhou was not on the sea, but was vulnerable to attack from that direction. This forced the Song to look outward. Interior contemplation, once the hallmark of Chinese polity, was sharply revised. The assault from the north intensified, now coming directly from the Mongols. In a few short years after the elevation of Genghis Khan in 1206, the Liao, the Xia, and the Jin were all conquered. The Southern Song fell in 1279.

These disturbances produced enormous population shifts. The Chinese were uprooted as never before. The census of 1080 listed no less than a third of the Chinese population as "transients," rather than "settled" people. Most of them were northerners fleeing from the invading outsiders (Lo 1955, 497–498). Driven by these forces, people poured into the six southeastern seaboard provinces, much of it old Nan Yue territory. These provinces came to hold no less than half the population on a mere 10 percent of China's land. By the time of the Yuan (Mongol) census of 1330, some two-thirds of the taxpayers of China lived in that region (Lo 1955, 497–498).

Whatever the ultimate reasons for this unprecedented movement of people, the results are not hard to see. Crowded into provinces bereft of vast lands to support agriculture, the people squeezed into cities; Hangzhou became the largest urban conglomerate in the world at the time.[8]

The only hope of economic growth was industrialization and an export drive. To these tasks the Chinese applied themselves. Shandong was an especially fruitful region for developing its natural resources. It also had fine transportation opportunities with the Yangtze, the Grand Canal, and the ports of its coast. Large metallurgical and ceramic establishments were only the most visible aspects of this expansion. A wealthy middle class arose, demanding the luxuries once reserved for the court. This required increased output to pay for increased imports. The cycle fed upon itself and transformed China. Chinese ceramics and cash were widely distributed, all the way to Africa (Gernet 1982, 320–322). Glass beads were another such commodity.

There are a few written accounts of Chinese glass beads being exported to specific places. They are sparse, but there are records from the Southern Song (1127 to 1279), Yuan (1280 to 1368), and Ming (1368 to 1644) periods.

In 1225 Zhao Rugua, the chief customs officer at Quanzhou, Fujian, wrote *Zhu Fan Zhi (Chu-fan-chï)* as a guide to Chinese mariners trading with the outside world. In the work, some of which was based on older compilations, he described the people living in countries where travelers visited and listed the goods foreign countries produced and those they would take in exchange. To the Philippine islands of Mindoro or Luzon, likely Palawan, and certainly the Visayas he advised taking "colored glass beads" (Hirth and Rockhill 1911, 160). He also told sailors to take glass beads to Borneo, though the type was not specified (Hirth and Rockhill 1911, 156) (Figure 7.2).

A little more than a century later (1349) during the Yuan dynasty a work by Wang Dayuan listed even more places where beads should be taken for commerce. Beads of unspecified types were to be taken to Annam, Thailand; Majapahit in Java; the Moluccas Islands; the northern Philippines; and two places not identified (Rockhill 1915, 86, 100, 238, 255, 260, 269, 464). He also suggested that yellow beads and red beads should go to Cambodia, colored beads to Ligor (Nakhon Si Thammarat, Thailand), red beads and green beads to Kelantan (eastern Malay Peninsula) and an unidentified site, dark red beads to the Jung people (possibly in the Malay Peninsula), red beads to eastern Sumatra, small colored *Menbang (Mên-pang)*[9] beads to Palembang and/or Jambi in Sumatra, yellow beads to Danmo (an unidentified place), blue ones to the Sulu Archipelago, and red ones and white ones to what might be Bombay (Rockhill 1915, 107, 109, 122, 128, 129, 134, 136, 255, 271, 467)[10] (Figure 7.2).

However, China's maritime career was soon abruptly halted. Ming China turned its back on the world, asserting that nothing from elsewhere was needed. Private maritime trade was forbidden by the first Ming Emperor, Zhu Yuanzhang (Tai Zu; reigned 1368 to 1398) in 1372. He renewed the prohibition several times, "not even allowing a wooden plank to drift to sea," and made it part of the "ancestral laws," requiring every successor to follow it (Blusse and Zhuang 1991). Not only was private commerce forbidden, but state-sponsored trade was also effectively halted.

Exactly why this happened is not clear. Duyvendak (1949, 27–28) ascribed it to the age-old feud between the eunuchs and the official classes. Chang (1934, 30–31) offered no explanation, but charted a drifting, purposeless official attitude toward maritime trade. Blusse and Zhuang (1991) suggested that resources, including those that once supported the southern naval troops, were required along the Mongolian border for most of this time. G. Wang (1991, 125–126) noted the pressures on

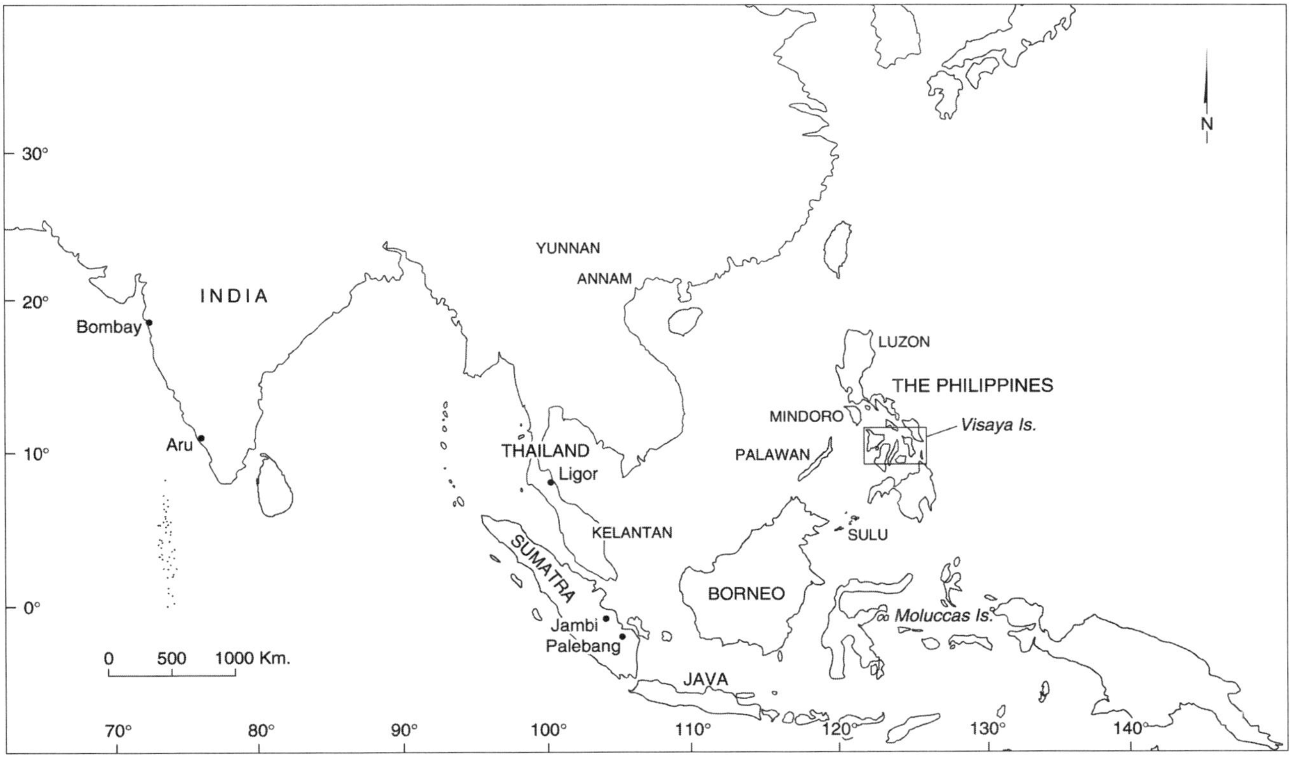

Figure 7.2. *Map of Southeast Asia showing places mentioned in the text.*

the northern borders, but concluded that it had more to do with the revived Confucian outlook on the nature of the state. The ban was not lifted until 1567.

While the ban was in effect, coastal dwellers, merchants, and mariners were hard-pressed. Many turned to smuggling (Chang 1934, 67–85; Blusse and Zhuang 1991). Others concentrated on developing their local industries, as happened at Quanzhou (G. Wang 1991, 84–85). Still others left China and settled in Southeast Asian and Japanese ports, including Banten, Manila, and Malacca. These "runaways," as the court saw them, are invisible to history until the coming of the Europeans. No official histories recorded them. They did not record their own dealings either because of illiteracy or prudence, nor did those in China who traded with them write anything about them (G. Wang 1991, 86–87).

There was also a major official exception to this ban. The eunuch Zheng He (Cheng Ho) was commissioned by the Emperors Cheng Zu (ruled 1402–1424) and Xuan Zung (ruled 1425–1435) to undertake and supervise a total of seven voyages between 1405 and 1431, the last one returning in 1433. At its peak, his fleet consisted of several hundred ships and tens of thousands of men. The fleet was at least sometimes divided into squadrons going to different places. These remarkable voyages of discovery were the largest that had been undertaken to that time—by some measures the largest ever undertaken (Mills 1970, 10–15).

The first three voyages visited only Southeast Asia and India. The fourth went all the way to Hormuz and the last three made it to East Africa. The fleet visited Arabia three times (Zheng He was a Muslim, but at least one Chinese scholar believes he converted to Buddhism) (Bai 1982, 334; Y. Liu 1991). The second voyage involved 249 ships and the third thirty thousand troops. The visits were intended to learn about other countries, forge ties with their kings, buy exotic goods, pay homage (to the Buddha's relics in Sri Lanka), perform the hajj, and in some cases use the fleet's military power to effect changes in the political systems of the countries visited.

Several books were written about these voyages.[11] *Yingyai Shenglan (The Overall Survey of the Ocean's Shores)*[12] by Ma Huan (also called Ma Zongyuan) was published around 1451.[13] Ma Huan was a Muslim and was taken on the voyages as an interpreter, traveling on the fourth, sixth, and seventh voyages (why he did not go on the fifth is unknown). It is probably the best of the books written about these voyages, but has its shortcomings, too.

Although Ma Huan's account is rich in details about organic gem beads (see chap. 15), he hardly mentioned glass beads given to places the fleet visited. He only noted beads being exchanged at Champa (central Vietnam) (Mills 1970, 85) and Java. The latter notice is translated variously, as "The people of this country are fond of Chinese porcelain with green flowers, musk, flowered and plain linen or silk, glassbeads [*sic*], etc." (Groeneveldt 1876, 53) and "The people of the country are very fond of the blue patterned porcelain-ware of the Central Country, also of such things as musk, gold-flecked hemp-silks, and beads" (Mills 1970, 97). It is likely that "beads" rather than "glass beads" is in the original.

Another book on these voyages, *Xingcha Shenglan (The Overall Survey of the Star Raft)*[14] by Fei Xin (Fei Hsin), is dated 1436.[15] Fei Xin borrowed heavily from other writers, including Ma Huan, but was on three of these voyages (the third, the fifth, and the seventh) as well as another voyage under the eunuch Yang Chi. Fei Xin provides us with many more notices of bead trading or gifting. He noted the export of beads to Thailand, Cambodia, Aru (Sumatra), and Calicut (India) and colored beads to the Moluccas and Palembang (Rockhill 1915, 105, 108, 118, 140, 142, 462). Colored glass beads were also to be taken to a place Rockhill (1915, 76) identified with Quilon, on the Malabar Coast of India. However, the description[16] of the place fits Groeneveldt's (1876, 78) identification of Belitung Island (Indonesia, north of Java) much better. Another place to which glass beads were to be taken was discussed by Groeneveldt (1876, 115), but not listed in Rockhill. It is clearly Karimata, a small island near Borneo (Figure 7.2).

After Zheng He's monumental undertaking the Ming reverted to their ban on sea travel. Their xenophobic attitude was rekindled when Europeans (Portuguese) began trading in China in 1519. In Chinese eyes, they offended local customs and flaunted the import laws.

This led to the expulsion of all foreigners and cessation of trade for three decades (Chang 1934, 32–85). The predicament was finally resolved with the granting of Macao as a trading port; the same solution was adopted centuries later with the British at Hong Kong.

After the lifting of the ban in 1567, maritime trade increased and became lucrative again. During at least part of the long reign of Kang Xi, the second Qing (Manchu) emperor (reigned 1661–1722), more than a thousand seagoing ships were built annually at Suzhou, the majority of which were sold abroad (Bai 1982, 410). Most important for our story is the Chinese trade with Spain via Manila. Inland trade remained a mockery, as attested to by visitors to Beijing in the early 1600s:[17]

> The Merchants come usually from the West to this Citie, which with fayned [feigned] Embassage, by ancient leagues of seven, or eight Kingdomes with that of China, have obtayned, that every sixth yeare seventie two in name of Legats should pay Tribute to the King, that shining Marble,[18] pieces of Diamonds, blue color and other things; thence they go to the Court at publike charge, and likewise returne. Their Tribute is rather by way of honour or homage than any way profitable; for no man payes dearer for this Marble than the King himselfe, who esteemes it a dishonour to take any thing of Strangers for nothing. (Father Matthew 1906, 234–235 [insertion mine])

Although the Han Chinese did not enter the Asian maritime bead trade until the Song period, the twelfth century was the critical period for China in this trade. It was also a significant period for the whole bead trade because of two other events in other parts of the world that changed the shape of commerce.

One of these was the demise of Srivijaya, more precisely of the capital at Vijaya (modern Palembang), between 1079 and 1082. This corresponds with the collapse of the Southeast Asian Indo-Pacific beadmaking industry, but exactly why is unknown. Certainly the most common bead made by the Chinese is superficially very similar to Srivijayan Indo-Pacific beads. Tiny Chinese "coil" beads (see chap. 8) are also small monochromes.

The other event took place a long way from China: the Crusades. This, coupled with the final, fatal blow of the Mongols in the early fifteenth century, crippled the once mighty West Asian glass bead industry (see chap. 9) so badly that it never again attained its old prominence and allowed Chinese glass beads to dominate this branch of commerce for centuries.

8

Chinese Beads in the Asian Maritime Trade

How are glass beads identified as Chinese? The answer is superficially simple. They are identified in the same way one identifies the origin of any artifact:

1. By direct evidence of manufacturing. As we have seen, there is little documentation for Chinese glass beadmaking. Save for Boshan, no bead production sites have been found or reported within China. There is, however, one type of bead known to be Chinese because Chinese artisans made them outside China.
2. By recognizing diagnostic technical attributes. Some technical characteristics point to Chinese production, the most important being the use of lead glass. Certain colorants are also an important clue, as are the ways in which beads were made.
3. By their distribution. Beads found at times and in places that mirror periods and areas of intensive Chinese trade as discussed in the last chapter could be Chinese, especially if not found elsewhere. This, however, is the weakest of these three lines of reasoning because distributions can be misleading and it relies on negative evidence of other production and distribution. (By itself, this is an argument for a global approach to bead studies.) Such distributions provide clues, but if this is the only characteristic met, it must be treated with caution until more data are available.

When all three elements are present, identifying particular beads as Chinese is a virtual certainty. Knowing that particular beads were made in China or by Chinese and not by anyone else is sufficient. Unhappily, such positive identification is rarer than we may wish. The technical clues are the next strongest evidence for beads being Chinese.

Technical Features in Chinese Glass

Lead Glass

The first studies of Chinese glass beads (Beck and Seligman 1934; Ritchie 1937; Seligman and Beck 1938) revealed that those from the Late Zhou period had a distinctive composition. The glass was high in both lead and barium. As noted in chapter 2, lead is a glass former with several advantages to the glass worker. Barium acts in much the same way. Gan (1991, 2) suggested that barium was used as an opacifier to make the glass look more like jade. It may also have occurred naturally in the lead ore.

Although lead was used in some Western glasses, it was rare. Turner (1956b, 175T) and Caley (1962, 65–66) both noted that only a few Western glasses contained even as much as 0.5 percent lead. Only a fraction of that number contained enough lead to have been purposely added, generally put at 5 to 10 percent. Lead was used in the West almost exclusively for bright-colored glass for enamels, especially yellows, oranges, and red (Brill 1967,

255–256; Biek and Bayley 1979, 16–17; Henderson 1985, 276–277). It was hardly ever used for beads.

In addition, virtually no other ancient glass contains barium. The few exceptions from medieval Georgia (Engle 1976, 1) and India (Dikshit 1969, 160–161) could have been imports from China. Otherwise, the earliest known purposely-added barium in glass is not recorded until J. W. Döbereiner experimented with it in 1829 (Turner 1956a, 48T). It was not commercially used until Schott of Jena offered it in 1884 (Seligman and Beck 1938, 8), though it may have been used slightly earlier in America (Honey 1937, 212 n. 101).

Seligman and Beck (1938, 21–22) thought that barium was an accidental additive, because it is often present in lead ore from northern China. They proposed that glass of the Han period indicated different factories or (they thought less likely) the same factory using different lead sources. Needham (1962, 103, 105), on the other hand, believed that the concurrent presence of barium and nonbarium glass indicates that the element was purposely introduced.

So extraordinarily rare was lead-barium glass that Seligman and Beck immediately recognized it as a marker for ancient Chinese glass, at least through the Han period (202 B.C. to A.D. 220). Nothing has changed that assessment since.

Ritchie (1937, table III) analyzed glass supposed to be later than Han, from "approximately" the third to the fifth centuries. The first notable difference between it and earlier glass was that the barium content had greatly diminished. Of the forty-three specimens of pre-Han and Han glass, barium was present in thirty-five (81.4 percent) pieces and in thirty-three (76.7 percent) in amounts of 1 to 10 percent. (He used arc spectrometry, which gives only a range of elemental concentrations.) In contrast, third- to fifth-century glass had only traces (less than 1 percent) of barium in three of ten specimens, two of which were doubtful in date.

Lead was not as prominent in this later glass. Among the forty-three pre-Han and Han samples, only one had no lead; 97.7 percent was lead glass. Among the ten later specimens, five had moderate amounts of lead, three had traces, and two had none. Thus, only half were true lead glass. Moreover, four of these five specimens were dated only tentatively by White, from whom they were obtained, and could have been earlier.

The latest glass in this analysis (Ritchie 1937, table IV) was supposed to have been Tang (a.d. 618 to 906). Their dates were not well attested, though one of the lead glass specimens was said to be "definitely T'ang" (Ritchie 1937, 218). Of the nine specimens said to be of Tang date, only two (22.2 percent) were lead glass; barium was all but nonexistent.

These analyses suggested to some scholars (Caley 1962, 91; Chen 1968, 361–366) that lead and barium marked Chinese glass until the end of the Han period, when barium was abandoned. It was further supposed that lead had disappeared a few centuries later. However, this supposition needs to be revised.

No early Chinese literature on glassmaking is scientific or technical, but we have brief descriptions of glassmaking, which might be called short recipes. There are at least six of these dating from the twelfth to the seventeenth centuries (emphases and insertions are mine):

1. *The Cloud Forest Lapidary,* an anonymous work of A.D. 1133,[1] says: "And at the western capital [Kaifung], in the Lo River, they find pieces of bluish white stone with spots of five colours in it. The whitest of these are compounded with *lead,* and mixed with other minerals, then after heating it is all changed into 'false jade' or liu-li [opaque] glass for use" (Needham 1962, 109).
2. Zhao Rugua's *Zhu Fan Zhi* (variously translated as *A Description of Barbarian Nations* and *Records of Foreign People*) of 1225 contains the passage: "Liu-li comes from several of the countries of the Ta-shï [Arabs]. The method followed in melting it is the same as that of China,[2] that is to say, it is made by burning *oxide of lead,* nitrate of potash and gypsum" (Hirth and Rockhill 1911, 227).
3. Brown and Rabiner's (1987, 76) extracts from the *Gazetteer of Qingzhou Prefecture,* written during the Jiajing reign of the Ming

dynasty (1522 to 1566), show that the glassmaking materials at Yanshenzhen were feldspar, fluorite, *yellow lead, white lead,* and copper.

4. They (Brown and Rabiner 1987, 76) noted that *lead* was an ingredient in glass of Yanshenzhen in the late Ming and early Qing period.
5. During the reign of Qian Long (1736 to 1796) *white lead* was added in the amount of 5.1 percent to the glass batch (Brown and Rabiner 1987, 76).
6. *The Creations of Nature and Man* by Song Yingxing of 1637 (Sun and Sun 1966, 308) described glassmaking in more poetic terms: "Nitre is a non-substantial material and is capable of transforming itself into nothing when heated with fire. In contrast, *black lead* is heavy-bodied material. When these two materials are heated together, nitre will strive to induce *lead* to become nothing, while *lead,* on the other hand, will strive to keep nitre in creation of a translucent and lustrous appearance."

The colors of lead mentioned in these notices refer to different compounds. White lead ($PbCo_3$) is found in nature as the mineral cerussite. Yellow lead (PbO) is a natural ochre, but is more often produced artificially, and usually called litharge[3] (Brady and Clauser 1977, 422–427). Several lead compounds are black in color; and "black lead" may refer to the lead ore galena, though it is usually not very high in lead content.

Gray (1875) left a detailed description of glassmaking in Guangzhou, during his "walks" in the city, especially at a factory that made flat glass for mirrors or painting upon (Gray 1875, 236–239). When discussing bangle making (Gray 1875, 241–242; insertions mine) he gave slightly different amounts of ingredients than for the flat glass: "ten catties [one catty equals one and a third pounds; ca. 600 g] of pewter, forty catties of lead, six catties of Yin tak [Guangdong Province] sand, and forty catties of saltpetre." The most unusual of these ingredients is pewter, though we are not told what percentage of tin it contained.[4]

Apart from literary notices, analyses of archaeologically derived materials have confirmed that lead glass was an important product of China long after the Han period. Shi et al. (1987) analyzed glass from several periods. Four of the seven samples (57 percent) of Tang date (618 to 906) and nineteen of the thirty-one samples (61 percent) of Northern Song date (960 to 1127) were lead glass. Lead glasses are known from the Ming and Qing dynasties (1368–1911) (England et al. 1991, 103; Gan 1991, 2), and lead glass is still being made in Beijing (Sprague and An 1990, 9–10). Lead glass did not disappear before or during the Tang period.

Glass often has a small amount of lead in it, because there are many constituents of glass. However, it is not considered to have been purposely added until it is at least 5.0 percent by weight. Glass analyses are complex and expensive, but lead can usually be detected by determining specific gravity. The specific gravity of ordinary leadless glass is in the range of 2.40 to 2.65. Higher weights may reflect different colorants, but as the specific gravity approaches and exceeds 3.00, it indicates that lead (or some other heavy metal) has been purposely added to the batch.

Recently there has been some discussion of the appearance of potassium-rich glass in southern China during the Han period, roughly 200 B.C. to A.D. 220 (Glover and Henderson 1995, 158–159; An 1996, 131). It is not yet clear if this glass was locally made, consists mostly of potassium-rich Indo-Pacific beads (at least some of the samples appear to be), or was the product of some Southeast Asian glassmaking center (see chap. 13). There are also some potassium-rich vessels reported from the Northern Song period (Shi et al. 1987, 44, nos. 44–46)

There was always Chinese glass without lead, but it was in the minority. The late Chinese glass examined by Ritchie (1937) and reported by Seligman and Beck (1938, 47) was leadless. However, the glass found at the fourteenth-century factory at Boshan had a very low lead content (Yi and Tu 1991). Leadless glass is a signature of

Shandong production and thus grew in importance over time. It is much more common than leaded glass from the Ming period onward because Boshan and its neighbors increasingly dominated Chinese glass production.

Ruby Red Glass

Metal oxides are added to glass to impart colors. An understanding of these additives aids in the identification of glass origins.

Most colorants in Chinese glass were similar to those used elsewhere. One, however, is distinctive and even diagnostic: copper produces a translucent red, commonly known as "ruby red." This color is highly desirable, but rather difficult to make. Most old translucent red glass, as for example in most European medieval stained-glass windows, is simply clear glass painted red[5] (Color Plate 15).

Early translucent red glass is very rare and is not a pure ruby color. Four vessels from fourth-century A.D. Rome are dichroic, exhibiting different colors when viewed in different lights. When light is reflected from their surfaces, they are green. However, when light is transmitted through them, they appear red. The colorants include gold (Harden 1987, 246–247). Henderson (1991, 73) reported on some Roman enamels that are dichroic in another way. They are dull red in reflected light and semitranslucent blue green in transmitted light. Again, these are not true "ruby reds."

Ruby red glass colored with copper is dusky rather than bright (Color Plate 15). This was used in Europe for some stained-glass windows of Gothic cathedrals in the twelfth through fourteenth centuries (Turner 1956b, table VII). After that time, however, no copper ruby glass was made in Europe for centuries. The loss of the secret may have been related to the Reformation and the movement away from stained-glass decoration. Read (1942, 293) emphasized the effects of the mid-fourteenth-century Black Death on the community of Christendom's artists. He mentioned the loss of knowledge of several glass colors, though he did not specify which ones.

Europe did not rediscover how to make copper ruby glass until the nineteenth century. France's Société d'Encouragement offered a prize to duplicate the popular Bohemian "colored glass" (ruby red made with gold to imitate their pyrope garnets). It was claimed in 1836 by the famous glassmaker George Bontemps and one de Fontaney (Sauzay 1868, 212–213; Thorpe 1935, 239). At least that is the official story. Lardner (1832, 221–222), who is not always reliable, gave an amusing account of a copper ladle accidentally dropped into a glass batch at the works of St. Gobain. One could discount the tale, except that it was published four years *before* Bontemps won his prize. Eball published the first scientific investigation of copper ruby glass in 1870 (Weyl 1959, 423–425).

The Europeans had a better substitute. Antonio Neri included a formula for making gold ruby glass in a book first published in 1612 (Mentasti 1980, 108–109), but his work was ignored until much later. Andreas Cassius usually gets credit for exposing the secret in *De Auro* in 1685. The formula was quickly developed by Johann Kunckel (died 1705). Bohemian glassmakers were also making red glass before 1700.[6] Since then, it has been widely used, though copper and selenium (introduced in 1891) have also been employed (Morazzoni 1953, 57–58; Weyl 1959, 380–381) (Color Plate 15).[7]

However, the story was different in China. Translucent red glass beads are on the complex reliquary pillar from Suzhou dated to 1013 discussed in chapter 6.[8] Many Southeast Asian sites have translucent red beads. David Killick helped me analyze two beads, one from Calatagan (the Philippines) and the other from Fort Canning Hill (Singapore), with X-ray fluorescence at the McKay Laboratory at Harvard. They were colored with copper (gold and selenium were absent), and both had significant levels of lead.

Copper ruby glass beads fit the characteristics we consider for identifying Chinese beads. They were likely to have been made by the Chinese, possibly at Suzhou; they are of lead glass; and their distribution is consistent with a Chinese origin, as discussed in chapter 6.

Hence, copper ruby is another technical marker of Chinese glass. It dates from at least the early eleventh century. For a long time, the Chinese were the only ones producing translucent red glass beads or, indeed, translucent red glass of any kind.

Chinese Beads in the Asian Maritime Trade

We have now reviewed the lines of evidence needed to identify Chinese glass beads in the Asian maritime trade. The review of glassmaking and glass beadmaking in China in chapter 6 showed us that there is little evidence thus far from China itself as to what beads may have been produced there. The understanding of Chinese trade patterns in chapter 7 gave us an idea of where we might expect to find Chinese beads. The immediately preceding section outlined some important technical markers of Chinese beads. We now move to a discussion of the actual beads.

Coil Beads

The most common Chinese glass beads are the most diminutive. They were made by winding a small amount of glass around a wire in one or more turns. Rey Santiago of the National Museum of the Philippines coined the name "coil bead" for them.[9] They look as though they were cut from a piece of coiled spring (Figure 8.1; Color Plate 16).

These monochrome beads are often 3 mm or less in diameter. They were the most numerous beads made by the Chinese and as far as we know the longest lived. Thus, the Chinese industry is similar to both the Indo-Pacific industry and modern glass bead industries (Japan, the Czech Republic, and, until recently, Venice) in that the smallest beads accounted for the largest and longest production.

Most coil beads that have been analyzed have high lead contents. Those in the Philippine National Museum have specific gravities ranging from 2.48 to 3.423, with a mean average of 2.948. Coil beads from Fort Canning Hill, Singapore (Temasek), are also high in lead (Miksic et al. 1994).[10] A strand of *mutiraja*[11] (opaque orange red coil beads) in the collection of the Center for Bead Research has a specific gravity of 3.50. Of four colors of coil beads from Fustat (Old Cairo),[12] the black ones and dark blue ones had low specific gravities. The light blue ones had a specific gravity of 2.89 and fluoresced under a short-wave ultraviolet lamp, indicating a small amount of lead. The opaque red ones had a specific gravity of 3.19. The low specific gravity of a few coil beads from the Philippines and Fustat shows that lead glass was not always employed to make these beads. However, most are made of lead glass.[13]

In addition to the technical marker of lead, their distribution is instructive. Long examples of coil beads, with as many as a dozen turns, are found in Korea. Blair (1951b, 403–404) suggested a fourth- to seventh-century date for them, but had no evidence to indicate that age. The earliest documented coil beads are in the Shōsō-in in Nara, Japan, dating to the eighth century (Blair 1973, 381)[14] and the Seungan Temple in Kyongju, Korea, dating from the ninth or tenth centuries (Francis 1985b, 22).

At Barus, North Sumatra, excavations by the National Center for Archaeological Research in Jakarta uncovered both coil and Indo-Pacific beads. The coil beads outnumbered the Indo-Pacific beads by a ratio of about five to one. The ceramics associated with them were all of Northern Song (960–1127) date. As discussed in chapter 7, their early presence here is due to the camphor trade. They were brought by traders of either Srivijaya or the Middle East or both.

The small, unpretentious coil bead was thus the vanguard of Chinese glass beads in the Asian maritime bead trade. They are the earliest identifiable Chinese glass beads found outside China.

Coil beads flooded the market just as Indo-Pacific beads were disappearing in the twelfth century. Perhaps they were even instrumental in the latter's disappearance. They are so similar in color and size that modern researchers and collectors often confuse them. The

Figure 8.1. *Drawings of coil beads. The smaller examples are twice actual size.*

smaller, shinier, and heavier coil beads may have driven Indo-Pacific beads out through competition. Both beads play the same role in decorative schemes, even in beadwork (Hector 1995, 10–11).

The expansion of trade by the Southern Song has been termed "disastrous" for Srivijaya (Wolters 1970, 42). The coil beads may simply have been filling the vacuum caused by the demise of the Southeast Asian Indo-Pacific bead industry. This was also the period during which the South Indian guild system, upon which the Indo-Pacific industry may have relied, was in decline (K. D. Morrison 1997, 10).

Whatever the reason or reasons, the shift from Indo-Pacific beads to coil beads is evident in the archaeological record. The end of Indo-Pacific bead preeminence was discussed in chapter 5 by comparing assemblages in the Philippines, Sarawak, and Indonesia. The same data show the growing trade in coil beads after around A.D. 1100.

In the Philippines (see Appendix A) among all excavated beads of all types in the Developed Metal Age (perhaps 200 B.C. to A.D. 1200) Indo-Pacific beads account for no less than 66.2 percent of the total. In stark contrast, in the Early and Middle phases of the Age of Trade and Contact with the East (ca. 1200 to 1450) the percentage of Indo-Pacific beads drops to 1.2 percent. Coil beads were not present in the earlier period, yet account for 32.8 percent of all excavated beads in the later period (Francis 1989d, 8–9).

The same pattern exists at Sarawak sites, though we lack statistics for them. Coil beads are in the Kain Hitam (in the Niah Cave complex) assemblage in Sarawak, East Malaysia. Two corrected radiocarbon dates from this site are A.D. 825 and 1000 (Solheim 1983, 42–43, 49). The early date is tenuous because the site was less than scientifically excavated (Solheim 1983, 42–43, 49). There are also bead intrusions in the collection (personal observation). There are no Chinese ceramics in Sarawak before the tenth century (L. Chin 1988, 8). Coil beads are not found at other Sarawak sites until the twelfth century.

Ninth- to tenth-century Sungai Jaong along the Sarawak River had Indo-Pacific beads and some beads from the Muslim West. Bongkissam, also along the Sarawak River (twelfth to thirteenth century), and Gedong in Kuching District (thirteenth to fourteenth century) had no Indo-Pacific beads and mostly coil beads. At Bukit Sandong in Kuching District (fourteenth to seventeenth centuries) there were no Indo-Pacific beads and fewer coil beads, because their trade had tapered off by then.

In Indonesia, only Indo-Pacific beads are found on early first-millennium sites, Srivijayan sites, and in "megalithic" burials (see chap. 5). Coil beads then become the rule, though most sites where they are found have not been excavated. Among those that have been, Barus has already been discussed. They are also the most common bead at Trowulan, East Java, founded in 1292.

Coil beads are also found in East Africa. At Zimbabwe, one of translucent red and apparently eight of white glass were in the sealed "bed-rock" layer (Beck 1931, 232–234). This has been radiocarbon dated to 1085–1450 or even 1550 (Robinson 1961a, 234). The eight white beads (no. 8a) had specific gravities of 3.2, which Beck recognized as being a sign of the presence of lead. He said such beads were common at Pemba (near Zanzibar). Beck did not say if the white beads were wound, but neither did he mention that the translucent red bead (no. 6d) was, though that is clear from the color illustration. At Kilwa, the three translucent red beads were apparently coil beads. Chittick (1974, 471) called them "single wound." As noted earlier, coil beads have been found at Fustat (Old Cairo), likely dating earlier than the fire that destroyed the tent city in 1168.

There is an unusual aspect of the distribution of coil beads, though its significance is not yet understood. One color often eclipses all others in a given assemblage. In the Philippines (Middle phase of the Age of Trade and Contact with the East) 62.8 percent of those excavated are white. At roughly contemporary Gedong, Sarawak, 61.7 percent are yellow (Nyandoh and Chin 1969, 86). At Sungai Mas, Malaysia, they are nearly all translucent red. At Kuala Selinsing, Malaysia, they are all white. At Sungai Lumet, Brunei, they are 52.3 percent blue and 40.5 percent white (L. Burke 1971–1972, 92) or 53 percent blue and 38 percent white (Harrisson 1973, 120), depending upon who was counting what.[15] At Kota Batu, Brunei, they are 75 percent blue (Harrisson 1973, 121). In the Sarawak River delta sites of Bongkissam and Buah, red accounts for about half the beads and yellow for one-fourth (Harrisson 1973, 122).[16] In Nusa Tenggara Timur and Timor opaque reddish orange dominates (the *muti-raja*). At Temasek (Singapore), yellow is most common. In the one trade cargo known, on the *Royal Captain* wreck no. 2[17] off Palawan, 61.0 percent are translucent red (Cuevas 1985).

It is difficult to suggest what this means. There is no similar pattern among Indo-Pacific beads.[18] In the Sarawak River delta at Jaong, the (mostly Indo-Pacific) beads were 27 percent blue, 32 percent red, 16 percent yellow, and 17 percent black, whereas at Bukit Maris, 17 percent were blue, 25 percent red, 37 percent yellow, and 15 percent green (Harrisson 1973, 122).[19] Lamb (1965b, 114–115) made a census of the colors at two Malaysian sites: at Kuala Selinsing they were 32 percent dark blue, 29 percent red, 13 percent orange, 13 percent yellow, and 11 percent opaque green and at Pengkalan Bujang there were 32.5 percent red, 30.0 percent dark blue, 17.5 percent black, and 14.0 percent yellow ones. My counts at Mantai were 30.06 percent blue green, 26.55 percent orange, 12.25 percent red, 11.40 percent translucent green, and 10.83 percent yellow. At Oc Eo[20] they were 40.14 percent red, 24.48 percent dark blue, and 18.97 percent black. The Arikamēḍu beads in the Pondicherry Museum are 41.08 percent dark blue, 31.94 percent red, and 11.93 percent black. There were different favored colors at each site, but no color among Indo-Pacific beads was in the majority anywhere, and "minority colors" were much more numerous than among coil beads.

Why would coil bead assemblages, but not those of Indo-Pacific beads, so overwhelmingly favor a single color? One possibility is that the beadmakers tended to make a single color for an extended period. The one bead trade cargo known to date had one color dominating its assemblage. Another possibility may have been local demand. Here it is pertinent to recall that Wang Dayuan in the fourteenth century often specified colors of beads to be taken to particular places. A third possibility is that we may not have sufficient data.

Coil beads are still being produced in China, but they began to wane as an important trade item by the fifteenth or sixteenth century, at least to most destinations. As noted earlier, there was a decrease in their number at Bukit Sandong, Sarawak, dated to the fourteenth to seventeenth centuries, compared with earlier Sarawak sites. In the Philippines, in the Late phase of the Age of Trade and Contact with the East (ca. 1450 to 1600), coil beads declined from about a third to only 7.4 percent of the total of excavated beads.

They were still being traded in and around Borneo. They were the most numerous beads on the *Royal Captain* wreck no. 2, dated between 1573 and 1620, presumably bound for that island. In 1780, Thomas Forrest (1971, 329) enumerated the typical cargo of the two junks that went annually from Amoy (Xiamen) to the Sulu Archipelago.[21] The goods included "beads of all colors, like swan shot." Both the size and relative weight of "swan shot" are fair matches for the attributes of coil beads.

Combed Polychrome Beads

Another early type of Chinese bead in Southeast Asia is polychrome decorated (Color Plate 14). These have a base of one glass color and other colors applied to the surfaces. The color was added as lines while the bead remained hot. A tool (commonly the edge of a metal paddle) was frequently dragged through these lines to form waves. This glass-decorating technique is known as "combing" (Figure 8.2). Glass objects decorated by combing have not been found in China, but are known from many other glass industries.

The editor of *Ornament* magazine (R. K. Liu 1991, 62) has argued against combed beads being Chinese. However, there is simply no other likely explanation of their origin (Francis 1991b).[22] Moreover, as discussed in chapter 6, their distribution is restricted to the eastern route of China's southern trade. These beads may have been made in Quanzhou only for export.

There are ten combed polychrome beads in the type collection of the Philippine National Museum found at three sites with different dates. Each group differs in appearance. The earliest ones are large suboblates and barrels with ogee designs (combed alternately up and down through the lines) found at Bubulungun, dated to the twelfth to thirteenth centuries. The next group came from Santa Ana (fourteenth to fifteenth centuries) and is barrel-shaped with simple combed waves. The last group is from Calatagan (fifteenth to sixteenth centuries). They are rather small oblates with combed waves (Francis 1989c, 16). All these beads have a significant lead content, with specific gravities ranging from 3.183 to 3.984 (mean average 3.529). It is tempting to suggest changes in styles of these beads over time, but this sample is not adequately large to do that with any certainty.

A translucent red barrel bead with a combed white, wavy design was uncovered at Banten Girang, West Java. The glass color alone indicates a Chinese origin. Combed beads that may be Chinese are also found at Bongkissam and Bukit Sandong, Sarawak.

A notable style of polychrome beads is cylindrical with several colors combed into waves in the center and one or more trailed at the ends; they have black perforation deposits, indicating that they were furnace-wound (Color Plate 14). These are particularly popular in Taiwan as heirlooms among the Paiwan people (Francis 1992a, 4–5). Chen (1968, 365–366) suggested that they were brought to the island early in the Christian era. De Beauclair (1970) put forward a possible Dutch origin, but they are nothing like known Dutch beads (Francis 1988b, 46). Miyamoto (1957) opted for West Asia and East Europe as sources, but failed to cite any parallels. However, their lead content points to China, as does their distribution. They are also found in Sarawak, and the single dated example known (between 1292 and 1520) was recovered at Trowulan, the Majapahit capital in East Java, with its strong Chinese influence.

Figure 8.2. *Techniques of the combing decoration on glass. A second color of glass is trailed onto a bead while it is still somewhat hot. The corner of a paddle is then drawn through the trailed glass (in the direction the arrows point), raking it into a design. The ultimate design depends on the initial application of glass and the direction in which it is combed. Sketch by Cynthia Schave.*

Another group of polychrome beads is curious, because they were obviously made in imitation of a European import, the multilayered chevron[23] (*rosetta* in Italian). The imitations could not have predated European beads in the area (Color Plate 14). The earliest imitation chevrons look quite like small examples of the earliest true chevron beads.[24] They are cleverly made with thick stratified bands of red, blue, and red applied from one end to the other over a white core. The bands were combed to interlock with each other in waves. At the juncture of the red and blue bands, mostly on the blue, a thin, wavy line of white was applied. Once decorated, the beads were paddled on the ends to give them the appearance of the faceting of early chevrons.

Later examples of imitation chevron beads are mostly oblate in shape, reflecting later chevron styles that have fewer layers with their ends ground round. These are particularly evident in Sarawak (Beck 1930a, pl. K, 17) and are known from Taiwan. What may be the last step in imitating chevrons are some beads of simple cylindrical shapes that retain nothing of their chevronlike quality save the wavy zones at the ends (Francis 1992a, pl. 3D).

Polychrome beads may be the "colored" beads advocated by the writers of the mariners' manuals cited in the last chapter. Zhao Rugua in 1225 advised taking colored beads to the Philippines. Wang Dayuan in 1344 said colored beads should go to Ligor, and Fei Xin in 1436 said they should go to the Moluccas and Palembang. Of course, beads traded to one place may be sold elsewhere as well. Nonetheless, the early mention of colored beads exported to the Philippines and the early appearance of polychrome beads in the Philippine archaeological context may be more than coincidental.

Copper Ruby Red Glass Beads

As discussed earlier in this chapter, a dusky translucent red glass can be produced with copper. As far as beads are concerned, this was exclusively a Chinese product until the nineteenth century.

The earliest ruby red beads known in China adorn the reliquary pillar found in Suzhou dated to 1013. Gernet (1962, 188) said that Suzhou was famous for its glass lanterns made of five different colors. Though he does not name the colors (and the Suzhou Museum has none of colored glass), ruby red is a good candidate for one of them. Suzhou may, therefore, have been the origin of at least some of these beads. The date of their first production is not known. No such beads are in the eighth-century Shōsō-in in Nara, Japan (Blair 1973, 103). This is, of course, negative evidence, but it is likely that if these beads were then in circulation some would have been added to this collection. Not everyone agrees, however.[25]

Copper ruby beads are high in lead content. Lead is not only a marker of Chinese glass of this period but would have aided the dissolving of the copper colorant. The specific gravity of the red beads in the Philippine National Museum collection ranges from 2.305 (unusually low for any glass) to 3.976, with a mean average of 3.387. Lead was confirmed in two specimens tested at the McKay Laboratory at Harvard by X-ray spectrometry: a bead from Calatagan has less than 10 percent lead and one from Fort Canning Hill has more. A ruby coil bead from Fustat, Egypt, has a specific gravity of 3.54.

In the Philippines, copper ruby beads are numerous in the Late phase of the Age of Trade and Contact with the East, about 1450 to 1600. Only one such bead is recorded in the earlier phases, but 95 are found in this period, constituting 14.1 percent of all beads excavated (Francis 1989d, 9). They were found principally at the cemetery site of Calatagan. These are oblate, square cylinder, and biconical in shape. A square cylinder from Cebu is in the Fox collection (see Appendix A). (Similar square cylinders of blue and a few other colors are common on the Philippines antiquities market.) Copper ruby beads have also been found at Sungai Mas, Malaysia (coil beads); Buah Cave, and Gedong, Sarawak (a suboblate and a square bicone); Banten Girang, West Java (a barrel with a combed white decoration); and Fort Canning Hill, Singapore (coil beads).

In addition, ruby red beads have been uncovered from two shipwrecks associated with the Asian maritime trade. They were the principal beads in the vessel now called the *Royal Captain* wreck no. 2 that sank on a reef near Palawan, the Philippines. This Chinese junk was apparently headed toward Borneo after having stopped in the northern Philippines. The ceramics aboard date it to between 1573 and 1620 (Cuevas 1985; Goddio et al. 1987; Goddio 1988). Fragments of copper ruby glass beads were also in the wreck of the Spanish galleon *Nuestra Señora de la Concepción* that sank off Saipan in 1638. It had finished its business at Manila and was bound for Acapulco[26] (Mathers 1990). These beads must have been on more than one galleon: a few were uncovered at Santa Catalina de Guale, a Spanish colonial mission on St. Catherines Island, Georgia (United States) (personal observation).

Wang Dayuan in 1349 listed several places where "red beads" were to be taken. They included eastern Sumatra, Kelantan, perhaps Bombay, and an unidentified place. Dark red beads were also traded to the Jung, presumably in the Malay Peninsula; these could have been either translucent or opaque red beads.

Ruby red beads are also found in East Africa. At Kilwa, twenty-seven wound spherical and apparently three coil ("single wound") beads were dated to the late thirteenth or fourteenth century (Chittick 1974, 471). At Zimbabwe, Robinson (1961a, 228) uncovered one from Period III, dated to A.D. 1085 to 1450 or perhaps as late as 1550. As already mentioned, a ruby coil bead had also been found earlier in the "bed-rock" layer at Zimbabwe in Caton-Thompson's excavation (Beck 1931, 234). Two from Fustat (Old Cairo) are in the Awad collection.

Translucent red beads have been reported from several sites in India, but all appear to have been intrusions or false leads. Beck (1930a, 174–175) examined one found in a midden near "megalithic" tombs at Sulur, Tamil Nadu, by Colonel Tucker. Most of the beads found there seem to have been Indo-Pacific types. However, there was nothing to date the midden, and the presence of two colorless glass beads suggests that some of the assemblage was late in date.[27] Dikshit (1969, 58) reported several sites with beads with white cores and a translucent red coat. The bead from Maski, at least, has a gold-red coat and is Venetian. V. N. Misra at Bagor, Rajasthan, found a small, drawn ruby red bead. It is very likely colored with selenium,[28] a modern product (Misra believes that one of his workers playfully contaminated the trench; there were even plastic beads present).

As a final note, Hirth and Rockhill (1911, 73) cited Zhao Rugua as saying that translucent red glass came from Ceylon. However, Chinese scholars at the Singapore National Museum who reviewed this passage for me translated it as "colored cloth and glass beads," with no mention of red glass.

Blue Barrel-Shaped Beads

A source of one type of bead's origin comes from historical records. John Saris, cited in chapter 6, indicated that some Chinese were making beads at Banten, Java, around 1600 for trade to Borneo. The first passage below is from a letter written to the East India Company on 4 December 1608 and the second is from his journal written between 1605 and 1609 under the heading "Commodities vendible and in request here."

> I have many times certified your worships of the trade the Flemings follow to Soocadanna (Sukadana) which place yieldeth great store of diamonds, and of their manner of dealing for them for gold principally which comes from Beniermassen (Banjarmasin) and *blue glass beads which the Chinese make* and sell 300 for a ps [piece] of eight, and they are there worth a mas a 100 which is 3/.s [three shillings] and sometimes more sometimes less according as gold doth rise and fall. I have delivered one of these beads unto our General to show unto your worships, to the end that if we shall trade these, we may have the like beads brought out of England at a cheaper rate. (Danvers 1896, 22 [insertions in brackets and emphasis mine])

> All sorts of *small Bugles,*[29] *Bugles which are made in Bantam, of colour blue,* and in fashion like a Tunne [a barrel], but of the bigness of a Beane, and cost at Bantam foure hundred a Riall of eight, worth at Soocodanna, a Masse the hundred, the Masse beeing three quarters of a Riall of eight. . . . (Saris 1905, 513–514 [insertion and emphasis mine])

Saris was a careful observer with a considerable knowledge of local conditions and trade. He was writing about the same kind of bead made in Banten (Bantam) and exchanged in Sukadana (Soocadanna), Borneo, for diamonds. In both passages, they are blue and had the same price in Borneo, though their cost fluctuated in Banten. A merchant could make a 300 to 400 percent profit by taking this bead from Java to Borneo. Despite Saris' best mercantile instincts, there is no evidence that the bead was ever replicated in England.

A type of bead matching the physical description given by Saris—blue, the size of a bean, and barrel-shaped—is well known in Borneo. They are the most prized heirloom beads among the Kelabit of Sarawak and Kalimantan (see chap. 17). Western writers usually call them *let,* though that is a general term for valuable beads among the Kelabit; to the Kelabit they are *let silo mau'hun* (or *mo'hun*). The beads are most often dark blue, but black and green ones are also known. They are usually 8.5 to 10 mm long and barrel-shaped with flat ends. Some from the Kelabit that have been analyzed have from 15.25 percent to 30 percent lead (Harrisson 1968, 129), even up to 37.2 percent (Munan-Oettli 1981, 25). Visually similar beads have been found at Kabwan

Cave (Palawan) and Calatagan (Luzon) in the Philippines. The specific gravity of the Philippine beads is 3.204 and 3.650, respectively, indicating lead glass.

However, Harrisson (1968, 127–130) analyzed other beads that were said to be visually similar to these from the Sarawak sites of Sungai Jaong, Tanjong Kubor, the west mouth of the Niah Cave, the Painted Cave of the Niah complex, and Kota Batu, Brunei. None had any appreciable amounts of lead. Two beads from Sungai Jaong (about the tenth to the thirteenth centuries) at the Center for Bead Research are visually similar to *let silo mau'hun* (at least to the staff of the Sarawak Museum and myself, though perhaps not to a Kelabit). They have specific gravities of 2.49 and 2.55 and lack lead.

The dates of the excavated beads from the Philippines are close to the period of beadmaking in Banten and they may very well have originated there. The Sarawak beads without lead are older. Whether they are Chinese-made cannot be said yet.

Multiple Wound Monochrome Beads

These oblate beads are distinctive in appearance. They were wound from a tapering stream of glass usually with four turns to build up the bead (Color Plate 14). By far their most common color is opaque light turquoise blue, though white and occasionally green ones are found. The glass tends to corrode to white at the edges of the glass streams, producing an effect that resembles a white spiral decoration. The specific gravity of one of these beads from Calatagan is 3.181, indicating a significant lead content. Their distribution also points to a Chinese origin.

These beads are on the antiquities market in northern Thailand and found in Kalimantan and Johore Lama (Malaysia), but none of these is from stratified contexts. Archaeological finds include Calatagan and Santa Ana (Luzon, the Philippines), the *Royal Captain* wreck no. 2 off Palawan (Goddio et al. 1987: groupe 724), and Trowulan, East Java.

Calatagan is dated from the late fourteenth to early sixteen centuries, Santa Ana less exactly from the twelfth to the sixteenth centuries, the *Royal Captain* wreck no. 2 from 1573 to 1620, and Trowulan from 1292 to 1520. The sixteenth century may have been the most productive period for these beads.

Early Opaque Low-Lead or Leadless Beads

These beads are only tentatively identified as Chinese. The evidence pointing to a Chinese origin is their distribution. They are found at a few sites in Southeast Asia and along the East African coast. The glass has little or no lead and comes in a small range of opaque colors: red, yellow, green, and blue. The beads tend to be small, commonly a centimeter or less in diameter. They are shaped as oblates or very short bicones (the more distinctive form) (Color Plate 14).

In the Philippines, a yellow short bicone and some yellow oblates were found at Bubulungun-I, chamber B, on Palawan, dated to the twelfth to thirteenth centuries. The short bicone has a specific gravity of 2.481, and two yellow oblates had specific gravities of 2.440 and 2.602. These beads have also been found at two Sarawak sites: Bongkissam, tentatively dated to the eleventh to twelfth century, and Gedong, thirteenth and fourteenth centuries. X-ray spectrometry tests on two short bicones from Gedong at the McKay Laboratory showed that the red one had no lead, and the yellow one had perhaps as much as 10 percent. If there is any lead in these beads, it is at a very low level.

In East Africa, Chittick (1967, 9) called the short bicones "lenticulars" and said that they were the same as Beck's (1928, pl. I) convex bicone disks.[30] This term is now common in the regional literature. Chittick (1967, 9) also recognized a "cone-lenticular" type, uneven in cross section, with one side shorter than the other. He initially thought they were imperfect examples of the other beads. They probably are.

At Kilwa, Tanzania, "lenticular" and "cone-lenticular" beads were 26.5 percent (18 percent + 8.5 percent) of the assemblage in Period II (late twelfth to late thirteenth centuries). They were rare at other times, except in Period IV (sixteenth to seventeenth centuries) when "lenticulars" were 11 percent of the assemblage. Yellow accounted for more than half of the Period II beads, with blue green, red, and light green each accounting for 16 percent or less. In Period IV red beads were in the majority. At the related site of Manda, H. M. Morrison (1984, 182) noted that "cone-lenticular" beads were found in blue green and light green colors from the mid-eleventh to the late thirteenth centuries.

Van der Sleen (1958, 210–201) wrote, "These [short bicones] I should like to call the 'guide beads' of the Trade-winds."[31] He noted that they were common at Zanzibar and Pemba and that at Kilwa some as large as 15 mm in diameter were found. He suggested that they might have come from Brahmapuri (Kolhapur), India. However, the few beads of this shape found there are not indicative of local manufacture, no red ones were found, and the glass worked at Kolhapur is different from that used for the beads in Africa. In addition, the Brahmapuri site was occupied during the Sātavāhana period, which ended in the third century A.D., and then again in the Bahmani period, which began in 1347. Neither date accords well with the dates of the African finds.[32]

Beck (1931, 234) described a blue short bicone and oblate from the "bed-rock" layer of Zimbabwe. The layer in which these beads were found was reported by Robinson (1961a, 234) to have a radiocarbon date of 1085 to 1450. Similar beads are found in Fustat, dated to before 1168.

These beads are clustered between the eleventh and thirteenth centuries, with possible later appearances at Gedong (Sarawak), Period IV at Kilwa, and the Zimbabwe "bed-rock" layer.[33] If they are Chinese, they predate other known Chinese leadless glass beads, discussed next. Without further information, little more can be said about them except that they were widespread in the Asian maritime bead trade for a few centuries.

Leadless Beads

The only beads universally identified as Chinese in the literature[34] are still being made in large quantities. Apart from the lack of lead, they have several identifying characteristics. These include distinctive glass colors, very bubbly glass, large perforations often with clay deposits, and irregular outlines, frequently including a small "peak" of glass at one or both ends (Chu and Chu 1973, 141; R. K. Liu 1975c, 10). These attributes are typical of many later Chinese beads.[35] There were, however, contemporary beads made for the Qing-mandated court chains that are made of better-quality glass and have more regular shapes and smaller holes (Francis 1986c, 24) (Color Plate 14).

Descriptions of modern Chinese beadmaking (Chu and Chu 1973, 138; Kan and Liu 1984; Sprague and An 1990; E. T. Lewis 1994) confirm that beads are both furnace- and lamp-wound by relatively crude methods. A variety of separators is used, sometimes different ones at one factory on the same day (Sprague 1992). The low heat of the lamp-winding operation and the process of dripping glass over a coated bamboo (Chu and Chu 1973, 138) account for the bubbly glass, imperfect shapes, and peaks on the ends of the finished beads.

All but one of these characteristics are found in the earliest leadless glass beads in the Southeast Asian trade. The missing trait is the distinctive glass coloring. These colors were the result of experimentation encouraged by the Emperors Kang Xi (1662–1722) and Qian Long (1736–1796) in the early years of the Qing dynasty. Both were patrons of the arts and inspired the development of new glass colors and glazes, some of which likely came from the imperial glass workshop on the grounds of the palace. The distinctive palette of glass colors developed under them was used especially for the mandated "court chains," worn by all officers and their immediate families.[36] This is an important chapter in Chinese glass bead history, but confined mostly to China itself.

Before the new colors were developed, the "typical" Chinese leadless glass beads with bubbly glass, large holes, and eccentric shapes were staples in the trade. They are widely distributed throughout Southeast Asia and beyond. They are not reported archaeologically very often because many are still in circulation or on sites of relatively recent date. Most, if not all, of them were made at Boshan.

In the Philippines, these beads are first recorded in the Early phase of the Age of Trade and Contact with the East, tentatively dated to between 1200 and 1300. This phase is represented in the Philippine type collection only by the site of Bubulungun, where a clear bead and a translucent dark blue bead of this type were uncovered. In the Early and Middle phases of this period (ca. 1200 to 1450) beads of this description account for 16.9 percent of all beads recovered in the archipelago. In the Late phase (ca. 1450 to 1600) they make up 9.5 percent. In addition to clear and cobalt blue, light opaque blue, light amber (translucent yellow brown), light translucent green, and an unusual blue green shade are also found. Such beads have been uncovered at Calatagan (Batangas Province, Luzon), Santa Ana (Manila, Luzon), Bungiao (Zamboanga Province, Mindanao), and Misibis (Albay Province, Luzon). These are mostly late sites, with Calatagan dated from the late fourteenth to the sixteenth centuries and Santa Ana from the twelfth to the sixteenth.

In Sarawak, these beads are first recorded in any numbers at Bukit Sandong, fourteenth to sixteenth centuries, where clear and blue green ones were common. They are present, but not very common, at the East Javanese site of Trowulan, dated from 1292 to 1520.

Leadless glass beads are the dominant Chinese type found in the Americas. They were common in Alaska and opaque blue ones were the most desired beads there for a century and traded as far south as Washington State (Francis 1994c, 285–287). Opaque white ones are heirlooms in isolated Mixe villages in Mexico (Francis 1994b).

In short, leadless Chinese glass beads are found widely on late sites, corresponding with the rise of Boshan as China's major beadmaking site. Their recent appearance accounts for their sketchy archaeological occurrences. In the ethnographic context, they are very numerous, making up major portions of some of the collections in Southeast Asia, as discussed in chapter 17.

Chinese glass beads in the Asian maritime trade have several characteristics in common. They were all wound glass beads, and most seem to have been wound alongside rather than directly in a furnace. The smallest Chinese beads, the coil beads, were the most common. As the Indo-Pacific bead industry collapsed in Southeast Asia, coil beads came to fill the same ornamental and symbolic roles the older drawn beads had. Chinese immigrants into Southeast Asia brought their skills with them. Although a relatively late player in the Asian maritime bead trade, China has made important contributions to it, especially since the twelfth century.

Part Four: Beads from the Middle East

9

Middle Eastern Glass Beads

The Middle East,[1] in particular Egypt and the Levant (Syria in the historical sense),[2] played a crucial role in the history of glass. This is so because of its pioneering status, persistence of production, innovation of technique, and marketing shrewdness.

Glass is generally acknowledged to have been invented in Mesopotamia in the middle of the third millennium B.C.[3] Virtually all early glass products were beads. What are commonly referred to as Phoenician[4] beads are spread around the Mediterranean littoral. Innovative glass beadmaking techniques were initiated in Hellenistic times and persisted through the Roman Empire, into the Byzantine-Coptic periods, and until the end of the Early Islamic period.

Major Middle Eastern beadmaking locales from 300 B.C. to A.D. 1200 included Rhodes (Davidson Weinberg 1971); Alexandria (Rodziewicz 1984), Fustat (Old Cairo) (Francis 1989e, 27–29), and possibly Thebes (Francis 1999, 5) in Egypt; Tyre (Miquel 1963, 219; Schefer 1970, 42 n. 1) and Damascus in Syria (Francis 1990d, 20); one or more Greek colonies on the Black Sea coast, most likely at least Hylaea (Venclová 1990, 59; Solovev 1998, 214); and possibly Acre, Aleppo, Antioch, and Samarra (Engle 1973). By the twelfth century the Crusades had destroyed the glass bead industries in most of these places. The Mongols ravaged the rest (Francis 1990d, 19–20; 1999, 9). Later remnants at Hebron, Armenaz (Syria), Samarkand, and their offshoots never attained the heights of beadmaking that had flourished for the preceding 1,500 years (Figure 9.1).

Middle Eastern glass beads played two roles in the Asian maritime bead trade. Those sold to Asia are treated in this chapter. Beadmaking methods transferred to Southeast Asia during the Early Islamic period is the theme of the next chapter.

The Asian trade was only one segment of Middle Eastern bead commerce. The Middle East looked north, west, and south as well as east. The beads discussed here do not constitute the entire repertoire of those made in the Middle East, but only those involved in the eastern branch of its trade.

All too often, Middle Eastern beads in the Asian trade have been identified as "Roman." At its height, the Roman Empire included the major glass beadmaking regions of the Middle East; however, few beads in this trade were products of the Roman Empire.

The Roman Glass Bead Problem

Children of the Western Renaissance tend to look upon the Roman era as a Golden Age, and it was long common to assign a Roman origin to any attractive, rare object not otherwise understood. The bead literature is replete with "Roman" or alternately "Phoenician"[5] or "Early Islamic"[6] beads without any evidence for such ascriptions. Dealers' identifications account for at least some of them, paralleling the infamous case of the Ziwiyah treasure (Muscarella 1977; Goldman 1989).[7]

A typical example is Dubin (1987, 55, 238), who located Roman glass beads in Mali, Ethiopia, and Borneo. No true Roman beads have ever been found in Mali or Borneo (Ethiopia is more likely). She (Dubin 1987, 56) also featured a "typical" group of glass beads bought on the antiquities market. Some "beads" in the plate are not even beads[8] (Plate 33).

Beadmaking in the Middle East is ancient. There is also enduring archaeological interest in the region. It is surprising that few details were known about this industry. On one hand, Middle Eastern beadmaking was conservative, producing visually identical beads for more than a millennium. On the other hand, it has been innovative, making beads of stunning complexity and beauty. "Roman" beads may actually be Hellenistic, Byzantine, Coptic, or Early Islamic in addition to Roman.

Clarifying this problem has been a major, long-term project at the Center for Bead Research. Data was collected from published and unpublished sources, dating from about 300 B.C. to A.D. 1200, concentrating on beads with distinct technological or stylistic features.[9] By collating that data and filtering it through the field of glass history, a coherent, albeit preliminary, picture of Middle Eastern glass beadmaking has been developed (Francis 1999).

In sum, the pioneer glassmaking techniques of Mesopotamia were transferred to Syria and the method of furnace-winding always remained standard in that region. The Hellenistic world was much more inventive, making segmented beads (including gold-glass beads), single- and double-strip folded beads, pierced and pierced-and-folded beads, torus folded beads, fused beads, fused rod beads, mosaic glass, and "agate" glass (Color Plate 18). The center of production for these beads was Egypt from the Hellenistic through the Early Islamic period (roughly 300 B.C. to A.D. 1200). Some of these beads had short production runs and can be used as chronological indicators. Others were essentially unchanged for some 1,500 years and are worthless for dating purposes.

These techniques are so diagnostic that when they

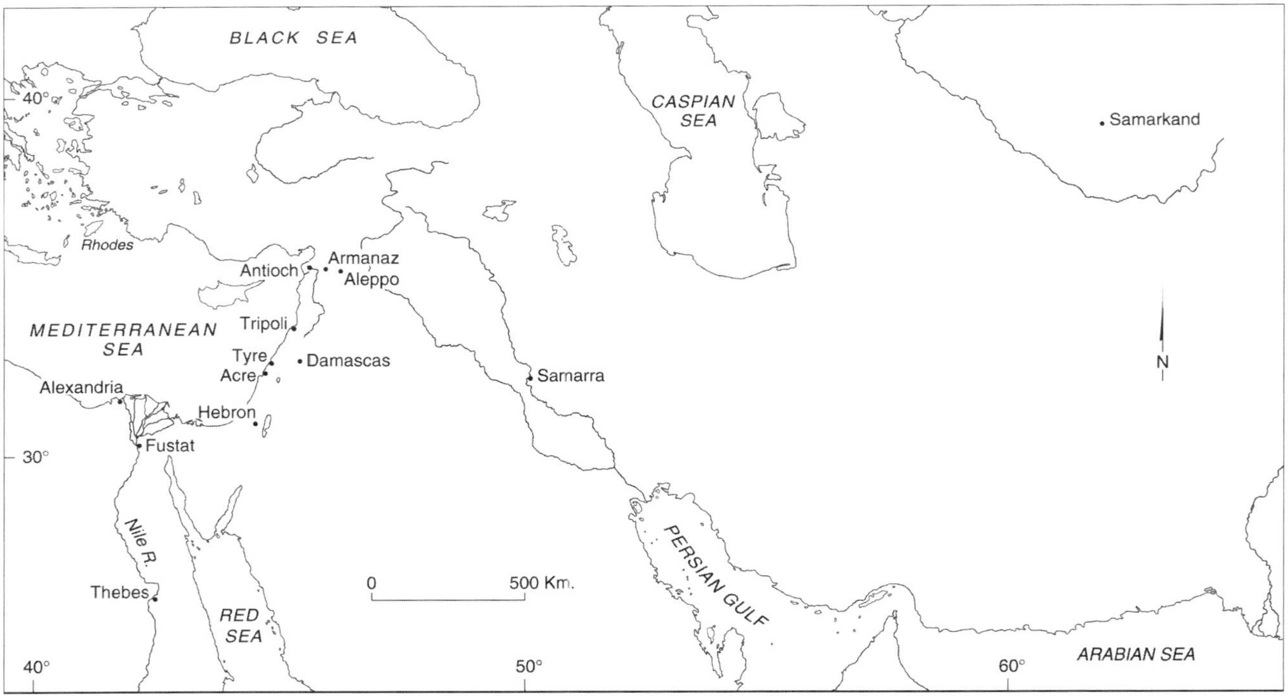

Figure 9.1. *Map of the Middle East showing the known and presumed locations of glass beadmakers.*

are found being employed outside the Middle East, the argument is strong that a technology transfer took place.[10] These techniques disappeared around the end of the twelfth century.[11] Mosaic glass was revived later in Venice, but by using different processes.

Were there Roman glass beads in the Asian maritime bead trade? There were very few. There is a mosaic eye bead at Mantai (Color Plate 19); a mosaic tabular at Arikamēḍu (Color Plate 20) (Francis 1987b, 6); a few mosaic beads at Oc Eo (Malleret 1962a, 269–271); and several face beads at Khlong Thom (A. Srisuchat 1987).[12]

A few other Roman beads in Asia arrived via land routes. These include eye beads in Northwest India (Beck 1941, 23–26) and North China (R. K. Liu 1975b, 11); a mosaic face bead from the King Michu's tomb area near Kyongju, Korea, dated to the early sixth century (B.-S. Han 1973, 26; Francis 1985b, 13–14); and gold-glass and silver-glass beads in several sites, as discussed later in this chapter.

It is not surprising to have some Roman glass beads in the region. What is surprising is that they are so scarce. They are concentrated along the land Silk Routes and in the emporia of Arikamēḍu, Mantai, Oc Eo, and Khlong Thom.

Many other descriptions of "Roman" glass beads in Southeast Asia have been published. Often writers are simply quoting each other when citing them, and many of the identifications can ultimately be traced back to Horace Beck. (For a more detailed consideration of the beads discussed in this chapter, see Francis 1989a, 12–16.)

Ranee Margaret (Queen Margaret Brooke) of Sarawak sent a necklace to Beck (1930a, 173–181), who identified several of the beads as Greek or early Roman. However, they either are of such universal types that one cannot pinpoint a source from a superficial examination or are now known to be Early Islamic or modern European. It is odd that Beck did not discuss the large checker mosaic bead (K 21, L 19) that is probably Early Islamic.[13] Dubin (1987, 238) alleged that it is a "Roman-period bead" from 300 B.C. to about A.D. 100.[14]

G. B. Gardner also sent Beck beads that he had picked up at Kota Tinggi and along the Johore River in southern Malaysia. Gardner (1937) did not mention Beck's report when he published the descriptions of these beads. It remained unknown that Beck had anything to do with their identification until his report to Gardner was rediscovered and published by Lamb (1964c).

Beck had written the report in his usual careful manner, tentatively suggesting that eight of fifty-eight beads might be Roman, with the rest modern trade beads. He was very cautious. For example: "I can see no reason why they should not have continued being made until a much later period"; "I do not know for certain how long this process was carried on, but probably to the present day"; "This looks very like a Roman bead, but it may be more recent." These comments (Lamb 1964c, 92) cover five of the first seven beads he described. It is odd that he was quite definite about a steatite (soapstone) bead, saying it is "called Hittite . . . not likely to be later than 700 B.C." (Lamb 1964c, 92). This is highly unlikely in the context of southern Malaysia.

Gardner (1937) ignored Beck's restrained remarks and unhesitatingly accepted some 20 percent of the six hundred beads he had gathered as Roman. He linked the Empire with Malaysia via Cōḷa India. This "evidence" was good enough for other scholars to elaborate on Roman-Malay trade (e.g., Wales 1940, 63; Braddell 1947; W. T. Han 1948, 19; Hsu 1948, 2).[15] Gibson-Hill (1955, 184) argued that old beads could have been brought to the site later. Lamb (1965b, 117–118) agreed with that and noted that the ceramics at Kota Tinggi were Ming in date.

Most of Gardner's beads are in the Museum of Archaeology and Anthropology at Cambridge University. G. Sieveking, Gertrude Caton-Thompson, W. G. N. van der Sleen, and I have examined them at different times. Van der Sleen (1956b) mounted them on cards and prepared a typescript describing them. Some he thought were Coptic. Other small collections gathered from Kota Tinggi are in the Peabody Museum at Harvard and the National Museum in Kuala Lumpur. All the collections are a mixed group, with mostly Indo-Pacific beads and recent Czech and Chinese beads.

In Gardner's collection, one strand is exceptional. It is of small faience beads, looking very like ancient Egyptian material. Attached to it is a first-century Roman mosaic glass bead similar to the one found at Arikamēḍu. If these beads are ancient, and they appear to be, they stand alone. One wonders whether the collection may not have been "salted" with a single strand, perhaps as a joke: the Piltdown Hoax of the bead world?[16]

Without going into tedious detail, other identifications of "Roman" beads in Sarawak (Harrisson 1950, 203–204; L. Chin 1984, 49; Dubin 1987, 238), the Philippines (Beyer 1947, 221, 289; Villegas 1983, 30), and Indonesia (Nieuwenhuis 1904; Raats 1958) were also ill informed. Except for the few genuine Roman beads mentioned earlier, the earliest Middle Eastern glass beads in the Asian maritime trade date to the Early Islamic period.

Middle Eastern Beads in the Asian Maritime Trade

Segmented Beads

Segmented beads were made from drawn tubes constricted along their length while hot, forming bulges. Various methods for constricting the tubes have been proposed (Francis 1989e, fig. 3). However, the only one known archaeologically was by rolling the heated tubes along grooved stone blocks (Figure 9.2) (Rodziewicz 1984, 241–243, pl. 72). The bulges were then cut apart as single or multiple beads. The beads might be further finished by reheating or grinding or be left rough on the ends.

Segmented beads were a key product of the Middle Eastern glass bead industry and are common throughout the region (e.g., at Siraf, Nishapur, Fustat, Berenike, Aqaba, Quseir al-Qadim), in Viking (Callmer 1977, 88–89) and Slavic territories, and early West African kingdoms (Vanacker 1984, 38–39). There is a considerable variety in their shape, color, method of segmenting, and thickness of walls (Color Plate 21; Figure 9.3) (Francis 1995a, 8). There is not yet enough data to sort out most chronologies or origins. Their manufacture is now documented from three places in the Middle East: third-century B.C. Rhodes (Davidson Weinberg 1971); late Roman Alexandria (Rodziewicz 1984, 241–243); and Early Islamic Fustat (Francis 1989e; 1995a). There may be other places of manufacture yet to be uncovered.

The most widespread of the segmented beads in Europe, the Middle East, and Africa are small, monochrome oblates. They date from about 300 B.C. to A.D. 1200 and were an important staple in the trade.

In Asia, a few have been found at Arikamēḍu, both in the early period (ca. 25 B.C. to A.D. 20) and in medieval levels. One each has been recovered at Sungai Mas (Malaysia), Takua Pa (Thailand; it might have been locally made), Sungai Jaong (Sarawak), and Sragen (Central Java). One from Khlong Thom (Thailand) was analyzed by Salisbury and Glover (1997, bead no. 38) and was made of typical Middle Eastern soda-lime glass.

The scarcity of small, monochrome, segmented

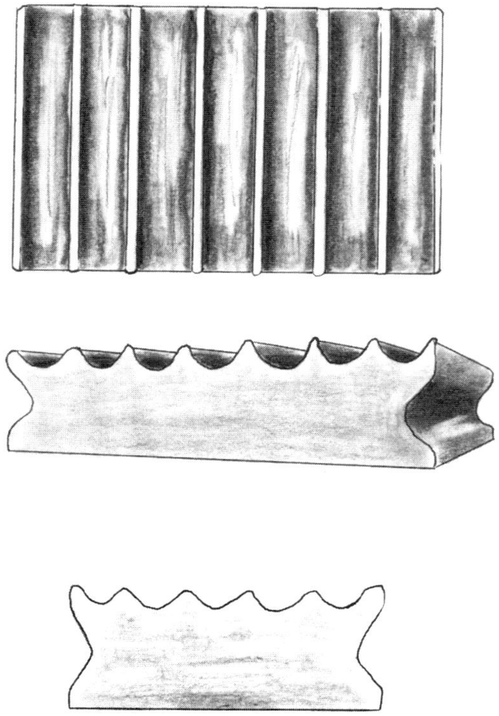

Figure 9.2. *Views of stone molds used to segment tubes uncovered in excavations in late Roman Alexandria. Stone blocks were grooved along one face. A heated glass tube rolled along the grooves created constrictions along the tube's length. The bulges between the constructions were then cut apart to be used as segmented beads. After Rodziewicz (1984); sketch by Lynda Dinneen.*

oblates in the Asian maritime bead trade contrasts with their ubiquity in other regions. There is an explanation for this. In Asia they would have competed directly with the numerous and inexpensive Indo-Pacific beads. There was probably little demand for a similar, more expensive imported bead. Other types of segmented beads, including those with multiple segments, striped ones, larger ones, and melon-shaped ones, found more acceptance because they had no or few local counterparts.

There are thin-walled single segmented beads of various sizes at Vijaya/Palembang. The most varied assemblage of segmented beads is at Sungai Mas, Malaysia. It includes small oblates, thick-walled segmented melons, striped ones, and some multiple disk-shaped beads, a type made at Fustat. Striped segmented beads were also found at nearby Pengkalan Bujang (Lamb 1966a, 89). Segmented melons have been found at Mantai, Oc Eo, Sungai Mas, Sungai Jaong, and Gedong (the last two in Sarawak) and in several sites in central and southern India.[17] Multiple segmented beads have been found at Khlong Thom and Takua Pa (Thailand), Sungai Mas (Malaysia), Muara Jambi (Sumatra), and Bukit Maras (Sarawak).

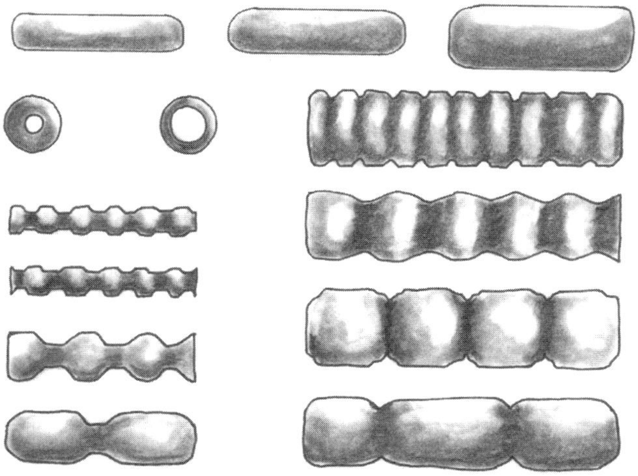

Figure 9.3. *Different forms segmented beads can assume depending upon the shape and the spacing of the device used to create the bulges along the tubes. Sketch by Bo Breda.*

Gold-Glass Beads

These are a variety of segmented beads, variously called gold-glass, gold-in-glass, gilt glass, goldfolium, gold-foil, and sandwich gold-glass beads. They were usually[18] made from two tubes of clear glass. The one with the smaller diameter was covered with gold foil and slipped into the larger one. The combined tube was heated and crimped along its length, producing bulges to be cut into beads. The finished product is quite bright, with gold shining through the protective outer layer.

Gold-glass beads are widely assumed to have been Egyptian products, at least originally. The technique may have spread to other parts of the Middle East (Boon 1966; 1977). However, some Indian writers believe that they were made in India:

> In India, we had almost contemporary production of gold-glasses, which was certainly an indigenous innovation. The gold glass technique, combining the skill of a gold-smiths [*sic*], a potter, and a glass-maker needs a well developed insight of technology. Ancient Indians attained all these technological perfections to compete [with] the old world. (Singh 1980–1981, 159 [insertions mine])

Singh based this statement on the work of Dikshit, who first asserted an Indian source for these beads. As evidence, Dikshit quoted a passage from Kauṭiliya's *Arthaśāstra*[19] that he believed to be a garbled account of their manufacturing:

> In some pieces mica may be firmly laid inside with wax and covered over with a double leaf (of gold or silver); when such a piece of mica or glass inside is suspended in water one of its sides dips more than the other, or when pierced by a pin, the pin goes very easily in the layers of mica in the interior. (Dikshit 1965, 67)

The passage appeared in a section of the *Arthaśāstra* devoted to discovering fraud in gold objects. Dipping in water and piercing with a pin are tests to see if mica was deceptively put between two layers of gold. A more recent translation of this passage reads:

> Or, a layer of mica is fixed in an article with a double base [between two sheets of gold] by means of lac. Of that, in which the fixing has been covered, one part sinks down when it is placed in water, or it is pierced with a needle in the spaces between the layers. (Kangle 1972, 120)

Dikshit (1965, 67) linked the phrase "pierced with a needle" to the piercing of glass globules to perforate into beads. He said this method was "somewhat unusual to a foreign scientist who is not well acquainted with the manner in which some of the old Indian glass is perforated. But to a student of Indian beads this method is quite familiar since many old specimens of glass are found pierced in this manner." He also reported that he, "has seen it [the technique] favoured by some craftsmen working in a small factory near Ghodegere near Belgaum in Karnataka who used muffled furnaces and dropped the ferrules [*sic*] on an earthen slaver for puncturing them" (insertions mine).[20]

In a footnote, Dikshit (1965, 67 n. 41) referred the reader to beads in his reports on Koṇḍāpūr and Ahichchhatrā. In the Koṇḍāpūr report (Dikshit 1952a, 16) bead number 188 is a flattened collar bead; it is very difficult to see how this could be a pierced bead as he suggested. He commented, "Similar beads occur very frequently in the Satavahanna layers at Brahmapuri near Kolhapur (cf. bead No. 1377)." No mention of this technique was made in the Brahmapuri report (Sankalia and Dikshit 1952), and bead number 1377 is not listed in the report or catalog.[21]

For the Ahichchhatrā report, Dikshit (1952b, 53–56) directed us to beads 95 and 58 in that order. Number 95 is described as a circular cylinder, but on fig. 5 is shown as a hexagonal cylinder. Dikshit said that it was "probably folded" and "bored by a sharp instrument." No. 58 is made of chalcedony, and apparently no. 98 was meant. No. 98 is an irregular or pear-shaped tabular. Again, he reported that it was folded and, "bored by a sharp instrument." Both beads have been clearly mixed up and in no case is it necessary to bore a hole into a folded bead.

In his final publication, Dikshit (1969) discussed these two issues again. Concerning the piercing of beads he averred (1969, 56): "Many beads are made in this way and this mode of making beads is mentioned in the Artha-śāstra. The mode therefore seems to have a very remote antiquity in India and according to some scholars seems to be peculiar to this country." As for gold-glass beads, he (1969, 57) stated, "From a vague reference in Kauṭiliya's Artha-sastra, it may be supposed that the technique was a familiar one in India in the Mauyran Age."

This leads nowhere. The *Arthaśāstra* was concerned with detecting fraudulent practices of goldsmiths. It mentions neither pierced glass beads nor gold-glass beads. Dikshit misused this passage to try to account for two very different processes. The references he cited as evidence have nothing to do with the *Arthaśāstra*, gold-glass beads, or pierced beads. The case for gold-glass beads being made in India thus evaporates.

Gold-glass beads are found in many parts of South, Southeast, and East Asia. Only the importing dates can help determine whether they were products of Hellenistic Egypt, the Roman Empire, or later. They are on many Indian sites in small numbers. Singh (1980–1981) compiled a list of them, some from Roman times and others from the Early Islamic period. Since his paper was published, several have been excavated from early and later levels at Arikamēḍu. None has yet been recorded from other early South Indian capitals or ports. They are also found at Mantai, Sri Lanka, and Mahastangarh, Bangladesh.

Other Roman gold-glass beads are at Oc Eo (Malleret 1962a, 268) and late Western Han or Xin (32 B.C. to A.D. 24) tombs in Guangzhou (Lam 1983, 214–215). They are also in fourth- to fifth-century royal tombs of the Paekche and Silla Kingdoms in Korea (Francis 1985b, 12, 14); Kuala Selinsing, Malaysia (Evans 1928, pl. XLIV), and at Ban Tha Kao (near Lopburi), Thailand (Basa 1992a, 86).

In the Early Islamic period, these beads remained

popular in India, Sri Lanka, and Southeast Asia. They are concentrated in Indonesia and especially in Srivijayan sites, such as Vijaya and Air Sugian, both in Sumatra. They are surface finds near Punung in Pacitan District, East Java. Punung is not dated, but its beads are a typical Srivijayan assemblage (red Indo-Pacific tubes and crude carnelian oblates and pentagonal barrels). These beads have also been found at Guning Wingbo, an early Iron Age settlement on the Yogyakarta coast; Jatiagung in East Java; and Laem Pho Chaiya, Thailand (Basa 1992a, 88).[22] Sungai Mas, Laem Pho Chaiya, and perhaps Guning Wingbo were associated with Srivijaya.

A gold-glass bead in the Fox collection is from Laguna, Luzon, the Philippines. Laguna (Laguna Lake) has been tentatively dated to the fifteenth to sixteenth centuries, but may be older. A "Takua Pa eye bead" was also found there, probably of the ninth century (see chap. 10). Both beads suggest an earlier date than that currently proposed for the site.

Imported gold-glass beads were desirable and expensive. A good imitation would have a ready market. Most false gold-glass beads in Asia were made with a small tube of semiopaque white and a larger, outer tube of amber-colored glass. They lack any gold.

False gold-glass beads were made in the Middle East. They are found at Siraf, Aqaba, and Berenike, ports serving Asia. Some were made at Takua Pa, Thailand, as discussed in the next chapter.

False gold-glass beads are found at Laem Pho Chaiya (Takua Pa's trading partner across the peninsula) and Ban Lum Khao, Utthani Province (both in Thailand); Sungai Mas; Kuala Selinsing; various Dvaravati sites in Thailand; Cicalugka (near Bandung, West Java); and Guning Mas (East Java). These sites date from the seventh to the tenth centuries, except for Guning Mas, which has Southern Song (beginning A.D. 1127) to eighteenth-century Qing ceramics;[23] Kuala Selinsing, which is somewhat earlier; and Ban Lum Khao, whose dates have not been fixed.

To summarize, genuine gold-glass beads reached India, China, and Korea via the land Silk Routes and Roman emporia via the maritime route in Roman times. In Early Islamic times, they were exported principally to Srivijaya. False gold-glass beads are found mostly in and around Thailand. Some were produced there, likely through the cooperation of Srivijaya and Middle Eastern beadmakers (see chap. 10).

Folded Glass Beads

Folding glass into a bead involves heating a small plaque and bending it around a mandrel or core. There are several ways to do this, but the only one that concerns us here is the "single-fold," in which a piece of glass is wrapped around the mandrel, leaving one seam.

This technique is a Hellenistic one, used by the third century B.C. at Rhodes.[24] Davidson Weinberg (1971, 144) distinguished three folded bead types at Rhodes: bicones, long bicones, and heart-shaped beads. They were all made in several colors, though translucent blue dominated. Some were striped.

The long, translucent blue, folded bicone is a persistent type. Such beads are found at Fustat (Old Cairo) in enough numbers that this may have been one place of their production in the Early Islamic period. This type of bead is fairly common at Sungai Mas. They are also found at Sengiran (West Java), Muara Jambi, and Vijaya/Palembang. They are rare in India, but two were uncovered at Karur, Tamil Nadu.

Another type of folded glass bead imitates onyx. It is made from a black or dark glass with one or two white stripes. When folded, the stripes encircle the bead. These are fairly common beads in the Middle East. They are known from several South Asian sites, including Arikamēḍu, Mantai, and Karur. In Southeast Asia, they are only recorded at Vijaya. A single-folded blue green bead with a yellow swirled decoration was found at Sungai Jaong.

A more complex kind of folded bead is made from a mosaic plaque of glass folded around a mandrel. One type is tubular with end zones and complex eyes. They have been found at Sungai Mas and Takua Pa and are on the antiquities market in the Philippines and Sarawak. Another type is round with complex mosaic eyes. They have been excavated or collected at Takua Pa, Laem Pho Chaiya, and Sungai Mas and are on the antiquities market in Indonesia.

In sum, Middle Eastern folded beads are not numerous in the Asian maritime bead trade. Onyx imitations were welcomed in South Asia. Blue bicones were distributed to Srivijaya. Folded mosaic beads have only been excavated in the Srivijayan sites of northern Malaysia and southern Thailand, though they have apparently been looted in other parts of Southeast Asia.

Mosaic Glass Beads

Mosaic glass is made by fusing different-colored glass to form patterns. The patterns appear on the end of a cylinder. The cylinder is then stretched out, reducing the size of the pattern along the length of the cylinder without distorting it. The result is a long rod (cane) with the pattern running through it. Small segments cut from the cane become the units of decoration. They are either fused together to form a bead, added individually onto the surface of a bead (usually as an "eye"), or fused into a plaque that can subsequently be folded or pierced to make a bead.

Mosaic glass is an old art that developed slowly (Harden 1967). The technique was revived in a much more sophisticated form at Alexandria in the late centuries B.C. and was continued later at Islamic Fustat (Francis 1999, 4–7). Rhodes (Davidson Weinberg 1971, 145), the Levant (Goldstein 1979, 40–41), and the city of Rome (Grose 1983) have also been suggested as centers of production. The glassmakers probably sold canes to beadmakers who employed various means of forming them into beads. The Egyptians apparently did not export eye canes to Syria until the early centuries A.D. In central Europe, at least, there are no wound beads with cane eye decoration until that time (Venclová 1983, 12).

Mosaic beads are known in very small numbers in the Asian maritime bead trade from the first century or so. As mentioned earlier, they have been found at the four emporia—Arikamēḍu, Mantai, Khlong Thom, and Oc Eo. There is also a simple type at Kauśāmbī, in North India. A mosaic face bead with a design of a duck on the opposite side was found in a sixth-century royal tomb in Korea (B.-S. Han 1973, 26).

The distribution of folded mosaic beads in the Early Islamic period was noted earlier. Wound beads decorated with mosaic glass "eyes," most likely made in Syria with Egyptian eye mosaics, are widely scattered around Southeast Asia. They have been uncovered at Takua Pa (Thailand), Muara Jambi (Sumatra), Sungai Mas (Malaysia), Bukit Sandong (Sarawak), Kejajar (Central Java), and in Cebu (the Philippines [Fox collection]). Fused mosaic beads (Egyptian or possibly Viking) are heirloomed by the Kayan of Sarawak and Kalimantan (see chap. 17).[25] Although scarce, mosaic glass beads of various types are found in the region, especially in sites connected with Srivijaya.

Ribe, Denmark, should be considered as a possible source of the heirloomed checker mosaic beads. From the eighth to the early ninth centuries glass beads were made there that parallel Middle Eastern beads. These included mosaic and checker mosaic glass. The glass and probably the workers must have come from the Middle East (Bencard et al. 1979, 124–133; Bencard 1983, Jensen 1991, 37–39). The mechanics of trade suggest that Scandinavia is a less likely source than the Middle East for glass beads in Southeast Asia. However, the oft-observed movement of glass beadmakers should always be borne in mind when attempting to pinpoint the origins of given beads.

Agate Glass Beads

I have coined "agate glass" to indicate a combination of opaque white and translucent dark blue and/or translucent brown glass. The blue and white variety is the glass of the Portland Vase.[26] In beads, the colors are sometimes in regular stripes and at other times swirled together in various ways. Beads were made with this glass by several processes, most notably winding and folding. They differ from beads simply decorated with lines by having all the colors penetrate to the interior (the perforation) of the bead.

These beads are not found in any numbers, if at all, in Southeast Asia. They are, however, rather common in South Asia through the first millennium. They are in the Gangetic Valley, the Deccan Plateau, southern "megalithic" (Pandukal) tombs, Sri Lanka (Mantai had ten and Tissamaharama had one), and Bangladesh.

Their origin is problematical. The earliest one on

record is a triangular pendant in white, blue, and brown from Taxila (now in Pakistan) dated to the first century A.D. (Beck 1941, 30). My initial impression was that they were made in India ("The Beads from Mantai," my chapter in John Carswell, ed., "Excavations at Mantai," unpublished). However, I now believe that the Middle East is a more likely source. Several pieces of evidence make me postulate this. The folding technique was unknown in India and there is no evidence for the combining of glasses this way, as there is for the Middle East, again citing the Portland Vase as an example (Turner 1959). These beads are also on the antiquity markets of West Africa (as well as Afghanistan and Iran), dating generally later than their appearance in South Asia. These beads have not been found at Fustat, Berenike, or Siraf, but they may have had an unusual origin and trading pattern.

A passage in the anonymously written *Periplus Maris Erythraei* of the mid-first century A.D. has been translated as "millefiori[27] glass of the kind produced in Diospolis" being imported to Adulis, Ethiopia (modern Zula, Eritrea) (Casson 1989, 53). The word Casson translated as "millefiori" was μορροης, usually written as "myrrhine." *Myrrhinê* has a long, convoluted history of scholars trying to discern what it was. It was a valuable import to Rome. According to Pliny it was imported from the East, often made into exorbitantly expensive cups, and soft enough for one ex-consul to damage his cup by gnawing on its edge (Eichholz 1962, 177–181). The *Periplus* tells us that it was an export from Barygaza (modern Broach), Gujarat, India (Casson 1989, 80–81).[28]

Without going into the whole thread of argument, the consensus is building that *myrrhinê* is neither agate nor glass, but fluorspar, also called fluorite (Harrell 1999, 112–113). The one drawback of this in the view of several writers (Harrell 1999, 112–113) was that they did not believe that India has fluorspar deposits. However, it does have substantial deposits in Gujarat and neighboring Rajasthan (Wadia 1990, 466), so Broach could easily have exported it.

This brings us to the notice in the *Periplus* where Rome was importing *myrrhinê* to Ethiopia. Because of the exceedingly high value placed on the material at the time (Pliny and the writer of the *Periplus* were contemporaries), it is quite likely that this *myrrhinê* was a substitute (that is, an imitation, as Casson suggested [1989, 112]). However, mosaic (millefiori) glass is not a good imitation of fluorite, whereas agate glass is. The *Periplus* tells us that *myrrhinê* was produced in Diospolis. Diospolis ("City of God") was the alternate Greek name for Thebes in Egypt (as opposed to Thebes in Greece). If this were the case, it would explain the absence of these beads at Fustat and Berenike. They were made at Thebes and not Fustat and the closest Red Sea port was Quseir al-Qadim (Leukos Limen in Roman times) and not Berenike. Unfortunately, we have no data from Alexandria, because so little excavation has been done due to the position of the modern city. Equally unfortunately, I have not been able to see most of the material from Quseir.

Despite their relative scarcity, Middle Eastern glass beads play an important role in the story of the Asian maritime bead trade. Not only were they items of commerce, but they also inspired new industries in the region. This is the subject of the following chapter.

10

Middle Eastern Beadmaking Techniques in Southeast Asia

In this chapter seven bead types found in Southeast Asia are examined. They are grouped together for two reasons. One is that they are roughly contemporary and, with one exception, are connected to Srivijayan sites. The other is that their manufacturing methods were unknown to South, East, or Southeast Asia until the appearance of this group. The beads include several types of mosaic glass, folded beads, segmented beads, and wound stratified eye beads.[1] Although their manufacturing techniques were unknown in India and to the east, they were standard in the Middle East.

These beads were apparently made in Sri Lanka and Southeast Asian sites connected to the Srivijayan polity. Evidence with various degrees of certitude for their manufacture exists at places we have already discussed in the context of Indo-Pacific beads: Mantai, Sungai Mas, Takua Pa, and Vijaya/Palembang.

Sites of Middle Eastern–Style Beadmaking

Mantai, Sri Lanka

Rather unusual beads were made at Mantai. The base color is black or dark blue and the beads are striped longitudinally, usually with white lines, but also with yellow or red ones. What is exceptional about these beads is that they were both folded and segmented. They began as a ribbon of glass folded (probably along a wire) into tubes. They were then treated as segmented beads, probably rolled along a grooved stone block to form bulges. The tubes with a series of bulges were cut into single or multiple beads of two to five segments. The ends were later reheated to smooth them (Color Plate 22).

Evidence at Mantai for making these include three incompletely folded beads, one having a perforation blocked with glass, and a group of three oblates fused together during the final reheating step. Altogether, Carswell recovered thirty of these beads from the upper layers of the site, dated to the eighth to tenth centuries. What may be similar beads were reported from Kuala Selinsing and Sarawak (Beck 1930a, 180, pl. L 25), from about the same time. The folding was not reported, but it is often difficult to detect.

This operation of folding and then segmenting beads has not yet been reported anywhere in the Middle East. Nonetheless, both operations separately are well known and at Mantai (and perhaps somewhere in the Middle East) were combined.

Sungai Mas, Malaysia

Two bead types at Sungai Mas, both composed of mosaic glass, appear to have been locally made by foreign techniques (Color Plate 23). The more abundant type is large (2 cm or so in diameter). They are deep translucent blue oblates with opaque white rings with blue centers, forming "eyes." These beads have no cores. They were made by directly joining canes or plaques of mosaic glass together and fusing them (Figure 10.1).

The other type are smaller beads, usually a centimeter or so in diameter. Again, they are formed of mosaic eye motifs fused to make a bead without a core (Color Plate 23). The eyes on these beads have opaque yellow centers surrounded by an opaque red ring. Small dots of opaque white were arranged in the surrounding matrix, which is either blue or green. As the mosaic cane was heated and manipulated into a bead, the dots (actually short sections of white glass canes) spread out as short rays or dashes radiating from the eyes.

There are three lines of evidence for local production of these beads. On one hand, there are a large number of these beads found at Sungai Mas, more than are found at any other recorded site, though they are seen on the Indonesian antiquity market. Second, these beads are always in a broken condition, as though they were wasters. These two observations alone do not prove beadmaking, but they suggest it. The third piece of evidence is the presence of several small pieces of plaques of mosaic glass matching the designs of the beads.

It appears that these plaques were the raw material for making the beads. They would have been cut up into appropriate shapes to meld together to form the beads. The plaques themselves must have come from Middle Eastern glassmakers and were exported as flat plates that could be turned into vessels by being slumped, furniture decorations, or whatever the artisan buying it wanted to make. If the plaques are the raw materials and the broken beads the wasters from this industry, no other evidence for local beadmaking would be expected.

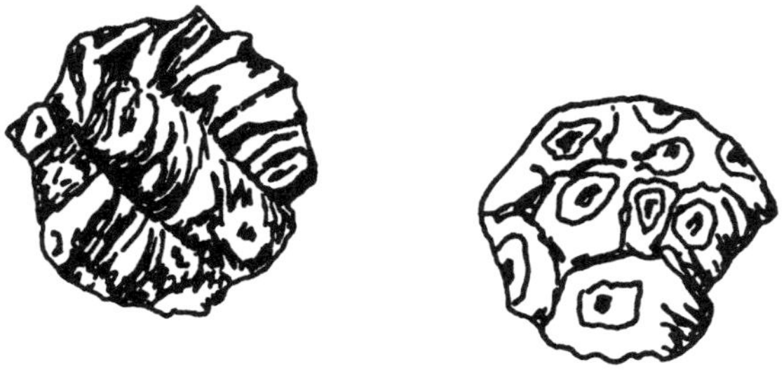

Figure 10.1. *Different views of a fused mosaic bead made of elements of blue "eyes." Sketch by Jacqui Steinberg.*

Takua Pa, Thailand

At Takua Pa, two entirely different types of beads are of interest. One is a wound oblate about a centimeter in diameter made of dark blue or green glass (Color Plate 24). The color is often dense enough to appear black in reflected light. On the surface are fifteen or so large, irregular, and irregularly spaced circular patches of opaque white surmounted by a smaller round patch of dark blue. The effect is that of an eye. Because the eye is built by superimposing patches of different colors, it is called a "stratified eye bead."

This particular style of stratified eye bead is known as the "Takua Pa eye bead" (Francis 1989c, 16). Even if they were not made there, they were first described from there (Lamb 1961, 52). They have been found elsewhere in Asia, including Mantai, Morong Rizal (the Philippines), Sungai Mas, and Laem Pho Chaiya (Thailand). They are, however, most numerous at Takua Pa, far more than anywhere else. Moreover, they are often, but not invariably, in a broken condition at Takua Pa. Again, this suggests, but does not prove, local manufacture.

The other type of bead, however, was more clearly made at Takua Pa. They are false gold-glass beads made by combining two tubes of glass, a thin inner one of whitish glass and an outer one of amber-colored glass. The tubes were fitted together and crimped along their lengths to make bulges and then cut into beads. The finished product shines rather like gold.

Evidence for local making comes in the form of a number of short tubes so crimped that the perforations were blocked and they could not be worked into beads (Color Plate 25).[2] Lamb (1961, 53) found and published one such closed tube. Several others have been found at the site since. Lamb (1966a, 93) had one analyzed and, because it contained no gold, said that there was a "mystery here that require[s a] solution."

Vijaya/Palembang, Indonesia

Vijaya was a noted site of beadmaking on several fronts. Its role as a center of Indo-Pacific beadmaking was already discussed in chapter 4, and in chapter 14 stone beadmaking there is examined. In addition, two types of folded glass beads were produced there, using two different folding techniques.

For one type, the operation was quite simple. A piece of glass with white and black stripes was heated and folded over a wire until the two edges met and fused into a single-strip folded bead (Plate 34).

The other type required a more complex piercing-and-folding operation, starting with a glass plaque. One side of the plaque was monochrome green, and the other side had stripes of red, white, black, and sometimes green (Color Plate 26). The plaque was heated, then pierced through the green side with a tapered metal rod. The glass was then folded up the rod until a bead formed. This produced a bead with a conical perforation. The green core is visible at the larger aperture, but not at the smaller. The multicolored stripes served as the decoration for the bead (Color Plate 27).

In the Kambang Unglen area of Palembang, several bead wasters from both these operations were found by the team led by Manguin. The wasters were in the form of imperfectly made beads, usually collapsed upon themselves. In addition, a piece of flat glass plaque matching the striped pattern of the pierced-and-folded bead was uncovered. As at Sungai Mas, it appears that the decorated glass was shipped to Vijaya in the form of a flat piece or pane, then cut apart to the appropriate size and shape to be made into a bead.

The Western Connection

We now have four sites that produced seven different types of beads by six different processes. The processes—fused mosaic glass, wound stratified eyes, segmented beads, single-strip folding, folding-and-segmenting, and piercing-and-folding—are otherwise unique to Southeast Asia, India, and China.[3]

The evidence is very strong that four of these bead types (the false gold-glass beads at Takua Pa, the single-strip folded and the pierced-and-folded beads of Vijaya, and the folded-and-segmented beads at Mantai) were made locally. It is less certain, but still quite likely, that the two mosaic eye bead types at Sungai Mas were locally made. It is probable, though not yet proven, that the Takua Pa eye bead was also locally made. In other words, these are foreign beadmaking techniques introduced to the region.

All these are Middle Eastern techniques, as discussed in the last chapter, with two exceptions. One is that "piercing-and-folding" was not discussed earlier. This technique has rarely been reported, perhaps because it is rarely recognized. Beck (1928, 62) outlined it, but cited no specific examples of beads made by it.

However, the technique might be more common than now appears. Nine pierced-and-folded beads have been uncovered from Berenike, Egypt, and the satellite town of Shenshef (Francis 2001) from the fourth to the sixth centuries. One was found in Nubia (B. B. Williams 1991, 232, fig. 45n) from the early centuries A.D. (personal observation). Another was recovered at Ribe, Denmark, from the ninth century (personal observation). There probably was also one found at Shabwa, Syria (H. M. Morrison 1991, 383, fig. 1.21). This suggests a long period of production, though perhaps not very abundant. All the foregoing beads have different color combinations than the ones made at Vijaya.

The other exception is the Mantai combination of folding-and-segmenting. This has never been reported or described before from any place. However, both operations are typical of the Middle East and the technique is simply a combination of the two.

The beadmaking techniques and at least some of the raw materials were obviously imported from the Middle East, mostly Egypt, to Southeast Asia. It is possible that people from Southeast Asia journeyed to Egypt, learned the techniques, and brought them home, or that people from a third place (for example, Indians) transferred the beadmaking methods.

However, it is more plausible that Middle Easterners took their skills with them to make beads in Mantai and Southeast Asia, as they apparently did to parts of Europe (Francis 1996a). Glassmaking and glassworking are often kept secret and there is little likelihood that Egyptian beadmakers would have taught their craft to strangers.

Why would glass beadmakers have gone abroad? Several scenarios might be considered:

1. Egypt magnanimously desired to share its technologies with its trading partners. On the face of it, this seems unlikely. Neither Egypt nor any part of the Arab world was likely to have done that at the time we are considering. Moreover, no other craft seems to have spread along these routes during this period.
2. Beadmakers were enticed to come to Mantai and the Srivijayan cities. Glassmakers are known to have been invited to ply their craft at other cities or in other nations. However, this opens the question as to why so many places (including the Viking region and probably Spain) solicited beadmakers at this time and not at others.
3. Beadmakers were forced to leave home and settled in new places that had commercial relations with their homelands. A study of the not infrequent movement of glass beadmakers concluded that there were various motives for beadmakers to relocate, but the overwhelming one was that they were forced to do so—that is, they were refugees from political or economic strife (Francis 1994a, 77).

In 832 the Baghdad-based Persian-oriented Abbasid government of Egypt harshly terminated a revolt of the Arab and Coptic[4] population of Egypt and was especially severe against the Copts. Could the beadmakers (as opposed to the glassmakers) have been Copts? By the tenth century only Jews and Muslims are mentioned as glassmakers in the letters of the Cairo Geniza (Goitein 1961; 1963; 1973). Had the Coptic glassmakers and glassworkers fled persecution?

This is something that may never be learned with certainty. It is set out here as a hypothesis. One way of testing it would be to have tighter chronological control over the sites of beadmaking at Mantai and in Srivijaya.

In any case, the existence of major trade routes would have facilitated the transfer. Trade between the Muslim West, Mantai, and Srivijaya was lively. Mantai was an essential port in the Asian maritime trade even after the shift to the "southern route." The three Srivijayan cities involved were all major stops on the "southern route." Sungai Mas was almost certainly the port of Kalah so often mentioned by Arab geographers. Vijaya was the capital of Srivijaya and a principal stop for Arab merchants. Takua Pa was a western terminal of the transpeninsular trade, albeit for a short period.

In addition, Indo-Pacific beads were made at all four sites. The relevance of this observation is that glass technology and tools would have been available where the beadmakers settled. A similar pattern can be seen in the Viking region, where Middle Easterners moved to places where glass beads of more simple style were already being made.

It appears, furthermore, that the raw materials were imported from the Middle East for most of these small industries. These include tubes for the false gold-glass beads (no clear glass was worked at any Indo-Pacific beadmaking site), and mosaic and other plaques for all the other beads except the Takua Pa eye bead. This is also what has been assumed to have happened at Staraja Ladoga, Russia, a Viking site of the eighth to early eleventh centuries, where beads were made to sell to the then barbaric Finns (L'Vova 1970; Rjabinin and Galibin 1995).

The discovery of this technology transfer parallels that of a similar transfer to the Viking region and Spain (Francis 1999, 8–9). Thus, the expansion of Arab trade paralleled the expansion of certain aspects of manufacturing. However, whether this was an outreach on the part of Egyptian beadmakers or a result of them becoming refugees is yet to be understood. Although the new beadmaking did not seem to last long in Southeast Asia, it did continue in Spain at least until the seventeenth century.

Color Plate 1. *Releasing a furnace-wound bead from the mandrel at Cairo, Egypt. The iron of the mandrel contracts faster than the glass and for a short time the bead is loose and may be knocked off into an annealing (cooling) chamber.*

Color Plate 2. *Drip-winding (a variation of lamp-winding) in Seoul, Korea. Glass rods are heated and allowed to drip onto a wire. The wire is rotated to give the bead a rounded shape. The wire is mounted on a pulley and moved along to make room for the next bead. Variations of this technique have been used in China and Japan for centuries.*

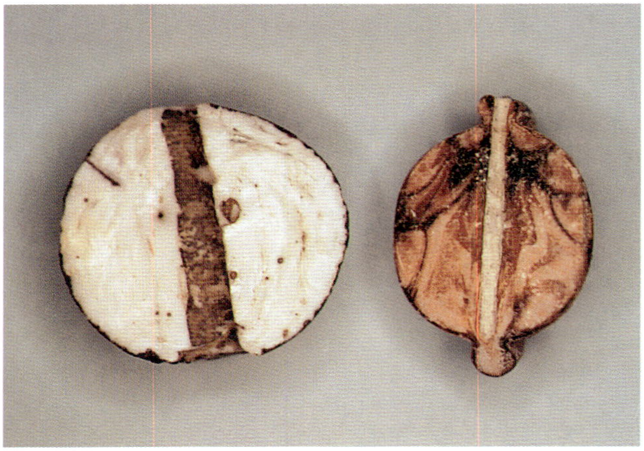

Color Plate 3. *The coatings of perforations often reveal how a glass bead was made.* Left, *a furnace-wound bead from Purdalpur, India, showing a thin layer of black iron oxide from the mandrel.* Right, *a Korean drip-wound bead with a white powdery deposit.*

Color Plate 4. *Chipping stones at Cambay to produce roughouts. The stone is rested against an iron stake driven into the ground and hit with a hammer of water buffalo horn mounted on a thin bamboo stick.*

Color Plate 5. *Drilling stone beads at Nagara, near Cambay, India. The bead is held in the split board in front of the worker, who bores it with a bow drill. The pot on the tripod at the right drips water slowly down a reed onto the bead to keep it cool.*

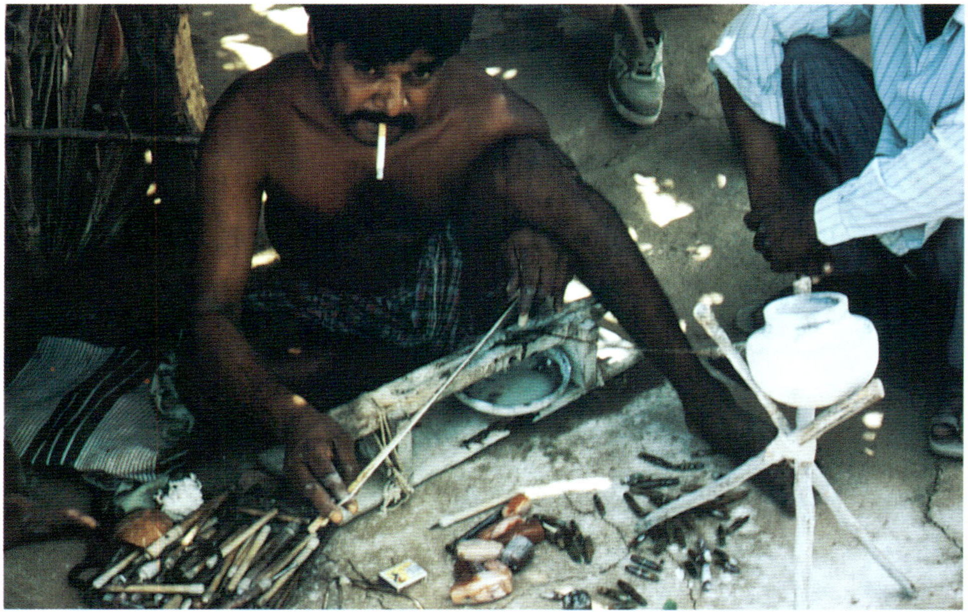

Color Plate 6. *Polishing quartz beads against bamboo at Pacitan, East Java.*

Color Plate 7. *The colors of carnelian and onyx are nearly always humanly induced.* Top (left to right): *roughout eventually to become a round carnelian bead; chip of babāghoria agate; carnelian bead.* Bottom (left to right): *sardonyx cylinder; brown onyx bead; black onyx round tabular. The sardonyx cylinder is 22 mm long.*

Color Plate 8 (Left). *Reddening finished carnelian beads in a small furnace at Cambay.*

Color Plate 9. *Indo-Pacific beads from several sources, showing varieties of the beads. The red strand at the bottom was purchased in Sumatra. The strand of small beads toward the top was purchased in Bangkok. The larger beads in the middle with yellow and orange prominent were picked up on a beach in southern Sri Lanka. The reddish tube in the center is 4.2 mm in diameter.*

Color Plate 10. *Bead-making wasters from modern Papanaidupet* (top row) *and Arikamēḍu* (second row). *From left to right they are:* a, *horns;* b, gedda paru *flakes;* c, *unperforated, pulled pieces (two from Papanaidupet; three from Arikamēḍu);* d, *bead clumps;* e, *bead with knots;* f, *large knots in tubes.*

Color Plate 11. *The archaeological site of Arikamēḍu, across a bend in the Ariyankuppam River.*

Color Plate 12. *A complex multiple eye bead from the Late Zhou (Warring States) period in China. Toledo Museum of Glass.*

Color Plate 13. *A court chain of a nobleman. National History Museum, Taipei.*

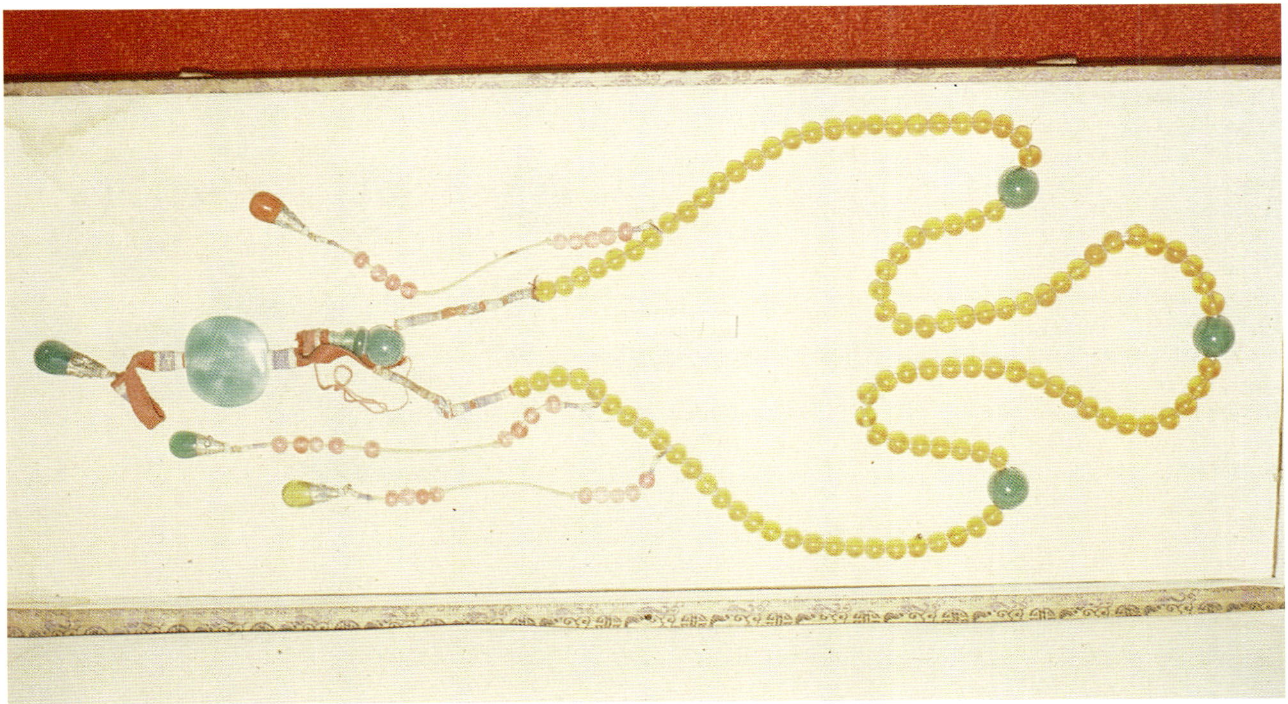

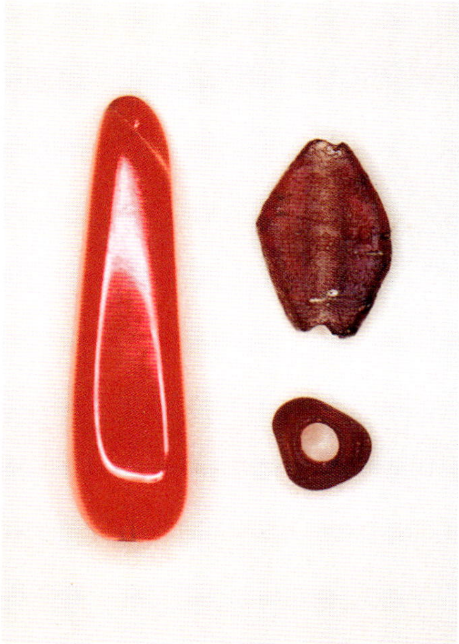

Color Plate 14. *Chinese glass beads.* Top left (left to right): *combed polychrome bead (a similar bead was excavated at Trowulan, Java); light blue multiple wound bead (from Calatagan, the Philippines); blue barrel bead similar to those made at Banten (from Sungai Jaong, Sarawak).* Bottom (left to right): *imitation chevron bead; opaque leadless glass bead (from Bongkissam, Sarawak); translucent leadless glass melon bead. The polychrome bead is 19 mm long.*

Color Plate 15 (Top right). *Two types of translucent red glass. The large, modern German bead on the left is colored with selenium. The two Chinese beads on the right are colored with copper, yielding a more dusky hue. The German bead is 27 mm long.*

Color Plate 16. *Chinese coil beads of various sizes. These were heirloom beads among the Akha of Thailand. The smallest beads are 3 mm in diameter.*

Color Plate 17 (Top left). *Chinese combed polychrome beads. National Museum of the Philippines.*

Color Plate 18 (Top right). *Two types of glass beads produced in the Middle East for some 1,500 years became staples in the trade. These are a single-strip folded bicone and a segmented gold-glass (actually silver-glass) bead. Note the seam on the folded bead and the joint where the foil does not quite meet on the silver-glass bead. The bicone is 17 mm long.*

Color Plate 19. *A wound glass bead decorated with mosaic elements and stripes from Mantai.*

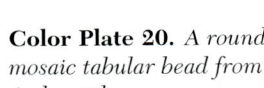

Color Plate 20. *A round mosaic tabular bead from Arikamēḍu*

Color Plate 21. *A variety of segmented glass beads from Sungai Mas, Malaysia.*

Color Plate 22. *Folded and segmented beads from Mantai.*

Color Plate 23. *Mosaic glass beads and related plaques from Sungai Mas.*

Color Plate 24 (Below). *A stratified "Takua Pa eye bead," 13 mm in diameter.*

Color Plate 25. *The end of a false gold-glass bead from Takua Pa, constricted so much that it cannot be strung.*

Color Plate 26. *Glass plaque found at Kambang Unglen (Vijaya) similar to the pierced-and-folded beads from the site and apparently used to make them.*

Color Plate 27. *Fragments of pierced-and-folded beads from Kambang Unglen (Vijaya). Evidence of the operation is visible in the perforation of the broken bead at bottom left. The diameter of the bead at bottom right is 10 mm.*

Color Plate 28. *A Bhil miner in a shallow mining pit at Damlai.*

Color Plate 29. *The shrine of Babā Ghor on Babā Ghor Hill. The shrine is apparently built on the tomb of Pir Kiste rather than that of Babā Ghor.*

Color Plate 30. *Nineteenth century sources indicate that this site is the final resting place of Babā Ghor (see Color Plate 29). The shrine on top of Babā Ghor Hill today is thought to be for the minor local saint, Pir Kiste.*

Color Plate 31. *Dressed stones from the Hindu temple atop Babā Ghor Hill. The temple was dismantled and the stones used as a walkway. By 1995, nearly all the stones had been cemented over by a new walkway.*

Color Plate 32. *Three charm case beads made from babāghoria agate. All are pierced through the top. The top bead is 38 cm long.*

Color Plate 33. *Etched carnelians.* Clockwise from upper left: *white design on red, black on whitened stone, the broken side of a whitened bead showing the red interior, broken etched bead from Arikamēḍu.* Center: *Islamic-period etched plaque, 22 mm long.*

Color Plate 34 (Above). *Some common bead shapes from the western Indian industry. In the center is a variety of the flat pendant discussed in the text.* Clockwise from upper right: *two cornerless cubes; round tabular; a stone charm case bead; a ring broken as it was being cut (a surface find at Limudra). The center pendant is 28 mm wide.*

Color Plate 35. *A pecked quartz bead blank from Arikamēḍu. Photo by Jonathan Mark Kenoyer.*

Color Plate 36. *Glass beads from Southeast Asia.* Clockwise from upper left: *dark blue bicone bead associated with Ban Chiang; long hexagonal green bicone from Java; a worn example of a bird bead, dark green cornerless cube bead. The longest bead is 29 mm long.*

Color Plate 37 (Above). *Long glass tubular bead and earring of the Ban Chiang type. Note the fold at the end of the tube that penetrates a few millimeters into the perforation. Lent by Ian Glover. The earring is 21 mm wide.*

Color Plate 38 (Below). *Two East Javanese glass beads.* Top: *small striped bead;* bottom: *mosaic bead. The striped bead is 13 mm in diameter.*

Color Plate 39. Stūpa *beads: surface finds from Rajangana, Sri Lanka. The larger one is 17 mm in diameter.*

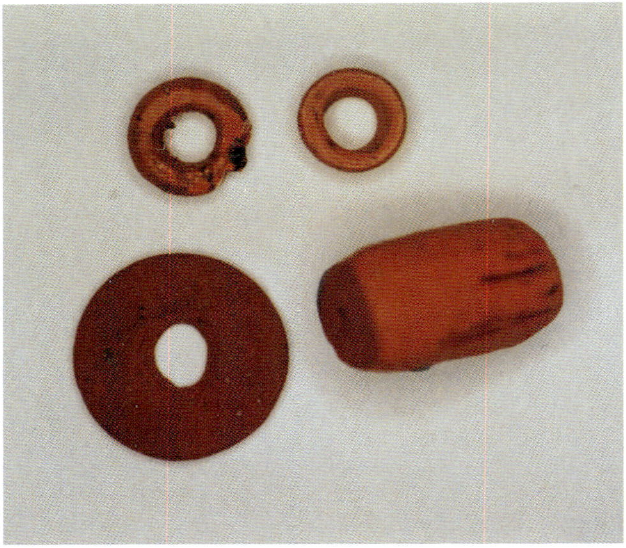

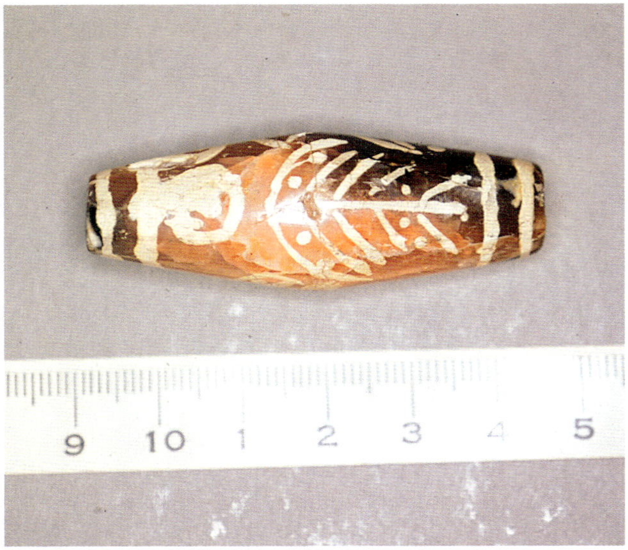

Color Plate 40 (Top left). *Some orange and red beads from Asia.* Top: *two slightly tapering orange beads from India. The one on the left shows the rounded end and the one on the right the flat end.* Bottom, *from Karaikadu: a small red disk and an orange-on-red bead, tilted to show the core. The disk bead is 8.5 mm in diameter.*

Color Plate 41 (Top right). *Unusual etched carnelian from Go Hang, Tan An District, Vietnam.*

Color Plate 42. *Etched carnelians, typical South Indian types, from the Pandukal site of Koḍumaṇal.*

Color Plate 43 (Top left). *Sixteenth-century Venetian chevron and Nueva Cádiz beads. The small Nueva Cádiz bead is the size of those excavated in the Philippines. The chevron is 14 mm in diameter.*

Color Plate 44 (Top right). *Some heirloom beads of the Ifugao at Kiangan, northern Luzon*

Color Plate 45 (Left center). *Heirloom beads of the Kalinga, at Luplupa, northern Luzon. The blue ground beads average a little under 10 mm in diameter.*

Color Plate 46. *A strand of heirloom beads of the Gad-dang of northern Luzon in the National Museum of the Philippines. The white beads decorated with blue loops came from the Kalinga, as did several other beads on the strand.*

Color Plate 47. *A strand of heirloom beads from the Toraja of Sulawesi, Indonesia. The beads range in date from the fifteenth to the late nineteenth or early twentieth centuries. They include beads from China, Holland, Venice, and Bohemia. The long blue bead at bottom is 25 mm long.*

Color Plate 48. Mutisalah *of the Lesser Sundas in Indonesia. The upper strand is* mutiraja *(Chinese coil beads) of the elite; the widest bead is 3.0 mm wide. The lower strand is* mutitanah *of the commoners; the widest bead is 6.7 mm wide.*

Part Five:
Stone Beads in the Asian Maritime Trade

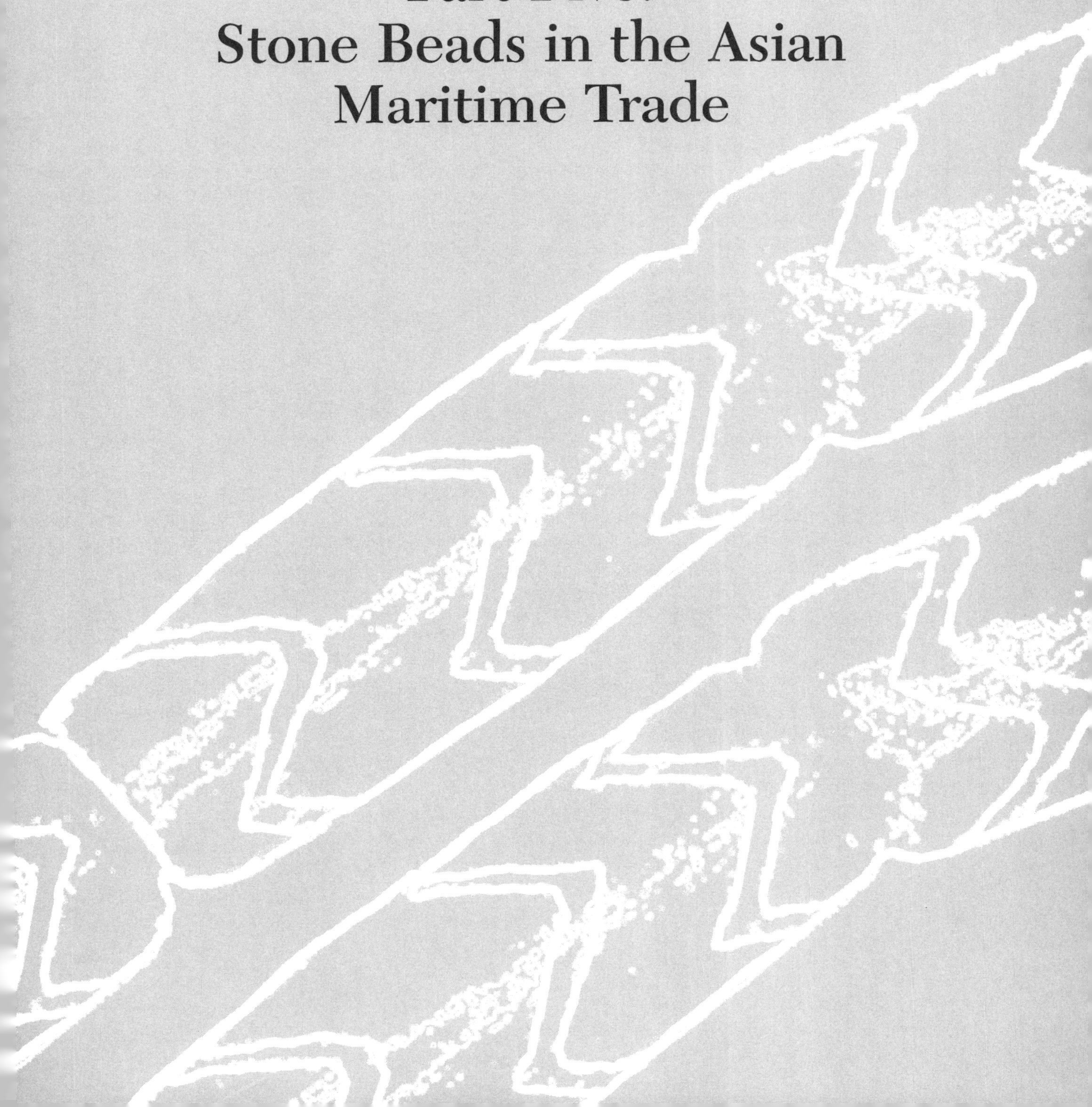

11
The Western Indian Stone Bead Industry

Quartz is the most abundant mineral on Earth. Many varieties are considered semiprecious and suitable for beads. Although quartz is found all over the globe, India has long been a major source of gem-quality stones. This is due to its geological history. Some sixty million years ago India experienced a lengthy episode of volcanism. Enormous amounts of lava flowed from fissures in the earth, forming the immense and deep "Deccan trap"[1] deposit (Wadia 1990, 275–286). Superheated water with dissolved minerals seeped into cavities and rifts in the lava to form massive (agate, carnelian) or crystalline (rock crystal, amethyst) quartz nodules and veins. In time, many of the nodules were washed out of the trap and brought downstream by riverine action.

With this wealth of minerals and the antiquity of civilization in India, it is no surprise that the subcontinent should be home to a major stone beadmaking tradition. It is, in fact, home to two. One is in western India, centered in the state of Gujarat. It has been extensively researched and is the topic of this chapter. The other, based in South India, has only recently come to light and is the subject of the next chapter. Together they ensured that India's position as stone beadmaker for the Asian maritime bead trade was unrivaled.

Prehistory

Making beads from hard stones such as carnelian and agate requires an appropriate technology, especially a method of drilling. In the Indian subcontinent this was first mastered at Mergarth (now in Pakistan), where carnelian beads were made about 4000 B.C. (Jarrige and Meadow 1980, 130–131). The stones were not locally obtainable and must have been imported. Because this predates any metal age, the drill bits were also made of stone. In the succeeding Harappān period, drill bits were principally of jasper, a quartz mineral somewhat "tougher" than the agate group. The microcrystals of jasper are arranged granularly rather than linearly, as in the agate group.

The Harappān (Indus Valley) civilization arose in this region. The Harappāns were very fond of beads. They made quartz minerals into beads at several centers, including Harappā (Beck 1940, 399–400), Mohenjo-Daro (Mackay 1938, 501–503), Chanhu-daro (Mackay 1943, 210–214), and Lothal (Rao 1973, 68–70).[2]

Of these, only Lothal was located outside the Harappān heartland, in modern Gujarat, not far from the head of the Gulf of Cambay. The stones for the Lothal beadmakers were probably found along the banks of the Narmadā River,[3] the source of stones for Cambay today. This may have been the origin of most of the agates and carnelians worked at Harappān and pre-Harappān sites. The Harappāns exported stone beads, at least to Mesopotamia (Chakrabarti 1982).

The Narmadā is India's major westward-flowing river, cutting through the Sātpurā Range. Historically, geographically, and culturally it has long been the boundary between North India and the peninsula (Figure 11.1). As far as North Indians were concerned, virtually nothing of interest existed south of this river for a long time. The early Purāṇic literature, such as the *Matsya Purāṇa*, saw the world ending at the north bank of the Narmadā. Only some later Purāṇas make brief references to the land south of the river (Ali 1966, 146–148).

Over eons, the Narmadā eroded agate nodules from the Deccan trap and deposited them near its mouth. The major deposition, in a layer of red silt or sand, ended around 22,000 to 23,000 years B.P. (K. T. M. Hegde, 1981, personal communication).

The mining of the stones is currently done by Bhils, a tribal group numbering several million concentrated in Gujarat (Color Plate 28). The center of this mining has been for centuries, if not millennia, Ratanpur ("Village of Gems"),[4] a tiny hamlet not far from the river along an old course.[5] Ratanpur is near the southern bank of the Narmadā River, a few kilometers upstream from where it empties into the Gulf of Cambay. It is the "fixed point" in the history of the western Indian agate bead industry, because it is the source of raw material. In contrast, the centers of stone cutting and the exporting harbors changed over time for various economic and political reasons.

Early Historic References

The first historical references to trade in Gujarat agates are found in two Western sources. The earlier is the mid-first century *Periplus Maris Erythraei (Periplus of the Erythraean Sea),* written by an anonymous Greek mariner. The second is *Geographia* by the Roman Claudius Ptolemy, written in the first half of the second century A.D.

The author of the *Periplus* described the great port of Barygaza (modern Broach) and in so doing discussed the workings of the bead industry, "There is in this region [sc. Of Barygaza] towards the east a city called Ozênê, the former seat of the royal court, from which everything that contributes to the region's prosperity, including what contributes to trade with us, is brought down to Barygaza: onyx; agate (?) . . . ." (Casson 1989, 81 [insertion Casson's]).[6] Although the *Periplus* author said that the raw stones were from Paithana (Paithan, Maharashtra), this seems highly unlikely. Ratanpur was much closer to Ujjain (Ozzene or Ozene) than Paithan and was under its

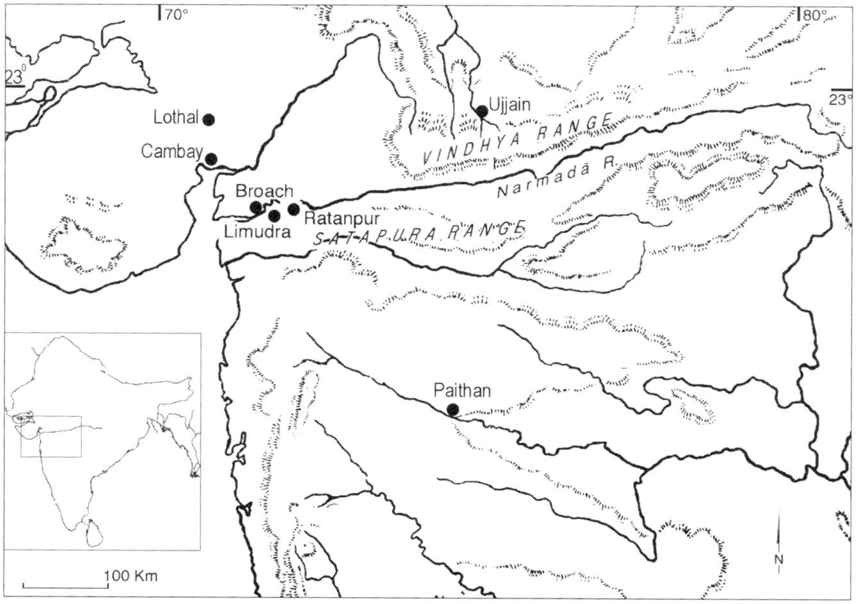

Figure 11.1. *Map of part of western India showing the Narmadā River valley and sites connected with the stone beadmaking industry.*

sway. Conversely, Paithan was in the hands of dynasties generally hostile to Mālwa (of which Ujjain was capital) and was for some time the capital of the rival Sātavāhanas.

Beadmaking at Ujjain during the late centuries B.C. has been confirmed archaeologically. Bannerjee (1959, 190–191) reported that evidence there was strongest during Period II (ca. 500 to 200 B.C.) and in the earlier levels of the succeeding Period III. Beadmaking may have moved out of the urban center some time in the second or first century B.C. It was also done in villages around Ujjain (Jain 1972, 132; Vishnu S. Wakankar, 1986, personal communication), though no details have been published.

Around 200 B.C., Ujjain was the second city of India (Chandler 1987, 462). The wealth of urbanized Ujjain was aptly described in the third-century Sanskrit play, *Mṛicchakaṭika (The Toy Clay Cart),* traditionally said to have been written by King Śūdraka. The character Mait speaks:

> The arched gateway is of gold and many-coloured gems on a ground of sapphire, and looks like the bow of Indra in an azure sky. What is going forward here so busily? It is the jewellers' court: skillful artists are examining pearls, topazes, sapphires, emeralds, rubies, the lapis-lazuli, coral and other jewels;[7] some set rubies in gold, some work gold ornaments on coloured thread, some string pearls, some grind the lapis-lazuli, some pierce shells, and some cut coral. Here we have perfumers dying the saffron bags, shaking the musk bags, expressing the sandal-juice and compounding essences. Whom have we here? Fair damsels and their gallants laughing, talking, chewing musk and betel, and drinking wine. Here are the male and female attendants, and here are the miserable hangers-on—men that neglected their own families and spent their all upon the harlot, and are now glad to quaff the drainings of her wine-cup. (Wilson 1835, 85–86)

It is not known how long Ujjain and its surrounding villages continued to be the center of stone beadmaking. As with all cities, Ujjain had its periods of expansion and contraction. Chandler (1987, 462–469) listed it as the second city in India and ninth in the world with a population of about 100,000 in 200 B.C. By A.D. 100 it had slipped to twelfth place in India and fifty-first in the world, with a little more than 40,000 people. Yet in A.D. 361 it had again become India's second city and eleventh in the world with some 80,000 people. It did not figure at all on the lists for 500, 622, or 900, but in 800 and 1000 was tenth and ninth in India and forty-fifth and sixtieth in the world.[8]

The second early Western document is the *Geographia* of Claudius Ptolemy.[9] He recognized the political connection between Ujjain, Broach, and Ratanpur, as shown on his map of India (Plate 35).[10] He placed them within the same kingdom (Mālwa [not named]). This indicates an early understanding of the relationship between the localities involved in the trade, if not their exact locations. Barygaza (Broach) is correctly shown on the north bank of the Namadus (Narmadā River) near the sea. The Narmadā runs a long distance from its "source," the Vindius Mons (Vindhaya Mountains). These are not actually its source, but form its northern valley wall. Ozzene (Ujjain) is recognized as the capital, though it is incorrectly placed on the Narmadā. Ratanpur is represented by the "Sardonyx Mountain" at the eastern rather than the western end of the Sātpurā Range and well beyond Ujjain.

The remote misplacement of the Sardonyx Mountain was likely the result of Indian "disinformation." Had the Romans known that the stones were so close to Broach they may have been tempted to go there and buy them directly. Several similar cases of Indians misleading Westerners about their geography are discussed in the next chapter.

The first Indian record to refer to the agate region was carved on a large rock at Girnar (Junāgadh), Gujarat. The same rock carries an earlier Aśōkan inscription. The

Sanskrit inscription of about A.D. 150 is roughly contemporary with the *Geographia.* It proclaimed Rudradaman I, the Saka King of Ujjain, as holder of many lands, beginning with *Purvaparna Akarvanti* ("East-West Akara and Avanti"). Avanti is a synonym for Mālwa (Indraji and Bühler 1878, 259; Kielhorn 1906). For many years, there was speculation on where Akara was. Bannerjee (1959, 190) pointed out that *Ākara* is Sanskrit for "quarry" or "mine." Although this could refer to iron mines,[11] the most famous quarries in Avanti or Mālwa are the agate mines around Ratanpur.

The next reference to the mining areas is in the "Agastya Saṃhitā" section of the *Garuda Purāṇa,* probably completed in the first half of the first millennium A.D. It tells the story of how the gods tricked the evil demon Velā into playacting the part of a sacrificial victim. They then turned on him and slew him. His body was transformed into gem-seeds, and the gods rushed in to claim their shares. Velā's bones became diamonds, his bile emeralds, his eyes sapphires, and so on. The fire god Agnī[12] took the skin:

> The fire-god, having picked up the complexion of the lord of the demons, cast it into the waters of the Narmada, a portion of which fell into the low-lying lands of the vicinity, occupied by the communities of vile caste. From the complexion so cast about [arose a stone], coloured like the hue of the Indragopta insect [Coccinellidae; ladybug] blended with that of the mouth of a parrot, and is characterized by a uniform elevation and brightness in all its parts.
>
> Blood-stones of various colours have been obtained on different occasions, some of which are extremely clear and coloured pale red and like the disc of the half-moon . . . [they are] looked upon as possessing the mystic value of increasing the wealth and number of servants of the wearer. (Shastri 1968, 207 [insertions mine])

Two glosses on this passage are required. Bloodstone (Sanskrit *rudhirkhys*) in modern mineralogical parlance is green jasper speckled with red. However, in this passage the term clearly refers to carnelian, which has been called "bloodstone" in many other contexts (Francis 1993c). As for the "community of vile caste," the word translated as "caste" is *jāti,* which is either caste or tribe. This is the first reference to the Bhil agate miners.

The sixth-century *Ratnaparīkśa* by Buddhabatta apparently postdates the *Garuda Purāṇa.* It repeats the story of the origins of gem stones from the body of the slain Velā, but is endowed with a wider geographic sense. It says that the carnelians fell in the Narmadā, "and a few in China and other countries"[13] (Finot 1896, 243–245). It also noted that carnelian stones were small, about the size of a *pilu* fruit (*Salvadora oleoides* Dcne. or *S. persica* L.),[14] which is only about a centimeter in diameter. The raw stones are usually several times larger than that. Perhaps Buddhabatta was looking at a finished bead.

Both Indian and foreign sources affirm a lively agate bead industry in western India in the early centuries A.D. There were three nodes of production: raw stones dug around Ratanpur, beads cut in and around Ujjain, and finished beads exported from Broach. This system was reorganized in time. First the lapidaries were moved, then the port, and then the lapidaries again.

Medieval History

Limudra succeeded Ujjain as the beadmaking center. It is only 5 km from Ratanpur and was once a place of note. Its ruins include two stone temples, stone and brick drains, a large scatter of iron slag, and an extensive area indicating stone beadworking. At nearby Babā Ghor Hill there was once a fine temple at the summit made of limestone or marble blocks held together with iron pins. There is also a large water tank with steps on all four sides nearby (Plate 36).[15] Current residents[16] remember that the region was once called "Maṇipur" ("Bead Place") and Limudra itself "Maṇipur Shahr," roughly "Bead City."[17] It is the only known place for working Ratanpur stones between the time Ujjain ceased being the lapidary center until the moving of operations to Cambay.

The precise date and circumstances of the move of

the lapidaries from Ujjain are not fully understood. It may have happened when the Soḷaṅkīs of Gujarat completed the conquest of Mālwa under Jayasiṁha in Vikram Saṁvat (V.S.) 1193 or A.D. 1135–1136 (Acharya 1922, 322–324).[18] Mālwa and Gujarat were long-standing enemies. Mālwa had come under control of the Rājput Paramāras by A.D. 800 (Bühler 1892). The warrior-king Bhoja I (ca. 1000 to 1055) directed his aggression toward Gujarat. He so ravaged the capital, Aṅhḷiwāṛ, which Chandler (1987, 469) rated as India's largest city in A.D. 1000, that the phrase "the sack of Aṅhḷiwāṛ" became proverbial (Dodwell 1969, 127). The Soḷaṅkīs of Gujarat got their revenge. After a twelve-year campaign, Jayasiṁha Siddharāja conquered Ujjain in 1137 and paraded the Paramāra king around his newly restored capital in a wooden cage (Luard and Lale 1908, 32–33).

The route of the Soḷaṅkī conquest went through the Narmadā Valley, and the valley was one of the spoils of war. After the conquest of Mālwa, the Soḷaṅkīs appointed two feudatory families in turn to rule the area south of the river.[19] The first were cousins of the Soḷaṅkīs, the Chahumānas (Fleet 1889, 81). The Viajavapāyaṇas, whose last king was ruling in 1290 (Ram 1962, 220), replaced them.

There are other ways the lapidaries may have moved from Ujjain to Limudra. Beadmaking could have been set up there between A.D. 580 and 735, when the Gujara dynasty, allied with the Pratihāras of Gujarat, controlled the Ratanpur region from their capital at Nandod, 35 km east-southeast of Ratanpur (Francis 1982c, 15–17). Some lapidary work apparently went on at Valabhi, across the Gulf of Cambay, either using Ratanpur stones (Francis 1982c, 17) or local stones (R. N. Mehta, 1981, personal communication).

The Paramāras of Mālwa could also have set up Limudra as the lapidary site during a period of decline at Ujjain. The Paramāras were devotees of Siva, but also worshipped a mother goddess and other minor gods. They encouraged ironworking and built temples and water tanks (Jain 1972, 405–421, 499). Such activities are evident in and around Limudra. Arguing against this possibility, however, is the fact that Limudra is more closely connected to Jainism than Hinduism.

Allchin (1975, 101) identified a Jain temple at Limudra that she dated to around A.D. 800 to 900. There was a Jain idol of Rikhadevji dedicated during the 1060s[20] in the town. The Jain tradition lives on in the area. On 5 February there is a Jain fair held very close to Limudra (*Gujarat State Gazetteer* 1961, 754). The deity said to have been vanquished by the Muslim Babā Ghor was called Mākkhan Devī and had her counterpart in Vaghan Devī, the mother goddess of Limudra. Mākkhan Devī is also referred to as a *"rakshiśa"* (Francis 1985a). A *rakshiśa* is a demon in Hindu mythology, but a minor god in the Jain pantheon (van Lohuizen–de Leeuw 1976, 234, 348).

It is difficult to say how far the Jainite connection might take us. Jainism was important in much of western India for many centuries (Majumdar et al. 1978, 95). The Soḷaṅkī conqueror of Mālwa, Jayasiṁha Siddharāja, was himself converted to Jainism in 1125.[21] The later Soḷaṅkīs were also known for being builders in stone and builders of wells, as well as for a policy of winning over the Bhils (Commissariat 1938, lvii, lxi, lxiv). However, the datable period of building activity at Limudra seems to predate Soḷaṅkī influence.

Whatever happened, late in the first millennium or so a new lapidary site was founded at Limudra. Limudra remained the bead-cutting center for centuries thereafter. Duarte Barbosa, who visited the then flourishing port of Cambay (variously spelled)[22] about 1505, mentioned the export of beads from Cambay and beadmaking at Limudra:

> Beyond this City of Cambaya, further inland is a town called Limadura. Here is found an *alaquequa* (carnelian)[23] rock, which is a white, milky or red stone, which is made much redder in the fire. They extract it in large pieces [this is not correct (insertion mine)], and there are cunning craftsmen here who shape it, bore it and make it up in divers fashions, that is to say; long, eight-sided, round and olive-leaf shapes, also rings, knobs for hilts of short swords and daggers, and other ways. The

> dealers come hither from Cambaya to buy them, and they [thread them and] sell them on the Red Sea coast whence they pass to our lands by way of Cairo and Alexandria. They take them also to Arabia and Persia, and to India [Goa (insertion mine)] where our people buy them to take to Portugal. And here they find great abundance of *babagoure,* which we call *calsadonia* (calcedony), which are stones with grey and white veins in them, which they fashion perfectly round, and after they are bored the Moors wear them on their arms in such a manner that they touch the skin, saying that they are good to preserve chastity: as these stones are plentiful they are not worth much. (Dames 1918, 142–145)[24]

Modern History and the Rise of Cambay

The destinies of Cambay and Ratanpur-Limudra eventually merged. Cambay was founded around the sixth century (Mehta 1968, 181; 1975, 20; Momin 1977, 177). It was first mentioned in a land grant from Kavi by the Rāshṭrakūta Govinda II in the year Saka 749/A.D. 827 (Altekar 1925, 47). It prospered under the Soḷankīs, being their major port, and was an early target of Muslim penetration into India. It has the oldest Muslim inscriptions anywhere in the country, except for the Punjab and Delhi (Desai 1961, 352). 'Ala ud-Din Khalji captured Cambay in 1297, and thereafter it expanded and became the port from which the hajj pilgrims embarked for Mecca (Mehta 1975, 21, 27).

Cambay was mentioned by Masu'ud, Al-Idrisi, Ibn Battuta, and Marco Polo, among others. However, none of the early visitors[25] mentioned beads or gems. Cambay traded with the Middle East, East Africa, and Southeast Asia. Tomé Pires (before 1515) said, "Cambay chiefly stretched out two arms, with her right arm she reaches out towards Aden, and with the other towards Malacca, as the most important places to sail to, and the other places are held to be of less importance" (Cortesão 1967, I: 42).

From the late fifteenth century, European visitors to Cambay began to mention agates. The Italian Nicoli Conti (1444) noted that sardonyx was found there (Major 1857, part II, 5). In 1501 Gasper Correa wrote that Sancho de Toar sent to Sofala, "cloth of Cambaya and red beads, these being the principal articles used in that trade" (Theal 1898, 26), likely referring to the export of carnelians from Cambay. In 1503 the Italian Ludivico di Varthema was the first European to note that the "carnelian hills [lie] seventy miles from Cambay" (Bose 1908, 176).

The first writer to say unequivocally that Cambay exported beads was Pires, who visited some years before 1515. He said that they were sold to Aden (Cortesão 1967, 16, 43), though Aden had finer (albeit fewer) of its own (Cortesão 1967, 18). Barbosa (Dames 1918, 12, 15, 55) noted the export of Cambay beads to Sofala and Angoche in East Africa and to Aden. He also listed them as products bought by traders from Arabia, Persia, India, Malacca, Sumatra, Malinde, Mogadishu, and Mombasa (Dames 1918, 154). Münster (1559, 1083) only mentioned precious stones in the Kingdom of Cambay.[26]

Caesar Frederick (1905, 90) in 1563 described Cambay as being in such a terrible state that the people were selling even their children for a pittance. Innumerable small boats came out to meet the European ships, selling, among many other things, "great stones like to Corneolaes, Granats, Agats, Diaspry, Calcidonii, Hematists and some kinde of naturall Diamonds."[27]

At least some stone workers moved to Goa to continue their trade. John Huyghen van Linschoten (1905, 258)[28] in 1583 said that the Gujaratis who were settled in Goa and elsewhere in India dealt in "all kinds of precious Stones wherein they have great skill." His contemporary, François Pyrard, said of the trade from Cambay to Goa, "They bring good stores of precious stones, not of the fine sorts, such as diamonds and rubies, but other kinds, which they know how to cut skillfully, and to work into a thousand pretty things" (Gray and Bell 1888, 247).

Some time between 1505 when Barbosa saw beadmaking at Limudra and 1638 when Mandelslo was the first to stipulate that the industry was located in Cambay (Commissariat 1931, 15), the industry was transferred from one place to the other. This probably happened before Akbar incorporated Gujarat and Nandod (then the capital of the realm encompassing Ratanpur and Limudra) into the Mughal Empire in 1572, because the Mughals did not favor Cambay and were unlikely to have enriched it with a new industry (Mehta 1975, 28). The Gujarat king Bahādur (1526–1536) had previously conquered both Mālwa and Nandod. He patronized Cambay (Anonymous 1879, 11), and because he controlled the industry, the transfer could have been made in his reign.

In 1592, Akbar issued an order requiring that all stones used to weigh coins and jewels in his realm be made of babāghoria agate (Blochmann 1927, 1:36, 2:60). Babāghoria agate is the gray and white banded agate of Ratanpur, named after the patron saint of the bead industry, Babā Ghor.

Babā Ghor is revered by locals of all religions at a shrine built in the 1870s on the westernmost hill of the Sātpurā Range. He was most likely a scion of the Ghors of Mālwa or a nobleman who took their name and died fighting against Ahmed of Gujarat during Ahmed's incursions in 1416 or 1431 (Campbell 1880, 99). Homage paid to Ghor's tomb was first recorded by the seventeenth-century historian ad-Dabir. He said that the young Gujarat king, Qutbuddin Ahmed Shah, in 1452: "paid a visit of respect to the saint of God, Babā Ghor, may his grave be sanctified. He then proceeded to Broach" (Lokhandwala 1970, 4). The name *babāghori* was in common use for the agate when Barbosa visited Limudra a half century later, around 1505.

A strong case can be made that Babā Ghor is not buried where his shrine is located, but that the current shrine (Color Plate 29) was built over the tomb of an older saint, Pir Kiste (Color Plate 30) (Francis 1989b). In any case, the worship of the enigmatic Babā Ghor is of great local importance and his canonization marks the coming of the power of Islam to the area.

Babā Ghor is credited with destroying the goddess or *rakshiśa* Mākkhan Devī and throwing her temple down, though it was more likely destroyed by Ahmed Shah of Gujarat.[29] The temple foundation remains on the summit of the hill. The blocks forming the temple were used as a walkway to ascend the hill, but most have now been covered over with cement pavement (Color Plate 31).

Stories about Babā Ghor abound and several brothers and sisters were eventually added to the pantheon. The local Siddis (descendants of the slave-revolt "Abyssinian dynasty" of Bengal) have made him one of their own, greatly bolstering their own status. Although the history and ethnology of the Babā Ghor story are fascinating, it goes beyond our interest here (see Francis 1982c, 22–28; 1985a; 1989b).

Cambay has now declined as a port with the silting up of the Mahi River, but beadmaking continues in the older quarter (Teen Darvaja) around the Friday Mosque. The first detailed account of the mining, of Limudra (therein Neemoodra),[30] and of Babā Ghor Hill was published by Copland in 1819. The first detailed description of bead working at Cambay was written by Summers in 1851. Since then, many accounts have appeared on both places, particularly in India.

Europeans did not become generally aware of the industry until Arkell (1936) published an answer to a note by Beck (1930b) on the origins of babāghoria barrel-shaped beads. Arkell (1936, 305) suggested that the region might have been a center for beadmaking as early as the Harappān period. The assumption has proven to be correct, but popularizers have exaggerated it. For example, "It is interesting to record that a factory [*sic*] making cornelian, quartz and other stone beads has been working in Cambay, Gujarat, for at least 7000 years and is still active" (van der Sleen 1973, 18). Most recently, intensive ethnoarchaeological projects have been conducted at Cambay, expanding our understanding of the mechanics of the industry (Roux and Pelegrin 1988–1989; Kenoyer et al. 1991).

Identifying Western Indian Stone Beads

Beads of agate, carnelian, and onyx are found on many sites throughout the Eastern Hemisphere. India, and often western India, is commonly identified as their source in most of the literature. In truth, however, we do not know enough at this time to be certain of the origin of all of these beads.

As discussed briefly in chapter 2, far less work has

been done on stone beads than on beads of glass. An intensive, international program is required to determine the origins of mineral beads at various sites. A limited program centering on Southeast Asia has been conducted (Robert Theunissen, 1998–1999, personal communication), but it is only a small beginning.

With these constraints, this section cannot be too dogmatic about identifying western Indian stone beads. The best that can be done now is to point out the characteristics that have been used to identify beads from this source and discuss their usefulness or validity.

The color of the carnelians and the patterning on babāghoria agate (Color Plate 32) are often invoked as diagnostic. However, both are variable and neither is unique. The red color seen on the plaque in Color Plate 33 matches that of most Ratanpur carnelians. However, the material of the plaque (which is likely from western India) is not monochrome, fading on the left-hand side.

Similarly, the attractive babāghoria agate in Color Plate 32 exhibits considerable variation. Other agate sources produce material very similar in appearance to babāghoria. Not all of these were exploited in antiquity, such as "Botswana agate," but some may have been.

Technical considerations may provide clues to the origins of stone beads, but for the most part they are now most useful to help date them. The earliest report of double-tipped diamond drills used on hard stone beads is from Hajar ar-Rayhani, Yemen (Gwinnett and Gorelick 1991, 192).[31] Among the nine hard stone beads dating from the seventh to the fifth century B.C., "some" were apparently drilled that way, and "some others" were bored with copper drills and abrasives. This is tentative and suggests a transition period, but it fits well with what is known about the introduction of this technique in India. The double-tipped diamond drill was established in both western and southern India by the time our period of interest opens.

Polishing of stone beads was done in one of two ways: by tumbling or by abrasion. The tumbling of round beads extends back well before the period considered here. Gwinnett and Gorelick (1991, 189–190) found evidence for tumbling in ninth- and eighth-century B.C. levels. However, faceted beads were not tumbled that early, because the process dulls the edges of the facets and makes the beads less attractive. They are tumbled today.[32]

Evidence from Viking graves in Scandinavia gives us the most likely date for this transition. The carnelian beads in these burials are almost certainly from western India. Beginning with the period dated 915 to 950 A.D. and then always after 950, the faceted carnelians are tumbled rather than polished by abrasion (Callmer 1977, 91).[33] This date appears to be a little earlier than the same transition in the South Indian industry (see chap. 12), where faceted forms were heavily favored.

The shapes of beads may provide some clues about their origin or dates. Some forms, of course, are virtually universal, but others are more restricted. Early reports of the industry listed some bead shapes. Barbosa around 1505 listed "long, eight-sided, round, and olive-leaf shapes" (Dames 1918, 143). Summers (1851, 325) noted "cut beads, diamond cut, almond shaped, oblong, flat spear shaped, round, etc." Some of these are more easily envisioned than others are. Neither of these lists is complete. The modern industry can and does make a wide variety of shapes.

Dikshit (1952a, 95; Francis 1982c, 42) attempted a chronology of stone bead shapes from the data then available to him. Few of the chronological distinctions he made have held up to later investigation. Nonetheless, a few shapes do appear to have some chronological value (see Color Plate 34).

The cornerless cube, a square prism with its corners cut off, became a popular bead shape a few centuries B.C. The assumption has long been that glass ones appeared in the West and that the style was transferred to India by this medium. A blue glass one at Taxila (now in Pakistan) dated to the fifth century B.C. (Beck 1941, 27) is an early example. Glass cornerless cubes are known from many sites in Europe and the Middle East, especially from Roman times though the Early Islamic period (ca. first century B.C. to ca. A.D. 1200).

Arguing against this presumed origin, however, are two considerations: (1) Faceted translucent stone beads have additional beauty because of the play of light resulting from multiple surfaces. The fourteen facets of a cornerless cube are technically fairly easy to accomplish. (2) Of the seven glass cornerless cubes found at Berenike, Egypt (275 B.C. to the sixth century A.D.), through the 1998 season, five were wound and paddled into shape. However, the other two had been worked from a piece of glass in the manner of stone, having been ground to shape and drilled. These facts suggest that the stone might have been the original cornerless cube material. The case is still open; more accurate reporting and dating are needed to settle the matter.

Undecorated (that is, not etched, see chap. 14) round tabular beads appear in Muslim times in India (Sankalia and Dikshit 1952, 89). They were particularly popular in Iran (personal observation). They were apparently made by perforating the edges of the cores left over from the production of agate rings, which were cut from flat pieces of stone with a hollow (probably copper) drill (Francis 1982c, 42). These cores/bead blanks are common surface finds at Limudra (Color Plate 34).

Pendants resembling a horizontal charm case (Color Plates 32, 33) also appear to be medieval in date. The earliest one reported is from early Muslim Dwarka, Gujarat, about the tenth century (Ansari and Mate 1966, 41). The original charm cases were made of metal and were hollow to hold some sacred writing. They are found in Egyptian, Buddhist, and Muslim contexts.

Finally, flat pendants perforated through a small loop on top and very difficult to describe in words (see Color Plate 34) are usually made of babāghoria agate.[34] Budge (1968, 67, pl. VI) pictured an acid-etched carnelian one with intricate designs (it may have been made in Iran) referring to them as Persian or Shiite amulets. The earliest dated example of the form is on a stucco figure at Nishapur, Iran, from the eighth or ninth century (Wilkinson 1986, 262, fig. 4.2). A pendant of this type made of babāghoria was also found at Nishapur. Akbar issued a gold coin in this shape in A.D. 1573 (P. L. Gupta 1979, pl. XXVI.274), and Mogul jade pendants were carved into the form (Brunel 1972, pl. 67). Whatever its origin and meaning, this interesting type of pendant is closely connected to Islam, and the design has found its way at least to Egypt.[35]

It is noteworthy that certain bead shapes are much more common in one region than another: round tabulars in Iran; large, scaraboidal tabulars in Afghanistan; and short, wide bicones and uneven square bicones ("date beads") in parts of Africa. Whether these differences are a function of time or the choice of traders or customers (see the Madagascar section in chapter 16) is not known.

Once analytical procedures for pinpointing the origins of stone beads are established, information regarding trading patterns can be gleaned from a study of their distribution. Eventually, research into stone beads may be as fruitful as that into glass beads.

Western Indian stone beads spread all over the world (in the Western Hemisphere since 1492).[36] There will be no attempt here to list their occurrences. As a rule of thumb, most imported carnelian and agate beads found west of India are probably from this industry. A few exceptions in the Asian maritime bead trade are discussed in chapter 14.

The western Indian bead industry has received a great deal of attention. Arkell's work has been particularly influential among Western scholars for the last half-century and more. What has not been suspected was the existence of a parallel stone bead industry as great as that of western India in the south. That is the subject of the next chapter.

12
South Indian Stone Beadmaking

The South Indian stone bead industry contrasts with the western Indian industry in subtle but important ways. The basic materials of the western industry—carnelian and agate—played a much smaller, though still significant, role in the south. Crystalline quartz (rock crystal, amethyst, and prase) and non-quartz minerals (beryl, garnets, diamonds, and corundum) were far more important in the south than in Gujarat.

Rajan (1997–1998, 59–60) collected references to this industry from what is popularly known as the *Sangam* literature,[1] collections of classical Tamil poems. They are not precisely dated, but are mostly from the first to the fourth century A.D., with some a century or two later. At times they reflect events earlier than the date at which they were written (Ramachandran 1996, 244–245). The literature identifies beadmakers or gem workers as *tirumaṇi kuyinar* and *maṇi vinaiar* (Rajan 1997–1998, 60), *maṇi* being "bead" or "gemstone."

The South Indian industry has been hidden from scholarly view. Classical western sources note that precious stones were bought at southern ports, but there was no understanding of the basics of the industry as there was for western Indian beadmaking. There are no accounts from early European visitors of the southern industry, and although it has survived to the present, it has only recently been recorded. Stone beadmaking in South India has a history of over two millennia, and in some periods it was the outstanding gem industry of the world.

The Arikamēḍu Clue

As early as the 1930s, it was obvious that there was a stone bead industry at Arikamēḍu. Judging from the number of beads and wasters found there, stone beadmaking was as important as the Indo-Pacific glass bead industry.[2]

The most notable fact about Arikamēḍu stone beads is that there were two different sequences of production (Francis 1988c). In one, beads were made in the way familiar for millennia in western India and the Chalcolithic period in the Deccan (Figure 12.1).[3] After chipping

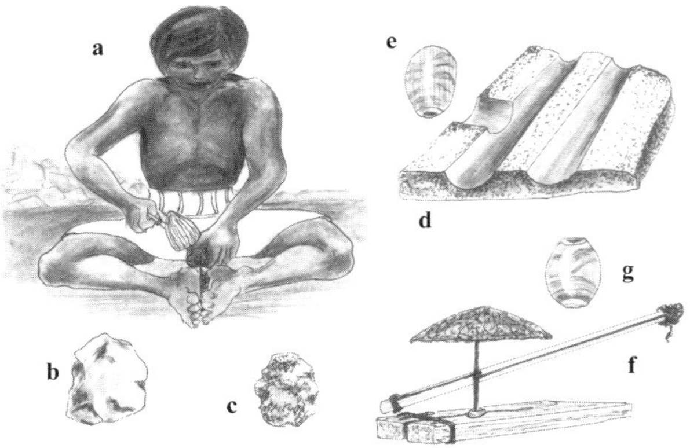

Figure 12.1. *Sketch of the basic steps used for stone beadmaking in western India. The initial chipping* (a) *turns a pebble* (b) *into a roughout* (c). *This is ground on a stone* (d) *or wheel (not shown) into a blank* (e). *Then the blank is drilled with a bow drill* (f) *and polished into a finished bead* (g). *Sketch by Lynda Dinneen.*

a stone into a roughout, a worker ground it into a blank. The blank was perforated and finally polished. At Arikamēḍu, this was used on about 80 percent of the chalcedonic material, but only half of the crystalline quartz material.[4] The rest of the beads, about a fifth of the chalcedony and half the crystalline material, were made differently. They were pecked[5] from a roughout into a blank by repeated hitting, perhaps with a diamond tip.[6] Then they were polished, against a wheel (see later in this chapter), before being bored (Figure 12.2). In some cases a final sheen was given to them after being bored.

Thus, there were two ways to make beads, the "grinding" (grinding, drilling, polishing) and the "pecking" (pecking, polishing, drilling) complexes.[7] At first, there was no ready explanation for the difference. The 1989–1992 Arikamēḍu excavation confirmed that both methods were used simultaneously. It may be easier to peck crystalline quartz than to grind it, but why is not clear. Nor would this explain why the polishing and drilling steps were reversed.

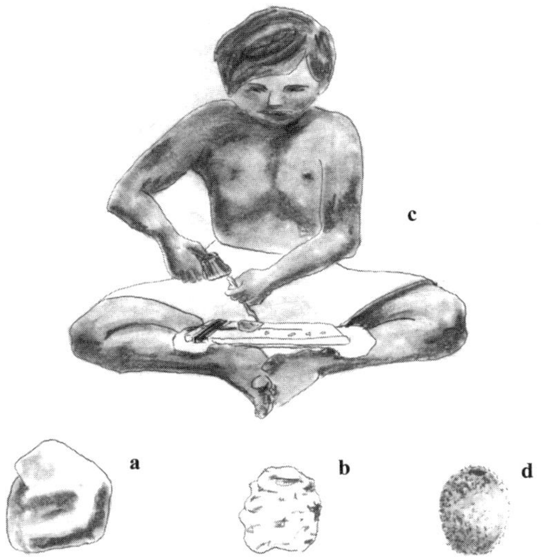

Figure 12.2. *Stone bead preparation using the pecking complex. A stone nodule* (a) *is chipped into a roughout* (b). *This is then pecked all around the surface, most likely by indirect peccussion* (c). *The pecked blank* (d) *is then ready to be polished and drilled. Sketch by Lynda Dinneen.*

The evidence now points to an ethnic difference. Urban Arikamēḍu no doubt saw people emigrate from other parts of India, and these perhaps included western Indian beadmakers. However, the pecking complex is associated with people who have long been a mystery in Indian archaeology.

The Pandukal Connection

The stone bead industries of Arikamēḍu and the rest of South India were largely in the hands of Pandukal people. These people are often called "Megalithians" in the literature, but "Pandukal" (Leshnik 1974, 1–2) is a better term and is adopted here.[8] Scholars knew little of the Pandukal people for a long time. Only their "megalithic" burial sites, often in isolated, prominent places, such as the tops of hills, had been investigated.

Although this is not the forum to discuss the "megalithic problem" in detail, a summary of recent evidence is useful. Early antiquarian notions linked the Pandukal people with West Asia or even Europe. By the mid-twentieth century it was acknowledged that they were a product of the Indian milieu, though how they fit into it is still not understood.

The remote nature of many of their burials made it difficult to identify their habitation sites. Even as recently as the compendium by Leshnik (1974), no Pandukal occupation sites were known. That picture has changed dramatically in the last quarter-century. Habitation sites have been identified in the Vidarbha region of eastern Maharashtra (Deo 1973, 1983; Mohanty and Walimbe 1996), western Tamil Nadu (Rajan 1990), eastern Tamil Nadu (Rajan 1998), and elsewhere in the south (Moorti 1994). Meanwhile, the significance of the "megalithic" component at Arikamēḍu has evolved from a mere ceramic assemblage (Casal 1949), to an appreciation of Pandukal participation in the economy of the site (Francis 1993d), and into a synthesis of development in Early Historic times throughout South India (S. Gupta 1995–1996).

The perception of the socioeconomic life of the Pandukal people has also undergone change. They were once considered nomadic pastoralists, in contrast to their settled agricultural neighbors (Deo 1983). Their "heartland" was thought to be north of the classical Tamil Kingdoms (Leshnik 1974, 19–21). Although it is still believed that young Pandukal men rode horses to herd cattle, the society is now recognized as having a mixed economy, including a strong agricultural base (Mohanty and Walimbe 1996, 138; Harishankar 1997–1998, 115), and perhaps a warrior element (Mohanty and Walimbe 1996, 141).

As studies intensify, it is clear that the Pandukal people were not confined to the "tribal belt" north of the Tamil Kingdoms. Rajan (1998) identified 143 Pandukal sites in South Arcot District, Tamil Nadu, alone, including fifty-four habitation-cum-burial sites or habitation mounds.[9] The patterns formed by differing burial practices were interpreted as indicating three distinct, contiguous clan territories.

Several cultural traits are associated with the Pandukal people, often unique for their time and place. The best-known one is the interment of the dead in secondary burials marked with megaliths or stone circles, contrasting with burial practices of their neighbors. They introduced horses into South India and held them in esteem. Many horses were buried, sometimes with numerous grave goods.

The Pandukal people were skilled metalsmiths. Settlements were often chosen for their proximity to iron or gold deposits. Iron production is attested to by a crucible at Takalghat (Moorti 1984–1985), a smelting furnace (Gogte 1981; Gogte et al. 1982) at Naikund,[10] both in Vidarbha, and several furnaces and extensive slag heaps at Koḍumaṇal, Tamil Nadu (Rajan 1990, 98). They may have introduced iron to South India. Koḍumaṇal was celebrated for its goldsmiths (Champakalakshmi 1990, 13; Rajan 1990, 93 n. 1). They also worked copper on a lesser scale; two daggers at Mahurjhari, Maharashtra, were composites with copper hilts and iron blades (Mohanty and Joshi 1996, 160).

Artifacts associated with the Pandukal people in graves and habitation sites include a wide range of iron instruments, particularly for horses and warfare, sometimes gold or copper items, and distinctive stone beads, including "etched carnelians."[11] The ceramic affiliated with them is black-and-red ware, a finely polished pottery achieved by firing pots in a reverse position. Although similar ceramics are known from other cultures at other times, in South India this type is almost always associated with Pandukal sites. Graffiti on these ceramics are exclusive to Pandukal centers. They have not yet been interpreted.[12]

To these traits, we may now add another: the making of stone beads. These are diagnostic in two ways. In the manufacturing realm, the "pecking" complex was employed to make the beads. In terms of style, the use of certain patterns on "etched" carnelians is unique. Dikshit (1949, 26–30) referred to these patterns as the "southern group" of etched carnelians, noting that they were found in "megalithic" and Sātavāhanan sites (Dikshit 1949, 14–15). However, they are not merely southern, but distinctly Pandukal.

The earliest known settlement dates for the Pandukal people are between the Tungabhadrā and Kṛishṇā Rivers, in the area Leshnik designated the "tribal belt" (Figure 12.3). They range from the middle to the late second millennium B.C. Another early date is at Korkai, later the seat of pearl fisheries, 905–780 B.C. after calibration (Moorti 1994, 4–5). Sites in Vidarbha (northern Maharashtra) are also old. Two radiocarbon dates from burials at Naikund (BS 92, BS 93) are 545 ± 105 B.C. and 505 ± 100 B.C. (Deo and Jamkhedkar 1982), and the oldest date (BS 265) from the habitation mound II is 690 ± 110 B.C. (Mohanty and Joshi 1996, 165). Even earlier dates, beginning with one (BS 536) at 750 ± 100 B.C., have been obtained for Bhagimohari (Mohanty and Joshi 1996, 165).

An early date in Kongu (northwest Tamil Nadu) is at Koḍumaṇal, around 250 B.C. (Rajan 1990, 93). All late Pandukal dates are in South India, within the Tamil Kingdoms. They indicate a dispersal of the culture (or the assimilation of the people with the surrounding population) beginning in the second or third century A.D. Yet, dates as late as A.D. 1040 ± 90 and 1175 have also been recorded (Moorti 1994, 5).

The relationship between the Pandukal people and the Tamils (or Dravidians) is not yet understood. Some scholars equate them and others draw a sharp distinction between them, even making them enemies. I am in no position to clarify the picture. The paradigm used here is that the Tamils were ancient inhabitants of the region and Pandukal people entered at a later (though still early) date. Reciprocity between the two spurred the urban development of the Tamil Kingdoms (Korkai, the traditional home of the three brothers who founded the kingdoms, has very early Pandukal associations). Over time, the two groups assimilated. This is not far from the construct of Soundara Rajan (1996), who maintains that the "hero stones" of South India echo the ancient megaliths.

The picture is not quite as simple as painted above. Although much of this development was independent of North India, northern elements were incorporated into the south, including, scripts, religious ideas, and other traits. There also is a contemporaneous "megalithic" or Iron Age presence in Sri Lanka (Begley et al. 1981). The impetus must have come from India, but this was largely a local development (Seneviratne 1984).

Pandukal Beadmaking Sites

Three Pandukal habitation sites are known to have had lapidaries (Figure 12.3). They are Mahurjhari in Vidarbha, Koḍumaṇal in Kongu, and Arikamēḍu in Pondicherry.

In Mahurjhari beads were made chiefly for local consumption. Hunter (quoted in Deo [1973, 32]), perceiving a similarity in material and shape, suggested that Mahurjhari may have supplied beads to central Asia.

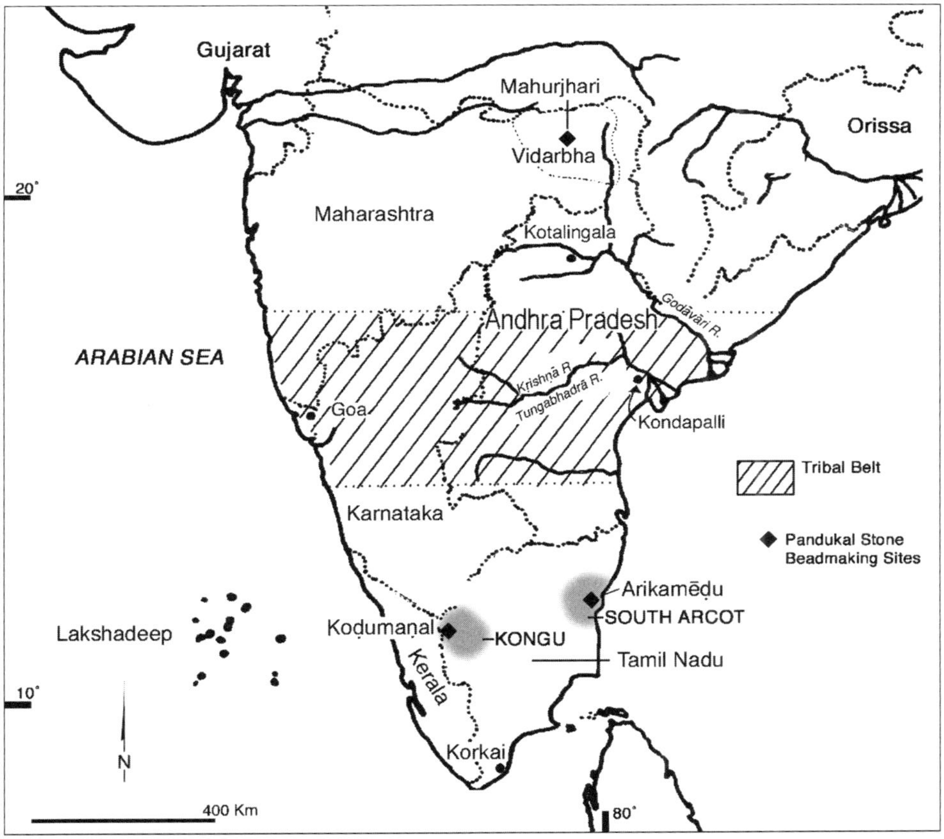

Figure 12.3. *A map of peninsular India showing early Pandukal settlements and Pandukal beadmaking sites.*

However Deo (1973, 32) observed that Mahurjhari is too old for such trade and its beads have closer affinities with South India.

There is a substantial amount of beadmaking refuse at Mahurjhari. Beads of chalcedony, crystalline quartz, and garnet were made by the pecking complex. Mahurjhari apparently did not export its beads outside its neighborhood. Its importance lies in its early age, judged to be from the seventh or sixth century B.C., and the continuity it shows of the Pandukal beadmaking tradition. To date it has only been surveyed and a 1-m^2 trench dug, but further work is anticipated (Mohanty 1999).[13]

In Kongu, 150 Pandukal burial sites have been identified; more than twenty of them are associated with habitation areas (Rajan 1990, 93). The most important is Koḍumaṇal, identified with Koḍumaṇam, mentioned in the *Patirruppattu (The Ten Tens),* an early work of the *Sangam* literature. The *Sangam* Koḍumaṇam was famed for its goldsmiths (Champakalakshmi 1990, 13; Rajan 1990, 93 n. 1). Workers at Koḍumaṇal also used the pecking complex exclusively on a variety of stones (Color Plate 35). Its products were no doubt widely exported, as discussed in the next section.

Arikamēḍu has not generally been considered a Pandukal site, but it may have been exclusively Pandukal at its founding, with other people coming later. A "megalithic" ceramic component was first recognized by Casal (1949), who later explored Pandukal burials in the region (Casal and Casal 1956). These and other Pandukal burials contain etched carnelians and red and blue Indo-Pacific beads.

The 1989–1992 excavation at Arikamēḍu demonstrated that typical Pandukal ceramics and graffiti are found almost exclusively at its lower levels. At these levels the range of shapes in these ceramics, exceeding one hundred different forms, is far greater than would be expected at a simple fishing village (Vimala Begley, 1994, personal communication). As discussed earlier in this chapter, pecking was one of two beadmaking complexes used at Arikamēḍu. Its industry was apparently devoted to export.

The *Sangam* literature describes some beadmaking or gem-cutting operations, in particular polishing or initial smoothing. A specialist *(sanaikal)* made a wheel, which he prepared with lac[14] and a material that was probably emery or crushed corundum. The stones were fixed onto a short stick (a dop) with lac to be ground against the wheel. The same method is still employed at Kangayam (Rajan 1997–1998, 60–61). Dops are not employed at Cambay, nor is there any record of them being used. It appears to be another aspect of the Pandukal pecking beadmaking complex.

This indicates an unbroken stone beadmaking tradition. Historically, the pecking complex is restricted to Pandukal sites.[15] It was exclusively used at the two purely Pandukal lapidary sites of Mahurjhari and Koḍumaṇal. At cosmopolitan Arikamēḍu, other beadmakers using the grinding complex worked alongside Pandukal beadmakers. The pecking complex survives at Kangayam. Pandukal society also had the means and motives for scouting out, retrieving, and supplying the raw materials used in the industry.

Sources of Raw Materials

The *Sangam* literature describes several ways of collecting gem materials, including simply picking them up from the ground. In some cases, they are naturally on the surface and at other times they emerge following a rain or after a herd of deer has passed over, unearthing them with their hooves. They are also discovered when digging for roots or in pits excavated by wild boars. They were gathered by the *kovalḷr* (cattle-rearing people) and the *kaṃavas* (hillock people), who sold them in the markets (Rajan 1997–1998, 59–60). Both names suggest Pandukal people. Although these methods may have provided some stones for lapidaries, they are unlikely to have contributed sufficient raw material for the major beadmaking sites of Koḍumaṇal and Arikamēḍu.

Arikamēḍu has no mineral resources. It is located on a deep alluvial deposit. A bore at nearby Bahur struck a lignite bed under 240 feet (about 74 m) of silt. Pascoe (1973, 1896–1897) interpreted this as evidence of the subsiding of the east coast.

Koḍumaṇal, on the other hand, is in a very rich mineralogical zone. There are major deposits of rock crystal quartz 5 km north of the village at Vengamedu ("quartz mound") and 5 km south at Arasampalayam. There is beryl at Padiyar 15 km south and sapphires at Śivamalai, 15 km to the southeast. Śivamalai is identified in the *Sangam* literature as a source of precious stones, exploited by the "cattle-raising people" (Rajan 1997–1998, 59). Although not yet quantified, rock crystal was the most common stone worked at Koḍumaṇal. This was also true at Arikamēḍu, where it accounts for 49.8 percent of all worked stone material in the Pondicherry Museum holdings. The links between Koḍumaṇal, Arikamēḍu, and crystalline quartz may help explain why these minerals were so often more pecked than chalcedonic materials.

The dominance of quartz at these two sites is indicative of the importance of this material in South India, unlike North India. A tally of beads from ten North Indian sites[16] of the Early Historic period (about. 500 B.C. to A.D. 500) shows that carnelian beads always outnumbered quartz. The quartz:carnelian ratio ranged from a low of 1:1.3 at Rājghāt to a high of 1:23 at Taxila, averaging 1:8.1. The reverse is true in the south. Koṇḍāpūr (Dikshit 1952a) has a 2:1 ratio; Mantai, Sri Lanka ("The Beads from Mantai," my chapter in John Carswell, ed., "Excavations at Mantai," unpublished) 1.5:1; and Arikamēḍu (Pondicherry Museum collection) 2.9:1.

An even more striking pattern is the distribution of amethyst beads. They were lacking altogether at six of the ten North Indian sites and never exceeded 4.7 percent (at Taxila) of the total of stone beads. At Koṇḍāpūr they were 46.7 percent of the total and at Arikamēḍu 14.3 percent. No amethyst deposits have yet been identified near Koḍumaṇal, but they may be there or were once there and are now exhausted.

Carnelian was the second most important stone bead material at both Arikamēḍu (17.1 percent of the Pondicherry Museum holdings) and Koḍumaṇal. There are no sources of carnelian near either site. Rajan (1990, 102) assumed that they had been imported to Koḍumaṇal from Gujarat, but this is unlikely for several reasons. Raw stones have never been recorded as an export from the region. The monopolistic tendency of the early Indian state, as outlined in Kauṭiliya's *Arthaśāstra,* argues against the exportation of anything but finished, value-added products. Also numerous at Arikamēḍu (5 5 percent of the Pondicherry Museum holdings) was banded agate, apparently always worked into black onyx. Agate/onyx was less common, but present, at Koḍumaṇal.

There are sources closer than Gujarat for carnelian and agates. Nodules washed from the Deccan trap are found along the lower courses of major southern rivers, especially the Godāvarī and the Kṛishṇā. Captain Newbold (1846, 37 [insertion mine]) listed: "Chalcedony, &c., Onyx . . . Plasma [crystalline prase?] . . . In the beds of the Kistnah, Godavery, and Bhima." Later writers noted the same thing (Wheeler et al. 1946, 123; Bauer 1968, 517). The stones are found in deposits that mirror those along the Narmadā River in Gujarat (Figure 12.3).

Lapidary activities at Kotalingala, Karimnagar District, Andhra Pradesh, are instructive (Figure 12.3). Excavated by the Andhra Pradesh State Department of Museums and Archaeology under V. V. Krishnasastry, it awaits full publication. The ancient city is rectangular, about a kilometer long by half a kilometer wide. On three sides, massive stone walls were erected, with watchtowers at each corner. The fourth side faced the Godāvarī River, into which stone jetties were built. It is tentatively dated to the fifth through second centuries B.C.; no first-century B.C. coins have been found there. The identifiable coins are of Sātavāhana kings, four of whom were previously unknown and appear to be earlier than the others. Kotalingala may have been the home of this powerful Deccan dynasty that expanded as Mauyran power waned (V. V. Krishnasastry, 1981, personal communication).

Brown onyx and amethyst beads were made at Kotalingala (Francis 1986f, 1990e). The onyx was made from banded agate. There was an initial processing center for agate near the eastern interior wall of the city, where quite large pieces are still to be found. Chunks of similar banded agate, rather than small pebbles from fluvial deposits, as at Arikamēḍu were also worked. A vein of banded agate may be located near Kotalingala or near the Godāvarī for easy transport to the site. This could also have been the source of Arikamēḍu's agate.

Although not worked at Koḍumaṇal, garnet was important at Arikamēḍu, constituting 10.1 percent of the Pondicherry Museum holdings. Most was of the reddish violet almandine (almandite) type,[17] but some reddish brown hessonite[18] was also present. The source of the almandine garnet was most likely near Kondapalli in Guntur District, Andhra Pradesh (Figure 12.4). The village has "long been famous" (Bauer 1968, 354) for this stone. Diamond mines along the lower reaches of the Kṛishṇā River within the Golconda (Ellore) diamond region also yield agate, carnelian, and other chalcedonies (Bauer 1968, 149). This area is also a source for wad[19] and copper, which with iron were the principal glass colorants employed at Arikamēḍu.

Almandine garnets, diamonds (for drilling stones), carnelian pebbles, wad, and native copper are found in the lower Kṛishṇā-Godāvarī doāb. This is the most likely source for these stones sent to Arikamēḍu and Koḍumaṇal for processing. It is also possible that the source of agates worked at Kotalingala was the same as that for these two centers.

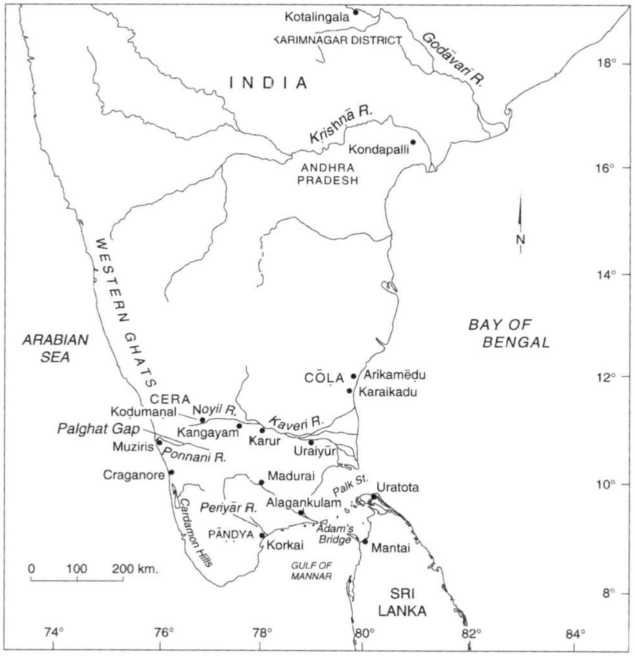

Figure 12.4. *Map of southern India showing the major locations for raw materials, processing, and overland trade routes making the region the treasure chest of the ancient world.*

However, stones do not leap out of the ground and propel themselves to a lapidary shop or a glass factory. Someone has to discover, mine, and transport them. Other scholars (Wheeler et al. 1946, 121–124; Rajan 1990) have considered the location of sources, but the question of the human actors in this operation has not been addressed. We may never know who was involved in this work, but a hypothesis is proposed here.

Young Pandukal men tending their free-ranging herds would have been in a position to scout out and detect economically important minerals, including precious and semi-precious stones, glass colorants, iron deposits, and gold. The importance of iron to the Pandukal people cannot be overstressed. Etched and plain carnelians had cultural meaning, certainly in burial contexts. Pandukal goldsmithing is a matter of historical record. Glass colorants gave life to Arikamēḍu's Indo-Pacific beads.

If Pandukal horsemen found deposits of interest, who mined them? The image of martial equestrians hammering out stones from a vein or digging through the mud of the Kṛishṇā-Godāvarī doāb does not ring true. Nor are there many Pandukal settlement sites in the region (Moorti 1994, maps). It is likely that they employed local residents to do the dirty work, periodically meeting with them to purchase their finds. They would then transport the stones to their settlements on horseback. This has long been the situation in western India at Ratanpur. Tribal Bhils do the hard work, and urbanized Hindus and Muslims carry the stones away and turn the material into beads elsewhere.

Treasure Chest of the Ancient World

With enormous resources in raw materials and lapidary skills, South India was well positioned as a source of semiprecious and precious gems and beads. Some of these treasures traveled eastward, particularly those made at Arikamēḍu. As early as the first century A.D., Indo-Pacific and stone and glass collar beads were traded as far as Java and Bali, as discussed in chapter 5. Flat onyx "shield" pendants, perforated along one thin edge, were made in Arikamēḍu and have long been common in Thailand as well as in Oc Eo. Most are likely to have been locally made, but Arikamēḍu may have been their inspiration.[20] As mentioned in chapter 14, there was probably movement of Arikamēḍu lapidaries to several sites in Southeast Asia.

However, there are more data available about the export of South Indian gems and beads to the Mediterranean region, especially the Roman Empire. Pliny the Elder (A.D. 23–79) appreciated the role of India in the world gem trade: "The rivers that produce gems are the Chenab[21] and the Ganges, and of all the lands that produce them India is the most prolific" (Eichholz 1962, 327–329). Neither the Indus system nor the Ganges produces many gemstones. The Chenab-and-the-Ganges phrase simply encompasses India. There is no question of India's importance to Rome in the ancient gem trade (Francis 1990f).

The Romans knew that carnelian and sardonyx were products of western India. Ptolemy even had a sketchy picture of the relative locations of key sites and the setup of the industry, as discussed in the last chapter. However, most of the important stones imported from India were products of the south. Note what Pliny said about them:

1. Beryl. "Beryls are produced in India and are rarely found elsewhere" (Eichholz 1962, 225).
2. Rock crystal. "That of India is preferred to any other" (Eichholz 1962, 181).
3. Amethyst. "Here the first rank is held by the amethysts of India" (Eichholz 1962, 263).
4. Almandine garnets. "The best [garnets] are the 'amethyst-colored stones'. . . Many writers state that the Indian stone is brighter than the Carthaginian" (Eichholz 1962, 239–241).
5. Prase.[22] "There are also many other kinds of green stones. A member of the commoner class is the prase. . . . India produces . . . these stones . . ." (Eichholz 1962, 255–7).
6. Onyx. "Formerly, as is clear from the very name, sardonyx meant a stone with a layer of carnelian resting on a layer of white. . . . Those stones that have now usurped the name although they lack all trace of the carnelian of the Indian stones come from Arabia . . ." (Eichholz 1962, 233). This is actually Pliny recording the change in fashion from the West Indian sardonyx to the South Indian (not Arabian) black onyx.[23]
7. Pearls. "Next [second only to diamond] in value in our estimation come the pearls of India and Arabia" (Eichholz 1962, 213 [insertion mine]). Only this gem had a rival source to India, the Persian Gulf.

Pliny mentioned Indian diamonds (Eichholz 1962, 207), but also several other sources. In fact, India was the chief supplier to the world for millennia. As Bauer (1968, 140 [insertion mine]) put it, "Diamonds have been known in this country [India] longer than in any other, and the most beautiful, famous and many of the largest stones were found here."

The Port of Muziris

The major South Indian port for the export of gems in the first few centuries A.D. was Muziris on the western or Malabar Coast.[24] The *Periplus* described it: "Muziris, in the same kingdom [Kêprobotes; the Cheras], owes its prosperity to the shipping from Ariakê [roughly Gujarat] that comes there as well as Greek shipping. It lies on a river. . . ." (Casson 1989, 83–85 [insertions mine]). Among its exports were "all kinds of transparent gems, diamond, sapphires . . ." (Casson 1989, 85). "All kinds of transparent gems" has been assumed to include beryl (Casson 1989, 222) or garnets (Warmington 1928, 252). The phrase no doubt included these as well as rock crystal, amethyst, and citrine. Diamonds and sapphires were also South Indian products.

Ptolemy placed *Muziris emporium* north of the mouth of the Pseudostomus River (Stevenson 1991, 149) (Plate 37). *Pseudostomus* means "false mouth or inlet." All rivers flowing into the Indian Ocean on the Malabar Coast originate in the Western Ghats. Western sailors must have been frustrated knowing that great riches were being shipped down (or along) a river to Muziris, but unable to find one to navigate inland. All they knew of the interior was "Punnata[25] in which is beryl . . . [and] *Carura regia Ceronrothi* [Karur, capital of the Cheras]"

(Stevenson 1991, 154 [insertions mine]) (Plate 38). The placing of the beryl source far inland, when it was really an easy trip through the Palghat Gap, was another form of Indian disinformation.[26]

Sangam poems mention Muziris several times. The *Puṟanāṉūṟu (The Four Hundred Stanzas of War)* described it as a bustling, rather wild, port city where interior goods were exchanged for imported gold:

> With its streets, its houses, its covered [fishing] boats, where they sell fish, where they pile up rice—with the shifting and mingling [crowd] of a boisterous river-bank where the sacks of pepper are heaped up —with its gold deliveries, carried by the ocean-going ships and brought to the river bank by local boats, the city of the gold-collared Chera king, [the city] that bestows [wealth] to its visitors indiscriminately, and the merchants of the mountains, and the merchants of the sea, the city where liquor abounds, yes, this Muziris, where the rumbling ocean roars, is given to me like a marvel, a treasure. (Méile 1940, 93 [insertions mine])[27]

Another Tamil poem[28] placed Muziris on the Periyār River (Méile 1940, 90). In Casson's translation it reads:

> the city where the beautiful vessels, the masterpieces of the Yavanas [Westerners], stir white foam on the Periyār, river of Kerala, arriving with gold and departing with pepper—when that Muçiri, brimming with prosperity, was besieged by the din of war. (Casson 1989, 296 [insertion Casson's])

Muziris has never been located. It has been strongly (Casson 1989, 296–299) or less certainly (Begley 1991b, 2 [map], 7) identified with modern Cranganore. *Periyār* literally means "the big river" and it identified several rivers, even in the same kingdom. The same poem placed the Chera capital on another Periyār, "'Karūvār [Karur] is a vast city . . .' on the porūneī-Periyār" (Méile 1940, 96 [insertion mine]). The Periyār on which Muziris was located was the "Periyār with cullis." *Cullis* is dead twigs, cinnamon, or various trees (Méile 1940, 90–91).

Cranganore is on the modern Periyār River, but no Roman antiquities have ever been found there. The Malabar Coast is infamous for its shifting rivers and sandbanks. Perhaps the "great river" of the past is not the "great river" of the present.

There may be another reason why Muziris is difficult to locate today: it may not have functioned as a port for very long. The *Sangam* poems have not been securely dated, but a recent assessment of them dated the *Puṟanāṉūṟu* to around A.D. 60, though later dates have also been proposed (Ramachandran 1996, 245). Zvelebil (1973, 29) also included it as one of the earlier works. Zvelebil (1973, 35) noted the lack of references to the Yavanas (Westerners) in the *Sangam* literature after the first century A.D.

The *Periplus* and Ptolemy are the only Western sources to refer to Muziris unambiguously. Muziris is featured on the Peutinger Table;[29] indeed, it the most important city east of Antioch (Stuart 1991). The map is perhaps a fifth-century copy of a third-century chart. Musaeus, a lawyer from Thebes, is recorded as writing, "Muziris the Mart of all India on this side of the Ganges . . ." (Ambrose 1905, 240). This Latin version of the narrative was associated with the fourth-century St. Ambrose, but even Samuel Purchas in 1625 questioned the ascription. It is now understood to be a literary fraud; the original version did not mention Muziris (Weerakkody 1997, 119–120).

Although Muziris was undoubtedly an important port in the first century A.D., it disappeared from the literary record as quickly as it appeared. The admittedly scant descriptions of it suggest that it was more of a frontier town than a city with substantial architecture (the "Augustian Temple" on the Peutinger Table is ambiguous as to its location or even identification). The Roman port that was its chief partner was Berenike. Trade between Rome and the East was moribund by the end of the second century. When Berenike started trading again in the fourth century, the bead evidence shows that it was going to Mantai (Francis 2001).

Muziris might have been little more than a fishing village that seized the opportunity to become wealthy through trade with the West. When that trade ceased, the boom was over and when the Westerners returned more than a century later, there was nothing left. The river and the sea may have washed away whatever remained.

Korkai and the Pearl Trade

Before summarizing the South Indian gem trade with the Classical West, one other gem that is not a stone must be brought into the picture: the pearl (see also chap. 15). In Early Historic times pearls were dived for in the Gulf of Mannar. Korkai, the original Pāṇḍya capital, was the center of the fishery. The *Sangam* poem *Maturaikkāñci* (*The Good Council [given to the King of] Maturai or Madurai,* early third century) sang its praises, "Oh lord of good Korkai, where the famous marvels, highly esteemed in the vast world, the precious pearls, the largest and most mature from the brilliant sea shells, lord of the city with suburbs of [pearl] fishing-grounds"[30] (Méile 1940, 97).

The *Periplus* says: "Beyond Komar [Cape Comorin] the region extends as far as Kolchoi [Korkai], where diving for pearls goes on; it is carried out by convicts. The region is under King Pandiôn [Pāṇḍya]. After Kolchoi . . . comes the Strand [Adam's Bridge], bordering a bay, with, inland, a region named Argaru [Uraiyūr, the Cōḷa capital]. In one place . . . along it . . . pearls are gathered" (Casson 1989, 87–89 [insertions mine]). Ptolemy listed "Colchi emporium," but did not mention pearls, only commenting, "the bay of Colchicus in which are pigeons" (Stevenson 1991, 150). His "Argari city" corresponds to the Periplus' "Argaru" (Casson 1989, 226–227) (Plate 39).

A limited excavation at Korkai by Nagaswamy (1970) identified three periods. Of these, "Period I is characterized by the occurrence of urns of megalithic variety and its associated black and red ware, black ware and red ware, shell bangle pieces, carnelian beads and bone ornaments" (Nagaswamy 1970, 52). In trench KRK I, he found an urn burial and a "finely facetted crystal bead" (Nagaswamy 1970, 52).[31] The following period was dominated by typical Tamil urban material of the Pāṇḍya type, including "sawed conches," probably for bangle making.[32]

The South Indian Bead and Gem Trade

We are now in a position to form a hypothetical reconstruction of the South Indian bead and gem industry in the first few centuries A.D. Young Pandukal riders would have established a network to bring gems to Arikamēḍu and Koḍumaṇal lapidaries and glass colorants to Arikamēḍu. Koḍumaṇal furnished rock crystal (and probably amethyst), beryl, and sapphires. Beryl was probably always bored at Koḍumaṇal,[33] but rock crystal and amethyst were also sent to Arikamēḍu. Pearls were found and processed at Korkai.

A second-century A.D. Brāhmī inscription at Archchalur (Erode District) calls gem and bead dealers *manivanakkan* (Rajan 1997–1998, 60). Who were they and how did they move their treasure to Muziris for export? There are three possibilities:

1. The distribution and sale of these gems was in the hands of Tamils, who shipped the goods overland between southern urban cities. Inscriptions and passages in the *Sangam* literature are full of references to Tamil merchants. Of course, not everyone with a Tamil name was necessarily an ethnic Tamil.

   The rivers of South India are not generally suitable for the transport of merchandise, nor is there any indication that canals were used for any purpose other than irrigation. At least in the period of the Imperial Cōḷas, there was a well-developed road system, consisting of *vadis*, which were little more than locally maintained footpaths, and *peru-vaḷi,* large roads suitable for wheeled vehicles, as much as 24 feet (7.3 m) wide, presumably maintained by the state. One such road *(Kongapperuvaḷi)* ran to the Kongu region (Nilakanta Sastri 1975, 594–595).

   In this scenario, the gems of Arikamēḍu and the pearls of Korkai would be funneled to Koḍumaṇal, where drilled beryl, rock crystal, and amethyst beads and perhaps gold jewelry[34] were added. The cargo would then cross through the Palghat Gap, to float down or be taken along the Ponnani River to Muziris, the famed port (Figure 12.4).

2. Alternately, Tamils may have employed a sea route, shipping Arikamēḍu gems via Alagankulam or Uratota and Mantai (where pearls could be added) and north to Muziris. Koḍumaṇal was near enough to Muziris to easily add its gems. The route would avoid the three Tamil capitals, where extra taxes or payments would have been demanded. The *Periplus* described trade between the two coasts and beyond:

   "Of the ports of trade[35] and harbors in these parts at which vessels sailing from both Limyrikê and the north call, the more important, lying in a row, are the ports of trade of Kamara, Podukê, and Sôpatma. They are the home ports for local boats that sail along the coast as far as Limyrikê and others, called *sangara*,[36] that are very big dugout canoes held together by a yoke, as well as for the very big *kolandiophônta*[37] that sail across to Chrysê[38] and the Gangês region. There is a market in these places for all the [sc. Western] trade goods imported by Limyrikê, and generally speaking, there come to them all year round both the cash originating from Egypt and most kinds of all the goods originating from Limyrikê and supplied along this coast." (Casson 1989, 89 [insertion Casson's])

3. Finally, there is the possibility that the land route was used by the Pandukal people, rather than Tamil merchants. Moorti (1994, 17) pointed out the importance of a belt of heavy concentrations of Pandukal settlement running from the Palghat Gap to the delta of the Kāverī. He identified over thirty sites, many of them large. To him it "seems to indicate that it [the belt] had become a commercially active route" that he specifically linked to Indo-Roman trade.[39] He further noted, "The location of several Megalithic sites on known ancient trade routes might not be without any significance. They probably served as exchange centres/places, which seems to have been a main factor in the development and growth of these sites." Transportation would also be speedy, given the Pandukal horses.

Each scenario requires the cooperation and coordination of Pandukal and Tamil people and all three Tamil states. The Tamil states often quarreled and sometimes went to war, but they acknowledged each other as relatives. Their founding myth speaks of three brothers whose fortune was based on the pearl trade (Maloney 1969, 13). Both Koḍumaṇal and Arikamēḍu suggest an acculturation of Pandukal artisans into Tamil society.

Except for the *Periplus* describing sea trade between the coasts, there is no other Western reference to the mechanics of this trade. Ptolemy made no connection between the two coasts; all his rivers flowed away from each other (Plate 59). The Peutinger Table is even less detailed.

The Later Industry

Stone beads continued to be made at Arikamēḍu for a long time, apparently down to the seventeenth century, as revealed by the 1989–1992 excavations.[40] In late Roman times (fourth century A.D.) Dionysius Periegetes wrote in his poem *Description of the Whole World:*

> [The Indians] are variously occupied;
> some by mining seek for the matrix of
> gold, digging the soil with well-carved
> pick-axes, others ply the loom to weave
> tex[tiles] of linen, others saw the tusks of
> elephants and varnish them to the bright-
> ness of silver, and others along the course
> of mountain torrents search for precious
> stones, the green beryl, or the sparkling

> diamond, or the pale green translucent jasper, or the yellow stone, or the pure topaz, or the sweet amethyst, which with a milder glow imitates the lure of purple.[41] (Prasad 1977, 199; van de Woestijne 1953, 95 [insertions mine])[42]

This fits South India well. Gold was usually exported from India as finished jewelry. Both gold and ivory were obtainable in many parts of India, but beryl, diamonds, the "pale green translucent jasper" (prase), the "yellow stone" (citrine), and amethyst are all decidedly South Indian products. Topaz, by which the Romans usually meant peridot (Eichholz 1962, 250–253), is not Indian, but Dionysius called this the "pure topaz." It apparently meant something else, not now identifiable.

In the mid-ninth century, Ibn Khurdadhbeh noted along the western Indian coast that "Crystal is obtained from Mulay and Sandan" (Nainar 1942, 198). Nainar identified Mulay with Quilon in Kerala. However, it is a wider geographic term. Mulay, Male, Malé and other variations are transliterations for *malai* or "mountain," the local name for the western coast, becoming Malabar (Yule and Burnell 1989, 539–542). Cosmas Indicopleustes (sixth century) said that "Male" had five ports for pepper exportation (McCrindle 1897, 367).

The twelfth-century *Book of the Balance of Wisdom* by 'Al-Khâzim' suggested that South Indian onyx was the most prized semiprecious gem in the Islamic world. He wrote:

> This whole class of stones [carnelian, onyx, lapis lazuli, and rock crystal, along with glass] is not highly prized; excepting the onyx, for a certain value is attached to specimens with ox-hoof circles, and likewise to those in which there happens to be presented the form of an animal, or some strange shape. Men have been long tired of the cornelian, so that it has ceased to be used as a stone for seal-rings, even for the hands of common people, to say nothing of the great. The lapis lazuli is employed on account of its tinting and variegation of its several species. (Khanikoff 1862, 64 [insertion mine])

Wang Dayuan (1349) wrote that precious stones *(yahu)* were available at Fandaraina (Rockhill 1915, 464). *Yahu* may be a transliteration of the Arabic/Farsi *yaqut*. In colloquial Arabic, it refers to precious stones, especially corundum. In modern Farsi it is specifically corundum. Appadorai (1936, 599) and Hardie (1985, 18) identified Fandaraina as Pandarani, south of Mangalore, to which the stones would have came across the Western Ghats. Pandarani (Pantalāyani) was once a flourishing port frequented by Chinese traders. Al-Idrisi and Ibn Battuta mentioned it, the latter commenting on its good harbor. Its trade with China was apparently the key to its success. After that stopped, it declined and by the early sixteenth century Varthema said that it was a miserable place without a harbor (Appadorai 1936, 598–599).

In the fifteenth century, the Russian Athanasius Nikitin wrote, "From Kulburga [Golbarga] I went to Kooroola (Kurula), where the akhik [agate] is produced and worked, and from whence it is exported to all parts of the world. Three hundred dealers in diamonds reside in this place. . . . I stopped there five months and then proceeded to Calica [Calicut]" (Major 1857, 3: 30 [insertions mine]). In a note Major (1857, 3: 30 n. 1) quoted a certain Stroef that says Kooroola is Kulura, but Kulura was not identified. There is a "Curula city" in Ptolemy's *Geographia* (Plate 40). When plotted on a modern map it is on the east coast south of Arikamēḍu (Figure 12.5). Could the name have survived for so long without being recorded elsewhere?

In tracing Nikitin's steps from Golbarga to Calicut, my assumption is that he stayed on the eastern side of the Western Ghats and crossed over to the coast through the Palghat Gap. Kurula might then have meant Kolar (but without any mention of gold it seems unlikely), Karur, or Kangayam, the last remaining beadmaking center in South India. The latter two seem more probable on this route. The very limited excavations at Karur have uncovered nothing indicating bead working, neither does surface evidence suggest it (K. Rajan, 1995, personal communication). We do not know how long Kangayam has been functioning. Kooroola remains an intriguing mystery.

In 1498, when the Portuguese first sailed to India, the Zamorin of Calicut gave a letter to Vasco da Gama to carry back to the king of Portugal. It read in part: "Vasco da Gama, a nobleman of your household, has visited my Kingdom, and has given me great pleasure. In my Kingdom there is an abundance of cinnamon, cloves, ginger, pepper, and precious stones in great quantities. What I seek from thy country is gold, silver, coral and scarlet" (Birdwood 1891, 163). Of the products the Zamorin claimed to have in abundance, only cloves were not Indian (Wit 1979, 216–217).

Münster[43] (1559, 1065), writing his compilation in 1544, highlighted the gem wealth of India in his introductory section. He did not specify the port or ports where they were obtained, but the list reflects South Indian production: "Abundant beryl, crystophrase, diamonds, carbuncles [garnets], many pearls and gems [my translation from Medieval Latin; insertion mine]." The last phrase *(margaritis multis & gemmis)* could also be read as "many beads and gems."

The Dutchman John Huyghen van Linschoten

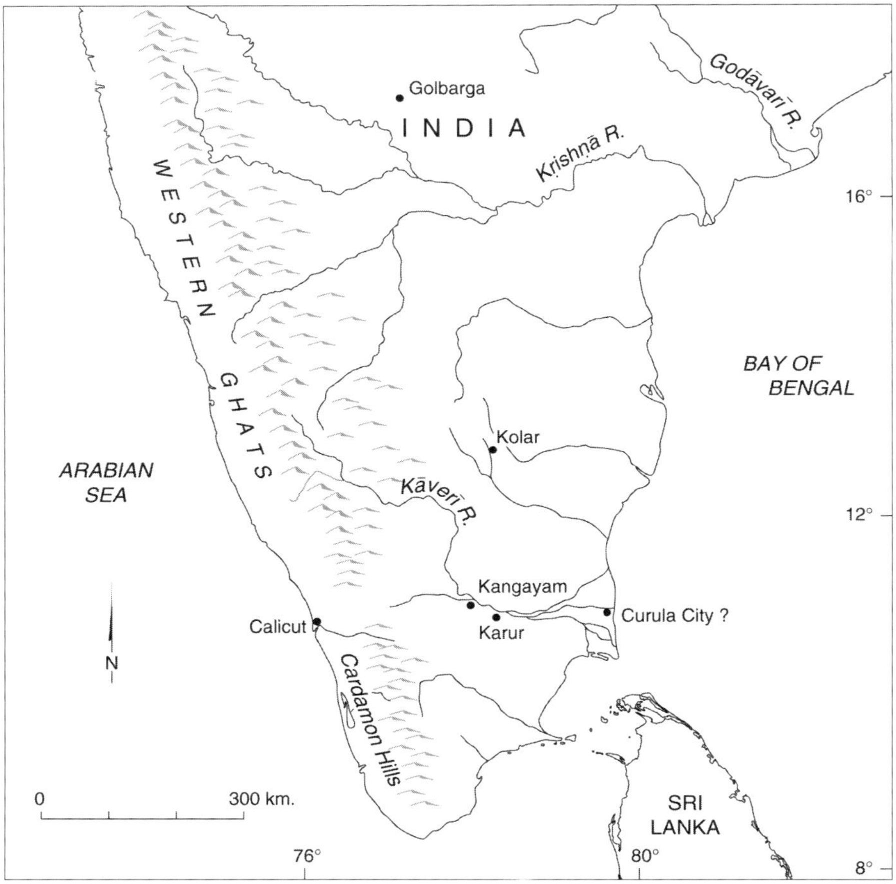

Figure 12.5. *Map of southern India showing places associated with Athanasius Nikitin's travel to Kooroola.*

(1598) made the outrageous statement that there was no rock crystal to be found in India ("nor in any of the oriental countries") and that what passes for it is actually "berylo." This was supposed to be found in Cambay, Pegu (Myanmar), and Sri Lanka (Tiele 1885, 138). However, he went on to say:

> Chrisolites and Amatiates are many in the Island of Seylon, Cambaia, and Ballagatte, [and] the stone called Alakecca, [which] is also called Bloodstone, because it quickly stauncheth blood, and other stones called Milke stones, which are good for women that give milke or sucke. These and such like stones are in great numbers found in Cambaia, and Ballagatte, and are brought to Goa, to bee solde, whereof they make Beades, Seales, Ringes, and a thousand such like curiosities. . . . (Tiele 1885, 141 [insertions Tiele's])

Chrysolite is now the name of a form of peridot, but historically the word was used for other minerals as well, including chrysoberyl, topaz, and corundum. Ceylonese chrysolite is a tourmaline (Bauer 1968, 619). "Alakecca" or bloodstone is carnelian, and milk stone is white chalcedony. "Seylon" and "Cambaia" are easily identified, but where is "Ballagatte"? *Bālāghāt* is a common place name in peninsular India referring to the land "above the passes" (that is, the upper Deccan plateau after the passes in the Western Ghats [Yule and Burnell 1989, 51]). It is difficult to say how far these notes can be taken, but they are suggestive. Certainly, the beryl mines operated a long time. The Englishman J. M. Heath held the last lease to them in 1818 (Jhingran 1962, 168).

By 1611 the Portuguese were well established at Goa. François Pyrard wrote, "The ships leave Goa towards October, and touch at Cochin for precious stones and spices . . . leaving there the merchandise of Europe or of the northern parts of India. Thence they sail for Malaca *[sic]* . . ." (Gray and Bell 1888, 175).

Stone beadmaking in South India was recorded in the late nineteenth century. Bauer (1968, 477), writing in 1903, said that Vellur (Tanjore District, Tamil Nadu) was known for rock crystal cutting. W. Francis (1985, 67) in the *Imperial Gazetteer* cited quartz working at Settipalaiyam (Coimbatore District) and said that amethyst was exploited around Vellur. Tanjore (Thanjavur) (Jhingran 1962, 167) and Tiruchchirappalli in Tamil Nadu are jewelry-making centers. Investigations at all these places by John Anthony and me in 1993 and 1995 turned up only negative evidence for stone beadmaking. K. Rajan (1997–1998) was the first to investigate and publish on the beadmaking village of Kangayam.

The South Indian stone bead industry has functioned for over two thousand years, but today it is a shadow of its former glory.

Part Six: Some Minor Bead Industries

13

Glass Beadmaking in Southeast Asia and Sri Lanka

Southeast Asia and Sri Lanka were frequently at the center of the Asian maritime trade. Many raw materials, including spices and jungle products, originated from the region. Commerce between India and the West with China passed through Southeast Asia and/or Sri Lanka.

In terms of beads, Southeast Asia was a major importer. Glass and stone beads from India and China and glass beads from the Middle East (and later Europe) dominate most assemblages. Nonetheless, there is evidence for independent glass beadmaking in parts of the region. Sri Lanka, in contrast, was largely self-sufficient in terms of beads. The two areas took different roads to glass beadmaking and are discussed separately.

Earlier chapters laid out cases for glass beadmaking being introduced to Southeast Asia and Sri Lanka from the outside. These include the Indo-Pacific industry in chapter 4; emigrant Chinese making beads in Java in chapter 6; and beads made via the transfer of technology or technicians from the Middle East in chapter 10. In this chapter glass beadmaking with local roots is discussed. Glass was not first created in Southeast Asia or Sri Lanka, and no one has suggested an independent invention for it in either place. Some degree of outside help or inspiration may be postulated. However, several indigenous glass bead industries can be identified.

The oldest of these are on the mainland. In south-central Vietnam from around 700 B.C. to the second century A.D. the Sa Huynh culture flourished. The Sa Huynh produced distinctive glass beads and other related ornaments. Some (perhaps all) were made at Giong Ca Vo in Can Gio District, Ho Chi Minh City.

Two sites in Thailand have yielded unusual glass beads that cannot be linked to known beadmaking industries: Ban Don Ta Phet in Kanchaburi Province in west-central Thailand and Ban Chiang in Udon Thani Province in the northeast. The former is a secondary burial site, apparently used for a short period in the fourth century B.C. (Glover 1990b, 37). The latter was occupied for a long time, though not as long as once thought. The glass beads date from the last few centuries B.C. to about A.D. 200 (see later in this chapter).

The other independent glass beadmaking center in Southeast Asia is much later, dated to the middle to late centuries of the first millennium A.D., concentrated in eastern Java. Several of its beads resemble Middle Eastern types and some transfer of inspiration or raw material probably took place. The beads differ enough technically from Middle Eastern products that it is unlikely they were made by Middle Eastern émigrés or processes taught by them.

Two glass bead types were all but certainly made in Sri Lanka in the first few centuries A.D. The evidence for them is more circumstantial than for the Southeast Asian industries, but is rather convincing.

Finally, there are several bead types with no or few parallels outside Southeast Asia and no obvious technological antecedents from elsewhere. Their origin is a mystery because they cannot be ascribed to the Middle East, India, China, or the industries discussed in this chapter.

There are not yet enough data to establish the precise location of their manufacturing.

The fact that a certain type of bead is only found in a particular area does not, of course, mean that it was manufactured there. It might simply have found a receptive clientele. Notwithstanding this caveat, the distribution pattern and confirmation of independent glass beadmaking (as opposed to Indian, Chinese, or Middle Eastern production within Southeast Asia) bolster the idea of local origins. Final judgments must await more data.

Glassmaking in the Sa Huynh Culture

The Sa Huynh people were great mariners. There is evidence that they sailed around much of Southeast Asia, especially in the Philippines. Solheim (1959) identified a Sa Huynh–Kalany pottery complex, with very similar ceramics made in both Vietnam and the archipelago. Some distinctive artifacts also mark their influence.

Among Sa Huynh artifacts, ornaments are prominent. Not all of these ornaments are beads and not all are made of glass. They are considered together because they are stylistically or otherwise related. One class of these ornaments consists of bangles, closed rings for the wrist. Some were decorated with protrusions or budlike knobs on the outside and others were slit to break up the round profile. Smaller versions of the slit bangles were worn as earrings (Figure 13.1).[1]

Another type of earring comes from the same source. It has a drop-shaped section and is called *ling-ling-o* in the Philippine literature.[2] It also may be plain or decorated with budlike bosses and is sometimes rotated, fitting on the ear via a small loop.

A third type of ornament has a thick horizontal bar hanging from a loop with identical animal heads on either end and a projection underneath the bar (Figure 13.3). This is usually known as a "bicephalous" pendant, though they were mostly or exclusively worn as earrings. The latest assessment of these earrings (Reinecke 1996, 6–7) identified the animal with the recently discovered *Pseudoryx nghetinensis,* an ungulate unknown to science until 1992.[3]

Figure 13.1. *Typical glass earrings of the Sa Huynh culture. Sketch by Bo Breda.*

Figure 13.2. *A golden* mamuli *earring from Sumba, Indonesia. Sketch by Bo Breda.*

One or more of these ornaments have been found archaeologically in many places outside Vietnam, including Hong Kong (Finn 1958, 147–151), Taiwan (Lien 1991, 345–348), the Philippines (Fox 1970, 123–139; Loofs-Wissowa 1980–1981), Thailand (Suchitta 1984, 152–153; Glover 1990a, 166; 1990b, 24), and Sarawak (Bellwood 1985, 276). What are presumably the earlier ones are of stone, commonly nephrite jade. In the Philippines, shell and clay imitations were made (Fox 1970, 140; Thiel 1986–1987, 250–258).[4]

The *lingling-o* earrings in metal have the longest history. They have been found at post–Sa Huynh sites, such as Oc Eo (Malleret 1962a, 73–74, 81–82) and Chansen, Thailand, from the second half of the first millennium A.D. (Bronson and Dales 1972, 40, fig. 12). Wire was sometimes formed into the shape. Moreover, the style persists. The Ifugao of northern Luzon make them and wear them as pendants, trading them to their neighbors, the Bontoc, Kalinga, and Gad-dang, who wear them as earrings (Francis 1992a, 6–7). The style is also known ethnographically from Java (Malleret 1962b, pl. XX), Sumatra (Gerlach 1971, pl. 21.1, 18), among the "Sea Dyak" (Iban) of Borneo (Roth 1968, 68), and Sumba, Indonesia (Keane 1988). In Sumba, highly elaborate gold ones are valued, but are no longer produced (Keane 1988, 12 n. 8) (Figure 13.2).

Figure 13.3. *Bicephalic earring of the Sa Huynh culture. Sketch by Bo Breda.*

Loofs-Wissowa (1980–1981, 61–62) suggested that the *lingling-o* with projections might be as early as the eighth or ninth century B.C. Vu (1991, 6) indicated that stone bangles, including ones with four bosses, are found at least in early Sa Huynh contexts. He noted that glass beads (the type was not specified) appear in the middle period and the bicephalic earrings only in the late Sa Huynh.

Glass versions of all three of these ornaments—the plain bangles, the *lingling-o* earrings, and the bicephalic earrings—were produced in the late Sa Huynh period. The glass bangles have a wide distribution in Southeast Asia.[5] On the other hand, the only glass *lingling-o* known outside Vietnam is from Rio-Fabian Cave in Palawan (Fox 1970, 139), and no glass bicephalic pendants have been found outside Vietnam.

At Giong Ca Vo, Vietnam, there are Indo-Pacific beads in red, orange, dark blue, opaque yellow, and opaque green, but there is no evidence for local manufacture of them. The site has been dated to between the fourth and second centuries B.C. (Glover 1994, 9–10). The blue are high in potash and colored with cobalt and manganese (Dussubieux and Gratuze 2000), suggesting that they came from Arikamēḍu.

There is, however, evidence of local glassmaking in the form of fritty waste and three pits in the ground that contained sand suitable for glass (Nguyen Thi Kim Dung, 1995, personal communication; Francis 1995b, 4–6). Most of the locally made glass is black or dark green, doubtless colored with iron. Triangular-sectioned bangles of the same color (and some colored violet with manganese) were found at the site. They were made by expanding "beads" into rings.[6]

There were also bottle green rods of glass and drawn tubular beads. The drawn green beads were not further heated to round them off or perhaps just barely heated. They are unlike Indo-Pacific beads in that sense, as well as in shape, size, and color. They are long, with a diameter of about 4 mm and length of 8 to 12 mm. They appear to have been cut from rather short tubes, judging from the length of the entrapped air bubbles.

Finally, there were three complete and one partial bicephalic earrings. These were made by joining the five parts of the pendant (the loop, the horizontal bar, the bud projection and the two heads) together after they had been fashioned independently.

Analyses of glass from Giong Ca Vo (Salisbury and Glover 1997) showed a mixed pattern of components. Two translucent green beads and two bangles of similar color were of soda glass with high levels of aluminum, and in two cases, high amounts of antimony. On the other hand, an opaque light blue, opaque dark blue, and translucent green bangles, as well as a broken ear or horn of the bicephalous pendant, were potassium glass with normal levels of the other elements. One bead had very low levels of either alkali, but was heavily corroded and they had probably leached out. Whether both types of glass were local or one was imported has not yet been determined.

Ban Don Ta Phet, Thailand

This cemetery site was discovered by schoolchildren in 1975 and the Thai Fine Arts Department under Chin You-di excavated it soon thereafter (Glover et al. 1984, 319). Later seasons were devoted to it as a joint project of the Fine Arts Department and the Institute of Archaeology, London. Radiocarbon dates of ca. 390 to 360 B.C. were obtained from temper in pottery, an unusual technique.

The site is rich in many antiquities, including beads of all sorts (Glover 1990a, 167–169; 1990b). These include a large number of Indo-Pacific beads. If the high date for this site is correct, the opening date of Indo-Pacific bead production must be pushed back. This may mean that Arikamēḍu is older than currently known, which is possible,[7] or that an even earlier site made Indo-Pacific beads before Arikamēḍu.

The most interesting glass beads at Ban Don Ta Phet were worked by lapidary methods. These included some hexagonal cylinders of translucent green glass, rather resembling emeralds (Glover 1990b, 13–14), and at least one diamond tabular (Basa et al. 1991, 371).[8] From another site another glass bead was treated as though it were stone (ground and cut into shape and drilled from both sides). It is a collar bead, an undated surface find from Ban Don Luang, Lopburi Province, in central Thailand. It has been published with an analysis, though the manufacturing method was not mentioned (Salisbury and Glover 1997).

The emeraldlike glass beads of Ban Don Ta Phet were made of soda glass (Glover 1990b, 14). However, at least four other faceted beads from the site (Basa et al. 1991, 376, nos. 1293, 1432, 1435; Salisbury and Glover 1997, 11), as well as the collar bead from Ban Don Luang (Salisbury and Glover 1997), are of potash glass.

Glass beads made by lapidary techniques are found in small numbers at many sites, including Berenike, Egypt; Arikamēḍu, India; Mantai, Sri Lanka; Aqaba, Jordan; Nishapur, Iran; and Palawan in the Philippines (Fox 1970, 137).[9] They are never numerous or at least rarely reported. They are perhaps more prevalent than the foregoing list indicates, because all of those known to me are from sites I have examined. It is easy to understand why what is perhaps the first piece of glass in the Philippines was locally turned into a bead. The others, however, seem to be random occurrences, with no pattern of their production discernible.

However, in Thailand such a pattern may be emerging. More archaeological work and more attention paid to the manufacturing processes of beads are needed to determine whether a regular industry of working glass beads by lapidary methods was a feature of prehistoric sites in Thailand.

There is no evidence for local glassmaking at Ban Don Ta Phet, and none would be expected from a cemetery. However, the use of potassium-rich glass and of lapidary techniques to make beads suggests that there may have been a small, localized industry for cutting and drilling glass beads. The comma-shaped earring found there may also have been locally made, though not by lapidary means, as has been suggested (Basa et al. 1991, 371–372; Glover and Henderson 1995, 147).

Ban Chiang, Thailand

Ban Chiang, Thailand, is a village of about 4,000, settled historically in 1787 by people from Chiang Khang. Chin You-di of the National Museum conducted a limited excavation there in 1967.[10] Two years later, MASCA (Museum Applied Science Center for Archaeology at the

University of Pennsylvania) announced that a thermoluminescent test (PT-104) done on some decorated buff potsherds yielded a date of 4363 ± 520 B.C. (Y. Chin 1976, 5–6; Charoenwongsa 1982; Na-Nakhonphanom 1982, 93).

This extremely early date aroused great interest, but proved untenable; the thermoluminescence process was then in its infancy. The earliest date for the appearance of bronze is now calculated at around 2000 B.C. (J. C. White 1997) and the painted buff pottery at 1000 to 500 B.C. (Na-Nakhonphanom 1982, 93) or even later. Nonetheless, the rush was on, and collectors and dealers began to loot the site avidly. The Thai Ministry of Education asked the University of Pennsylvania to help excavate and analyze the finds. The campaign was conducted from 1974 to 1979, but the analysis was delayed by the death of the director, Chester Gorman, in 1981.

Rather few glass beads have been excavated at Ban Chiang. Most "Ban Chiang beads" were looted from the site or elsewhere. The excavated beads were principally orange drawn disk beads (J. C. White 1982, 82), discussed in the section on Drawn Orange and Red Beads later in this chapter. The beads considered here include the biconical beads that White (1982, 88–89; fig. 161) placed under the rubric "Unprovenienced Artifacts Possibly of the Ban Chiang Tradition" and a long tubular type in the National Museum and private collections.[11] A third glass object, an earring of open circular form, is also discussed here.[12]

Before these beads are discussed, it should be kept in mind that none of the examples that have been analyzed and none of the ones I describe here have been excavated from the site of Ban Chiang. Nor were any of them even found on the surface or looted from the site, as far as anyone knows. Although I use the term "Ban Chiang," here, it refers to the region and the "Ban Chiang Culture" rather than any more precise place or date.

Ban Chiang beads have been reported principally in popular works (Labbé 1985, 67–69; R. K. Liu 1985; 1995a, 84–87). Excavated examples are from Late Period X (Late Bronze 2), dated 200 B.C. to A.D. 300 (J. C. White 1983, 55; 1990, 128) with a few from Middle Period VIII (Mid Bronze Period 2) of 800 to 400 B.C. (J. C. White 1983, 55; 1990, 128; Nikon 1979, 47), but none is earlier than 500 B.C. (Pisit Charoenwongsa, 1984, personal communication).

All of these glass objects have several characteristics in common. The five that have been analyzed (two bicones, two long tubes, and an earring) are potassium glass, with moderate to high levels of aluminum and low levels (less than 1 percent) of lime (Basa et al. 1991, 376; Salisbury and Glover 1997, 11). The glass is always very bubbly and contains much refractory material, perhaps clay, which renders it weak and subject to breakage. The objects have all been manipulated into shape in some way, rather than being simply wound or drawn.

The wound truncated bicones are dark blue, light blue, or green (Color Plate 36). These beads were wound on a thick (7.5 mm) mandrel and worked into shape. The patterns of the bubbles near their equators suggest that each hemisphere was shaped into a cone separately.[13] These beads have only been found at Ban Chiang and contemporary neighboring sites, suggesting they were either made locally or especially for this market.

The other distinctive Ban Chiang beads are long (7 cm or more) tubes with a smaller perforation (3.1 mm) and perhaps somewhat better glass (with less refractory material) than used for the bicones. They are among the longest glass beads known. Again, their distribution is restricted to Ban Chiang and related sites.[14]

Long, tubular beads are markers of prehistoric cultures in Thailand; they are hardly found elsewhere.[15] At Kok Charoen, long, tubular stone beads were associated with organic material radiocarbon dated to 880 to 1480 B.C., though the excavators thought they might be older (Loofs and Watson 1970, 76). At Ban Kao, a skeleton had a necklace of shell disk beads with two long, stone tubular beads in the center. The burial was dated 3720 ± 140 B.P. and 3310 ± 140 B.P. (Sørensen 1957, 9, pls. 25, 27.12, 126.a).

These long, tubular stone beads are common and distinctive enough that Nikon (1979, 47) referred to them as "magic beads," though why was not specified. Whether magical or not, they are distinct for this part of the world. Hence, the unusually long, tubular glass beads at Ban Chiang would have been made for that particular market.

Precisely how they were made is difficult to assess. The ends are beveled and at the short side of the bevels there is a fold that extends a millimeter or more into the perforation (Color Plate 37). My initial thought was that the bead was folded, and perhaps it is, though I am unable to detect any more evidence of a seam either on the exterior or down the perforation.[16] The bubbles in the glass are elongated along the perforation, but not as uniformly as they would have been if the tube had been drawn by any known method.

The making of the earring was initiated by pulling out some glass in a slightly tapered shape. The ends were then rounded and the glass was twisted around a mandrel of the same size (probably the same tool) as that used to wind the bicones. Both outer sides of the earring are slightly flattened, but whether this was done purposely or was an effect of the manipulation is not known.

Who made these glass beads and earring? Their lack of lead[17] rules out China, because virtually no leadless Chinese glass is known in this period. There are no parallels for their shapes in India or the Sa Huynh culture. The glass composition and manipulative nature of their shaping recalls the Sa Huynh bicephalous pendant, but it is difficult to determine how far this analogy can be taken. Another possibility is local production. Whether local or not, they must have been made by someone who was aware of the demand for long, tubular beads.

Early Glass Beadmaking on Mainland Southeast Asia

The material presented above indicates that at times between the fourth century B.C. and the second century A.D., glass beads and other ornaments were made in Vietnam and probably Thailand. They were not widely distributed, and few of them can be said to have entered the Asian maritime bead trade. Yet they are important for indicating the manufacture of glass beads in peninsular Southeast Asia at a rather early date. The impetus, and some or most of the raw material, may have come from outside.

Each of these small industries is similar in that they were satisfying local tastes. In the case of Sa Huynh, glass bangles and earrings were a reflection on the same objects made of nephrite jade. The glass objects at Ban Chiang, at least the long tubes, are a continuation of a style with an extended history. The faceted glass beads of Ban Don Ta Phet (and perhaps the collar bead from Ban Don Luang) echo stone beads, which were also popular at the site, though the extent of this beadmaking industry is not yet known.

At this point we do not know where the glass for these beads was made. Only Giong Ca Vo in Vietnam is recognized as a glassmaking site, but we do not know if the site made soda glass, potassium glass, or both types. The potassium glass seems to stand out, because it was used for the bicephalous earring, but only half the glass objects analyzed from there are of this type. All five specimens thus far analyzed from Ban Chiang are of potassium-rich glass, as are some (though not all) of the faceted beads at Ban Don Ta Phet.

The techniques used to make these glass objects were also unusual. Except for the bangles and drawn green beads at Giong Ca Vo (and even with the latter, we do not know how they were drawn out), the manufacturing methods cannot be considered standard beadmaking techniques. The Sa Huynh bicephalous pendant and the Ban Chiang ornaments were manipulated while hot. At least some beads from Ban Don Ta Phet (and the collar bead from Ban Don Luang) were worked by lapidary methods. None of these processes is totally unique, but they do differ from the more usual winding or drawing methods of glass beadmaking.

East Javanese Glass Beads

These beads are grouped together chronologically and geographically. They are called "East Javanese" or "Jatim"[18] beads. They were once thought to have been made in the Kediri Kingdom (Francis 1993e), but it is now established that they are older than that, probably between A.D. 600 to 900 (Adhyatman and Arifin 1993, 65, 69).[19] They have been published in both popular and scholarly works (Molsbergen 1925, pl. 5; Seligman and Beck 1938, pl. IV.10; van Heekeren 1958, pl. 13; Yoshimizu 1980, 58–60; R. K. Liu 1985; 1986; 1995a, 90–91; Francis 1991c, 225–229; Adhyatman and Arifin 1993, 47–72).[20] There are several types (Francis 1991c, 225–

226; 1993e, 8), depending upon how finely one categorizes them. They include:

1. East Javanese mosaic beads. Relatively large beads (about 2 cm in diameter) decorated with fancy mosaic cane eyes (Plate 41; Color Plate 38).
2. *Pelangi* (Indonesian for "rainbow"). Similarly large beads with a multistriped combed decoration (Plate 42).
3. White spotted beads. Beads of similar size decorated with simple white spots embedded in a blue green matrix (Plates 43, 44).
4. "Big yellows." Quite large beads (an example in the Trowulan Museum weighs 175 g) with a yellow surface (Plate 45).
5. Twisted striped beads. Smaller beads (about 1.5 cm in diameter) with colored stripes twisted in a candy-cane pattern (see Adhyatman and Arifin 1993, pl. 55–70; R. K. Liu 1985, 1986) (Color Plate 38).

The attractive East Javanese mosaic eye beads were made by applying slices of mosaic canes onto cores.[21] Some have been found in Malaysia (Evans 1932, 111–112) and the Philippines, as well as Sumatra and Kalimantan, but they are by far most common in Java. They are among the heirloom beads on Palau (Belau)[22] (Osborne 1958, 171, pl. 16; Thijssen-Etpison n.d., 42) (see chap. 17).

They have caught the fancy of bead collectors. Speculations on their dates once ranged from the early centuries A.D. to the twentieth century and on their origins from Persia eastward. They are vulgarly called "Majapahit beads" (Dubin 1987, 340), probably a dealer ascription (R. K. Liu 1986, 65). There is no evidence for such an association. None has been excavated at the Mahapahit capital, Trowulan, and all dated examples are earlier than the A.D. 1292 founding of the kingdom. The high prices that these and associated beads fetch have sadly assured the looting of many archaeological sites in Indonesia.

A striking feature of the mosaic beads is how they were made. Very thin slices of mosaic canes were placed on different sorts of cores. In addition to cores of sintered or fritty glass (Francis 1991c, 225), there are several wound glass cores visible on beads in the National Museum, Jakarta. J. D. Allen (1994) reported drawn glass cores. Apparently, any glass bead of the desired size was used as the core. The thinness of the mosaic canes (Plate 41) suggests they were scarce and valuable (R. K. Liu, 1988, personal communication).

The white spotted beads are among the most important heirloom beads in Palau (Thijssen-Etpison n.d., 42).[23] They were made in a puzzling way. The perforations have a bulging hollow in their centers, with several encircling ridges (Plate 43). Van Heekeren (1958, 42) assumed that they were wound on a stick that left an impression. It is doubtful that a stick could withstand the heat of molten glass. The configuration is not that of a bamboo joint. What might have caused this feature remains to be learned. On the inside walls of some perforations are traces of the exterior color. This is not surprising, but it is extraordinary that bits of the exterior white and blue green glass are also found *within* the cores of the beads.

Misshapen beads of this type, overheated and slumped, have been found at Jatiagung in East Java near Jember (Plate 44), suggesting nearby manufacturing. On Palau good ones are part of the "bead currency" (Osborne 1958, 171; Palau Community Action Agency 1976, 36). They have not been reported from elsewhere.

The "big yellows" are large monochromes with thin layers of yellow over darkly colored cores (Plate 45). In some cases a yellow coat was applied over a mosaic eye bead. Why this was done is unknown and rather perplexing.

The combed *pelangi* (rainbow) beads may also have been made at or near Jatiagung, because overheated examples have also been found nearby (Adhyatman and Arifin 1993, pl. 67b). They come in a variety of color schemes and cores (Adhyatman and Arifin 1993, 65–66). They are also heirloom beads in Palau (Thijssen-Etpison n.d., 43).[24]

The smaller twisted striped beads are the most widely distributed of the group. They have been found in the Philippines, at Oc Eo (Malleret 1962a, 269, no. 1238, first type; 1962b, LV); they are heirloom beads in Palau (Thijssen-Etpison n.d., 42),[25] and have been found in Japan (Tokyo National Museum 1978, 145, no. 561). The Japanese specimen is dated to the late sixth century, but the Oc Eo connection suggests that these beads could have been circulating at least to the eighth century.

There remains much to learn about these East Javanese glass beads. They likely originated in or around Jember, about A.D. 600 to 900. Unfortunately, Indonesian archaeological resources are stretched thin and these beads are "hot" on the antiquities market, so that we have learned little more about them.

They were made in odd ways. The mosaic beads have different cores. The white spotted beads have strange configurations in their perforations and the exterior glass was somehow occasionally incorporated into the cores. Some mosaic beads were coated with yellow, obliterating their complex designs. All of these are most unusual features. It appears that the beadmakers were inspired by Middle Eastern mosaic, eye, and combed beads. The mosaic glass itself was likely imported from the Middle East. However, the manufacturing techniques did not come from there. Middle Eastern mosaic beads, for example, were made without cores. Nor are there parallels for the other manufacturing peculiarities found in the East Javanese beads.

East Java was not in close contact with the Middle East until after these beads were made. The first reference to East Java (Mul-Java) among Arab geographers was by Wassaf around 1300, when reporting that Kublai Khan had "conquered" it (Tibbetts 1979, 60).[26] Ibn Battuta, who died in 1377, mentioned it (Tibbetts 1979, 151–152). Unlike Srivijaya, East Java was not an important trading partner for the Arabs when these beads were made.

The distribution of these beads is spotty outside Java. The one exception is Palau. The "bead money" of this Micronesian island has attracted much interest.[27] It shares some beads with Yap, from which many apparently came to Palau. The bead money includes pieces of glass bangles and various glass beads (see chap. 17), and it is surprising to find the whole range of East Javanese beads[28] there. Because of the antiquity of these beads, it is all but certain that East Javanese traders or settlers brought them to the Micronesian Islands. They may have been circulating in Micronesia for some time. The people of Yap and especially Palau are fond of them and they have built up considerable inventories. They are among the oldest heirloom beads known anywhere.

Rare and beautiful glass beads imported from the Middle East probably encouraged the birth of an industry. Without outside technical help (except mosaic canes) the East Javanese devised ways of making beads largely on their own. Many of the resulting beads are quite stunning. Middle Eastern methods or workers were not imported to make them, as they had been into Srivijaya. The East Javanese glass beads are a triumph of artistic vision over technological barriers.

Glass Beadmaking in Sri Lanka

As discussed in chapter 4, Mantai, Sri Lanka, was an Indo-Pacific beadmaking center. The two types of beads discussed here were certainly not made there, though the raw material for them (glass tubes and canes) might have been. The two bead types have some similarities. Both began as drawn pieces of glass, in one case a tube and in the other a solid cane. Both were then worked in somewhat unusual ways, at least for their time, and both seem to be rather widely distributed. One seems rather certain to have been made in Sri Lanka. The other might possibly have been made elsewhere.

Thin Red and Orange Lapidary-Made Disks

These beads were made from disks cut from relatively wide (about a centimeter), solid canes.[29] The disks are thin, usually not more than a millimeter thick. On one (sometimes both) sides the perforations are tapered. The perforations vary in size, but are larger than a double-tipped diamond bit would have made. They are also asymmetrical, indicating that whatever was used to drill them (likely a quartz or similar stone drill) was not being used in conjunction with a bow drill or any similar mechanical device. In some cases, the perforations appear to have been chipped or pecked (Plate 46).

The ends of the beads were ground flat and the edges rounded or tapered by grinding, often leaving a sort of polish. These operations were done in some cases before perforating and in others after. The beads are found in shades of opaque red and orange glass.

These beads are common on many sites all over Sri

Lanka. They were by far the most numerous beads in the Gedige area of the citadel at Anurādhapura, the ancient northern capital, located in the inland "dry zone" (Deraniyagala 1972, 137, type 10b(i)), where they accounted for nearly three-fourths (297 of 404) of all beads excavated.[30] In the south at Tissamaharama (the remains of Mahagama, the capital of Ruhuna from the second century B.C.) the joint KAVA/Archaeological Department of Sri Lanka team excavated a large number of these beads, 253 of 2,800 beads of all kinds (Weisshaar and Wijeyapala 1993, 160). In the far north on the Jaffna Peninsula, Pieris (1921, 64) was probably the first person to report on them. He said, "The red discs which first led me to look for beads are exceptionally abundant and are of different sizes and shades of red."

They seem to have a fairly wide distribution, if all of these beads are, in fact, the same. One was found on the surface at Karaikadu and they may be widespread in South India.[31] Similar beads have been excavated at Ban Chiang, Thailand (J. C. White 1982, 77–78), and visually similar ones are offered in the antiquities markets of Thailand and Afghanistan. They are absent or at least scarce at Mantai (see note 31).

Three of these beads have been analyzed. One was done by Mellor on a bead found by Pieris (1921, 64) in the Jaffna Peninsula, and two from Tissamaharama were analyzed by Rösch (Rösch et al. 1997, table III; see color plate e). All three have similar characteristics in that potassium is the dominant alkali (more than twice the soda in two cases) and there is a large amount of copper (13.5 to 17.3 percent) present. Thus, they do not resemble the red glass of any known Indo-Pacific beadmaking site (see Appendix B), though they could conceivably (though perhaps unlikely) match Mantai's glass, which has yet to be published.

Pieris (1921, 65) wrote, "As to the glass, it is now proved that glass beads were made in Ceylon, but I hesitate to make the assertion that they were made in the [Jaffna] Peninsula itself, though there is reason to believe that they were so made. I have found both unperforated and also unseparated glass beads." It is difficult to draw any firm conclusions from this. On the preceding page he discussed a number of glass beads, without being explicit enough to identify any of them except for the red disk beads. "Unperforated glass beads" strongly suggests the disk blanks before they were drilled. "Unseparated" could refer to partly cut red canes, but may also be his description of multiple segmented beads.

Stūpa Beads

These are among the most astonishing beads in this whole study because they alone (save for some very late Czech beads) were molded into shape. The nature of the molding device, whether a two-part mold or two applications of a single half-mold cannot yet be determined. In most cases they were molded from drawn tubes, but others were made from a wound bead or a small amount of glass.

The beads are round tabulars, flat and pierced through the edges. They are unique in having the rims of both sides raised and a low swelling at the center of each face, sometimes with an additional small knob atop the swelling (Figure 13.4; Color Plate 39). Some have thin collars around the apertures. Those without collars may have simply lost them, because they are easily broken off. They come in various colors, dark translucent blue being the most common.

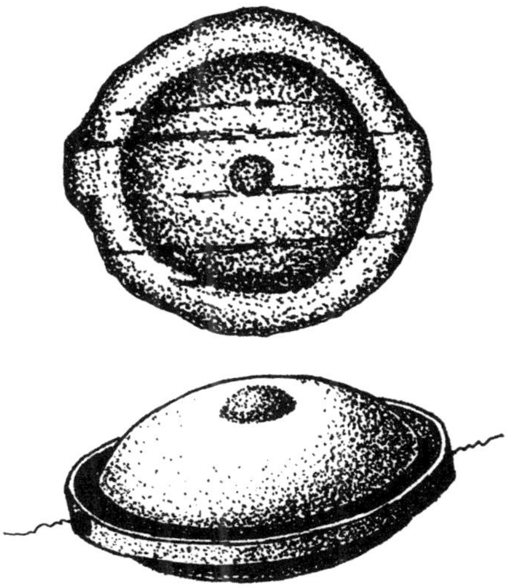

Figure 13.4. *Two views of a* stūpa *bead. Sketch by Cynthia Schave.*

The shape of these beads immediately recalls that of a *stūpa,* the quintessential contribution to architecture by Buddhism. A *stūpa* consists of a rounded mound (the *aṇḍa*) on a circular platform surrounded by a railing, usually with four elaborate gates, and surmounted by a structure (the *harmikā*) that holds a mast *(yashṭi),* which usually supports several umbrellas. The *aṇḍa* is built over a casket that holds relics of the Buddha. Although two of these beads were found at Mantai and one at Sungai Mas, they are far more common in southern Sri Lanka and the Dvaravati sites of Thailand, including U Thong. Both of these areas were strongholds of Buddhism. The cultural ties between Sri Lanka and Thailand are old and tenacious, principally based on the Buddhist connection (Dewaraja 1990b; Guruge 1990).

The style seems to have been long-lived. One of the beads from Mantai was found in a context that suggests a first century A.D. date. The other was from nearer the end of the site's occupation, about the eighth century. Tissamaharama is dated from the first two centuries B.C. to the fifth or sixth centuries A.D. (Weisshaar and Wijeyapala 1993). Sungai Mas and the Dvaravati Kingdom suggest seventh to ninth or tenth century dates. Except for the early one from Mantai, a date between the fifth and tenth centuries seems most plausible. Because they appear to have been made for a Buddhist clientele, their production in Sri Lanka or perhaps Dvaravati is very likely.

Beads Whose Origins Are a Mystery

The following beads are found principally or exclusively in Southeast Asia. Whether this indicates local production is not known with our current state of knowledge. Some appear to be Southeast Asian, but more research is necessary to clarify their origins.

Standard Pressed Hexagonal Bicones

These beads are called "standard" in Beck's system (1928, 4, 6) because they are approximately equal in length and diameter. They were made by winding glass on a mandrel and paddling twelve facets onto the bead to form a hexagonal bicone shape (Plate 47). They are translucent in either dark blue or medium to gray green.

One blue and sixty-seven light green examples were found at Oc Eo (Malleret 1962a, 254, 256). All but one of the green ones were melted together. Malleret (1962a, 246, 256) assumed that they were from a nearby workshop. Two were analyzed, and they conformed to the general composition of Indo-Pacific beads on the site (Malleret 1962a, 466–467).

Elsewhere in Southeast Asia, a dark blue hexagonal bicone is in the Wat Khlong Thom museum, Thailand. A blue one was found at Kejajar on the south slope of the Dieng Plateau, Java, Indonesia, but whether it was associated with the kingdoms based on the plateau is difficult to say. They are on the antiquities markets in the Philippines (Villegas 1983, 35, row 3.5). They have also been found in Han China (Osborne 1958, 171) and are "common" on Palau (Osborne 1958, 171).

They are also known from sites in South India, from the early centuries A.D. Three green ones were uncovered at Uraiyūr, the old Cōḷa capital. A dark blue one was found at Alagankulam, on the southern tip. A clear one and a green one were found at Karur, the Chera capital. Three from Mantai, Sri Lanka, were surface finds or in disturbed levels. Basa (1992b, 97) noted a green one also from Kāñchī.[32]

Considering the age of the datable beads and their absence in later contexts, an origin in the first half of the first millennium A.D. may be assumed. The most likely source for them may be Oc Eo. However, there are other explanations for a group of beads being melted together. Nothing suggests Indian manufacture. China is also unlikely, because the beads contain no lead.[33] Their wide distribution in urban areas is notable.

Long Pressed Hexagonal Bicones and Cornerless Cubes

These are similar to the beads in the preceding group, being made by pressing wound glass into faceted shapes (Color Plate 36). However, their distribution and age sets them apart. The more common shape is a long (length exceeding diameter by at least 25 percent) hexagonal bicone. The other is a cornerless cube: a cube with the eight corners cut at an angle. They were principally made of translucent light green glass and secondarily translucent dark blue. Dark green and opaque turquoise blues ones have also been recorded (Adhyatman and Arifin 1993, 60).

Two long, blue cornerless cubes were found at Calatagan, Luzon, the Philippines, dating to the late fourteenth to early sixteenth centuries. A long octagonal bicone of light opaque blue glass, which may be related to this group, was also found there. A standard blue cornerless cube was found at Laem Pho Chaiya, Thailand, dated to the ninth century.

These paddled faceted beads are most numerous in Indonesia,[34] but not from stratified contexts. For example, twenty-two light translucent green standard cornerless cubes are in the Trowulan Museum, having been picked up at Jember, East Java. A string of long hexagonal bicones in a similar green glass is in the National Museum, Jakarta. It came from Candi Laras, Kalimantan. Both sites may date to the eighth or ninth centuries. These beads are popular on the Indonesian antiquities market, so much so that they are currently being imitated by contemporary Indonesian glass beadmakers.

The few beads of this type that can be dated are later than the short hexagonal bicones of the preceding section. Their origin cannot be deduced at this time, though the large numbers in Indonesia might suggest they were made in the archipelago. Adhyatman and Arifin (1993, 60) suggested that they were by-products of the Indo-Pacific bead industry, but there is no evidence for their production at any Indo-Pacific beadmaking site, and they are wound rather than drawn beads.

Bird Beads

These are made of dark blue or black glass, usually oblate shaped, but sometimes flattened into ellipsoidal tabulars. Their most obvious feature is a trailed white design of two "frames" formed by crossing two loops of glass. Within each frame is a motif. The most common combination is a standing bird in one frame and a star burst pattern in the other. Other observers see different figures or there are different figures to be seen. Sometimes a squirrel replaces the bird and flowers substitute for the star-burst (Figure 13.5; Color Plate 36).

Several bird beads were excavated at Oc Eo (Malleret 1962a, 266–267; 1962b, liv). Other locations include Khlong Thom, Dvaravati sites in Thailand, and places in Indonesia, among them Candi Laras, Kalimantan. They have not been found in well-stratified loci, but they seem to date from the middle of the first millennium A.D.

Malleret (1962a, 266) compared the bird design to one on an etched carnelian from Kosam (Kauśāmbī), Uttar Pradesh, India (Dikshit 1949, 69, no. 10). It is difficult to draw any conclusions from the resemblance. Glass bird beads have never been recorded in India.

Drawn Orange and Red Beads

Opaque orange glass is similar to the more common opaque red because both are colored with a colloidal solution of cuprous oxide (Cu_2O_3). All Indo-Pacific beadmakers made red beads, but only some made orange beads. Orange beads were not purposely made at Arikamēḍu.[35] This section concerns orange and red drawn beads other than Indo-Pacific beads and the Sri Lankan disk beads discussed earlier in this chapter.

Beck (1941, 23–24; Dikshit 1969, 7) described a small drawn orange glass bead from fourth-century B.C. Taxila. He noted that it was valuable along the Malabar (southwestern Indian) Coast. Exactly what bead was being discussed is now difficult to say. It may have been an Indo-Pacific bead or the bead described as type 1 below.

The beads considered here are all drawn, but they are not Indo-Pacific beads. Two of the types were finished differently than Indo-Pacific beads. The other type has an unusual composition. Three different types of

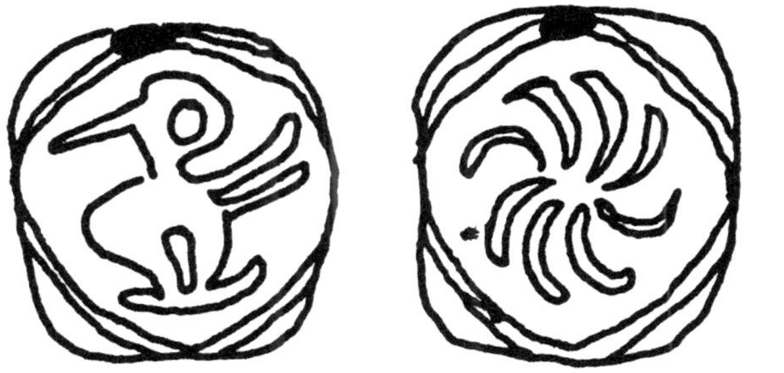

Figure 13.5. *Two views of a bird bead. Sketch by Jacqui Steinberg.*

beads are involved (see Color Plate 40): (1) small beads with a slightly tapered shape; (2) cylinders with dark interiors and orange exteriors; (3) large unreheated orange disks.

Type 1. Small drawn orange glass beads are found at South Indian sites and elsewhere. They differ from Indo-Pacific beads by having conical profiles and usually one rounded and one flattened end. Two sites in Andhra Pradesh yielded one hundred of these beads. Dhulikotta, occupied from the first century B.C. to the second or third century A.D., had forty-seven, and Peddabonkur, occupied from the first to the third centuries A.D., had fifty-three.[36]

To test my observation (Francis 1982b, 3) that these beads have tapered holes, I measured the apertures, the lengths, and the diameters at both ends of the beads from these two sites. Only eight have tapering perforations, but eighty-nine (89 percent) have tapered sides. The beads are slightly conical. Most are rounded at the smaller end and flat at the larger end.

The beads were made by cutting segments from a tube. Their shapes indicate that the segments were reheated for only a short time while resting on a flat plate without being stirred. This would have barely melted the beads, causing the exposed end to slump and become rounded and the end sitting on the plate to retain a flat surface. The slight heating would have caused the bead to become somewhat conical. The only other beads recorded finished in this way are "nila" beads (see chap. 5).

In addition to South Indian occurrences, there are similar beads on the antiquities markets in Thailand, said to be, but not necessarily, from Ban Chiang. From the South Indian data, they may be presumed to date to the first few centuries A.D.

Type 2. These are barrel or cylindrical in shape with two layers of glass. The exterior is orange, and the interior or core is of a darker glass. There are two subtypes, one with a red core and the other with a dark, perhaps black or green, core. Whether they are related is not yet clear. Neither type is very common.

The earliest of these is a red-cored surface find from Karaikadu. It is 5.6 mm in diameter and 9.1 mm in length. Pilditch (1992, 174–175) found ninety smaller, similar beads at Ban Bon Neon, Thailand, as yet with no dates.[37]

At Khlong Thom, Takua Pa, and Sungai Mas were a few beads the size of the Karaikadu one, but with very dark cores. The Sungai Mas examples are the largest. These sites (and Karaikadu) were all Indo-Pacific beadmaking centers, but there is no evidence (no matching wasters) for local production at any of them. Pilditch (1992) suggested that Ban Bon Neon might have been an Indo-Pacific beadmaking site, but concluded that it was more likely simply involved in the trade. The only such bead beyond India and Southeast Asia that has come to my attention was excavated by Paul Yule at Samad al Shan, Oman, dated around 400 to 600 A.D.

Type 3. These beads were cut from tubes of orange glass with diameters from a half centimeter to a centimeter or more. They were subsequently reheated to smooth off their sharp edges, but their profiles remain undulating. They were numerous at Mantai, where they were apparently made. One was found at the cemetery site of Calatagan, the Philippines (Francis 1989d, 34, bead 119-AT). If these beads were made only at Mantai, which seems likely, the one at Calatagan is probably an heirloom, because the earliest date for the cemetery is in the fourteenth century.

The scant evidence for many of the beads in this chapter means that conclusions about their origins and even dates are less secure than those in other chapters. Much work is needed to clarify points raised here. Some conclusions drawn here will surely be revised. They are offered as hypotheses to lend clues into the nature of Asian glass bead industries and to stimulate further research.

14

Minor Stone Bead Industries in the Asian Maritime Trade

Because of the limitations outlined in chapter 2, the origins of many stone beads will always be enigmatic. Small-scale stone bead industries can be identified at several places in this region. It had long been assumed that quartz-family beads, especially carnelian in Southeast Asia, were direct imports from India (e.g., Lamb 1965b, 91–93; Bellwood 1985, 279, 347; Francis 1989c, 21–28; 1989d, 5; Glover 1990b, 17; Ray 1996, 43). Some alternatives have also been suggested, as in the works just cited of Glover and Francis. It appears that in the case of Iron-Age Thailand, at least, locally made carnelian beads outnumber imported products (Theunissen and Grave 1998; Theunissen et al. 2000). More geochemical analyses like those used by Theunissen are certainly desirable. A few were involved in more than local trade.

One group of minor stone-working centers consists of Indo-Pacific beadmaking sites. There are not enough data to tell whether lapidary arts were transferred to these sites in the same way as Indo-Pacific beadmaking, but there is stone beadmaking at so many of them that it may have been. China stands apart; it was only a small and late contributor to stone beads in the Asian maritime trade because of its focus on jade, serving the domestic market. A miscellaneous group includes two important classes of beads, lapis lazuli and "etched" carnelians.

Stone Beadmaking at Indo-Pacific Beadmaking Sites

There is evidence for stone beadmaking at all Indo-Pacific beadmaking sites except Takua Pa and modern Papanaidupet. The data for Sungai Mas and Mantai are limited. However, the other sites, beginning with Arikamēḍu, made stone beads on a significant scale.

Arikamēḍu has been recognized as a stone beadmaking site since the first collection of its antiquities was made in the 1930s. Its beadmaking in relation to South India is discussed in chapter 12. The principal materials used were rock crystal, carnelian, amethyst, almandine garnet, agate, crystalline prase, and hessonite garnet. In addition, Arikamēḍu lapidaries were notable for producing black onyx from banded agate and the first recorded citrine from amethyst. The industry continued throughout the occupation of the site, though citrine and hessonite garnet are not found in the later stages of occupation.

Stone was also worked at Karaikadu, just south of Arikamēḍu and probably a satellite town. The materials were similar to those at Arikamēḍu, except that garnets and citrine have not been identified and prase seems to have been used more often. Excavations have not been extensive, and the schedule of industrial building will prevent any further archaeological work there for a long time (Raman 1975; 1991, 128–129).

Malleret (1962a, 152–165 passim) recognized Oc Eo as a stone beadmaking site. Rock crystal, amethyst, carnelian, agate, sardonyx, plasma/crysoprase, and garnets were worked. Beads and ring settings of other stones were present, some of which may have been locally fashioned. The industry resembles that of Arikamēḍu, except for the minor minerals.

One difference between Arikamēḍu and Oc Eo is the relative proportion of garnets. The 1989–1992 Arikamēḍu excavation uncovered 227 garnet pieces, of which almandine accounted for 209 pieces,[1] and hessonite accounted for only eight pieces,[2] 3.6 percent of all garnets. In the Oc Eo material at the History Museum in Ho Chi Minh City, however, there are forty-one[3] pieces of almandine garnet and thirty-two of hessonite.[4] Hessonite accounts for 43.8 percent of the garnets. This might indicate a source somewhere within or near Funan. Lam Dong Province in southern Vietnam is today a source of this garnet variety.[5] It could have furnished raw material to Oc Eo and perhaps also to Arikamēḍu.

Kuala Selinsing was actually the earliest identified stone beadmaking site in this group, having been reported on by Evans (1932, 90–91). He said that local rock crystal was made into beads, but saw no evidence for working of carnelian or agate. Wasters of these two minerals have been found since and are deposited in the National Museum in Kuala Lumpur. The current excavators (Nik Hassan Shuhaimi and Ab. Latib B. Ariffin) have found a grooved stone that may have been used for grinding beads.

Carnelian and to a lesser extent onyx (derived from agate) and rock crystal were worked in Khlong Thom. Bronson (1991, 216–217) reported on roughouts and waste material that he had collected there, including carnelians with attached cylinders of resin. He suggested that the resin was used to secure the stone onto a short stick (a dop) for grinding or polishing. As discussed in chapter 12, this was (and still is) the practice of South Indian lapidaries, though never recorded in the western Indian industry.

Mantai is the least impressive stone beadmaking site among the early Indo-Pacific sites. The evidence appears late, only around the seventh or eighth centuries A.D. Rock crystal and carnelian were the most important stones worked there, and there are single examples of green feldspar (amazonite), flint, and agate being made into beads. The crystalline beads (rock crystal and amethyst) were polished before being drilled, indicating the pecking complex of beadmaking.

Among the later Indo-Pacific beadmaking sites associated with Srivijaya, only a single carnelian chip was uncovered at Sungai Mas. Although this suggests very limited activity, the site has been briefly excavated only once by a SPAFA team (ASEAN 1985, 51–68).[6] Nearly all of the rich collection of beads in the Merbok Museum from this site have been surface finds made by local farmers. They may not have considered stone flakes or small chunks to be of any interest, though one would think that roughouts or blanks would have been gathered. The one trench opened by the SPAFA team yielded only glass beads.

At Vijaya/Palembang, two stone bead materials dominate: carnelian and a friable white flint with black bands. Both were probably locally worked.

The white flint is also found in Thailand, especially at Chaiya, a northern Srivijayan city. Analysis done on one example indicated that it is a silicate (A. Srisuchat, 1991, personal communication). Two beads of this material were uncovered at Arikamēḍu (Francis n.d.). It is called "flint" here for lack of a better term, though it might also be deemed chert or banded jasper.

A large, broken spherical bead of this material found at Muara Jambi and now in the Jambi Museum was dyed a violet color that penetrated only a millimeter or so under the surface. A fragment of a cylindrical bead found at Kambang Unglen was also dyed, this time to blacken the natural gray lines (Plate 48).

Besides the use of white flint, the outstanding mark of Vijaya production is the crudeness of the carnelian beads. They come in two principal shapes: oblates and long faceted beads. The latter vary from barrel to bicone in profile and are square, pentagonal, and hexagonal in section. Most seem to have been meant to be pentagonal barrels. All the carnelian beads were poorly finished. They had not been tumbled and have uneven surfaces with many depressions. They were bored with a double-tipped diamond drill, but their final appearance is quite coarse.

These stone beads, especially the carnelian ones, along with typical long Indo-Pacific tubes produced in Vijaya, are found in the bead assemblages of several related sites. These include nearby Jambi (Jambi Museum) and Air Sugian, South Sumatra (Palembang Museum), and as far removed as Punung in Pacitan District, East Java (Museum Negeri, Surabaya).

Thus, of the known Indo-Pacific beadmaking sites, only Takua Pa and Papanaidupet lack evidence for stone beadmaking. Arikamēḍu, Karaikadu, Oc Eo, and Vijaya have quite strong evidence. The first three are contemporary and their industries look similar. About the seventh or eighth century, stone beads began to be made at Mantai and Vijaya. The white-banded flint and the polishing of carnelian beads at Vijaya set it apart from the other sites.

China

The nature and extent of Chinese stone bead production are something of a mystery. The Chinese were not especially interested in beads of quartz minerals and there are few references to them in the literature. This is due to the overwhelming role of jade, the "stone of heaven." It was such a favorite that all other minerals were secondary or minor. As an example, during the Tang dynasty (A.D. 618 to 906), it was decreed that plaques were to be added to girdles, previously made only of leather. Only jade and metal ones were authorized. It was not until the Qing dynasty (after 1644) that lapis lazuli and coral were added to the repertoire (Laufer 1974, 286–293).

The literature regarding jade is extensive because of its prominence in Chinese culture. However, it was almost always an internal product and it rarely entered international commerce. To evaluate China's role in the Asian maritime stone bead trade we need more data on stone beadmaking in China.

The evidence suggests that the quartz family minerals were principally imported into China, as either raw material or finished articles. A survey of the classical literature bolsters this supposition.

In the *Zhou`li (The Rites of Zhou),* jade is all but exclusively mentioned as a precious material, with only occasional references to ivory (e.g., Biot 1851, 127)[7] and gold. Other early Chinese writings,[8] including *The Book of Odes* and the works of Confucius (551–479 B.C.) and Mencius (372–289 B.C.), refer almost exclusively to jade. Sometimes vague terms such as "gem," "precious stone," or "jewels" are used. There were also some stones named, but they have not been identified. The only exception is in *Lessons from the State,* of the Late Zhou or later. A young woman pined:

I escorted my mother's nephew,
Long, long did I think of him.
What did I present to him?
A precious jasper, and gems for his
girdle-pendant.
(Legge 1972, 4: 203)[9]

It is interesting that a poem from the *Minor Odes of the Kingdom,* of the Early Zhou period or before, indicated an awareness of working precious stones:

The crane cries in the ninth pool on
the marsh
Pleasant is that garden
In which are the sandal trees;
But beneath them are only withered leaves
The stones of those hills,
May be made into grind-stones.
The crane cries in the ninth pool on
the marsh
Pleasant is that garden
In which are the sandal trees;
But beneath them is the
paper-mulberry tree
The stones of those hills,
May be used to polish gems.
(Legge 1972, 4: 297)[10]

Sima Qian's *Shi ji,* an account of the Western (Former) Han dynasty, is also vague on identifications of precious stones, with one notable exception. The section entitled *Shanglin Park* is a long poem written and then revised by Sima Xiang to be presented to Emperor Wu Di (141 to 87 B.C.). It is a satirical fantasy describing the Emperor's pleasure garden and the activities therein. The garden was full of exotic animals (zebra, tapir, rhinoceros, peacock, and so on) and plants (betal nut or areca palm, pomegranate, date palm, sandalwood, and so on). It also contained precious stones including carnelians, garnets, white quartz, amethyst, turquoise, chalcedony, beryl, onyx, figured agate, pearls, chrysoberyl, and clear quartz (Watson 1961, 297–321).[11] Thus, by the Western Han period, the Chinese were familiar with a wide range of stones, though they were not necessarily exploited in China itself.

Agate, carnelian, rock crystal, amethyst, and other semiprecious quartz stones are found archaeologically in China, including provinces commonly under central control (F. Wang 1979, 696; Keller and Wang 1987). They were exploited from an early period; the archaeological record is a little more prolific than the literary.

Nephrite jade was by far the most common stone used for ornamental or mortuary purposes. However, as early as the Shang period (1523 to 1027 B.C.)[12] both softer and harder stones were worked by the Chinese (Chêng 1960, 109–113). This trend continued into the following Zhou period (1027 to 256 B.C.), when rock crystal, amethyst, carnelian, turquoise, malachite, marble, serpentine, soapstone, and other materials are reported (Chêng 1963, 185–190).

Nonetheless, these stones played a minor role. Turquoise, probably from Hubei Province (Team for Technical Research 1985, 416), and marble are most common after jade. Agates, chalcedony, quartz, and amethyst were quite rare, even being outnumbered by glass beads during the Zhou period (Chêng 1963, 50–255 passim).

It is only in the Western Han dynasty (202 B.C. to A.D. 9) that other hard stones, especially the quartz minerals, become common. Displays in the National Palace Museum in Beijing include a large number of onyx, agate, rock crystal, carnelian, and turquoise beads. Many of them appear[13] to be Indian in origin, though a few have shapes not found in India. Jenyns (1982, 185–220) said that various hard stones had been carved regularly since the Han period and illustrated a few early examples, but did not specify what the sources of the stones were. Unfortunately, the great majority he cited date from the eighteenth century.

By Tang times, there are references to Buddhist prayer beads of rock crystal. One reads:

Good craftsmen rubbed and scrubbed, and
formed a string of beads,
Limpid through and through, pellucid,
void and clear—look, and they seem
not there,
Star flashing, moon beaming, nothing
surpasses them. . . .
(Schafer 1963, 227)

At least one quartz prayer strand in the period was a gift from a Japanese monk. Other gifts of crystal objects were recorded from Samarkand and Bactria (Schafer 1963, 227). Carnelian, too, was known in Tang times, but most examples were gifts given by neighboring countries, including raw materials from Persia and Japan. Japan sometimes sent a false carnelian, the composition of which would be interesting to learn (Schafer 1963, 228–229).

In the Song period, the *Song Shi* (completed by 1345) recorded tribute missions (see next section) to China from Srivijaya in 971 and 974 that included "crystals" and crystal finger-rings (Groeneveldt 1876, 64). A list of imports to China drawn up around A.D. 999 contains both carnelian and rock crystal (Hirth and Rockhill 1911, 19).[14] A ship wrecked off Sha Cui (High Island) in Hong Kong, dated to the eleventh century, was importing Indo-Pacific beads and a square bicone bead of carnelian.[15] Zhao Rugua discussed carnelian and rock crystal in several passages.[16] Both were said to be products of the Arab world (Hirth and Rockhill 1911, 16, 19, 103), and both were said to have been made into pillars in the palace of the Arab king (Hirth and Rockhill 1911, 102, 115). Arab or Persian merchants were importing the stones from India. The story of the pillars is doubtless an exaggeration (Hirth 1885, 238–241).

In the late Yuan period, the *Chuogenglu* (*The Interrupted Plowing*, 1366) included a section called *Precious Stones of the Muslims* that discussed *guluman*, a stone with "an irregular color; it is red, mixed with dark yellow. This stone is found in large pieces, and is the least valuable of the above mentioned [including rubies and garnets]" (Bretschneider 1910, 174 [insertion mine]). On rather flimsy linguistic grounds, Bretschneider identified the stone as opal, but the description fits carnelian much better.[17] In the succeeding Ming period we meet with *guloman* as one of the stones of Sri Lanka (Mills 1970, 128). Mills (1970, 128 n. 1) cited Bretschneider and a couple of dictionary entries for this and *kumulan*. He also argued that it is not opal because opal does not come from Sri Lanka. There is also a question of whether carnelian is found in Sri Lanka.[18] Not all items the Chinese said were produced in various countries were actually produced there.

During the Ming dynasty around 1515, Tomé Pires observed that "a great many carnelians from Cambay" were among the goods the Chinese bought at Malacca (Cortesão 1967, 123). The *Ming Shi* (*History of the Ming*, 1735) recorded tribute of agate and crystal from Sumatra in the period 1573–1619 (Groeneveldt 1876, 91–92). Agate was also listed as a tribute from Malacca, though at what date is difficult to tell (Groeneveldt 1876, 134).

By late Ming times, Chinese lapidaries were exploiting their own mineral wealth. In 1637, Song Yingxing wrote in *Diangong Kaiwu (The Creations of Nature and Man)* that agate "is abundantly produced in China itself, the merchants do not trouble themselves with purchasing it from distant places" (Sun and Sun 1966, 307). The variety he called "red-flower" may be carnelian. This passage shows that there had been a time when merchants did "trouble themselves" to import agates.

As for export, the only permitted outward trade during much of the Ming period was the galleon trade, and Chinese hard stone beads were part of the commercial stock. In 1609 de Morga observed Chinese ships bringing "*tacley*,[19] which are beads of all kinds, strings of cornelians, and other beads and stones of all colours," to Manila to trade to the Spanish (Cummins 1971, 306). The 1638 wreck of the Spanish galleon *Nuesta Señora de la Concepción*, lost off Saipan on its way from Manila to Acapulco, included Chinese glass beads and carnelian beads (personal observation).[20] Unfortunately, we cannot tell whether the carnelians were Chinese or Indian.

To recapitulate, China was involved in the Asian maritime stone bead trade from an early period, as an importer via the tribute system. Then in the late Ming period China began to exploit its own deposits of nonjade hard stones, especially for export to Manila. China may have been a major supplier of carnelian, quartz, and agate beads found in Southeast Asia from the seventeenth century onward, but the evidence is limited. As with glass beads, more work within China, both archival and archaeological, is needed before the picture can be clarified.

China and Tribute Missions

There have been several references to "tribute" being paid to the emperor of China in this chapter, and there are even more in the following chapter, which mentions amber, coral, ivory, and pearls being sent as favors. The nature of tribute in this context needs to be understood. Tribute is usually defined as the payment from a king or nation to another monarch to acknowledge the receiver's superiority and to secure his protection.

In the Chinese view, the Son of Heaven ruled the Middle Kingdom. The emperor was the center of the world, and China was superior to all other nations in technical, intellectual, economic, and moral realms. The "barbarians" of less-developed countries would naturally want to pay homage to the emperor and bring him presents of the exotic goods they produced or acquired. The generous emperor in turn would shower the lesser king with tangible and intangible presents: girdles of precious stones, royal seals, and proclamations that so-and-so was king of such-and-such a place, as well as silks and other fine Chinese products.

That is how the Chinese saw it, at least officially. It is doubtful that any of the nations paying tribute to the emperor saw themselves as vassals. They were independent entities and only on rare occasions (most notably during the Yuan period when Mongols were in charge) did China interfere directly with the affairs of other countries. There were other reasons to participate in this pretense.

If one were to do business in Asia, it was always a good idea to have China approve of your activities. In this sense, tribute missions meant insurance against the possibility that the strongest nation in the region would retaliate against a weaker one. However, there were other considerations, too. Many tribute missions were designed not to please China but to gain an advantage either at home or regionally. For example, two areas (such as Java and Srivijaya) might have been vying for trading rights, or several pretenders to a throne might have sought the imprimatur of the emperor. Changes in dynasties, either in China or in the "subordinate" nation, might have engendered missions. The seals, rich robes, and girdles of precious stones legitimized the authority of the person who received them and usually secured kingship for them at home.

Then, too, the tribute and reciprocal gifts were a form of trade. Most Chinese dynasties officially eschewed trade, but still wanted the goods that commerce brought. Tribute was a way to hide or circumvent the situation. Many of the ambassadors were really just merchants. It seems likely that merchants backing a claimant would have financed many tribute missions that were designed to outdo a rival.

As mutually beneficial as the tribute system was, it was expensive. Tributary nations had to journey long distances and present presents worthy of the emperor. Financially, however, they may have made the better bargain, because they were not only receiving goods but also were hosted by the Chinese government in what were likely more sumptuous surroundings than they had at home. As trade increased significantly with Southeast Asia under the Southern Song, the tribute system became a burden and in 1178 was abandoned. During the rest of the dynasty the many merchants who were flocking to China to take advantage of the new free trade policy did not go to the court, but were housed in a hostel in Quanzhou (Groeneveldt 1876, 67). The tribute system was reinstated by the traditionalist Ming.

Other Stone Beadmakers

It is likely that there have been several other Asian sites that at one time or another housed stone beadmaking industries. Making beads from stone requires some skill, but it is not as challenging as making glass from its raw materials. The tool kit of stone beadmakers is relatively simple and, except for diamonds for drilling, readily available. Diamonds, of course, are small and easily transported. Apart from technical knowledge and the necessary tools, only the raw material is required for stone beadmaking to exist.

Quartz Mineral Beads

In 1982, twenty-five[21] Indian sites with evidence for quartz mineral beadmaking were known (Francis 1982c, 39). This seems impressive, but once the Pandukal sites, those connected with the Gujarat industry, and older sites (1000 B.C. and earlier) are eliminated, the number is reduced to ten. Several of these have only scant evidence for beadmaking. Thus, even India, as rich as it is in stones and as old as stone beadmaking is there, had relatively few lapidary centers, mostly meeting local demands.

There were other stone beadmaking centers elsewhere, but their importance in the Asian maritime bead trade has yet to be understood. Only five[22] other sites in this region have been clearly identified as having had quartz-working lapidaries.

The most evidence for beadmaking comes from Siraf, Iran. The assemblage[23] in the British Museum includes two small carnelian pebbles large enough to be made into beads, a chipped chunk or large flake of carnelian, five carnelian roughouts (oval, barrel, disk, and sub-oblate in shape), a perforated but unpolished carnelian barrel, and an abraded but unperforated cylinder of gray chalcedony.

Some material excavated from the Red Sea port of Quseir al-Qadim, Egypt, is available for study at the Oriental Institute in Chicago.[24] It shows that carnelian and amethyst may have been made into beads there. There are four chunks of carnelian, all with traces of the cortex of the original pebbles. There are also four chunks or crude roughouts of amethyst. Quseir was occupied in Roman (then called Leukos Limen) and Early Islamic times, and it has not yet been determined to which period(s) the stone chunks belong.

At Berenike, Egypt, soft stones were made into beads and there is some evidence that hard stones were as well. A carnelian oblate was drilled but not pierced through; the drill bit was not a double-tipped diamond. There is a carnelian bead broken while being drilled and one polished but not drilled. There were also four carnelian[25] and one rock crystal bead that were crudely made, most drilled from only one side. Most of the stone beads were technically well done, similar to Indian beads, and were probably imports (Francis 2001).

At Bukit Maris, in the Santubong region of Sarawak, East Malaysia, carnelian is locally available (Everett and Hewitt 1908, 7). In the Sarawak Museum are a ground but undrilled carnelian barrel and an oblate with an incomplete hole. A vinyl silicate impression of this hole confirmed that the bead was being drilled with a double-tipped diamond drill.

Demak, central Java (fifteenth and sixteenth centuries), was an early Muslim center on the island. Ambary et al. (1977, 46) published an account of square bicone carnelian roughouts they excavated.

"Etched" Carnelian Beads

The term "etched carnelian" is a misnomer. Etching involves the eating away of a surface with acid. These beads (also known as "decorated" and "soda-etched") had a pattern applied with alkali that did not erode the surface, but produced indelible white lines. Black lines were also made with a metal salt (Color Plate 33).

These distinctive beads were first noticed in India. Probably the earliest reference to them is contained in a rambling footnote[26] published in 1819 by Bowdich (1966, 268–271). He said a "gentleman lately returned from India" described beads from Pandukal tombs, "those in India, which appear to be of a red glass, very like red carnelian . . . with white lines of enamel, inlaid, as it were, in the body of the bead" (Bowditch 1966, 270 n).

The first scientific accounts of etched carnelians were in two papers by Bellasis (1856a, b) reporting on his excavation at Brahminabad. Initially they greatly puzzled him, but he pursued them.

> I am not aware that lapidaries of the present day are able to produce figures and patterns upon cornelians without making an incision in the stone,—no process of burning, no application of acid, will leave a permanent mark upon a cornelian; but yet at Brahminabad many of the cornelian ornaments are found figured with various patterns in white lines on a perfectly smooth surface, and, after having withstood the damp of ages, are, when dug up, quite fresh. (Bellasis 1856a, 418)

> Respecting the cornelian ornaments found figured with patterns in white lines, on a perfectly smooth surface, and which I thought were so curious in my first paper, I have made further inquiry; and while at Sehwan, in upper Sind, an old city famed for cornelian engravers, I found some stones figured in exactly a similar manner. On examination, it was ascertained that the chief ingredients used were potash, white lead, and the juice of the Kirar bush *(Capparis aphylla)* made into a thick liquid and applied with a pen on the cornelian, which, on being exposed to a red heat in charcoal, rendered the device indelible. (Bellasis 1856b: 471)

N. G. Majumdar located Sahebdino (or Saheb Dino) in Sehwan (now in Pakistan).[27] Except for his son, he was the last person to know the process. He had learned it as a young boy, but was in his seventies by the time that Mackay (1933) visited him. He had not used it for fifty-five years. Sahebdino crushed the shoots of the *kirar*[28] bush in a bowl until he obtained a greenish paste. To this he added soda (he used washing soda, but advised natural soda with a little vinegar) mixed in water. He applied it to a carnelian plaque with a reed pen, put the plaque in a small clay holder, and heated it in the embers of a charcoal fire for about five minutes. After allowing it to cool for another ten minutes, he wiped the soot off and the process was complete.

Mackay (1933, 145) conducted subsequent experiments and ascertained that the kirar juice had no chemical effect, but helped the soda adhere to the carnelian.

He also discovered that the addition of any soluble lead aided the work by rendering the transparent solution opaque so that the lines could be seen as they were being "painted on." Finally, he realized that adding a little borax to the mixture lowered the temperature at which the solution dried and prevented the stones from losing their original deep color.

Beck (1933, 384–388; 1934, 193) examined thin sections of etched carnelians and deduced that in "most, if not all cases" the alkali penetrated the surface and spread out just under it in many small opaque white particles. This forms a permanent line that cannot be felt on the surface. There are, however, etched beads with lines very slightly raised above the surface. Different ingredients may account for the differences between the smooth and slightly raised lines, though this has not been scientifically investigated.[29]

Many papers have been written about etched carnelians. The seminal work was by Beck (1933). He identified two types of applications (white figures on the natural surface, black ones on whitened stone) and three periods in which different patterns were in use that would now be called Harappān, Early Historic, and Early Islamic. In his monograph on Taxila, Beck (1941, 3) identified a third application: black figures on the natural surface. Dikshit (1949) added two subtypes of decorations (black on whitened patches and black and white figures directly on the stone). He also separated the Early Historic period beads into North and South Indian groups. The latter is now identified as Pandukal. Margabandhu (1971; 1978, 35–40; 1985, 231–239) expanded the geographical range of some of Dikshit's beads, without negating the North/South dichotomy.

Outside India, the monograph by Reade (1979) made a strong case for etched carnelians of certain patterns being made in Mesopotamia contemporary with or earlier than Harappān levels.[30] Etched carnelians were produced in Iran at least from Sasanian times (Francis 1980) and this continued into the Early Islamic period, accounting for most, perhaps all, of Beck's Period III beads (Francis 1989e, 26). Beck (1933, 393) reported that inscribed carnelian plaques were being made in Iran in the 1930s. Mohammed Gorbanzedah, a knowledgeable Iranian dealer, informed me in the mid-1970s that this had ceased about fifty years before (Color Plate 33).

Charoenwongsa (1984)[31] surmised that the process was transferred to Thailand based on designs unknown in the Indian corpus. There are certainly a large number of etched beads in Myanmar, Thailand (e.g., Glover et al. 1984, 328; Glover 1990a, 167; 1990b, 17), and Vietnam that do not match any in India (Color Plate 41). Although no direct archaeological evidence has been found in Southeast Asia for etching carnelians, almost none would be expected. The bowl that held the alkali, the organic pen, and the little clay holder would be very difficult to recover, if they even survived. Only when the beads were etched before being perforated (see next paragraph) would there be direct evidence. It is not certain that all etched beads were made this way.

In addition to Sehwan, a few other North Indian manufacturing sites have been identified. At Sabaur, Bihar, etched and ordinary carnelian bead blanks, polished but unperforated, were found when a college was being built (Beck 1933, 386). Kosam (Kauśāmbī) yielded many etched carnelians, including blackened beads later etched with white designs[32] and decorated beads not yet perforated (Dikshit 1949, 5, 10–11).

Dikshit's (1949) "Southern Group" is now understood to be Pandukal production. Unperforated etched beads were found in Pandukal levels at Kaundinyapura (Dikshit 1968, 88–89) and Mahurjhari (Deo 1973, 32). K. Rajan (1992, personal communication) believed that the numerous etched carnelian beads at Koḍumaṇal were made locally. The beads were certainly made there, and he thought it unlikely that they were fashioned, shipped elsewhere to be decorated, and then shipped back to be used.

In the same vein, etched carnelians were probably made at Arikamēḍu. There is no evidence of production (Francis 1987b, 8), but none would have survived had they been etched after being drilled. A few etched carnelians have been found casually at Arikamēḍu, identical with beads from nearby Pandukal graves[33] (Color Plate 33).

Green Stone Collar Beads

Collar beads made of a soft opaque green stone (perhaps steatite) have been found at three early Indo-Pacific beadmaking sites. They have irregular outlines and are often decorated with seemingly random short incisions. Arikamēḍu yielded four, three in the Pondicherry Museum and one from the 1989–1992 excavation. Three were uncovered at Oc Eo (Malleret 1962a, 224). The largest number recorded is seven from Khlong Thom (A. Srisuchat 1987[34]; Francis 1989c, 27; personal observation at Wat Khlong Thom Museum).

Beads of this material (but not this shape) come from the surface and level III–IV at Karur, Tamil Nadu, and four beads, three of them collars, two with incisions, were found at Koḍumaṇal. Surface finds from the medieval site of Gangaikondacholapuram, Tamil Nadu, include many beads of various shapes in a similar stone. The source of the stone may be South India, but no evidence for making these beads has yet surfaced.

Lapis Lazuli

Lapis lazuli has long been desired in much of Eurasia. The only known ancient source is in Badakshan, northerneastern Afghanistan. Lapis lazuli beads appear sporadically at many North Indian sites[35] and may have been used in China.[36] In both cases, it reached these markets through overland routes; Schafer (1963, 231) was explicit about this in the Tang period.

Of the West Asian ports considered here, lapis lazuli was found only at Siraf (nine beads in the British Museum). None was at Aqaba, Quseir al-Qadim, or Berenike.

Lapis lazuli beads are much more common in South India.[37] Long square cylinders are most frequent, but there are a variety of shapes at Arikamēḍu. Uncut pieces at Koḍumaṇal suggest local working. The material was exported from Barbarikon, as confirmed in the *Periplus Maris Erythraei* (Casson 1989, 75), shipped to Muziris, and thence sent to Koḍumaṇal for cutting. One product involved in the commercial exchange was the typical Pandukal etched carnelian[38] (Figure 14.1; Color Plate 42).

Mantai had four lapis lazuli beads from the later period of the site, the fifth to the tenth centuries. These must also have arrived by sea. Three Mantai beads (a cornerless cube, an octagonal drop pendant, and a diamond tabular, though perforated differently) are paralleled in

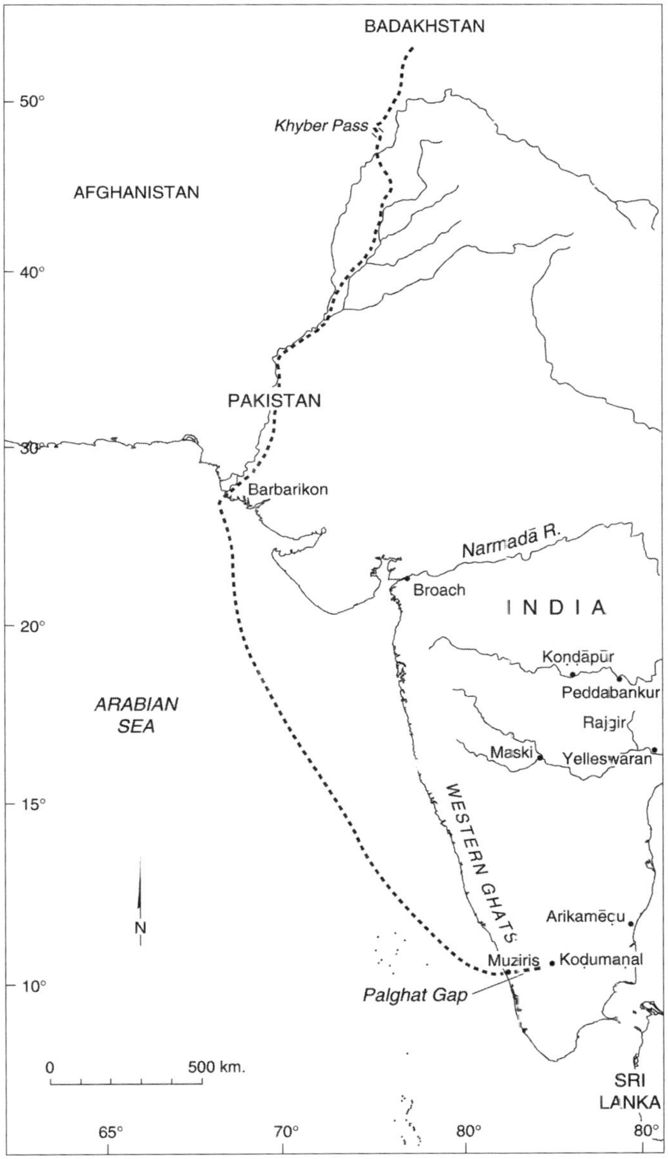

Figure 14.1. *Map of the Arabian Sea showing the route of exchange of South Indian etched carnelians for lapis lazuli.*

the Nishapur, Iran, assemblage, where they may have been cut (Francis 1987c, 35). No lapis lazuli beads are known from anywhere in Southeast Asia.

Jade

Jade, as already discussed, is the premier stone of the Chinese. Most jade in Asia is connected with Chinese culture and the trade was principally land-based and internal. The one exception is the Philippines. In the period Fox called the Early Metal Age (about 700 to 200 B.C.), jade beads make up 79 of 241 beads (32.8 percent) excavated from seven of nine sites (Francis 1989d, 7). It was much rarer in the preceding and following periods.[39]

Nephrite jade exists in the Philippines, and Fox (1970, 131) and Solheim (1981, 80 n. 5) suggested that the beads were of local origin. Jade axes are no doubt local, but the material is much different from that used for the beads. Villegas (1983, 17, 24) suggested Taiwan as a source. The most spectacular jade object in the Philippines is a bicephalic ear pendant from Duyong Cave, Palawan (Fox 1970, 129). It is certainly a Sa Huynh object (see chap. 13). Nephrite jade circular earrings of the *lingling-o* type, another Sa Huynh product, are also found in the Philippines.

Some of the Philippine beads have grooves on one end. Fox (1970, 116) thought these were an artifact of breaking the stone apart, but they are probably "dimples" to allow the drill a place to bite (Francis 1989d, 4, 12). Such grooves are found on some beads from Trang Kenh, Vietnam, dating to ca. 1000 B.C., as well as on one in the Seligman collection in the British Museum from "China." The similarities of beadmaking technology, the long evidence of jade ornament and beadmaking in Vietnam (Glover 1994, 7–8; Francis 1995b, 4; Nguyen 1996), and the bicephalic and *lingling-o* earrings all point to trade from Vietnam to the Philippines.

15

Organically Derived Gem Materials

Before glass and stone became staple luxuries, people employed materials from plants or animals for beads. There is an embarrassment of riches when considering organic bead materials. In the interest of conciseness, most are omitted here. This chapter concentrates on those that have been most important in the Asian maritime bead trade. Some have been passed over because they are used only coincidentally for beads. King fisher feathers[1] and camphor[2] are two examples. Another is "tortoiseshell,"[3] a trade item often mentioned in the literature, but with limited use as a bead.

A prominent bead material is marine shell.[4] Since Jackson (1917), there has been much written on its use as ornaments. Shell beads germane to this study include *Conus* shell spires traded from Iran to East Africa (Francis 1989e, 31); cowries, especially the "money cowry" (*Cypraea moneta*) from the Maldives; and shells in the Kula ring (Malinowski 1922). Although these are engaging topics, they are not expanded upon here. Most shell trade is not intramaritime but from the shore to the interior, as in New Guinea (Hughes 1977). Moreover, shell bead use in many places had waned by the end of the last millennium B.C. For example, in the Philippines before about 700 B.C., shell accounted for 85.7 percent of all excavated beads, but never more than 5.0 percent thereafter, and usually less than 0.5 percent (Francis 1989d, 7–9).

Four organic materials—amber, coral, ivory, and pearls—have been selected for attention. They were chosen because they have played critical roles in the bead trade, they have been universally honored as precious materials, and they have long been articles of commerce. Except for ivory, their principal use was for beads. Each of these materials also has rather (or as with amber and coral, very) restricted source areas. Because of their frequent appearance in the Asian maritime bead trade, their trade patterns often paralleled those of stone and glass beads.

This chapter terminates at the seventeenth century. The next chapter deals with the cessation of the old model in the Asian maritime bead trade in the nineteenth century and includes a few notes on these materials in that context. These four materials remained important items until that time, especially in China.

A word of caution should be entered before the discussion of specific organic gems. As in our day, especially with plastic so easily passed off as amber, there were attempts in the past to substitute materials of lower value for those more esteemed. Because of the nature of texts and translations, it is not always clear that the name of one or more of these actually refers to the item in question. Where a clarification can be made, it is; otherwise the texts are taken literally. Even if some imitations were successfully substituted, they would not change the overall picture.

Amber

Amber is the fossilized resin of certain trees. Upon burial, the exudation undergoes polymerization that renders it solid and resistant to some chemicals. As with many precious substances, small amounts of amber, and sometimes large deposits,[5] are found in many parts of the world. However, the chief deposit exploited since high antiquity has been under and adjacent to the Baltic Sea (Figure 15.1).

Amber has been admired for millennia and was widely traded (Todd 1993). Its ancient trade is complex and still being unraveled (see C.W. Beck and Bouzek 1993). Although it was obvious to many that amber was the sap of a tree, its precise nature was not understood for some time. In the fifth century B.C., Ktêsias wrote of trees in India that "supply the Indians with their amber" (McCrindle 1882, 21). He was apparently referring to lac.[6]

Pliny wrote at length about amber, "although, as yet it is fancied only by women" (Eichholz 1962, 186–203). He used his writing as "an opportunity for exposing the falsehoods of the Greeks" (Eichholz 1962, 187). Amber's origins had been ascribed to everything from lynx urine to the tears of the grieving sisters of Phaethon, who was transformed into poplar trees when he was struck by a thunderbolt. However, Roman conquests had gone far enough in Pliny's time that "It is well established that amber is a product of islands in the Northern Ocean, that it is known to the Germans as 'glaesum'" (Eichholz 1962, 195). This is the root of the English word "glass." The Greeks, who called the material *"electron,"* from which "electricity" is derived, had established the static electrical properties of amber.

Although amber has been identified in some tombs of the Eastern Han period in China (Yü 1967, 116–117), it has not been confirmed that it was Baltic amber, if, indeed, it was amber at all.[7] The Chinese knew about amber at an early date, and its true nature was discerned by the third century. The Tang poet Wei Yingwu wrote of it:

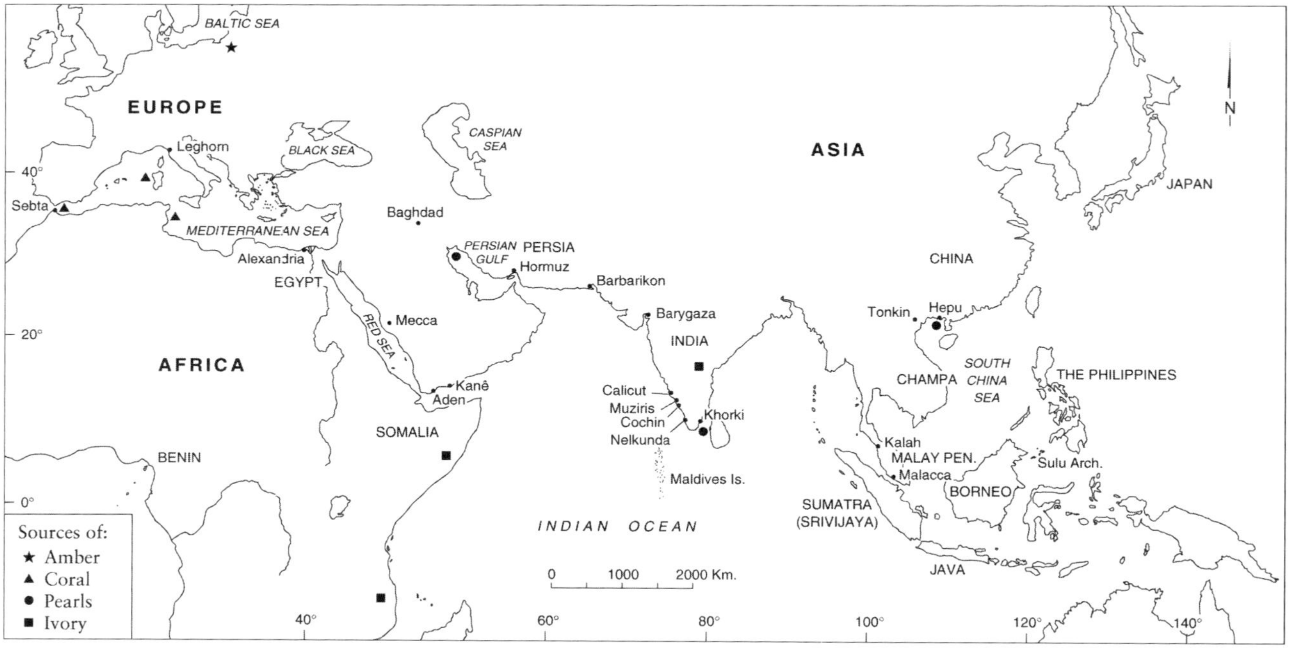

Figure 15.1. *Map showing the major sources, processing sites, and distribution of amber, coral, ivory, and pearls in the Eastern Hemisphere.*

Once it was the old "deity of chinaroot,"
But at bottom it is the sap of a cold pine tree.
A mosquito or gnat falls into the middle of it,
And after a thousand years may still be seen there. (Schafer 1963, 247)

Most amber entering China in Han and Tang times came across the overland route via Persia (Schafer 1963, 248). The overland bias is evident in works of the Northern Dynasties during the fifth and sixth centuries. The *Wei Shu,* written in A.D. 554, listed amber among the products brought by the *Bosi,* possibly in this case really meaning Persians, over the Silk Roads (Hirth and Rockhill 1911, 16 n. 1). The *Hou Zhou Shu,* of the Northern Zhou dynasty (557 to 581), also contained amber in an impressive tribute roll brought by Persians over the Silk Road (Wolters 1967, 72).

Sea routes were also employed. In Han and Tang times, amber was imported via Champa, Japan, and the South China Sea (Schafer 1963, 248). It was among the tributes sent to the southern Wei dynasty from central Vietnam (G. Wang 1958, 52). Later this route became the norm. The amber listed as an import in the *Song Shi,* written about 999 (Hirth and Rockhill 1911, 19), probably came in ships. The *Lingwai daida* (1178) said amber was obtainable on the Coromandel coast of Southeast India (Hirth and Rockhill 1911, 100 n. 8). Zhao Rugua (1225) noted that it was imported from Srivijaya, but was ultimately from the West or *Dashi* (Hirth and Rockhill 1911, 61).

In Ma Huan's account of Zheng He's voyages he first described the resin damar at Malacca and continued, "The sort of [damar] which is bright, clear and good, resembles golden amber; its name is *sub-tu-lu-ssu.* The foreigners make it up into cap-buttons and sell them. The 'water-amber' of this present day is this substance" (Mills 1970, 111 [insertion mine]). In a footnote (Mills 1970, n. 2), Mills suggested that this might be copal.[8] This seems to be the case, and it is interesting that the Chinese were distinguishing between copal (which is available in China) and amber at this date. Aside from the Malacca reference, Ma Huan noted the sale of amber only at the western ports of Aden and Hormuz and at Mecca (Mills 1970, 155, 171, 176). The products of Hormuz were described in greatest detail, and they included, "golden amber, amber beads, rosary beads, wax amber, black amber (of which the foreigner name is *sa-pai-chih*)" (Mills 1970, 171). Golden amber is clear amber, and wax amber refers to the opaque variety.[9] "Black amber" is a fairly common term for jet,[10] another precious organic gem, and Ma Huan may have been transliterating *sabaj,* the Arabic word for jet (Mills 1970, 171 n. 1).

Amber was also popular in India, but the first recorded experience of Europeans importing it there was a disappointment. William Edwards wrote to the (British) East India Company that at Ajmere in 1614 all the goods in "the great trunk of French wares" were acceptable "except the crystal,[11] amber and other beads and fans, which are nothing worth here" (Foster 1899, 16).

Amber had a better reception elsewhere in India. It sold out at Burhanpur in 1622 (Foster 1908, 66). It was in great demand at Agra in 1625 (Foster 1909, 175). It made a 25 percent profit at Ahmadabad in 1628, though less than in earlier years; "A smaller quantity should be sent, and the balance made up with rough amber" (Foster 1909, 196). In 1629, amber fetched twenty-nine shillings the pound at Ahmadabad or "Rs. 9 1/4 per seer"[12] (Foster 1909, 326). "A similar quantity will sell yearly; but the people here seem to prefer the amber 'rough and unwrought'" (Foster 1909, 334). Raw amber was demanded at Ahmadabad so that it could be worked in India and sold for a much cheaper price.

The British trade in amber reached beyond India. It was sent, along with coral, to Banten, Java, in 1646 (Sainsbury 1912, 134) and to the "King of Tywan" in 1671 (Sainsbury 1932, 58). In Indonesia under Dutch rule, the trade in amber was restricted to the Dutch East India Company (Vereenigde Oostindische Compagnie), also referred to as the "United Company" (Meilink-Roelofsz 1962, 238).

All true amber would have come from around the Baltic Sea. Richard Hakluyt wrote for the East India Company, "[Amber is] found on the coaste of Africa, about Gofala [Sofala], Mozambique and Malinde" (Birdwood 1891, 203 [insertions mine]). The Portuguese traded amber from Mozambique (Foster 1902, 250). The African product referred to here is a semifossilized gum (Brady and Clauser 1977, 212), a type of copal.

Amber is the softest of the materials under discussion here and is the first to disintegrate. It was also burned as incense. Consequently, archaeological discoveries of amber in tropical or semitropical regions are relatively rare.

Coral

Coral is a secreted limy or horny material produced by countless small sea polyps to build a structure to which they attach themselves. Precious coral, *Corallium rubrum,* is particular about where it lives, requiring a specific combination of salinity, depth, and temperature. Although it and some related species are found in small amounts elsewhere, the Mediterranean Sea is by far its most important source (Figure 15.1). The word for coral has given rise to the general word for "bead" in eastern Slavic Russian *(korolek,* pl. *koral'ki),* western Slavic Czech *(korálek,* pl. *korálo)* and Polish *(koralik),* Dutch *(kraal,* pl. *kralen),* and Yiddish *(krel).*

Coral processing centers are located along the Mediterranean littoral. They include towns in Italy, France, and on several islands. Except during the Roman period and more recent times, these places did not process the coral for export to Asia. On the western end of North Africa are other coral beadmaking centers. Tunisia is currently a major producer. In the past, Sebta (Ceuta)[13] in Morocco was important (Levtzion and Hopkins 1981, 130). The Sebta/Ceuta products went mostly to sub-Saharan Africa, in particular Benin, which lies outside the scope of this work, where they were of great cultural importance.

Again, the exact nature of coral was long misunderstood. It was referred to as a plant in many early sources because of its branching tendencies. In Europe, this was believed at least as late as 1633 when Gerard (1975, 1575–1578) listed coral and sponges in his *Herbal.* They were both considered mosslike plants.

The poet Sima Xiang, who died about 117 B.C, wrote the earliest reference to coral in China. In Han times, coral was known to be a product from the West (Wheatley 1959, 78). Its importation into North China overland by Persians parallels that of amber. It is mentioned in this context both in the Wei Shu, written in A.D. 554 (Hirth and Rockhill 1911, 16 n. 1), and in the roughly contemporary *Hou Zhou Shu* (Wolters 1967, 72).

On the other hand, by the fifth century, coral was being imported by sea from Funan (G. Wang 1958, 58). The *Sui Shu* (*History of the Sui,* 656 A.D.) noted only a single tribute mission from Boli, situated on the northern Sumatra coast, in 616. The description of the country says "they get corals from the sea" (Groeneveldt 1876, 83), but it is not immediately apparent whether that means that the people of Boli dived for coral themselves or got them from "across the sea," or even what sort of coral was meant.

The *Song Shi,* discussing the period of about 999, included mention of coral imports, probably entering via a maritime route (Hirth and Rockhill 1911, 19). Zhao Rugua (1225) recognized that coral "trees" were Western products sent to Srivijaya for sale to China (Hirth and Rockhill 1911, 61). He listed Baghdad and Mosul as sources (Hirth and Rockhill 1911, 103, 140), as well as the Cōḷa Kingdom in Southeast India (Hirth and Rockhill 1911, 96). He also understood that these were only transit stops. Its true source was where "The sea is two hundred feet deep, and the coral-tree is found in it." (Hirth and Rockhill 1911, 154) If Hirth and Rockhill correctly identified this "country" as al-Maghreb al-Aksa, the Chinese understood the true origin of coral by the thirteenth century. Al-Maghreb al-Aksa, "The Farthest West," is the Arabic name for Morocco.

The land-based Silk Roads functioned when China could suppress the western barbarians. The alchemist Zhang Zhun saw coral on one of his trips ordered by Genghis Khan. On his way from the khan's summer camp in northern Afghanistan to Samarkand he wrote: "On the road we met people coming from the West, carrying a lot of coral. Some of the officers in our escort bought fifty branches for two bars of silver. The largest was over a foot long. But as they were on horseback, it was impossible to prevent it from getting broken" (Waley 1931, 103–104).

Ma Huan's references to coral are very interesting. No coral is mentioned in Southeast Asia except at Aceh in northern Sumatra, which may be the same area as Boli discussed earlier. However, here the coral is not the Mediterranean variety:

> In the shallow water, about two *chang* [20 feet; 6.2 m] deep, at the side of the mountain there grows a marine tree; the people there recover it, and sell it as a valuable commodity; this is coral [and] the largest trees are two or three ch'ih [2 or 3 feet; 60 cm to 1 m] in height. At the top of the roots, there is a single large root as big as [one's] thumb; it is deep black like ink, and has a soft sheen like jade-stone; a little higher up it forks out into attractive fluttering branches; [and] the large piece at the tip of the roots can be cut into hat-buttons [and other such] articles. (Mills 1970, 123–124)[14]

This black coral is a gorgonian or horny coral, consisting principally of the complex protein gorgonin, rather than lime, which is the chief constituent of precious red coral. It is likely to be *Antipathes* sp., which has found limited use in jewelry. It is found in many parts of the world, but Southeast Asia remains an important source for it.

The other times Ma Huan mentioned coral it was precious red coral and was available only on the western coast of India and the Middle East, at Cochin, Calicut, Aden, Hormuz, and Mecca (Mills 1970, 136, 141–143, 155, 170–171, 176). Again, Hormuz had the greatest variety, "coral-tree beads, branches, and stems" (Mills 1970, 170–171). It is at Cochin, however, that we are given a short description of coral beadmaking:

> The people called 'Che-ti' are all property-owners; they specialize in purchasing such things as gem-stones, pearls, and aromatic goods; [then] they wait until visitors from the gem-ships of the Central Country[15] or from foreign ships of different countries come to buy. . . .
>
> [In the case of] coral-stems, the Che-ti reckon the weight in *chin* when they purchase them; they hire craftsmen, who cut up [the stems] into pieces, and on a lathe fashion them into beads, which are washed and polished until they are bright and clean; they, too, are bought [according to] their weight in *fen* and *liang*. (Mills 1970, 136 [insertions Mills'])

The *chin* was equal to 1.31 pounds (779 g), a *liang* was one-sixteenth of that weight, and a *fen* was 0.0119 troy ounces (0.37 g). In other words, the coral was bought in bulk and sold at jeweler's prices. The "Che-ti" are the Chetti,[16] a wealthy trading caste of South India, which Hutton (1977, 12) described as "a caste of bankers, brokers, shopkeepers, moneylenders and traders . . . being in general wealthy and of much business acumen, their social importance is greater than mere numbers would warrant."

Following the Portuguese conquest of Malacca in 1511, the *Ming shi* lamented that "coral-trees" were "among the goods that Malacca was accustomed to bring as tribute" (Groeneveldt 1876, 134). The strikingly long tribute list in which coral is only one item follows passages that describe the "Franks'" (Portuguese) conquest of Malacca and the Chinese emperor's unsuccessful attempt to get them to leave. Not only did the Portuguese not leave, but they proceeded to Guangzhou. According to Chinese sources, the governor imprisoned them, because their country was not recognized as a tributary kingdom. The emperor told the governor to buy their goods (rather than receive them as tribute) and send them away (Groeneveldt 1876, 133–134). The Portuguese histories, however, speak only of the ships being detained at Guangzhou while the men roamed freely, including doing some spying on defenses, and were allowed to trade (Chang 1934, 35–46). Later, of course, the Portuguese were admitted to Macao, "where some of them are always found" (Groeneveldt 1876, 134).

A few Portuguese did make it to Beijing, including

Tomé Pires, whose visit was not very successful (Cheng 1934, 48–53). A later mission to the capital in 1669, after being detained in Guangzhou for two years, brought a branch of coral as well as coral beads (and amber beads and ivory) in tribute (Fu 1954–1955, 86).

Coral has long been favored in India, as well. It is one of the few easily identifiable gems in the *Mahābhārata* epic, where it occurs frequently. It was specifically worn on strings or gold chains (Lad 1979, 191–192). The *Vāyu Purāṇa,* one of the earliest Purāṇa,[17] speaks of obtaining coral from Aṅgadvīpa, "famous for its mines of gold and for coral, being near the salt sea" (Wheatley 1961, 178). The place has not been identified further than being somewhere in the Malay-Indonesian world. The coral may have been either a Southeast Asian variety related to *Corallium rubrum* or transshipped from the Mediterranean.

The first-century *Periplus Maris Erythraei* recorded the importation of coral to Barygaza (Broach), Muziris, and Nelkynda in India (Casson 1989, 81, 85); Kanê in Arabia[18] (Casson 1989, 67); and Barbarikon on the Indus (Casson 1989, 75). It was being drained away from the Roman Empire especially to India. The people of newly conquered Gaul could no longer afford it, so great was the demand abroad (Warmington 1928, 263). Coral beads at Berenike, Egypt, are in contexts suggesting that they were being exported, not locally used (Francis 2001).

Coral always maintained its importance in the Asian maritime bead trade. In the tenth and eleventh centuries it was a major commodity. Coral from Sardinia and North Africa was shipped through Alexandria to Asian markets (Goitein 1973, 247–248). The "eastward pull" in coral sales is evident in a mid–eleventh century fragment found in the Cairo Geniza. "Corals are weak in Jerusalem, for it is a poor town. In any case, bring them or a part of them, for success is in the hand of God. If Persians happen to arrive, they may buy them" (Goitein 1973, 107). It was among the most important exports from Egypt to India, and its sale was stable over time (Goitein 1961, 170; 1963, 198).

It was still a requisite when Europeans arrived in India. When Vasco da Gama reached Calicut in 1498, the Zamorin gave him a letter for the Portuguese king requesting gold, silver, coral, and scarlet (Birdwood 1891, 163). Around 1620, the Mogul court forbade coral imports by the British to their factory in Surat, so the British just sent it to other ports (Gokhale 1962, 276).

The role of the coral trade was underscored in a letter from the officers of the East India Company in Surat to London in 1639: "Next to broadcloth, coral is 'the most stable and vendible commodity' that Europe produces" (Foster 1912, 208). In the next year, the minutes of the Company in London recorded: "a double provision of coral (which yields more advantage than all other commodities) [is] to be sent [to India] . . . no commodity [is] offering so much profit as coral" (Sainsbury 1909, 54–55 [insertions in brackets mine]). The minutes of the Company on 1 November 1641 listed goods to be sent to India, among them ivory and "ammell" (enamels). However, coral still reigned supreme: "The court taking into consideration the good to be reaped by having such a commodity ready bought, which never yields less than eighty percent profit, sometimes even a hundred" (Sainsbury 1909, 204).

A few decades later the French jeweler Jean-Baptiste Tavernier observed:

> Although coral does not rank among precious stones in Europe, it is nevertheless held in high esteem in the other quarters of the globe. . . .
>
> The common people wear it and use it as an ornament for the neck and arms throughout Asia, but principally towards the north in the territories of the great Mogul, and beyond them, in the mountains, of the Kingdoms of Assam and Bhutan. (V. Ball 1889, 132, 136)

With the lucrative nature of the coral trade and the fact that Britain did not produce it, the East India Company had to search for the perfect supplier. Several Mediterranean ports, presumably with cutting facilities, were contacted, especially between 1635 and 1637: Venice

(Sainsbury 1907, 76, 97), Marseilles (Sainsbury 1907, 84, 120, 148), Genoa (Sainsbury 1907, 263), and even Rouen (Sainsbury 1907, 173–174) were tried. On 27 January 1636 it was recorded, "Mr. Bowen ordered to write to Messers. Cogill and Honnywod and express the Company's displeasure at being charged 8,000 crowns for coral which they have not received" (Sainsbury 1907, 148). Finally, a supplier in Leghorn (Lugarno, Italy) was found that met the Company's satisfaction. Leghorn was recorded as the coral supplier from then on (Sainsbury 1909, 1912), except for one notice of Genoa (Sainsbury 1912, 134).

The economics of the coral trade was not unlike that of amber. There was a demand for the raw product to be processed in India, which, as we have seen, was very much in evidence in the early fifteenth century and no doubt much earlier. President Breton and others at Swally Marine (Surat) reported on 30 March 1646 that the Portuguese imported coral to India:

> [The coral beads are] 'exceedingly well liked, but so dear that no man dares venture upon them, rendered so (we conceive) by the extraordinary charge of their making, whereas in these parts those artifacers [artisans] labour for little, and of the [raw] coral they buy of us make beads which, being cheap, are of readier vend than these' [made in Europe]. (Foster 1914, 36 [insertions in brackets mine])

Ivory

Ivory is derived from the teeth of large mammals, especially elephants. These magnificent creatures once roamed most of the world, but their range has been seriously decreased, due principally to the demand for ivory.

Modern elephants are of two species, different enough to be classified as separate genera. The larger African elephant, *Loxodonta africana,* is nearly impossible to domesticate and produces the biggest and best tusks. The Asian species, *Elephas maximus,* remains an important beast of burden and work. It rarely breeds in captivity and the domestic stock must be replenished through newly captured animals. The ranges of both species of this intelligent creature are wide (Figure 15.1). Walrus and other ivories were used in northern Europe in early times (Clark 1986, 14).

Ivory has been exploited for beads and other ornaments since the Upper Paleolithic period in Europe. In China, its use dates as far back as about 5000 B.C. It continued to be popular there even as the elephant became locally extinct (D. Liu 1984). It has been employed largely for carvings and furniture fittings. Beads were often a side product, utilizing the small and otherwise discarded bits of the tusk. Specialized uses included belt toggles (Cammann 1962) and sometimes seals (Lai 1976, xii, 21). Elephants disappeared from West Asia and North China by the mid–first millennium B.C. They became rare, if not extinct, in South China around 300 B.C.[19] (Bishop 1921).

In Tang China at least some walrus ivory was brought from eastern Russia via Korea (Laufer 1913, 323, 338). Narwhal and whale ivory were also used in China, as was fossil ivory (Cammann 1962, 64–66). On the latter, the *Shi lu* of Kang Xi in 1720 reported: "Now in the Arctic regions of Russia there are rats as huge as elephants, which travel underground and die whenever they meet the wind and sun. Their bones are similar to ivory. The aborigines use their bones to make bowls, saucers, combs and the like. We have seen these utensils, and therefore, We believe the account is true" (Fu 1966, 133).

Once local sources of ivory were exhausted, the Chinese imported it from farther and farther away. North China obtained it from the Persians, as stated in the *Wei Shu,* completed in A.D. 554 (Hirth and Rockhill 1911, 16 n. 1). However, the maritime route was used even earlier. In late Han times, ivory was imported from Tonkin (Yü 1967, 177–178) and in the fifth century from Funan (G. Wang 1958, 52). By the Tang period, the Chinese had information about African ivory. The *Yuyang Zazu* by Duan Zhengshi (died A.D. 863) described a place Persian merchants visited where the people drank the blood of their cattle and sometimes sold their women into slavery. It produced ambergris and ivory. It can hardly be any place other than Somalia (Duyvendak 1949, 12–13).

By Song times, the Chinese maritime trade in ivory was so well developed that sources were numerous. The amounts of ivory and other luxury goods (rhinoceros horn, strings of pearls, aromatics, and incense) increased dramatically. From 1049 to 1053 the annual importation of such goods amounted to 53,000 units (whatever a unit was) and by 1175 had reached more than 500,000 units (Duyvendak 1949, 16). Tributes of ivory are recorded twice from Srivijaya and once (six tusks) from western Borneo (Groeneveldt 1876, 64–65, 109). The latter was acting as a middleman, because there are no elephants on the island. Similarly, Java sent ivory as tribute during the Yuan dynasty (Groeneveldt 1876, 27).

During the Southern Song period, ivory was also a staple in the maritime trade beyond tribute missions. Zhao Rugua (1225) listed many sources: Tonking, Cambodia, Annam, places on the Malay Peninsula, Sumatra, Java, Southeast India, and the Arab countries (Hirth and Rockhill 1911). The best was the Somalian variety (Hirth and Rockhill 1911, 128). Big tusks are recorded from Pemba or Madagascar (Hirth and Rockhill 1911, 149). Srivijaya imported African ivory from the Arab world (Hirth and Rockhill 1911, 61), because it was judged superior to that from Southeast Asia, particularly Annam and Cambodia (Hirth and Rockhill 1911, 232).

Zheng He's voyages in the early Ming period brought a few notices of ivory or elephants' teeth. Fei Xin said that the Chinese imported it from Cambodia and Thailand (Rockhill 1915, 75, 110) and reexported it to the Moluccas (Rockhill 1915, 66). Ma Huan also listed only Southeast Asia sources: Champa (central Vietnam), Java, and Srivijaya (Mills 1970, 81, 85, 88, 106).

Arab traders, who forged important links between Africa and China, mentioned ivory only occasionally. Abu Zaid in 916 wrote that Kalah, identified herein with Kedah in Malaysia, was the most important port for ivory (Tibbets 1979, 33). Kalah would have been a key distribution center, as it was for other goods. Ibn Said (died 1274) noted ivory from Langabalus, one of the Andaman-Nicobar Islands, which is unlikely (Tibbets 1979, 58). Ja'far ibn Rashid is quoted in the *'Aja'ib al-Hind* as saying that in 945 he sailed to Waqwaq, and found many things desired both by the locals and the Chinese, including ivory (Tibbets 1979, 160). Waqwaq has never been identified.[20]

In Japan, ivory came to be widely used for netsuke (Okada 1976, 5–6) and *ojime* (Okada 1976, 45; Mikoshiba and Bushell 1979), especially from the Tokugawa period, beginning in 1603. The Japanese used ivories of different types, all of which reached the island nation by sea. Ivory carving was elevated to an important minor industry (Griffis 1888, 710). Until the recent ban, Hong Kong was the chief carver and Japan by far the biggest consumer of the material in the world (*New York Times* 1989; Stevens 1990).

Indonesia continued its role as a merchant in ivory, even from islands that had no elephants. As with amber, in colonial times the Dutch East India Company controlled the trade in raw ivory (Meilink-Roelofsz 1962, 238). It was principally concentrated at Banten, to which tusks had to be imported (Meilink-Roelofsz 1962, 148).

In India, ivory's documented use is much later than in China. No ivory ornaments are known from the Upper Paleolithic or Mesolithic periods (Francis 1981, 1982e). Sankalia (1974) recorded none in his survey of prehistoric India. Only one ivory bead is recorded in the Harappān period (Beck 1940, 408),[21] though combs (Mackay 1938, 542; 1943, 196), box and chest decorations (Mackay 1938, pl. CIX 3, CX 14; 1943, 233), and dice (Marshall 1931, pl. CXXXII; Mackay 1938, pl. CXLIII 18–54; 1943, 171) have been found.

Ivory's use was well established by Early Historic times (Margabandhu 1985, 80–82). India was an exporter for centuries. An ivory figurine found at Pompeii is assumed to have come from there (Margabandhu 1985, 80–82). The *Periplus* noted ivory as an export from Barygaza (Broach), Limurikê (South India, whose main port was Muziris), and Dêsarênê (on the east coast, north of the Kṛishṇā estuary) (Casson 1989, 81, 85, 89). Dêsarênê produced a particular type of ivory, called "bosare" or "bôsarê," perhaps the product of an esteemed black elephant (Yule and Burnell 1989, 489).[22] Indian ivory is shown being brought into Byzantium on a carved ivory object dated to about A.D. 500 (Clark 1986, 17–18).

First via the Arabs and then via the Europeans, India began to import the larger and superior African ivory. A letter from Francis Fetiplace and Robert Hughes from Agra to the East India Company in London, in December 1617, gave a short account of the then current trade:

> Elephant's teeth will also sell in Agra in good quantities; that which is sold in Guzeratt is brought hither, and yet little of it spent here, only is trimmed and so sent to Lahore, where the women wear them for manacles or bracelets for their arms, which is the greatest occasion of the venting of that commodity. It is worth in Agra a better price than in Suratt; but the way is long, and they are subject to cracking with the heat of the sun. Those which buy them there saw them off in short pieces before they bring them hither. Hereof is much landed this year, and more than we think will be suddenly sold. (Foster 1902, 250)

Pearls

Pearls result from marine or freshwater mollusks depositing successive layers of nacre over something that irritates their bodies. The final pearl may be connected to the inner lining of the shell or be detached. Pearls have been so long esteemed and in such widespread use as ornaments that the word for "pearl" is synonymous with "bead" in many languages.[23] Pearls are found in many places (Figure 15.1), but the chief locations in Asian waters have been the Persian Gulf and the Gulf of Mannar. The estuary of the He River in Guandong, China, was an important pearling station, but principally served the Chinese market (Schafer 1952). As with all natural resources, pearl beds can be overexploited. However, if not completely destroyed, they will recover in time.

The pearl fisheries of the Persian Gulf, especially those around the island of Bahrain, probably have a very ancient history. Bibby (1969, 156–157, 163–165) contended that the hero Gilgamesh dived for pearls to ensure his immortality. He averred that pots with snakes and beads, in at least one case a pearl,[24] were buried under houses in memory of this exploit. If he was correct in identifying "fish-eyes" with pearls (Bibby 1969, 189),[25] then Babylonian texts dating from the nineteenth century B.C. indicate trade in them from Bahrain to Mesopotamia.

In the Indian context, Maloney (1969, 14) believed that the pearls in the *Atharva Veda,* of about 800 B.C. (Shende 1949, 367), either were imports from the Persian Gulf or came from the Gulf of Cambay. This may have been too early for the exploitation of the Gulf of Mannar. The legendary Pandiya brothers, the traditional founders of the three South Indian Tamil Kingdoms, are supposed to have established their empire on the strength of the pearl trade (Maloney 1969, 13). Pearls are naturally interwoven into the Sangam Tamil literature. Those inside a hollow golden anklet mark the climax of one of the most popular of the poems, the *Cilappatikāram (The Lay of the Anklet)* (Zvelebil 1973: 177–178). It is significant that the Tamil word for pearl, *mutu,* whence comes the Hindi word *moti,* has no Prakrit form. It is apparently Dravidian (Tamil) in origin (Subramoniam 1961, 299; Maloney 1969, 15).

The pearl trade in Roman times involved different parts of India. The *Periplus Maris Erythraei* spoke of pearls being exported from Oman and Kanê in Arabia to Barygaza (Broach) in India (Casson 1989, 73). They were said to be inferior to (South) Indian pearls and were apparently destined for a North Indian market.

In South India at Limurikê (Dravadian country), particularly Muziris, an outstanding export was "good supplies of fine-quality pearls" (Casson 1989, 85). Sri Lanka and the Ganges estuary are also credited with pearl fisheries (Casson 1989, 89–91). Indian pearls were highly esteemed in Rome. Pliny (Eichholz 1962, 213) listed them as the second most valued gemstones in the Empire, particularly those from India and Arabia.

The import of pearls to Rome caused disgust among several commentators. Pliny (Eichholtz 1962, 173–177) attributed the beginning of the excessive use of the "effeminate" gem to Pompey's defeat of Mithradates VI (66 B.C.). He mourned, "To think that it is of pearls, Great Pompey, those wasteful things meant only for women, of pearls, which you yourself cannot and must not wear, that your portrait is made!" (Eichholtz 1962, 175). The pearls of Pompey's portrait may have come from the Persian Gulf, but those worn by Gaius and Nero were likely from the Gulf of Mannar. St. Paul also thought that pearls were excessive: "women should adorn themselves modestly and sensibly in seemly apparel, not with braided hair or gold or pearls or costly attire. . . ." (1 Tim. 2:9, RSV).[26]

By Marco Polo's time (Komroff 1953, 280–281), Korkai (see chap. 12) was no longer the seat of pearl fishing in South India, because it was situated several miles from the sea as a result of the silting of the Tambaraparni River. The business had moved to Kayal, now Palaiyakayal (Old Kayal). Several writers, including Marco Polo (Komroff 1953) and Le Beck (1799) for the Gulf of Mannar (see also Streeter 1996) and Belgrave (1934) for the Persian Gulf, left eyewitness descriptions of the old methods of diving for pearls and processing them.

On the other side of the Gulf of Mannar, Sri Lanka also exploited its pearl wealth. It is frequently noted as being rich in pearls in Chinese accounts (see below) as well as several Arab sources (Imam 1990, 174). We have noticed the close Sri Lankan–Persian connections in regard to Mantai. While Mantai was still flourishing, the king of Sri Lanka sent Khusraw I (ruled A.D. 531–578), the Sasanian king of Persia, ten elephants, two hundred thousand pieces of teakwood, and seven pearl divers (Imam 1990, 173). The Persian Gulf and the Gulf of Mannar were the two leading pearl-yielding regions, so it is interesting to see that one would shift highly skilled workers to the other. Was it merely a mark of friendship or was there some practical necessity for it? Were the Persian Gulf beds recovering from a period of low production, creating a sudden need for more divers? Or did the Sri Lankans bring some special skill with them?

In China, Guanzi (693 to 642 B.C.) wrote of trade with outside countries involving jade, pearls, and gold, of which the first two were most esteemed (Laufer 1974, 190). The *Han Shu* of the Western (Former) Han dynasty said:

> The trading boats of the barbarians which carried them from one place to another were also engaged in trade as well as in rapacity. It was a great danger to sail on these boats. Besides, the seas were rough and often times they perished on the sea. It took those who did not quit the round trip several years to return [to China]. [They brought back] large pearls with a circumference of slightly below two inches. (Yü 1967, 172 [insertions Yü's])

During the Eastern (Latter) Han, the desire for pearls was fulfilled in two ways. One was from the pearl fisheries at Hepu, at the estuary of the He River. The other was trade from Tongkin, perhaps modern Hanoi. Hepu provided most pearls, but large and rare ones were imported via Tongkin; a tribute mission from Japan included especially "white pearls" (Yü 1967, 177–186). The Southeast Asian connection continued; in the fifth century, there was a report of pearls coming from Funan (G. Wang 1958, 52).

In Tang times, foreign pearls were still greatly valued. They were imported by tribute-bearers from India (A.D. 642), Champa (749), Ceylon (750), and Japan (839) (Schafer 1963, 244). The *Xin Tang Shu (New History of the Tang)* by Ouyang Xiu in 1063 noted that a king in northern Sumatra wore "a piece of flowered silk or cotton, adorned with pearls" (Groeneveldt 1876, 84). This is a rare mention of wearing pearls by sewing them onto cloth, a fashion that was to grip Europe a few centuries later. The exotic and somewhat dangerous nature of the regions in which these pearls were supposed to be caught is revealed in Wang Jian's poem, *The South:*

> *In the southern land many birds sing;*
> *Of towns and cities half are unwalled.*
> *The country markets are thronged by*
> *wild tribes;*
> *The mountain-villages bear river-names.*
> *Poisonous mists arise from the damp*
> *sands;*
> *Strange fires gleam through the night-rain.*

> *And none passes but the lonely seeker of pearls*
> *Year by year on his way to the South Sea.*
> *(Schafer 1963, 244)*

Pearls figure prominently among goods imported in Song times (Duyvendak 1949, 16). They were tribute items from Srivijaya in the late eleventh century, according to the *Song Shu* (Groeneveldt 1876, 66). In 1156 the king of Srivijaya sent a present of pearls to a Chinese minister. The minister had died before they could reach him, so the emperor took them, paying what was perceived to be their full value (Groeneveldt 1876, 67).

Zhao Rugua, quoting the *Lingwai daida* by Zhou Qufei (1178), said that the best pearls came from Ceylon, the Arab countries, and eastern Sumatra, though South China also produced them (Hirth and Rockhill 1911, 229). He listed many pearl producers, including eastern Sumatra, Java, the southeast and southwest coasts of India, Baghdad, the Arab world, Oman, Kish, and Luzon in the Philippines (Hirth and Rockhill 1911). He said that they were sacred on Borneo (Hirth and Rockhill 1911, 160) and noted that Srivijaya obtained them from the Arab world and was a major collecting center. Zhou Qufei had said that only seed pearls were a product of Srivijaya (Hirth and Rockhill 1911, 61, 63 n. 1).

Arab traders in the region placed pearl origins within Indonesia. Al-Idrisi (died 1165) identified Srivijaya as having pearl fisheries, as did Ibn Sa'id (died 1274) a century later (Tibbetts 1979, 51, 58). Wassaf (ca. 1300) said Java was a source (Tibbetts 1979, 60). The *'Aja'ib al-Hind* (ca. A.D. 1000) related a charming story in which one Sa'id gave a traveler going to Kedah enough goods to buy a fish. When the fish was being dressed, an oyster with a fine pearl was found inside (Tibbetts 1979, 48). Burini (973–1048) came to the conclusion that there were no more pearls in the Gulf of Mannar because the oysters had migrated to Sofala, where they were then being fished (Tibbetts 1979, 166).

Without assuming an immigration of oysters, Sofala, now in Mozambique, was apparently a pearl source for some time. In the late sixteenth century the Friar Joaõ Dos Sanctos described pearl fishing around the island group now controlled by France, the Bassas da India, a short distance east-southeast of what was then Sofala:[27]

> There are many Oysters which breede the Pearle, which they take with diving, fastning a Cord to their middle, and holding stones in their hands (which when they are at the bottome they let goe) and fill a Basket, which is let downe from the Boat with a Cord, having a stone in it to make it sinke, which being full is drawne up; and then to it againe. They are so used to it that they will continue halfe a quarter of an houre under the water. (Dos Sanctos 1905, 229)

Ma Huan mentioned pearls several times, and his entries are of interest. He said that the king of Bengal sent "men to travel on board ship to the various foreign countries to trade," for pearls, among other things, "which are presented as tribute to the Central Country" (Mills 1970, 165). At Sri Lanka he said:

> In the sea there is a stretch of snow-white floating sand; when the sun or moon shines on the sand, it sparkles brilliantly like ripples on the water; [and] every day the pearl-oysters collect together on the sand. The king has constructed a pearl-pond; [and] once in two or three years he orders men to take pearl-oysters and pour them out into the pond; he sends men to guard over this pond; they wait until the [pearl-oysters] are decayed and rotten, then with water they scour out the pearls, and take them to the officials; [but] it also happens that they are stolen and sold in other countries. (Mills 1970, 128 [insertions Mills'])

This account is contrary to all other accounts of fishing pearls at the Gulf of Mannar. Pearl oysters don't habitually gather on sand, no matter how brilliantly it sparkles. They could have been dived for and put into a pond in which they would eventually die. Waiting several years for this to happen seems a waste of time, not to mention being risky, as the notice of them being stolen attests. Neither Marco Polo in the early 1290s nor Le Beck in 1797 mentioned anything like that.

At Hormuz, Ma Huan saw pearls as large as a longan fruit and one weighing some 69 grains (4.5 g) (Mills 1970, 170). In Cochin the Chetti merchant caste handled them. Ma Huan reckoned that a pearl weighing 5 carats (1.3 g) was worth 3.73 kg of silver (Mills 1970, 136 n. 2).

Pearls as tribute were mentioned several times in the *Ming Shu*. In 1321 Java gave eight large ones (Groeneveldt 1876, 36). In 1417 Sulu sent pearls and in 1421 gave one weighing seven *taels* (more than 9 ounces avoirdupois or about 260 g) (Groeneveldt 1876, 105). Pearls were in the long list of items Malacca formally sent to China composed in 1537 (Groeneveldt 1876, 136).

The *Ming Shu* said that the Chinese had not heard of the Sulu Archipelago before the Ming period. The first entry on Sulu was "shortly after the year 1368" (Groeneveldt 1876, 105); that is, the first year of the Ming dynasty. Sulu raiders attacked Borneo, only to be driven back by the Javanese of Majapahit (Groeneveldt 1876, 103). At the end of the entry on Sulu is the following: "There is a pond with pearls in it and at night their light is seen on the surface of the water; the natives sell pearls to the Chinese and on the large ones enormous profits are made. When the (Chinese) merchant-vessels leave, a few of their men are detained as hostages for their coming back again" (Groeneveldt 1876, 105).

Ignoring the night-lights and the poor hospitality shown to Chinese merchants, we again have a pearl pond as described for the Gulf of Mannar. The use of this pond is not elaborated here and it is not clear if it was the same as at Sri Lanka. It is suggestive (though not definitively) of some sort of cultivation of pearl mollusks. Much depends upon the attributes of the pond.

The Chinese had ample opportunity to learn about Sulu. In 1417 three "kings" and 340 retainers paid their respects to the emperor, who granted them status equal to that of Malaccan envoys. They stayed nearly a month, but one of them died. His wife, concubines, and eighteen followers remained for three years to mourn him. The wife later sent the large pearl mentioned above. The last "tribute mission" was in 1423, but the Chinese kept in touch, noting the unsuccessful attack on Sulu by the "Franks" between 1573 and 1619 (Groeneveldt 1876, 103–105).

The *Song Shu* offers us one more interesting story about a pearl. This time, it is the tale of a war fought over one. In this account, Polo and Bruni are approximately modern Brunei and Pu-ni about where Kuching, Eastern Malaysia, is located; both are on Borneo. Pahang and Djohore (Johore) are on mainland Malaysia:

> In the period Wan-li (1573–1619) the son of the viceroy of Djohore was to marry the daughter of the king of Pahang. When the marriage was about to take place, the viceroy brought his son to Pahang and the king of the country gave a feast, where all his relatives were present. The son of the king of Polo (Bruni) was the son in law of the king of Pahang; he offered a cup of wine to the viceroy, who then saw that he had on his finger a large pearl of great beauty, and wanting to have it, he offered a very high price. The prince would not part with it, on which the viceroy became angry, went home and came back with soldiers to attack the country. The people of Pahang were taken unprepared; they dispersed without fighting and the king fled to the gold-mountains, along with the Prince of Bruni. The king of Pu-ni (western coast of Borneo) was the elder brother of the king's wife; when he heard of all this, he came with his people to assist those of Pahang and then the viceroy of Djohore was compelled to retire, after having burnt and plundered very much. (Groeneveldt 1876, 137–138)

Knowledge of the precise nature of pearls was very slow in coming. Aristotle thought they were oyster hearts (Martiere 1555, 95r). Arrian noted that "Some writers allege that in swarms of oysters, as among bees, individuals distinguished for size and beauty act as leaders" (McCrindle 1960, 115). Pliny the Elder wrote,

> [W]hen the season of the yeare requireth that they should engender, they seeme to yawne and gape, and so do open wide; and then (by report) they conceive a certaine moist dew as seed, wherewith they swell and grow big, and when time commeth labor to be delivered hereof; and the fruit of these shell fishes are the Pearles, better or worse, great or small, according to the qualitie and quantitie of the dew which they received. (Newsome 1964, 94)

Both the Chinese (Schafer 1952, 156, 160) and Indians (Shastri 1968, 186–187) conceived of pearls as coming from any number of animals. When Balboa discovered pearl fisheries in the Caribbean, he was full of age-old questions (Did oysters move about in swarms? Was the pearl soft in the shell?), and he recorded all the information he could gather pertaining to their fishing (Martiere 1555, 94v–95v, 139v–142v).

Of these four materials, only ivory and pearls are found in the seas and lands adjoining the Asian mainland.

Part Seven: Drawing to a Close

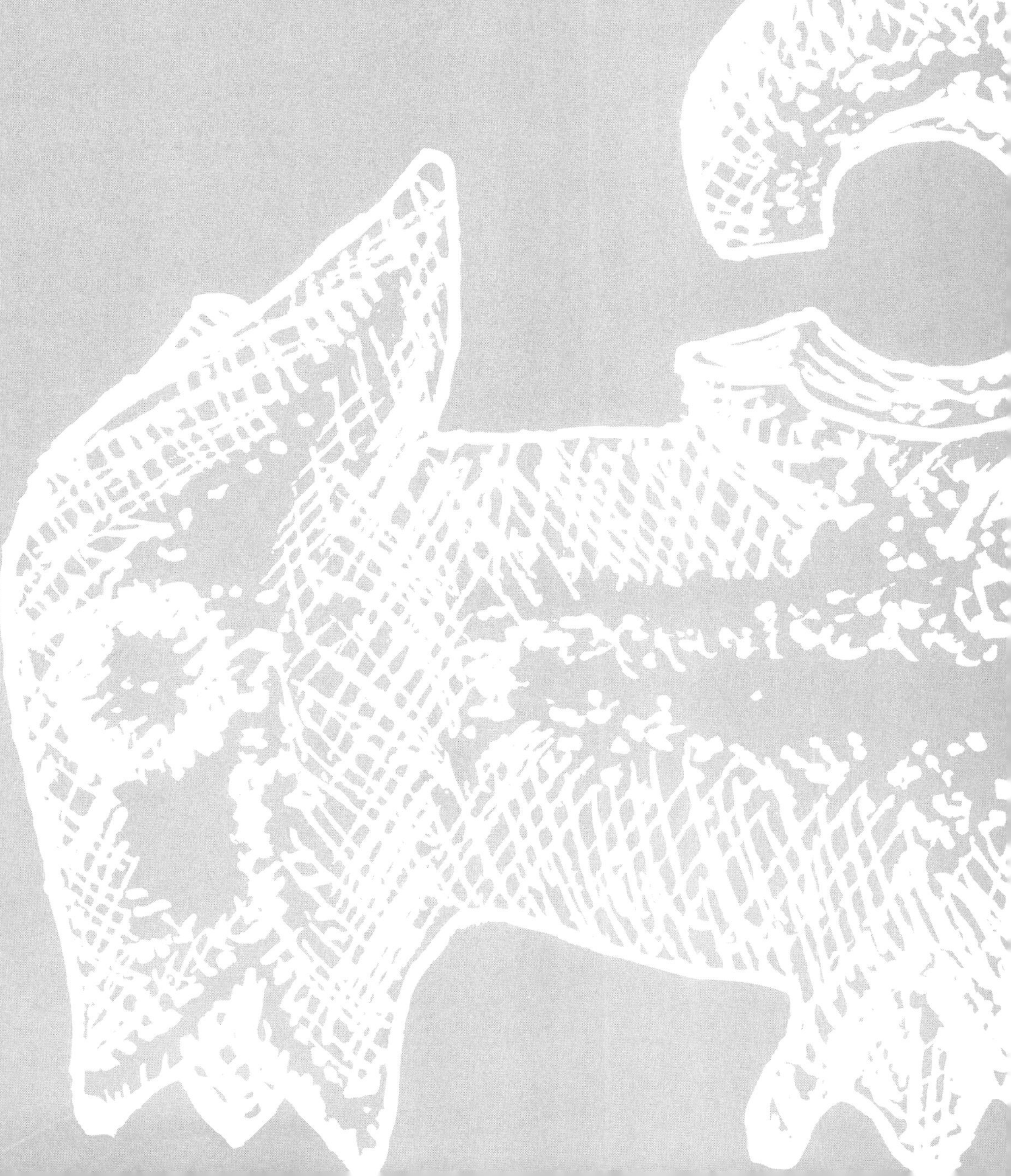

16

The End of the Asian Maritime Bead Trade

This chapter deals with the end of the bead trade in the Asian maritime region as controlled by Asians themselves. That is, we shall try to define the point at which European beads and traders supplanted Asian traders and beads. The Europeans followed the ancient inter-Asian trade routes and eventually came to dominate them by making themselves the principal merchants and their beads the predominate ornamental commodities. They also became politically ascendant in the region.[1]

Earlier studies on American (Francis 1986g; 1992c) and West African (Francis 1993a) bead trade networks found that commercial patterns were affected quite rapidly after the arrival of the Europeans, though in different ways. The 1490s began an extensive shift in worldview and trade routes. In 1492, Christopher Columbus sailed to what he thought were "the Indies" (as most of Asia was then known). His contemporaries soon recognized that he had found a New World. Five years later, Vasco da Gama rounded the Cape of Good Hope, sailed to Zanzibar, took on an Arab pilot, and crossed over to Calicut, India. These events affected the bead trade everywhere

In the civilizations of Mesoamerica and the Andes the bead trade had consisted of moving raw materials to a central locale, processing them, and distributing finished products to outlying regions. The Spanish quickly seized the centers of these civilizations. They destroyed the old bead industries and introduced outside beads. Soon both native and Spanish traders were using the old trade routes but carrying new beads (Francis 1992c).

In less culturally advanced northern America, Europeans moved into the heartland slower, settling first on the coasts and ever pushing back the "frontier." From its edge, native traders took European beads through the old trade routes. They swiftly became staples across the continent (Francis 1992c).

In West Africa, trade routes traditionally went north to south, communicating with Arab North Africa. As Europeans visited, traded, and settled along the coast, the direction of trade was reversed. European beads moved north and east via native coastal dwellers, replacing the old beads at a swift rate (Francis 1993a).

In each case, the old trade routes (the most efficient lines between population centers for a given mode of transport) became the new ones. Native traders remained in charge except where colonies were founded. New beads (Venetian glass, Baltic amber, Indian carnelians, and Chinese glass) rapidly replaced the beads that had dominated for millennia (catlinite, jade, turquoise, and shell in the Americas; Middle Eastern and Indian glass and Indian stone beads in Africa). Did this happen in Asia?

Van Leur (1955, 159–162) pointed out the strength of the Asian powers when the first Europeans sailed into the Indian Ocean. Asia was more organized than Africa or America, immune to European diseases, and advanced in weapons development. The continent resisted European encroachment commercially and politically for a long time. He suggested a date of about 1650 for the triumph of European commerce in Asia. More recently, Simkin (1968, 252) suggested that Asian trade remained in Asian hands until the late eighteenth century. How accurate are those assessments as applied to the Asian maritime bead trade? To answer this question we shall consider five representative geographic areas in the Asian littoral (Figure 16.1):

1. The Philippines, the western terminus of trade for the Spanish across the Pacific.
2. Indonesia, especially the Greater Sundas (Borneo, Sulawesi, Sumatra, and Java), the eastern end of the Indian Ocean, and the southern end of the South China Sea.
3. China, the great power on the eastern edge of Asia.
4. India, the great power in the center of the Asian maritime trade.
5. Madagascar, as an example of the western border of the trade.[2]

By examining the transformation of the bead trade in these areas we can form an idea of the momentum of change from the "old way" (products, routes, traders all Asian in origin) to the "new way" (products and most traders outsiders, with extended trade routes).

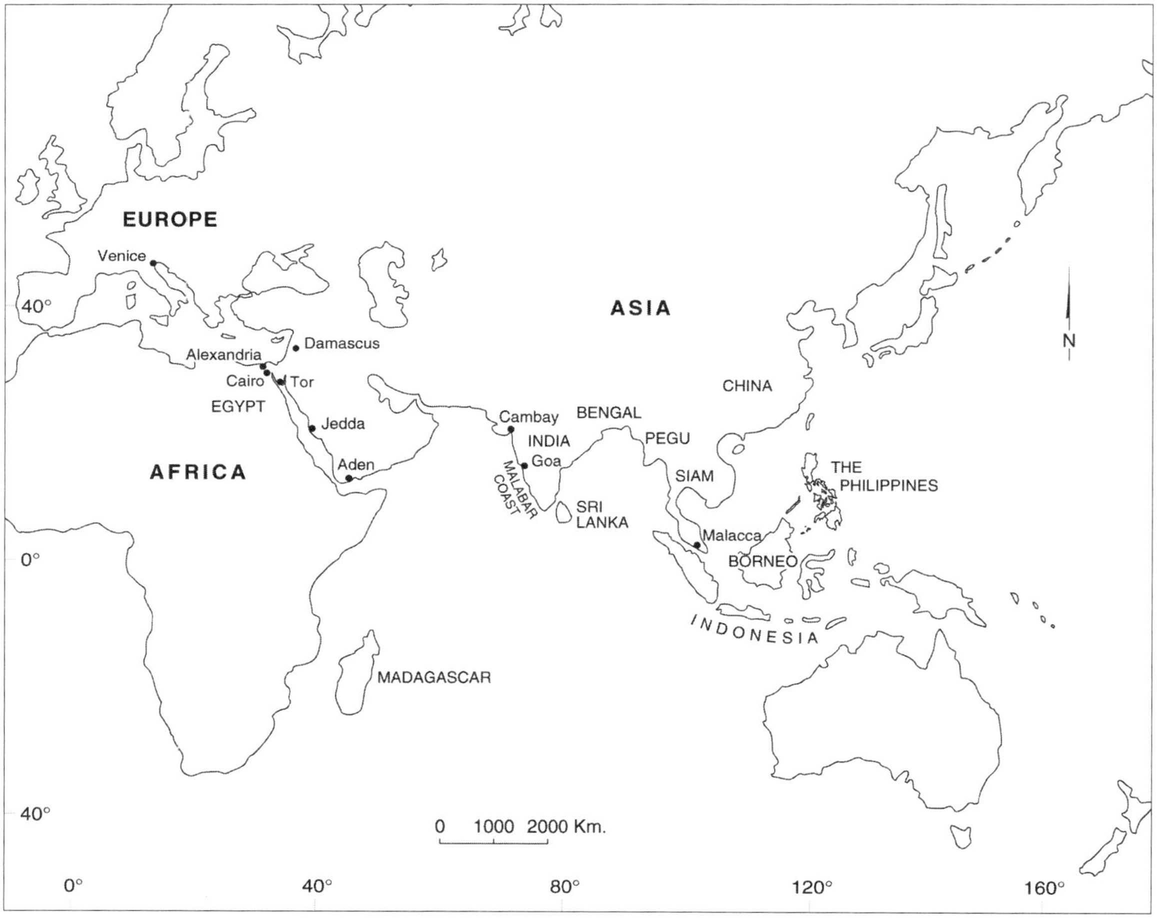

Figure 16.1. *Map showing places between Madagascar and the Philippine Islands that are mentioned in the text, including major trading posts as described by Tomé Pires in 1515.*

The Philippines: The Western Terminus

Soon after Columbus' return from his first voyage, Pope Alexander VI issued two bulls on 4 May 1493 that drew a line of demarcation to divide the world into Spanish and Portuguese spheres.[3] The Treaty of Tordesillas signed between Spain and Portugal revised the line on 7 June 1494. The line was drawn down what was thought to be the center of the Atlantic Ocean (the first voyage of Columbus was the only reference) and the bulge of Brazil ended up on the Portuguese side. All new lands west of the line belonged to Spain; all those to the east were Portuguese. In practice, it meant that Spain could continue exploring in the direction Columbus took and Portugal could continue exploring the western coast of Africa. When it was later confirmed that the world was round, the line was extended around the globe.

This "Line of Demarcation" ("The Pope's Line" to the Protestants) had immense ramifications. Alexander's Spanish homeland gained Church support for control of all the Americas, save Brazil. Moreover, the fixed routes of exploration and commerce affected the Asian maritime trade. The Protestant powers ignored the line, but Portugal and Spain honored it for centuries.

Portugal's claim over all lands east of the Line of Demarcation allowed it to sail along and soon around Africa to the Orient. Being a small power, its strategy was to settle only principal ports along the way to form a network of possessions across the globe. Protestant Europe quickly followed with the same strategy as Holland, Britain, France, Denmark, and others established their enclaves in Portugal's "half of the world."

Spain inherited a huge landmass no one had envisioned. It lost the northeastern part to aggressive Protestant powers, but held on to most of Latin America until the early nineteenth century. However, Spain was still far removed from the riches of Asia. In 1519 Ferdinand Magellan, a Portuguese sailing for Spain, rounded the southern tip of South America and sailed ninety-eight days until he reached the eastern Philippines. His death[4] on Mactan Island (Cebu) did not detract from his accomplishment of finding a way to Asia by sailing west.

Thus, Spain could reach Asia, albeit with some effort. To do so, galleons were sent out from Acapulco, Mexico, carrying silver from the mines of Taxco and Zacatecas, Mexico, and Potosí, Bolivia. They sailed to Manila, the Philippines, where the silver bought goods from merchants from all over Asia. The Asian luxuries were sent to Acapulco, carried on the "China Road" to Mexico City, and distributed. Much remained in Nueva España, but the most precious items were dispatched to Veracruz and loaded onto another galleon, which rendezvoused with galleons from South America and the Caribbean to form an armada for protection against pirates. Thus, the riches of Asia were delivered to Seville (see Schurz 1939).

From the beginning, the Spanish took beads with them to the Philippines. Pigafetta (1905, 97) wrote that Magellan gave the king of Butuan "Beades of Crystall." Whether these were rock crystal or Venetian "cristallo"[5] is not known. Magellan stopped a barter involving beads between one of his men and a native: "One man offred for six threds of Crystall Beades a Crowne of massie Gold, with a Collar: but the Generall [Magellan] would not permit such bartering, that they should not perceive more account to be made of their Gold by the one, then by the other of the Spanish Wares" (Pigafetta 1905, 98 [insertion mine]).

In 1565 Legazpi gave away or traded beads in two villages in the Ladrones (Blair and Robertson 1973, 109, 110), at Leyte (Blair and Robertson 1973, 115), and on Cebu (Blair and Robertson 1973, 136). A memorandum of 1665 from "His Majesty's Camp" on Cebu requested from Nueva España a number of products, several of which were specifically Spanish. Among them were:

> A great quantity of beads, blue, green, and yellow; ten breadths of each sort
> Four pounds of fine coral of all sorts
> Three quintals of glass, (one blue)[6]
> One thousand bundles of glass beads—green and yellow,
> Five hundred dozen hawks' bells[7] (Blair and Robertson 1973, 191)[8]

It is impossible to tell exactly what the requested glass beads were. Columbus took small yellow and green beads with him, now identified as wound annulars found in America until about 1550 (M. T. Smith and Good 1982,

3) or perhaps later. Brill and Hoffman (1987) judged these as Spanish based on their lead isotopes. A glass industry was founded in Puebla, Nueva España, in 1542, but whether beads were made there is not known (Francis 1987d).

Archaeologically, the earliest European beads in the Philippines were excavated from the cemetery at Calatagan on Luzon. This early contact site has yielded five Venetian glass beads: three chevrons[9] and two small Nueva Cádiz[10] beads (Color Plate 43). These two bead types are common on early Spanish contact sites.[11] Yet, the bead trade in the Philippines was dominated for many more centuries by Asian beads.

The Chinese were well established as beadmakers and traders to the archipelago before the Spanish arrived. As Manila became a pivot in the world system that linked Asia with Europe via America, the Chinese extended their trade with the islands. About 1570 Gonzales de Mendosa[12] (1906, 148) reported more than twenty Chinese junks a year coming to Manila. In 1588, the Englishman Francis Pretty (1905, 175) counted twenty to thirty junks. In 1609, Antonio de Morga (Cummins 1971, 305) put the number at thirty to forty.[13]

De Morga told us that the galleon trade attracted many people, some of whom were resident at Manila and others who sailed there periodically. The list of merchant homelands is impressive: China, Japan, the Moluccas, Malacca, Siam, Cambodia, Borneo (Cummins 1971, 304), Patani (Cummins 1971, 318), and even Portugal, bringing Portuguese wine and fruits (some prepared in Goa) and Indian, Persian, Turkish, and Macao goods (Cummins 1971, 307–308). One item the Portuguese took back to Malacca was Colombian emeralds (Cummins 1971, 309).

However, the Chinese dominated the trade. Although admitting that Manila could not function without them, de Morga (Cummins 1971, 314–315) wished to see their number diminished. Chinese junks brought the most impressive products (Cummins 1971, 305–306), including, "*tacley,*[14] which are beads of all kinds, strings of cornelians, and other beads and stones of all colours" (Cummins 1971, 306).

Many beads were distributed among the bead-loving people of the Philippines. Chinese interisland trade was considerable. De Morga complained that some Chinese "go trading from island to island in large or small sampans" (Cummins 1971, 314). If only their number were reduced: "Nor would there be so many Sangleyes[15] wandering about the Islands under cover of being traders among the natives, but in fact committing innumerable crimes and villainies. For, at the very least, these people are spying out the land, reconnoitering the river creeks and ports, *which they know better than do the Spanish themselves* . . ." (Cummins 1971, 315 [emphasis mine]).

Archaeologically, a shipwrecked Chinese junk off Palawan showed commerce in Chinese beads. The *Royal Captain* wreck no. 2, dated by its ceramic cargo to between 1573 and 1620, was probably on its way to Borneo from Manila. It carried copper ruby red coil beads and multiwound blue and white lead glass beads. Ethnographic investigations show that Chinese glass and Indian agates dominated in the islands for a long time (Francis 1992a, 5–8). The earliest European beads used as heirlooms date only from the nineteenth century (chap. 17).

Another destination for Chinese beads was America as the Asian maritime trade expanded across the Pacific. A Spanish galleon, *Nuestra Señora de la Concepción,* sank off Saipan in 1638 when headed for Acapulco. Its cargo included carnelian beads of undetermined origin, Chinese blue glass beads high in lead (Dussubieux and Gratuze 2000), and copper ruby glass beads from China.[16] Most Chinese glass beads remained in Nueva España. The Spanish had little use for beads (save coral and pearls for rosaries), but Native Americans would buy them. Blue beads American collectors call "Padre beads"[17] are certainly of Chinese manufacture. The older white heirloom beads among some Mixe, specifically in the villages of Mixistlan and Yacoche, Oaxaca, Mexico, are also Chinese (Francis 1994b).[18] Hexagonal bicones in copper ruby red glass at St. Catherines, Georgia (United States), show that Chinese beads were traded to the very outposts of Spanish America (personal observation).

European beads did not significantly penetrate the Philippine market until the nineteenth or early twentieth centuries. The old beads, the old traders, and the old routes persisted for a long time. Was this a result of the lack of interest in beads on the part of the Spanish or the relative isolation of the archipelago? A contrast with Indonesia should be instructive.

Indonesia: The Eastern Terminus

In the early sixteenth century, the Portuguese Tomé Pires visited much of Asia and wrote a detailed description of trade between Europe and Asia while staying in Malacca and India between 1512 and 1515 (Figure 16.1). Venice was its Western hub, as it had been for centuries. Goods from all over Europe went from there to the East. Venice also added its own goods, including "all sorts of glass beads" (Cortesão 1967, 12). These were new products, because the technical breakthrough of drawing glass beads happened there around 1480 (Francis 1988b, 13). Pires wrote:

> The merchandise which these people take to India comes from Venice in Italy. It comes to Alexandria, and from the Alexandria warehouses it comes by river to the factors in Cairo, and from Cairo it comes in caravans with many armed people. It comes to Tor,[19] but this is not often, because on account of the nomad robbers they need many armed people to guard the merchandise. But at the time of the Jubilee *(Jubileu)*,[20] which is held every year in Mecca on the first day of February,[21] when many people come, [the merchandise] is sent to Mecca with them. And from there it comes to Jidda and from Jidda it comes to the warehouses they have in Aden and from Aden it is distributed to Cambay, Goa, Malabar, Bengal, Pegu and Siam.[22] (Cortesão 1967, 12–13 [insertions Cortesão's])

Thus, the earliest European beads entered the Asian maritime bead trade via Muslim traders based in Aden. The Europeans themselves were mere observers.

As Pires moved eastward, he visited other nodes in this network. At Aden, Egyptian merchants traded their goods for ". . . glass beads,[23] beads from Cambay, many carnelians[24] of all colours . . ." (Cortesão 1967, 16). They also "bring the merchandise which comes from Italy and Greece and Damascus to Aden, such as . . . glass beads . . ." (Cortesão 1967, 43). The merchants of Aden took the goods from Egypt, Europe, and other trading partners to Cambay where they traded them for the goods of Malacca and the products of India, including carnelians (Cortesão 1967, 43).

Malacca most impressed Pires: "Whoever is lord of Malacca has his hand on the throat of Venice" (Cortesão 1967, 287). Malacca, not Cairo, Aden, nor Cambay, was the heart of the Asian maritime trade. The Cairo-Venice link plugged Europe into the system.

Pires' enumeration of "countries"[25] from which traders came to Malacca includes no less than sixty-three, with the added provision that the Indonesian archipelago has "a thousand other islands" (Cortesão 1967, 268). It was to Malacca that "Those from Cairo bring the merchandise brought by the galleasses of Venice, to wit, . . . coral, . . . glass and other beads, and golden glassware" (Cortesão 1967, 269). It was from Malacca that the Chinese obtained "elephant's tusks, . . . red beads . . .they buy a great many carnelians from Cambay . . ." (Cortesão 1967, 123). It was also at Malacca that Borneo traders "take a great deal of coloured glass beads from Cambay, and pearl beads;[26] they ask for red beads;[27] and with these they go about the islands where there is gold and take it in exchange for the cloth, and for the beads only" (Cortesão 1967, 133).

European beads penetrated the islands slowly. This is evident when considering the heirloom beads in the lesser Sundas, of the Southern Toraja of Sulawesi, and of groups living in Borneo (see chap. 17). Except for a few seven-layer chevrons in the National Museum and in private hands (Adhyatman and Arifin 1993, 91) and seventeenth- to early eighteenth-century Dutch beads, European beads in Indonesia are principally nineteenth century.

Malacca eventually lost its position to Singapore, which the British built up from the early nineteenth century as the hub of trade east of India. As late as 1882, the old networks were still functioning with the same traders and articles of commerce. Bock (1882, 187–188), writing about interior Borneo, said that agate beads traded inland had been brought to the coast by Malay traders, who had bought them in Singapore.

There was no dramatic change in the bead trade at Singapore until early in the twentieth century. Data gathered from import and export lists of governmental publications[28] (Francis 1989a, 22–23) showed that bead exports went mainly to Sarawak, the Dutch Indies (Indonesia), Borneo, Sumatra, and Java, with Brunei/Sabah, Indochina, China, and Thailand as minor customers.

Between 1909 and 1922, the percentage of European beads (mostly German and Italian) rose from 57.5 to 69.0 percent, while Indian beads dropped from 28.2 to 16.3 percent. From 1927 to 1934, European imports rose from 65.5 to 76.4 percent, though Germany's slid badly and Italy's disappeared. The percentage of Indian beads dropped from 8.2 to 4.6 percent, reaching a nadir of 0.8 percent in 1933. The Czechs accounted for the increase in European beads and there was a new Asian player: Japan, whose share was 20.5 percent in 1927, 17.0 percent in 1933, and 18.8 percent in 1934.

At the beginning of the twentieth century, European beads accounted for only half the Singapore trade to Indonesia and Indian beads for more than a fourth. Twenty-five years later, European imports rose to three-fourths, the Indian trade had dropped dramatically, and Japan was ascendant.

The Eastern Giant: China

When Europeans first came to Asia, China was insulated from outside influences. In 1372 the first Ming Emperor forbade private maritime trade, "not even allowing a wooden plank to drift to sea," a policy not reversed until 1567, with few exceptions (see chap. 7). The first Europeans to gain a foothold in China (and the last to let go) were the Portuguese at Macao. The prospects were good, but never fulfilled. Macao was marginalized in 1640 by the loss of Malacca to the Dutch and the severing of ties with Manila (Chang 1934). However, trade flourished from Fujian and other littoral states (Blusse and Zhuang 1991). Projected translations of important Chinese documents may give us much more data on the Chinese role in the Asian maritime bead trade.[29]

The succeeding Qing dynasty had a different outlook. Emperor Kang Xi (1662–1722) was open to foreign knowledge. Kang Xi favored Jesuit missionaries for their spiritual outlook and technical skills. They established themselves in China and in 1782 published a multi-volume description of the Middle Kingdom. This included a notice of 1774 on what to import to China. In the first rank were "All that which is the province of the jewelers, such as rings, ear pendants, hair pins and head ornaments in false stones for the women . . ." (Missionnaires de Pe-kin 1782, 269–270 [my translation]).

As delighted as court women may have been with European gewgaws, the bulk of trade continued in the traditional way. Crawfurd (1820, 444–445) recorded that the "Indian Archipelago" (Indonesia) sent an annual cargo of pearls to China worth twenty-five thousand Spanish dollars[30] and mother of pearl worth seventy thousand Spanish dollars.

Ivory was a most important import to China. "Elephants' teeth" came from South Africa, Siam, and Burma, especially the latter two. A Chinese artisan could turn a 3-pound ivory piece into a "toy" worth $100 (*Chinese Repository* 1834, 460).

A new trading partner, New Zealand, figured into the bead commerce. J. H. Gray (1875, 241) noted that jade was imported to China from several quarters, including New Zealand. The Chinese were said to have found it inferior to their own.

These brief, scattered notices over several centuries do not give us a complete picture of China's participation in the Asian maritime bead trade. Later European (particularly British) records are more detailed. Among the earliest are commercial reports of the import and export trade from Canton (Guangzhou) in the first half of 1863 (Irish University Press 1972, 300–312).[31] This information is summarized in Table 16.1.

Table 16.1 shows that even at this late date China was still involved in the bead trade patterns that had existed for centuries. The major imports were organic gems: amber, coral, ivory, and pearls. The stone imports were old favorites: carnelian, quartz, and jade (whether from Burma, New Zealand, or elsewhere). Amber, carnelian, jade, and quartz were mostly consumed in China.

TABLE 16.1
Import and Export of Beads and Bead Materials through Canton, First Half of 1863

Article	Import in Piculs[a]	Export in Piculs	Reexport in Piculs	Value of Imports[b]	Value of Exports[b]
Amber					
Raw	101.1	2.0			
Beads	0.24	8.8			
Refuse		6.36			
Total				26,444	15,234
Coral					
Beads		16.54			
Fragments	2.94	0.83	0.90		
Ware		0.10			
Total				83	1,453
Carnelian					
Beads	35.71	7.10			
Stones	466,324[c]				
Ware		9.48			
Total				30,359	8,197
Glass					
Raw	50.54[d]				
Beads		213.24			
Bangles		747.30			
Total				177	39,490
Ivory					
First sort	207.91	3.71	10.27		
Second sort	32.51	2.47	2.25		
Ware			44.70		
Total				38,433	34,652
Jade	24.50	841[c]		10,547	1,199

Continued on next page

TABLE 16.1 (continued)

Import and Export of Beads and Bead Materials through Canton, First Half of 1863

Article	Import in Piculs[a]	Export in Piculs	Reexport in Piculs	Value of Imports[b]	Value of Exports[b]
Pearls					
Large	0.4	0.2			
Seed	0.12				
Total				1,197	1,046
Quartz	37.47			281	0
Imitation coral		0.1			141
False pearls		17.75			
Scented beads		12,939[e]			

[a] A picul is 133.3 pounds avoirdupois or 60.4 kg.
[b] Apparently in Spanish dollars.
[c] Pieces, not piculs.
[d] All imported from other parts of China, not Europe.
[e] Strings

Imports and exports of pearls and ivory were about even; pearls had local sources and the added value of reexported ivory kept the monetary figures in balance. The only anomaly is coral; the Chinese were possibly then working down an earlier imported surplus.

The most telling figure is for glass. No European glass beads were reported. The only imported glass is refuse from other parts of China. Canton had a large export surplus of glass beads and especially bangles. To this can probably be added "imitation coral" and "false pearls." It would be interesting to learn what the relatively cheap "scented beads" were.

Statistics from the *China Year Book* (Bell and Woodhead 1912, 120–137; 1916, 152–183; 1919–1920, 159–193) covering 1906 to 1917 show the import of ivory, jade, and pearls, and the export of fewer pearls than were imported. European beads may be hidden under "Jewellery, Real and Imitation," and Chinese export glass beads may be with "Glassware, Bangles, etc."

China was late to receive Europeans and even later to receive their beads. It continued to import traditional bead materials, working them into value-added goods for internal use and export. As late as 1863, Chinese glass beads were an important export. European glass beads had yet to make an impression in Chinese commerce.

The Central Giant: India

India is different from the other regions considered here because of its overwhelming dominance in beadmaking. It remains important to this day. Apart from dozens of smaller and larger industries making beads from organic materials, India still has traditional glass and stone beadmaking industries. Historically there have been four major industries:

1. Stone beadmaking in western India (now concentrated around Cambay) still operates.
2. Glass beadmaking in the south (Indo-Pacific beads) continues to the present.

3. The southern stone bead industry was weakened during the last several centuries, though it still operates on a small scale.
4. The northern glass bead industry (Francis 1982b) still produces beads. It was not discussed earlier because it did not participate significantly in the maritime bead trade. Its fate as a competitor of European imports to India concerns us here.

As with China, the fate of the European bead trade was linked to the health of the Indian industry. Europeans hardly ever [32] succeeded in exporting stone beads to Asia, but became successful traders of Indian stone beads. European glass beads sent to Asia had to compete with local products.

Detailed records of the British in the bead trade in the early seventeenth century are found in the documents of the (British) East India Company.[33] Queen Elizabeth I incorporated the "Governor and Company of Merchants of London Trading into the East Indies" (the British East India Company or simply "the Company") on 31 December 1600.

The Company first directed its efforts toward the lucrative trade with the Spice Islands (the Moluccas of Indonesia). However, Dutch influence was very strong there, and English attention was soon deflected elsewhere. It attempted to establish a "factory" (trading station) in India as early as 1608. This bore fruit when one was granted at Surat, between Bombay and Cambay, in 1612. The proximity to Cambay was important.

Before Surat opened as the first factory, another site considered was Gogha (Goga) on the Kathiawar Peninsula opposite the mouth of the Narmadā. The Cambay port was silting up,[34] and oceangoing vessels anchored at Gogha, from whence small boats took goods to Cambay. In the winter of 1617–1618, Sir Thomas Roe inspected Gogha, but deemed it unsuitable. He argued that ivory was already being sent from Surat to Cambay and the coral trade would suffer, though he did not explain why (Foster 1900, 151–153). Cambay's port was thus ignored.

Initially, the British paid little attention to Cambay, much less its beads. The city appeared in the Company papers first in conjunction with cloth (Danvers 1896, 9–15, 18; Foster 1899, 256). Cambay was inhospitable to the British, largely because of Portuguese intrigue (Foster 1899, 38). There were also unpleasant incidents, such as throwing Englishmen in chains on a flimsy excuse and a fierce exchange with robbers on the Cambay road (Danvers 1896, 116–121).

The first mention of stone beads in the Company's letters appeared in 1619 and did not mention Cambay. Thomas Kerridge and Thomas Rastall at Surat wrote the Company on 9 and 15 February 1619 to say that bloodstones[35] were difficult to get in Ahmadabad though "Aggat or babagoria beades can be furnished and they have sent some crystal beads and agate cups" (Foster 1906, 52). This suggests a bead industry at Ahmadabad, which is not out of the question, because there was contemporary work there in precious stones and jewelry for the Mughal court (Gokhale 1967, 193). However, the Ahmadabad dealers may have bought the beads from Cambay.

The earliest reference to Cambay agates was by Joseph Salbank and Nicholas Crispe, merchants who had settled there. In a letter to Surat on 22 November 1622, they said: "[We sent] 48 strings (24 corge)[36] of beads suitable for barter in Madagascar, costing half a rupee per corge. Will produce a further supply if these are approved" (Foster 1908, 154). Two weeks later, Salbank sent fifty-two strings to Hodeida, a port near Mocha "as desired" (Foster 1908, 161).

Madagascar is discussed later in this chapter, but the reference to Mocha, Yemen, is also of interest. Yemen is a carnelian source. Niebuhr (1774, 125) noted natives digging a fine red carnelian near Damar in the 1760s, and in Egypt first-class carnelian was called *Akik Yemani* (Tagore 1879, 2: 954). Agate is also found there (Rihani 1930, 167). Why would anyone send Cambay carnelians or agates there? Twentieth-century reports on Yemeni lapidaries only mention producing cabochons to be mounted in jewelry, not beads (Rihani 1930, 170–171; Ingrams 1963, 22). Yemen may have made only cabochons and seal stones.

As the British sold more stone beads, the quality began to concern them. On 13 April 1630, a letter by President Wylde and others said that they paid seven rupees a maund[37] for first-class "bloodstone" (carnelians) and four rupees a maund for second class at Cambay. The beads received were inferior to the samples and the merchants were rebated one and one-fourth and one rupee per maund, respectively. They concluded that "[beads] being made in Cambaia will not bee soe well ordered as when wee have a residency in that place" (Foster 1910, 21).

In 1632 the fleet commanded by Captain Weddell at St. Augustine, Madagascar, bought cattle for five to seven beads per bullock. However, most beads they had with them "were so bad that they could hardly put them off" (Foster 1910, 223). Again, on 12 December 1639, President Fremlen and John Wilde wrote that they were sending 920 "long red beads" on the *Discovery* "though the number is small and the quality is poor." For these, they had paid seven rupees a hundred.[38] They promised better beads later (Foster 1912, 220).

A 1631 proclamation of Charles I outlined the flow of goods to and from Britain and India (and points east). English exports were manufactured woolens, pewter, saffron, silk manufactures, roses edged with gold lace, beaver hats with gold or silver bands, felt hats, strong waters, knives, Spanish leather shoes, iron, and looking glasses. Imports to Britain included peppers, sugar, nutmeg, ginger, myrabolans, bezoar stones, drugs, *agate beads, bloodstones (carnelians),* musk, aloes, soccatrina,[39] ambergris, carpets of Persia and Cambay, satin quilts, taffeta, calicoes, benjamin, damasks, satins and taffetas of China, quilts of China embroidered with gold, silk-embroidered quilts of Patania,[40] (silk?) worm-seeds, sugar candy, China, and porcelain (Birdwood 1891, 37 n).[41]

The Company's papers also give insight into who was carrying the goods. By 1650 merchants (and sailors?) trading on their own account began to worry the Company; after all, they were competing with it. Because the Company provided transport to India, any private trade conducted there reduced its profits.

Between 23 January and 16 September 1650 the Company's court met on at least four occasions to consider this problem (Sainsbury 1913, 5, 9, 33, 59). Throughout the discussions, the same six commodities were exclusively reserved. A notice of 27 March said, "It is resolved that no man shall be allowed to carry out [to India] vermillion, quicksilver, lead, elephant's teeth, broad cloth or coral,[42] and that this prohibition shall be inserted in all charter-parties" (Sainsbury 1913, 33 [insertion mine]). On 16 September, the final list was drafted with these products. Pearls, diamonds, rubies, cowries, and "agate ware of all sorts" were not prohibited (Sainsbury 1913, 59). Therefore, the trade in carnelian and agate beads passed into private hands. India continued to sell beads to Europe, where they were both worn and reexported.

The glass bead industry fared differently.[43] By the 1790s, House of Commons reports showed that the bulk of exports to India was cloth (including woolens), metals (tin, lead, copper, silver), and naval and military supplies. The Company reserved the exclusive right to trade in these commodities and "clocks, toys, etc. decorated with jewels" (Russell 1793, 26–27). On 3 January 1793 items that could be traded privately included glass beads and jewelry, the latter to China (Russell 1793, 28). None of Russell's (1793) lists mentioned amber, coral, or ivory. They were no doubt still items of commerce, but no longer as lucrative as they once were because they were likely being sold to India as raw materials. The Company's trading rights were abolished in 1833.

Britain increased its political power in India, eventually annexing it in 1858. British policy was to make India a consumer rather than a producer. British-made or British-brought goods flooded Indian markets. Manchester broadcloth was cheaper than locally made cottons, and Sheffield steel replaced Mysore steel. Indian industry, being labor-intensive and village-based, could not compete (Gadgil 1929, 46; H. L. Gupta 1960, 92; Simkin 1968, 287–288; Majumdar et al. 1978, 799–805).

This applied to the glass bead industry as well as any other. It was neither well organized nor technologically advanced. Mill (1826, 42) described Indian glassmaking this way: "Though the Hindus know the art of making a species of rude glass, which was manufactured into trinkets and ornaments for the women, they have never possessed sufficient ingenuity to apply it to the many useful purposes for which glass is so admirably adapted." Of course, this is not entirely true, but it is not a mean assessment of northern Indian bead and bangle makers.

By 1889, Watt (1889, 429) reported that glass beads were being made at Kaira (Gujarat), Jaipur and Bundi (Rajasthan), Sagor (Madhya Pradesh), Multan (Sind, now in Pakistan), and Delhi. Purdalpur (Uttar Pradesh), the only surviving site of glass beadmaking in northern India today, must have been overlooked. Glass beads and/or false pearls were exported from Bombay to East Africa via Aden around this time (Hunter 1877, 93). Concurrently, glass beads became an increasingly valuable import item to India (see Table 16.2).

The statistics are impressive, not only because the amount of imports nearly doubled in five years, but also because the sheer volume and the value of the trade were high. The 23,243 hundred weight of 1883–1884 is equal to 1,056.5 metric tons. The rupee was then worth about one U.S. silver dollar or a British crown, so well over a million (silver) dollars a year was being spent. Roughly, this is a thousand tons of glass beads worth a million dollars.

TABLE 16.2
Import of Glass Beads into India,
1879–1880 to 1883–1884

Date	Hundredweight	Value in Rupees[a]
1879–1880	13,751	879,895
1880–1881	15,483	1,168,060
1881–1882	16,724	1,184,148
1882–1883	19,897	1,279,023
1883–1884	23,243	1,618,728

Source: Watt (1889, 427).

[a] The value in rupees in this and Table 16.3 was recorded by Watt using the Indian style, with a comma between the fourth and third digits (1,234) and the next comma between each subsequent two digits (1,23,456). The latter number is read "one lakh, twenty-three thousand, four hundred and fifty-six." A hundred lakh is a crore (10,000,000 or 1,00,00,000). I have converted these into the more widely used "million" system.

By far the major supplier in the 1883–1884 period was Italy, with 77.3 percent of the volume and 44.7 percent of the value. China and Austria (Bohemia) accounted for less than 8 percent of the volume each, but Austria's beads were worth four times those of China and more than three times those of Italy by weight (Watt 1889, 428).

At the beginning of the twentieth century, Italy remained the major dealer of beads to India, followed by Austria (Bohemia), Germany, and the United Kingdom, the latter probably re-exporting beads from elsewhere. The volume was lower than it had been several decades before, but the value was equal or greater (see Table 16.3).

India eventually reversed the trend as Europeans began to build modern glass factories. This had a two-fold effect on traditional village-based industries. On one hand, it crushed many of the smaller ones, and bead and bangle makers began to converge into Purdalpur (Purdilpur, Purdilnagar), the last remaining heir to the industry (Francis 1982b, 12–13). On the other hand, Firozabad (Uttar Pradesh) emerged as the major producer of ornamental glass for the whole country, even supplying glass and glassmakers to Papanaidupet (Francis 1982b, 12–13).[44]

The revival of India's glass bead industry began during World War I, expanded during World War II, and grew after Independence in 1947. The number of glass workers (excluding those who decorate and close bangles) swelled. In 1923, there were 2,318. In 1939, there were 8,934. In 1943, the number had increased to 18,328. By 1970 there were 55,181 (Francis 1982b, 7). By the

TABLE 16.3
Import of Glass Beads into India,
1902–1903 and 1906–1907

Date	Hundredweight	Value in Rupees
1902–1903	14,437	1,651,325
1906–1907	22,540	2,402,442

Source: Watt (1908, 122).

mid-1970s, India was self-sufficient in glass and exported glass products, including beads. By the 1990s, the country had again become a major player in the world bead trade, with production at Purdalpur[45] extending into neighboring towns. Benares[46] became a glass beadmaking site with Czech help in the 1940s and has grown into a major producer.

The most important beadmaking country in Asia only slowly accepted European beads. Only British mercantile policy imposed after India became the "jewel in the crown" had an appreciable effect on the old trading system. It was devastating to India's glass bead industry. Only Purdalpur and Papanaidupet survived; the latter has recently been much weakened by the installation of Japanese drawing machines in Benares. In recent decades, the downward trend in the glass bead industry in the North has been reversed.

Madagascar and East Africa

The history of the Madagascar bead trade reveals interesting details on the western side of the Indian Ocean. The Portuguese Diego Diaz accidentally landed at the world's fourth largest island when blown off course on his way to India in 1500.[47] The Portuguese named it "St. Lawrence," but were unsuccessful at proselytizing there and eventually abandoned it.

During the third voyage of the East India Company, the *Consent* and the *Hector* stopped at St. Augustine Bay (adjacent to a river and an island of the same name) on the southeast coast near present Tollara. The halt was short, meant to load water, wood, and food, yet three accounts of it survive. David Middleton (1905, 53) on the *Consent* noted that there was "great plenty of victualls, both Sheepe and Beeves for little value." The captain of the *Consent,* William Keeling (1905, 511–512), was more explicit. On 20 August 1607, Captain Hawkins of the *Hector* went ashore with some men. The natives had fled, so the British left some beads and other goods in a boat. Two days later, Keeling went ashore and met "a subtill people, their bodies strong, and well framed; their privities onely carelesly covered, with cloath made of the rindes of trees."[48] He bought a calf, a sheep, and a lamb, but "they would not deale save for silver, by any meanes." After two days, the British secured three cows, two steers, and four calves: "they cost us nineteene shillings sterling, besides a few beads." Keeling concluded that St. Augustine was not fit for "refreshing" (Keeling 1905, 513).

The merchant William Finch (1905, 11–13) wrote the most detailed account of this first encounter. He described the people in much the way Keeling did and added, "neither had they bad smels on their bodies." He observed their "darts," alligator teeth hanging from their girdles, hairstyles, and knives. The cattle were strange to him, being humpbacked *(Bos indicus),* and he commented on the local bats, birds, insects, spiders, and foliage. He also discussed commerce. "They therefore regard no Iron, nor will barter for any thing but Silver, for which we bought a sheepe for twelve pence, a Cow for three shillings and sixe pence, they asked Beades into the bargaine, for which yet alone they would give nothing, save a little Milke brought down in gourds, excellent sweet and good" (Finch 1905, 11).

The British were not likely paying in silver coins but in silver trinkets. In August 1614, Captain Thomas Elkington (1905, 252) on the *Vice-Roy* wrote about St. Augustine, ". . . we bought Cattell in exchange of Silver Chaines, they taking the value of twentie pence, or two shillings in a Chaine for an Oxe, which in money would cost five or sixe shillings." As for the beads in these accounts, they were undoubtedly European (likely Venetian), because the convoy was sailing east. Because they were unknown at St. Augustine, they had no local value.

The letter from Joseph Salbank and Nicholas Crispe of 22 November 1622 cited earlier said: "[We sent] 48 strings (24 corge) of beads suitable for barter in Madagascar, costing half a rupee per corge. Will produce a further supply if these are approved" (Foster 1908, 154). The British bead trade to Madagascar had opened.

During the reign of Charles I (1625–1649) the British attempted to build a plantation on Madagascar, and a short-lived colony was established (Sibree and Cana 1942, 605). Traditionally, Arab merchants dominated the trade. The desirable beads on the island were Indo-Pacific beads and carnelians. During the years the British were there, carnelian beads continued to be in demand. The British began to appreciate the value of Cambay products.

On 13 April 1630, President Wylde and traders at Swally Marine wrote the Company that they had just "unexpectedly procured 216,550 red cornelian beads." They remarked that the Portuguese and Dutch were trading heavily in them and sent some to the *New Stock* and 2,400 to two other ships for barter at St. Augustine. They complained, however, that ship captains often exchanged ten times more than necessary, giving the beads away too freely. "This should be reformed" (Foster 1910, 39–40). An account of the "homeward" voyage of the *Charles* by Nicolas Sharpe, entered on April 1630, showed the bead trade in full swing at St. Augustine:

> And after some five weekes being here we had a great stor of lemons and oringes brought us every other day, howle pras [whole prows] full; which att first we had for a rund bead apeece, and afterwards we had them for long beads, 12, 16, 20 for one bead. The people, both men and weomen, are well favored, and they will trad for nothing but for read beads. Our Captaine had half a scour of them abord, and ther Captains name being Ander Pilow which he [the captain of the *Charles*] clad from top to toe, sword and belt hanging about his neck; but the next day, some of our men being att his towne, he sould all away for one string of beads; which showeth the little esteame of cloths. . . . The beves [plural of beef] we had all this whill for 7, 8, and 10 or 12 beads apeece the best, and sheep and goots for 2 and 3 apeece. If ther had bene ships that had neded a thousand head of cattell thes three mounths they might have bene suplied. (Foster 1910, 42 [insertions mine])

The exchange of such good food for a few beads continued unabated, with little apparent inflation. In 1630, John Vian wrote that the *Jonas* bought a cow for six or eight beads and a sheep for four or five (Foster 1910, 44). In 15 May 1644, Robert Bowen, Henry Olton, and Humphrey Pinson at St. Augustine wrote "To the Commanders of Subsequent Ships." They noted, "Beefe may be bought on the other side of the [St. Augustine] river for 10 rangoes a beefe, or 8 rangoes and 20 samma sammas." (Foster 1913, 182 [insertion mine])

Both "samma-samma" and "rangoes" can be identified. Burton (1860, 529) described a bead in East Africa as "Samsam (Ar.) sámesáme (Kis.)[49] . . . names for the small coral bead, a scarlet enamelled upon a white ground" (that is, the popular "Cornalaine d'Aleppo" or "white heart").[50] However, "white hearts" were not being made in 1644, so it is unclear what beads had that name at that time. They might possibly have been "green hearts," with a translucent green core and an opaque red coat, then manufactured in Venice and Holland.

Rangoes (also arango, arrango) figure in documents written about Malagasy (Madagascar), the Cape of Good Hope, Gambia, Mali, and Sierra Leone, dating from 1644 to 1805–1806. Both editions of the *Oxford English Dictionary* cite "arango" first only from 1715.[51] It is defined as: "A species of beads made of rough carnelian . . . formerly imported from Bombay for re-exportation to Africa." Foster (1913, 182 n. 1) said that "rango" meant "long," but in what language he did not state. Perhaps not all beads called "rango" were the same, but the weight of evidence suggests that they were long carnelians and often valued relatively highly. The etymology of the word remains unknown (Francis 1992d).

There were changes in consumer demand in the trade by the end of the 1630s. Archaeologically, the most important carnelian beads in Madagascar were hexagonal cylinders (Thierry 1961, 106–116). These are apparently the "long beads" or "rangoes" in the Company's records. In December 1639, President Fremlen and others at Surat wrote to the Company that the *Francis*, which had visited Mozambique and Madagascar, had reported that round carnelian beads were preferred there (Foster 1912, 289). In early 1640 the *Francis* returned to Mozambique with the traditional long beads (Foster 1912, 226), but by December Surat was sending out long and round carnelian beads (Foster 1912, 289). The round beads were more desired than the long ones, "Which are not here [Surat] (unlesse forebespoake) procurable without much difficulty and those scarce worth the buying" (Foster

1912, 289–290 [bracketed insertion mine]). The Englishman Richard Boothby wrote in 1644 that the people of Madagascar liked "the red carnelian beads sold by India, the round ones and the spindle shaped faceted ones [hexagonal bicones], and which are, in their eyes, of great value" (Thierry 1961, 135 [insertion mine]).[52] He also noted that coral was worth forty times more than carnelian.

Along with round carnelian beads, the other new bead Surat sent to Madagascar was "a small sort of glasse beads called by the Portugalls contaria"[53] (Foster 1912, 289). The *contaria* (also *conterie*) were small, drawn glass seed beads that were also popular along the coast of Sofala (Foster 1912, 289). They were European competitors to the established Indo-Pacific beads.

Archaeologically, the most important site in Madagascar is the Muslim cemetery at Vohémar (Thierry 1961; Vernier and Millot 1971). It has mixed material and is not yet firmly dated. Most numerous there were small glass beads locally called *jijikely,* evidentially Indo-Pacific beads. Carnelian beads, mostly hexagonal cylinders, were very common. Quartz beads (indicating trade with South India?) were also popular, as was coral. European beads were also found, most notably early, seven-layered chevrons and Nueva Cádiz beads.

The Madagascar trade mirrors the late Asian maritime bead trade. Initially Arabs, Malays, and Indians imported Cambay or South Indian carnelians and Indo-Pacific beads. Fancy Venetian glass beads (chevrons and Nueva Cádiz) found favor in the first century of European contact, at least among Muslims. Arabs or the early Portuguese could have brought them.

Among the natives of Madagascar, the first European beads were not highly regarded, fetching only milk. Silver chains, trinkets, and perhaps coins[54] were all the British had to trade until they discovered the value of Cambay beads. In a few decades, changes in taste at Sofala and Madagascar favored round carnelian beads over long ones (hexagonal cylinders). Newly introduced Venetian seed beads became popular, eventually overtaking Indo-Pacific beads.

In the Americas and West Africa, the new European beads were accepted quite quickly. In North America, European settlers had more technical resources than Native Americans did and the new beads became all the rage. In Latin America, Europeans destroyed the old dispensation. In West Africa, it was easier to bring beads on ships involved in the slave and gold trades than to take them across the Sahara from the Arab world.

We see the same pattern in Madagascar. In the first few decades only silver and Cambay long beads were welcomed, but the major traders had changed. Soon there was a demand for round Cambay beads, Venetian seed beads, chevrons, and Nueva Cádiz beads.

However, in Asia, whether China, India, the Philippines, or Indonesia, a different pattern emerged. The large producing nations continued the commerce they had built up over millennia, but hardly made adjustments to their traditional pattern of trade until the mid- or late nineteenth century, and then only because of European political influence.

As with the core nations, so with the two peripheral archipelagoes. European beads were introduced early into both the Philippines and Indonesia. However, they continued to play secondary roles in trade until the end of the nineteenth or beginning of the twentieth century.

In sum, the cessation of the Asian mode of commerce in the bead trade of the region is quite late. The Asian bead manufacturers were industrious and the demand for their beads in far-flung regions was enormous. They were able to maintain their superiority over imported (European) beads until they were crushed politically and economically.

It is significant to note that the mid or late nineteenth-century date we have arrived at here is much later than van Leur's date of 1650 and also about a century later than Simkin's late eighteenth-century date for the end of the Asian mode of trade. Either these dates need to be reconsidered or the bead trade was unusually conservative.

17

Heirloom Beads in Southeast Asia and Micronesia

The concept of handing down property from one generation to the next is ancient. At times, formal institutions were developed to regulate the practice. Britain has codified this law in considerable detail. In the United States, the custom is less formal. Any object may be considered an heirloom providing it was inherited.

Formal patterns of heirloom succession still exist among many minority groups, including those in Southeast Asia. Many of these people have been marginalized.[1] In most cases, they were literally driven from the lowlands into less bountiful but more protective mountainous regions by newcomers who seized their old territories. They have kept themselves apart, and their beads play an active role in this isolation. Nonetheless, it will probably not be many decades before these people are better integrated into the fabric of their nations and even electronically connected to the rest of the world.

The term "heirloom bead" is found scattered in the bead literature, both in popular and scientific writings. Scholars have recognized that particular beads are very important to certain people. Rouffaer (1899) composed a book-length (266 pages) paper aimed at explaining the origins of *mutisalah* a century ago.[2] The "heirloom" concept has often been invoked since.[3]

My initial study of this topic (Francis 1989a) was based mostly on museum collections and concentrated on Sarawak and the Philippines. It pointed out an overlap between some excavated beads and heirloom beads as well as the role heirlooming played in the history of many of these beads. A later study of fourteen Southeast Asian ethnic groups was based on fieldwork, interviews, ethnographic literature, and museum holdings (Francis 1992a) (Figure 17.1). Most recently, data on the beads of Palau in Micronesia have been added.

The methodology used in the preceding chapters was to trace a phenomenon from its beginning to the period of European domination in the Asian maritime trade. In this chapter we look in the other direction, as it were, from the present to the past.

One facet of Southeast Asian heirloom beads may be posed as questions. Do the oldest beads date to a period of cultural crisis in the history of their owners? Did heirlooming begin when the people involved experienced a traumatic event, such as being driven into the uplands?

There are no comparative studies of heirloom beads available. Indeed, there is only one scientific study of such beads in a single context, that of Lubo, Kalinga-Apayao, the Philippines (Abellera 1981). Lacking precedence, I developed a specialized vocabulary to describe certain phenomena:

1. Inheritance patterns. This involves determining who receives the beads from whom, on which occasion, and under what circumstances.
2. Curating versus splitting. Beads are usually found on strings. These can potentially be passed down as a whole (curating) or the strings can be disassembled and individual beads divided between some or many sur-

vivors (splitting). Each community decides how this is done.

In at least two cases (the Paiwan of Taiwan and the Kalinga of Luzon) a change in bead distribution must have taken place. Both groups pass on complex multistrand jewelry with only a few old, valued beads at the center of each strand. Initially, both groups were probably splitters, but eventually there would have been no beads left to divide. They then became curators, anointing the jewelry as the unit of inheritance, and giving it to only one child.

3. Closed versus open-ended collections. A closed collection involves the transfer of only one or a few types of beads. No other types can ever be added to the original stock. By contrast, an open-ended collection accepts new beads, no doubt after a lag of time so that even the new beads seem old. (Beads probably become true heirlooms only after they are irreplaceable.)
4. Use as social diacritical marks. A "diacritical mark" is a symbol that distinguishes one person or group from another. This is an important role for beads, because they often announce their owner's social status, religion, wealth, gender, age, birth order, position in the family, marital status, and so on. Heirloom beads are always social diacritical marks, especially indicating one's ethnic group.

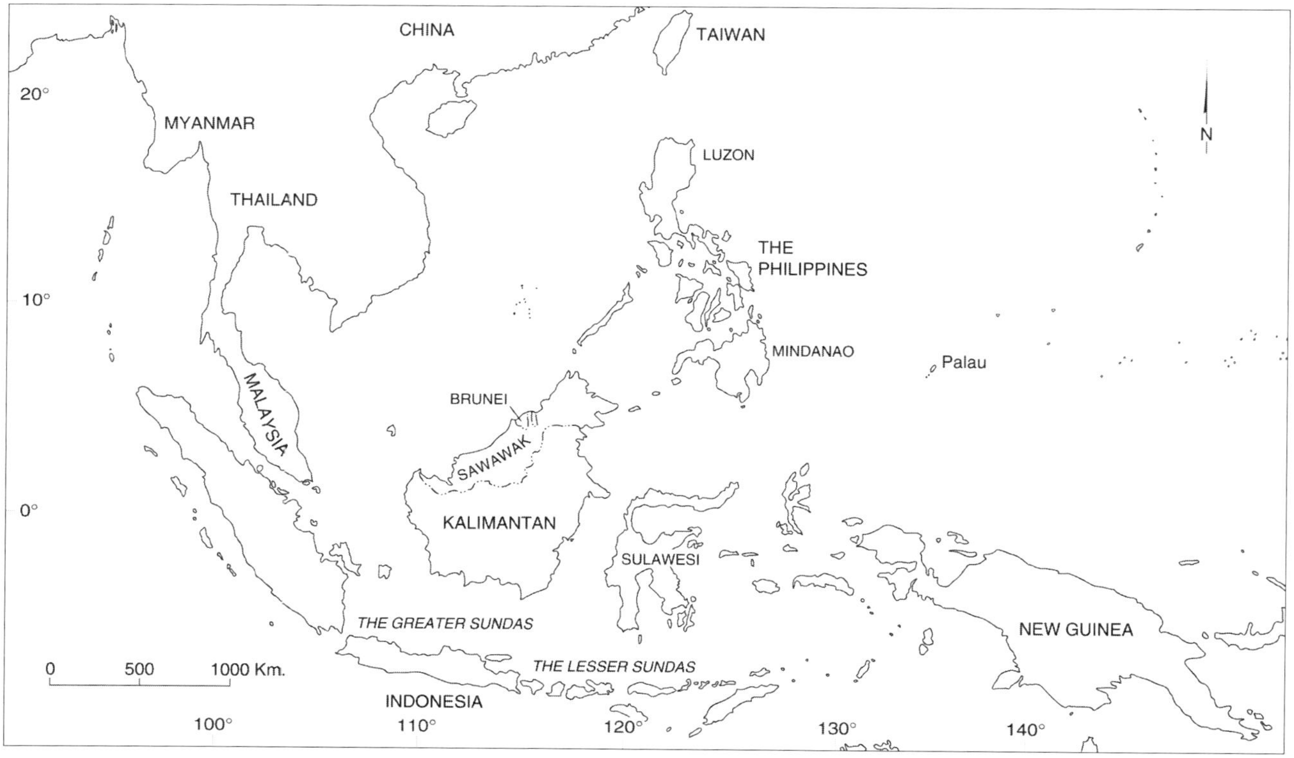

Figure 17.1. *Map of Southeast Asia showing the location of places discussed in the text.*

Heirloom Beads in Southeast Asia and Micronesia

Of the fifteen groups considered here, five are in the Philippines. Four of these are in northern Luzon: the Kalinga of Kalinga-Apayao Province, the Bontoc of Mountain Province, the Ifugao of Ifugao Province, and the Gad-dang of Isabel Province and neighboring regions of Kalinga-Apayao and Mountain Provinces. The fifth group is the T'boli of South Cotabato Province, Mindanao.

Sarawak and western Kalimantan (both on Borneo) are home to three of these groups. The Kelabit live in the uplands of Sarawak and Kalimantan beyond the navigating limits of the rivers. The Kayan live downriver. The Bidayuh (formerly labeled Land Dyaks) live to the southeast of them. Three other Indonesian groups are included: the Southern Toraja of Sulawesi and two groups divided by a deep, traditional class structure, the commoners and nobles of Nusa Tenggara Timur and Timor.

The other peoples are the Paiwan of southeastern Taiwan, the Akha of northern Thailand and adjacent countries, the Chin of southwestern Myanmar (they are called Kuki on the Indian side of the border), and the natives of Palau in the Pacific Ocean. The Chin and Akha did not receive their heirloom beads through the Asian maritime trade, but they are still of interest.

The Ifugao

The Ifugao have the oldest and most valuable beads in Luzon. Their most prized heirlooms are wound gold-glass beads, usually called *pang-o (pang-aw)*[4] (Color Plate 44). These beads have been excavated from a fifteenth- or sixteenth-century Philippine context (see Appendix A). They are no doubt Chinese. Another type of Chinese bead of considerable age is the false chevron of the sixteenth century (Appendix A). Most of the remaining beads are Indian carnelians and Chinese leadless glass beads, all of which may be a few centuries old.

Ifugao collections are not entirely closed. There are European beads of the nineteenth century or so, but they are neither numerous nor especially valued. Uniquely among the people surveyed here, heirloom beads go to the eldest child, who decides how to distribute them. If the eldest is a man, he often divides them among his siblings, but is under no obligation to do so. If it is a woman, she frequently curates the collection, but may decide to apportion it among her siblings. The strand is the unit of distribution, so collections are curated. Beads are not worn daily, but reserved for special occasions.

The Ifugao were strong, independent people whose complex rice terraces brought them surpluses with which they traded. From coastal people they received shells and beads and from people in the Benguit region they imported gold. The oldest heirlooms mark the campaign by the Spaniards to win over the lowlanders and the subsequent dwindling of trade between the coast and the mountains.

The Ifugao are inheritors of one of the oldest ornamental devices in Southeast Asia, the *lingling-o* (see chap. 13). Introduced in the first millennium B.C. from the Sa Huynh culture, the ornaments were originally of jade or glass and used as earrings. Subsequent examples are found in metal in much of Southeast Asia for a long time. Only the Ifugao make them now. Most are bronze and worn as pendants. Gold ones are highly esteemed. Neighboring groups buy them from Ifugao smiths and wear them as earrings.

The Kalinga

The beads of the Kalinga are worn in spectacular multistrand necklaces and bandoliers (Color Plate 45). Their most valuable ones are onyx and carnelian. These are mostly Indian, but difficult to date. Among their glass beads are large onyx imitations, some possibly Chinese, and others nineteenth-century Czech. Large, six-layered chevrons are valued. They are most likely nineteenth-century products, though they might be earlier. Beads popularly called "Ming" are actually Venetian and probably were not made before 1830.[5]

One of the most common and interesting type of Kalinga beads is a deep translucent blue barrel with flat ends. It is a nineteenth-century Czech product made from a drawn tube with six sides. Segments were cut from the tube and then ground at the twelve corners, giving the bead eighteen facets.[6] These were very popular on the world market for about a century. The Kalinga[7] accepted these beads and did their own grinding, smoothing off the facets to make a barrel-shaped bead.[8]

This is one of two recorded examples of altering beads in Southeast Asian. Bead altering is an important, but long-ignored segment of bead history. It is defined as the systematic[9] changing of beads after they have left the manufacturer (Francis 1993f). Examples of the practice are known from the middle of the sixteenth century onward and have been uncovered in Asia, America, and especially Africa. At least in the African context, it persists because it transforms an exotic item into one that embodies local handiwork.

Kalinga women inherit their beads when they marry. The mother gives hers to her oldest daughter, who wears them daily. Only a very rich family has enough to give to younger daughters as well. The names of beads[10] constitute lore known only by elderly women. As discussed earlier, the Kalinga probably began as splitters and once likely maintained open collections. Today they are curators with closed collections. Their beads are more recent than Ifugao ones. Most that can be dated are from nineteenth-century Europe.

The Bontoc

Bontoc women wear three strings of beads on their heads. One consists of a couple of strings of seed beads that end in the back in a large tassel with larger glass beads, pierced teeth, and other ornaments. These are apparently personal to each woman, and their fate after her death is unrecorded. The second strand is a *duli,* made from the center vertebrae of a python, which is captured and eaten. The *duli* is believed to prevent lightning from striking the woman while working in the rice fields. The male equivalent is a belt of a thick strip of cloth on which *Conus* shells and large ivory annulars are strung.

The most valued beads are on the third string. They are round or cylindrical carnelians and large white beads called *fukas* (also *fuk-as* and *fokash*). Most writers assumed that *fukas* were made from shell (Francis 1992a, 7). However, Bontoc men cut them from white marble obtained from the lowlands to the south. The last *fukas* maker is said to have died in Besao in the late 1980s. *Fukas* are large, rectangular spacers, with two holes running their length.[11] Thus, one type of the heirloom beads of the Bontoc is an import: carnelian, mostly from India of indeterminate date. The other was locally made with little prospect of future production.

The heirloom beads are used in the marriage ceremony, but do not pass to the bride. Her mother retains them. All Bontoc heirlooms are contested after death. Inheritors are usually the largest contributors to the funeral banquet. Bontoc beads are not as spectacular as those of the Ifugao or Kalinga, probably because of their long isolation and their reputation for ferocity.

The Gad-dang

The Gad-dang differ in their bead habits from their three neighbors already surveyed. They have been the most isolated of these four groups and began to heirloom beads only recently. They are the only group that uses small, drawn seed beads to decorate costumes and articles of daily life. These are strung in open patterns using only red, white, yellow, and black. The Gad-dang have also devised a distinctive short tassel composed of these beads.

The heirloom beads among the Gad-dang are larger ones, mostly of recent European make. The Gad-dang tend to be quite eclectic (Color Plate 46). They prize the beads of their neighbors, including *pang-o* beads, “Ming” beads, and *fukas.* Many of their beads are similar to those of the Kalinga, including drawn ocher-colored glass tubes, round carnelians, chevrons, and imitation onyxes. The ornaments they make from these beads also resemble Kalinga pieces. Some objects they value are of mixed construction, such as a Bontoc bachelor’s hat embellished with Ifugao shell earring pendants and decorated all over with seed beads in the collection of the National Museum of the Philippines. Heirloom beads pass to each child when they marry.

The Gad-dang are in the process of developing their own heirloom system. Their interest in beads is relatively new (Artemio Barbosa, 1995, personal communication). Their system is still open and they are still splitters. Their isolation (until recently embodied in insurgency) is now being broken and they seem to feel a need to set themselves apart during this turbulent period in their history.

The T'Boli

The T'Boli live on the southeastern slopes of the Cotabato Mountains in Mindanao. They resisted the influx of Islam into the southern Philippines as well as later Catholic influences. They remain animists. They may not have worn many beads until the 1940s (Artemio Barbosa, 1991, personal communication). Their heirloom necklace is the *lieg* and the T'Boli rarely part with them.

The *lieg* is so valuable that they are scarce or missing in museum and private collections. An initial assessment of them (Francis 1992a, 8) was based on a few written descriptions and the plastic imitations they made of them in the early 1980s.[12] Bucklee Bell (1997, personal communication) visited the T'Boli to document and photograph their ornaments, and a clearer picture of them has emerged. The beads on the *lieg* are nineteenth- or twentieth-century Venetian and Czech, metal beads, *Conus* shell disk tops, and plastic imitations of the glass and shell beads.[13]

The Kelabit

The Kelabit are one of the most remote people considered in this survey. They inhabit west-central Borneo in lands above the point of navigation on westward-flowing rivers. They live in Indonesian Kalimantan and across the border in Malaysian Sarawak.

The Kelabit only honor monochrome beads. These include those made of shell, carnelian, and glass. In at least one case, there is evidence for altering beads among them. In the Sarawak Museum is a *pata,* a woman's heirloom hat. One section is decorated with polychrome beads, some of which have been ground to remove their decorations.

The most important Kelabit bead is a blue (sometimes green or black) barrel, commonly called *let* by Western scholars. The blue ones are *let silo mau'hun (mo'hun). Let* is the general word for bead, and *mo'hun* means "old."[14] These beads are high in lead and fit the descriptions written by John Saris around 1600 of beads made in Banten, Java, by immigrant Chinese (see chap. 8). They are also found archaeologically in the Philippines (see Appendix A). Their presence on Borneo is a result of the gold and diamond trades, which were very active when the beads were made. How they passed from southern Borneo to the interior is not yet understood.

Both men and women wear these beads, especially to symbolize wealth and status. Their elite owners may lend them to others on special occasions. Beads are normally passed through the female line at death. However, other relatives may scheme or make a big show at a funeral and obtain what they would not have otherwise received.

The Kayan

The Kayan are the greatest bead collectors in Southeast Asia. Their geographic and historical position and an element in their cultural behavior might explain this phenomenon. They live mostly in Sarawak along the same rivers as the Kelabit, but their villages can be reached by boat, so they are in touch with coastal dwellers. A young Kayan man traditionally spends several years along the coast working, for example, at a Brunei oil rig or a Chinese sawmill. At the end of his sojourn, he has enough money to retire to his native village, where little currency changes hands. The money is used to pay taxes.

This is an excellent conduit for the bead trade. The Kayan are the bead traders of the region and their collections suggest the assembling of beads over a long period. Their most valued beads are priced at several thousands of (US) dollars each. The three most valued are the *lukut sekala,* the *lukut kong ba,* and the *lukut sak badak* (*lukut* is "bead"). The latter two are mosaic beads. The *lukut kong ba* is a checker mosaic, and the *lukut sak badak* is an eye bead without a core. The *lukut sekala* is a small, wound oblate with rosette decorations.

The mosaic beads have parallels in the Middle East during the Early Islamic period. The checker *lukut kong ba* could also have been made in Scandinavia at that time by Middle Eastern immigrants (Francis 1996a, 10). No precise parallel for the *lukut sekala* is recorded. They are most likely Middle Eastern.

The Kayan also value many other beads. These include Indo-Pacific, single- and double-folded Early

Islamic, sixteenth-century Chinese, seventeenth-century Dutch, nineteenth-century Czech and Venetian, and twentieth-century Japanese beads. Theirs is obviously an open collection, which is probably split rather than curated.

Along the northwestern Borneo coast, a pattern in bead use can be discerned archaeologically. Beads were commonly buried with the dead until around Song times (A.D. 960 to 1279). After that they are rarely found in burials (Francis 1989a, 30). These coastal people were not Kayan, but heirlooming (no longer important among the coastal people) may have developed about the same time within both groups.

The Bidayuh

The Bidayuh live southeast of the Kelabit and Kayan and are being integrated more quickly into modern Malaysia because of their closer access to the state capital, Kuching. Some now grow cash crops and others have abandoned their traditional longhouses. There are no heirloom beads among the general population, but healing specialists rely on them to communicate with the spirits during ceremonies.

One such healer is Raseh of Mentu Tapuh.[15] Magical beads are handed down through both the male and female lines; Raseh received his from his grandfather. They are particularly powerful during ceremonial times. No one else can touch them then, but the healer may restring them (in no particular order) and add new beads. Beads do not lose their power if they break. A wildcat tooth for healing and a few brass bells to prevent the other beads from quarreling are necessities. The remaining beads are mostly glass: leadless Chinese, opaque Chinese beads with waves, and some European ones. None is more than two centuries old (Francis 1989g, 79, fig. 4).

I pointed out the difference between an Indian carnelian and a Czech glass imitation on the strand to Raseh. Edmund Kurui, who grew up in Mentu Tapuh, actually communicated this. However, Raseh did not seem to care. This "boy" and this stranger had nothing important to tell him about his beads.

The Southern Toraja

The Toraja inhabit the southwestern peninsula of Sulawesi and are notable for their love of ornamentation. However, ethnographers have overlooked their use of heirloom beads. No such beads are in any public collection, nor had any been published before this project (Francis 1992a, pl. 3D) (Color Plate 47). It is possible that they had not been sold to outsiders until recently. In Jakarta in 1991, strands of heirloom beads were being offered at several antique shops. After examining many of them, I purchased a typical one for the collection of the Center for Bead Research from a Bugis trader, selecting it for the widest range of identifiable beads. These strands are excellent examples of the result of "splitting" heirloom beads. Of the seventy-four beads on this strand, there are no less than fifty-two different types.

The collection is open-ended. The beads range from fifteenth-century Chinese (copper ruby and a combed polychrome bead) and seventeenth-century Dutch (drawn and wound) to nineteenth-century Czech. There are several Chinese wound beads of the nineteenth century or earlier, and Venetian and Czech beads of the nineteenth century.

At the death of a parent, all children may inherit property. The shares they receive depend upon the number of water buffaloes they slaughter at the funeral. Splitting may occur at that time.

The Elite and the Commoners of the Eastern Lesser Sundas: *Mutisalah* Beads

This section involves two of the fourteen groups considered here. Although of the same ethnic stock, they are deeply divided by class. The government of Indonesia discourages the division into the elite and commoners (and sometime slaves) in the eastern islands. However, the practice persists, and heirloom beads are important social diacritical markers in the interior of Timor, Flores, Sumba, Roti, Alu, and smaller islands.

Heirloom beads are known as *mutisalah*.[16] This and related terms were recorded by early Dutch explorers and merchants in these islands. The search for their origins inspired Rouffaer's (1899) lengthy paper on the subject.[17] The misunderstanding of their use created the debate between Lamb and van der Sleen over what they were, a debate with wide ramifications (see chap. 3).

The problem with all previous investigations has been the assumption that *mutisalah* were a particular type of bead. They are not. The term is a general one designating heirloom beads. Such beads are always small and reddish brown to brownish orange (Color Plate 48).

The most numerous *mutisalah* are opaque red and worn by the commoners. They are called *mutitanah* (*tanah* means "earth"), in reference to their color. There is also a more valuable type, the orange *mutibata,* derived from *bata* (meaning "brick"), again because of their color. These are both Indo-Pacific beads. The elite, however, wear *mutiraja* (*rajā* is "king"). These are not Indo-Pacific beads, but Chinese coil beads.

Both groups treat their *mutisalah* in different ways. A young man of the common class borrows from his mother or buys a few strands of *mutitanah* or *mutibata* to give to his bride on their wedding day. On the other hand, among the elite the bride brings *mutiraja* to the marriage and receives water buffaloes and gold in exchange. All members of the elite wear these beads, with distinctive styles for married and unmarried women. The princes don them on special occasions and one may bedeck a servant with them to attend a function in his stead. Commoners are not even allowed to touch *mutiraja.*

The *mutitanah* Indo-Pacific beads are quite inexpensive. Strands are currently available in many parts of Indonesia for a few dollars. The *mutitanah* are older than the *mutiraja.* They were likely products of the Srivijayan branch of the Indo-Pacific bead industry and are at least eight hundred years old.

In contrast, a strand of *mutiraja* is quite valuable. It costs a water buffalo, estimated to be worth $200 to $250 in the early 1990s. Yet, the *mutiraja* are newer than the *mutitanah.* They most likely reached the islands after the Chinese began direct trade for their most prized product, sandalwood. At first, the Chinese bought sandalwood through Javanese go-betweens. By 1225, Zhao Rugua's description of these islands showed that the Chinese were already acquainted with the islands themselves:

> The natives . . . are strong fellows, but savage and of a dark bronze colour. They wrap (a cloth round) their limbs and tattoo their bodies. They cut the hair and go barefooted. They use no vessels in eating or drinking; in their stead they bind leaves together, which are thrown away when the meal is finished.
>
> As a standard of exchange the people use only pecks and pints of sago. They do not know either how to write or how to count.
>
> They erect stages with wooden poles stuck in the ground and reaching to a height of twenty feet or more; on the top they build houses with walls and roofs of the same type as those made by the Sin-t'o people [western Javanese.][18]
>
> The native products include sandalwood, cloves, cardamoms, fancy mats, foreign cotton cloth, iron swords and other weapons. (Hirth and Rockhill 1911, 84 [insertion in brackets mine]).

The islands had many trading centers, each under its own leader. Trade was not carried on if the leader was not present, "for fear of disturbances." From the fifteenth century the direct trade appears to have ceased (Meilink-Roelofsz 1962, 102–103). At a minimum, the commerce involved contact with foreigners and the marshaling of labor to cut and transport the trees. Chinese coil beads would have been part of the payment for sandalwood, and the elite had first choice over its distribution. Because of their lead content and the way they were made, coil beads are shinier and heavier than the older Indo-Pacific beads. It is not much of a leap to imagine the leaders reserving them for themselves as a differentiating mark of their status.

The Paiwan

As Austronesian-speaking natives of Taiwan, the Paiwan were steadily driven into mountainous regions by the major influx of Chinese beginning in the seventeenth century. Their beads are principally Chinese, as their lead content confirms. One variety is a combed polychrome cylinder, one of which was excavated at Trowulan, East Java, dated to between 1292 and 1510. Another type is a chevron imitation that resembles seventeenth-century European chevrons. Both were likely made in Quanzhou.

The beads are arranged in strands that recall the Kalinga strands. A few old, valuable beads are in the center and more numerous and less-valued ones form the rest of a single or multistrand necklace. The collections are now closed and curated, but it appears that they were once open and split among inheritors. The beads are women's property and function in marriages, but their precise inheritance patterns do not seem to have been recorded.

The Akha

The homeland of the Akha is Yunnan, China, where a million still live. During the last few centuries, some have migrated southward, most recently to Thailand, where about twenty-five thousand are officially recognized as "mountain people." Akha participation in the Asian maritime trade is minimal, but their treatment of beads is instructive.

Akha culture emphasizes continuity. Ancestor worship is important, and the male line is traced back to the beginning of time. The Akha wear many silver ornaments, as do their neighbors, though in different styles. The women are fond of beads. They sew them onto clothes and headdresses and wear them as necklaces and bandoliers. They prefer to use only one type of bead per strand, which might be very long. An Akha woman collects beads until she is older. She then slowly gives them away to her daughters and daughters-in-law. Elderly women may not have many at all.

The Akha attitude toward beads is a living example of open collections that are split during inheritance. All their oldest beads are Chinese. They include leadless glass beads that predate the Qing "color revolution" and coil beads, including rather large ones. Their most valued type of bead must be several centuries old. It is an oblate decorated with random dots in the "crumb" technique.[19]

The family determines what will become heirloom beads. Most beads now used are European seed beads, especially the popular "white heart" (translucent red over opaque white drawn beads), and Chinese beads of current production, some made in Yunnan.[20] The Akha are active bead traders, operating in neighboring countries, including Myanmar (Dunning and Dunning 1992). Today old beads are often sold and replaced by new beads, including those of plastic.

The Chin

The heirloom bead tradition of the Chin is one of the more remarkable in this survey. Their beads are called *pumtek (pumték, pum-tek),* meaning "buried thunderbolts," and were made from opalized palm wood *(Borassus flabellifer)* decorated so that they have white designs on a purposely darkened base. The decorations sometimes recall those on etched carnelians found in Myanmar and Thailand. They were made in Wadi (Waddi), a walled town of the Pyu, the Indianized founders of the first state in what is now Myanmar.[21] The first written Pyu script comes from the fifth century A.D. and the last from 1297. The Chinese referred to the Pyu Kingdom as late as 1369–1370 (Francis 1992a, 4; 1992e; 1993g; Moore and Myint 1993).

The Pyu and Chin coexisted peacefully for centuries. Fan Chuo, writing in A.D. 863, described the Chin as "by nature polite and respectful," living in cities with neither inner nor outer walls (Luce 1985, 78). From 851 to 1120, Arab writers referred to three kingdoms in Burma, now identified as the Pyu, the Chin, and the Mi-ch'en, probably Old Pegu (Minorsky 1942, 149–150; Luce 1985, 79). Luce (1985, 79) cited a corrupt passage from Fan Chuo that apparently says of the Chin, "The *Man* barbarians are friendly with them and closely trust (?) the kingdom." When the Burmese (the Mranma) entered the region in the ninth century, they were forced to fight many peoples, but the Chin were not among them. The very name Chin *(Khyan; K'yaṅ)* is Burmese for "mates" or "comrades."

The Burmese eventually absorbed the Pyu. The Chin lived peaceably along the Chindwin River ("the hole of the Chin") until the Shan overran northern Burma in

1301. The Chin evacuated, most settling in the Chin Hills, taking their beads with them.

At least until recently, the Chin were most reluctant to part with their *pumtek*. Selling them was believed to cause the end of the family line. *Pumtek* are used in marriage and other ceremonies and are part of the complex inheritance systems, the *hlawn* of the women and the *ro* of the men (Head 1917, 14; Lehman 1963, 128–129). The finest examples belong to chiefs. Their wives wear them except on special occasions, when the chiefs put them on and exhort their sons never to part with them. *Pumtek* are thus the oldest heirloom beads in Southeast Asia and perhaps the purest example anywhere of curating a closed bead collection. In this century, looted ones from Wadi and imitations made by lowlanders (recognized as such) have joined the stock.

The Palauans

Palau (Belau) Island is the westernmost island of the Carolines, themselves the westernmost large island archipelago in Micronesia (the "tiny islands") in the Pacific Ocean. It is directly north of Irian Jaya (the Indonesian part of New Guinea). Linguistically, Palauan is one of only two languages (the other is Chamorro, spoken on Guam) in Micronesia related to the Western Austronesian group, spoken in Indonesia (but in New Guinea only in the extreme west), Malaysia, the Philippines, and Madagascar (Crystal 1987, 317–319).

The "bead money" of Palau *(udoud ra Belau)* has often been written about since Captain Henry Wilson wrecked the *Antelope* off the island in 1783. Most recently, Thijssen-Etpison (n.d., 38–53) synthesized earlier reports on them and added a wealth of new information in the form of color photographs and plates.[22] Her work is remarkable for revealing many collections, because most owners are very secretive about them. Among the beads are monochrome ones difficult to identify from the photographs alone, but there are three groups distinctive enough to be identified from the plates. They are:

1. Indo-Pacific beads. These are the "trade wind beads" (Thijssen-Etpison n.d., 41) and the *balang*, which have been out of circulation (probably because of the influx of small Japanese and later American coins) since the 1920s.
2. The *bachel*. These are the most valued beads. They were made by cutting thick glass bangles into pieces and drilling them at two edges so they sit as a gorget on the neck (Figure 17.2). The bangles probably originated in China or mainland Southeast Asia, but without more study (including analyses) they cannot be dated. They were altered into beads by local artisans, apparently to increase the money in circulation (Thijssen-Etpison n.d., 40).
3. East Javanese glass beads, the focus of the following remarks.

All the spectacular East Javanese beads are found in Palau. (For a more detailed description of these beads see chapter 13.) The most valued ones are the white-

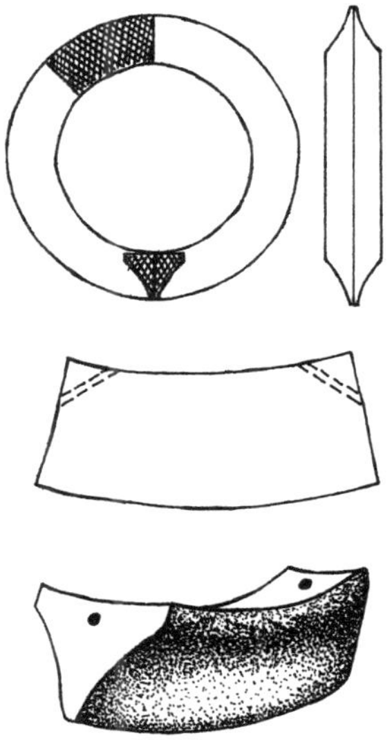

Figure 17.2. *The* bachel, *an important "money bead" in Palau made from glass bangles. A bangle (reduced top and side view at top) was cut, usually into six short sections. These were drilled along the paths shown in the cross-section view in the center. At the bottom is a completed* bachel, *which is worn close to the neck in the manner of a gorget. Sketch by Cynthia Schave.*

spotted eye beads with a yellow center, a *chelbucheb*, specifically the *meringel chad*, "precious" (Thijssen-Etpison n.d., 42). These are apparently the most widely owned beads on Palau. The large combed beads called *pelangi* by Indonesians and *kluk* on Palau and the smaller twisted striped beads called *smesmob* of the *chelbucheb* class (Thijssen-Etpison n.d., 43, 42) are in circulation, as are mosaic beads or *ngirbidul* (the right bead labeled "unknown types") (Thijssen-Etpison n.d., 42). The "big yellows" might be the *bleob* of the *kldait* group (Thijssen-Etpison n.d., 43).

There must have been contact between the Palauans and East Java between ca. A.D. 600 to ca. 900, when these beads were produced. Although beads travel widely and remain in circulation for a long time, the presence of so many of these beads on Palau strongly suggests that they were obtained when they were current in Java and have been circulating since.

An interesting phenomenon is that some *chelbucheb* and *kluk* beads were altered by being sliced into rings (Kubary 1889, 18–19). This was done to increase their circulation for a food-paying ritual from a wife's family to the husband's. The ritual was stopped in the 1920s during the Japanese occupation, and these beads are now out of circulation Thijssen-Etpison n.d., 43).

To summarize Thijssen-Etpison (n.d., 38), the largest collections of these beads are in the hands of powerful, older men or the clan as a whole. They can be sold; some of the bangle-gorgets have brought up to US$30,000. However, this devalues the bead, because its worth lies in its known history (sometimes several centuries old) and its use in rites and ceremonies. Women wear only a single or a few beads on most days. These are usually loans from her husband's clan or indicate her natal clan's wealth. A woman can own them individually, inheriting them from her mother or husband. They are vital as symbols of social status, though they are often secreted away.

All the heirloom beads function as money. Some suffered devaluation after the Japanese occupied Palau in 1914. During the 1920s the sliced ring-beads, the Indo-Pacific beads, and the bottle green *cheldoech* bangle-gorget pieces were devalued. The bangle-gorget pieces were imitated by using the heels of bottles (Thijssen-Etpison n.d., 42). It is not clear who produced these imitations.

The old ornaments of Palau are interesting case studies in heirlooming. The collection is closed, with two exceptions. One is the increase of circulating beads by cutting and drilling bangles and slicing beads to form more units. The other is the recent importation of illegally excavated East Javanese beads sold by antique dealers in Jakarta and Kuta (Bali). Older Palauans insist that even if they are the same kind of beads from the same place (and they are, unless they are recent imitations)[23] they will never have the value of the genuine old resident beads, because they have no history attached to them. The acculturation of these newly introduced beads will be fascinating to observe. It is also, unfortunately, another motive for looting archaeological sites.

Palauans show a mixed tendency in splitting or curating collections. There is constant splitting, as new adolescent girls and wives are added to a clan. Older men, presumably chiefs, are curators of their own or the clan's collection and seek to enlarge their holdings. The desire to own particular beads generates lawsuits and various nefarious schemes.

Kubary (1889, 24–28) discussed four legends current on Palau about the origin of the bead money. All ascribe the origin to the same legendary far-off land. These beads and drilled and undrilled bangles are found accidentally on Yap and used in exchange by the people of Yap who come to Palau to cut the stones they use for their own peculiar money. It was widely believed on Palau that the inhabitants of Palau originally lived on Yap and were driven to Palau by newcomers to Yap.

If this is correct, it means the inhabitants of Yap obtained these beads from East Java between about A.D. 600 and 900, later bringing most of them to Palau when they were forced off Yap. The people themselves may have been from Indonesia, as many elements of their culture suggest (Kubary 1889, 28), including their language.

Variations in Practices

Heirloom beads in Southeast Asia and Micronesia are governed by a variety of rules and practices. Inheritance patterns differ substantially. What might be thought of as the "normal" custom of a mother giving beads to her daughter is only followed in five of these fifteen cases. The timing and circumstances of passing on beads also vary greatly.

If the collections are viewed through the lenses of the split-and-curated dichotomy, spectra rather than neatly separated behavioral patterns emerge. Collections that were once split are now curated (the Kalinga and Paiwan). Collections can be split and still curated as long as they are completely closed (the Palau money beads and the *mutisalah*). A group may adopt both practices (the Ifugao).

This spectrum is even more evident when ascertaining if a collection is open or closed. It runs from completely closed collections (the Chin, the Kelabit, and the people of the Lesser Sundas[24]) to recently closed (the Kalinga and perhaps the Toraja), barely open (the Bidayuh), and still wide-open ones (the Gad-dang and the Akha). East Javanese beads on the Indonesian antiquities market may be accepted slowly in Palau, and not as readily as newly excavated *pumtek* were by the Chin.

None of this is surprising. It merely reflects the diversity among people. Although many of these groups are ethnically related, they live under quite different circumstances.

Certainly, an essential function of heirloom beads is to serve as an external diacritical mark to distinguish one group from another. Neighbors in Luzon, Borneo, and the Lesser Sundas never wear the same kind of beads. Even inheritance patterns differ radically among them. We should not be surprised if there is an exception to this rule, and there is. The Gad-dang are currently adapting the beads of their neighbors and are in the process of building their collections. On the other hand, the eclectic nature of their ornaments is itself a distinctive feature. Within communities, heirloom beads also serve as diacritical marks to distinguish wealth, power, political, and marital status of individuals.

The "Cultural Crisis" Hypothesis

At the beginning of this chapter I posed questions about links between the age of the oldest heirloom beads and historical events that caused a "cultural crisis." A review of the fifteen groups surveyed with these questions in mind can serve as a test of this hypothesis.

In Luzon this pattern fits very well among the four groups. The Ifugao were the most active traders with coastal people and felt the impact of the Spanish earliest. Their oldest beads (especially the *pang-o*) date to the period when they were being cut off from coastal trade. The *pang-o* is even found in coastal graves.

The Kalinga and Bontoc were more remote and the outside world did not impact on them much until American "pacification." Their beads are mostly nineteenth century (the stone beads are hard to date). They are also partially self-sufficient in beads: the Bontoc made *fukas* and the Kalinga alter beads. The Gad-dang are the most isolated of the four, with little outside contact until Independence. They are still building their collections.

On Borneo, however, this pattern is more obscure. The Bidayuh do not heirloom beads in the usual way. They are the property of only a few people—probably only one man and one woman in each village. The collections are still open. If Raseh's strand is typical, heirlooming began in the last century, when the "white Rajah" came to rule.

The Kayan seem to have merged their once-in-a-lifetime sojourn with their position as "bead traders to the jungle." Their oldest beads date to the Early Islamic period. This suggests that heirlooming began about the time coastal dwellers stopped burying their beads with the dead, roughly the tenth century. Kayan collections are still wide open and rare beads are very expensive. Thus, Kayan bead heirlooming seems to have evolved rather than having been the result of a community trauma.

The Kelabit are another story, but there is no evidence for what it might be. Their most valued beads were made by Chinese around 1600 in Java.[25] They were traded to the Philippines, but their most important destination was the southern Borneo coast to be exchanged for gold and diamonds. Learning how the beads got to the Kelabit would give some insight into their uncharted history.

In the Lesser Sundas we have a chicken-and-egg problem. We do not know if the elite began heirlooming and the commoners followed the fashion or if everyone used Indo-Pacific beads until the Chinese coil *mutiraja* arrived. Indo-Pacific beads were made in such enormous quantities for such a long time that the *mutitanah* and *mutibata* are impossible to date. They may have become heirloom items after the collapse of the Southeast Asian branch of the industry, around the beginning of the eleventh century. At that time, China opened an active bead trade throughout the archipelago. The elite ended up with the Chinese coil *mutiraja,* because they are more attractive and much rarer.[26] The princes received them because they controlled the sandalwood trade. Heirlooming began as a result of events far away from the Lesser Sundas, not because of cultural clash.

More information is needed on the settling of Palau. The East Javanese beads may have entered as trade or have been brought by settlers. To determine whether they became important because of a "cultural crisis" requires more data about the prehistory of Palau. If the people were forced off Yap to resettle in Palau, then the "cultural crisis" idea does apply to them. The beads at least give an approximate date of contact between East Java and the people of Palau and maybe a hint of the island's history.

The "cultural crisis" hypothesis fits the remaining five groups well. The Paiwan received their earliest beads from the Chinese and divided them among many heirs. When the Chinese came to colonize, the Paiwan were driven into the hills and the old beads became reminders of old times.

In Burma the last Pyu inscription is A.D. 1297 and the Shan invasion that drove the Chin to the hills happened four years later. Whether the Pyu, who were being slowly acculturated by the Burmese, made *pumtek* beads that late is unknown. Heirlooming may have started before the 1301 invasion, as the Chin memorialized the old dispensation.

The Akha, migrating southward, brought Chinese beads with them. The Toraja saw their world disappearing as Dutch influence penetrated. The T'boli were untouched until the American occupation and have some of the newest heirloom beads in the region.

The hypothesis that a significant lifestyle change can be correlated with the oldest beads of a particular group fits about two-thirds of the examples studied here. That is, it has been identified among nine of fifteen groups, eleven if one counts the special situations of the Bidayuh and the Palauans. The three groups it does not fit (the Kayan and the two classes in the Lesser Sundas) have the oldest beads except for those of the Chin and the Palauans. The prehistory of the Kelabit is so imperfectly known that a relationship between heirloom beads and an important event in their past is unclear.

I conclude this chapter with the words used to summarize my earlier study, because they are still valid:

> The study of heirloom beads has only commenced. Much more work is needed before we can build a global theory about this most interesting cultural trait. The work that has been done, however, shows much promise. It indicates the importance of beads to many people, suggests areas in which further investigation may prove profitable and demonstrates the crucial role formal heirlooms play in the lives of many people. Moreover, it shows that an understanding of heirloom beads can reveal much about the people who have them; their social systems, values and even something about their history, as yet so imperfectly understood.
>
> This is, indeed, a contribution bead studies can make. The ubiquity of beads and their universal employment mean that they can serve as markers for our greater understanding and appreciation of other peoples, other places and other times. (Francis 1992a, 15)

18

Conclusions

There was nothing extraordinary about beads in the Asian maritime trade. Calculated by weight or bulk, they composed a very small part of any cargo. Yet, they have two traits that make them particularly useful in tracing the history of this trade.

One is that they went everywhere. Ancient traders were eclectic and dealt in a wide variety of products. Beads are highly portable because they are relatively small and easily packed. Whether of glass, stone, or organic materials, beads were exotic luxuries to their recipients. Traders appreciated their high value for low volume. Thus, they were all but ubiquitous in the Asian maritime trade.

The other is that beads were often made of durable materials. With the exception of certain organic substances, they last a long time. This allows us to excavate and compare them with historical accounts. It also allows them to be heirloomed and studied ethnographically.

However, the mere acts of excavating or recording beads and subsequently cataloging and publishing them does not guarantee that something will be learned about the Asian maritime trade. The data from one site must be combined with those from many other sites and with data from other disciplines. Someone must then collate this information to generate hypotheses and the means to test them.

This is not the first attempt to trace the bead story over large geographic and chronological spans. It differs, however, from earlier exercises in being more scientifically rigorous and drawing on a much larger database. It differs in another way as well, because it has two goals. One is to discover the beads and the people involved in their trade, and the other is to trace the Asian maritime trade through the bead evidence. These missions are complementary, but have different emphases.

Beads and People in the Asian Maritime Trade

Beads

The beads in this trade have been discussed in detail in the foregoing chapters. Our interest is not primarily in the beads themselves, but what they can tell us about the actors in the trade. Because many of them carry technical or stylistic signatures that furnish clues about where and by whom they were made, we can assign them to particular industries, lending insight to the people involved. The vast majority of beads in this trade came from only a few sectors that can be easily outlined.

1. Indo-Pacific and related beads
2. Western Indian agates
3. The glass beads of the Middle East and its technical affiliates
4. Chinese glass beads
5. South Indian gems
6. Organic materials
   (a) Amber
   (b) Coral
   (c) Ivory
   (d) Pearls
7. Southeast Asian beads
   (a) Sa Huynh glass and nephrite
   (b) East Javanese glass

(c) Sri Lankan glass
(d) Unidentified origins (e.g., Ban Chiang glass, green stone collars)

The people involved in making and trading these beads can often be deduced from the origin and nature of the bead industries in question. Before discussing them in detail, a point should be made about this list.

All but two of the foregoing sectors (amber and coral) originate along the Asian littoral itself. Moreover, the first four sectors are among the six bead industries with a truly global reach[1] (Francis 1991d, 8–9). Thus, much of the world's ancient bead trade was incorporated in Asian commerce, and, indeed, many of the beads have Asian origins.

Two groups of people involved in this trade are of particular interest—beadmakers and bead traders. They are the principal actors in this commerce and deserve particular attention. Their ethnic affiliations, religious backgrounds, and genders are important, but often not recognizable through the tools employed in this study. However, we can glean details about the organization of their occupations and sometimes their status. Because beadmakers have been covered in some detail elsewhere (Francis 1994a), more attention is paid here to bead traders.

The Organization and Status of Beadmakers

In all but a few industries in the Asian maritime bead trade, guilds played a decisive role in the development of beadmaking, a common pattern around the world (Francis 1994a). This was true for China, Japan and Korea, pre-Roman and the Roman Middle East, South India and Sri Lanka, and Europe. In North India, the caste system took the place of guilds. Only in the Islamic world were guilds less important. Islam developed a rather modern approach to labor: anyone could do anything. The rules were so flexible that Jewish and Muslim glassmakers could use each other's tools on each other's respective holy days (Goitein 1973, 24), and scions of glassmaking families became renowned scholars (e.g., Cohen 1973, 34). Even so, Middle Eastern cities were (and are) divided by occupation, and sons generally followed their fathers' professions.

Without doubt, the most outstanding guild was the one involving the makers of Indo-Pacific beads (and perhaps stone beadmakers). It must have been based in South India and was most likely the Maṇikgrāman, at least in the later stages. If the hypothesis that all or most moves of these beadmakers were done under the direction of guilds proves to be correct, then they were the most important organizations involved in the Asian maritime bead trade.

The social rank of beadmakers has also been covered in an earlier publication (Francis 1994a). On the global stage, status varied between places and over time. In some circumstances, as with glass beadmakers in India, the status of the beadmakers was associated with the status of the material (in this case, both were held in low esteem). Nor is the status of stone beadmakers (as opposed to the major dealers) in western India very high.

This seems to be in contrast to the situation in ancient Sri Lanka. The word *maṇikara* (literally "bead worker") occurs several times in cave and other inscriptions found in Sri Lanka from the third century B.C. to the first century A.D. (Paranavitana 1970, 6, 17, 42, 60, 62, 64, 81, 88). Paranavitana translated it in all cases as "lapidary." That may be valid, though as we have seen in chapter 13 there is also a good case for glass beads being made on the island.

In several of these inscriptions only a name or the word *maṇikara* can be read. In others, small presents to the *Saṅgha* (the association of Buddhist monks) are dedicated, such as some steps or, in partnership with other donors, a complete cave. In one case, the beadmaker must have been a person of some wealth: "The cave of the householder, the lapidary Tissa, [is given] to the Saṅgha" (Paranavitana 1970, 42). In another inscription three people of interest to us are listed: "[The cave] of lord Sumana, of Tissa, of the female lay-devotee Sumanā, of the female lay-devotee Tissalā, of the lay-devotee . . . Kumāra, of the householder Dutaka, of the potter Soṇa and of the ivory worker Sumana. The lapidary Datta is a partner. The lapidary Cuḍa is a co-partner" (Paranavitana 1970, 62).

Another inscription shows us that the life of a beadmaker was not always joyous or even safe. It also attests that at least in this case the *maṇikara* were lapidaries who held a high position: "The lapidaries of king Mahācūḍika, who came here on account of brick-(shaped blocks) of stones, went to their death" (Paranavitana 1970, 64).

A rock inscription at Galgirikanda, the site of a Buddhist temple, discusses the upkeep of a *vihāra* or monastery named *maṇikāragall* (Paranavitana 1983, 118). The monastery was likely built by the beadmaking guild, which lobbied King Bhātiya (probably Bhātiya II, second century A.D.) to grant fields and other lands for its support. It begins with the word "Success!" and continues to list the land donated by the king. The same inscription refers to the village of Maṇikaraviya. There are also two villages recorded in inscriptions and the epic *Mahāvaṁsa* named Maṇikāragāma and Maṇikaragamaka, distinguished by their geographical locations (Paranavitana 1983, 106). Thus, there were at least three beadmaking villages in Sri Lanka in the last century B.C. and the first few centuries A.D.

It might be argued that a *maṇikara* did not work with his (or less likely her) hands, but was the owner of a shop employing laborers to make the beads. However, this would not explain why the king's *maṇikara* died in an attempt to secure raw materials. Taken at face value, the inscriptions imply that beadmakers must have enjoyed some status and even wealth in ancient Sri Lanka.

The Organization and Status of Bead Traders

It is not as easy to discuss the social history of bead traders as it is of beadmakers. Beadmakers form discreet groups, but trade is a more widely diffuse activity and many people participate in it. In social status, they range from the loftiest emperor to the lowest hawker going from village to village.

Merchants were intermediaries, and there was always more than one involved in the trade of any bead in the Asian maritime context. Someone had to move the bead from the beadmakers' shops to the ships. Someone took them across the sea. Then someone distributed them from the ships to the ultimate customers.

Commerce generates wealth, and the wealthy usually exercised control over international maritime trade. Customs duties were an important share of government revenue. Rome, India, and China established port masters, customhouses, and similar institutions at early dates, and other kingdoms evolved comparable mechanisms in time. In dealings with China, trade was usually subsumed under the term "tribute." Beads are also a sign of wealth. The exotic beads buried with Han noblemen in southern China, with Korean royalty, or those still circulating within the princely classes of the lesser Sundas reflect not only trade but also social stature.

Aside from the nobility, wealthy individuals, families, castes, and guilds were involved in trade. They alone had the capital to build large ships and launch major expeditions. Long-distance maritime trade required large, strong ships that could carry ample quantities of goods. One person rarely owned the cargo. Most was on consignment. Sometimes merchants went with their cargo, but more often not. Casson (1991, 10) discussed a single consignment of 700 to 1,700 pounds (318 to 773 kg) of nard, over 4,700 pounds (2,136 kg) of ivory, and 790 (359 kg) of textiles sent from Muziris to Alexandria. When sold in Egypt it could have bought 2,400 acres (about 1,000 ha) of prime farmland, yet it was only a fraction of the entire cargo of the ship; a 500-tonner (not uncommonly large) would have held 150 such consignments.

Traders may be involved in more than just the commercial side of the equation. In several examples, most notably in India, traders financed or organized beadmaking production. That has long been the case in the western Indian agate bead industry and is the situation in modern Papanaidupet, perhaps reflecting an older social system associated with Indo-Pacific beads. The Chetti in South India fulfilled this role in regard to coral. As the British East India Company began to wrest control of trade from Asians, Indians requested that amber and coral be imported in a raw state.

Alongside the major traders were smaller entrepreneurs. Captains, officers, and sailors bought and sold on their own account. Others worked from small boats along the shore or upriver or added their cargoes to seaworthy ships. The division of labor in China was minute. This is probably true elsewhere as well. In tenth-century Java, taxation was levied on finely divided groups of craftsmen and traders. The traders were distinguished by what they sold and by how they moved their goods, whether on their backs, by oxcart (water buffalo), by packhorse, or by boat (Jones 1984, 37–38, 50).

South Indian trading guilds were major players in the Asian maritime trade. The Indian guild known simply as "the 500" is praised on an inscription of perhaps the early eleventh century found in the old Mysore state. It claimed to do business from Gujarat to Cambodia. Its goods were elephants and horses, spices and medicines, and "large sapphires, moonstones, pearls, rubies, diamonds, lapis lazuli, onyx, topaz, carbuncles, coral, emeralds *karkkētana* and various such articles . . ." (Nilakanta Sastri 1932, 323),[2] and it boasted about enriching the coffers of the king and giving generously to holy men.

At Cambay, caste Hindus and Muslims were in charge. They were the "Baniyan and Borahs" of Summers (1851, 318) and the "few financiers who work as dealers and run their own factories" of Trivedi (1964, 26).[3] They have been the principal merchants for centuries.

Once a ship arrived, goods had to be taken to market. The Romans had a well-regulated system to transport cargo from Red Sea ports to the cities of Egypt (Rostovtzeff 1957, 155–157). Casson doubted that a Roman shipload was ever owned by a single merchant, but the Seṭṭhi family of India is described in the *Chullaka Seṭhi Jātaka* as buying an entire cargo and selling it to smaller traders at a great profit (Prasad 1977, 202). Secondary dealers further distributed merchandise, as with the Chinese in the Philippines. There are also specialist bead traders, such as the Akha of Thailand, the Kayan of Borneo, and the Hausa of Africa. Others dealt in whatever they could sell.

Diversity is the key to understanding bead traders. The trade involved many movements from the maker to the final customer. Many people, high and low, participated. They are those that van Leur (1955, 197–208) characterized in the Indonesian context as "Peddlers," "Merchant Gentlemen," and the "Lords of the Land."

The Asian Maritime Trade as Seen through the Bead Evidence

The scholars cited in the first chapter and others drew the outlines of the Asian maritime trade long before this study. Beads are a detail within the larger picture. However, focusing on them opens a rich source of new insights and generates leads for possible future research. The Asian maritime bead trade teaches us much about the people involved in it. It highlights roles that had only previously been suggested and identifies areas in which more investigation is likely to prove fruitful.

The Roman–South Asian Trade

Much has been written about trade between the Roman Empire and South Asia, particularly India. Most of it comes from the Western viewpoint, perhaps because most documentary sources have been located there. Views from the other direction prove enlightening (e.g., Weerakkody 1997). In this study I seek to examine the phenomenon from several perspectives.

One intriguing detail is that Indians seem to have succeeded in purposely misleading Western sailors and merchants about the facts of their luxury goods industries. The assignment of the sources of precious stones (sardonyx in the west and beryl in the south) to remote areas when they were actually close to major ports was one way Indians could keep their valuables secure. They also did this with stories of gold dug by ants and diamonds retrieved by eagles. The greatly exaggerated size of Sri Lanka and the monsters in the surrounding sea also helped retain Indian control over the lucrative exchange at Adam's Bridge.

What is striking is the ignorance about the source of most Roman gems. Those most prized were all products of South India.[4] They were involved in a system that linked raw material sources to lapidaries and then to merchants. There is nothing in Classical Western literature to hint at the role Arikamēḍu and Koḍumaṇal played in this trade. In terms of trade the region was terra incognito and has remained mostly so, even to later scholars.

The pivotal role of Muziris in the first century A.D. ensured it being celebrated probably long after it was gone. Earlier scholars recognized the standing of the port, but the reason for its preeminence had never been explained beyond the obvious proximity to the pepper crop. Gems, whether they reached Muziris via land or sea, were also key commodities. The port's power lay in what was happening in its hinterland. Pandukal riders probably gathered raw materials for Arikamēḍu and Koḍumaṇal, and Koḍumaṇal shared some of its materials with Arikamēḍu. Karur may have been a key transit point. The Chera Kingdom, of which little is ever written, and the Pandukal people, who have hardly been discerned, were at the heart of this trade.

The Early Islamic Middle East and the Eastern Trade

The "Arab" trade with Asia has been studied with some intensity. The important eastern outposts of the system were Kalah (the bead wealth of Kedah, Malaysia, seems to confirm their equation) and Zabaj (Vijiya/Palembang). Both were prominent in the bead trade.

New to the story is the technological transfer from the Middle East to Sri Lanka and Srivijaya. Glass beadmaking was transferred to Mantai, Sungai Mas, Takua Pa, and Vijaya. Beads never before (or since) made in South or Southeast Asia were introduced: mosaic glass, segmented (false gold-glass), folded, pierced-and-folded, folded-and-segmented, and stratified eye beads. Malays or Tamils could have learned these techniques in the West, but it is more likely that Westerners went east, possibly as exiles. The concentration in Srivijaya, the apparent short chronological period of the production of these beads,[5] and similar transfers to the Viking territory and Spain suggest a coordinated spreading of glass bead industries. A minimum of six different glass beadmakers was involved in this transfer to Southeast Asia, though none seems to have flourished very long.

South India and Sri Lanka as Pivots of the Trade

With a few exceptions, scholars have ignored South India as a dynamic participant in world trade. Most histories of India stress political events in the north. In terms of beads, though the western Indian agate bead industry has received attention for a century and a half, the gem industry and trade of the south has only come to be recognized recently.

The centrality of South India in the Asian maritime bead trade may be mirrored in other aspects of the trade. Within the bead context, it is undeniable. The glass bead industry (Indo-Pacific beads) and the stone bead industries functioned for two millennia or more, exporting their products both east and west. The long reach of Arikamēḍu's beads to Southeast Asia is remarkable. Its beads in Iron Age Thailand and in first-century sites in Java, Bali, and Vietnam indicate a widespread trade in these products at an early period.

Although the mechanism was not understood in the West, South India was the treasure chest of the ancient world. It lost its title to Sri Lanka in the mid-first millennium, but thereafter the two neighboring regions shared the honor.

Perhaps the most remarkable result of this study is the recognition of the role of the Pandukal people. They introduced stone beadmaking to South India and Sri Lanka. They selected habitation sites to take advantage of gold, iron, and gem deposits and were likely the people who brought stones to the lapidaries and colorants to the glassmakers of South India. Most of the lapidaries were themselves Pandukal. It is no longer adequate to focus on their burial practices. Their participation in world commerce must now be assessed. They were responsible for producing many gems sold to Rome, and the exchange with the Parthians (lapis lazuli for etched carnelians) is an example of their extraordinary scope.

Southeast Asia as the Crossroads of Trade and Culture

Southeast Asia's role in trade between India and China had been acknowledged previously. Beads furnish evidence of very early ties between Southeast Asia and India. Indo-Pacific and certain stone beads may now be added to early exotic industries or products on the mainland and islands. These are South (not North) Indian, often specifically Pandukal.

The apparent connections between Arikamēḍu and Funan via their beadmakers and later between South India and Srivijaya offer clues to the role of these states in Asian history. The movements of beadmakers, particularly glass beadmakers, are often accurate barometers of social conditions (Francis 1994a, 77). The migrations of Indo-Pacific and probably stone beadmakers may have much to tell us about events in the region.

Heirloom beads of some peoples also highlight certain historical processes. Many people with heirloom beads were marginalized, some before the coming of Europeans. The ages of some of these beads demonstrate the long "lives" they can have. Many are centuries old, and even newer ones let us trace trade patterns down to the consumer level.

China as a Player in the Bead Trade

The role of China in the Asian maritime bead trade parallels its emergence in Asian trade and politics. Chinese glass beads in Southeast Asia and East Africa reflect Chinese ceramic distributions, especially beginning with the Southern Song. Chinese glass beadmakers in Java are an example of the Chinese diaspora.

For a long time, scholars resisted the idea that China made much glass or glass beads, or exported them. Its role in the world bead trade is now acknowledged, and Chinese glass beads join ceramics and coins as evidence of contact, direct or not. The glass bead industry also ties the Western Hemisphere into the Asian maritime bead trade, with links to Alaska and Mexico. Perhaps this demonstration of the wide distribution of Chinese beads will inspire glass historians to take another look at Chinese glass history.

Final Thoughts

Henry Augustus Fox-Lane Pitt-Rivers wrote, "Common things . . . are of more importance than particular things (i.e. rarities), because they are more prevalent" (quoted in Atkinson 1953, 168).[6] Beads are common things. Small and often understated, they have long been overlooked. When they are studied, however, they begin to assume considerable importance. Their ubiquity alone makes them worthy of attention. Pitt-Rivers' maxim can also be applied to beads as a whole. Indo-Pacific and coil beads are the leading players in this study, and small, monochrome segmented beads were staples among Middle Eastern glass beads. East Javanese glass beads, etched carnelians, Middle Eastern mosaics, and other more "particular" beads can be informative, but only when the backgrounds of the "common" beads are appreciated.

Beads join other intensely studied artifacts in the tool kits of archaeologists and other scholars. Whether they will mirror ceramics as a backbone of investigation or become almost an independent discipline similar to numismatics cannot be predicted, but their richness deserves the attention of those who would learn about other cultures.

Bead studies can be useful in larger debates about the nature of the past. Bead evidence may be useful in testing Bronson's (1977) "upstream/downstream exchange" model. The core-periphery-hinterland hypothesis (Rowlands et al. 1987; Gills and Frank 1991, 86–89) looks especially useful for the Asian maritime bead trade. The debate over the world system (see Frank 1993) may also profit from their study. It would certainly confirm a world system operating well before A.D. 1500 or even 1250 (Abu-Lughod 1989). However, a global bead trade (excluding the Western Hemisphere) cannot be documented before the rise of cohesive empires that ensured merchants and producers a stable atmosphere for commerce.

Beads are not the most important things on Earth. Yet neither are they trivial. They are survivors of a great variety of human behaviors.

Appendixes

Appendix A

The Type Collection of Beads in the National Museum of the Philippines

Robert B. Fox served in the U.S. Navy during World War II. His assignment took him to the Philippines. He was so captivated by the land and the people that he returned in peacetime.

The Philippines was then a newly independent country. During the previous half century it had been an American possession, after having been in Spanish hands for 350 years. During the early twentieth century, archaeology and ethnography had grown into respectable disciplines. Fox and other American scholars introduced them to the Philippines (Conklin 1986).

Fox had some formal training in the United States after the war and soon returned to the archipelago. He spent most of the rest of his life there and became a leading scholar in the region.[1] He was one of a generation of European and American scholars who worked in Southeast Asia after World War II, many of whom recognized the importance of beads.

Fox conceived of building two bead type collections. One would preserve an example of every different type of bead that he had excavated. The other was to include every bead in use by different ethnic groups in the archipelago. The ethnographic collection was not very successful, perhaps because of the high price many Filipinos place on their heirloom beads.[2]

The archaeological collection proved to be more easily constructed. Each new excavated bead type was assigned to a broad pre- or protohistoric period and given an accession number. When similar beads were found at a site, they were strung together and attached to heavy pieces of cardboard, each representing a single site or portion of a site.

Fox enlisted the help of two Filipinos to work with the beads. Rey Santiago, then a young museum technician, had a background in—and a flare for—graphic arts. He painted a dozen plates showing all the beads in the collection with such skill that the details of the beads are often more easily seen than on a photograph. Some are reproduced in Fox (1977). After Fox died in 1985, Santiago became the curator of the collection.

The other collaborator was Jose B. Lugay, a chemist at San Miguel Breweries. Among other enterprises, San Miguel is the largest glassmaker in the Philippines. Lugay's (1974) chemical studies of the glass beads were carefully done. However, he freely admitted that some of the beadmaking techniques he described (in particular "dipping" to make a tube)[3] were highly speculative (Jose B. Lugay, 1989, personal communication).

The data gathered on each bead are maintained in extensive records in the National Museum. Their provenience, the identification of materials (often down to species and mineral types), shapes, sizes (in tenths of millimeters), and colors (with Munsell cross-references) were all recorded. Glass beads had their specific gravity reported to three decimal places. This information, illustrated with Santiago's plates, was to have formed the basis of a book. Claire Davison, then a doctoral candidate at the University of California, Los Angeles, visited the Philippines in search of material for her thesis on glass beads in Africa (Davison 1972). She agreed to help write the book. It was not to be. Fox suffered a debilitating stroke in 1975.

By late 1988, more than three hundred bead types[4] had been used to catalog over ten thousand beads from seventy-five sites. As Santiago said (1989, personal communication), they had all the data, but they did not know what it meant. Details of the collection were first published in 1989 (Francis 1989d). In 1991, data from Fox's private parallel collection maintained by Fernande Fox were added. Anyone who has read this book knows how useful the type collection has been. The figures in the tables in this appendix result from combining the two collections.

Despite the wealth of information on the beads themselves, the dates of the sites at which they were found are not well established. Radiocarbon dating has not been widely available in the Philippines until recently. Using other means, Fox divided Philippine prehistory into lengthy periods with tentative dates bracketing them. This is now changing, but it will take some time before Philippine archaeology has a useful series of radiocarbon dates. It will take even longer to reform the bead collection. Here Fox's chronology is used, with occasional adjustments when it seems appropriate.

Fox divided the prehistoric era into a Neolithic period, an Early Metal Age, and a Developed Metal Age. He called the protohistoric period the Age of Trade and Contact with the East. By this he primarily meant China, which actually lies northwest of the Philippines. This period is often shortened here to the Age of Trade.

The Chronology of Bead Use in the Philippines

The following tables divide beads in each period by several criteria. The material of the beads is the initial division, with finer divisions for different types of glass beads.

The tables include the number of beads of each type and their percentage among all beads excavated from the period. They also show the number of sites at which these beads were found followed by the percentage of sites where the beads were excavated. The final row gives the sum of the beads excavated in that period, the percentage of those beads represented in the table,[5] and the total number of sites excavated from that period.

The tables begin with the Late Neolithic period in Table A-1. Only one bead is recorded from the Early Neolithic, a pendant of a crocodile tooth with a triangular, gouged perforation.

These sites contained no metal; all tools were stone. The beads resemble those from pre-metal sites from other parts of the world.[6] Organic materials, especially shell, dominate overwhelmingly. *Conus*, *Cypreae* (cowry),

TABLE A-1

Beads from the Philippine Late Neolithic (to ca. 700 B.C.)

Material	Number of Beads	Percentage of Beads	Number of Sites	Percentage of Sites
Total organic	7,927	96.8	14	73.7
Whole shells	2,668	32.5	9	47.4
Cut shells	5,165	63.2	13	68.4
Teeth	93	1.1	3	15.8
Soft stone	251	3.1	9	47.3
Nephrite jade	11	0.1	8	42.1
Totals	8,185	100.0	19	

Nassarius, and *Tridacna* shells have been specified. Next in importance, though constituting only a small percentage, were those cut from locally available soft stones. These are probably mostly steatite, chlorite, and calcite.

The most interesting beads are of nephrite jade. As discussed in chapter 14, these came in trade from Vietnam, brought by Sa Huynh mariners. These people left their mark on the Philippines in many ways, including jewelry styles—especially the *lingling-o* (Francis 1995b, 4–6)—burial practices, and ceramic techniques. The beads add to the list of exchanges between the two areas.

During the Early Metal Age (Table A-2), imported beads were the most numerous. Indo-Pacific beads are found in relatively large numbers, at not quite half the sites. Nephrite beads were next most common and were more widespread. Beads from the quartz family (all likely to be from India) are in fourth place; a zonal banded etched carnelian barrel is in this group. Beads of organic materials have virtually disappeared. The only locally made beads in any significant numbers are of soft stones, found at only two sites.

Fox (1977, 761) called attention to a broken glass specimen from Uyaw Cave in Palawan. He maintained that it was the earliest glass bead found in the country. He believed that it was a cicada, but Santiago contends that it is bud-shaped, and he is very likely correct.[7] This bead was made by the lapidary methods of grinding and drilling. It appears to be a local product made from scrap glass.

Gold was more bountiful in this period than Table A-2 indicates. The Philippines has long been a major gold producer. The wealth of early gold jewelry is evident in private collections and that of the National Bank (Peralta 1983, Villegas 1983; Villareal 1988, 1991; Escobar 1991). Gold from scientific excavations is scarce because of illicit looting.

The terminal date (200 B.C.) proposed for this period by Fox fits the Sa Huynh nephrite bead data well. However, it seems a little too early for the importation of so many Indo-Pacific beads. They were being made at Arikamēḍu at that time, and they are found in Thailand and Vietnam by then, but they did not reach Java or Bali until around the first century A.D. A calibrated radiocarbon date for Manunggul Cave, Chamber B, where the

TABLE A-2
Beads from the Philippine Early Metal Age (ca. 700 to 200 B.C.)
(Revised to ca. 700 B.C. to A.D. 1)

Material	Number of Beads	Percentage of Beads	Number of Sites	Percentage of Sites
Total organic	3	0.1	3	33.3
Shell or coral	2	0.1	2	22.2
Bone	1	0.04	1	11.1
Soft stone	25	10.4	2	22.2
Nephrite	79	32.8	7	77.8
Quartz family	16	6.6	7	77.8
Indo-Pacific	111	46.1	4	44.4
Gold	5	0.2	2	22.2
Other glass	3	0.1	1	11.1
Totals	241	96.3	9	

earliest Indo-Pacific beads have been excavated in the Philippines, ranges between 390 and 15 B.C. (Glover and Henderson 1995, 148).

The Developed Metal Age (Table A-3) stretches over an uncomfortably long time span. In Fox's reckoning, it is 1,400 years long. Even if we bring down the upper date to around A.D. 1 (because of the Indo-Pacific beads in the last period) and the lower date to about A.D. 1150 (see the discussion on the next table), we are still dealing with a large chronological dimension.

It is clear, however, that India or Indians provided the bulk of beads to the Philippines throughout the first millennium A.D. Most of the Indo-Pacific beads, which make up two-thirds of all beads found, were probably made in Funan and Srivijaya. Those of the agate family would most easily have come from South India. Though they were relatively numerous, they were not as widely distributed as Indo-Pacific beads.

Some individual stone beads during this period are notable. A black and white etched oblate with a white net design is likely North Indian. A bead made from "mudstone" is shaped exactly like the *nelli*[8] beads of Sri Lanka (Dissanayake 1985). A spherical chert bead ground into a cube (retaining rounded edges) is paralleled in a bead of milky quartz from Oc Eo (Malleret 1962a: 197).

The Early (1200 to 1300) and Middle (1300 to 1450) Age of Trade and Contact with the East period were combined in Table A-4. Only one site (Bubulungun-I) was accredited to the Early Phase, and the fine dating suggested by their division is questionable. Bubulungun had mostly stone beads.

The beginning of this period might be earlier. The disappearance of Indo-Pacific beadmakers in Srivijaya may be linked to the transfer of power to Jambi (1079 to 1082). Unlike Vijaya, there is no evidence for beadmaking there, though it may have continued at Vijaya and Sungai Mas for some decades. In addition, Chinese beads were probably reaching the archipelago soon after the fall of Kaifung (1127).

This period is more closely dated than the preceding ones, thanks to the presence of Chinese ceramics. They were not the only goods coming from China. Chinese beads far outnumber all other beads. Quartz family beads and Indo-Pacific beads are now scarce and at only a few sites. Chinese glass beads constitute more than half the assemblage. Among the "Other Chinese" beads are polychrome combed beads and a wound bead with interior gold foil, known as *pang-o* among the Ifugao (see chap. 17). Many of the "wound glass" beads and the "glass onyx" imitations are probably also Chinese. They

TABLE A-3

Beads from the Philippine Developed Metal Age (ca. 200 B.C. to A.D. 1200)
(Revised to ca. A.D. 1 to 1150)

Material	Number of Beads	Percentage of Beads	Number of Sites	Percentage of Sites
Organic	14	4.6	4	25.0
Soft stone	1	0.3	1	6.7
Nephrite	1	0.3	1	6.7
Quartz family	62	20.5	6	37.5
Indo-Pacific	200	66.2	13	80.0
Other glass	24	7.9	3	20.0
Totals	302	99.8	16	

are leadless and may be early Shandong products. The European glass beads are chevrons found at Calatagan, Luzon. They cannot date before 1480.

Identifiable Chinese glass beads still dominated the trade during the Late Phase of the Age of Trade and Contact with the East (Table A-5). Some of the most interesting ones are grouped in the "Other Chinese" category. Combed polychrome beads continued, including imitation chevrons that cannot date before 1480. The light opaque blue oblates wound with several turns of glass were popular. Cobalt blue barrel beads of heavy lead glass were apparently made in Banten, Java, around A.D. 1600. Leadless dark blue glass was pressed into square bicones. Similar beads, also in red and clear glass, are found elsewhere in Southeast Asia as well as Alaska (Francis 1994c, 290).

Indian (or by now perhaps Chinese) beads of the quartz family are also notable. A hexagonal cylinder is made of a banded agate, western India's babāghoria agate. The nephrite beads may indicate heirlooming.

Indo-Pacific beads appear to make a comeback, but this is probably illusory. Most (82.5 percent) come from Butong and Tres Reyes. Fox (1967, 47) dated these sites to the fourteenth and fifteenth centuries, but they could

TABLE A-4
Beads from the Philippine Early and Middle Phases of the Age of Trade and Contact with the East (ca. A.D. 1200 to 1450) (Revised to ca. 1150 to 1450)

Material	Number of Beads	Percentage of Beads	Number of Sites	Percentage of Sites
Organic	0	0.0	0	0.0
Soft stone	0	0.0	0	0.0
Nephrite	0	0.0	0	0.0
Quartz family	6	0.6	3	21.4
Indo-Pacific	12	1.2	3	21.4
Total Chinese	556	54.6	12	85.7
Coil beads	334	32.8	9	64.3
Leadless Chinese	172	16.9	4	28.8
Copper ruby	1	0.1	1	7.1
Other Chinese	41	4.1	6	42.9
Glass onyx	246	24.2	6	42.9
Wound glass	196	19.3	10	71.4
Drawn glass	7	0.7	2	14.3
European glass	7	0.7	2	14.3
Copper	2	0.2	1	7.1
Totals	1,018	101.5	14	

be earlier. At least one Indo-Pacific by-product, a large, opaque orange reheated disk from a grave at Calatagan, is an heirloom. These were made at Mantai (see chap. 13) no later than the tenth century. The "Takua Pa eye bead" (ninth century) found at Morong was either heirloomed or the date for the site needs to be reconsidered.

European chevrons and Nueva Cádiz beads require some consideration. As discussed in chapter 16, these had been viewed as markers of early Spanish penetration. However, their occurrences in Egypt, Madagascar, and Jamestown, Virginia, show that other nations traded with them. Arab, Portuguese, or third-party traders could also have brought them to the Philippines, even before the arrival of the Spanish.

The Geographic Distribution of the Beads

There is not yet enough archaeological data to construct a definitive distribution of beads in the Philippines. This is largely an artifact of where Fox and his successors excavated. Rather little work has been done in the south. Most excavations have been on Luzon and Palawan. There is virtually no information on beads from Mindanao or the Sulu Archipelago. The Visayas also need to be better served.

Locally made beads, especially of organic materials, are universal on sites of the Late Neolithic throughout the archipelago. The introduction of foreign glass and nephrite beads is recorded first in the Early Metal Age in

TABLE A-5

Beads from the Philippine Late Phase of the Age of Trade and Contact with the East (ca. A.D. 1450 to 1600)

Material	Number of Beads	Percentage of Beads	Number of Sites	Percentage of Sites
Organic	2	0.3	1	5.0
Soft stone	0	0.0	0	0.0
Nephrite	11	1.6	3	15.0
Quartz family	67	9.9	6	33.3
Indo-Pacific	194	28. 7	3	15.0
Total Chinese	344	50.9	15	75.0
Coil beads	50	7.4	4	20.0
Leadless Chinese	64	9.5	5	25.0
Copper ruby	95	14.1	5	25.0
Other Chinese	120	17.8	8	40.0
Glass onyx	2	0.3	1	5.0
Wound glass	25	3.7	5	25.0
European glass	28	4.1	1	5.0
Gold	12	1.8	1	5.0
Totals	676	101.0	20	

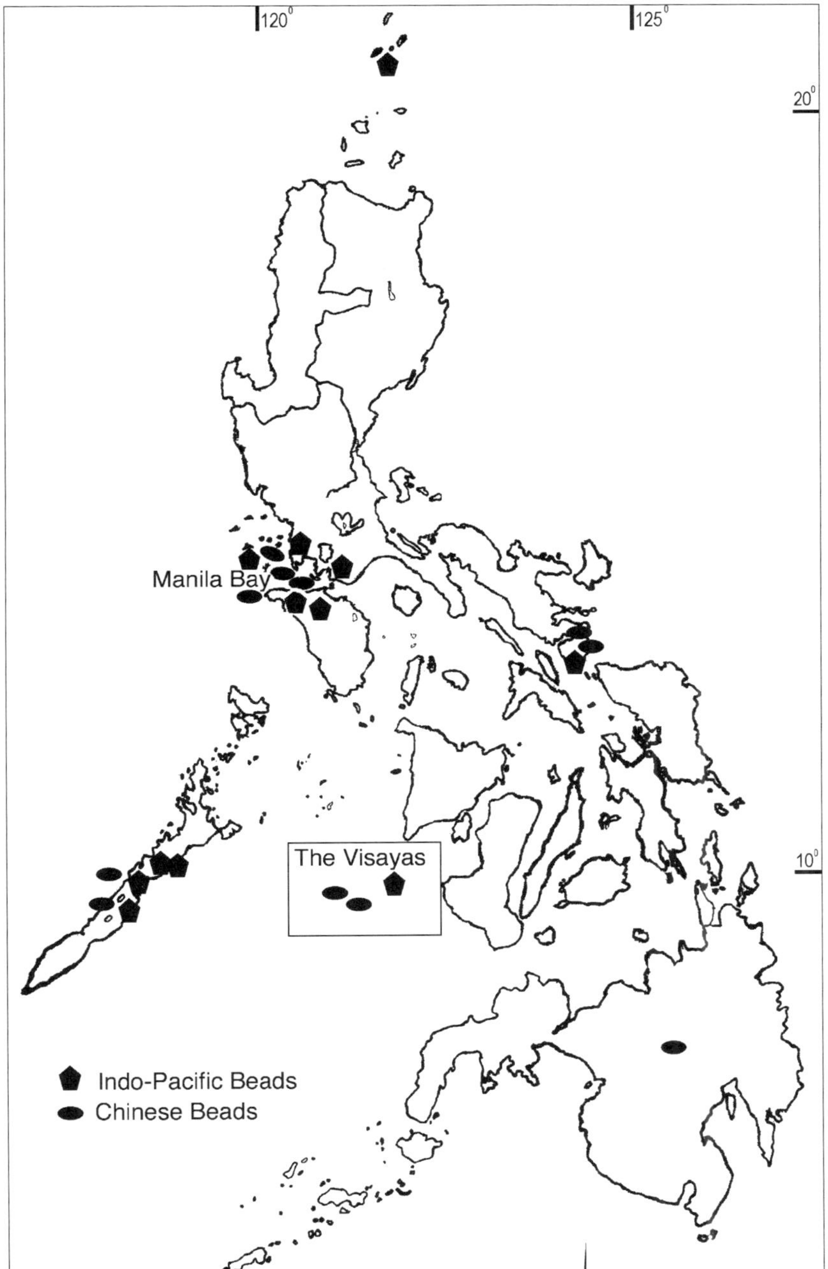

Figure A.1. *Map of the Philippines showing the geographic distribution of imported beads up to ca. 1450. The centrally located Visaya Islands are represented by the small rectangle.*

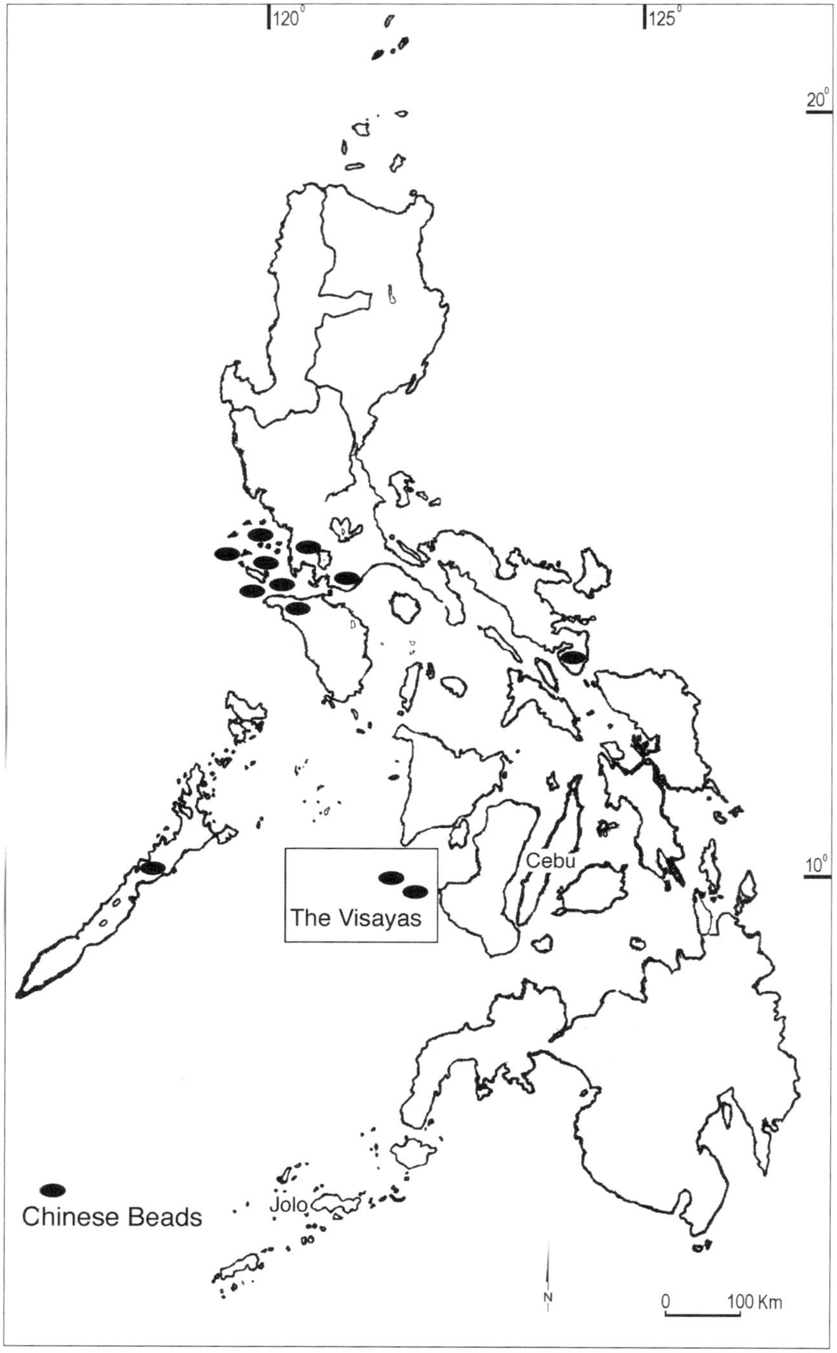

Figure A.2. *Map of the Philippines showing the geographic distribution of imported beads between ca. 1450 and 1600, indicating the concentration of imports at the emerging entrepôts. The centrally located Visaya Islands are represented by the small rectangle.*

Palawan. This is perhaps due to the intensive archaeological work done in the well-preserved caves of that island.

In the long Developed Metal Age (revised to ca. A.D. 1 to 1150) Indo-Pacific beads were most popular. They have been found in sites all around the archipelago: four in Palawan, five around Manila Bay, one in Albay, one in the Visayas, and one in Batanes. In the succeeding Early and Middle Phases of the Age of Trade, Chinese beads were by far the most important. They are also found at scattered sites: two in Palawan, four around Manila Bay, one in Albay, two in the Visayas, and one in Mindanao (Figure A.1).

The wide distribution of Indo-Pacific beads in the Developed Metal Age and of Chinese beads thereafter confirms Fox's (1967, 55–58) hypothesis that until about A.D. 1450 there was no dominant entrepôt in the islands. Malay traders with their Indo-Pacific beads and then Chinese traders with their own beads visited many harbors to conduct their business.

Fox (1967, 55–58) averred that this pattern changed during the fifteenth century, and the bead evidence confirms this. Just before the coming of the Spanish, Chinese beads continued to be the most common, but were more concentrated in their distribution. They have been found at one site each in Palawan and Albay, at two in the Visayas, but at eight around Manila Bay (Figure A.2). Fox indicated that Jolo in the Sulu Archipelago and Cebu became focal points of trade at that time. Their bead evidence will be most interesting to study.

It is important to record some beads that are absent from the National Museum but held in private collections. These include Middle Eastern or Srivijayan beads (Legarda 1977, 69, center plate; Villegas 1983, 34[9]) and East Javanese beads (Legarda 1977, 68, top plate; Villegas 1983, 34, row 4, nos. 4, 5). There is an even greater variety on the antiquities market. They are said to come from various parts of the country, and Bicol and Cebu are most often mentioned as sources. How far this can be trusted is difficult to say. A primarily southern distribution for both types would be expected and would explain their absence (except for the "Takua Pa eye bead") in the museum's collection.

The Type Collection of Beads in the National Museum of the Philippines is a unique resource. It is the only countrywide data bank on beads anywhere in the world. The building of similar collections elsewhere is encouraged. Notwithstanding its considerable value, there are limitations on its use. One is the loose assignment of dates. This will be corrected in time, but three modifications have been suggested here: (1) extending the end of the Early Metal Age forward to about A.D. 1; (2) putting the start of the Early Phase of the Age of Trade a half century or so earlier; and (3) combining the Early and Middle Phases of the Age of Trade until more sites of the Early Phase have been excavated.

The Age of Trade and Contact with the East should perhaps be renamed the Age of Trade and Contact with China. China was "the East" only from Fox's natal viewpoint, and the Philippines had been in contact and trading with other parts of Asia long before this period.

The other problem is the paucity of excavations outside Palawan and Luzon, especially in the south. In recent times, this has largely been the result of political problems. One can only hope that the era of confrontation is coming to an end. With new excavations in other parts of the archipelago, much new bead data can be expected. A Southeast Asian–Middle Eastern element may well be discovered in the south.

The occurrence of beads in the Philippines matches what one would expect from the study of beads elsewhere in Southeast Asia and along the Asian maritime routes. In the Neolithic period shell predominates. The first imports were nephrite beads from Sa Huynh, followed by Indian-made or -inspired Indo-Pacific beads and Indian beads of the quartz family. Around 1150, there was a significant change, and for centuries thereafter Chinese beads dominated the assemblage, even after the coming of the Spanish. The only important missing elements are the beads of the Middle East and the industries of Southeast Asia. These will likely emerge as archaeological activity expands in the island nation.

Appendix B

Analyses of Indo-Pacific Beads

Glass analysis is a labor-intensive, time-consuming, and expensive proposition. Several different physical and chemical analytical techniques have been employed for the task. They all require considerable expertise and, increasingly, very complex tools.

No analytical method is perfect. Some destroy samples. Others test only the surface or near-surface layers, where corrosion is most likely, though surfaces can usually be cleaned or ground before testing begins. None reports all elements present. Some do not search for crucial elements and others combine elements. Older analyses and those done by arc spectrography are usually less informative than newer ones such as neutron activation, XRF, and microprobe techniques.

Glass is rarely homogeneous, and different parts of the same piece may yield different results. Because of calibration problems, analyses done on the same piece of glass may differ from laboratory to laboratory or even between two different testing runs at the same facility.

The interpretation of glass analyses is also complicated. Results are given in percentage of weight. Some analyses report oxides, and others only elements. The percentage will be higher in the former than the latter. Total percentages almost never equal 100 percent because not all elements were sought. When the totals equal 100 percent, the silica was usually determined by subtracting the other detected elements from that base. Nor do all analyses seek and report the same elements.

With all these problems, one must sift carefully through available analyses to determine their meaning. In this appendix I examine the results of sixty analyses made on Indo-Pacific beads or glass pieces by various investigators. Of these, other authors had published forty, some of which were discussed in an earlier paper (Francis 1988–1989, 4–9). Ron Hancock, using the SLOWPOKE Reactor Facility of the University of Toronto, did the other twenty specifically for this project. I supplied him with samples from seven Indo-Pacific beadmaking sites and one importing site; the beads were given to me for this purpose by the excavators of the respective sites.[1]

Further analyses have been done on 151 glass beads and wasters from fifteen sites in South and Southeast Asia that I supplied Laura Dussubieux and Bernard Gratuze at Institut de Recherches sur les Archéomatériaux, Centre Ernest Babelon in Orléans, a unit of Centre National de la Recherche Scientifique. These samples came both from Indo-Pacific beadmaking sites and from importing sites. Before this volume went to press, a preliminary report on these beads was sent to me (Dussubieux and Gratuze 2000); I have made use of some of the data here, but the full analyses are not yet available.

Interpreting Glass Analyses

Ancient and modern glasses are composed of many different elements. Glassmaking was traditionally an art, not a science, and early glassmakers did not have the ability to purify their ingredients completely. Some elements in glass are important in tracing the origin of the raw materials, but others are not considered significant. The constituents of glass may be grouped into six categories:

1. Glass formers. All glass considered here is silica-based. The silica contents vary from less than 55 percent to nearly 75 percent. The difference depends on the amount of other ingredients; it is rarely crucial to understanding glass samples. The other important glass former is lead, which by virtue of its high specific gravity can register up to 90 percent of the weight of ingredients. No Indo-Pacific beads were made of lead glass. However, the lack of lead in some of these glasses is important.
2. Alkalies. Silica melts at a very high temperature, too high for any ancient furnace to reach. A flux, employed to lower the melting point of silica, needed to be added to the batch. Lead can serve as a flux, but more often alkalies were used, principally sodium (as soda) and potassium (as potash). They were derived from soil deposits, evaporated seawater or saline lakes, or the ashes of plants.[2] Plant ash is usually a mixture of these two alkalies. In fact, most alkalies in ancient glasses are mixed to some degree. The ratio of alkalies in glass is often an important clue to their association and their sources.
3. Secondary ingredients. Calcium, aluminum, iron, manganese, and magnesium are usually present in older glass in concentrations from 1.0 to 10.0 percent; the higher concentration is rare. Lime (calcium) is necessary to stabilize glass, though ancient glassmakers may not have realized this (Turner 1956a, 45T–46T). Manganese and iron may be added as colorants (discussed next); otherwise, along with aluminum and magnesium, they are impurities introduced with the sand, the alkalies, colorants, or the crucibles (especially in the case of aluminum).
4. Colorants. Metal salts are added to the batch to impart various hues. Upon firing they convert to oxides. All but the purest modern glasses have some color. Iron and copper, both common by the time glass was invented, can impart a wide spectrum of colors, depending on their amounts and how the glass is worked. Manganese and cobalt are powerful colorants that have been known for a long time.
5. Opacifiers. Arsenic, antimony, and tin have been used as opacifiers, as have salt, bone, and fluorides. The elements in these ingredients are also commonly found in trace amounts. Purposeful addition is not usually assumed until a concentration of 1.0 percent or so is reached.[3]
6. Trace elements. Tiny amounts of other elements enter the glass batch inadvertently. Titanium, vanadium, gold, silver, and others are nearly always present in amounts of 0.1 percent, 0.01 percent, or even less. Combinations of trace elements may provide a "fingerprint" to help identify particular glasses, but the validity of that expectation has not yet been demonstrated. There are still not enough analyses revealing such "fingerprints" to be useful in comparing them. Differences in trace elements may be attributed to any of the primary or secondary constituents of glass, and the sources of these ingredients may vary widely, even at one glasshouse.

Analyses of Indo-Pacific Beads

Indo-Pacific beads were made at several sites over a long period. Beadmakers do not need to make glass to make beads. Broken glass can be recycled, and glass "cakes" have been articles of commerce for millennia. Because there are several possible origins for Indo-Pacific bead glass, various questions arise.

The first is whether the glass for Indo-Pacific beads was imported from outside, in particular the West. An earlier work in which analyses of these beads were compared with glass from various Western sources showed that glass of Indo-Pacific beads is unlike any contemporary Western glasses[4] (Francis 1988–1989, 4–9). The results from the SLOWPOKE-Toronto analyses confirm that assessment.

This leaves us with other questions. If the glass was made within the Indo-Pacific beadmaking system, where was it produced? Was it made in one place and exported to other beadmaking sites? Were there regional glass-making centers? Did each beadmaking locale make its own glass?

We cannot answer all these questions with absolute certainty yet, but we are beginning to see some patterns. No patterns could have been recognized before Indo-Pacific beads were acknowledged as a discrete type of bead nor before it was understood where they were made. Earlier investigations grouped Indo-Pacific beads and glass from beadmaking sites with beads from importing sites, and sometimes even with other kinds of beads or glass, making it impossible to discern any trends. Here we concentrate only on glass from Indo-Pacific beadmaking sites.

To make real comparisons between Indo-Pacific beads made at different sites, it was necessary to choose only analyses that were certainly of these beads or their wasters. This limited the number of analyses used here, but ensures that we are comparing like with like.

Several published analyses, indeed twenty-five of sixty-five, that might otherwise have been included here[5] were eliminated because vital information about the beads was not presented. Even Indo-Pacific beadmaking sites have beads from other sources. When only a color or an ambiguous description (such as "bead") is given without any indication of the manufacturing technique, it is unwise to assume that the analyzed items are Indo-Pacific beads. In addition, especially in the case of Arikamēḍu, when color is omitted, the analysis is not useful.

Rather than include beads that may not be of the Indo-Pacific type, I have preferred to exclude these analyses, including those published by Lamb (1965b) and Lal (1987). This is unfortunate, but the responsibility of reporting all relevant facts about beads rests on those who analyze and publish their findings.[6]

Of the ten known Indo-Pacific beadmaking sites, there are analyses available for eight of them. None has been made for modern Papanaidupet, because its glass is made at or with technical help from Firozabad. Analyses of Mantai glass are being done in conjunction with the excavation and are unfortunately not yet available.

The only analyses for Karaikadu, Sungai Mas, and Vijaya/Palembang were done at SLOWPOKE-Toronto; there are several analyses done by different investigators for the other five sites. There are nineteen available for Arikamēḍu, twelve for Kuala Selinsing, eleven for Oc Eo, six for Khlong Thom, and five for Takua Pa.

The results are not strictly comparable. In the SLOWPOKE-Toronto analyses, silica and iron were not recorded, because of nuclear activation property problems. The results are also reported as elements and not oxides. In the tables comparing data on beads from several different types of analyses (Tables B-1 through B-7), only major elements are listed. All elements from the SLOWPOKE-Toronto analyses are given in Table B-8. Some other analyses (e.g., Salisbury and Glover 1997) also searched for minor constituents not listed in the tables in this appendix. The interested reader is referred to the publications involved. The tables also do not take into account the work done by Dussubieux and Gratuze (2000).

The analyses for Oc Eo were done at the Office Indochinois du Riz (OIR), Saigon. It did not distinguish between soda and potash, which is most unfortunate in this context. The beads from Kuala Selinsing for both Harrisson and Lamb were analyzed by the Eastern Mining and Metals Co., Ltd. At least with some of them, silica, aluminum, calcium, and copper were analyzed chemically, but other elements were determined spectroscopically (Lamb 1961, 54).

No ancient glass object, even when produced at the same place, can be expected to be precisely like another piece. There are often wide deviations in the amounts of particular elements present. This is only to be expected. In general, these variances are not significant unless they differ by an order of magnitude[7] or fall outside the recorded ranges of concentrations. "Recorded ranges" usually refers to European and Middle Eastern glass. The fact that many of these samples do fall outside those ranges confirms that they do not belong to those glass

TABLE B-1

Glass Analyses (Percentage of Total) from Arikamēḍu

Sample No.	SiO_2	Na_2O	K_2O	CaO	Fe_2O_3	Al_2O_3	CuO	MnO	MgO	Other
1	64.81	11.35	4.32	4.81	1.20	3.41	0.72		2.25	P_2O_3 = 5.00; Cu_2O = 1.33
2	64.64	17.0	3.5	4.0	1.2	5.8	1.7	0.25	1.6	PbO = 0.05
3	66.45	13.50	3.9	5.0	1.5	5.1	1.9	0.15	2.1	PbO = 0.C
4	66.69	14.3	4.0	4.6	1.3	4.5	2.1	0.14	2.0	PbO = 0.01
5		8.72	4.21	2.56		1.89	1.24	0.15	≤0.84	Co = 0.003
6	67.6	12.4	3.76	5.61	0.69	3.36	4.02	0.26	2.12	Pb = 0.01
7	63.6	0.9	16.6	4.0	1.9	2.9	3.5	0.1	3.2	P_2O_3 = 1.4; Cl = 0.4
8	65.9	12.8	3.0	4.6	1.6	5.1	1.6	0.1	2.0	P_2O_3 = 0.8; Cl = 0.9
9	61.5	12.6	6.2	4.5	1.5	3.6	3.6	0.2	3.0	P_2O_3 = 1.0; Cl = 0.9
10	75.81	1.0	15.0	2.0	1.2	2.4	0.04	1.5	0.45	
11	73.6	2.2	13.4	3.9	1.1	1.9		0.4	1.4	FeO = 2.0
12		≤0.26	12.4	≤0.62		0.90	≤0.10	1.5	≤1.55	Co = 0.04
13	72.49	0.20	14.14	2.94	6.50	1.12		1.99	0.68	
14	72.9	0.7	12.9	1.3	1.9	1.8	ND	2.1	0.3	Co = 0.1
15	75.90	4.27	3.93	1.84	2.58	2.88	1.50		1.31	
16	73.62	1.30	12.78	1.96	3.84	1.38		5.01	0.30	
17	66.9	14.5	0.6	8.1	0.5	1.6	ND	4.0	0.5	Co = ND
18		2.06	5.78	3.87		2.69	≤0.03	0.09	1.88	Co = 0.001
19		≤0.54	14.9	≤0.86		1.40	≤0.12	4.8	≤3.21	Co = 0.01

Sources: Red glasses: 1, bead (Tornati and Sleen 1960, 23); 2, lump (Lamb 1965b, 99); 3, long bead (Lamb 1965b, 99); 4, short bead (Lamb 1965b, 99); 5, chunk, from VI.106, an early locus (SLOWPOKE-Toronto); 6, tube (Brill 1987, 17); 7, waste fragment (Glover and Henderson 1995, 162); 8, waste fragment (Glover and Henderson 1995, 162); 9, waste fragment (Glover and Henderson 1995, 162). Dark blue: 10, lump (Lamb 1965b, 101); 11, beads (Subramanian 1950, 19–20); 12, chunk from VII.106, an early locus (SLOWPOKE-Toronto); 13, lump (Lal 1952, 25); 14, waste fragment (Glover and Henderson 1995,162). Green: 15, bead (Tornati and Sleen 1960, 23). Deep violet/purple: 16, lump (Lal 1952, 25); 17, waste fragment (Glover and Henderson 1995, 162). Black: 18, chunk from XI.055, an early locus (SLOWPOKE-Toronto); 19, chunk from XII.014, a late locus (SLOWPOKE-Toronto). ND, not detected.

groups. Unless there is a reason to do otherwise, I cite components of the glass as elements (aluminum) rather than oxides (alumina), whatever the tables may show. With these caveats in mind, let us first consider the glass from Arikamēḍu in Table B-1.

The glass of Arikamēḍu (ca. second or third century B.C. to A.D. 1600) is unusual. The red glass (nos. 1 through 9) is made without lead, an extremely rare occurrence in the West (Brill 1970, 120; Henderson 1985, 281-282).[8] More telling is that the other colors—dark blue, purple, violet, manganese black, and probably iron black—have potassium as their chief alkali.[9] Only the opaque green bead (no. 15) has more soda than potash, but by a very small margin.[10] Soda was exclusively used for Western glasses through the first millenium (Turner 1956b, 177T).

The Arikamēḍu red, on the other hand, is a soda glass; the one exception is no. 7.[11] This points to different alkali sources, either soil efflorescence or shore-dwelling

TABLE B-2

Glass Analyses (Percentage of Total) from Karaikadu
(all SLOWPOKE-Toronto)

Sample No.	Na	K	Ca	Al	Cu	Mn	Mg	Other
1	10.8	1.41	1.41	3.08	1.53	0.1	≤0.43	
2	0.56	11.8	≤0.71	1.19	≤0.14	1.45	≤1.68	Co = 0.04

1, Red; 2, dark blue.

TABLE B-3

Glass Analyses (Percentage of Total) from Oc Eo

Bead Color	SiO_2	Na_2O	CaO	Fe_2O_3	Al_2O_3	CuO	MnO	MgO	Other
Dark red	59.3	20.60	3.60	1.59	9.40	2.3	0.13	1.81	S = 0.89
Orange red	55.5	20.92	3.80	4.31	6.33	5.27	0.09	1.88	S = 1.30, Co = trace
Dark blue	59.4	23.34	10.80	0.64	2.16	0.63	0.03	2.60	Co = trace
Dark blue	61.0	23.90	8.00	1.20	3.42		0.14	1.44	Co = trace
Light blue	61.9	22.95	3.20	0.80	8.79	1.26	0.08	1.15	S = 0.37, Co = trace
Yellow	58.6	25.04	3.80	0.48	10.02		0.08	0.57	S = 0.61
Bright yellow	57.2	22.42	4.00	0.48	12.54	0.31	0.11	1.66	S = 0.68
Greenish yellow	59.5	21.70	3.00	0.64	11.61	0.63	0.11	1.73	
Light green	56.4	20.35	5.80	0.48	4.84		0.04	1.44	S = 0.75
Translucent green	62.2	26.45	5.40	0.48	2.46		0.04	2.17	
Black	63.5	22.81	3.60	0.80	6.90	trace		0.57	S = 1.02

Sources: Malleret (1962a, 465–469).

plants for the red glass and plants from inland for the other colors. Moreover, the dark blue glass is colored with manganese with a small amount of cobalt in a potash glass. This pattern is also seen in dark blue glass from Gilimanuk and probably Sembiran (see chap. 5), Bali, where Arikamēḍu beads were imported (see Table B-8).

The glass from Karaikadu (Table B-2) of the first few centuries A.D. is so similar to that of Arikamēḍu and the two sites are so geographically proximate that the glass was either made at Arikamēḍu or made with the same formula at both places. Again, most telling is the potash-manganese-cobalt dark blue specimen.

Oc Eo (Table B-3) in the first to seventh centuries was one of the first sites outside India to make Indo-Pacific beads. The lack of separation of the alkalies in these analyses is a major drawback. The difference in alkalies between different colors was important at Arikamēḍu and Karaikadu. Because the alkalies were not separated at Oc Eo, we are prevented from comparing this aspect of its glass. The high percentages reported for sodium at Oc Eo are suspect. They are never less than 20 percent and in two cases are over one-fourth of the total elements. The *combined* alkali figure in all other Indo-Pacific beads reaches 20 percent in only two beads and then just barely.

The aluminum concentration of Oc Eo beads is high.[12] Turner (1956b, 176T), discussing Western glasses, said that alumina is commonly present in amounts of 1 to 5 percent. He noted only three exceptions (1.85 percent of his samples) having more: 7.2, 9.8, and 14.5 percent. Seven of the eleven Oc Eo specimens have more than 5.0 percent and three exceed 10.0 percent. No Arika-

TABLE B-4

Glass Analyses (Percentage of Total) from Kuala Selinsing

Sample No.	SiO_2	Na_2O	K_2O	CaO	Fe_2O_3	Al_2O_3	CuO	MnO	MgO	Other
1	64.3	12.7	1.7	3.1	0.05	16.4	1.37	0.006	0.16	Pb = 1.2
2	67.0	2.0	6.0	4.7	2.7	5.7	1.1	trace	trace	
3		10.3	1.15	1.79		4.48	1.45	0.05	≤0.93	
4	76.0	1.3	3.4	4.7	2.9	4.2	5.7	0.01	1.3	Pb = 0.05
5		10.7	1.60	2.94		5.91	7.01	0.04	≤0.22	
6	66.0	16.5	3.2	4.2	2.6	4.1	0.3		0.5	
7	69.1	1.8	5.2	6.5	2.6	11.0	0.6	trace	0.4	Pb = 0.30
8	69.5	2.9	3.2	6.3	1.5	11.5	1.6	0.04	trace	Pb = trace
9		11.3	2.21	1.08		5.03	0.64	0.02	≤0.03	
10	67.0	2.4	6.0	8.3	1.3	12.0	1.2	trace	trace	Pb = 0.46
11	71.0	5.0	1.4	9.0	1.3	6.0	0.6	0.46	trace	Pb = 0.46
12	64.0	5.0	trace	7.3	3.0	10.0	0.2	trace	6.0	Pb = 2.7

Sources: Red beads: 1, Lamb (1965a, 36); 2, Harrisson (1964, 38); 3, SLOWPOKE-Toronto. Orange beads: 4, Harrisson (1964, 38); 5, SLOWPOKE-Toronto. Blue beads: 6, Colani (1935, 305); 7, Harrisson (1964, 36); 8, light blue (Harrisson 1964, 36); 9, light blue (Lamb 1965b, 105); 9, light blue (SLOWPOKE-Toronto). Green beads: 10, dark green (Harrisson 1964, 38); 11, light green (Harrisson 1964, 38). Yellow: 12, Harrisson (1964, 38).

mēḍu glass approaches these high levels. The Oc Eo dark blue glasses were not colored with the potash-manganese-cobalt combination. Arikamēḍu did not make glass for Oc Eo.

Kuala Selinsing (Table B-4) during the early first millennium was apparently related to Funan. Its glass is quite different from that of Arikamēḍu and Oc Eo. The alkalies as shown in Table B-4 are notable. They present a mixed picture, with soda dominating in seven cases and potash in five. Moreover, the total alkali content is generally lower than that of any other Indo-Pacific glass. Five of the twelve samples had 7 percent total alkali content or less. No other glass considered here has such low levels. However, this may be an anomaly.[13]

There is no cobalt-manganese-potash dark blue glass at Kuala Selinsing. In fact, there may not have been any dark blue glass beads there. Harrisson listed one; Colani only called a bead "blue." Lamb reported only a light blue bead, and there were no dark blue beads available to me when I collected samples from the site.[14] There may be a few, but nearly all the blue glass is light in hue and colored with copper.

Two orange beads have been analyzed from Kuala Selinsing. Their analyses agree with that of the orange bead from Oc Eo because they all have higher concentrations of copper than do the related red beads.

The elevated amount of alumina is especially noticeable at Kuala Selinsing. Nine of the twelve samples have more than 5.0 percent and five have more than 10.0 percent. The aluminum in the two samples tested by SLOWPOKE-Toronto is also high and would be even higher if calculated as alumina. Sample no. 1 has more alumina than any glass reported by Turner.

Yet another marker of Kuala Selinsing glass is the very low concentration of magnesium. Turner (1956b, 176T) reported that the usual magnesium concentration is from 2.0 to 5.0 percent. Only 33 of the 162 (20.4 percent) samples he considered had less than 1.0 percent. Yet, at Kuala Selinsing only two had more than 1 percent, and the yellow one looks as though the magnesium might have been a coloring agent.[15] Sayre and Smith (1967, 283–285) identified a low-magnesium glass common during the first millennium in the West. Yet, even with that glass, at least 0.6 percent of the element was present, more than nearly all of the Kuala Selinsing glasses.

TABLE B-5
Glass Analyses (Percentage of Total) from Khlong Thom (Khuan Lukpad)

Sample No.	Na_2O	K_2O	Al_2O_3	CaO	PbO	Sb_2O_3	CuO	MnO	MgO	FeO
1	9.93	2.24	6.23	1.42			1.33	0.06	1.32	
2	12.00	3.88	6.36	3.01	0.49	1.32	1.34	0.22	1.42	3.12
3	12.08	1.65	4.28	1.89	0.81	<0.5	3.56	<0.1	0.55	1.25
4	12.53	2.60	10.18	2.59	0.66	<0.5	1.76	<0.1	0.16	1.28
5	9.56	≤0.90	2.37	2.72			≤0.13	1.7*	≤1.55	
6	11.99	3.36	10.05	2.30	4.57	<0.5	<0.1	<0.1	<0.1	1.10

Sources: 1, Red bead (SLOWPOKE-Toronto); 2, square red tube (Salisbury and Glover 1997, 12, bead 29); 3, square red tube (Salisbury and Glover 1997, 12, bead 36); 4, red bead (Salisbury and Glover 1997, bead 39); 5, dark blue bead (SLOWPOKE-Toronto); 6, yellow drawn tube (Salisbury and Glover 1997, 12, bead 37).

* Also contains 0.04 Co.

TABLE B-6

Glass Analyses (Percentage of Total) from Takua Pa

Sample No.	SiO_2	Na_2O	K_2O	CaO	Fe_2O_3	Al_2O_3	CuO	MnO	MgO	Other
1		11.0	1.37	2.57		5.44	0.71	0.05	≤0.12	
2	76.9	9.6	1.5	6.0	0.06	4.2	0.22	0.06	0.25	Pb = 0.75
3		10.7	1.56	3.72		0.81	≤0.11	1.1	3.70	Co ppm = 443
4	72.6	12.6	1.5	5.2	0.03	5.6		0.05	0.37	Pb = 1.5
5	71.1	7.0	1.5	9.3	0.06	10.1	0.36		0.02	Pb = 0.20

Sources: 1, Red bead (SLOWPOKE-Toronto); 2, dark blue bead (Lamb 1961, 55); 3, dark blue bead (SLOWPOKE-Toronto); 4, yellow bead (Lamb 1961, 55); 5, light blue bead (Lamb 1961, 55).

TABLE B-7

Glass Analyses (Percentage of Total) from Vijaya and Sungai Mas (all SLOWPOKE-Toronto)

Sample No.	Na	K	Ca	Al	Cu	Mn	Mg
1	9.44	1.07	2.49	5.10	1.03	0.05	≤0.15
2	13.2	≤0.64	1.32	2.41	0.45	0.03	≤0.48
3	12.9	1.35	3.75	4.68	0.53	0.05	≤0.26
4	9.71	1.34	2.30	5.50	0.31	0.05	≤0.08
5	10.7	3.13	2.88	2.58	≤0.07	0.17	≤0.59

1, Vijaya, red; 2, Vijaya, dark blue; 3, Vijaya, chunk of green blue; 4, Sungai Mas, red; 5, Sungai Mas, dark blue.

In sum, the Kuala Selinsing glass does not resemble that of Arikamēḍu, Oc Eo, the Western world, or any other known glass industry at the time. It apparently made its own glass.

Khlong Thom (Table B-5) from about the first to seventh centuries was contemporary with Oc Eo, Arikamēḍu, and Kuala Selinsing. Its red glass is similar to that of these sites. The one dark blue specimen analyzed has the manganese-cobalt combination seen in Arikamēḍu dark blues, though without being a potassium glass (a dark blue bead from Takua Pa has the same signature). The aluminum level is high, but not as high as at Kuala Selinsing. The magnesium level is generally higher than at Kuala Selinsing and is more in line with that of most other ancient glasses. The manganese level is quite low, except in the dark blue bead, which not only has a high level of manganese but also some cobalt. It may have been colored with wad, either imported from Arikamēḍu or found locally.

The ninth-century glass from Takua Pa (Table B-6) is less distinctive than that from the other sites examined.[16] The aluminum level is elevated; three of the five samples have more than 5.0 percent, but only one had more than 10.0 percent. Four of the samples have less than 1.0 percent magnesium. What is striking is the low level of iron, a universal contaminant. The analyses by Dussubieux and Gratuze (2000) confirm the high aluminum and low magnesium levels of four beads at Takua Pa. However, the low level of iron as reported by Lamb (see Table B-6) was not confirmed. It ranged from 1.42 to 2.36 percent. Unfortunately, iron was not detected by SLOWPOKE-Toronto. It is interesting that one of the dark blue beads from Takua Pa has the same manganese-cobalt combination as seen in Arikamēḍu glass, though it is a soda glass. Was some wad imported from India?

The two other Indo-Pacific beadmaking sites have had glasses analyzed only by Ron Hancock at SLOWPOKE-Toronto and by Dussubieux and Gratuze (2000). Only those done by Hancock were available for Table B-7.

Vijaya (ca. seventh to eleventh centuries) and Sungai Mas (ca. ninth to eleventh centuries) (Table B-7) were contemporary and within the same polity. Their glasses are similar to each other and to that of the related site of Takua Pa. The lack of lead in the red glasses and the very low magnesium concentrations distinguish it from Western glass. At Vijaya there are many chunks of a distinct blue green color, not seen at any other Indo-Pacific beadmaking site and apparently not made into Indo-Pacific beads. Copper, cobalt, and perhaps iron may have been responsible for its color. Dussubieux and Gratuze (2000) place it in a different group than the beads from Vijaya they analyzed because the alkali was derived from a mineral rather than a vegetal source. Exactly what role this glass had in Indo-Pacific beadmaking, if any, needs further investigation.

Table B-8 presents the complete results of the SLOWPOKE-Toronto analyses of Indo-Pacific beads and glass. The magnesium has been corrected for the aluminum influence.[17] As a check, the tests gave two values for sodium and they have been averaged; in all cases, both values were very close. One site here, Gilimanuk, Bali, was not an Indo-Pacific beadmaking center. It was included to see if a source could be found for its glass. The data for the dark blue bead confirm that it came from Arikamēḍu.

Miscellaneous Notes

The amount of lime in a few specimens is unusual. Turner (1956b, 176T) reported 2.11 percent as the lowest amount in his data bank. Henderson (1985, 277) suggested an upper limit of about 8.0 percent. A few Indo-Pacific beads have both less and more of these limits. Two from Arikamēḍu and one from Karaikadu have less than 1.0 percent of elemental calcium, and two others from Arikamēḍu have less than 2.11 percent lime. One from Takua Pa has 9.3 percent lime, and one from Kuala Selinsing has 9.0 percent. Oc Eo goes to both extremes: the lime content ranges from 0.48 to 10.80 percent. There is no significant pattern in this, except that Arikamēḍu seems to have employed less lime than most other glassmaking sites.

The suggestion that an approximate 1:1 ratio of calcium and magnesium[18] indicates the use of dolomite for lime has been discussed on several occasions since first proposed by Matson in 1949 (e.g., Turner 1956b, 176T; Henderson 1985, 277). One bead each from Kuala Selinsing, Khlong Thom, and Takua Pa and perhaps a couple from Arikamēḍu fit that pattern. However, this idea has several weaknesses, aside from those pointed out by Turner and Henderson. "Dolomite" refers to both a mineral (Sinkankas 1969, 369–371) and a sedimentary rock (Pettijohn 1977, 416–425), and the amount of magnesium in either one is quite variable. Ron Hancock (1997, personal communication) suggested that dolomite can have as low as an 8:1 ratio for calcium:magnesium. On this basis, most of the glass from Arikamēḍu and Oc Eo might have included dolomite. On the other hand, calcium and magnesium can enter the batch in other ways.

Tin did not play a major role in any of these glasses, including those that came from the Thai-Malay Peninsula where the metal is abundant. Indeed, the glass highest in tin, with only 0.5 percent, was from Arikamēḍu.

Sayre and Smith (1967, 307–309) reported that some Western glasses have copper, tin, and lead ratios that match those of contemporary bronzes. They suggested that oxidized bronze may have been used as a glass colorant. To see if this was the case among Indo-Pacific beadmakers, copper and tin ratios were compared.

Red Indo-Pacific beads all have more copper than the dark blue, light blue, and blue green beads from the same site. If bronze were used, a corresponding increase in tin should be recorded for the red beads.[19] A 10:1 copper:tin ratio was used as a rule-of-thumb. Among the beads from Arikamēḍu (and Karaikadu and Gilimanuk) there is less tin in the red beads than in the other colors, suggesting that tin was a minor constituent in wad.[20] Only the red and orange beads from Kuala Selinsing and the beads of Srivijaya had 10:1 increases in copper and tin.

TABLE B-8

SLOWPOKE-Toronto Analyses (Percentage of Total) of Indo-Pacific Beads and Glass

Sample No.	Ca	Cl	Co	Cu	Al	Mg	Mn	Na	Sn	Ti	V	As	K	Sb
1	2.56	0.79	≤0.003	1.24	1.89	≤0.54	0.15	8.72	≤0.09	≤0.01	0.008	≤0.007	4.21	≤0.008
2	3.87	0.78	≤0.001	≤0.03	2.69	1.45	0.09	2.06	≤0.04	0.02	0.003	≤0.002	5.78	≤0.003
3	≤0.62	0.19	0.04	≤0.10	0.90	≤1.41	1.5	≤0.26	≤0.27	≤0.37	0.006	≤0.002	12.4	≤0.003
4	≤0.86	≤0.23	≤0.01	≤0.12	1.40	≤2.99	4.8	≤0.54	≤0.53	≤0.48	≤0.002	≤0.003	14.9	≤0.003
5	1.08	0.68	≤0.002	0.64	5.03	≤0.03	0.02	11.3	≤0.07	0.21	0.007	≤0.008	2.21	≤0.009
6	1.79	0.67	≤0.003	1.45	4.48	≤0.21	0.05	10.3	0.25	0.28	0.007	≤0.007	1.15	≤0.13
7	2.94	0.27	≤0.004	7.01	5.91	≤0.22	0.04	10.7	0.34	0.28	0.009	0.02	1.60	≤0.011
8	1.87	0.39	≤0.003	1.68	3.13	≤0.50	0.13	11.2	≤0.1	≤0.14	0.005	≤0.008	1.68	≤0.011
9	≤0.29	≤0.03	0.02	≤0.06	2.28	≤0.34	0.5	0.24	≤0.1	≤0.17	0.004	≤0.01	13.5	≤0.012
10	2.49	1.05	≤0.003	1.03	5.10	≤0.15	0.05	9.44	0.2	0.31	0.005	≤0.005	1.07	≤0.008
11	1.32	0.65	≤0.002	0.45	2.41	≤0.48	0.03	13.2	≤0.07	0.29	0.01	≤0.009	≤0.64	≤0.015
12	3.75	0.58	≤0.003	0.53	4.68	≤0.26	0.05	12.9	≤0.09	0.32	0.01	≤0.008	1.35	≤0.011
13	2.30	0.69	≤0.003	0.31	5.50	≤0.08	0.05	9.71	≤0.09	0.32	0.01	≤0.006	1.34	≤0.01
14	2.88	1.05	≤0.003	≤0.07	2.58	≤0.59	0.17	10.7	≤0.09	≤0.14	0.003	≤0.006	3.13	≤0.008
15	2.57	1.14	≤0.002	0.71	5.44	≤0.12	0.05	11.0	≤0.08	≤0.12	0.01	≤0.007	1.37	≤0.008
16	3.72	0.53	0.004	≤0.11	0.81	3.70	1.05	10.7	≤0.2	≤0.27	≤0.002	≤0.004	1.56	≤0.005
17	1.42	0.82	≤0.003	1.33	6.23	1.32	0.06	9.93	0.24	≤0.14	0.005	≤0.007	2.24	≤0.01
18	2.72	0.78	0.03	≤0.13	2.37	≤1.55	1.71	9.56	≤0.29	≤0.40	0.01	≤0.01	≤0.90	≤0.014
19	1.41	0.69	≤0.003	1.53	3.08	≤0.43	0.12	10.8	0.21	0.30	0.006	≤0.006	1.41	≤0.009
20	≤0.71	≤0.08	0.04	≤0.14	1.19	≤1.68	1.46	0.56	≤0.3	≤0.47	0.01	≤0.004	11.8	≤0.004

Sources: 1, Arikamēḍu red chunk, early; 2, Arikamēḍu black chunk, early; 3, Arikamēḍu dark blue chunk, early; 4, Arikamēḍu black chunk, late; 5, Kuala Selinsing, light blue; 6, Kuala Selinsing, red; 7, Kuala Selinsing, orange; 8, Gilimanuk, red; 9, Gilimanuk, dark blue; 10, Vijaya, red; 11, Vijaya, dark blue; 12, Vijaya green blue; 13, Sungai Mas, red; 14, Sungai Mas, dark blue; 15, Takua Pa, red; 16, Takua Pa, dark blue; 17, Khlong Thom, red; 18, Khlong Thom, dark blue; 19, Karaikadu, red; 20, Karaikadu, dark blue.

Glassmakers at these sites could have used bronze as a source of copper, but further work is needed to demonstrate if they did.

Conclusions

The glass for Indo-Pacific beads was not made at a single center. Some from a few sites looks similar, but they are the sites for which we have the fewest analyses. There are four and perhaps five distinct chemical signatures among these glasses:

1. Arikamēḍu and Karaikadu. The use of potash in all but the red glasses (with one exception in nine) sets them apart from both Western and other Indo-Pacific glasses. The use of wad for dark blue, violet, and some black is also distinctive, though some wad may have been exported to Khlong Thom and Takua Pa.
2. Kuala Selinsing. The elevated amounts of aluminum, the very low amounts of magnesium, and the lowered amounts of alkalies make this glass virtually unique.
3. Oc Eo and Khlong Thom. Contemporary with early Arikamēḍu-Karaikadu and Kuala Selinsing, Oc Eo has glass that does not match that from the Indian sites. Its aluminum content is relatively high and its manganese concentration very low, as with that of Kuala Selinsing, but its higher magnesium concentration sets it apart from the glass from that site.

   Khlong Thom glass is similar to that of Oc Eo. The exception is the elevated manganese content in the dark blue bead, but the presence of cobalt suggests that it might have been colored with wad.
4. Takua Pa. There may be a distinctive signature if the very low iron concentration can be confirmed. The high aluminum and low manganese levels are not as evident as at Oc Eo and Kuala Selinsing.
5. Vijaya and Sungai Mas. At these two sites, levels of magnesium are also low, though the aluminum content is not excessively elevated. Except for a single bead with high aluminum content at Takua Pa and one bead high in magnesium, the glasses from these three sites look rather similar. More analyses for these sites are needed to draw any firm conclusions, however.

In sum, Arikamēḍu and Karaikadu shared the same glass or the same ingredients and recipes. Oc Eo and Khlong Thom may also have had glass from one place. Kuala Selinsing stands alone. The three Srivijayan sites (Vijaya, Sungai Mas, and perhaps Takua Pa) may have had one glassmaking center. On the other hand, the distinctive blue green glass of Vijaya and the possible low iron content of Takua Pa glass may argue against that. Unquestionably, there is more work to be done.

Notes

Preface

1. More accurately, in 1979 I founded the Bead Research Bureau, as well as the publishing firm of Lapis Route Books and the book distributor, Cornerless Cube. In 1984, these and other branches of the operation were combined into the Center for Bead Research, in Lake Placid, New York, which provided permanent quarters for the bead study collection, library, photo archives, and other affiliated facilities.

Chapter 1: The Scope of This Work

1. The anonymous author of *Periplus of the Erythraean Sea* credited the Greek Hippalos, around A.D. 50: "by plotting the location of the ports of trade and the configuration of the sea, [he] was the first to discover the route over open water . . ." (Casson 1989, 97).
2. This phenomenon is often discussed. See, for example, Wheatley (1961, xviii–xix).
3. Two legends account for this name. One is that Adam and Eve walked across it to Sri Lanka, eventually to be buried on Adam's Peak. The other is that they descended from heaven on Adam's Peak and *left* Sri Lanka via Adam's Bridge to populate the world.
4. Nicholas (1990a) contended that the route was open in ancient times, based on calculations of the silting up of the Mannar Passage in recent centuries. It could be that the Mannar Passage was open during some periods, but the weight of evidence from shipping routes suggests that it was closed to large ships most of the time.
5. This danger has not abated. During the Madras-Bangkok leg of the United Nations Educational, Scientific, and Cultural Organization (UNESCO) Maritime Silk Roads: Roads of Dialogue Project in early 1991, passengers on the *Fulk-al-Salamah (Ship of Peace)* were warned of the possibility that pirates might attempt to take over the ship. The crew was prepared for the contingency, but we were spared any action.
6. The initial report on Alagankulam (Nagaswamy 1991) has received some useful criticism indicating that the ceramics do not derive from as far away as first suggested (Begley 1994) and that its antiquity has been exaggerated (Ramachandran 1996–1997). It appears to date from the first century B.C.
7. This site has not been excavated.
8. The differences between these two today are botanical. In Classical times it was mostly qualitative, with cinnamon being considered the better grade.
9. For the early Middle Eastern chronology, I follow Mellaart (1979, fig. 1).
10. The alternate spelling is cornelian, used in British English. The two words have different etymologies, which need not be explored here. Carnelian is favored in American English and by the pioneer bead researcher, Horace C. Beck, even though he was English. At least one English authority (Sax 1996, 66) regarded it as the "accepted term in mineralogy."
11. The identification of places and products in much of the Old Testament is difficult. I may be accused of using those that suit me, but I do think they are the most logical. Quotations are from the Revised Standard Version (*Oxford Annotated Bible* 1962) and dates from introductions to books in that volume and Albright's chronology in the appendix.
12. Tarshish may or may not have been an actual place. Some passages suggest that it was west of Israel: Italy or Spain or perhaps a mythical locale at the end of the world. However, the term "ships of Tarshish" referred to the largest and strongest ships of the day, just as "East Indiaman" referred to large ships, whether they sailed to India or not (Müller 1911).
13. Was Ophir India? Many, including the editors of the Septuagint Bible, think so. Flavius Josephus in the first century wrote, "the land that was of old called Ophir, but now the Aurea Chersonesus, which belongs to India. . . ." (Whis-

ton n.d., 226) Others disagree, suggesting that Ophir was the east coast of Africa (at one time even identified with Great Zimbabwe) or the Arabian Peninsula, particularly along the Persian Gulf.

The precise spot may never be fixed with enough certainty to please everyone, but several elements can be used to locate Ophir. The three-year journey is too long for a voyage to the Persian Gulf, despite Price's (1911, 628) assumptions. Moreover, why bother to construct ships to sail to the Persian Gulf when the land route was much shorter?

The products provide other clues. *Almug* (perhaps correctly *algum*) wood has been tentatively identified with red sanderswood, *Pterocarpus santilinus* (Schafer 1957, 130), though often confused with sandalwood *(Santalum album)*. Both are Indian. The word for ivory in the passage (*shen habbin* [*shen* is "teeth" in Hebrew]) has been linked with *ibha*, "elephant" in India, known in the *Ṛig Veda* and apparently Dravidian in origin (Joseph 1963). Peacock *(takkiyyin)* is said to be cognate with *tokei*, the Tamil name for the stately bird (Post 1911). These Tamil connections are mirrored by the distribution of red sanderswood, sandalwood, and precious stones in the western and southern Deccan. Gold is concentrated in the south and east of India, and silver in the northwest.

None of this is conclusive. Ophir could have been a port receiving goods from India or elsewhere. Only the woods and peacocks are exclusively Indian, though the latter is not universally accepted as being in the original text (Buttrick 1962, 605). Complementing this evidence is the lack of the mention of frankincense and myrrh, important Arabian products. Ophir is probably India, particularly the west coast and Dravidian territory.

14. These may not be what we call emeralds. It is possible that they were beryls from South India, though it seems too early. The Greek *smaragdus* anciently connoted various green stones (Eichholz 1962, 168 n. a) or rock crystal (Petrie 1911, 620).
15. The coral must have been in transshipment from the Mediterranean. Compare Ezekiel 27:15, which mentions ivory being brought by the merchants of Rhodes.
16. The four Aryan holy books, the Vedas, are the earliest surviving Indian texts and some of the earliest books in the world. The oldest, the *Ṛig Veda*, may have been completed by 1500 B.C. The latest, the *Atharva Veda*, is dated to about 800 B.C.
17. The *Mahābhārata* was compiled over several centuries after the Vēdic period. Its core may go back to 1000 B.C., but precise dates cannot be assigned to particular passages.
18. The assumption is that precious red coral, *Corallium rubrum*, from the Mediterranean, is meant here. See chapter 15.
19. This may have had much to do with the development of money. Coins were first used in the seventh century B.C. in the eastern Mediterranean (Lydia and Ionia) and in China and in India by at least the fourth century. The introduction of large, valuable (gold or silver) coins authorized by extensive empires would have expedited international commerce. Such coins appear under the late Achamenids and Alexander in the fourth century, and Greek influence brought them to India by the second. Chinese coins are of a different type, being always of bronze, cast rather than struck, and usually with holes to string them into multiples. The first large bronze coin in China was cast for the First Emperor, Qin Shi Huang, in 221 B.C. (Allan 1942, 616–632; Grierson 1977). The reader will find Wicks (1992) a valuable work on the development of money in the Southeast Asian context.
20. Francis, lecture delivered at Denver Museum of Natural History, 1994.

2: Beads, Bead Materials, and Beadmaking

1. Without a stabilizer, "water glass" results from the combination of silica and an alkali. This substance dissolves in water, making it impractical for most glass applications.
2. This was tiny bits of seashells or flecks of dolomite or other calcium-rich rocks.
3. Manganese is present in both the divalent and trivalent forms, with the trivalent imparting the color. When manganese-clarified glass sits in the sun for several years, ultraviolet radiation solarizes it by knocking some electrons off the divalent atoms. Because this increases the proportion of the trivalent form, the glass turns violet. This does not happen to most modern glass, because it is usually clarified with selenium rather than manganese.
4. At Arikamēḍu, India, all three types of black glass were made. The opaque glass was probably colored much as is done at Purdalpur, Uttar Pradesh, India, where goat dung is added to the batch; the blackening matter is carbon.
5. This is by weight, not volume. The specific gravity of cast lead is 11.34 and of rolled lead 11.37. Thus, lead is more than four times heavier by volume than quartz, with a specific gravity of 2.65.

6. When an object is being made from hot glass, it is constantly reheated while being shaped or decorated. This often requires several reheating operations for each bead.
7. This term has been used to describe drawn segmented beads, glass beads with segments made by winding, glass and plastic beads blown into molds, and nonglass beads cut or molded into segments. Here it is used only for drawn segmented beads.
8. Unless some other heavy element, such as gold, is present in large quantities, lead is assumed to have been added to glass when its specific gravity is 3.00 or more.
9. However, the Venetians, the dominant glass beadmakers of the last five centuries, did not have noticeable perforation deposits in their lamp-wound beads. They glued a lime and white clay separator to the wires (Karklins and Adams 1990, 74).
10. There are several ways of dividing this group. See Sax and Middleton (1992) or Sax (1996).
11. Some carnelians turn red upon the initial heating to make the material easier to work. Virtually none is red when mined. German carnelians, made of chalcedony from Minas Gerais, Brazil, and most other carnelians do not contain iron naturally and must be soaked in an acid bath into which iron has been dissolved to turn them red upon heating.
12. "Onyx," derived from the Greek for "fingernail" because of its banding, has several meanings. Mineralogists refer to a banded form of compacted gypsum, also called alabaster, as onyx. (Egyptian alabaster and Mexican onyx-marble are travertine.) In this book I use the gemological definition of onyx, a strikingly banded chalcedony. The modern jeweler's "onyx" is not banded but is blackened chalcedony. It is a misnomer because it has no banding.
13. The banded agate from western India is called babāghoria agate, after the patron saint of the industry, Babā Ghor. The name has been applied at least since Akbar's time. Babā Ghor's exact identification is still not known (Francis 1985a), and he is not even buried where he is worshipped today (Francis 1989b) (see chap. 11).
14. Glass also corrodes, especially on the surface. This sometimes makes it difficult to analyze the glass and often to identify a bead's manufacturing technique or even color.
15. The unauthorized reprint of 1973, which is more generally available than the original article, has the same pagination as the 1928 article.
16. Beck's nomenclature has stood the test of time, but his classification has not. He fixed (in some cases must have coined) some 450 bead names, most of which are still current. His classification, based almost entirely on form, has proven less practical and has been adopted by only a few scholars. New classification systems are currently being devised.
17. The unauthorized American reprint (n.d.) of this book follows the same pagination as the Liege edition of 1973.
18. Writers differ on the ratio to be used for these designations. I suggest at least a 25 percent variation.

3: Introduction to Indo-Pacific Beads

1. These three accounts are almost identical; the section in the 1956 paper was reprinted verbatim in the 1958 paper. The 1973 reference is *A Handbook on Beads* for which little editing was done. The first edition of this widely known work was in 1967. It was printed in a very short run and is rarely encountered. The 1973 edition and the more easily available but unauthorized U.S. edition (n.d.) are paginated identically.
2. At first, I called them Indo-Pacific Monochrome Drawn Glass Beads or IPMDGB. Soon I saw no reason to insist upon this clumsy term and shortened it to "Indo-Pacific."
3. So exceptional is the process that after I returned to the United States from my first visit to Papanaidupet, several glass historians to whom I outlined the technique flatly told me that it was impossible and did not exist.
4. I did this with the help of John Anthony and the staff of the Pondicherry Museum. We also classified the equally numerous stone beads and wasters, discussed in chapter 12.
5. Although not totally. In 1984, after the tube-drawers' strike, discussed later in this chapter, work was resumed and continued through the day to make up for lost production.
6. As discussed in chapter 2, glass needs to be constantly heated while being worked. At Papanaidupet the glass is inserted into the furnace several times during this process.
7. Stern (1987) observed the workers throwing some crushed brick into the *lada* before piercing the glass cone, apparently to help the process. This does not account for all "knots," as she claimed. Torben Sode (1998, personal communication) has also seen this.
8. The question arises as to whether there was some connection between the two industries at some time. Most of the details of these operations and even the tools used are so strikingly similar that one might conjecture that an early European visitor to India saw the process and brought news of it back to Venice. The tube-drawing technique was not

adopted, but it is quite complicated. Certainly, the doctrine of independent invention could also be invoked, but a whole complex of processes is involved here. See Francis (1998c).

9. Unfinished segments of Indo-Pacific beads were never sold as far as I can tell. They do not appear at importing sites. The modern seed bead industry sells tubular beads known as "bugles," which are often left untumbled.
10. At the time of this writing in late 1999 three people who had recently visited Papanaidupet independently after learning about it from me have told me that the operation has nearly shut down. Whether this is a temporary lull or the beginning of the end cannot be determined, though the prognosis does not look good. Apparently the competition of Banaras Beads, Ltd. which bought automated equipment from Toho of Japan, has seriously disrupted the Papanaidupet market.

4: Indo-Pacific Beadmaking Centers

1. For example, the recent finds of some glass chunks, drips, a knot, and some bead clumps at Bãi Lãng in Vietnam may suggest such an industry. Glover (2000) remained cautious about drawing this conclusion on the basis of only a few artifacts.
2. For details on the *Sangam* literature, see chapter 12.
3. There have been many arguments put forward to explain the meaning of Podouké and Arikamēḍu. No others have the benefit of Mahadevan's scholarship and none had previously sought information in the vast Tamil *Sangam* literature.
4. Wheeler's account of how he identified Arikamēḍu as a significant site and obtained permission to dig there is detailed in Wheeler (1955, 187–218) and has been excerpted by Rapport and Wright (Wheeler 1969, 269–274).
5. One wonders whether Wheeler would have described fish in English waters as "gullible."
6. As Wheeler himself might have said (or should have known), this last entry and most of the glass would have been a case of "carrying coals to Newcastle."
7. I joined this excavation during the last (1991–1992) season as the "small finds man."
8. The idea of brick-robbers leaving behind imported Chinese celadon apparently did not strike Wheeler as incongruous. Perhaps they brought a table set with them for a picnic.
9. The so-called "rouletted ware," of which so much has been written, was not decorated with a small wheel, as this term implies, but by a technique called "chattering" (Begley 1985).
10. The date of the invasion was put at 993 by Carswell and Prickett (1984, 60), though earlier Carswell (1983, 85) had cited 959. Nilakanta Sastri (1975, 172–173) said that 993 is the date of the first inscription to include Sri Lanka among the conquests of the Cōḷa King Rājarāja I. He further suggested that it happened after 991 because it is not mentioned in the *Mahāvaṁsa*. In 991 the annals of the Sri Lankan king Mahinda V became confused as a result of an internal military uprising. Hence, the event most likely happened between 991 and 993.
11. Vietnamese scholars now refer to this polity as the "Oc Eo Culture."
12. The amount of recognizably Western objects from Oc Eo compared with that at Arikamēḍu, because it is much farther east, has always surprised me. I tallied some artifacts from the two sites and Oc Eo does seem to be richer in Roman items than Arikamēḍu. Oc Eo had twice as many gold-glass beads as Arikamēḍu (twenty-one compared with ten), substantially more segmented beads (thirty compared with nineteen), and two each of pierced and folded glass beads and gold medallions (Arikamēḍu had none). Other classes were less strikingly different. There were thirty-seven folded beads at Oc Eo and thirty at Arikamēḍu, and both had two intaglios. How significant this may be is difficult to say without more data. However, it might lend credence to the idea of the "Cinnamon Route" (see chap. 1) proposed by Miller (1969), assuming that Oc Eo played a role in that trade.
13. I examined the Oc Eo material in the National Museum in Ho Chi Minh City. I was not shown everything and was not given much time to examine what I was shown. There were few wasters in the material I saw, though I had specifically asked to see them. There were some pulled pieces, perhaps from close to the end of the draw, and some cut ends of tubes. There are other wasters reported in Malleret's account.
14. In addition to this collection, I also investigated Khlong Thom material at the Department of Archaeology/Fine Arts Department and Thamasat University, both in Bangkok.
15. The site is located on an island (*pulau* in Malaysian) near a promontory (*tanjong*, now spelled *tanjung*) in the estuary (*kuala*) of the Selinsing River (Sungai Selinsing) near the village of Kuala Selinsing. It has thus been variously called

Kuala Selinsing, Tanjong Rewa, Tanjung Rewa, and Pulau Kelumpang. These are all the same site or groups of mounds.

Not only is the nomenclature difficult, but so is the geography. The original site is now believed to have been a low island, the structures of which were on piles over the mud (Glover 1998, 30). It currently consists of shell middens surrounded by mud in the midst of a mangrove forest planted by the Forest Department (Taha 1987, 32). When Evans started work in the 1920s the sea was cutting into it, but by 1951 the mangroves had grown out to sea about 100 m. By 1963 they extended out more than a mile (1.6 km) (Lamb 1964a, 167). Lamb (1966a, 81) published an aerial photograph of the site. Most recently, eight middens, some of which may have originally been on the shore, have been identified; the complex geomorphologic history of the area is now better understood (Nik Hassan 1991, 141–45).

16. Peacock (1979, 210) has a more abbreviated account of this exploration. He agreed with Lamb's interpretation of the site.
17. While lecturing for the SEAMEO-SPAFA Training Course in Archaeological Beads Analysis (National University of Malaysia, 1992), Rey Santiago of the National Museum of the Philippines and I examined the specimens reported as a variety of gemstones. One (Tan and Samsudin 1990, fig. 1a) was carnelian, of a distinctly nonberyl color. The rest were Indo-Pacific glass beads. This was so visually obvious that we read the laboratory notes and asked for Tan to be consulted. What apparently happened was that a not very skillful student was assigned to conduct the mineralogical tests (hardness, specific gravity, refractive index) upon which the false identifications were based.
18. I made this identification in 1986 or 1987 when working on a chapter "Western Geographic knowledge of Sri Lanka and Mantai" for the excavation report (John Carswell, ed., "Excavations at Mantai"), which has not yet been published. In the meantime, this connection has apparently been widely recognized in Sri Lanka. The authors of at least six of the papers in Bandaranayke et al. (1990), that is virtually everyone who mentions Mantai, made the same identification. The following was originally in the text of this book, but because I do not need to make the case so strongly, I have relegated it to this note.

    Both Mantai and Modutti are at the northern end of Taprobane (Sri Lanka) on a small promontory east of Cape Comorin. Both are on the right bank of a river on which the capital Anuradhapura is located upstream on the left bank. Linguistically, the modern Singhalese name *(Matota)*, the Tamil name *(Mantottam)*, the Greek *(Modouttou)*, and the Latin *(Modutti)* are all quite close. The phonemes /t/ and /d/ are both dental plosives, the /t/ being aspirated and voiceless, the /d/ being voiced. An /n/ (and sometimes an /r/) were added later, a not uncommon linguistic occurrence.
19. This refers principally to the ceramics. There were several beads imported from the Mediterranean region ("The Beads from Mantai," my chapter in John Carswell, ed., "Excavations at Mantai," unpublished), but none from China because the export of Chinese beads had not begun before Mantai was abandoned or had at least stopped its major phase of trade (see chap. 7).
20. However, there was glassmaking and -working in southern Vietnam before Funan, in the Sa Huynh culture, as discussed in chapter 13. How or whether this industry interacted with Indo-Pacific beadmaking or Indo-Pacific beadmakers is currently unresolved.
21. Caste is shrinking in importance, but retains its grip on much of India. In general, anyone who works with his or her hands is low caste or Sūdra, though there are exceptions, such as Brāhman cooks.
22. In the north the largest beadmaking caste is the Maṇihar (*maṇi* is bead). They converted to Islam during the reign of Aurangzeb, who died in 1707 (Gode 1949, 13). Next in size is the Curihar, also Muslim (Baines 1912, 97, 150). Most Indian Muslims were outcastes or of low caste before converting. They were attracted to Islam because it does not recognize caste. The Muslim connection suggests a historically low status for them.
23. SPAFA was originally an acronym for SEAMEO *P*roject on *A*rchaeology and *F*ine *A*rts. SEAMEO is *S*outh*e*ast *A*sian *M*inisters of *E*ducation *O*rganization. The SEAMEO Regional Centre for Archaeology and Fine Arts is headquartered in Bangkok and retains the name SPAFA. The final reports of the four SPAFA conferences dealing with Srivijaya were published as SPAFA (1979, 1982, 1983, and 1985).
24. Most writers do not distinguish between Srivijaya as a state and Srivijaya as the capital city. However, Takakusu (1966, xxx n. 2) pointed out that Yijing (I-tsing; I-Ching), the Chinese pilgrim who first described Srivijaya, used "Vijiya" (Bhoga in Takakusu's transliteration) as the city and Sribhoga as the country, though sometimes he interchanged

them. This is a most useful distinction and, because it has the blessing of historic use, is adopted here.

25. In earlier reports (Francis 1989c; 1990b) Sathing Pra, in southeastern Thailand, was included here, based on discussions with Thai archaeologists in 1988. Since then, I have searched for physical evidence of beadmaking from the site, examining the collections in the Songkhla Museum, the Songkhla branch of the Fine Arts Department, and the Bangkok headquarters of the Division of Archaeology/ Fine Arts Department. I found no evidence, thus Sathing Pra is not confirmed as a site of Indo-Pacific beadmaking.

    Muara Jambi in Sumatra was also once considered a beadmaking site (Francis 1989c) because some drips and bead clumps were found there. Since then, I have visited the site. Nothing in either the Jambi Museum or in the site museum resembles beadmaking wasters.

    I had initially included Kuala Selinsing in this later group, but its position was always problematical. Now it appears that it was allied to Funan and not Srivijaya.

26. Evidence for Indo-Pacific beadmaking is clear at Sungai Mas, but not at Pengkalan Bujang. This is at variance with the conclusions reached by Lamb (1965a, b; 1966a, b), but I have not seen any Indo-Pacific wasters from Pengkalan Bujang. The glassware at Pengkalan Bujang is mostly imported, but its Indo-Pacific beads have compositions that match Indian rather than Middle Eastern glass (Francis 1988–1989).

27. SLOWPOKE stands for *S*afe *LOW*-*P*ower *K*ritical *E*xperiment.

28. Bead no. 1157. This table is based on spectrographic examination. Both the cobalt and manganese contents were rated *beaucoup,* or over 10 percent, an extremely high amount. The bead immediately following from Arikamēḍu (Virampatnam) has the same characteristics, though it is lower in cobalt. Both also have very small amounts of soda, suggesting that they may have had more potassium.

29. Caley (1962) reported no such glass. Turner (1956b, 172T–174T) listed only a blue window glass from Reims Cathedral and an Eighteenth Dynasty Egyptian piece with this formula. Sayre and Smith (1967, 295) referred to a manganese-cobalt combination, but not in association with potassium.

30. Ardika suggested that these beads were drawn on the questionable grounds that the ends were not symmetrical, as suggested by Bronson (1990, 220). Distinguishing between drawn and wound beads is not as difficult as Bronson believed, and the reheating of cut, drawn segments to round them off does not facilitate elongated bubbles to assume spherical shapes. In any case, I have seen the beads from Sembiran at the Dempasar branch of the National Center for Archaeological Research and can confirm that they are Indo-Pacific beads.

    Cobalt was not looked for in the analyses done for Ardika by K. Basa, but both the dark blue and the purple bead had elevated amounts of manganese. Ardika's suggestion that the potassium content might point to a South Chinese or Southeast Asian origin cannot be accepted. The potassium-based glasses of those regions do not include drawn Indo-Pacific beads.

31. There was a suburb of Kāvēripaṭṭinam in Southeast India named Maṇikgrāmman (Rao 1969). It is likely that it was home to many guild members. Beads were found there, but no glass beadmaking wasters. For spelling variations see Indrapala (1990, 159 n. 15) and Christie (1998, 2 [Wilson-Select printout]).

32. As far as I can trace it, the ultimate source is the Indo-Iranian *mani,* which means "seed," "sperm," or "precious stone."

33. Virtually all precious stones in antiquity were made into beads. Setting stones is a relatively recent phenomenon, and our notion of precious and semiprecious stones did not operate in the past. Most precious stones of antiquity are today's semiprecious stones. Stone beadmaking took place at several Indo-Pacific beadmaking sites (see chap. 14).

34. The Portuguese referred to these beads as *barros miudas* or "earthenware beads" (van der Sleen 1956a; 1973, 82). The error of identifying these glass beads as clay has been made often. Not only does it appear in the literature, but I have also personally known several people who made the same mistake.

35. São Tomé is the Portuguese form of St. Thomas. The legend is that the doubting apostle brought Christianity to this part of India in the first century A.D. His purported tomb may be visited atop St. Thomas Mount. Mylapur was the original settlement at Madras and is still a section of the old city. Madras has since been renamed Chennai.

36. For many years I looked for an alternative site, which I called "Site X." Archaeological reports, gazetteers, and local archaeologists and historians were consulted, all with no results. With the now-recognized long occupation of Arikamēḍu, it is no longer necessary to postulate Site X.

5: Indo-Pacific Bead By-Products and the Distribution of the Beads

1. One by-product is not discussed here because it has yet to be recognized outside of Arikamēḍu, where it was apparently made. It was formed by taking a short segment of a drawn rod (a "cane"), heating it, and piercing it through its length to form an oblate. This may have been done in molds; a clay mold with depressions of the right size is in the Pondicherry Museum. The beads were mostly black, though a few blue ones and red ones have also been found. Piercing glass to make a bead is usually associated with the Middle Eastern glass bead industry (Francis 1999). There are beads imported from that region to Arikamēḍu, but the evidence strongly suggests that these were locally made. There are at least sixteen of them (more numerous than any imported bead type), there are canes of the right size, and there is the clay mold in the Pondicherry Museum.
2. The precision of the dates of Taxila is open to question.
3. The excavation at Berenike, Egypt, the major Red Sea port for trade with the East, helps to confirm this. Gold-glass collar beads do not appear before there was extensive trade with India (personal observation).
4. The only exception is a larger glass type that may have been made at Oc Eo.
5. Kurt Nassau (1996, personal communication) has examined some of these pieces and agrees that this was the cause of this color.
6. In this, they are somewhat similar to segmented beads. However, they were pinched for the technical reason described in the text, which did not apply to the smaller-diameter segmented beads, and it is unlikely that a mold was used for this operation. Moreover, they are never found as multiple tubes, always as individual beads.
7. Sara Young (1989, personal communication), a glass beadmaker of Providence, Rhode Island, told me that this was her personal experience. It has since been confirmed by other beadmakers.
8. For example, their known distribution is now confined to the Eastern Hemisphere. However, they might have been brought to the New World. If the Portuguese took them to their colonies in Africa, might they not have taken them to Brazil?
9. I computed this from Bronson and Glover's figures.
10. At least this is what was reported. Indraningsih had trouble distinguishing bead materials. Her analyses of eight beads from Gilimanuk (1985a, 8; 1985b, 139) include one that must be shell (49.05 percent calcium oxide and 39.40 percent lost in combustion) and another that is clay (55.74 percent alumina and 21.40 percent silicon dioxide). Why analyses were performed on these is not explained, nor was it mentioned that they were not glass.
11. There are also a few clear or colorless beads, which are not found at Indo-Pacific beadmaking sites. Their origin is a mystery.
12. The red specimen (S5) has much more copper (14.2 percent) than do other red Indo-Pacific beads. Of course, it could be something other than an Indo-Pacific bead. The red samples (S2 and S6) have potash as their major alkali, an unusual but not unknown ingredient for Arikamēḍu red Indo-Pacific beads.
13. Colani (1935, 157, 305) had a dark blue bead analyzed from Sa Huynh, Vietnam. It has the potash-manganese combination; cobalt was not looked for. This analysis mixed green and blue beads, and assuming they were evenly divided, the manganese concentration would be similar to that in Arikamēḍu blues. Sa Huynh predates Funan and Oc Eo.
14. No one was available to discuss the beads in the Guangzhou City Museum, so there was no way of ascertaining how accurate the dating was. If the large blue beads are from the Western Han, they probably came from Arikamēḍu, because no other Indo-Pacific beadmakers were active at that time, as far as is known.
15. Many occupants of tombs in Kyongju have not yet been identified. Hence, tombs are commonly named after an outstanding feature such as the "Gold Crown Tomb" or the "Flying Horse Tomb" (after a mural) or simply given a number.
16. *Boli (po-li)* is translucent glass, derived from the Sanskrit *vaidūrya*, a precious stone. See chapter 6.
17. Robert B. Fox founded the type collection. For more on him and the collection see Appendix A. The figures used here are slightly altered from those published earlier (Francis 1989d), because excavated beads in Fox's private collection have been factored in.
18. The beads from Pasemah and Matesih were not well enough identified in the reports to conclude that they were Indo-Pacific beads. However, I have examined them at the National Centers for Archaeological Research at Jakarta and Yogyakarta and confirmed that they are Indo-Pacific beads.
19. I have seen only one stone and two (wound Chinese) glass beads from Banten Girang. Edwards McKinnon (1991, 10)

found two stone and seven glass beads. In private discussions, we concluded that some of them might be Indo-Pacific beads.

20. Most beads from Quseir al-Qadim had been returned to the Cairo Museum by the time I studied them at the Oriental Institute in Chicago, in turn, just after my most recent trip to Egypt. There may have been more Indo-Pacific beads in the assemblage. This circumstance also prevented me from confirming the status of the collar bead discussed in the next paragraph.
21. Unlike beads from Arikamēḍu, those from Berenike have a large proportion of green blue beads and some orange ones. Dark blue, red, black, and violet ones are rare or absent; these colors make up the bulk of Arikamēḍu beads. The color palette at Berenike is much more similar to that at Mantai, especially the unusual green blue.
22. The one exception may be Fustat. There were no Indo-Pacific beads excavated by Scanlon, nor are there any in the Fustat material in the Islamic Museum, Cairo. However, the Awad collection (Francis 1995a) contains a few short drawn beads, dominated by red. They are similar to Indo-Pacific beads. It is difficult to confirm if they are, however, because tubes were made at Fustat. These were usually used for segmented or long, tubular beads but could have been cut into shorter beads.
23. Sharma Saitowitz has been studying these beads, and her preliminary papers (Saitowitz 1994; Saitowitz et al. 1996) indicated that she believes in an Egyptian origin for them. I cannot agree with her (Francis 1998a, 8 n. 5).
24. The Kingdom of Ghana is not the same as the modern country that bears its name. It was located principally in what is now southern Mali and was succeeded by the more extensive Kingdom of Mali by the thirteenth century. Modern Ghana (formerly the Gold Coast) has always been or aspired to be a democracy.
25. The translation from the French is mine. I have omitted "ou rangée," which Defrémery and Sanguinetti inserted after *nazhm*. The French *rangée* means "a file of things placed in a row." Neither Littré (1961) nor Robert (1966) defined it as a string of beads, though this is what the translators had in mind. The Arabic *nazhm* is derived from the verb meaning "to string," especially when used with *lulu*, "pearls." It also means "to put in order; to array; to classify, file" (Madina 1973, 675).
26. The American trade offers "nila" beads from Mali. The name is not related to the Nile River, as some assume. *Nīla* is Sanskrit for indigo and used by many Arabic speakers for the color blue. They are small, drawn blue or blue green beads with one rounded end heated while lying flat on a plate. The other end is flat with small pits where the bead sat on the plate. They either were made in the Middle East or are heat-altered Indo-Pacific beads.

    A dealer told me that he was present during an illegal excavation and saw "nila" beads being recovered. The Awad collection of Fustat beads contains several "nila" beads. Perhaps the heating was done in Egypt rather than West Africa. Only chemical analysis can tell us whether the original bead was an Indo-Pacific specimen.
27. Size, color, shape, and technique (where mentioned) were considered when identifying Indo-Pacific beads in the reports. Similar descriptions are found in the Asian literature, and when they are examined, they nearly always turn out to be Indo-Pacific beads.

    I have seen quite a lot of looted material from West African sites, and Indo-Pacific beads are common. My impression is confirmed by the properly excavated assemblages from Ghana that I have studied directly.

    Most scholars cited in this section have assumed that these beads were Venetian. However, they were working before the Indo-Pacific bead phenomenon was recognized and before it was understood that Venice did not make drawn beads until the 1480s or later (Francis 1979, 6; 1988b, 13).
28. The translation from the French is mine.
29. Begho is the only site in this subsection whose beads I have personally examined. The radiocarbon sample N-2142 was dated A.D. 1045 ± 80 and N-2141 was dated A.D. 1120 ± 80 (Anquandah 1982, 143).
30. The trade of Indo-Pacific beads through Siraf, Iran, went principally to East Africa, though some may have been sent on to Egypt (Francis 1989e, 30–31).

6: Glassmaking and Glass Beadmaking in China

1. We have also learned much about Middle Eastern, Venetian, and Czech glass beadmaking by studying their exports. Once we are able to identify the beads coming from a particular source, their chronology and stylistic and technical developments are often more easily seen in the archaeological records of importing sites rather than at the manufacturing sites themselves.
2. A useful summary, including material not yet published by Needham, is in Temple (1986).

3. It apparently did not convince everyone. R. K. Liu (1995a, 54), referring to Francis (1986c), still thought the history of Chinese glass and glass beadmaking was "probably discontinuous." He did not cite Francis (1990c), a report that strengthened the earlier work concluded after a trip through China.
4. This is a pseudonym of Ge Hong. The book is commonly known by this personal name.
5. Curiously, Hirth did not mention the movable palace, which apparently could be taken apart and reconstructed elsewhere.
6. In the French transliteration of the day, Jaubert called this city Djankou (the "dj" combination in French is equivalent to the English "j").

   Hirth and Rockhill (1911, 228, n) said that this was the only Arab source they knew that mentioned glassmaking in China and identified the city with Kanfu or Hangzhou. Hangzhou is not directly on the sea and Kanfu is its port. However, Kanfu ("Khanfou") is mentioned separately by al-Idrisi.

   Tibbetts (1979, 72) equated the city in question with Canton (Guangzhou), but it is more realistic to ascribe that to Jaubert's "Khançou" (Moroccan Arabic has no sound like the "hard g" in English), said to be "end of the journey for Westerners" (Jaubert 1836, 85). The glassworking center was three days from Guangzhou (Jaubert 1836), though precisely where is not possible to say without further evidence.
7. It was (understandably) common for Chinese ships to carry locally made goods, as is demonstrated by the ceramic assemblage of a shipwreck recovered at Ningbo (S. Liu et al. 1991, 308–309). A few combed polychrome vessels (perhaps core-formed, though this seems unlikely) have also been found at Pengkalan Bujang, Malaysia; Singapore; and Mindoro Island, the Philippines. Seidel (2000) linked these and a few beads for which she had references to glassmaking at Quanzhou (Ch'üan-chou).
8. Several foreign communities lived at Quanzhou, including Tamils (Christie 1998, 17–18). They, however, would not have been familiar with the combing technique.
9. The reader who wishes to follow the complications of the use of this word in various languages may refer to the references cited in the text. The English word "beryl" is another product of the linguistic changes undergone by the original.
10. Ayers assumed that by Yen-ching, Boshan was meant, but Du Halde's Yen-ching is more likely Yanshen, even though Du Halde put the town in Jinan Prefecture.
11. There are various ways to make glass bangles. They are often produced by winding a bead of glass on the tip of a mandrel, expanding it by hitting the mandrel until it begins to slump, and then widening it into bangle size either by pulling it up a clay cone (*kalgood* in North India) or manipulating it with two mandrels. Traditionally, North Indian beadmakers and bangle makers worked side by side, though bangles made on the Japanese-introduced *balen* are now more common (Francis 1983a; Koch and Sode n.d.). The *balen* method and the Roman-Islamic technique of heating a rod and bending it over to join are not so closely connected with beadmaking.
12. There was once confusion over the authorship of the first of five books in this journal. They are now understood to have been Ricci's work, written in Italian and translated into Latin and published by Nicholas Trigualt (Gallagher 1942, v; 1953, xviii).
13. The glass workshop was documented by Jesuits living in Beijing (Missionnaires de Pékin 1777, 261–266, 463, etc.), though some scholars have had trouble finding the source (Ayers 1965, 19). Glass scholars have discussed this workshop for a long time without much detail. Nesbitt (1879a, 134–135; 1879b, 651) was probably the first to cite it. Bushell (1914, 2: 62–63) mentioned it next, and Honey (1937) and Ayers (1965, 22) identified objects made there. Warren (1977, 87 n. 7) noted that Bushell never divulged the source of information on the other twenty-six imperial workshops, but allowed that the famous sinologist may have had access to books that discussed them.

    Engle (1982) elaborated on Verbiest's role in the glass workshop, but without documentation. A Belgian Jesuit, Verbiest was a polymath who captured Kang Xi's attention when he pointed out an error in the official calendar in 1669 (Fu 1966, 42–43). By 1674 he had become the director of the Imperial Board of Astronomy and was ordered to cast "light but effective cannons" for the army (Fu 1966, 48). His success with the cannons earned him the title of "junior vice-president of the Board of Works" in 1682, added to those of director of the Imperial Board of Astronomy, supervisor of the Administration of Calendar-calculation, and commissioner of the Office of Transportation (Fu 1966, 58). After he died in 1688 he was given a sacrifice and a state funeral and canonized as Qin Mian ("Diligent and Clever"), a unique honor for a Westerner (Fu 1966, 99, 476 n. 276). Nothing in the state papers so meticulously edited by Fu (1966) connect him with the glass workshop.

John Bell said that the German Jesuit Kilian Stumpf (or Stumpff [1655–1720]) was in charge of the glass factory at the palace, although Stumpf had died after Bell's visit in 1720. Mention of Stumpf appears in only one court document edited by Fu (1966, 172), where he is accused of destroying astronomical instruments more than four hundred years old. The closeness to Kang Xi and the fame throughout China attributed to Stumpf by Bell seem more appropriate for Verbiest. Perhaps Bell confused the two, especially because there was such a lag between his visit and the publication of the account of his travels. Brown and Rabiner (1990, 21–22) assumed that Bell meant that the imperial glass workshop had been begun by Stumpf, but Bell (1788, 42) said only that Stumpf was "employed to superintend and carry on" the workshop.

14. Glass and porcelain factories were listed together. Sometimes it is impossible to tell them apart. Here I count only those that are obviously for any glass product, including mirrors, chimneys, and bottles.
15. This apparently happened to at least one type of Chinese bead. Long (2.5 cm), thin drawn beads, most commonly dark or satin blue, were sold for many years by G. B. Fenstermaker, who obtained them from the Sing Chong Company of San Francisco, a Chinese merchant house (see Fenstermaker and Williams 1979, 46–47). Similar beads, brown in color, decorate items in the National History Museum, Taipei. Visually similar beads were also produced in Japan (Klamkin 1976, pls. 450, 451). The Center for Bead Research has a package of these beads marked "Made in Japan." The technique was likely developed in Japan and transferred to China, with many of the beads shipped to and exported from Japan.
16. During the Yuan and Ming dynasties, a diaspora of Chinese, mostly from the south, took place, settling in Southeast Asia. Many were artisans, disturbed by the attitude of the Yuan and Ming toward their crafts and later by the dwindling fortunes of China under the Ming. During the Yuan dynasty (1280 to 1368) selected families skilled in various crafts had been given special status, many of them being separated from the rest of the population. This was extended under the Ming, and the discontent it caused led many to emigrate. Official dynastic histories often referred to them as "runaways" (e.g., Groeneveldt 1876, 49). We cannot say for certain that this was the origin of the Banten beadmakers, but it is at least possible.
17. In several earlier papers I reported that coil beads were made at Fort Canning Hill, Singapore, the site of fourteenth-century Temasek. John Miksic, the director of the Fort Canning Hill Project, called my attention to an area that included a fire pit; drips of glass; broken pieces of glass, some of which had melted; bangles; and coil beads. At the time, he assumed that the coil beads were being made there and it certainly looked as though that were the case. However, after having the material analyzed it transpired that the bangles were being made there, not the coil beads (see Miksic et al. 1994).

7: Export of Chinese Beads

1. There were two Han dynasties. The Former or Western Han dates from 202 B.C. to A.D. 9. The Latter or Eastern dates from A.D. 25 to 220. Between the two was a period of much confusion named after the Xin dynasty.
2. As Wolters (1967, 285 n. 27) pointed out, both Hirth and G. Wang had made previous translations of this passage. Wolters' argument in favor of his own interpretation seems justified.
3. Most of the "evidence" for Persians involved in this trade comes from the frequent use of *Bosi (Po-ssi, Po-ssu)* in Chinese texts describing ships, mariners, or products. This word refers to the *Parsa,* the *Fars,* whose name lives on as Persia, the province of Fars (Iran), and the language of Farsi. Most early scholars assumed that the use of this word in Chinese texts pointed directly to Persians (Ferrand 1913, 1–3; H. Hasan 1928, 81–83). However, starting with Laufer (1919, 468–487), others have noted that the term had much wider meanings, particularly when applied to products that were mostly Southeast Asian. The consensus has grown that *Bosi* did not usually mean Persian when applied to the maritime trade (G. Wang 1958, 124–127; Wolters 1967, especially chap. 10), though a few maintain that position (Schafer 1963, 281 n. 50). I have retained the term "Persian" when quoting sources, but reserve doubt that actual Persians are meant very often.
4. Could they possibly have been Vikings?
5. Javanese and Tamils also frequented Barus (Christie 1998, 11). They may also have been players in this trade, although there is no record of that.
6. See note 3.
7. Dashi (Ta-shih) is derived from "Tajik," a name that lives on in modern Tajikistan; it referred to Arabs in general (Hirth and Rockhill 1911, 282).
8. Chandler (1987, 470–477) listed Hangzhou as the world's

largest city in A.D. 1200, 1250, 1300, and 1350, though it never quite surpassed the size of Kaifeng in 1100, then the world's largest city. First place went to Nanjing in 1400 and Beijing in 1450.

9. Is this the Chinese name for the small "coil beads," a staple in this trade? See chapter 8.
10. Except for Ligor, which is now believed to be near Nakhon Si Thammarat, these identifications are Rockhill's. He had put Ligor farther south; some of the other identifications may also need review, though this source is still considered fairly accurate (Ptak 1998, 15).
11. Several books, most of which have only recently been rediscovered, other than those discussed in the text describe one or more of these voyages. They are not yet available in Western languages (Y. Liu 1991, 1–3).
12. In a more poetic vein, Bai (1982, 334) translated this as *Vision in Triumph in a Boundless Sea.*
13. The precise date of publication is not known. Mills (1970, 36) accepted Pelliot's date of 1451. In some works (e.g., Groeneveldt 1876) the publication date is given as 1416. However, that was the date of the preface that Ma Huan wrote after his first (the fleet's fourth) voyage. He joined the sixth and seventh voyages as well and added to the body of the work (he was assisted by another traveler, Guo Chongli), but did not alter the preface.
14. Bai (1982, 334) translated this as *Vision in Triumph: Ships Sail under Starry Sky.* The *Star Raft* was the name of the ship that carried the emperor's ambassador (Mills 1970, 59–60).
15. As with Ma Huan's book, this is the date of the preface, but the actual date of publication is unknown. The first known version was printed in 1544 (Mills 1970, 60).
16. It was only ten days from the sacred mountain in Champa and the Yuan fleet was blown off course to this island when they were beginning to attack Java in 1293 (Groeneveldt 1876, 78).
17. Zhang (1993, 108) quoted some of this passage from a secondary source saying that Benedict Goes (Goez) wrote it. However, Goes, a Portuguese nonclerical Jesuit, was the main protagonist of the story. He died in 1606 in Beijing, the suspicion being that rival "Saracens" poisoned him, just as "Saracen spies" stole his journal. The tale was related by one Isaac, apparently a Persian, to Father Matthew [Ricci?], who wrote it in the third person and reported that Isaac was still alive in 1615 (Father Matthew 1906, 237–238).
18. The "shining Marble" is referred to several times in this report. In one passage it becomes clear what it is, even though it is described as "a certaine shining Marble, which wee are wont to call Jasper" (Father Matthew 1906, 228). The passage describes it being fished out of the River Khotan and brought as great boulders from the mountains. It further discusses its "inexorable hardnesse" and that it is made into "divers ornaments for Vessels, Garments, Girdles, with leaves and flowers artificially [artfully] engraven." It is obviously jade, and this is one of the earliest Western accounts of its importance in China.

8: Chinese Beads in the Asian Maritime Trade

1. This is apparently *Yunlin shibu* by Du Wan, ca. 1126.
2. Actually, it is not the same formula.
3. *Encyclopaedia Britannica,* 14th ed., s.v. "lead."
4. Pewter is principally tin. China was a net exporter of tin, at least in the early twentieth century. The *China Year Book* (Bell and Woodhead 1912, 132–133) listed the price of tin in 1905 at 51.11 Hong Kong dollars per picule (100 catties), whereas lead was worth 7.74 per picule and pig and manufactured iron only 1.55. Thus it was relatively expensive. Tin has uses in glass, but is hardly necessary. Why would it have been used in such quantity for the bangles that Gray (1875, 242) reported were "very cheap"? Perhaps his identification of the alloy was wrong.
5. Two objects in the Center for Bead Research collection are red-painted glass. One is a small window element from Iran, either Safavid or Qajar in date. The other is a fringe of glass beads bought in Madras, India, probably made in the north during World War II.
6. For many years the story was that the Bohemian red glass (locally called "composition") was developed by two brothers who had worked in Venice as "spies" some time after their return to Bohemia in 1711 (Vávra 1954, 182; Urban n.d., 3). However, the Venetian glass historian Astone Gasparetto located documents that show that this glass had been developed at least by 1709 (Maternova 1991, 371). Moreover, two beads in excellent context were recovered from St. Catherines Island, Georgia (United States), by a team from the American Museum of Natural History in New York under David Hurst Thomas. They are ruby red and tong molded (personal observation). Because they cannot date later than 1680, the date for Bohemian "composition" must be put back a few more decades. The Bohemians followed (or independently developed) Neri's recipe,

which called for lead in the glass, rather than Cassius' formula using a pigment involving tin and gold.

7. Needham and Lu (1974, 268–270) put a different slant on the history of red glass in the West. I have not located the fifteenth-century manuscript "Segreti per Colori" nor the works of Ganzenmüller, on which they based their notes. Both Ganzenmüller and Campbell Thompson (1936, xxxi–xxxiv) claimed an ancient origin for gold ruby glass, but this is doubtful. Needham and Lu quoted Ganzenmüller as saying that Theophilus used copper ruby glass. Theophilus did not mention red glass, though a red copper *stain* was discussed in *On Divers Arts* (Hawthorne and Smith 1979). Needham and Lu were not looking at beads (they had enough to look at) and did not see the long use of copper ruby glass in China.
8. Here is a case of a researcher fooling himself. They were translucent red. In my notes on this pillar I called them "pink-violet" beads. I later altered that to "opaque red" and published it that way (Francis 1986d, 6). "They had to have been opaque red," I told myself, "because there was no translucent red glass made then." Now I realize that I should have believed my eyes.
9. Some have objected to this term, on the misunderstanding that it labels the manufacturing process. That is in error. The beads are wound. The term "coiling" has been used by some writers as a substitute for "winding," but that is not how the word is employed here. "Coil bead" is a nominative, not a verb. It is also incorrect to say that I coined the term. Rey Santiago did.
10. As discussed earlier, a translucent red one from this site showed a lead content of more than 10 percent in an X-ray spectrometry test at the McKay Laboratory at Harvard University.
11. *Mutiraja* is a term designating heirloom beads on some islands in Indonesia. They are discussed in detail in chapter 17.
12. These are in the Awad collection. See Francis (1995a).
13. Coil beads are still being made in China from lead glass. There have been no reports of their production at Boshan, but Sprague and An (1990, 8–9) saw them in Beijing, apparently made there. Strands in the collection of the Center for Bead Research purchased in China in 1986 also have coil beads on them.
14. Blair assumed that these beads were Japanese. Certainly the Japanese made glass beads, but her assumption that nearly all glass in Japan was made there is too sweeping, especially in the light of recent research. Her contention (Blair 1973, 44, 48) that the *magatama* is Japanese in origin and borrowed by Korea is likely wrong. The Koreans have the stronger case for its origin (Francis 1985b, 9). Blair (1973, 103) said that beads of the Nara period have a lead content near or exceeding 70 percent and that such levels are not found in Chinese glass. However, both Tang and Northern Song glass pieces do contain as much lead (Shi et al. 1987, 44). She (Blair 1973, 57–58) even suggested that "opaque reddish brown beads" (Indo-Pacific beads) could have been made in Japan, because they are colored with copper, which is abundant there.

   The few beads from the Tomb period that I have examined are Indo-Pacific beads. S. Gupta (1999) made a thorough study of these beads and found that they were mostly Indo-Pacific beads. This renders Blair's (1973, 53–54) discussion of tube production in Japan dubious. Despite these critiques, most of her work is quite good, but the problems of glass beads in Japan need a fresh review.
15. These figures are not strictly comparable for several reasons. Burke counted only coil beads and divided the blues into turquoise (the great majority) and cobalt (1.7 percent). Harrisson counted the dark ones with amethyst-colored beads. The color differences are of considerable importance, probably indicating different ingredients, not mere shading. Harrisson lumped all beads together, including some wound zone and melon beads and 79 (of 2,503) Indo-Pacific beads. Harrisson (1973, 119) was irked that Burke did not refer to his earlier published account, but his reliance on color to the exclusion of manufacturing technique was ill founded. Burke did the better job of reporting on the beads.
16. It is little use quoting Harrisson's more precise figures, because he again combined all beads at these sites for his count. See note 15.
17. So called because it was found beneath the wreckage of an English ship, the *Royal Captain*.
18. The numbers reported in this paragraph represent only those colors in concentrations of 10 percent or more.
19. Again, all beads were massed together, but the great majority was Indo-Pacific beads.
20. I have tabulated these from Malleret (1962a).
21. Amoy (Xiamen) is a fine, natural port in Fujian Province. In the eighteenth century, it monopolized the Chinese trade to the Strait of Malacca and Java. The Sulu Islands, situated between Mindanao and northern Borneo, are now part of

the Philippines. In the eighteenth century they were ruled by Moro (Muslim) sultans and did not become part of the (Spanish) Philippines until the following century.

22. Neither R. K. Liu nor anyone else has even ventured an alternative origin for these beads since the publication of this exchange of views.
23. Chevrons are drawn glass beads made with layers of different-colored glass, each (except the outer) with a cogwheel or starburst shape in cross section. When their ends are beveled, the layers appear as a series of chevrons, hence their English name. Most were made in Venice. The earliest, from about 1480 to 1610, had faceted ends to expose the layers.
24. So visually alike are the European drawn chevrons and the early wound imitations that no one had noticed their differences in the Philippine National Museum before my work on them.
25. The origin of the objects in this famous and heavily protected collection has been hotly debated. Blair opted for Japanese origins for all the glass, but her enthusiasm for things Japanese is not entirely justified. Choi (1996) argued that most things came from Korea. There is probably a mixture of Chinese, Korean, and Japanese items in the treasure.
26. Correspondence (1988–1989) from Michael Flecker, Pacific Sea Resources, Singapore, to the Center for Bead Research, Lake Placid.
27. Beads were also found in a tomb, but did not include any ruby reds. Dikshit's (1969, 54) account of the beads from the tomb is muddled. Not all the glass beads, but only six white ones were brought to Tucker while he was having lunch (Beck 1930a, 175 [not 171 as in Dikshit]). The high specific gravity of these white beads (3.43) might suggest that they were not legitimately from the tomb, because "megalithic" (Pandukal) tombs are usually earlier than coil bead export. Further suspicion might be raised if the workers were being paid for finds, a common practice of the day. Could the beads have been Chinese?
28. Unfortunately, the person who was supposed to have analyzed it carelessly misplaced it.
29. The term "bugle" denotes a small, drawn tubular bead used in beadwork. It is derived from a confusion of two different words in Old French and French, one meaning "trumpet" and the other "pipe." Its first literary appearance was in Edmund Spenser's *The Shepherd's Calendar* in 1579, followed by William Shakespeare's *As You Like It* in 1599. This is one of the few types of beads ever made by the English. Saris was not talking about the embroidery bead, as his description clearly shows. Rather, he used the term in a more general way, because it had only recently come into the English language (Francis 1997, 10).
30. Beck (1931, 234) did not call these beads "convex bicone disks," but "short bicones," the term also used by van der Sleen and adopted here.
31. This inconsistency of placing both drawn and wound beads into his "Trade Wind" bead group (not to mention stone beads) was responsible for my rejection of this term as descriptive of any specific bead. See chapter 3.
32. No matter how carefully dug Brahmapuri may have been, its beads are of little use to later researchers. Dikshit's discussion and listings are less than exemplary and impossible to reconcile with the collection now housed in the Kolhapur Museum. Dikshit was in possession of the collection for a long time; it was not sent to the museum until after his death. No documentation of any type is available to separate the beads into the two widely spaced periods of occupation. At least some beads never made it to the museum.
33. The date of the sealed "bed-rock" layer at Zimbabwe has been the subject of contention for a long time, most of it revolving around the bead evidence. Beck (1931, 235–237) based his eighth- to ninth-century date on the similarity of beads from Tangal, India, and Kuala Selinsing, nicely agreeing with Caton-Thompson's eighth- to tenth-century date. However, these were Indo-Pacific beads, which we now know had a very long life span. The bead that has caused the most discussion from this layer is an opaque red on translucent green drawn bead, known as a "green heart." The earliest date for them in the American context is 1600 (Brain 1979, 106). They were made in Venice and in seventeenth-century Holland. They are well-known European trade beads. Being aware of this, African archaeologists have had a hard time reconciling their presence in the "bed-rock" layer. The bead was at the center of the debate between Laidler (1934) and Caton-Thompson (1936). Robinson (1961a, 230–231, 235; 1961b, 93–95; 1963, 167) often discussed it. Unfortunately, the infamous specimen is no longer available for inspection (Robinson 1963, 167).

    With the recognition of Chinese coil beads and opaque leadless beads in this "bed-rock" assemblage, a date later than originally proposed makes sense. The radiocarbon dating put the layer between A.D. 1085 and 1450 or even 1550 (Robinson 1961a, 234). The latter date is close to the earliest known date for a green heart and would accommodate the apparently Chinese beads as well.

34. That is, in the older literature. This statement also excludes Late Zhou and some Han period beads.
35. Collectors often call these "Peking glass beads." There is no indication that they were made in Beijing. The colors, however, most likely derived from the imperial glass workshop developments, so it would not be amiss to call them "Beijing color beads" or some such term.
36. The beads used for "court chains" were finer made and much more regular than those used for export. They were specifically for the elite and are easily recognized as such. After the Revolution of 1911–1912, the symbols of the hated Manchus were abolished. Pigtails were cut off and "court chains" torn apart. The beads from the "court chains" were sold in shops with exterior advertisements consisting of frames strung with beads (Crane 1926, no. 41).

9: Middle Eastern Glass Beads

1. This term and its substitutes—the Near East, West Asia, and WANA (West Asia and North Africa)—are all imprecise and have various drawbacks. The Middle East and the Near East are from a West European perspective, which the rest of the world does not share. West Asia excludes Egypt, and WANA is very broad. Glass bead production was concentrated in an area roughly bound by Rhodes, Aleppo, Hebron, and Thebes, Egypt. To the east, Mesopotamia invented glass, but had stopped production by our period of interest. Farther east, Iran has been called a major center of glass beadmaking, but no evidence whatsoever has been put forward to indicate that. The term "Eastern Mediterranean" could have been used, but it would exclude the prominent traders of Iran and Oman.
2. That is, larger than the country named Syria today. It included what are now Syria, Israel, Lebanon, Palestine, and parts of Jordan and Turkey.
3. Dayton (1993) argued that glass was a by-product of silver smelting in Saxony. His thesis is provocative, but needs more testing.
4. The term "Phoenicia" is Greek for land of the "red-dye people," the city-states of Tyre, Sidon, Byblos, Arwad, and Ugarit. Of these, the first two made glass, and Tyre, at least, made beads. The term first appears in the Septuagent version of the Bible (third–second centuries B.C.). Kurinsky (1991, 81–109) argued that the glassmakers were Canaanites, not Phoenicians. In truth, many "Phoenician beads" are products of other workshops.
5. The most notorious example of this is Morlot's (1862; 1992) conclusion that the Phoenicians came to America because a Venetian chevron bead (which he thought was ancient) was found in an "Indian Mound" in Canada (Francis 1985d).
6. Since the wide acceptance of my contention that many of the older glass beads on the antiquities market (particularly those from West Africa and Southeast Asia) are Early Islamic rather than Roman, this term has recently become the "default date" for armchair bead scholars.
7. The "Ziwiyah treasure" was an eclectic collection of gold, silver, and ivory objects said to have been found near the village of Ziwiyah, Iran. Collectors and museums began accumulating them and art historians wrote glowingly about the "treasure." Much of what was once ascribed to this find came from other places or are modern reproductions. There may or may not have been any finds at Ziwiyah. Certainly many objects given the Ziwiyah label do not deserve it. Controversy about the nature of the "treasure" still exists.
8. The square tubular "beads" that dominate the second strand from the bottom on her plate are made by antiquities dealers, who buy ancient broken glass vessels and cut beads from folded-over rims, the hollow in the rim becoming the "perforation." The Eye of Horus on the strand may be from a similar source; arrowhead "pendants" were made this way (Francis 1985d). There are a few cases of vessel rims used for beads in antiquity in Europe (Henricsen 1995, fig. 3; Anton Dieselburger, 1995, personal communication). However, none has been scientifically excavated in the Middle East. Moreover, the large number of these "beads" and the new breaks on most edges point to recent "recycling."
9. The principal database contains eighteen bead types from forty-five sites. Only beads with adequate descriptions or illustrations from well-stratified contexts were used from the literature; these are depressingly scarce. Well-stratified assemblages from Middle Eastern and Asian sites I have personally cataloged were added. They include Siraf, Iran, in the British Museum; Nishapur, Iran, in the Metropolitan Museum of Art, New York; Aqaba, Jordan, and Quseir al-Qadim, Egypt, in the Oriental Institute, Chicago; Fustat, Egypt, in the Islamic Museum, Cairo, with George Scanlon, and in the Awad collection; Berenike, Egypt, from the Delaware-Lieden Berenike Project; Mantai, Sri Lanka,

from John Carswell; Sungai Mas, Malaysia, at the Merbok Museum; Kyongju, Korea, at the National Museum, Kyongju; Sungai Jaong and Gedong, Sarawak, at the Sarawak Museum; and Takua Pa and Laem Pho Chaiya, Thailand, at the Division of Archaeology Fine Arts Department in Bangkok. Much of the data from these sites is from personal observation. Therefore, earlier and less-complete published descriptions are rarely cited here.

10. This happened in Southeast Asia, the subject of the next chapter. It also took place in Viking territory in North Europe (Francis 1996a, 7, 9) and at some date in Spain (P. Francis and L. Pendleton, "The Beads at St. Catherines," American Museum of Natural History Anthropological Papers, in preparation). See note 11.
11. Not completely, however. The site of St. Catherines Island, Georgia (United States), the northernmost Spanish mission along the Atlantic coast excavated by David Hurst Thomas and Lorann Pendleton Thomas, has examples of both segmented and gold-glass beads (personal observation). They were most likely made by a beadmaker from the Middle East who migrated to Spain while it was still a Muslim country and whose (presumably Christian) descendents carried on the trade into the seventeenth century.
12. Srisuchat pictured three beads. The Wat Khlong Thom Museum has a photograph of fourteen of them, apparently found locally. They are first- or second-century A.D. pierced mosaic beads. Aléxéeva (1971, pl. 2) showed a number of similar designs, though not exact parallels.
13. At least it is Early Islamic in date. The possibility exists that these beads were made in a Viking beadmaking site, particularly Ribe, Denmark. They were most likely brought to Asia through the Arab trade, but see note 4, chapter 7.
14. On what authority is not revealed. She associated the bead with Alexandria, which was not Roman as early as 300 B.C. She also called it a *lukut sekala* of Kalimantan and Sarawak. It is not. It is the *lukut kong ba* (see Munan-Oettli 1988).
15. This is not so much a condemnation of these writers' scholarship (except, perhaps, for Gardner's wild speculation) as it is a commentary on the poor state of bead research that prevailed until recently.
16. Alternately, the strand could have been mixed into the collection at a later time. Beck did not see the faience beads or the mosaic bead.
17. Suboblate, dark blue, segmented melon beads are common particularly in the Deccan during Sātavāhana times (ca. 200 B.C. to A.D. 200). Dikshit (1969, 44) assumed that these were made by a Sātavāhana glass industry, but this has never been substantiated. A few were found on the surface at Arikamēḍu during the 1989–1992 excavations. Their origin is unknown, but they may have been imports from the Middle East. They are unlike segmented melons reported herein from South and Southeast Asia. They are shorter, with more lobes, and were often left as multiple beads. They are also many centuries older.
18. See Jönsson and Hunner (1995) for alternate ways of making these beads.
19. Dikshit quoted from the translation by Shamasastri (1915).
20. This was apparently the only time Dikshit saw any bead being made. It is difficult to interpret his account, especially the "ferrules," by which he apparently meant a drop of glass. No beads are known to have been made this way anywhere. If the glass were as hot as his account suggests, it would stick to the mandrel-punch and not form a bead. Cold glass can be heated and pierced with a cold mandrel-punch; this was done by the Chimu of Peru (Harris and Liu 1979; Francis 1983b), the Krobo of Ghana (Kirk Stanfield, 1993, personal communication), and in the Middle East, at least during Roman times (Francis 2001).
21. I have examined the beads of Brahmapuri, Koṇḍāpūr, and Ahichchhatrā. They have been curated so poorly that it is difficult, often impossible, to relate them to those in Dikshit's reports. In the Brahmapuri material at the Kolhapur Museum there is one green and one blue bead that may have been pierced. They are disk-shaped and have conical holes, but are very weathered and might have been made some other way. These alone might relate to the technique Dikshit reported at Ghodegere, but they are utterly unlike any beads he cited in his reports and are quite rare as opposed to being very common.
22. Basa (1992a) also mentioned a few other finds of these beads. Because these were surface finds on sites occupied during several periods, I have not tried to fit them into this scheme.
23. The evidence, however, is not very satisfactory, because only three potsherds have been excavated at Gunung Mas.
24. Vandiver (1983, 242) listed it among the techniques used to produce glass beads at Nuzi, Iraq, in the fourteenth century B.C. The Nuzi material (in the Semitic Museum at Harvard) is in a poor state of preservation. The technique was apparently only employed for the "Nuzi beads," ribbed

multiple spacers, unique to that site. It seems not to have been used thereafter for any bead until the Hellenistic period.

25. Three types of Kayan heirloom beads from this period can be identified. The *lukut kong ba* and *lukut bela daha* are both checker mosaics. The former has zones at the ends and the latter does not. The *lukut sak badak* is an eye mosaic bead made without a core (Munan-Oettli 1988; personal observation).
26. The Portland Vase is a two-handled glass amphora with a blue core overlaid with white (or opal) glass. The white was cut in relief to form scenes. The seminal study of the ancient object is by Turner (1959), whose introduction begins with, "The Portland Vase is probably the best known piece of ancient glass in existence." (Turner 1959, 263T) To bolster this statement he cited the skill with which it was made, its history, its reproduction in pottery by Wedgwood and in glass by various artists, and its frequent publication in books and related glass literature.
27. "Millefiori" is Italian for "a thousand flowers," and is a variety of Venetian mosaic glass. In this context, mosaic glass would have been a better choice.
28. Casson translated *myrrhinê* as "agate" in this passage for the reasons he gave on page 206. There is no justification for this, and now that fluorspar has been recognized in India, it is unnecessary.

10: Middle Eastern Beadmaking Techniques in Southeast Asia

1. Wound beads with stratified eyes were produced in the Late Zhou and Han periods in China. They are not known thereafter and those beads are quite different from the type being discussed here.

   As noted in the last chapter, segmented melon beads of blue glass and gold-glass beads are found on sites in India. Dikshit thought that both types were locally made, but this has never been demonstrated. They are most likely imports from the Middle East.
2. It is also possible that these were wasters imported to Takua Pa along with good beads. Some sites in Europe, such as Ribe, Denmark, suggest such a trade to some scholars (Torben Sode, 1996, personal communication). This assumes that the whole consignment was sold loose. However, I feel that this was not the case here. For one thing, such unusable gold-glass or false gold-glass beads have not been reported from anywhere else in the Asian littoral. Second, the concentration of false gold-glass beads in and around Thailand, as noted in the last chapter, lends weight to the assumption that they were locally made.
3. With the exception, of course, of the earlier production of wound stratified eye beads in China.
4. The Copts are the "Old Egyptians," the remnant of the original inhabitants of the land. Under the Hellenistic regime, they were the common people as distinct from the Greek-speaking upper class. They accepted their own brand of Christianity fairly early. They were generally lower class under the Romans, then stigmatized and sometimes persecuted by the Muslims after the Arab conquest. Many Arabs were moved into Egypt to tip the balance of population in their favor. Eventually, many Copts converted to Islam. Today they are the largest minority in Egypt. They are still under threat by extremists, but generally live in peace with and are indistinguishable from their Muslim neighbors.

11: The Western Indian Stone Bead Industry

1. The term "Deccan" is derived ultimately from the Sanskrit *Dakshiṇa,* originally meaning "on the right hand" (compare "dextrous") and later meaning "the south," referring roughly to peninsular India south of the Narmadā River (Yule and Burnell 1989, 301). "Trap" comes from the Swedish *trappa,* meaning "stairway," because of the steplike aspect of the flat, weathered basaltic hills of the formation (Wadia 1990, 275).
2. There are many newer studies of some of these sites, particularly Mohenjo-Daro (Moenjodaro) and Harappā. I have cited only the initial studies on these bead industries. Because the Harappān civilization lies outside the scope of this work, I cite newer works only when they are germane to the topics herein.
3. In 1986, K. K. Bhan, John Anthony, and I made field explorations of two sites south of the Narmadā that had been labeled "Harappān" and could have furnished raw stones to Lothal. Telod (K. P. Gupta 1972, 266) had no Harappān affinities that we could locate; it appears to be medieval in date. Bhagatrav (Rao 1973, 102) did, but we did not see anything relating to the bead industry. However, if it had been only a site to gather and ship stones to be worked at Lothal, little or none would be expected. Excavation at this large site would be most revealing (Francis 1986e, 8).
4. A Hindi word for gem is *ratna* (*pur* is village). How the letters were transposed is not known. It may have been the

British that did it, but Ratanpur rather than Ratnapur is found in the earliest literature on the place. There are other Ratnapurs or Ratnapuras in India, and also the famous Ratnapura of Sri Lanka. In Sanskrit *ratna* did not originally mean "precious stone," but any precious object. During Vēdic times, in relation to the king it meant his most trusted advisors. The use of the word for "precious stone" was a later development (Nilakanta Sastri 1978, 132–134).

5. Mining has also been conducted in other villages nearby. On three occasions between 1892 and 1961, visitors to Ratanpur found no activity there and proclaimed the mining dead (Francis 1982c, 31). Some may have visited at the wrong time of the year. Alternately, the Bhils may have moved elsewhere to work at another location. In 1995, John Anthony and I found that they had shifted to Damlai, about 15 km away, where they were digging in a sandy former course of the river. The Bhils also moved from Ratanpur to Damlai in the winter of 1907–1908 (Bose 1908, 181–183).

   Trivedi (1964, 10) listed eleven other mining villages in the region. None was active when he was writing, and Anthony and I did not find any of them working between 1981 and 1995.
6. Where Casson wrote "agate(?)" the Greek has *myrrhinê* (μορροη), which he identified as agate in this passage (Casson 1989, 206). However, as discussed in chapter 9 under agate glass beads, it is more likely fluorspar or fluorite.
7. Not all names used in the original text correspond to gem stone names used today. It is especially unlikely that emerald and topaz as we know them were circulating there.
8. These figures are, of course, estimates and there are many variables to be considered in such educated guesses. They result, however, from Chandler's extensive research and are not out of line. Cambay, incidentally, first showed up in A.D. 900 as India's fifth and the world's thirty-third city, with more than 50,000 souls.
9. What survives today of this book is the result of considerable editing by an anonymous Byzantine scholar.
10. More precisely, on maps constructed from his instructions in the *Geographia,* because none of his original maps exists. Two editions have been consulted for this analysis. One is a map printed by the Government Photozincographic Office in Pune, India, in 1880. The other is the text and the tenth map of the Ebner manuscript (Stevenson 1991, 153).
11. Iron mines and iron works were important segments of the Ujjain economy. This industry may have produced the famous Iron Pillar of Delhi, dated to about A.D. 500, which as yet shows no trace of rust. The technology for making such an object was well ahead of its time (Subbarayappa 1981). Iron was also exploited around Limudra, a village near Ratanpur, as evidenced by extensive slag tips, as yet undated.
12. This is related to the English word "igneous."
13. The translation from the French is mine.
14. *Pilu* is the name of the fruit of *S. oleoides* in Sanskrit and preserved in Punjabi for the fruit of *S. persica* (Chopra et al. 1956, 219).
15. The tank can hardly have served anything other than the temple, because no people live on top of the hill, nor is there any indication of past habitation. Copland (1819, 294–295) also observed the desolate nature of the hilltop and marveled that a tank was there at all (the temple was long gone by that time).
16. John Anthony and I interviewed Bukkar Bhai Balasingh Thakkur, Jina Bhai, and Antur Dipsingh, initially in 1981.
17. *Maṇi* is an old Indo-Iranian term meaning "seed, sperm, gem," and, by extension, "bead." *Pur* is "village" or "place," and *shahr* is "city." Maṇipur was defined by our interviewees as the stretch from the banks of the Narmadā to the Sātpurā Hills. Limudra was the de facto capital of this region.
18. This was my initial assumption (Francis 1982c, 18), although other dates are possible.
19. The region south of the river was then known as Antar-Narmadā (Sankalia 1945, 153) and/or Narmadātta-mandaḷa (Munshi 1955, 411).
20. Campbell (1880, 162) referred to the date of this statue as Saṁvat 1120 or A.D. 1064, whereas Bose (1908, 177) referred to it as Saṁvat 1126 or A.D. 1064. However, the Saṁvat era began in 58 B.C., which makes Campbell's date A.D. 1062 and Bose's A.D. 1068. Smart (Dames 1918, 143 n.*), commenting on Campbell and apparently using him as a source, reported that the statue was dated Saṁvat 1126 or A.D. 1004, probably a misprint. The statue is no longer to be found, so we shall never know the precise date.
21. *Encyclopaedia Britannica,* 14th ed., s.v. "Jains."
22. The current spelling is Khambhat. I have retained "Cambay" because it is better known outside India. Sternbach (1955, 103) listed no less than twenty-four different ways the name of the city had been spelled. To that list may be added Thevenot's "Cambage" (Sen 1949, 18), Hamilton's (1739, 142) "Cambaut," Tod's (1971, 247) "Cambayet,"

Abu' l-Fazl 'Allami's "Khambhayat" (Blochmann 1927, 2: 248), and my personal favorite, Tagore's "Kambalayet" (Tagore 1879, 884).

23. *Alaquequa* is derived from the Arabic *al-akik*, meaning "the agate." This is also the source of the English word. While translating, Dames correctly inserted "carnelian," the stone that reddens in the fire. Stanley (1866, 66) did not gloss the Portuguese term.
24. Dames' insertions are in parentheses, mine are in brackets except for "[thread them, and]." Dames substituted this for the wording that he (1918, 144 n. 2) noted was translated as "harden them" by Stanley (1866, 66). Stanley's translation was proper for the Spanish text he used. However, because one does not harden quartz mineral stones Dames chose "thread them" from Ramusio's early Italian translation. The Portuguese text Dames used for his translation did not have either phrase. The original Portuguese manuscript is lost.
25. Al-Idrisi was a geographer, not a traveler, and did not visit Cambay.
26. See note 43 in chapter 12 for more details on Münster.
27. That is, carnelian, garnet, agate, diaspore, chalcedony, hematite, and perhaps rock crystal. Diaspore is a minor gem mineral, hydrated alumina in composition. It and hematite are most unusual for Cambay exports. "Some kinde of naturall diamonds" is a puzzle, unless it refers to diamonds.
28. His name is spelled John Huighen van Linschoten in this edition.
29. Few Indian conquerors destroyed their enemy's temples. Ahmed Shah was infamous for doing this and apparently the only such ruler active in the region.
30. /L/ and /N/ are interchangeable in many Sanskrit-derived languages, including Gujarati.
31. The title of this paper, "Bead Manufacture at Hajar ar-Rayhani, Yemen" is misleading, because the authors themselves (Gwinnett and Gorelick 1991, 193) admitted that there is no evidence whatsoever for local production. They (Gwinnett and Gorelick 1991, 193–194) explored the idea that the beads may have come from India, and they most likely did.
32. That is, most faceted beads from Cambay are tumbled. There are a few exceptions, such as multifaceted rock crystal beads, which would lose all their attractiveness if tumbled. Beads made under the "revivalist" influence of Jonathan Mark Kenoyer (Kenoyer 1996) are also commonly polished by abrasion.
33. Callmer wrote of the rock crystal and carnelian beads (S-beads), "In the later bead periods . . . there is a very noticeable decrease in quality of the S-beads. The strict regularity of the early beads is replaced by uncertain forms and ground facets." Discussions with Callmer in 1995 confirmed my suspicion that this marked the polishing abrasion/tumbling transition.
34. In the early nineteenth century the Bohemian glass bead industry copied both this pendant and stone charm cases for sale to the regions where the originals were popular (Francis 1988b, 39, 42).
35. Acid-etched pendants of this type are on sale in Egyptian markets. The Petrie collection at the Institute of Archaeology, London, has a Bohemian glass reproduction with Egyptian hieroglyphs rather than the usual Arabic inscription.
36. On 30 December 1492 Columbus gave away carnelians to a local ruler, "And the Admiral took from his own neck a collar of fine agates and handsome beads of beautiful color that looked well in all its parts and put it on the king. . . ." (Dunn and Kelley 1988, 297). In the Spanish text "agate" is *alaqueques* (Dunn and Kell, 296), derived from the Arabic *al-akik*. It was not used by the Spanish, but only by the Portuguese (e.g., Barbosa at Limudra) (Dames 1918, 142). It referred not to agates, but to carnelians. Columbus no doubt picked up the word in the Guinea trade when he sailed for Portugal along the coast of West Africa (Francis 1993c).

12: South Indian Stone Beadmaking

1. *Sangam (caṅkam)* is Tamil for "academy." The legend is that three academies, whose tenure spanned 9,990 years and included 8,598 poets, sages, and, in the earliest, gods, were responsible for these poems. This late legend (first recorded in the seventh century A.D.) gave rise to this term being applied not only to a body of literature, but also to a grammatical system and even the period, "The *Sangam* Age" (Zvelebil 1973, 45–50). It is not strictly a proper term, but is used here for convenience.

   Unfortunately, these poems have been only sparsely translated into Western languages, often in editions difficult to find (Zvelebil 1973, 340–341). I have had to rely heavily on the work of others who have examined modern Tamil editions of the works. The dating of the works herein mostly follows Zvelebil (1973, 23–44), as does the spelling.
2. The Arikamēḍu bead census conducted by John Anthony

and myself at the Pondicherry Museum counted 22,889 stone beads and wasters, nearly matching the number in glass (25,945). In the 1989–1992 Arikamēḍu excavations, glass beads and wasters (3,489) outnumbered stone ones (1,231). However, 1,433 Indo-Pacific beads were found together. All but one was opaque red and they were either strung together or were going to be strung. When they are eliminated, the totals are much closer (1,648 and 1,231).

3. This complex of bead production has been well documented for Cambay, is evident in the material at Limudra, and was employed at Ujjain (Bannerjee 1959). Beads were also made this way in Inamgaon, a Chalcolithic site in the Deccan near Pune (Dhavalikar and Ansari 1988, 649, 711; personal observation).
4. More precisely, to 80.55 percent of the chalcedonic and 50.14 percent of the crystalline material. These figures vary slightly from those published in Francis 1988c, because it was then thought that the prase was chalcedonic. It has been determined to be crystalline prase by S. N. Rajguru and the Geology Laboratory of Deccan College, Pune, India.
5. Jonathan Mark Kenoyer (1999, personal communication) suggested that this stage is not pecking, but a finer chipping. Chipping in the Indian stone bead industry is a form of flaking using indirect percussion. For the very fine flakes to have been removed that way, a very small and sharp point would have had to be placed behind the bead being hit by a hammer. However, the contemporary beadmakers of Kangayam, Tamil Nadu, apparently the last survivors of this industry, use small chisels directly on the surface of the stones to form the blanks, a form of pecking (Rajan 1997–1998, 60).
6. Leonard Gorelick suggested this to me after examining a pecked roughout from Arikamēḍu.
7. Although I refer to these as "pecking" and "grinding," the variations in techniques are greater than these two operations alone and include all the subtle differences between them. Hence I have labeled each of them "complexes."
8. The term is derived from the Tamil *Paṇṭu,* meaning "old," and *kal,* meaning "stones." The reasons advanced by Leshnik (1974, 2) for substituting "Pandukal" for "Megalithians" were (1) many of their burials do not encompass large stones; (2) some large stone structures in South India are not burial complexes; (3) "Pandukal" is in use in South India to refer to these, because it is Tamil for "old stones"; (4) "megalithic" is easily confused with European megaliths, after which it was named, though there is no demonstrable connection between them; (5) "Pandukal" was used by many early English writers on the subject and Leshnik is thus "rescuing from oblivion a useful label"; (6) the better-known term produces strange constructions such as "megalithic pottery." His argument has great merit, especially because "megalithic stone bead" is even more absurd than "megalithic pottery."
9. Because of space limitations in the paper cited, it is not always clear whether each habitation site is Pandukal or not, though most of them are so identified. South Arcot District surrounds and is intermingled with the Union Territory of Pondicherry, where Arikamēḍu is located.
10. A reconstructed model of this furnace is on display in the Museum of Archaeology at Deccan College, Pune, India.
11. This widely used term is technically incorrect (or an extension of the usual definition), because etching involves the use of acid. For these beads, an alkali was applied to the surfaces and heat applied, imparting indelible, smooth, white decorations. See chapter 14.
12. Sadly, no one seems to have ever tried, in contrast to the many attempts (some of them quite laughable) at translating Harappān glyphs. Lal (1962) compared Pandukal marks with Harappān glyphs favorably. A connection between the Pandukal and Harappān people is at least possible, but has not been demonstrated.
13. Ravi Mohanty and I have frequently discussed the material from Mahurjhari, and I have examined it in some detail. Some of the information in this paragraph comes from personal communications with him and my observations.
14. Lac is the product of female insects, principally *Laccifer lacca,* that feed on resinous trees, especially *Ficus* sp., transforming the sap to build tiny cells or nests around themselves. The term is related to *lakh,* which in modern India is 100,000 (written 1,00,000), but which originally meant an enormous number, reflecting the swarming habits of these insects. Lac is still widely used for many purposes in India, but in the West it is today mostly recognized as shellac (shell lac). In the past, however, it was more common. It was employed as sealing wax, the red color being derived from the body of the same insect. Rajan (1997–1998) referred to "sealing wax" in his discussion of the Kangayam industry. Lac was also used for early cylindrical and disk records before the introduction of vinyl. It is distinct from lacquer, which is a quite different material.
15. Pecking, of course, has been employed for tools and sculp-

ture in many places. In the Harappān period and in some isolated sites in India, pecking was used to perforate thin disk beads (Francis 1988c, 57–58). Pecking, both to shape and perforate beads, is known from Neolithic West Africa and precontact Meso- and South America.

16. Taxila (Marshall 1951, 730), Rājghāt (Narain and Singh 1977, 21), Ahichchhatrā (Dikshit 1952b, 45–47), Ahar (Deo 1969, 163), Maheshwar and Navdatoli (Deo 1958, 178, 185), Nevasa (Deo 1960, 346), Nagara (Mehta 1968, 135–137), and two northern Pandukal sites, Khala and Gangapur (Moorti 1984–1985).
17. Cordelia Rösch of Würzburg University tested a surface sample with an electron microprobe. She determined that it was an unusually pure almandine (83 mol-%) with a small amount of pyrope (12 mol-%).
18. Also called "cinnamon stone," hessonite is the brownish red variety of grossularite. A small surface find was tested at the Center for Bead Research by the fusion method to confirm its nature, because both zircon and spinal often resemble this type of garnet. It may have come from Sri Lanka or Vietnam (Francis 1995b; see chap. 14).
19. Wad is the manganese ore likely used for the dark blue, violet, and black glasses made at Arikamēḍu (see chap. 4).
20. They have been found at many sites in Thailand from the Iron Age through the Dvaravati period (seventh to tenth centuries A.D.). Some are on display at the National Museum, Bangkok (see also Theunissen 1997). They are also found at Oc Eo (Malleret 1962a, 214–215). The scalloped bottoms of many of the Thai pendants and the long unfinished one at Oc Eo have no parallels at Arikamēḍu.
21. This is one of the rivers of the Punjab ("five waters"). They flow into each other to form the Indus, now in Pakistan.
22. This is *prasius* in Latin. Eichholz (1962, 254 n. c) identified it as "dark leek-green chalcedony," whereas S. H. Ball (1950, 93) equated it with "plasma or prase." The identification in Pliny's work of what we now call prase is all but impossible. Warmington (1928, 242–243) suggested that it might be what Pliny calls *iaspis* (jasper) or some other green stone. Then again, it just might be what he called prase.
23. No precise date can be affixed to the introduction of black onyx cameos into Rome. Ritcher (1971, 6) noted that nicolo (a synonym) occurred only occasionally before the establishment of the empire.
24. Gems were not its only export. It was then also the chief emporium for the shipping of black pepper and cardamom, both of which grow in the Western Ghats.
25. Warmington (1928, 250) placed Punnata in southwestern Mysore, apparently the only modern reference to this place, probably taken from Ptolemy.
26. This is another example of Indian counterintelligence, in addition to rumors about sea monsters around Sri Lanka mentioned in chapter 1 and the placement of agate sources far inland discussed in chapter 11. There were also stories of enormous, ferocious gold-digging ants related by Herodotus (Hutchins 1952, 111–113). Yet another story was that diamonds were in valleys so full of poisonous snakes that one had to throw raw meat to the floor and retrieve the diamonds from nests of eagles that took the meat (the diamonds stuck to the meat). The latter story was circulating by the fourth century and was known to Europeans, the Chinese, and the Arabs. It was still current in Marco Polo's day (see Francis 1990f, 34–35).
27. This is my translation from the French, with some help from Méile's commentary on it. The original Tamil was in poetic form and this would read better that way. Méile provided a translation into prose and, although tempting, I shall not attempt to restore it as a poem.
28. Méile reported this as being from the *Agananuru*.
29. The Peutinger Table is a map of the world drawn from a Roman perspective.
30. This is my translation from the French.
31. Beck (1930a, 175) reported on "two spherical beads of colourless crystal" found in urn burials in the Wynaad (now in Cannanore and Kozhikode Districts) remarking, "It is supposed that these beads were intended as passage money for the dead." On what grounds is not revealed. He further commented that they were worked in such a way "to leave a number of minute facets that run more or less at forty-five degrees with the axis. . . ." It is not known whether these are like the Korkai beads, but a beautiful, partly finished amethyst bead at Koḍumaṇal was worked in the way that Beck described, except that it had continuous rather than many small facets.
32. As at Arikamēḍu (see Francis 1996b), shell bangles were not made during the Pandukal occupation of a site. The holy conch is a northern idea.
33. Pliny said, "All of them [beryls] are cut by skilled craftsmen to a smooth hexagonal shape . . ." (Eichholz 1962, 225 [insertion mine]). However, as Eichholz (1962, 225 n. e) pointed out, this is not correct. Beryl crystals are naturally hexagonal in form. The beryl beads that became so fashionable in Rome (often strung with pearls) were merely

drilled, though they may have also been ground some to smooth their facets.

34. Champakalakshmi (1990, 15) paraphrased the *Paṭṭiṇappālai* as saying, "gold ornaments were exported to the western countries." Koḍumaṇal's fame as a goldsmith village has already been noted. Some of the gold may have come from Rome in the form of coins, at least during some periods.
35. "Port of trade" is Casson's (1989, 271) translation for *emporium.*
36. Small boats with a low draft that could navigate through Adam's Bridge. See Casson (1989, 229).
37. Apparently from the Chinese *kunlunpo. Po* is a large vessel; *kunlun* is said to be Southeast Asia (Casson 1989, 230). *Kunlun* is more usually considered to be some place in Southeast Asia, such as Pulau Condore (Ptak 1998, 2).
38. This is the Malay Peninsula.
39. Warmington (1974, 394 [insertion mine]) came to a comparable judgment in the revised edition of his classic work, after the discovery of Arikamēḍu. He said that the concentration of coins in Coimbatore District point to, "active overland trade between the Malabar coast and the eastern coast at Arikamedu . . .through the Coimbatore [Palghat] gap, thus avoiding, if such action was desired or necessary, the sea-voyage round Cape Comorin. . . ."
40. The 1989–1992 excavations showed that stones were still being worked at Arikamēḍu until its abandonment, assumed to be the seventeenth century from the data gathered from the glass bead industry (see chap. 4).
41. "Royal purple" or "Tyrian purple" was an expensive cloth dye of high status. It was obtained from shells of *Purpura* sp. and *Murex* sp.
42. The Latin version is in van de Woestijne. The translation in Prasad is quoted here.
43. Sebastian Münster (1489 to 1552) was a remarkable scientist. The most famous of his labors was *Cosmographiae universalis,* originally published in 1544. It was translated into German as *Beschreibung aller Länder,* the first methodical description of the world in German. Münster enlisted the aid of more than 120 collaborators, mined the classics, and added new information pouring in about the world on a regular basis. The book was reprinted long after his death; the last edition was in German in 1628. More detailed accounts of the world had then become available and Münster was forgotten. There was only one French translation and none in English. Although there were forty-six editions, it is rarely cited. The bibliophile Raymond D. Tomasso brought it to my attention.

13: Glass Beadmaking in Southeast Asia and Sri Lanka

1. At Phu Hoa, Dong Nai Province, Vietnam, small strings of beads were found hanging from the bosses of such earrings (History Museum, Ho Chi Minh City).
2. H. Otley Beyer (Fox 1970, 126) apparently introduced this term after an Ifugao name (Solheim 1981, 44). Beyer married an Ifugao woman and lived much of his life in Banaue. However, Ifugao men who make them, Ifugao women who owned gold heirloom ones, and the curator of the Kiangan Museum called them *bung* or *boong* (Francis 1992a, 6–7). Harold Conklin (1996, personal communication) informed me that the more properly written *buung* refers to something strung in the manner of a pendant.
3. These have been called "double-zoomorphic-heads" and "bicephalic pendants." That they were earrings rather than necklace pendants was confirmed by burials from Giong Phet, ca. 300 B.C. (History Museum, Ho Chi Minh City) and in two burials at Giong Ca Vo (Reinecke 1996, 8); both sites are in Can Gio District, Ho Chi Minh City. The identification of the animal heads was long a subject of debate. Fox (1970, 128) said that they were "probably horse[s]," Suchitta (1984, 153) thought they were calves, and Bellwood (1985, 276) opted for deer. Goat, pig, water buffalo, ass, dog, and fantasy animals have also been suggested (Reinecke 1996, 6).
4. Thiel (1986–1987, 258) excluded the clay ones she found from the class of *lingling-o,* but they are a variation on the theme.
5. They are common in the Philippines. Rey Santiago of the National Museum and I often considered where they might have originated. Beyer (1947, 283), who thought they were from Cambodia or Southeast Asia [*sic*], and Fox (1970, 139), who guessed South China or Indochina, were not far off.
6. This is a very common and probably the oldest way to make a bangle. The maker began with a bead wound from the furnace and expanded it, either by rolling it up a clay cone (called *kalgood* in northern India [Francis 1982b, 21–22]) or by manipulating it with two iron mandrels. The method was used in many places. It is the only way bangles found at Berenike, Egypt, were made during Hellenistic and Roman times. It is also the method suggested by Theophilus (Hawthorne and Smith 1979, 73–74) to make finger rings.

7. Glover (1990a, 169) noted this when reporting on Ban Don Ta Phet. At Arikamēḍu, the earliest levels reached were in the second century B.C. However, it is likely that the site is somewhat older than that. Digging was halted in the northern sector because the water table had been reached. Pumps were brought in, but the sandy nature of the soil made it impossible to proceed. However, the southern sector is believed to be much earlier, being the site of the Pandukal settlement. No trenches in this sector reached sterile levels. Work was cut short by at least two seasons because of the noncooperation of local Archaeological Survey of India officials and the unfortunate deteriorating health of the lead excavator, Vimala Begley.
8. It is not possible from the published literature on these beads (Glover 1990b, 13–14; Basa et al. 1991; Glover and Henderson 1995, 148–150; Salisbury and Glover 1997) to tell exactly how many of the faceted glass beads were worked in a lapidary manner. Perhaps a much larger percentage of them were than are now identified. On the other hand, Kishor Basa (1999, personal communication) told me that he thinks only a few of these beads were made by lapidary techniques.
9. This is Fox's "cicada," though it more likely represents a flower bud. Fox did not discuss how it was made. See Francis (1989d, 13).
10. Chin You-di was given some potsherds from Ban Chiang by Steven Young, son of a former U.S. ambassador to Thailand. Young had started fieldwork for his dissertation in the village. The villagers had been picking up the potsherds for a decade or more.
11. Ian Glover kindly loaned one to me for further study. It and an analysis of its glass were featured in a paper on Southeast Asian beads by Salisbury and Glover (1997).
12. Ian Glover also loaned this to me. See previous note.
13. By this, I do not mean that two cones were formed and then joined. Rather, the conical shapes of each half were fashioned separately. The equator is curved rather than sharp. Bubbles on each side converge toward it in a chevron pattern or form short dashes running parallel with the perforation. Both patterns can appear on the same bead, indicating hand manipulation rather than a mold or trough through which the beads were run.
14. The "parallel" from Korea suggested by Glover and Henderson (1995, 150) does not apply. The Korean beads are simply long glass tubes and technically unlike the Ban Chiang beads.
15. Perhaps the only other ancient people who used such long tubular beads were the Tairona of Colombia (Kessler and Kessler 1978).
16. In addition to looking down the perforation at both ends with a hand microscope, I made vinyl silicate impressions of the perforation at both ends.
17. A bead of the bicone type donated to the Center for Bead Research has a specific gravity of 2.37, relatively low for glass, perhaps because of its numerous bubbles. Published analyses have confirmed the lack of lead.

    As discussed in chapter 8, potassium-rich glass is reported in southern China from about 200 B.C. to A.D. 220. It is not certain that this glass was Chinese in origin.
18. Jatim is a contraction of Jawa Timur, or East Java. Indonesians are fond of contractions and acronyms. To avoid undue confusion, they are called East Javanese beads here.
19. In addition to the data in their book, correspondence with Adhyatman (letter on file, Center for Bead Research, 23 December 1993) clarified the picture. Adhyatman and Arifin examined the Dutch records to determine discovery locations and associated ceramics to help date the beads.
20. Some references cite these beads in Sarawak, but they seem not to be the beads in question.
21. Precisely how this was done is not yet understood. Jamey Allen, in a display for the Bead Museum, then in Prescott, Arizona, and in an unpublished manuscript, suggested that the canes were fused into a flat plaque and applied over a drawn tube subsequently constricted along its length to make the beads. He proposed the same method for the white spotted beads and the combed *pelangi*.

    I believe it is more likely that the mosaic chips were placed on the core individually. Perhaps some of the cores were drawn, but a bead of this type in the Archaeology Department of the National Museum in Jakarta was sawed in half at its equator to reveal its interior and another has broken in half in the same way. In both cases, the cores are clearly wound.
22. These are Osborne's "true *millefiori*" and Thijssen-Etpison's *ngirbidul* and the left one of "unknown types" among Palau beads. "Palau" means "island" in Malay tongues. The place is now known as Belau, but I have retained the earlier name because it is far more common in the literature and is still used by most governmental agencies (Paul Titchenal, personal communication, 2000).
23. This is a yellow-centered *chelbucheb*, the *meringel chad*, meaning "precious" on Palau.

24. They are among the *kluk* group of beads on Palau.
25. They are the *smesmob* on Palau.
26. This refers to the Chinese invasion of the Kediri Kingdom in 1292. This marked the foundation of Trowulan and the ascent of Majapahit. China did not annex Java.
27. Kubary (1889) did the first major study of these beads. Among recent studies are Osborne 1958, 168–171; Force 1959; De Beauclair 1963; Force and Force 1963; and D. R. Smith 1983, aside from Thijssen-Etpison. The latter book is undated, but it was probably published after 1990. It alone has profuse color illustrations.
28. The "big yellows" may be included in the *bleob* class on Palau.
29. I measured the 253 beads of this type excavated at Tissamaharama, thanks to the excavation team from Kommission für Allgemeine und Vergleichende Archäologie KAVA [Commission for General and Comparative Archaeology], Bonn, Germany. The diameters varied from 0.8 to 1.3 cm and averaged 1.0 cm. Smaller examples are also known, but this seems to be the standard size.
30. The Indian parallels cited for this type of bead by Deraniyagala (1972, 138) are not valid, because most or all of those beads are simply red Indo-Pacific beads.
31. At Mantai in the upper levels of Trench H were found fourteen thin, red disk beads in rather close conjunction, eight of them in the same loci. I cataloged them as red jasper, but I am no longer sure that they are. Their perforations were drilled and they were worked on the edges, but so are these glass beads. They are all smaller than the ones at Tissamaharama, about half a centimeter in diameter, but smaller glass ones are known from elsewhere. I have also seen these beads at Koḍumaṇal, Alagankulam, and Arikamēḍu and initially classified them all as red jasper. I need to revisit these assemblages in the light of what I have learned about the glass beads in Sri Lanka. Their presence in South India and at Mantai would not be a surprise, but they would still be surprisingly scarce at Mantai.
32. Basa also mentioned these beads from Arikamēḍu, Ter, and Paithan. His pictures of the ones from Arikamēḍu (Basa 1992b, 95, fig. 5) do not appear to be of this type. The one on the left looks quite different. The center one looks like a round bicone, though it is difficult to judge. The one on the right is not glass, but a naturally occurring crystal, one of many recovered and carefully marked by the earliest French excavators. I cannot comment on the ones from Ter and Paithan that Basa cited from Dikshit, but the drawing of at least one bead (Dikshit 1969, 42, fig. 10.19) does not resemble beads of this class.
33. I have been misquoted as saying that these are Han Chinese (Adhyatman and Arifin 1993, 60) in origin, but this misunderstanding was corrected in their second edition.
34. That is, unless many of the faceted beads from Thailand, discussed in the section on Ban Don Ta Phet earlier in this chapter, are paddled rather than ground to shape.
35. There are only five beads of this color among the 4,244 Indo-Pacific beads in the Pondicherry Museum. The color was probably accidental, due to an excess of copper.
36. I studied these beads in the Andhra Pradesh Department of Archaeology and Museums, thanks to V. V. Krishnasastry, the excavator of both sites.
37. These beads were made either by casing a red core with orange and drawing the gather out or through careful control of the glass melt. Some Indo-Pacific beads have an orange coat over red or vice versa, apparently accidentally resulting from the concentration of cuprous oxide particles or the conditions of the furnace. These methods are unlike that suggested by Pilditch. The red in the bead from Karaikadu is less homogeneous than Indo-Pacific reds, containing numerous small bits of green glass that had not been properly oxygen-starved to turn red. This is probably what Pilditch assumed was the "core" of the bead.

14: Minor Stone Bead Industries in the Asian Maritime Trade

1. These included eighty-eight unworked pieces, thirty finished beads, and ninety-one flakes.
2. There were four beads and three chunks. One locus had many small flakes, which I recorded simply as "many" and count here as one piece.
3. There were thirty-six beads and blanks and five flakes.
4. These had not been tested. They are called garnets in Malleret's notes. He had several minerals tested and did not record either zircon or spinel, the two minerals that might be confused for hessonite.
5. This information was obtained from a dealer at the Denver Gem and Mineral show in 1995 who dealt principally in Vietnamese gems. He was reluctant to give me his name.
6. For anyone referring to this report, note that the term "capped" bead was substituted in error for "oblate." This arose from a misunderstanding of the picture of a capped bead in van der Sleen (1973, 41, fig. 5.15), which was interpreted as a simple oblate.

7. "Perles" are mentioned in this French translation, but this apparently refers to jade beads (bead is *perle* in French) rather than the products of mollusks. Laufer (1974) made extensive use of Biot's translation.
8. To survey this material, I consulted the detailed indexes of Legge's (1972) *The Chinese Classics*, originally published in 1890 by Oxford University Press in seven volumes, looking for agate, bead, carnelian/cornelian, crystal, gem, gold, jade, jasper, jewelry, pearl, quartz, and silver.
9. *Lessons from the State*, Book XI: Odes of Ts'in, Ode IX, Wei yang, verse 2.
10. *Minor Odes of the Kingdom*, Ode X, Heh Ming, verses 1, 2.
11. The stones are mentioned on pp. 302–303 (white quartz through figured agate) and p. 310 (pearls through clear crystal). Birch (1965, 142–152) contains an abbreviated version of Watson's translation of this poem; it omits the first group of stones.
12. Dates for the Shang and the following Zhou periods have not been firmly fixed. Those used here are from Lee (1952).
13. I have observed these, but not personally examined them, so my conclusions as to their origins are tentative.
14. Hirth and Rockhill did not separate imports from exports when they published this list. However, it appears that they listed exports first and then imports. I have inserted "Exports" and "Imports" where they seem logical and correspond with known Song dynasty tribute lists. The passage would read: "[Exports:] gold, silver, Chinese cash, coined money, lead, piece-goods of all colours, porcelain-ware, [Imports:] cotton fabrics, incense and scented woods, rhinoceros horns, ivory, coral, amber, strings of pearls, steel, shells of turtles, tortoise-shell, cornelians, ch'ö-kü shell, rock-crystal, foreign cotton stuffs, ebony and sapan wood."
15. This material is in the Hong Kong History Museum in Kowloon.
16. Some of these passages were copied from the *Lingwai daida* by Zhou Qufei written in 1178.
17. Bretschneider (1910,174 n. 499 [insertion mine]) wrote: "I do not know what red stone is meant by *gu-mu-lan*. Kaferstein [*Mineralogia Polyglotta* (1849); from which Bretschneider made most of his identifications], p. 68 gives *kumala* as the Malayan name of a precious stone of extraordinary beauty. Perhaps opal." Carnelian fits the description of the stone much better than opal. Moreover, this would be the only place carnelian could be listed among the red stones, assuming that Bretschneider's (or Kaferstein's) other identifications, which were put forward with somewhat more assurance, are correct.
18. There is a problem when it comes to the question of "carnelian" beads in Sri Lanka. Red hard stone beads are found there and were locally made for a long time. However, it is not known whether carnelian actually exists in Sri Lanka, whether raw stones were imported from Gujarat in western India, or whether they came from South India. It is also not certain at the time of this writing whether the red stones are actually carnelian or red quartz.
19. This word may be derived from "tsáo chú" or "tú chú," which were used by Chinese traders for "glass beads" in the late nineteenth century (S. W. Williams 1966, 120).
20. Michael Flecker of Pacific Sea Resources, Singapore, sent me samples of the beads for identification. An account of *Nuestra Señora de la Concepción* is in Mathers (1990).
21. They were misnumbered in that publication, with no. 24 being recorded twice.
22. There are also several sites in Sri Lanka, including Ridiyagma in the far south (Bopearachchi 1995, 383–384) where carnelian or red quartz was worked. Until the issue of the identification and sources of these stones is straightened out, it is not fair to comment on this industry.
23. David Whitehouse kindly allowed me to examine the material he excavated. He has indicated to me in a personal communication (1989) that only about half of the excavated material is in the British Museum. The rest is in Iran.
24. More than half of the material excavated by Don Whitcomb had been repatriated to Egypt before I examined the beads at the Oriental Institute. Unfortunately, when I was last in Egypt I was not aware of this.
25. One of these was from the satellite town of Shenshef.
26. The footnote and the passage to which it is connected are infamous in the historiography of West African beads. See Francis (1990g, 4–5; 1993a, 7).
27. The industry made carnelian plaques, no doubt with passages from the Koran for use in jewelry, continuing an old practice. Beck (1933, 392) noted that plaques of "etched carnelians" were then still being produced in Iran. That has also ceased. The plaques made today in Iran are decorated by an acid technique.
28. Mackay identified this as *Capparis aphylla*, now recognized as *C. decidua* Edgew. The genus is the source of the pickled delicacy capers.
29. Beck (1934, 193) noted that the treatment slightly weak-

ened the stone and the lines tend to flake out, leading earlier writers to assume that they had been added as incised lines.

Several years ago a bead dealer specializing in Afghan material told me that the Afghans were etching beads again. I have since seen carnelians I believe were the ones he was discussing. They are usually faceted beads painted (not etched) along their edges in designs unlike any recorded etched carnelian styles.

30. I think it unlikely that the process originated in Mesopotamia. The Harappāns had the stones and they were quite inventive in the decorating and coloring of stone beads. It is possible that immigrant Harappāns made the Mesopotamian designs.
31. This is in an internal memo, "Sites of the Highest Possible Priority: Targets for Archaeological Reconnaissance in Thailand," for the Division of Archaeology/Fine Arts Department of Thailand, Bangkok.
32. Dikshit (1949, 10) called these "black agates." In fact, all appear to be chalcedony or carnelian artificially blacked in the manner of black onyx and then etched with white figures. Blackening parts of a bead, leaving some areas undarkened by using a resist, dates to late Harappān or post-Harappān times (Francis 1982d). When white lines are added, the technique is similar to dZi beads (Francis 1982d), which fall outside the scope of this work.
33. The casual finds are on the color plate in Francis (1987b, row 1: 4, 5). The beads from the burials have not been published. Those from Souttoukeny excavated by Casal are in the Museé Guimet, Paris. Others are in the Auroville Museum in Pondicherry from nearby tombs. In burials Indo-Pacific glass beads accompanied the etched carnelians.
34. Second color plate, lower picture. Most of these are glass collar beads, but at least the fourth one from the left in the center row is one of these green stone beads.
35. At Taxila, fairly close to the source of lapis lazuli, there were forty-five (Marshall 1951, 732, 734). Otherwise they are rare. S. J. Hasan (1983, 138) surveyed the archaeological literature on Gangetic Valley sites and listed only nine, mostly at Kauśāmbī. Margabandhu (1985, 198 n. 261) listed seventeen sites where lapis lazuli beads were found, concentrated in western India and the Deccan, especially in Vidarbha.
36. This assumes that Schafer (1963, 230) was correct in identifying *"se-se"* as lapis lazuli. He remarked that no identifiable name for the rock appeared until Mongol times. This name is not in Bretschneider's (1910) fourteenth-century source. This has also been identified as turquoise and balas ruby or spinel (Needham 1959, 672). No lapis lazuli appears in Watson's (1961, 301–321) translation of *Shanglin Park*.
37. At Koṇḍāpūr twenty-two were found (Dikshit 1952a, 10–11). In a single Pandukal grave at Raigir seventy-three were uncovered (Beck 1930a, 166–167), several times the total from all northern sites. They are widely scattered in the south and are especially numerous at Pandukal sites, such as Yeleswarum, Peddamaru, Peddabonkur, Maski, and Arikamēḍu. They are not found in Tamil urban centers. None is known from Karur, Uraiyūr, Kāvēripaṭṭinam, or Alagankulam.
38. A large number of these etched carnelians are currently coming onto the antiquities market from looted sites, reportedly from northern Afghanistan (Francis 1993d, 4).
39. In the Late Neolithic to about 700 B.C., jade accounted for 10 of 8,173 beads from eight of nineteen sites. In the Developed Metal Age, only 1 of 282 beads from fifteen excavated sites was jade (Francis 1989d, 7–8). All periods and dates are those proposed by Fox.

15: Organically Derived Gem Materials

1. The brilliant blue feathers of the Alcedinidae were used to decorate jewelry, including beads and pendants, and were employed at least since Han times (Hartman 1980, 76). The bird is mentioned in *Shanglin Park* of the Western Han (Watson 1961, 305). The Chinese eventually exhausted their own supplies (Hartman 1980, 75) and were importing the feathers by the Tang period (Schafer 1963, 16). They do not appear on a list of imports around 999 during the Northern Song (Hirth and Rockhill 1911, 19). However, they were being worn extravagantly enough to be banned by the emperor in 1107 on humanitarian grounds, though smuggling continued (Hirth and Rockhill 1911, 236). Zhao Rugua reported how the birds were captured and imported, mostly by sea, from Cambodia (Hirth and Rockhill 1911, 235).
2. The favored camphor, that of *Dryobalanops aromatica*, was important to the Chinese trade (Schafer 1963, 166–169). It came from Borneo and Sumatra; "barus camphor" is named for Barus, Sumatra, where the earliest Chinese glass coil beads appear in Southeast Asia. The Chinese

burned it, as do most people. In Puri, India, camphor was formed into beads for wedding *malas* (garlands) that sublimated overnight. Today these are made only on special request, having been largely replaced by paraffin (Francis 1983c, 20).

3. This is the shell of a turtle, *Eretmochelys imbricata*. It was often mentioned in the first-century *Periplus*. Later, there was considerable trade in it from Sri Lanka and Southeast Asia to China.
4. There has been more attention to shells than to many other beads, because the subject commends itself to many fields of interest. There has even been a shell bead conference (Hayes 1989). It is possible to source shells rather precisely (Claassen 1989), but little work has yet been done on this topic.
5. Small amounts of amber can be found in many places. The Baltic deposits dwarf all of them, especially historically. The most notable competitors are the Dominican Republic and Myanmar (Burma).
6. Lac is produced in the body of a female insect and is the source of shellac, sealing wax, pre-vinyl records, and so on. See note 14, chapter 12.
7. A semifossilized resin, known as "copal" is found in China and neighboring countries and may have been the substance listed as amber. It is also possible that it is amber from other than a Baltic source, though this is probably too early for the exploitation of Burmese amber.
8. True copal, *copalli* in Nahuatl (the Aztec language), is a recent, nonfossilized resin used for incense. In the modern gem trade, the word refers to various semifossilized resins found in several parts of the world.
9. The sap that eventually became amber was initially full of many tiny bubbles that rendered it opaque. However, if the sap was exposed to sunlight for some time, the bubbles were driven from it and it became translucent.
10. Jet is a form of coal, a type of fossilized wood.
11. This may have been rock or glass crystal. Britain imported 34,000 "crystal" beads from France in 1625–1626 and 80,000 in 1629–1630, and Kidd (1979, 29) assumed that they were glass. There was also then a rock crystal industry in Europe, at least in Venice (Alcouffe 1984) and perhaps elsewhere.
12. That is, rupees per seer. The rupee (tola) was the standard silver coin and weight for most of North India. It was worth between 175 and 180 troy grains (11 to 11.3 metric g) of silver (Yule and Burnell 1989, 775, 807). Sir Thomas Roe (1905, 346) in 1616 valued a rupee at 2 shillings, 2 pence, and in the same year Edward Terry (1905, 23) noted inconsistencies in rupee weights and valued rupees between 2/- and 2/9. The seer, though not always exactly the same weight, was usually equivalent to 80 tola or 2.5 troy pounds (0.9325 kg). Thus, the price of this amber was roughly £1/8/8 (£1.48) sterling per kilogram, using Roe's value of the rupee. This is cheaper by half than 29/- a pound.
13. Ceuta and Mellila are small Spanish possessions on the northern coast of Morocco. Sebta is a transliteration of the Arabic name for Ceuta.
14. I have converted the Chinese measurements into English and metric measurements. All other insertions are Mills'.
15. The "Central Country" in this and subsequent passages from Ma Huan is China. This term is equivalent to the perhaps better known "Middle Kingdom."
16. This widespread caste is known as *cheṭṭi* in Malayālam, *sheṭṭi* in Tamil, *seṭṭi* in Telugu, and *seḍḍi* in Sinhalese (Yule and Burnell 1989, 189).
17. The *Purāṇas,* "old tales" or "that which lives from ancient times," began as oral tradition akin to the epics. They were written down after the epics and amended over the centuries. They are sometimes called the "Vedas of the people" because they deal with many aspects of ordinary life. Parts of the *Vāyu Purāṇa* date back to 500 B.C. or so, but it was still being edited as late as the sixth century A.D. (Wheatley 1961, 204–205; Dandekar 1965, 4).
18. Warmington (1928, 263) suggested that the coral imported to Kanê was destined for reexport to India, a not-unlikely scenario.
19. Their disappearance from South China is in dispute. Cammann (1962, 63) said that they were still found south of the Yangtze as late as the eighteenth century, and two stray herds were reported in 1957. However, their effective extinction was much earlier.
20. Tibbetts (1979, 161–177) listed Waqwaq among the "legendary places" in Arab geography texts. Clearly, many stories have been mixed up in the telling, so that by themselves the accounts of Waqwaq are not reliable. It may be that more than one place was called by this name. In some cases it appears to be Indonesia. However, it is often described as a place east of China at the edge of the known world that produces gold. This brings to mind the Philippine Archipelago. There is a district in Manila called Wakwak. Wakwak is said to be a cult in some of the southern islands.

Were this the Wakwak cited here, the ivory, of course, would have come from somewhere else.

21. More recent excavations may have uncovered other examples.
22. Yule and Burnell quoted the seventh-century Chinese visitor Xuan Zang describing Kalinga (roughly Gunter to Cuttack), "The kingdom produces wild elephants of a black color, which are much valued in the neighbouring realms." In a footnote, they suggested that this was the subspecies referred to in the *Periplus*. Casson (1989, 233) concurred, noting that this region was celebrated for its elephants in Indian literature.
23. The word for bead is *perle* in French, *perla* in Italian, *Perle* (as in *Glasperle*) in German, and *pärla* in Swedish. In Greek and Latin, *margarite* served both purposes. The Tamil word for pearl, *mutu*, was adopted in Hindi as *moti* (Subramoniam 1961, 299). *Mutiara* is pearl in Bahasa Indonesia, but the word for bead is differently derived. In Timor and neighboring islands, the *mutisalah* group of heirloom beads is derived from this root (see chap. 17). In the older Australasian linguistic strata, "pearl" and "bead" is *ino* among the Kayan of Sarawak (Harrisson 1950, 211), *inu* on Flores, *hinu* on Roti (Rouffaer 1899, 413), and *hinau* in Visayan or Cebuano in the central Philippine Archipelago.

    Apart from words derived from "coral," discussed in the section of this chapter on coral, there are other roots for "bead." The Indo-Iranian *maṇi* ("seed, precious stone, sperm") became *maṇikya* in Hindi ("precious stone," along with *ratna*) and *maṇi*, which is "bead" and "gem." *Manik*, usually in its plural, *manik-manik*, is Malay/Bahasa Indonesia for "bead(s)."

    A common Spanish word is *cuenta*, for the beads' role in counting with a rosary. The English "bead" is from a similar source; *bede* in Old English meant the act of praying, a prayer, or a request (Francis 1989f, 1). Ultimately it is derived from Indo-European **bhidh*, originally "pot, tub, barrel," becoming *fides* and *fiscus* (Pokorny 1927, 185) or **bheudh*, "to be attentive, spiritually active, awake," from which are also derived *bo*, *bhodi*, and *Buddha* (Pokorny 1927, 147–148).

    Various Arab dialects, Farsi, and Dari use *akik* (agate) for "bead." In Arabic *nazhm* (to put into order) is sometimes substituted; *lulu nazhm* means "to string pearls."
24. Pearls do not survive long in most burial conditions, so many more may once have been buried in those pots.
25. Campbell Thompson (1936, 53 n. 2) also believed "fish-eyes" were pearls. Among other things, Mesopotamian "Ladies of Quality" powdered it to use as a cosmetic. Howard-Carter (1986) suggested that "fish-eyes" were eye stones: banded agates cut into low domes to reveal concentric bands and pierced side to side. These are otherwise known as "Aleppo stones." She traced them to western India.
26. *Oxford Annotated Bible* (1962).
27. The old city of Sofala as such no longer exists. The sea wore much of it away and it went into steep decline after the establishment of Beira a little to the north. Beira is today the capital of Sofala Province. The town of Nova Sofala marks the site of Sofala.

16: The End of the Asian Maritime Bead Trade

1. Although Europe did not actually colonize western Asia, it managed to administer most of it and made unilateral decisions of great importance. All of South and Southeast Asia (except for Thailand) was colonized and China was bullied into submission. Korea and Japan remained aloof and Afghanistan stubbornly independent.
2. Madagascar (Malagasy) is a surrogate for the East African coast. It has been chosen because there is considerable documentation for the early years of the trade.
3. Because "it is not common," Samuel Purchas (1905, 32–64) transcribed the bull sent to Spain (the other one was sent to Portugal). He wrote a short introduction to it and included "The same Englished," an English translation by Richard Eden. Purchas' "Animadversions" (censorious criticisms) follow in which he berated the "Parasite" Alexander VI for attempting to control the world.
4. Every schoolchild knows that Magellan was the first man (or captain) to circumnavigate the globe, but then soon learns that he died in the Philippines. He gets credit because he had earlier sailed from Europe to the Spice Islands (Moluccas, Indonesia), which are east of Mactan/Cebu. He had gone around the world one and a half times before he died.
5. "Cristallo" was the clearest glass made in Europe and the pride of the Venetian industry. It was invented by Angelo Barovier (1405–1460) and made with purified alkalis, worked with special care, and employed manganese as a decolorant. By 1612, marble pebbles from northern Italy had replaced sand as the silica, and the process was refined even further (Mentasti 1980, XLVI, LV–LVI, 1–2).
6. What were they going to do with this glass? The Spanish

later tried to set up a bottle factory at Santa Ana, near Manila, but at this time they were still encamped on Cebu. In the Americas, natives took glass (asked for it from Columbus on his first trip) to make tools. There are cases of raw glass made into beads by Native Americans in both North and South America.

7. Hawks' bells were common gifts from Europeans to natives in both the Americas and Africa, where they were used principally for decoration, most commonly as tinkling pendants.
8. In the original text lower-case Roman numerals followed each entry to confirm the number of items being requested. I have eliminated these; all were correctly entered.
9. Chevrons (*rosettas* in Italian) are (mostly) Venetian drawn beads with multiple corrugated layers (the outer layer is smooth) that reveal chevrons on the edges when beveled. The earliest ones usually had seven layers, the inner of "bottle green" glass and then white, blue, white, red, white, and blue layers. The edges were faceted to reveal the designs. This type was made from about 1490 to 1610.
10. These are named for the settlement on Cubagua Island, Venezuela, from which they were first archaeologically described (Fairbanks 1968). They are long, drawn beads with square sections, sometimes twisted. The core is usually dark blue, coated with a thin layer of white covered with a thin layer of light or dark blue (red examples are known in the American northeast). There are also smaller, shorter blue versions. They date from around 1500 to 1610. Their origin has been debated, but their sophistication and their discovery at Fustat (Old Cairo), Madagascar, and Jamestown, Virginia (Francis 1996c), point to Venice. The smaller types have been excavated at Calatagan; large ones (including twisted varieties) are in private collections in the Philippines.
11. In addition to the Philippines, they are found together in Venezuela (Fairbanks 1968), Florida (M.T. Smith 1983), Peru (M.T. Smith and Good 1982), and Mexico (Francis 1987e). However, other traders, including the English (e.g., at Jamestown [Francis 1996c]) and the Arabs or Portuguese (e.g., Madagascar, Egypt), also used them. Before these were identified as European, Filipino archaeologists had assumed that the cemetery was abandoned before Spanish contact.
12. His name is variously written as Ivan Gonzales de Mendoça, Ivan Gonzales de Mendosa, and Juan Gonzalez de Mendoza.
13. Although these observations suggest a steady increase in the number of junks coming to Manila, the trajectory was not always upward. The number varied from twenty to sixty (in 1616 there were only seven), but did increase in the early decades of the trade (Schurz 1939, 71).
14. As noted in chapter 14, *"tacley"* may be derived from "tsáo chú" or "tú chú." In the late nineteenth century S.W. Williams (1966, 120) said that this was a Chinese trade term for glass beads.
15. De Morga consistently referred to the Chinese as "Sangleyes." Schurz (1939, 63 n. 1) said this is derived from *sengli,* meaning "trade" in Amoy.
16. Bead fragments recovered from this wreck were sent to me by Michael Flecker of Pacific Sea Resources of Singapore, a treasure salvaging company. In addition to the types in the text, there was a deep red stone (garnet?) cornerless cube on a wire, likely of copper or bronze, possibly Indian, Sri Lankan, or even Bohemian, if it had been part of a Spaniard's rosary.
17. The unsubstantiated story is that they were introduced to the natives of the U.S. Southwest by missionaries (*Padre* is Spanish for "Father") coming north from Mexico.
18. Mexico has many souvenirs of this trade. *China-poblana,* the national dress, is said to have been invented by a Chinese (or Indian) princess (or not) brought up in Puebla; a bridge in the city honors her. Chinese textile patterns, embroidery, and jewelry had significant impacts on Mexican styles (Davis and Pack 1963, 58). There is even a tiny village called China in the Yucatán on the Campache-Edzna road.
19. Tor (El Tûr) is now a place of little account, but then it was an important port on the Gulf of Suez on the eastern coast of the Sinai Peninsula.
20. By this the annual hajj pilgrimage must be meant.
21. Of course, it is a movable feast. Cortesão (1967, 12 n. 2) pointed out that the nearest year in which the hajj began on 1 February was in 1481 and that in 1513 it fell on 7 February.
22. The Kingdom of Pegu is now part of Myanmar, or Burma. Siam is an old name for Thailand.
23. Because these beads were moving west, they must have originated in Asia, whether India, China, or Southeast Asia is not clear.
24. This is probably *alaquequas* in the original, which later meant carnelian (Francis 1993c), but at this early date could have meant agates; thus the reference to different colors.

25. Some of these were independent kingdoms. Others were port cities, and still others were ethnic groups. It is an impressive list; compare it with de Morga's at Manila.
26. Without the original Portuguese it is impossible to know what Cortesão translated as "pearl beads." The phrase may have meant pearls or simply beads.
27. The term "red bead" is unfortunately ambiguous in this context. It could have referred to Cambay carnelians, Venetian or Indo-Pacific opaque red glass, or Chinese copper ruby glass.
28. Government of Straits Settlements (1910, 1916); Government of British Malaya (1923); Government of Malaya (1930, 1935) (Francis 1989a, 22–23).
29. In particular the *Dongxiyang Kao* by Zhang Xie (1574–1640). This is one of three surviving works of fifteen by this resident of Fujian. It deals with the maritime trade of that province and is very detailed, though not without its faults. Its publication may be as important as that of Zhao Rugua. Blusse and Zhuang (1991) are preparing the translation.
30. The Spanish eight real (pieces of eight) and the "milled" dollar, mostly made in Mexico or Peru, were the standard unit of currency in much of Asia because of the influx of silver via the galleon trade. These coins, approximately the size of an American silver dollar or a British crown, were often divided into two, four, or eight segments and traded thus as smaller currency, a practice leading to the American expression "two bits" for a quarter dollar.
31. The voluminous Irish University Press Area Studies Series: British Parliamentary Papers: China has a wealth of information on this subject. Unfortunately, my time to work with it was brief. Volumes 6 through 21 contain commercial reports and Volumes 36 to 39 trade reports.
32. There are German-made stone beads in some parts of Southeast Asia, but they are late in date.
33. There are many published and unpublished documents in the British Library Oriental and India Office Collections. The information extracted herein results from consulting the following: (1) The 1879 summary made of the first collection by Birdwood (1891). (2) The six-volume *Letters Received by the East India Company from Its Servants in the East*. Volume 1 was edited by Danvers (1896) and the others by Foster until 1902. They contain verbatim correspondence from 1602 to 1617. (3) The first eleven (of thirteen) volumes of *The English Factories in India,* edited by Foster, the historiographer of the Indian Office. They contain abstracts of letters and the Surat factory's "Letterbook" from the years 1610 to 1654. They were published between 1906 and 1915 (Khan 1926, 273). (4) *A Calendar of the Court Minutes etc. of the East India Company,* edited by E. B. Sainsbury for the years 1634 to 1673 published between 1907 and 1932. The series ran to eleven volumes published through 1938. (5) *The English Factories in India (new series)* edited by Charles Fawcett covering the years from 1670 to 1684 and divided geographically into the Western Presidency and the Eastern Coast and Bengal, published between 1936 and 1955.
34. What was once the harbor of Cambay is now an immense mud flat extending for miles.
35. Far more likely to refer to carnelian than the green and red jasper now called bloodstone.
36. A "corge" is an old trade term meaning a score (Yule and Burnell 1989, 255). Thus, 480 beads were involved, ten beads per string.
37. Several "maunds" were then current. It was likely the Bombay maund, equaling 28 pounds (12.7 kg) (see Yule and Burnell 1989, 563–564). A rupee was worth between 2 shillings and 2/9 (see note 12 in chap. 15). The price would work out to £ 0/1/3 (£ 0.28) per kilogram for the first quality and 13 pence per kilogram for second-quality beads.
38. Compare this with seven rupees a maund nine years before.
39. This was perhaps some product of Socotra.
40. Patani, Thailand?
41. This is nearly verbatim, but reformed somewhat to make it more easily understood. The emphases and insertions are mine.
42. Vermilion (scarlet) and coral were also two of the items requested by the Zamorin of Calicut when Vasco da Gama landed there 150 years previously (chap. 15).
43. This discussion focuses on the northern glass bead industry. The southern (Indo-Pacific) industry, by this time at Papanaidupet, continued to export to Africa (for exactly how long has not been determined).
44. The glass factories of Firozabad (Uttar Pradesh) were set up by the British to consolidate the Indian glass industry. Only a few beads are made there, molded into segments from hollow tubes or tubes blown on the spot and subsequently silvered inside (Francis 1982b, 7–10). Japanese introduced this method, probably in the early 1970s. Banaras Beads, Ltd. farms out some work to villages surrounding the city (R. K. Gupta, 1999, personal communication). Demand at Purdalpur has caused work to be extended into

neighboring Sikandra Rao and even Agra (Torben Sode, 1998, personal communication). None of these is a traditional beadmaking place.

Glassmaking for beads and bangles at Jalasar reported by Koch and Sode (n.d., 7–9) never existed. The furnaces were built in an attempt to get the government to allot more fuel to the village (Torben Sode, 1999, personal communication).

Small mirrors to be sewn on dresses were still being made in Kapadvanj, Gujarat, in the early 1980s. After Partition in 1947, about half the beadmakers from North India went to Pakistan and were settled in Hyderabad, Sind, where the government built a large glass factory.

45. It is not clear why glass bead and bangle makers from North India settled at Purdalpur, but this village remains the only site of traditional glass beadmaking in North India.
46. This city is currently known as Varanasi. Banaras is a variation on the spelling and was adopted by what is probably the largest beadmaking concern in the world, Banaras Beads, Ltd.
47. Marco Polo had a chapter on Madagascar, but he did not go there, nor was he writing about this island. His information came from Arab informants. He mixed up the facts on Mogadisho, misheard and misspelled the name, and ascribed it to an island (Paxton 1977, 1148). Many kingdoms were called "islands" in Arab geography.
48. It must have been quite careless, because he also wrote, "The people are circumcised, as some affirmed to have seene" (Keeling 1905, 511).
49. Ar. is Arabic. Kis. is Kiswahili, the proper name for Swahili (Crystal 1987, 339).
50. These beads, first produced about 1830 when gold ruby glass was introduced into Venetian beads, have a clear red coat over an opaque core, usually white. "Cornalaine d'Aleppo" is a trade term that dates back at least to 1879 (Haldeman 1879, 269). Such beads were not made at Aleppo, Syria. The name comes from "Aleppo stone," a sardonyx cut so that it lies flat against the skin and shows a white center surrounded by red. It was supposed to prevent the "Aleppo boil" or "Oriental sore," a skin ulceration caused by the protozoan *Leishmania tropica.*
51. It did not enter American English. There are no listings for any form of this word in *Webster's Third New International Dictionary.*
52. Ironically, this is my translation from the French. Although Boothby was English, this was compiled in *Collection des Ouvrages anciens concernant Madagascar* and quoted by Thierry.
53. *Contaria* is Italian for fancy glassware; *conterie* refers to beads. It has been used for fancy lamp-wound beads (Gasparetto 1958, 188), but is usually reserved for small, drawn seed beads. Because these were small, and lamp beads were not made then, that is certainly what they are.
54. In which case they would most likely have been pierced and worn as pendants.

17: Heirloom Beads in Southeast Asia and Micronesia

1. Heirloom beads are not limited to Southeast Asia. They are found in Mexico (Francis 1992f; 1994b), Africa (Francis 1992f), and probably elsewhere. In Mexico, the Mixe were driven to the mountains from the valleys before their Chinese beads were imported. The beads of the Venda of South Africa seem to date from the time they were forced south of the Limpopo River. In West Africa, many heirloom beads are markers of the dominant ruling family. There is no evidence that the custom developed there because of a "cultural crisis."
2. Unfortunately, Rouffaer failed to identify their origins, nor did he understand the difference between *mutiraja, mutitanah,* and *mutibata.* The differences sparked the debate between van der Sleen and Lamb (see chap. 3) and are discussed later in this chapter. However, in a work I have not been able to locate published in 1915, Rouffaer at least recognized that the Chinese had complete control over the trade in *mutisalah* (Meilink-Roelofsz 1962, 392 n. 72).

   Rouffaer must be given credit for assembling as much literature as he could find for this paper. He is especially valuable for Dutch references. He also cited world literature on all types of beads, often at length in the original language. It is sad that the volume in which this remarkable paper was published cannot be located in at least three major American research libraries. It seems they were all stolen, but whether for Rouffaer's paper or not is unknown.
3. Individual beads are sometimes found that had been broken in some fashion and repaired, redrilled, or otherwise restored to their function. These are sometimes referred to as heirloom beads. These are perhaps better called "restored" beads, because it is rarely or perhaps never possible to determine archaeologically if they had been handed down to another generation.
4. Harold Conklin (1995, personal communication) informed

me that the terms *"pang-o"* and *"lingling-o"* (see chap. 13) connote the idea of an arrangement of elements of an odd number of beads or pendants, with the largest in the middle and those of declining size toward the back.

5. This is an urban collector's name for large, white barrel beads with blue end zones and a "squiggle" design around the equator, made by combing through a series of small circles. The "squiggle" device appears on small ellipsoidal beads from reportedly as early as 1725 (R. P. Burke 1936, 63) or a few decades later (Brain 1979, 113, variety WIIIB1). On some "Ming" beads gold ruby glass was substituted for the blue. The Venetians did not use this glass for beads much, if at all, before 1830.
6. The Czech glass bead industry was an outgrowth of its garnet industry. The grinding of pyrope garnets is still carried out in the village of Turnov. Glass, particularly a gold ruby introduced at least by 1680, was first worked into artificial garnets. As the Czech glass bead industry grew, grinding remained an important subsidiary branch. Beads were ground to remove their seams, to be faceted, or to be given special decorations (Francis 1994d, 65–67). In the source cited, the beginning of this industry was put around 1715. More recent evidence pushes the date back (see chap. 8, note 6).
7. It is a tentative assumption that the Kalinga did this themselves, because these altered beads are not found among their neighbors. In West Africa today (as was true five hundred years earlier) bead dealers do such altering as a service to their customers. Used grinding stones outside the house advertise the residence of a bead dealer (Francis 1993a, 4).
8. Could this have been done "in memory of" the blue barrel beads made by Chinese in Banten, Java? See chapter 8.
9. Individual beads manipulated to recycle them are not members of this class. Altering may be done by breaking larger beads into smaller ones, by grinding them to change their shape or remove decorations, or by several operations involving heat.
10. Several writers have mentioned that these differ from village to village, but without being explicit. I compared a dozen names I collected in Luplupa with those Abellera (1981, 167–168) gathered at nearby but remote Lubo. Only two types, an ocher-colored drawn tube and the "Ming" bead, had remotely similar names.
11. There are also long bicones of white marble, but I am not sure if they are classified as *fukas*.
12. The T'Boli have been transforming rulers, pens, and toothbrushes into beads since at least the late 1950s. Henry Beyer (1991, personal communication) recalled seeing the first group of Peace Corps volunteers assigned to the south wearing them in Manila while on break. The T'Boli were making imitation *lieg* at least by the early 1980s. They were so loath to sell the originals that they offered locally made imitations. Since the late 1980s, they have been making different styles of beads. The Kalinga also transform plastic items from the market into beads. The earliest example known was accessioned by the National Museum in 1969. In the early 1990s, they were making miniature Kalinga multistrand necklaces, worn only by children and the very poor.
13. This can be seen on http://www.thebeadsite.com/SEAC2-03.html.
14. There are *let silo* that are not old. *Let hitam* are considered as old as the *let silo mau'hun*, but are not as valued because they are black; *hitam* is "black" in Malay. See Harrisson (1950, 210).
15. This interview took place thanks to Heidi Munan, Lucas Chin, and Edmund Kurui of the Sarawak Museum. Raseh is the storyteller in Geddes' (1985) classic work *Nine Dayak Nights*. More details of the interview are in Francis (1992a, 10–11).
16. The term is derived from the Tamil *mutu*, meaning "pearl" and "bead." The cognate in Hindi is *moti*. On Flores, the Austronesian *inu* (compare Kayan *ino* and Cebuano *hinau*) was sometimes substituted for *muti*. *Salah* means "false."
17. See note 2 in this chapter.
18. Zhao Rugua (Hirth and Rockhill 1911, 70) said that in "Sin-t'o" (Sunda, West Java) the houses were, "roofed over with the bark of the coir-palm." His editors (Hirth and Rockhill 1911, 71 n. 2) noted that nipa palm leaves were "universally used by the Malays for thatching."
19. These are different from later Chinese crumb beads. They most commonly have a yellow or white base, with the crumbs prepared or melted in carefully to form nearly perfect circles. A string of these beads priced at 3,450 bhat (then US $138) was the most expensive item in the 1991 price list of a Chiang Mai shop, Thai Tribal Crafts. Even at that price, none was then available.
20. With technical help from Boshan, the Chinese set up a glass beadmaking factory in Gejiu, Yunnan, specifically to serve the demands of southern non-Han people (E. T. Lewis 1994).

21. From about 1900, the villagers of Payagyi, adjacent to the ruins of Wadi, began finding old beads on the site. They sold them to the Chin, anxious for new stock. As they ran out, the villagers bored unperforated, decorated blanks they found in Pyu burials. After these were gone, some villagers learned to imitate them, though they used a different sort of petrified wood. This ended around 1970, but international demand for these beads has prompted a revival. *Pumtek* beads are popular in contemporary bead markets, but the great majority are twentieth-century copies. For details see Francis (1992e; 1993g) and Moore and Myint (1993).
22. I am following her naming system, which does not always agree with that of Kubary (1889). Some names or attitudes toward some beads may have changed in a century.
23. The lively, new Indonesian glass industry has been reproducing heirloom beads for sale to Borneo. They apparently also produce a good imitation of the white spotted beads and the mosaic beads (Kathleen Kuzmitz, 1997, personal communication).
24. The Lesser Sundas are the small islands in a chain stretching eastward from Java, distinguished from the Greater Sundas (Java, Sumatra, Borneo, and Sulawesi). Not all people of the Lesser Sundas (for example, those of Bali and Lombok) have heirloom beads.
25. How long they were made there and whether they were also made in China are unknown.
26. Chinese coil beads of this color are very scarce. There are a few on a piece of beadwork from Lampung, Sumatra (Hector 1995, 25). Thirty (seventeen orange and thirteen red) were at Bolinao, Pangasian, Luzon, a thirteenth- to fifteenth-century site, but they are not recorded anywhere else in the Philippines. Perhaps only one artisan or family made them for a few decades.

18: Conclusions

1. The Mediterranean coral trade and European glass trade beads are the other two. The amber trade and the (newly appreciated) South Indian gem trade are candidates for inclusion. A "global bead trading network" has multiple sources and processing centers and complex distribution systems. Small-scale networks characterized prehistoric bead trading and still exist in isolated pockets today. Intermediate-sized networks were typical of early civilizations (e.g., nephrite in China, jadeite in Mesoamerica, and the early lapis lazuli trade).
2. Carbuncles were probably garnets. Topaz was either Egyptian peridot, South Indian citrine, or yellow corundum from Kashmir or Sri Lanka. What the emeralds were is impossible to say.
3. The western Indian stone bead industry is often described in terms of guilds rather than castes, because the industry has been in Muslim hands for a long time. Most guilds were essentially caste (or religious) based, and to move into a higher guild, especially the highest, required great expense.
4. Except, perhaps, ruby. Sri Lanka was also sometimes tied into this system.
5. At Mantai, the folding-and-segmenting technique (not yet documented from anywhere else) was concentrated in the "Early Medieval levels," perhaps the eighth or ninth century. Takua Pa was occupied only during the ninth century. The periods of exotic beadmaking at Sungai Mas and Vijaya have not been determined.
6. I have not located the original quotation and do not know who made the interpolation "(i.e. rarities)." The ellipsis results from the insertion of "as General Pitt-Rivers said," by Atkinson.

Appendix A: The Type Collection of Beads in the National Museum of the Philippines

1. This was not a unique experience. William Henry Scott (Conklin 1994) and Harold C. Conklin (1996, in a privately circulated resume) were also introduced to the Philippines during World War II via the U.S. Navy and subsequently devoted their lives to Philippine studies.
2. As of 1991, this collection was in the possession of Fernande Fox in Bagio. It consists of eighty-one beads mounted on eight cards and identified by provenience. Portions of it may be missing. The data on this collection are on file at the Center for Bead Research.
3. Not only is this method not recorded from any place, but it is also physically impossible. A tube of glass could not be slipped off a rod that had been dipped into a crucible of glass. A diagram of this method unfortunately appeared in Francis (1996d) because of an editorial error.
4. Each different color or shape of a bead was designated a specific type. Many numbers were assigned to beads that would now be considered a single class. For example, every different color of Indo-Pacific and coil beads received its own number.
5. These do not always add up to 100 percent. A few type

beads are missing from the collection, and rounding off percentages sometimes skews this number.

6. I have studied Neolithic assemblages from several other contexts. One was the proto-Neolithic "twin sites" of Shanidar Cave and Zawi Chemi Shanidar, Iraq, thanks to Ralph and Rose Solecki, then at Columbia University. Another was Jarmo, Iraq, thanks to Robert and Linda Braidwood of the Oriental Institute, Chicago. In the United States, I have examined the material from the Lindenmeier site in Colorado, thanks to Joyce Herold of the Denver Museum of Natural History and Dennis Stanford and Pegi Jodrey of the Smithsonian Institution.
7. Even the broken specimen does not resemble a Chinese jade cicada, an amulet put into the mouths of the dead. The bead is square in cross section; cicadas are flattened. In addition, cicadas were not perforated through their length as this bead is. A picture of a bud bead seen by Santiago is in Fox (1977, 758, bottom row, middle bead).
8. *Nelli* is the Tamil and Malayalam name for *Emblica officinalis,* a sacred tree in North India. The eatable fruit is called *amalaka* in Sanskrit; *amla* is a common cognate in North Indian tongues. Indian scholars use *amalaka* to describe what are called "melon" beads in English. The form is round and divided into lobes distinguished by grooves between them. The *nelli* beads of the Kandy District of Sri Lanka differ from others because the lobes are flattened rather than rounded; they are distinctive to the region.
9. These include at least the first and third beads in the fourth row and the third and fourth beads in the fifth row. The second bead in the fifth row looks as though it might be a pierced-and-folded bead. It could have come from the Middle East or Vijaya.

Appendix B: Analyses of Indo-Pacific Beads

1. The one exception is Karaikadu. The samples were obtained as surface finds.
2. The word "alkali" is derived from the Arabic *al-qili,* "the ash," referring to the ashes of the glasswort or saltwort *(Salsola kali),* used around the Mediterranean for glassmaking and other purposes. The botanical specific name has the same etymology.
3. This rises to around 5.0 percent in the case of lead, because of its higher specific gravity.
4. For the earlier centuries, the glasses of Arikamēḍu, Oc Eo, and several importing sites were compared with Roman and late Egyptian glasses. For the medieval period, glasses from Southeast Asian sites, including Kuala Selinsing and Takua Pa, were compared with glasses from the Islamic world, West Europe, Russia, central Asia, the Caucasus, Byzantium, and the Balkans.
5. Some of these ambiguous analyses were included in Francis (1988–1989), as well as some on beads from imported sites. I have been more rigorous here.
6. A case in point are the analyses done by Salisbury and Glover (1997). I could not tell from the descriptions which beads were Indo-Pacific or their wasters. After I asked him, Ian Glover kindly sent the samples from Khlong Thom (Khuan Lukpad) that he still had in his possession. Of the fifteen samples analyzed, only four could be used here. From the original descriptions it was evident that some were not of the Indo-Pacific type. Among those sent to me, one was a wound bead and another was a large drawn bead (a fragment, possibly a segmented bead), not of the Indo-Pacific type. Two masses of glass, one a bead clump, were analyzed, but the different colors of glass in them made the analyses useless for our purposes here, because color is often an important factor among Indo-Pacific beads.
7. Ron Hancock (1997, personal communication), who reviewed this appendix, noted that an order of magnitude was a "generous" allotment. In his work on European glass trade beads 30 percent or 40 percent differences in elemental concentrations may signify different glass batches. With older glass, however, we can expect more variation.
8. Perhaps the only exceptions are some tesserae or mosaic cubes of Roman date analyzed by Hughes (Biek and Bayley 1979, 12) and seven specimens listed by Sayre and Smith (1967, 304), two of which are Indian.
9. As this book was in press, S. Gupta (2000) published some new analyses of beads and wasters from Arikamēḍu. Two of the four dark blue specimens had potassium as their dominant alkali, but the other two had sodium as the chief alkali. In addition, Dussubieux and Gratuze (2000) found that two of thirteen blue beads from Arikamēḍu that they analyzed had soda as their chief alkali, but the other eleven had potash. Clearly, there was a slight variation in alkalies used in the blue glass, although potash was the overwhelming choice.
10. Moreover, the total amount of alkalies in this specimen is low (8.2 vs. 15.0–20.0 percent commonly found). This suggests some weathering of the piece, which will decrease and alter the alkali contents. Dussubieux and Gratuze (2000)

reported two different groups of opaque green glass beads from Arikamēḍu. One type (five samples) is colored and opacified with copper, lead, and lead stannate. Its major alkali is soda and it has a lime content of about 4.5 percent. The other type (four samples) has the same coloring and opacifying agents, but has potash as its principal alkali and a low amount of lime.

11. Two other exceptions are in the analyses reported by Lal (1987, 52). These are not in Table B-1, because it is not certain that these were Indo-Pacific beads. The high potassium concentration suggests that they might not be. After Brill read his paper at the Archaeometry of Glass conference in 1986, Lal questioned Brill about his (Brill's) analysis of red glass from Arikamēḍu being soda glass, because Lal's analysis had potash-rich red gloss. Brill replied, "All that can be said is that both potash and soda were used in Arikamēḍu glasses" (Brill 1987, 25). Yamasaki's (1987) analysis of a red bead from Arikamēḍu lacked details; soda and potash were found, but their ratios were not reported. Recent analyses by Dussubieux and Gratuze (2000) of ten additional red Indo-Pacific beads from Arikamēḍu show them all to have soda as their principal alkali.
12. The aluminum content of many glasses from mainland Southeast Asia tends to be higher than in most other glasses. This was true of some (but not all) of the beads from the Sa Huynh site of Giong Ca Vo near Ho Chi Minh City, Vietnam, and the beads from Ban Chiang, Thailand (see chap. 13). It is also true for several other sites in this region discussed in this chapter.
13. All of the samples with low total alkali and potash dominating were published by Harrisson (1964, 38) and were analyzed at the same facility. The analyses done for Lamb and for Colani and those done by SLOWPOKE-Toronto show a higher level of alkalies and soda dominating. Fourteen specimens from Kuala Selinsing analyzed by Dussubieux and Gratuze (2000) show equally high levels of alkalies, and in all cases the soda dominates.
14. I had specifically requested dark blue and red samples from the excavators of all the sites from which I gathered material because these were the dominant colors at Arikamēḍu and most everywhere else. I wanted to make as close comparisons as possible.
15. Soda-magnesia glass shifts the spectrum of the copper colorant from blue to green (Weyl 1959, 159, 167). Weyl did not mention yellow, but the shift is in that direction. Dussubieux and Gratuze (2000) reported levels of magnesium at less than 0.6 percent concentration from twelve of the fourteen beads they analyzed from Kuala Selinsing.
16. Lambert et al. (1996) analyzed fifty-nine pieces of glass from Takua Pa, as well as eighty-seven pieces from Laem Pho Chaiya, its trading partner across the Isthmus of Kra. Unfortunately, they were not concerned with glass connected to Indo-Pacific beads. They reported finding no evidence for glassmaking (Lambert et al. 1996, 11), though as seen in Table 4-1, there is evidence at least for glassworking. Their analyses were done entirely on fragments from glass vessels.
17. This was done by subtracting 0.16 percent of the value for aluminum from that of magnesium.
18. This translates into a 2.43:4.00 magnesium:calcium ratio on a mass concentration basis (Ron Hancock, 1997, personal communication).
19. Arsenic bronze is another possibility, but the amounts of arsenic are very low for all these beads.
20. There are also relatively high amounts of tin in the dark blue beads from Khlong Thom and Takua Pa, which may have been colored with wad.

References

The following abbreviations are used in the references:

AJA, American Journal of Archaeology

BDC(P)RI, Bulletin of the Deccan College (Postgraduate &) Research Institute

BEFEO, Bulletin de l'École Français d'extrême-orient

BIPPA, Bulletin of the Indo-Pacific Prehistoric Association

BSTN, Bead Study Trust Newsletter

CCBR, Contributions of the Center for Bead Research

Factories, The English Factories in India [dates]: *A Calendar of Documents in the India Office, Westminster.*

IFAN, Institute Français d'Afrique Noire

JAOS, Journal of the American Oriental Society

JBBRAS, Journal of the Bombay Branch of the Royal Asiatic Society

JESHO, Journal of the Economic and Social History of the Orient

JFMSM, Journal of the Federated Malay States Museums

JMBRAS, Journal of the Malaysian Branch of the Royal Asiatic Society

JSGT, Journal of the Society of Glass Technology

Letters, Letters Received by the East India Company from Its Servants in the East: Transcribed from the 'Original Correspondence' Series of the India Office Records

Minutes, A Calendar of the Court Minutes etc. of the East India Company

OPCBR, Occasional Papers of the Center for Bead Research

Purchas, Samuel Purchas 1905–1907 *Hakluytus Posthumus or Purchas His Pilgrimes.* James MacLehose and Sons, Glasgow. 20 vols.

RGH, Readings in Glass History

SPAFA, SEAMEO [Southeast Asia Ministers of Education Organization] Project on Archaeology and Fine Arts

WBMS, World of Beads Monograph Series

Abellera, Benjamin Cabrera
1981 The Heirloom Beads of Lubo, Kalinga-Apayao. M.A. thesis, Asian Center, University of the Philippines, Diliman.

Abu-Lughod, Janet L.
1989 *Before European Hegemony: The World System A.D. 1250–1350.* New York: Oxford University Press.

Acharya, G. V.
1922 Gala Inscription of Siddharaja Jayasimha (Vikrama) Samvat 1193. *JBBRAS* 25:322–324.

Adhyatman, Sumarah, and Redjeki Arifin
1993 *Manik-Manik di Indonesia/Beads in Indonesia.* Penerbit Djambatan, Jakarta. (Bilingual.)

Alcouffe, Daniel
1984 Rock-Crystal Candlesticks. In *The Treasury of San Marco, Venice,* ed. David Buckton, Christopher Entwistle, and Rowena Prior, 274–276. Milan: Olivetti.

Aléxéeva, E. M.
1971 Les Mosaïques Miniatures dans les Parures de Verre Datant du Ier Siècle Avant Nôtre Ère-du IIe Siècle de Nôtre Ère. *Soviet Archaeology* 4:185 (French resumé) + 2 plates.

Ali, S. M.
1966 *The Geography of the Puraāṇs.* New Delhi: People's Publishing House.

Allan, J.
1942 *Encyclopaedia Britannica,* 14th ed., s.v. numismatics.

Allchin, B.
1975 The Agate and Carnelian Industry of Western India and Pakistan. In *South Asian Archaeology, 1975,* ed. J. E. van Lohuizen–de Leeuw, 91–105 + 2 plates. Leiden: E. J. Brill.

Allen, Jamey D.
1994 Obscure Varieties of Glass Cane Beads. Paper read at Bead Expo '94: Glass Beadmaking and Trade, Santa Fe, N.Mex. (Copy available at the Center for Bead Research, Lake Placid, N.Y.)

Allen, Jane
1991 Trade and Site Distribution in Early Historic-Period Kedah: Geoarchaeological, Historic, and Locational Evidence. *BIPPA* 10:307–319.

Altekar, Anat Sadasiv
1925 A History of Important Ancient Towns and Cities in Gujarat and Kathaiwad. *The Indian Antiquity* 54: supplemental pages 9–54.

Ambary, Hasan Muarif
1991 The Role of Several Major Harbours in Sumatra on the Maritime Silk Road between the Seventh and Sixteenth Centuries. Paper read at International Seminar: Harbour Cities along the Silk Roads, Surabaya. (Copy available at Center for Bead Research, Lake Placid, N.Y.)

Ambary, Hasan M., Hasan Djafer, Moh. Romli, and Rokus Due Awe
1977 *Lamporan Ekskavasi Tridonorejo Demak, (Lamporan) No. 7.* Jakarta: Pusat Purbakala Dan Peninggalan Nasional.

Ambrose (Saint), Bishop of Milan
1905 The Travels of Musaeus, Thebaeus and Others Mentioned by Saint Ambrose; of Others also Mentioned in the Ecclesiasticall Histories of Eusebius, Ruffinus, Socrates and Sozomen. In *Purchas.* Vol. 1, 239–243.

An Jiayao
1996 Ancient Glass Trade in Southeast Asia. In *Ancient Trades and Cultural Contacts in Southeast Asia,* ed. Amara Srisuchat, 127–138. Bangkok: Office of the National Cultural Commission.

Annual Report on Indian Epigraphy
1986 *Annual Report on South-Indian Epigraphy for the Year Ending 31st March 1927.* Director-General of the Archaeological Survey of India, New Delhi. (Reprinted in *Annual Report on Indian Epigraphy [1926–1929]).*

Anonymous
1879 *The Rulers of Baroda.* Bombay: Education Society's Press.

Anquandah, James
1982 *Rediscovering Ghana's Past.* London/Accra: Longmans/Sedco.

Ansari, Z. D., and M. S. Mate
1966 *Excavations at Dwarka.* Poona: Deccan College.

Appadorai, A.
1936 Economic Conditions in Southern India (1000–

1500 A.D.). 2 vols. Madras University Historical Series No. 12. Madras: Madras University.

Ardika, I. Wayan

1995 Beads from Sembiran, Bali. *BSTN* 26:6–8.

Ardika, I. W., P. S. Bellwood, R. A. Eggleton, and D. J. Ellis

1993 A Single Source for South Asian Export-Quality Rouletted Ware? *Man and Environment* 18 (1): 101–109.

Arkell, A. J.

1936 Cambay and the Bead Trade. *Antiquity* 10:292–305 + 4 plates.

ASEAN (Association of South East Asian Nations)

1985 *Archaeological Excavation and Conservation, Bujang Valley, Kedah Malaysia.* Kuala Lumpur: ASEAN.

Atkinson, R. J. C.

1953 *Field Archaeology.* 2d ed. London: Methuen & Co.

Ayers, John

1965 Chinese Glass. *Transactions of the Oriental Ceramic Society 1963–64* 35:17–27.

Bai Shouyi, ed.

1982 *An Outline History of China.* Beijing: Foreign Language Press.

Baines, Athelstane

1912 *Ethnology (Castes and Tribes).* Gundriss band 2, haft 5. Strassburg: Karl J. Trubner.

Ball, Sydney H.

1950 *A Roman Book on Precious Stones: Including an English Modernization of the 37th Booke of the Historie of the World by G. Plinus Secundus.* Los Angeles: Gemological Institute of America.

Ball, V.

1889 *Travels in India by Jean-Baptiste Tavernier, Baron of Aubonne.* Vol. 2. London: Macmillan.

Bandaranayake, Senake, Lorna Dewaraja, Roland Silva, and K. D. G. Wimalaratne, eds.

1990 *Sri Lanka and the Silk Road of the Sea.* Colombo: The Sri Lanka National Commission for UNESCO and the Central Cultural Fund.

Bannerjee, N. R.

1959 The Technique and Manufacture of Stone Beads in Ancient Ujjain. *Journal of the Asiatic Society* 1 (2): 189–195.

Basa, Kishor K.

1992a Early Historic Glass Beads in Thailand and Peninsular Malaysia. In *South Asian Archaeology 1990,* ed. Ian Glover, 83–102. Hull, U.K: Center for Southeast Asian Studies, University of Hull.

1992b Early Glass Beads in India. *South Asian Studies* 8:91–104.

Basa, Kishor K., Ian Glover, and Julian Henderson

1991 The Relationship between Early Southeast Asian and Indian Glass. *BIPPA* 10:366–385.

Batchelor, John

1892 *The Ainu of Japan.* London: Religious Tract Society.

Bauer, Max

1968 *Precious Stones.* 2 vols. New York: Dover Publications. (Reprint; orig. published 1903 in German.)

Beck, Curt W., and Jan Bouzek, eds.

1993 *Amber in Archaeology: Proceedings of the Second International Conference on Amber in Archaeology, Liblice 1990.* Prague: Institute of Archaeology.

Beck, Horace C.

1928 Classification and Nomenclature of Beads and Pendants. *Archaeologia* 77:1–76. (Reprinted 1973 as a monograph, Liberty Cap Books, York, Pa.).

1930a Notes on Sundry Asiatic Beads. *Man* 30:166–182 + 2 plates.

1930b A Note on Certain Agate Beads. *The Antiquaries Journal* 10:149–151 + 1 plate.

1931 Rhodesian Beads. Appendix I in *The Zimbabwe Culture: Ruins and Reactions,* ed. G. Caton-Thompson, 229–242 + 4 plates. Oxford: Clarendon Press.

1933 Etched Carnelian Beads. *The Antiquaries Journal* 13:384–398 + 4 plates.

1934 The Use of the Microscope in the Study of Ancient Beads. *Journal of the Royal Microscopical Society* 54:189–194.

1937a Beads from Slab Graves in Malaya. Appendix A in H. D. Collings, Recent Finds of Iron-Age Sites in Southern Perak and Selangor, Federated Malaya

States, 91–93 + 1 plate. *Bulletin of the Raffles Museum,* ser. B, 1 (2): 75–93.

1937b The Beads of the Mapungubwe District. In *Mapungubwe,* ed. Leo Fouche, 104–113. Cambridge: Cambridge University Press.

1940 Report on Selected Beads from Harappā. In M. S. Vats, *Excavations at Harappā.* Vol. 1, 392–431. Delhi: Government of India Press. (Reprinted 1974, Bhartiya Publishing House, Varanasi.)

1941 *The Beads from Taxila.* Memoirs of the Archeological Survey of India No. 65. Delhi: Manager of Publications.

Beck, Horace C., and C. G. Seligman

1934 Barium in Ancient Glass. *Nature* 133:982.

Begley, Vimala

1983 Arikamedu Reconsidered. *AJA* 87:461–482.

1985 Rouletting and Chattering: Decoration on Ancient and Present-Day Pottery in India. *Expedition* 28 (1): 147–154.

1988 Rouletted Ware at Arikamedu: A New Approach. *AJA* 92:427–440.

1991a Ceramic Evidence for pre-*Periplus* Trade on the Indian Coasts. In *Rome and India: The Ancient Sea Trade,* ed. Vimala Begley and Richard Daniel De Puma, 157–196. Madison: University of Wisconsin Press.

1991b Introduction. In *Rome and India: The Ancient Sea Trade,* ed. Vimala Begley and Richard Daniel De Puma, 2–7. Madison: University of Wisconsin Press.

1993 New Investigations at the Port of Arikamedu. *Journal of Roman Archaeology* 6:93–108.

1994 Are There Imported Fine Wares at Alagankulam, South India? In *From Sumer to Meluhha: Contributions to the Archaeology of South and West Asia in Memory of George F. Dales, Jr.,* ed. Jonathan Mark Kenoyer, 315–321. Wisconsin Archaeological Reports. Vol. 3. Madison: University of Wisconsin.

1996 *The Ancient Port of Arikamedu: New Excavations and Researches 1989–1992. Vol. 1.* Mémoires Archéologiques 22. Paris/Pondichéry: L'École Française d'Extrême-Orient/Centre d'Historie et d'Archéologie.

Begley, Vimala, and Richard Daniel De Puma, eds.

1991 *Rome and India: The Ancient Sea Trade.* Madison: University of Wisconsin Press.

Begley, Vimala, John R. Lucas, and Kenneth A. R. Kennedy

1981 Excavations of Iron Age Burials at Pomparippu, 1970. *Ancient Ceylon* 4:48–132 + 5 plates.

Beijing Review

1980 Ancient Buddhist Column Found in Suzhou. *Beijing Review* 1980.9:29.

Belgrave, C. Dalrymple

1934 Pearl Diving in Bahrain. *Journal of the Royal Central Asiatic Society* 21 (3): 450–452.

Bell, H. T. Montague, and H. G. W. Woodhead

1912 *The China Year Book 1912.* London: George Routledge & Sons.

1916 *The China Year Book 1916.* London: George Routledge & Sons.

1919–1920 *The China Year Book 1919–1920.* London: George Routledge & Sons.

Bell, John

1788 *Travels from St. Petersburg in Russia to Various Parts of Asia.* 2 vols. Edinburgh: William Creech. (Orig. published 1763, as *Travels from St. Petersburg in Russia to Divers Parts of Asia,* Glasgow.)

Bellasis, A. F.

1856a An Account of the Ancient and Ruined City of Brahminabad in Sind. *JBBRAS* 5 (20): 413–425.

1856b Further Observations on the Ruined City of Brahminabad in Sind. *JBBRAS* 5 (20): 467–477.

Bellwood, Peter

1985 *Prehistory of the Indo-Malaysian Archipelago.* Sydney: Academic Press.

Bencard, Mogens

1983 Das Handwerk der Wikingerzeit in Ribe (Ripen) Eine Übersicht. In *Das Handwerk in vor- und frühgeschichtlicher Zeit. Teil 2. Archäologische und philologische Beiträge,* ed. Herbert Jankuhn, Walter Janssen, Ruth Schmidt-Wiegand and Heinrich Tiefenbach, 161–173. Göttingen: Vandenhoek & Ruprecht.

Bencard, Mogens, Kristina Ambrosiani, Lise Bender Jørgensen, Helge Brinch Madsen, Ingrid Nielsen, and Ulf Näsman

1979 Wikingerzeitliches Handwerk in Ribe eine Übersicht. *Acta Archaeologica* 49:113–138.

Best, Jonathan W.

1982 Diplomatic and Cultural Contacts between Paekche and China. *Harvard Journal of Asiatic Studies* 42 (4): 442–501.

Beyer, H. Otley

1947 Outline Review of Philippines Archaeology by Islands and Provinces. *The Philippine Journal of Science* 77 (3–4): 205–390.

Bhatnagar, S. S., chairman of the editorial committee

1957 *The Wealth of India: Industrial Products.* Vol. 4. Delhi: The Wealth of India.

Bibby, Geoffrey

1969 *Looking for Dilmun.* New York: Alfred A. Knopf.

Biek, Leo, and Justine Bayley

1979 Glass and Other Vitreous Materials. *World Archaeology* 11 (1): 1–25.

Biot, Feu Édouard

1851 *Le Tcheou-Li or Rites des Tcheou.* Tome 1. Paris: L'Imprimerie Nationale.

Birch, Cyril

1965 *Anthology of Chinese Literature from Early Times to the Fourteenth Century.* New York: Grove Press.

Birdwood, George

1891 *Report on the Old Records of the India Office.* London: W. H. Allen & Co.

Bishop, Carl W.

1921 The Elephant and Its Ivory in Ancient China. *JAOS* 41:290–306.

Blair, Dorothy

1951a East Asiatic Glass, Part I—China. *The Glass Industry* 32 (7): 347–350, 368–369.

1951b East Asiatic Glass, Part II—Korea. *The Glass Industry* 32 (8): 402–404, 428.

1973 *A History of Glass in Japan.* Tokyo/Corning, N.Y: Kodansha International/Corning Museum of Glass.

Blair, Emma Helen, and James Alexander Robertson

1973 *The Philippine Islands 1493–1898.* Vol. 2. Mandaluyong, Rizal, Manila: Cachos Hermanos. (Reprint; orig. published 1903–1909; 55 vols.)

Blochmann, M. A.

1927 *The Ain-i-Akbari by Abu' l-Fazl 'Allami.* 3rd ed. Delhi: Oriental Books Reprint Corporation. (1st ed. 1873; reprinted 1977.)

Blusse, Leonard, and Zhuang Guotu

1991 Fuchienese Commercial Expansion into the Nanyang as Mirrored in the *Tung Hsi Yang K'ao.* Paper read at International Seminar: Harbour Cities along the Silk Roads, Surabaya. (Copy available at Center for Bead Research, Lake Placid, N.Y.)

Bock, Carl

1882 *The Head-Hunters of Borneo: A Narrative of Travel up the Mahakkam and down the Barito; Also Journeying in Sumatra.* 2nd ed. London: Sampson Low, Marston, Searle & Rivington.

Boon, G. C.

1966 Gilt Glass Beads from Caerleon and Elsewhere. *Bulletin of the Board of Celtic Studies* 22 (1): 104–109.

1977 Gold-in-Glass Beads from the Ancient World. *Britannia* 8:193–207.

Bopearachchi, Osmund

1995 Sea-borne and Inland Trade of Ancient Sri Lanka: First Results of the Sri Lanka–French Exploratory Programme. In *South Asian Archaeology 1995: Proceedings of the 13th Conference of the European Association of South Asian Archaeologists.* Vol. 1. ed. Raymond Allchin and Bridget Allchin, 377–391. Cambridge: The Ancient India and Iran Trust.

Bose, P. N.

1908 Notes on the Geology and Mineral Resources of the Rajpipla State. *Records of the Geological Survey of India* 38 (2): 167–183.

Bowditch, T(homas) Edward

1966 *Mission from Cape Coast Castle to Ashantee.* 3d ed. Ed. W. E. F. Ward. London: Frank Cass & Co. (Reprint; orig. published 1819.)

Braddell, Roland

1947 Notes on Ancient Times in Malaya, 2: The Ancient Bead-Trade. *JMBRAS* 20 (1): 1–10.

1949 Notes on Ancient Times in Malaya, 4. Takola and Kataha. *JMBRAS* 22 (1): 1–16.

1980 Most Ancient Kedah. In *Lembah Bujang: The Bujang Valley,* ed. I. Chandran and J. Baharuddin, 32–54. Kuala Lumpur: Persatuan Sejarah Malaysia.

Brady, George S., and Henry R. Clauser

1977 *Materials Handbook: An Encyclopedia for Managers, Technical Professionals, Purchasing and Production Managers, Technicians, Supervisors, and Foremen.* 11th ed. New York: McGraw-Hill.

Brain, Jeffrey P.

1979 *Tunica Treasure.* Cambridge/Salem, Mass.: Peabody Museum of Archaeology and Ethnology, Harvard/Peabody Museum of Salem.

Bretschneider, E.

1910 *Mediaeval Researches from Eastern Asiatic Sources: Fragments towards the Knowledge of the Geography and History of Central and Western Asia from the 13th to the 17th Century.* Vol. 1. London: Kegan Paul, Trench, Trübner & Co.

Brill, Robert H.

1967 Lead Isotopes in Ancient Glass. *Annales du 4e Congrès de Journées Internationale du Verre,* 255–260.

1970 The Chemical Interpretation of the Texts. In A. Leo Oppenheim, Robert H. Brill, Dan Barag, and Axel von Saldern, *Glass and Glassmaking in Ancient Mesopotamia: An Edition of the Cuneiform Texts Which Contain Instructions for Glassmakers with a Catalogue of Surviving Objects,* 104–128. Corning, N.Y.: Corning Museum of Glass.

1987 Chemical Analyses of Some Early Indian Glass. In *Archaeometry of Glass: Proceedings of the Archaeometry Session of the 14th International Congress on Glass, 1986, New Delhi,* ed. H. C. Bhardwaj, 1–25. Calcutta: Indian Ceramic Society/Care; Central Glass and Ceramic Research Institute.

1995 Chemical Analysis of Some Glasses from Jenné-Jeno. In Susan Keech McIntosh, *Excavations at Jenné-Jeno, Hambarketolo, and Kaniana (Inland Nile Delta, Mali), the 1981 Season,* 252–256. University of California Publications in Anthropology. Vol. 1. 20. Berkeley: University of California Press.

Brill, Robert H., and Charles A. Hoffman

1987 Some Glass Beads Excavated on San Salvador Island in the Bahamas. *Annales de 10e Congrès de l'Association International pour l'Histoire du Verre,* 373–398.

Bronson, Bennet

1977 Exchange at the Upstream and Downstream Ends: Notes toward a Functional Model of the Coastal State in Southeast Asia. In *Economic Exchange and Social Interaction in Southeast Asia: Perspectives from Prehistory, History, and Ethnography,* ed. Karl L. Hutterer, 39–52. Michigan Papers on South and Southeast Asia, 13. Ann Arbor: Center for South and Southeast Asian Studies, University of Michigan.

1990 Glass and Beads at Khuan Lukpat, Southern Thailand. In *Southeast Asian Archaeology 1986,* ed. Ian and Emily Glover, 213–230. BAR International Series 561. Cambridge.

1991 Chinese and Middle Eastern Trade in Southern Thailand during the 9th Century A.D. Paper read at Integral Study of the Silk Roads: Roads of Dialogue, Bangkok. (Copy available at Center for Bead Research, Lake Placid, N.Y.)

1996 Chinese and Middle Eastern Trade in Southern Thailand during the 9th Century A.D. In *Ancient Trades and Cultural Contacts in Southeast Asia,* ed. Amara Srisuchat, 181–200. Bangkok: Office of the National Cultural Commission.

Bronson, Bennet, and George F. Dales

1972 Excavations at Chansen, Thailand, 1968 and 1969: A Preliminary Report. *Asian Perspectives* 15:15–46 + 2 plates.

Bronson, Bennet, and Ian Glover

1984 Archaeological Radiocarbon Dates from Indonesia: A First List. *Indonesia Circle* 34:37–44.

Bronson, Bennet, and Jan Wisseman

1976 Palembang as Srivijaya: The Lateness of Early Cities in Southern Southeast Asia. *Asian Perspectives* 19:220–239.

Brown, Claudia, and Donald Rabiner

1987 *The Robert H. Clague Collection: Chinese Glass of the Qing Dynasty 1644–1911.* Phoenix: Phoenix Art Museum.

1990 *Clear as Crystal, Red as Flame.* New York: China House Gallery/China Institute in America.

Brown, Lloyd A.

1977 *The Story of Maps.* New York: Dover Publications. (Orig. published 1949.)

Brunel, Francis

1972 *Jewellery of India: Five Thousand Years of Tradition.* New Delhi: National Book Trust.

Budge, E. A. Wallis

1968 *Amulets and Talismans.* New York: Collier Books.

Bühler, G.

1892 The Udepur Prasasti of the Kings of Malwa. *Epigraphia Indica* 1:222–238.

Burke, Lee

1971–1972 Beads from Sungai Lumut, Brunei. *Brunei Museum Journal* 2 (2): 89–95.

Burke, R. P.

1936 Check List, Glass Indian Trade Beads. *Arrow Points* 21 (5 & 6): 53–63.

Burton, Richard F.

1860 *The Lake Regions of Central Africa: A Picture of Exploration.* New York: Harper and Brothers.

Bushell, Stephen W.

1914 *Chinese Art.* 2d ed. 2 vols. Victoria and Albert Museum Handbooks. London/New York: H. M. Stationery Office/Brentano's.

Buttrick, George Arthur and Others, eds.

1962 Ophir. In *The Interpreter's Dictionary of the Bible.* Vol. 3, 605–606. New York: Abington Press.

Caley, Earle R.

1962 *Analyses of Ancient Glass 1790–1957: A Comprehensive and Critical Study.* Corning, N.Y.: Corning Museum of Glass.

Callmer, Johan

1977 *Trade Beads and Bead Trade in Scandinavia ca. 800–1000 A.D.* Acta Archaeologica Lundensia Ser. IN 4, Nr. 11. Bonn/Lund: Rudolf Habelt/C. W. K. Gleerup.

Cammann, Schuyler

1962 *Substance and Symbol in Chinese Toggles: Chinese Belt Toggles from the C. F. Bieber Collection.* Philadelphia: University of Pennsylvania Press.

Campbell, James M.

1880 *Gazetteer of the Bombay Presidency.* Vol. 6. Bombay: Bombay Government Central Press.

Campbell Thompson, R.

1936 *A Dictionary of Assyrian Chemistry and Geology.* Oxford: Clarendon Press.

Carswell, John

1983 Medieval Trading Post in the Indian Ocean. *Illustrated London News* October: 84–85.

Carswell, John, and Martha Prickett

1984 Mantai 1980: A Preliminary Investigation. *Ancient Ceylon* 5:3–68 + 13 plates.

Cartographic Publishing House

1985 *Map of the People's Republic of China.* Beijing: Cartographic Publishing House.

Casal, J.-M.

1949 *Fouilles de Virampatnam-Arikamedu: Rapport de l'Inde et de l'Occident aux environs de l'Ère Chrétienne.* Paris: Imprimerie Nationale.

Casal, J.-M., and G. Casal

1956 *Site urbain et sites funéraires des environs de Pondichéry: Virampatnam—Mouttrapaléon—Souttoukény.* Paris: Presses Universitaires de France.

Casson, Lionel

1989 *The Periplus Maris Erythraei.* Princeton, N.J.: Princeton University Press.

1991 Ancient Naval Technology and the Route to India. In *Rome and India: The Ancient Sea Trade,* ed. Vimala Begley and Richard Daniel De Puma, 8–11. Madison: University of Wisconsin Press.

Caton-Thompson, G.

1936 A Commentary on Dr. Laidler's Article on Beads in Africa South of the Zambesi. *Transactions of the Rhodesia Scientific Association* 34 (2): 10–18.

Chakrabarti, Dilip K.

1982 'Long Barrel-Cylinder' Beads and the Issue of Pre-Sargonic Contact between the Harappan Civilization and Mesopotamia. In *Harappan Civilization: A Contemporary Perspective,* ed. Gregory L. Possehl, 265–270 + 2 plates. Warminster, U.K.: Aris & Phillips.

Chakravarti, Adhir K.

1972 Early Sino-Indian Maritime Trade and Fu-nan.

In *Early Indian Trade and Industry*, ed. D. C. Sircar, 101–117. Calcutta: University of Calcutta.

Champakalakshmi, R.

1990 Sangam Literature as a Source of Evidence on India's Trade with the Western World: Problems of Methodology and Interpretation. Paper read at the UNESCO Silk Roads Conference, Madras.

Chand Chao Mom

1987 *Towards a History of Laem Thong and Sri Vijaya.* Asian Studies Monographs No. 034. Bangkok: Institute of Asian Studies, Chulalongkorn University.

Chandler, Tertius

1987 *Four Thousand Years of Urban Growth: An Historical Census.* Lewiston/Queenston: St. David's University Press.

Chandran, I., and Jazamuddin Baharuddin, eds.

1980 *Lembah Bujang: The Bujang Valley.* Kuala Lumpur: Persatuan Sejarah Malaysia.

Chang T'ien-Tsê

1934 *Sino-Portuguese Trade from 1514 to 1644: A Synthesis of Portuguese and Chinese Sources.* Leyden: Late E. J. Brill.

Charoenwongsa, Pisit

1982 Ban Chiang in Retrospect: What the Expedition Means to Archaeologists and the Thai Public. *Expedition* 24 (4): 13–16.

Chen Chi-Lu

1968 *Material Culture of the Formosan Aborigines.* Taipei: Taiwan Museum.

Chêng Tê-K'un

1960 *Archaeology in China.* Vol. 2. *Shang China.* Cambridge: W. Heffer & Sons.

1963 *Archaeology in China.* Vol. 3. *Chou China.* Cambridge/Toronto: W. Heffer & Sons/University of Toronto.

Chin, Lucas

1984 *Cultural Heritage of Sarawak.* Kuching: Sarawak Museum.

1988 *Ceramics in the Sarawak Museum.* Kuching: Sarawak Museum.

Chin You-di

1976 Ban Chiang Prehistoric Culture. *Sawaddi Special Edition* 20 (1): 5–8.

Chinese Repository

1834 Articles of Import and Export of Canton. *The Chinese Repository* 2 (10): 447–472.

Chittick, Neville

1967 The Description and Dating of the Glass Beads in Eastern Africa. Paper read at the Conference on East Africa and the Orient. (Copy available at the Center for Bead Research, Lake Placid, N.Y.)

1974 *Kilwa: An Islamic Trading City on the East African Coast.* Vol. 2. Memoir No. 5. Nairobi: The British Institute on Eastern Africa.

Choi Jai-seuk

1996 *Shōsō-in's Collections and Ancient Korea (the Unified Shilla)—Where Shōsō-in's Collections Were Made.* Seoul: Ilchisa (in Korean with English summary).

Chopra, R. N., S. L. Nayar, and I. C. Chopra

1956 *Glossary of Indian Medicinal Plants.* New Delhi: Council of Scientific and Industrial Research.

Christie, Jan Wisseman

1998 The medieval Tamil-language inscriptions in Southeast Asia and China. *Journal of Southeast Asian Studies* 29 (2): 239–268 [page numbers cited in text refer to pagination in WilsonSelect Internet printout, 29 pp.].

Chu, Arthur, and Grace Chu

1973 *Oriental Antiques and Collectibles, A Guide.* New York: Crown.

Claassen, Cheryl

1989 Sourcing Marine Shell Artifacts. In *Proceedings of the 1986 Shell Bead Conference: Selected Papers,* ed. Charles F. Hayes III, 17–23. Research Records No. 20. Rochester, N.Y.: Rochester Museum and Science Center.

Clark, Grahame

1986 *Symbols of Excellence: Precious Materials as Expressions of Status.* Cambridge: Cambridge University Press.

Cleuziou, Serge

1999 The Bronze-Age Cultures of Oman and Their Relations with India and Mesopotamia. Paper read at the Fifteenth International Conference on South Asian Archaeology, Leiden.

Coedès, G.
1918 Le royaume de Çrivōjaya. *BEFEO* 18:1–36.
1968 *The Indianized States of Southeast Asia.* Ed. Walter F. Vella, trans. Susan Brown Cowing. Honolulu: East-West Center Press.

Cohen, H. J.
1973 Early Islamic Scholars as Glassmakers. *RGH* 2:30–35.

Colani, Madeleine
1935 *Mégalithes du Haut-Laos (Hua Pan, Tran Ninh).* Tome Second. Paris: Les Editions d'Art et D'Historie.

Comfort, Howard
1991 Terra Sigillata at Arikamedu. In *Rome and India: The Ancient Sea Trade,* ed. Vimala Begley and Richard Daniel De Puma, 134–150. Madison: University of Wisconsin Press.

Commissariat, M. S.
1931 *Mandelslo's Travels in Western India (A.D. 1638–9).* London: Oxford University Press.
1938 *A History of Gujarat.* Vol. 1. London: Longmans, Green & Co.

Conklin, Harold C.
1986 A Bibliography of the Works of Robert B. Fox. *Pilipinas* 7:75–85.
1994 A Bibliography of William Henry Scott. *Pilipinas* 22:62–91.

Copland, John
1819 Account of the Cornelian Mines in the Neighbourhood of Baroach. *Transactions of the Bombay Literary Society* 1:289–295.

Cortesão, Armando
1967 *The Suma Oriental of Tomé Pires and the Book of Francisco Rodrigues.* Ser. ii, No. 89. London: Hakluyt Society. 2 vols. (Reprint, Kraus, Nendeln.)

Crane, Louise
1926 *China in Sign and Symbol.* Shanghai: Kelly & Walsh.

Crawfurd, John
1820 *History of the Indian Archipelago: Containing an Account of the Manners, Arts, Languages, Religions, Institutions and Commerce of its Inhabitants.* Vol. 3. Edinburgh: Archibald Constable and Co.

Crystal, David
1987 *The Cambridge Encyclopedia of Language.* Cambridge: Cambridge University Press.

Cuevas, Maharlika A.
1985 Typological Analysis of Beads from the Royal Captain Wrecksite Underwater Archaeological Project. (Manuscript, Philippine National Museum, Manila.)

Cummins, J. S.
1971 *Sucesos de las Islas Filipinas by Antonio de Morga.* Cambridge: Cambridge University Press.

Dames, Mansel Longworth
1918 *The Book of Duarte Barbosa, An Account of the Countries Bordering on the Indian Ocean and Their Inhabitants, Written by Duarte Barbosa and Completed about the Year 1518 A.D.* Vol. 1. *Including the Coasts of East Africa, Arabia, Persia and Western India as far as the Kingdom of Vijayanagar.* 2 vols. Ser. ii, No. 44. London: Hakluyt Society. (Reprinted 1967, Kraus, Nendeln/Liechtenstein.)

Dandekar, R. N.
1965 *Post-Vedic Literature.* Publications of the Centre of Advanced Study in Sanskrit Class A, No. 2. Poona: University of Poona.

Danner, Edward
1917 Patent 1,218,598. Process of Drawing Molten Material in Cylindrical Form. *Official Gazette* 6 March 1917: 245.

Danvers, F. C.
1892 *Report to the Secretary of State for India in Council on the Portuguese Records Relating to the East Indies, Contained in the Archivo da Torre do Tombo and the Public Libraries at Lisbon and Evora.* London: Registrar and Superintendent of Records, India Office. (Reprinted 1966, N. Israel, Amsterdam.)
1896 *Letters Received by the East India Company from Its Servants in the East.* Vol. I. 1602–1613. London: Sampson Low, Marsden.

Davidson Weinberg, G.
1971 Glass Manufacture in Hellenistic Rhodes. *Deltion* 24:143–151 + plates 76–88. (Reprint; orig. published 1969.)

Davis, Mary L., and Greta Pack
1963 *Mexican Jewelry.* Austin: University of Texas Press.

Davison, Claire C.
1972 Glass Beads in African Archaeology: Results of Neutron Activation Analysis, Supplemented by Results of X-Ray Fluorescence Analysis (LBL-1240). Ph.D. diss., University of California, Berkeley.

Dayton, John E.
1993 *The Discovery of Glass: Experiments in the Smelting of Rich, Dry Silver Ores, and the Reproduction of Bronze Age–Type Cobalt Blue Glass as a Slag.* American School of Prehistoric Research Bulletin 41. Cambridge, Mass.: Peabody Museum of Archaeology and Ethnology, Harvard University.

De Beauclair, Inez
1963 Some Ancient Beads of Yap and Palau. *The Journal of the Polynesian Society* 72 (1): 1–10 + 1 plate.
1970 A Note on the Dutch Period of Formosa 1622–1662: Dutch Beads on Formosa? *Bulletin of the Institute of Ethnography, Academia Sinica* 29 (1): 394–402 + 2 plates.

De Casparis, J. G.
1961 New Evidence on Cultural Relations between Java and Ceylon in Ancient Times. *Artibus Asiae* 24 (3/4): 241–248.

Defrémery, C., and B. R. Sanguinetti
1922 *Voyages d'Ibn Batouttah.* Tome 4. Paris: L'Imprimerie Nationale.

Deo, S. B.
1958 Beads. In *The Excavations at Maheshwar and Navdatoli (1952–53),* ed. H. D. Sankalia, B. Subbarao, and S. B. Deo, 177–191. Poona/Baroda: Deccan College/Maharaja Sayajirao University.
1960 Beads, Pendants, and Amulets. In *From History to Pre-History at Nevasa (1954–60),* ed. H. D. Sankalia, S. B. Deo, Z. N. Ansari, and S. Ehrhardt, 346–375. Poona: Deccan College.
1969 Beads. In *Excavations at Ahar (Tambavati). 1961–62,* ed. H. D. Sankalia, S. B. Deo and Z. D. Ansari, 163–175. Poona: Deccan College.
1971 Beads. In *Excavations at Navdatoli,* ed. H. D. Sankalia, S. B. Deo, and Z. D. Ansari, 351–372. Poona/Baroda: Deccan College/Maharaja Sayajirao University.
1973 *Mahurjhari Excavations.* Nagpur: University of Nagpur.
1983 The Megaliths: Their Culture, Ecology, Economy, and Technology. Paper read at International Conference on Recent Advances in Indian Archaeology, Pune. (Copy available at Center for Bead Research, Lake Placid, N.Y.)

Deo, S. B., and A. P. Jamkhedkar
1982 *Naikund Excavations (1978–1980).* Maharashtra, Bombay: Department of Museums and Archaeology.

Deraniyagala, S.
1972 The Citadel at Anuradhapura 1969: Excavations in the Gedige Area. *Ancient Ceylon* 2:48–169.

Desai, Z. A.
1961 Muslims in the 13th Century Gujarat, As Known from Arabic Inscriptions. *Journal of the Oriental Institute, Baroda* 10:352–364.

De Slane, Mac Guckin
1913 *De l'Afrique Septentrionale par El-Bekri.* Algers/Paris: Adolphe Jourdan/Paul Geuthner.

Dewaraja, Lorna
1990a Muslim Merchants and Pilgrims in Sarandib c. 900–1500 A.D. In *Sri Lanka and the Silk Road of the Sea,* ed. Senake Bandaranayake, Lorna Dewaraja, Roland Silva, and K. D. G. Wimalaratne, 191–198. Colombo: The Sri Lanka National Commission for UNESCO and the Central Cultural Fund.
1990b Thailand Repays Her Debt to Sri Lanka: A Study of the Cultural Contact between the Two Countries from the Fifteenth to the Eighteenth Centuries. In *Sri Lanka and the Silk Road of the Sea,* ed. Senake Bandaranayake, Lorna Dewaraja, Roland Silva, and K. D. G. Wimalaratne, 253–259. Colombo: The Sri Lanka National Commission for UNESCO and the Central Cultural Fund.

Dhavalikar, M. K., and Z. D. Ansari
1988 Other Artifacts. In *Excavations at Inamgaon.* Vol. 1, Part ii, ed. M. K. Dhavalikar, H. D. Sankalia, and Z. D. Ansari, 553–664, 670–724. Pune: Deccan College.

Dikshit, Moreshwar Gangadhar
1949 *Etched Beads in India.* Deccan College Monograph Series 4. Poona: Deccan College.
1952a *Some Beads from Koṇḍāpūr.* Hyderabad Archaeological Series 16. Hyderabad: The Archaeological Department of the Government of Hyderabad.
1952b Beads from Ahichchhatrā, U.P. *Ancient India* 8:33–63 + 5 plates.
1965 Studies in Ancient Indian Glass—I: Glass as Mentioned in Kautilya's Arthasastra I. *East and West* 15 (1 & 2): 62–68.
1968 *Kaundinyapura.* Bombay: Director of Archives and Archaeology, Maharashtra State.
1969 *History of Indian Glass.* Bombay: University of Bombay.

Dissanayake, Ellen
1985 Kandyan Mālē: Jewellery from fruits, seeds, and flowers. *Serendib* 4 (2): 12–15.

Dodwell, H. H., ed.
1969 *The Cambridge Shorter History of India.* Delhi: S. Chand & Co.

Dohrenwend, Doris
1980–1981 Glass in China: A Review Based on the Collection in the Royal Ontario Museum. *Oriental Art* 26 (4): 426–446.

Dos Sanctos, Joaõ
1905 Collections out of the Voyage and Historie of Friar Joaõ dos Sanctos his Aethiopia Orientalis, & Varia Historia, and out of other Portugals, for the better knowledge of Africa and the Christianitie therein. In *Purchas.* Vol. 9, 197–255.

Dubin, Lois Sherr
1987 *The History of Beads from 30,000 B.C. to the Present.* New York: Harry N. Abrams.

Dunn, Oliver, and James E. Kelley Jr.
1988 *The* Diario *of Christopher Columbus's First Voyage to America 1492–1493.* Norman: University of Oklahoma Press.

Dunning, Duangporn, and Steven Dunning
1992 Chinese (Peking) Glass: Interview with an Akha Bead Trader. *Hands of the Hills Newsletter* winter: 1–2.

Dussubieux, Laure, and Bernard Gratuze
2000 Indo-Pacific Beads. Orléans: Centre Ernest Babelon, Institut de Recherches sur les Archéomatériaux, Centre National de la Recherche Scientifique.

Duyvendak, J. J. L.
1949 *China's Discovery of Africa.* London: Arthur Probsthain.

East-Asiatic Economic Investigation Bureau (Toa-Keizai Chosakyoku)
1931 *The Manchuria Year Book 1931.* 2d. ed. Tokyo: East-Asiatic Economic Investigation Bureau.

Edwards McKinnon, E.
1991 Banten Girang and Banten Lama. Paper read at SPAFA Training Course on Conservation of Ancient Cities and/or Settlements, Banten. (Copy available at Center for Bead Research, Lake Placid, N.Y.)

Eichholz, D. E.
1962 *Pliny: Natural History.* Vol. 10. Loeb Classical Library. Cambridge, Mass.: Harvard University Press.

Elkington, Thomas
1905 Collections taken out of the Journall of Captaine Thomas Elkington, successour to Captain Nicholas Downton in the Voyage aforesaid, written by himself. In *Purchas.* Vol. 4, 251–257.

England, Pamela, James C. Y. Watt, and Lambertus van Zelst
1991 Analyses of Some Qing Period Chinese Glasses: An Interim Report. In *Scientific Research in Early Chinese Glass,* ed. Robert H. Brill and John H. Martin, 103–107. Corning, N.Y.: Corning Museum of Glass.

Engle, Anita
1973 3,000 Years of Glassmaking on the Phoenician Coast. *RGH* 1:1–26.
1976 Glassmaking in China. *RGH* 6/7:1–38.
1982 Father Ferdinand Verbiest and the Imperial Palace Workshops. *RGH* 15/16:47–55.

Ernawan, Yusuf
1987 Manik-manik Situs Matesih: Studi Pendahuluan Tentang Teknologi dan Peranannya. Thesis, Gadjah Mada University, Yogyakarta.

Escobar, Vicenta Mendoza

1991 *Philippine Antique Jewelry.* Manila: Privately published.

Evans, Ivor H. N.

1928 On Ancient Remains from Kuala Selinsing, Perak. *JFMSM* 12 (5): 121–131 + 8 plates.

1932 Excavations at Tanjong Rawa, Kuala Selinsing, Perak. *JFMSM* 15 (3): 79–133 + 20 plates, 6 maps.

Everett, Harold H., and John Hewitt

1908 A History of Santubong, an Island off the Coast of Sarawak. *Journal of the Straits Branch of the Royal Asiatic Society* 51:1–30 + 2 plates.

Fairbanks, Charles H.

1968 Early Spanish Colonial Beads. In *The Conference on Historic Site Archaeology Papers* 2 (1), ed. Stanley South, 3–21. Raleigh, N.C.

Father Matthew

1906 The report of a Mahometan Merchant Which Had Beene in Cambalu: and a Troublesome Travell of Benedictus Goes, a Portugall Jesuite, from Lahor to China by Land, Thorow the Tartars Countreyes. In *Purchas.* Vol. 12, 227–238.

Faucheux, L.

1946 *Une Vieille Cité Indienne près de Pondicherry: Virapatnam.* Pondicherry: La Mission.

Fenstermaker, G. B., and Alice T. Williams

1979 *The Chinese Bead and the Romance of the Bead-Jewelry Trail.* Lancaster, Pa.: Fenstermaker Books.

Ferrand, Gabriel

1913 *Relations de Voyages et Textes Géographiques Arabes, Persans et Turks Relatifs à l'Extrême-orient de VIIIe au XVIIe siecles.* 2 vols. Paris: Ernest Leroux.

Finch, William

1905 Observations of William Finch, Merchant, taken out of his large Journall. In *Purchas.* Vol. 4, 1–77.

Finn, Daniel J.

1958 *Archaeological Finds on Lamma Island near Hong Kong.* Ed. T. F. Ryan Jr. Hong Kong: Ricci Publications, University of Hong Kong.

Finot, Louis

1896 *Les Lapidaires Indiens.* Paris: Librairie Emile Bonillon.

Fleet, J. F.

1889 Sanskrit and Old Kanarese Inscriptions, No. 174: Copper Plate Grant at the time of Ajayapala—Vikrama Samvat 1231. *Indian Antiquary* 18:80–85.

Force, Roland W.

1959 Palauan Money: Some Preliminary Comments on Material and Origins. *The Journal of the Polynesian Society* 68 (1): 40–44 + 1 plate.

Force, Roland W., and Maryanne T. Force

1963 Palauan Money: Some Preliminary Comments on Material and Origins. In *Proceedings of the Ninth Pacific Science Congress, 1957.* Vol. 3, 52–54. Bangkok: Secretariat, Ninth Pacific Science Congress.

Forrest, Thomas

1971 A Voyage to New Guinea and the Moluccas, from Balambangan: Including an Account of Magindanso, Sooloo and other Islands. In *Travel Accounts of the Islands (1513–1787),* 209–361. No. 19. Manila: Filipiniana Book Guild.

Forsyth, Robert Coventry

1912 *Shantung: The Sacred Province of China in Some of Its Aspects, Being a Collection of Articles Relating to Shantung, Including Brief Histories with Statistics, Etc., of the Catholic and Protestant Missions and Life-Sketches of Protestant Martyrs, Pioneers, and Veterans Connected with the Province.* Shanghai: Chinese Literature Society.

Foster, William

1899 *Letters, Vol. III—1615.* London: Sampson Low, Marston & Co.

1900 *Letters, Vol. IV—1616.* London: Sampson Low, Marston & Co.

1901 *Letters, Vol. V—1617.* London: Sampson Low, Marston & Co.

1902 *Letters, Vol. VI—1617.* London: Sampson Low, Marston & Co.

1906 *Factories 1618–1621.* Oxford: Clarendon Press.

1908 *Factories 1622–1623.* Oxford: Clarendon Press.

1909 *Factories 1624–1629.* Oxford: Clarendon Press.

1910 *Factories 1630–1633.* Oxford: Clarendon Press.
1912 *Factories 1637–1641.* Oxford: Clarendon Press.
1913 *Factories 1642–1645.* Oxford: Clarendon Press.
1914 *Factories 1646–1650.* Oxford: Clarendon Press.

Fox, Robert B.
1967 The Archaeological Record of Chinese Influences in the Philippines. *Philippine Studies* 15 (1): 41–62.
1970 *The Tabun Caves: Archaeological Explorations and Excavations on Palawan Island, Philippines.* Monograph No. 1. Manila: National Museum.
1977 Ancient Beads. In *Filipino Heritage.* Vol. 3, ed. Alfredo R. Roces, 757–766. Manila: Lahing.

Francfort, H.-P., and M.-H. Pottier
1978 Sondage Préliminaire sur l'Établissement Protohistorique Harappéen et Post-Harappéen de Shortugaï (Afghanistan du N.-E.). *Arts Asiatiques* 34:29–57.

Francis, Peter, Jr.
1979 *The Story of Venetian Beads.* WBMS 1. Lake Placid, N.Y.: Lapis Route.
1980 Bead Report, II: Etched Beads in Iran. *Ornament* 4 (3): 24–28.
1981 Early Human Adornment in India, Part I: The Upper Paleolithic. *BDCRI* 40:137–140.
1982a *A Handbook of Bead Materials.* WBMS 5. Lake Placid, N.Y.: Lapis Route.
1982b *The Glass Beads of India.* WBMS 7. Lake Placid, N.Y.: Lapis Route.
1982c *Indian Agate Beads.* WBMS 6. Lake Placid, N.Y.: Lapis Route.
1982d Followup: dZi Beads. *Ornament* 6 (2): 55–56.
1982e Early Human Adornment in India, Part II: The Mesolithic. *BDCRI* 41:59–67.
1983a Bead Report, Part IX: Bangles and Baubles, Part I. *Ornament* 6 (4): 36–37.
1983b Early Post-Contact Native-Made Glass Beads. *Bead Forum* 2:5–6.
1983c Bead Report, Part VIII: Minor Indian Beadmakers. *Ornament* 6 (3): 18–21.
1984a Beadmakers' Strike in India. *Bead Forum* 5:7–8.
1984b Some Observations on the Glass Beads of Arikamedu. *Revue Historique de Pondichery* 30:156–161.
1985a Baba Ghor and the Ratanpur Rakshisha. *JESHO* 29:198–204.
1985b A Survey of Beads in Korea. OPCBR 1. Lake Placid, N.Y.
1985c Chinese Beadmakers in Java ca. 1600? *Margaretologist* 1 (1): 4–6.
1985d Bead Report, XIV: A Collection of "Phoenician" Beads. *Ornament* 8 (4): 42–45.
1986a Bead Report, XVIII: The Asian Bead Study Tour, Part IV: A Little Tube of Glass. *Ornament* 10 (1): 54–57, 74–78.
1986b Collar Beads: A New Typology and a New Perspective on Ancient Indian Beadmaking. *BDCPRI* 45:117–121.
1986c *Chinese Glass Beads: A Review of the Evidence.* OPCBR 2. Lake Placid, N.Y.
1986d Glass Beads in China: Further Evidence. *Margaretologist* 1 (3): 6–7.
1986e Sidetrips: Baroda, Ujjain, and Delhi, India. *Margaretologist* 1 (3): 8.
1986f Archaeology: Indian Antiquity. *Lapidary Journal* 39 (12): 45–55.
1986g *Beads and the Discovery of the New World.* OPCBR 3. Lake Placid, N.Y.
1987a Bead Report: The Endangered Bead. *Ornament* 11 (1): 64–73.
1987b *Bead Emporium: A Guide to the Beads from Arikamedu in the Pondicherry Museum.* Museum Publications 2. Pondicherry: Pondicherry Museum.
1987c *Report on the Beads from Nishapur, Iran, in the Metropolitan Museum of Art Obtained from the Museum's Excavations under Charles K. Wilkinson.* CCBR 2. Lake Placid, N.Y.
1987d San Pedro Quiatoni and Puebla Glass. *Margaretologist* 1 (4): 9.
1987e Chevrons and the Conquistadors. *Margaretologist* 1 (4): 6–7.
1988a Bead Report: Some News about Old Beads. *Ornament* 11 (4): 33–34, 70–76.
1988b *The Glass Trade Beads of Europe: Their Manufacture, Their History, and Their Identification.* WBMS 8. Lake Placid, N.Y.: Lapis Route.
1988c Pecking and Beads. *Lapidary Journal* 42 (5): 57–62.

1988–1989 Glass Beads in Asia, Part I: Introduction. *Asian Perspectives* 28: 1–21.

1989a *Heirloom and Ethnographically Collected Beads in Southeast Asia.* CCBR 6. Lake Placid, N.Y.

1989b Where Did They Bury Our Saint? *Margaretologist* 2 (4): 3–4.

1989c *Beads and the Bead Trade in Southeast Asia.* CCBR 4. Lake Placid, N.Y.

1989d *The Type Collection of Beads from Archaeological Contexts in the Philippine National Museum.* CCBR 5. Lake Placid, N.Y.

1989e Beads of the Early Islamic Period. *Beads* 1:21–39.

1989f BEAD. *Margaretologist* 2 (4): 1.

1989g Bead Report: Bead Peregrinations. *Ornament* 13 (2): 78–82.

1990a The Secret of Papanaidupet. *Glastechnische Berichte* 63:210–212.

1990b Glass Beads in Asia, Part II: Indo-Pacific Beads. *Asian Perspectives* 29:1–23.

1990c Glass Beads of China. *Arts of Asia* 20 (5): 118–127.

1990d Beadmaking in Islam: The African Trade and the Rise of Hebron. *Beads* 2:15–28.

1990e Two Bead Strands from Andhra Pradesh, India. *Asian Perspectives* 29:45–50.

1990f East and West: The Ancient Gem Trade between India and Rome. *Gemological Digest* 3 (1): 33–39.

1990g The Mysterious Aggrey Bead. *Margaretologist* 3 (2): 3–8.

1991a Beadmaking in Arikamedu and Beyond. *World Archaeology* 23 (1): 28–43.

1991b Letter to the Editor: Chinese Glass Beads. *Ornament* 14 (4): 4, 6.

1991c Beads in Indonesia: A Review of the Evidence. *Asian Perspectives* 30:218–241.

1991d Some Thoughts on the Bead Trade. *Margaretologist* 4 (2): 3–12.

1992a *Heirlooms of the Hills: Southeast Asia.* Beads and People Series 1. Lake Placid, N.Y.: Center for Bead Research.

1992b Mutisalah Beads: What Is Their True Story? *Margaretologist* 5 (1): 5–8.

1992c The Globalization of the Bead Trade: The Americas "Plug In" to the World Network. Paper read at The Bead Trade in the Americas Conference, Santa Fe, N.Mex.

1992d What's a Rango? *Bead Forum* 21:8–11.

1992e The Pumtek Bead: What Is Its Story? *Margaretologist* 5 (1): 3–5.

1992f Heirloom Beads. *Margaretologist* 5 (2): 3–6.

1993a *Where Beads Are Loved: Ghana, West Africa.* Beads and People Series 2. Lake Placid, N.Y.: Center for Bead Research.

1993b Sumatra's Lost Kingdom. *Lapidary Journal* 47 (7): 108–118.

1993c Bloodstone, Agate, and Carnelian. *Bead Forum* 22:16–20.

1993d South Indian Stone Beadmaking. *Margaretologist* 6 (2): 3–6.

1993e Southeast Asian Glass Beads and the Western Connection. *Margaretologist* 6 (2): 7–9.

1993f Bead Altering. *Margaretologist* 6 (1): 7–8.

1993g Common Intrigue. *Lapidary Journal* 47 (3): 41–44, 96–98.

1994a Toward a Social History of Beadmakers. *Beads* 6:61–80.

1994b Beads in Mexican Villages. *Margaretologist* 7 (2): 12–13.

1994c Beads at the Crossroads of Continents. In *Anthropology of the North Pacific Rim,* ed. William W. Fitzhugh and Valérie Chaussonnete, 281–305. Washington: Smithsonian Institution Press.

1994d *Beads of the World.* Atglen, Pa.: Schiffer.

1995a The Beads from Fustat in the Awad Collection. *Margaretologist* 8 (1): 7–11.

1995b Beads in Vietnam: An Initial Report. *Margaretologist* 8 (2): 3–9.

1996a European Glass Beads ca. 1000 BC to AD 1500. *Margaretologist* 9 (1): 3–12.

1996b Appendix C: Marine Shells at Arikamedu. In *The Ancient Port of Arikamedu: New Excavations and Researches 1989–1992,* Vol. 1, ed. Vimala Begley, 393–395. Mémoires Archéologiques 22. Paris/Pondichéry: L'École Française d'Extrême-Orient/Centre d'Historie et d'Archéologie.

1996c Beads at Jamestown: A First Look. *Margaretologist* 9 (2): 12.

1996d Beads, the Bead Trade, and State Development in Southeast Asia. In *Ancient Trades and Cultural Contacts in Southeast Asia,* ed. Amara Srisuchat, 139–152. Bangkok: Office of the National Cultural Commission.

1997 A Vocabulary of Seed Beads. *Margaretologist* 10 (2): 9–13.

1998a Glass and Glass Analysis. *Margaretologist* 11 (1): 3–8.

1998b Analyses of Indo-Pacific Beads. *Margaretologist* 11 (1): 9–14.

1998c The Venetian Bead Story, Part 1: History. *Margaretologist* 11 (2): 3–12.

1999 Middle Eastern Glass Beads: A New Paradigm. *Margaretologist* 12 (2): 3–11.

2001 Human Ornaments. In *Report of the 1998 Excavations at Berenike,* ed. Steven E. Sidebotham and Willemina Z. Wendrich. Leiden: Research School of Asian, African, and Amerindian Studies (CNWS), Universiteit Leiden.

n.d. The Beads and Other Small Finds. In *The Ancient Port of Arikamedu: New Excavations and Researches 1989–1992.* Vol. 2, ed. Vimala Begley. Paris: Mémoires Archéologiques, École Française d'Extrême-Orient. (in press.)

Francis, W.

1985 *Imperial Gazetteer of India: Provincial Series—Madras I.* New Delhi: Usha. (Reprint).

Frank, Andre Gunder

1990 A Theoretical Introduction to 5,000 Years of World System History. *Review Fernand Braudel Center* 13 (2): 155–248.

1993 Bronze Age World Systems Cycles. *Current Anthropology* 34 (4): 383–429.

Frederick, Caesar

1905 Extracts of Master Caesar Frederike [*sic*] his Eighteen Yeeres Indian Observations. In *Purchas.* Vol. 10, 88–143.

Fu Lo-Shu

1954–1955 The Two Portuguese Embassies to China During the K'ang-Hsi Period. *T'oung Pao* 43 (1/2): 75–94.

1966 *A Documentary Chronicle of Sino-Western Relations (1644–1820).* 2 vols. The Association for Asian Studies: Monographs and Papers No. 22. Tucson: University of Arizona Press.

Gadgil, D. R.

1929 *The Industrial Evolution of India in Recent Times.* 2d ed. Oxford: Oxford University Press.

Gallagher, L. J.

1942 *The China That Was: China as Discovered by the Jesuits at the Close of the Sixteenth Century.* Milwaukee: Bruce Publishing Co.

1953 *China in the Sixteenth Century: The Journals of Matthew Ricci: 1583–1610.* New York: Random House.

Gan Fuxi

1991 Introduction to the Symposium Papers. In *Scientific Research in Early Chinese Glass,* ed. Robert H. Brill and John H. Martin, 1–3. Corning, N.Y.: Corning Museum of Glass.

Gardner, G. B.

1937 Ancient Beads from the Johore River as Evidence of an Early Link by Sea between Malaya and the Roman Empire. *Journal of the Royal Asiatic Society* 34 (3): 467–470 + 3 plates.

Gasparetto, Astone

1958 *Il Vetro di Murano.* Venezia: Neri Pozza Editore.

Geddes, W. R.

1985 *Nine Dayak Nights.* 2d ed. Singapore: Oxford University Press.

Gerard, John

1975 *The Herbal or General History of Plants.* Ed. and rev. Thomas Johnson. New York: Dover. (Orig. published 1633.)

Gerini, G. E.

1905 Historical Retrospect of Junkceylon Island. *Journal of the Siam Society* 2:121–259.

1909 *Researches on Ptolemy's Geography of Eastern Asia (Further India and Indo-Malay Archipelago).* Asiatic Society Monographs No. 1. London: Royal

Asiatic Society/Royal Geographical Society. (Reprinted 1974, Oriental Books, New Delhi.)

Gerlach, Martin

1971 *Primitive and Folk Jewelry.* New York: Dover.

Gernet, Jacques

1962 *Daily Life in China on the Eve of the Mongol Invasion 1250–1276,* transl. H. M. Wright. Stanford, Calif.: Stanford University Press.

1982 *A History of Chinese Civilization,* transl. J. R. Foster. Cambridge: Cambridge University Press.

Gibb, H. A. R.

1929 *Ibn Battuta, Travels in Asia and Africa 1325–1354,* London: G. Routledge.

Gibson-Hill, C. A.

1955 Johore Lama and Other Ancient Sites on the Johore River. *JMBRAS* 28 (2): 127–197.

Giles, H. A.

1923 *The Travels of Fa-hsien (399–414 A.D.), or Record of the Buddhistic Kingdoms.* Cambridge: Cambridge University Press.

Gills, Barry K., and Andre Gundar Frank

1991 5000 Years of World System History: The Cumulation of Accumulation. In *Core/Periphery Relations in Precapitalist Worlds,* ed. Christopher Chase-Dunn and Thomas D. Hall, 67–112. Boulder: Westview Press.

Glover, Ian C.

1990a Ban Don Ta Phet: The 1984–85 excavation. In *Southeast Asian Archaeology 1986,* ed. Ian and Emily Glover, 139–183. BAR International Series 561. Cambridge.

1990b *Early Trade between India and Southeast Asia: A Link in the Development of the World Trading System.* 2d ed. Occasional Papers No. 16, Centre for South-East Asian Studies. Hull, U.K.: University of Hull.

1994 Bead Notes from Southeast Asia. *BSTN* 23/24: 7–11.

1998 The Role of India in the Late Prehistory of Southeast Asia. *Journal of Southeast Asian Archaeology* 18:21–49.

2000 Notes on Glass from Bâi Lãng Site, Culao Cham, Quang Nam Province, Vietnam. *BSTN* 35:12–13.

Glover, Ian, and Julian Henderson

1995 Early Glass in South and South East Asia and China. In *South East Asia and China: Art, Interaction and Commerce,* ed. R. Scott and J. Guy, 141–170. Colloquies on Art and Archaeology in Asia No. 17. London: Percival David Foundation of Chinese Art.

Glover, Ian C., Pisit Charoenwongsa, Bryan Alvey, and Nawarat Kamnounket

1984 The cemetery of Ban Don Ta Phet, Thailand: Results from the 1980–1 excavation season. In *South Asian Archaeology 1981,* ed. Bridget Allchin, 319–330. Cambridge: Cambridge University Press.

Goddio, Franck

1988 *Discovery and Archaeological Excavation of a 16th Century Trading Vessel in the Philippines.* Manila: World Wide First.

Goddio, Franck, Michel L'Hour, and Florence Richez, eds.

1987 Les perles de verre. In Revenement Archéologique sur les côtes des Philippines, 76–79. *Dossiers Histoire et Archéologie* 113.

Gode, P. K.

1949 Notes on the History of Glass Vessels and Glass Bangles in India, South Arabia, and Central Asia. *Journal of Oriental Studies* 1 (1): 11–16.

Gogte, Vishwas D.

1981 Discovery of Megalithic Iron Smelting Site by Three-Probe Resistivity Survey. *BDCRI* 40:211–215.

Gogte, V. D., S. M. Kanetkar, and A. A. Kshirsagar

1982 Efficiency of Megalithic Iron Smelting by Chemical Analysis. *BDCRI* 41:68–76 + 1 plate.

Goitein, S. D.

1961 The Main Industries of the Mediterranean Area as Reflected in the Records of the Cairo Geniza. *JESHO* 4 (2): 168–197.

1963 Letters and Documents on the India Trade in Medieval Times. *Islamic Culture* 37 (3): 188–205.

1973 *Letters of Medieval Jewish Traders.* Princeton: Princeton University Press.

Gokhale, B. G.
1962 Some Aspects of Early English Trade with Western India (1600–1650). *Journal of Indian History* 40 (2): 268–286.
1967 Ahmadabad in the XVIIth Century. *JESHO* 12:187–197.

Goldman, Bernard
1989 Ziwiyeh. Miscellany. *Bulletin of the Asia Institute* 3:1–13.

Goldstein, Sidney M.
1979 *Pre-Roman and Early Roman Glass in The Corning Museum of Glass.* Corning: Corning Museum of Glass.

Gonzales de Mendosa, Ivan
1906 First Discoverie of the Philippinas. In *Purchas.* Vol. 12, 142–148.

Gray, Albert, and H. C. P. Bell
1888 *The Voyage of François Pyrard of Laval to the East Indies, the Maldives, the Moluccas and Brazil.* Vol. 2. Ser. i, No. 77. London: Hakluyt Society.

Gray, John Henry
1875 *Walks in the City of Canton.* Victoria (Hong Kong): DeSouza & Co.

Grierson, Philip
1977 *The Origins of Money.* The Creighton Lecture in History 1970. London: The Athlone Press, University of London.

Griffis, William Elliot
1888 Japanese Ivory Carvers. *Harper's New Monthly Magazine* 76 (455): 709–714.

Groeneveldt, W. P.
1876 *Notes on the Malay Archipelago and Malacca Compiled from Chinese Sources.* Batavia: W. Bruining.

Grose, Davis
1983 The Formation of the Roman Glass Industry. *Archaeology* 36 (4): 38–45.

Gujarat State Gazetteer
1961 *Broach District.* Ahmedabad: Government Printing House.

Gunawardana, R. A. L. H.
1990 Seaways to Sielediba: Changing Patterns of Navigation in the Indian Ocean and Their Impact on Precolonial Sri Lanka. In *Sri Lanka and the Silk Road of the Sea,* ed. Senake Bandaranayake, Lorna Dewaraja, Roland Silva, and K. D. G. Wimalaratne, 25–43. Colombo: The Sri Lanka National Commission for UNESCO and the Central Cultural Fund.

Gupta, Hira Lal
1960 The Economic Impact of the West on Indian Industries. *Journal of Indian History* 38 (1): 77–100.

Gupta, K. P.
1972 Lower Narmada and Its Antiquities. *Journal of the Oriental Institute, Baroda* 21 (4): 265–274.

Gupta, P. Lal
1979 *Coins.* India: the Land and the People Series. New Delhi: National Book Trust.

Gupta, Sunil
1995–1996 Beyond Arikamedu: Micro Stratigraphy of the Iron Age–Early Historic Transition and Roman Contact in South India. *Purātattva* 26:50–61.
1999 Indo-Pacific Beads in Japan. *BSTN* 34:11–14.
2000 New Analyses of Indo-Pacific Beads and Glass Waste from Arikamedu, India. *BSTN* 35:8–9.

Guruge, Ananda W. P.
1990 The Sri Lankan Factor in the Development of the Art of Sukothai and Lanna Tai. In *Sri Lanka and the Silk Road of the Sea,* ed. Senake Bandaranayake, Lorna Dewaraja, Roland Silva, and K. D. G. Wimalaratne, 245–251. Colombo: The Sri Lanka National Commission for UNESCO and the Central Cultural Fund.

Gwinnett, A. John, and Leonard Gorelick
1981 Beadmaking in Iran in the Early Bronze Age, Derived by Scanning Electron Microscopy. *Expedition* 24 (1): 10–23.
1991 Bead Manufacture at Hajar ar-Rayhani, Yemen. *Biblical Archaeologist* (December): 187–196.

Haldeman, S. S.
1879 Beads. In Reports upon Archaeological and Ethnographical Collections from Vicinity of Santa Barbara, California, and from Ruined Pueblos of Arizona and New Mexico, and Certain Interior Tribes, ed. Frederick W. Putnam, 263–271 + plate XIII. In Geo. M. Wheeler (in charge), *Report upon*

United States Geographical Surveys West of the One Hundredth Meridian. Vol. 7—*Archaeology.* Washington: Engineer Department, U.S. Army.

Hall, Kenneth R.

1982 The "Indianization" of Funan: An Economic History of Southeast Asia's First State. *Journal of the Southeast Asia Society* 13 (1): 81–106.

1985 *Maritime Trade and State Development in Early Southeast Asia.* Honolulu: University of Hawai'i Press.

Hamilton, Alexander

1739 *A New Account of the East Indies.* Vol. 1. London: A. Butterworth and C. Hitch.

Hamilton, H. C., and W. Falconer

1912 *The Geography of Strabo.* 3 vols. London: G. Bell & Sons.

Han Byong-Sam

1973 *The Arts of Korea.* Vol. 2. Seoul: Dong Hwa.

Han Wai Toon

1948 A Study on Johore Lama. *Journal of the South Seas Society* 5 (2): 17–35.

Harada, Yoshito

1962 Ancient Glass in the History of Cultural Exchange between East and West. *Acta Asiatica, Bulletin of the Institute of Eastern Culture* 3:57–69.

Harden, Donald B.

1967 Some Aspects of Pre-Roman Mosaic Glass. *Annales du 4e Congrès de Journées Internationale du Verre,* 29–38.

1987 *Glasses of the Caesars.* Corning/London/Cologne/Milan: Corning Museum of Glass/British Museum/Römish-Germanisches Museum/Olivetti.

Hardie, Peter

1985 China's Ceramic Trade with India. *Transactions of the Oriental Ceramic Society 1983–1984* 48:14–31.

Harishankar, B. S.

1997–1998 Recent Trends in South Indian Megalithic Studies. *Purātattava* 28:114–116.

Harrell, J. A.

1999 Geology. In *Report of the 1997 Excavations at Berenike and the Survey of the Egyptian Desert, including Excavations at Shenshef,* ed. Steven E. Sidebotham and Willemina Z. Wendrich, 107–121. Leiden: Research School of Asian, African, and Amerindian Studies (CNWS), Universiteit Leiden.

Harris, Elizabeth, and Robert K. Liu

1979 Identification: Mold-made(?) Glass Beads from Ecuador/Peru. *Ornament* 4 (2): 60.

Harrison, John

1954 The Saghalien Trade: A Contribution to Ainu Studies. *Southwestern Journal of Anthropology* 10 (3): 278–293.

Harrisson, Tom

1950 Kelabit, Land Dayak, and Related Glass Beads in Sarawak. *Sarawak Museum Journal,* n.s., 5 (2): 201–220.

1964 Monochrome Glass Beads from Malaysia and Elsewhere. *Man* 64:37–41.

1968 New Analyses of Excavated Prehistoric Glass from Borneo. *Asian Perspectives* 11:125–133.

1973 Ancient Glass Beads from Brunei and Sarawak Excavations (Compared). *Brunei Museum Journal* 3 (1): 118–126.

Harrisson, Tom, and S. J. O'Connor

1969 *Excavations of the Prehistoric Iron Industry in West Borneo.* Vol. 2: *Associated Artifacts and Ideas.* Data Paper 72, Southeast Asia Program/Department of Asian Studies. Ithaca: Cornell University.

Hartman, Roland

1980 Kingfisher Feather Jewellery. *Arts of Asia* 10 (3): 75–81.

Hasan, Hadi

1928 *A History of Persian Navigation.* London: Methuen.

Hasan, S. Jamal

1983 The Distribution and Types of Beads in the Gangetic Valley. *Purātattva* 11:131–140.

Hawthorne, John G., and Cyril Stanley Smith

1979 *Theophilus On Divers Arts: The Foremost Medieval Treatise on Painting, Glassmaking, and Metalwork.* New York: Dover. (Orig. publication 1963, University of Chicago Press.)

Hayes, Charles F., III, ed.

1989 *Proceedings of the 1986 Shell Bead Conference: Selected Papers.* Research Records No. 20.

Rochester, N.Y.: Rochester Museum and Science Center.

Head, W. R.

1917 *Hand Book on the Haka Chin Customs.* Rangoon: Office of the Superintendent, Government Printing, Burma.

Hector, Valerie

1995 Prosperity, Reverence, and Protection: An Introduction to Asian Beadwork. *Beads* 7:3–36.

Heekeren, H. R. van

1958 *The Bronze-Iron Age of Indonesia.* The Hague: Matinus Nijhoft.

Henderson, Julian

1985 The Raw Materials of Early Glass Production. *Oxford Journal of Archaeology* 4 (3): 267–291.

1991 Technological Characteristics of Roman Enamels. *Jewellery Studies* 5:65–76.

Henricson, Lars G.

1995 Broken Glass Beakers Re-Used as Glass Beads. In *Glass Beads: Cultural History, Technology, Experiment, and Analogy,* ed. Marianne Rasmussen, Ulla Lund Hansen, and Ulf Näsman, 13–17. Studies in Technology and Culture. Vol. 2. Lejre, Denmark: Historical-Archaeological Experimental Centre.

Herrmann, Georgina

1968 Lapis Lazuli: The Early Phases of Its Trade. *Iraq* 30:21–57.

Hirth, Friedrich

1885 *China and the Roman Orient: Researches into Their Ancient and Medieval Relations as Represented in Old Chinese Records.* Shanghai/Hong Kong. (Reprinted 1966, Paragon Book Reprint Co., New York; 1975, Ares Publishers, Chicago.)

Hirth, F., and W. W. Rockhill

1911 *Chau Ju-Kwa: His Work on the Chinese and Arab Trade in the Twelfth and Thirteenth Centuries, Entitled Chu-fan-chï.* St. Petersburg: Imperial Academy of Sciences. (Reprinted 1966, Paragon Book Reprint Co., New York.)

Hobson, R. L.

1915 *Chinese Pottery and Porcelain: An Account of the Potter's Art in China from Primitive Times to the Present Day.* Vol. 1. New York/London: Funk and Wagnalls/Cassell and Company.

Honey, W. B.

1937 Early Chinese Glass. *The Burlington Magazine for Connoisseurs* 71:211–222.

Hourani, George Fadlo

1951 *Arab Seafaring in the Indian Ocean in Ancient and Early Medieval Times.* Princeton: Princeton University Press.

Howard-Carter, Theresa

1986 Eyestones and Pearls. In *Bahrain through the Ages: The Archaeology,* ed. Shaikha Haya Ali Al Khalifa and Michael Rice, 305–310. London: KPI.

Hsü Yün-Ts'iao

1948 Notes on Malay Peninsula in Ancient Voyages. *Journal of the South Seas Society* 5 (2): 1–16.

Huang Guangxi

1991 A Preliminary Study of Han Dynasty Glass in Guangxi. In *Scientific Research in Early Chinese Glass,* ed. Robert H. Brill and John H. Martin, 185–200. Corning, N.Y.: Corning Museum of Glass.

Hughes, Ian

1977 *New Guinea Stone Age Trade: The Geography and Ecology of Traffic in the Interior.* Terra Australis 3. Canberra: Department of Prehistory, Research School of Pacific Studies, Australian National University.

Hunter, F.

1877 *An Account of the British Settlement of Aden in Arabia.* London: Trübner & Co.

Hutchins, Robert Maynard, ed.

1952 *Herodotus: The History.* Great Books of the Western World 6. Chicago: Encyclopaedia Britannica Co.

Hutton, J. H.

1977 *Caste in India: Its Nature, Function, and Origins.* 4th ed. Bombay: Oxford University Press.

Huvelin, P.

1904 Mercantor, Greek. In *Dictionnaire des Antiquités Grecques et Romaines.* Tome Troisième, Deuxième Partie L–M, ed. Ch. Daremberg and Edm. Saglio, 1731–1736. (Reprinted 1969, Akademische Druck u Verlangsanstadt, Graz, 5 vols.)

Ikuta, Shigeru
1991 The Place of Srivijaya on the Maritime Trade Network of Southeast Asia: An Interpretation of Chinese Resources. Paper read at International Seminar: Harbour Cities along the Silk Roads, Surabaya. (Copy available at Center for Bead Research, Lake Placid, N.Y.)

Imam, S. A.
1990 Cultural Relations between Sri Lanka and Iran. In *Sri Lanka and the Silk Road of the Sea,* ed. Senake Bandaranayake, Lorna Dewaraja, Roland Silva, and K. D. G. Wimalaratne, 173–178. Colombo: The Sri Lanka National Commission for UNESCO and the Central Cultural Fund.

Indraji, B., and G. Bühler
1878 The Inscription of Rudradaman at Junagadh. *Indian Antiquity* 7:257–263.

Indraningsih, Panggabean Joyce Ratna
1985a Research on Prehistoric Beads in Indonesia. Paper read at the 12th Indo-Pacific Prehistory Association Symposium. (Copy available at Center for Bead Research, Lake Placid, N.Y.)
1985b Research on Prehistoric Beads in Indonesia. *Bulletin of the Indo-Pacific Prehistory Association* 6:133–141.

Indrapala, K.
1990 South Indian Mercantile Communities in Ceylon circa 950–1250. In *Sri Lanka and the Silk Road of the Sea,* ed. Senake Bandaranayake, Lorna Dewaraja, Roland Silva, and K. D. G. Wimalaratne, 153–162. Colombo: The Sri Lanka National Commission for UNESCO and the Central Cultural Fund.

Ingrams, Harold
1963 *The Yemen: Imams, Rulers, and Revolutions.* New York: Frederick A. Praeger.

Irish University Press Area Studies Series: British Parliamentary Papers
1972 *China 6: Embassy and Consular Commercial Reports 1854–66.* Shannon: Irish University Press.

Jackson, John Wilfred
1917 *Shells as Evidence of the Migrations of Early Culture.* Manchester: University of Manchester Press.

Jain, Kailash Chand
1972 *Malwa through the Ages.* Delhi: Motilal Banarsidass.

Janse, Olov R. T.
1947 *Archaeological Research in Indo-China.* Vol. 1. *The District of Chiu-Chên during the Han Dynasty, General Considerations and Plates.* Harvard-Yenching Institute Monograph Series, Vol. 7. Cambridge, Mass.: Harvard University Press.
1951 *Archaeological Research in Indo-China.* Vol. 2. *The District of Chiu-Chên during the Han Dynasty, Description and Comparative Study of the Finds.* Harvard-Yenching Institute Monograph Series, Vol. 10. Cambridge, Mass.: Harvard University Press.

Jarrige, Jean-François, and Richard H. Meadow
1980 The Antecedents of Civilization in the Indus Valley. *Scientific American* 244 (8): 122–133.

Jaubert, P. Amédée
1836 *Géographie d'Édrisi.* 2 vols. Paris: L'Imprimerie Royale.

Jensen, Stig
1991 *Ribes Vikinger.* Ribe: Den antikvariske Samling.

Jenyns, R. Soame
1982 *Chinese Art III.* Rev. 2d ed. Ed. William Watson. New York: Rizzoli.

Jhingran, A. G.
1962 Gem Stones of Lesser Importance. *Records of the Geological Survey of India* 90:166–171.

Jones, Antoinette M. Barrett
1984 *Early Tenth Century Java from the Inscriptions: A Study of Economic, Social, and Administrative Conditions in the First Quarter of the Century.* Verhandelingen van het Koninklijk Instituut voor Taal-, Land- en Volkenkunde 107. Dordrecht, Holland/Cinnaminson, N.J.: Foris Publications.

Jönsson, Maibritt, and Pete Hunner
1995 Gold-Foil Beads. In *Glass Beads: Cultural History, Technology, Experiment, and Analogy,* ed. Marianne Rasmussen, Ulla Lund Hansen, and Ulf Näsman, 113–116. Studies in Technology and Culture. Vol. 2. Lejre, Denmark: Historical-Archaeological Experimental Centre.

Joseph, P.

1963 Indian Ivory for Solomon's Throne. *Tamil Culture* 9 (3): 271–280.

Jouveau-Dubreuil, G.

1940 Les ruines Romaines de Pondichery. *BEFEO* 40 (2): 448–450.

Kan, Paddy, and R. K. Liu

1984 Chinese Glass Beadmaking. *Ornament* 8 (2) 38–40, 57.

Kangle, R. P.

1972 *The Kautiliya Arthasastra I.* 2d ed. Delhi: Motilal Banarsidass.

Karklins, Karlis, and Carol F. Adams

1990 Dominique Bussolin on the Glass-Bead Industry of Murano and Venice (1847). *Beads* 2:69–84.

Keane, Webb

1988 Ombres des Hommes et des Espirits: Les *Mamuli* de Sumba/Shadows of Men and Spirits: Mamuli of Sumba. *Tribal Art* 2:3–15. (Bilingual.)

Keeling, William

1905 A Journall of the third Voyage to the East India, set out by the Company of Merchants, Trading in Those Parts: in Which Voyage Were Imployed Three Ships, viz. the Dragon, the Hector, and the Consent, and in Them the Number of Three Hundred and Ten Persons, or Thereabouts: Writtten by William Keeling, Chiefe Commander Thereof. In *Purchas.* Vol. 2, 502–549.

Keller, Peter C., and Wang Fuquan

1987 The Gem Resources of China: The People's Republic's New Focus Is on Gemstone Exploitation. *Terra* 26 (1): 10–14.

Kenoyer, Jonathan Mark

1996 Bead Replicas: An Alternative to Antique Bead Collecting. *Ornament* 20 (2): 66–71.

Kenoyer, Jonathan Mark, Massimo Vidale, and Kuldeep Khan Bhan

1991 Contemporary Stone Bead Making in Khambhat, India: Patterns of Craft Specialization and Organization of Production as Reflected in the Archaeological Record. *World Archaeology* 23 (1): 44–63.

Kessler, Earl, and Shari Kessler

1978 Beads of the Tairona. *Bead Journal* 3 (3/4): 2–5, 81–86.

Khan, Shefaat Ahmad

1926 *Sources for the History of British India in the Seventeenth Century.* London: Oxford University Press.

Khanikoff, N.

1862 Analyses and Extracts of the Book of the Balance of Wisdom: An Arabic Work on the Water-Balance Written by 'Al-Khâzim' in the Twelfth Century. *Journal of the American Oriental Society* 6:1–128.

Kidd, Kenneth E.

1979 *Glass Bead-Making from the Middle Ages to the Early 19th Century.* History and Archaeology 30. Hull: National Historic Parks and Sites Branch, Parks Canada.

Kielhorn, F.

1906 Junagadh Rock Inscription of Rudradaman, the Year 72. *Epigraphia Indica* 8:36–49.

Klamkin, Marian

1976 *Made in Occupied Japan: A Collectors's Guide.* New York: Crown Books.

Koch, Jan, and Torben Sode

n.d. *Glass, Glassbeads, and Glassmakers in Northern India.* Vanlose, Denmark: THOT. (English translation; orig. published in Danish as a number of the magazine *BYGD* in 1994; no number or date appears on the issue.)

Komroff, Manuel

1953 *The Travels of Marco Polo.* The Modern Library 196. New York: Random House.

Kubary, J. S.

1889 *Ethnographische Beiträge zur Kenntnis des Karolinen Archipels.* Leiden: P. W. M. Trap.

Kurinsky, Samuel

1991 *The Glassmakers: An Odyssey of the Jews: The First Three Thousand Years.* New York: Hippocrene Books.

Labbé, Armand J.

1985 *Ban Chiang: Art and Prehistory of Northeast Thailand.* Santa Ana, Calif.: Bowers Museum.

Lad, Gouri

1979 Gems and Jewelled Articles: Chronological and Cultural Dimensions with Special Reference to the Mahabharata. *Indica* 16 (2): 191–200.

Lai, T. C.

1976 *Chinese Seals.* Seattle: University of Washington Press.

Laidler, P. W.

1934 Beads in Africa South of the Zambesi. *Proceedings of the Rhodesia Scientific Association* 34 (1): 1–27.

Lal, B. B.

1952 Examination of Some Ancient Indian Glass Specimens. *Ancient India* 8:17–27.

1962 From the Megalithic to the Harappa: Tracing Back the Graffiti on the Pottery. *Ancient India* 16:4–24 + 43 plates.

1987 Glass Technology in Early India. In *Archaeometry of Glass: Proceedings of the Archaeometry session of the 14th International Congress on Glass, 1986, New Delhi,* ed. H. C. Bhardwaj, 44–56. Calcutta: Indian Ceramic Society/Care; Central Glass and Ceramic Research Institute.

Lam, Peter, ed.

1983 *Archaeological Finds from Han Tombs at Guangzhou and Hong Kong.* Hong Kong: Guangzhou Museum/Art Gallery, Chinese University.

Lamb, Alaistar

1961 Some Glass Beads from Kakao Island, Takuapa, South Thailand. *Federation of Malaya Museums Journal,* n.s., 6:48–55 + plates 81–92, frontispiece.

1964a Miscellaneous Archaeological Discoveries. *JMBRAS* 37 (1): 166–168 + 4 plates.

1964b Takuapa: The Probable Site of a Pre-Malaccan Entrepot in the Malay Peninsula. In *Malayan and Indonesian Studies: Essays Presented to Sir Richard Winstedt on His Eighty-Fifth Birthday,* ed. John Bastin and R. Roolvink, 76–86. Oxford: Clarendon Press.

1964c Notes on Beads from Johor Lama and Kota Tinggi. *JMBRAS* 37 (1): 88–98.

1965a Some Glass Beads from the Malay Peninsula. *Man* 65:36–38.

1965b Some Observations on Stone and Glass Beads in Early South-East Asia. *JMBRAS* 38 (2): 87–124 + 2 plates.

1966a A Note on Glass Beads from the Malay Peninsula. *Journal of Glass Studies* 8:80–94.

1966b Old Middle Eastern Glass in the Malay Peninsula. In *Essays Offered to G. H. Luce.* Vol. 2. *Essays on Asian Art and Archaeology,* ed. Ba Shin, J. Boisselier and A. B. Griswold, 74–88. 2 vols. Ascona, Switzerland: Artibus Asia.

Lambert, Joseph B., Suzanne C. Johnson, Robert T. Parkhurst, and Bennet Bronson

1996 Analysis of Ninth Century Thai Glass. In *Archaeological Chemistry: Organic, Inorganic, and Biochemical Analysis,* ed. Mary Virginia Orna, 10–22. ACS Symposium Series 625. Washington: American Chemical Society.

Lamm, Carl Johan

1939 Glass and Hard Stone Vessels. In *A Survey of Persian Art.* Vol. 3. ed. Arthur Upham Pope and Phyllis Ackerman, 2592–2603. London: Oxford University Press.

Lardner, Dionysius

1832 *A Treatise on the Origin, Progressive Improvement, and Present State of the Manufacture of Porcelain and Glass.* Philadelphia: Carey and Lea.

Latourette, Kenneth Scott

1964 *The Chinese: Their History and Culture.* 4th ed. New York: Macmillan.

Laufer, Berthold

1913 Arabic and Chinese Trade in Walrus and Narwhal Ivory. *T'oung Pao* 14:315–364 (+ addenda by Paul Pelliot, 365–370).

1919 *Sino-Iranica: Chinese Contributions to the History of Civilisation in Ancient Iran with Special Reference to the History of Cultivated Plants and Products.* Field Museum of Natural History Publication 201, Anthropological Series 15 (3). Chicago: Field Museum.

1974 *Jade: A Study in Chinese Archaeology and Religion.* New York: Dover. (Orig. published 1912, Anthropological Series 10, Field Museum, Chicago.)

Le Beck, Henry L.

1799 An Account of the Pearl Fishery in the Gulph of Manar in March and April 1797. Communicated by Dr. Roxburgh. *Asiatic Researches* 5:393–403.

Le Gentil, G.

1779 *Voyage dans les mers de l'Indie fait par ordre du Roi à l'occasion du passage de Venus sur le disque de Soleil le 6 juin 1761 et le 3 du même mois 1769.* Tome 2. Paris: L'Imprimerie Royale.

Le Xuan Diem

1987 Archaeology in South Vietnam Provinces since 1975. *Vietnamese Studies* 23 (16): 50–74.

Lee Shao Chang

1952 *China's Cultural Development* [wall chart]. Princess Anne, Mich.: Michigan State College Press.

Leemans, W. F.

1960 *Foreign Trade in the Old Babylonian Period as Revealed by Texts from Southern Mesopotamia.* Leiden: E. J. Brill.

Legarda, Angelita G.

1977 Antique Beads of the Philippine Islands. *Arts of Asia* 7 (5): 61–70.

Legge, James

1972 *The Chinese Classics with a Translation, Critical and Exegetical Notes, Prolegomena, and Copious Indexes.* 5 vols. Taipei: Wen-she-je chu-ban-she. (Orig. published 1890, Oxford University Press, London, 7 vols.)

Lehman, F. K.

1963 *The Structure of Chin Society: A Tribal People of Burma Adapted to a Non-Western Civilization.* Illinois Studies in Anthropology No. 3. Urbana: The University of Illinois Press.

Leshnik, Lawrence S.

1974 *South Indian 'Megalithic' Burials: The Pandukal Complex.* Wiesbaden: Frans Steiner.

Leur, J. C. van

1955 *Indonesian Trade and Society: Essays in Asian Social and Economic History.* Selected Studies on Indonesia by Dutch Scholars. Vol. 1. The Hague: W. van Hoeve Ltd.

Levtzion, N., and J. F. P. Hopkins

1981 *Corpus of Early Arabic Sources for West African History.* Cambridge: Cambridge University Press.

Lewis, Elaine T.

1994 Beads of the Peoples of the Golden Triangle. Paper read at Bead Expo '94: Glass Beadmaking and Trade, Santa Fe, N.Mex. (Copy available at the Center for Bead Research, Lake Placid, N.Y.)

Lewis, Oscar

1949 *Sea Routes to the Gold Fields: The Migration by Water to California in 1849–1852.* New York: Alfred A. Knopf.

Lien Cheo-mei

1991 The Neolithic Archaeology of Taiwan and the Peinan Excavations. *BIPPA* 11:339–352.

Linschoten, John Huighen van

1905 John Huighen van Linschoten, His Voyage to Goa, and Observations of the East Indies. Abbreviated. In *Purchas.* Vol. 10, 222–318.

Littré, Émile

1961 *Dictionnaire de la Langue Français.* Tome 6. Levallois/Paris: Gallimand/Hachette.

Liu Daofan

1984 Ivory Carving in Ancient China. In *Recent Discoveries in Chinese Archaeology,* ed. Foster Stockwell and Tang Bowen, transl. Zuo Boyang, 59–60. Beijing: Foreign Language Press.

Liu Lai-ch'eng

1978 The Northern Wei Stone Coffin Unearthed at Tinghsien, Hopei Province. In *Chinese Archaeological Abstracts,* ed. Richard C. Rudolph, 308–313. Monumenta Archaeologia 6, Institute of Archaeology. Los Angeles: University of California.

Liu, Robert K.

1975a Chinese Glass Beads and Ornaments. *Bead Journal* 1 (3): 13–28.

1975b Ancient Chinese Glass Beads. *Bead Journal* 2 (2): 9–19.

1975c Cover Story. *Bead Journal* 1 (3): 10–12.

1985 Asian Glass Ornaments: Part I. *Ornament* 8 (4): 15, 25, 28–31.

1986 Followup: Indonesian Glass Beads. *Ornament* 9 (4): 64–65.

1991 Editor's Note. *Ornament* 14 (3): 62.

1995a *Collectible Beads: A Universal Aesthetic.* Vista, Calif.: Ornament.

1995b Ancient Chinese Ornaments: Zhou to Han. *Ornament* 19 (1): 46–55.

Liu Shimin

1991 Waterfront excavations at Dongmenkou, Ningbo, Zhe Jiang Province, PRC; ed. Jeremy Green, transl. Du Genqi. *The International Journal of Nautical Archaeology* 20 (4): 299–311.

Liu Yingsheng

1991 Recent Studies in China on Admiral Zhen He's Navigation. Paper read at International Seminar on Silk Roads: Roads of Dialogue, Malacca. (Copy available at Center for Bead Research, Lake Placid, N.Y.)

Liu Yingsheng and Adrian B. Lapian

1991 San Fu Qi, Its Dependent Port States, and the Trade Among Them (A Study of the Description by Zhao Rukua). Paper read at International Seminar: Harbour Cities along the Silk Roads, Surabaya. (Copy available at Center for Bead Research, Lake Placid, N.Y.)

Lo Jung-Pang

1955 The Emergence of China as a Sea Power during the Late Sung and Early Yuan Periods. *The Far Eastern Quarterly* 14 (4): 489–503.

Lohuizen–de Leeuw, J. E. van

1976 *Iconographic Dictionary of the Indian Religions.* Studies in South Asian Culture, Vol. 5. Leiden: E. J. Brill.

Lokhandwala, M. F.

1970 *An Arabic History of Gujarat.* Baroda: Oriental Institute.

Loofs, H. E. E., and William Watson

1970 The Thai-British Archaeological Expedition: A Preliminary Report on the Second Season, 1964. *Journal of the Siam Society* 48 (2): 67–78.

Loofs-Wissowa, H. H. E.

1980–1981 Prehistoric and Protohistoric Links between the Indochinese Peninsula and the Philippines, as Exemplified by Two Types of Ear-Ornaments. *Journal of the Hong Kong Archaeological Society* 9:57–76.

Luard, C. E., and K. K. Lale

1908 *The Paramaras of Dhar and Malwa.* Bombay: British Indian Press. (Reprinted from *Dhar State Gazetteer.*)

Luce, G. H.

1985 *Phases of Pre-Pagán Burma: Languages and History.* Vol. 1. London: Oxford University Press.

Lugay, Jose B.

1974 Determination of the Methods of Manufacture of Glass Beads. In *Proceedings of the First Regional Seminar on Southeastern Asian Prehistory and Archaeology,* 148–181. Manila: National Museum of the Philippines.

L'Vova, Zlata A.

1970 Les Perles en Verre de Staraja Ladoga. In *Premiere Congrès International d'Archéologie Slav, Warsaw,* 237–246.

Macartney, George

1963 *An Embassy to China, Being the Journal Kept by Lord Macartney during his Embassy to the Emperor Ch'ien-Lung, 1793–1794.* Hamden, Conn.: Anchor Books.

Mackay, Ernst J. H.

1933 Decorated Carnelian Beads. *Man* 33:143–146.

1938 *Further Excavations at Mohenjo-Daro.* 2 vol. Delhi: Manager of Publications.

1943 *Chanhu-Daro Excavations 1935–36.* American Oriental Series 20. New Haven, Conn.: American Oriental Society.

Madina, Maan Z.

1973 *Arabic-English Dictionary of the Modern Literary Language.* New York: Pocket Books.

Mahadevan, Iravatham

1970 The Ancient Name of Arikamēḍu. In *Paritimār Kalaiñar Nūṟṟāṇṭu Viḻā Malar: V. K. Suryanarayana Sastri Centenary Volume,* ed. N. Subrahmanian, 204–206. Madurai.

Major, R. H.

1857 *India in the Fifteenth Century.* Vol. 22. London: Hakluyt Society.

Majumdar, R. C.
1944 *Hindu Colonies in the Far East.* Calcutta: A. K. Majumdar.

Majumdar, R. C., H. C. Raychaudhuri, and Kalikinkar Datta
1978 *An Advanced History of India.* 4th ed. Delhi: S. G. Wasani for Macmillan of India.

Malinowski, Bronislaw
1922 *Argonauts of the Western Pacific: An Account of Native Enterprise and Adventure in the Archipelagoes of Melanesian New Guinea.* London: Routledge & Kegan Paul.

Malleret, Louis
1962a *L'Archéologie du Delta du Mékong. Tome Troisième. La Culture du Fou-Nan, Texte.* 4 vols. Paris: l'École Française d'Extrême-Orient.
1962b *L'Archéologie du Delta du Mékong. Tome Troisième. La Culture du Fou-Nan, Planches.* 4 vols. Paris: l'École Française d'Extrême-Orient.

Maloney, Clarence Thomas
1969 The Effect of Early Coastal Sea Traffic on the Development of Civilization in South India. Ph.D. diss., University of Pennsylvania. Ann Arbor, Mich.: University Microfilms.

Manguin, Pierre-Yves
1987 Etudes Sumatranaises: 1. Palembang et Sriwijaya: Anciennes Hypothèses, Recherches Nouvelles (Palembang Ouest). *BEFEO* 76:337–402.
1992 Le programme de fouilles sur les sites de Sriwijaya (Province de Sumatra-Sud, Indonésie). *BEFEO* 79:272–277.
1993 Palembang and Sriwijaya: An Early Malay Harbour-City Rediscovered. *JMBRAS* 66 (1): 23–46.

Margabandhu, C.
1971 Etched Carnelian Beads from Vidarbha. *Indica* 8 (2): 107–13.
1978 Some Etched Beads and Pendants from Kondapur—Their Cultural and Chronological Significance. *Journal of Indian History* 56 (1): 35–46.
1985 *Archaeology of the Satavahana-Kshatrapa Times.* Delhi: Sundeep Prakashan.

Markham, John
1869–1870 Notes on the Shantung Province, Being a Journey from Chefoo to Tsiuhsien, the City of Mencius. *Journal of the North-China Branch of the Royal Asiatic Society* 6:1–29.

Marshall, John
1931 *Mohenjo-Daro and the Indus Civilization.* 2 vols. London: Arthur Probsthain.
1951 *Taxila: An Illustrated Account of Archaeological Excavations, 1913–34.* Vol. 2. Cambridge: Cambridge University Press.

Martiere d'Anghiera, Pietro
1555 *The Decades of the Newe World or West India,* transl. Richard Eden. March of America Facsimile Series 4. Ann Arbor, Mich.: University Microfilms. (Reprinted 1966.)

Maternova, Vera
1991 The History of the Manufacture of Glass Stones and Costume Jewelry in Bohemia. In *Jewels of Fantasy: Costume Jewelry of the 20th Century,* ed. Deanna Farenti Cera, 371–373. New York: Abrams.

Mathers, William M.
1990 Nuestra Señora de la Concepción. *National Geographic* 178 (3): 38–53.

McCrindle, J. W.
1879 *The Commerce and Navigation of the Erythrean Sea.* Calcutta: Thacker, Spink & Co.
1882 *Ancient India as Described by Ktêsias the Knidian; Being a Translation of the Abridgement of His "Indica" by Phôtios, and of the Fragments of That Work Preserved in Other Writers.* Calcutta: Thanker, Spink & Co. (Reprinted 1973, Manohar Reprints, Delhi.)
1897 *The Christian Topography of Cosmas, an Egyptian Monk.* Ser. i, No. 98. London: Hakluyt Society. (Reprint, Burt Franklin, New York.)
1960 *Ancient India as Described by Megasthenês and Arrian,* ed. R. C. Majumdar. Calcutta: Chuckervertty, Chatterjee & Co. (Orig. published 1877.)

McIntosh, Susan Keech
1995 *Excavations at Jenné-Jeno, Hambarketolo, and Kaniana (Inland Nile Delta, Mali), the 1981 Season.* University of California Publications in Anthropology, Vol. 20. Berkeley: University of California Press.

McIntosh, Susan Keech, and Roderick J. McIntosh

1980 *Prehistoric Investigations in the Region of Jenné, Mali: A Study in the Development of Urbanism in the Sahel, Part i: Archaeological and Historical Background and the Excavations at Jenne-jeno.* 2 vols. Cambridge Monographs in African Archaeology 2, BAR International Series 89(i). Cambridge.

1982 Finding West Africa's Oldest City. *National Geographic* 162 (3): 396–418.

1984 The Early City in West Africa: Towards an Understanding. *African Archaeological Review* 2:73–98.

Mehta, R. N.

1968 *Excavations at Nagara.* Baroda Archaeological Series 10. Baroda: Maharaja Sayajirao University.

1975 Khambhat (Cambay): Topographical, Archaeological, and Toponymical Perspectives. *Journal of Maharaja Sayajirao University, Baroda* 24 (1): 17–28.

Méile, Pierre

1940 Les Yavanas dans l'Inde Tamoule. *Mélanges Asiatiques* [*Journal Asiatiques*] 232:85–123.

Meilink-Roelofsz, M. A. P.

1962 *Asian Trade and European Influence in the Indonesian Archipelago between 1500 and about 1630.* The Hague: Martinus Nijhoff.

Mellaart, James

1979 Egyptian and Near Eastern Chronology: A Dilemma? *Antiquity* 53:6–18.

Mentasti, Rosa Barovier

1980 *Antonio Neri: L'Arte Vetraria 1612.* Milan: Edizioni Il Polifilo.

Mesny

1899 Commercial Notes. *Mesny's Chinese Miscellany* 3 (3): 51–52.

Meyer, Carol

1992 *Glass from Quseir Al-Qadim and the Indian Ocean Trade.* Studies in Ancient Oriental Civilization No. 53. Chicago: The Oriental Institute of the University of Chicago.

Middleton, David

1905 The Voyage of M. David Middleton in the Consent, a Ship of One Hundred and Fifteene Tuns, Which Set Forth from Tilburie Hope, on the Twelfth of March, 1601. In *Purchas.* Vol. 3, 51–60.

Mikoshiba, Misao, and Raymond Bushell

1979 The Sōken Kishō and Ojime. *Arts of Asia* 9 (4): 59–69.

Miksic, John N.

1977 Archaeology and Paleogeography in the Straits of Malacca. In *Economic Exchange and Social Interaction in Southeast Asia: Perspectives from Prehistory, History, and Ethnography,* ed. Karl L. Hutterer, 155–175. Michigan Papers on South and Southeast Asia, 13. Ann Arbor: Center for South and Southeast Asian Studies, University of Michigan.

Miksic, John N., C. T. Yap, and Hua Younan

1994 Archaeology and Early Chinese Glass Trade in Southeast Asia. *Journal of Southeast Asian Studies* 25 (1): 31–46.

Mill, James

1826 *The History of British India.* Vol. 2. London: Badwin, Cradock & Joy.

Miller, J. Innes

1969 *The Spice Trade of the Roman Empire: 29 B.C. to A.D. 641.* Oxford: Clarendon Press.

Mills, J. V. G.

1970 *Ma Huan: Ying-yai Sheng-lan 'The Overall Survey of the Ocean's Shores' [1433].* Hakluyt Society Extra Series No. 42. Cambridge: Cambridge University Press.

Minorsky, V.

1942 *Sharaf al Zamān Tāhir: Marvasī on China, the Turks, and India, Arabic text* (circa *A.D. 1120*). London: Royal Asiatic Society.

Miquel, André

1963 *Al-Muqaddasī: Aḥsan at-Taqāsīm Fī Ma'rifat al-Aqālīm (les Meilleure Répartition pour la Connaissance des Provinces).* Damascus: Institut Français de Damas.

Missionnaires de Pékin

1777 *Mémoires Concernant l'Histoire, les Sciences, les Arts, Les Moeurs, les Usages, &c des Chinois.* Tome Second. Paris: Nyon.

1782 *Mémoires Concernant l'Histoire, les Sciences, les Arts, Les Moeurs, les Usages, &c des Chinois.* Tome Septieme. Paris: Nyon.

Miyamoto, Nobuto

1957 Glass Beads of the Formosan Aborigines. *Minzoku-Gaku Kenkyu (Japanese Journal of Ethnology)* 12 (4): 89–93 (in Japanese, English abstract).

Mohanty, R. K.

1999 A Bead Manufacturing Centre at Mahurjhari, Nagpur District, Maharashtra, India. *BSTN* 33:6–8.

Mohanty, R. K., and P. S. Joshi

1996 The Megalithic Problem of Vidarbha: Retrospect and Prospect. In *Spectrum of Indian Culture: Professor S. R. Deo Felicitation,* Vol. 1, ed. C. Margabandhu and K. S. Ramachandran, 157–169. Delhi: Agam Kala Prakashan.

Mohanty, R. K., and S. R. Walimbe

1996 An Investigation into the Mortuary Practices of Vidarbha Megalithic Cultures. In *Spectrum of Indian Culture: Professor S. R. Deo Felicitation,* Vol. 1, ed. C. Margabandhu and K. S. Ramachandran, 136–149. Delhi: Agam Kala Prakashan.

Molsbergen, E. C. Godee

1925 *Geschiedenis van de Nederlandsch Oost-Indische Compagnie en Nederlandsch-Indië, in Beeld.* Weltevreden: Topografische Inrichting.

Momin, K. N.

1977 Archaeology of the Kheda District (Gujarat) up to 1300 A.D. Ph.D. diss., Maharaja Sayajirao University, Baroda.

Moore, Elizabeth, and U Aung Myint

1993 Beads of Myanmar (Burma): Line Decorated Beads Amongst the Pyu and Chin. *Journal of the Siam Society* 81 (1): 54–87.

Moorti, Udayaravi (Ravi) S.

1984–1985 Socio-Economic Aspects of Megalithic Vidarbha. *Purātattva* 15:56–67.

1994 *Megalithic Culture of South India: Socio-Economic Perspectives.* Varanasi: Ganga Kaveri Publishing House.

Morazzoni, Giuseppe

1953 Le Conterie Veneziane dal Secolo XIII al Secolo XIX. In *Le Conterie Veneziane,* ed. Giuseppe Morazzoni and Michaelangelo Pasquato, 5–74. Venice: Società Veneziana Conterie e Cristallerie.

Morlot, A.

1862 On the Date of the Copper Age in the United States. *Proceedings of the American Philosophical Society* 9:111–114.

1992 On the Date of the Copper Age in the United States, ed. Karlis Karklins. *Beads* 4:39–48.

Morrison, Helen M.

1984 The Beads. In Neville Chittick, *Mande: Excavations at an Island Port on the Kenya Coast,* 181–189. British Institute in Eastern Africa, Memoir No. 9. Nairobi.

1991 The Beads and Seals of Shabwa. *Syria* 58:379–392.

Morrison, Kathleen D.

1997 Commerce and Culture in South Asia: Perspectives from Archaeology and History. *Annual Review of Archaeology* 26:87–108 [page numbers cited in text refer to pagination in WilsonSelect Internet printout, 22 pp.].

Müller, W. Max

1911 Tarshish. In *A Dictionary of the Bible,* Vol. 4, ed. James Hastings, 683–685. New York: Charles Scribner's Sons.

Munan-Oettli, Adelheid

1981 Bead Necklace 1593 in the Sarawak Museum Collection: An Itemized Checklist of 15 Common Sarawak Beads, Based on a Necklace in the Sarawak Museum's Bidayuh Section. *Sarawak Museum Journal* 29:18–26 + 2 plates.

1988 The Southwell Collection of Kayan Beads in the Sarawak Museum (An Annotated Checklist). *Sarawak Museum Journal* 39:105–110 + 1 plate.

Munshi, K. M.

1955 *The Glory That Was Gujaradesa.* Vol. 2. Bombay: Bharatiya Vidya Bhavan.

Münster, Sebastian

1559 *Cosmographiae universalis.* Basel: Henrichum Pettch. (Orig. published 1544 in Latin.)

Muscarella, Oscar White

1977 "Ziwiye" and Ziwiye: The Forgery of a Provenience. *Journal of Field Archaeology* 4 (2): 197–219.

Nagaswamy, R.

1970 Excavation at Korkai, District Thirunelveli. *Damilica* 1:50–54.

1991 Alagankulam: An Indo-Roman Trading Post. In *Indian Archaeological Heritage: K. V. Soundara Rajan Festschrift.* Vol. 1, ed. C. Margabandhu et al., 247–254 + 2 plates. Delhi: Agam Kala Prakashan.

Nainar, S. Muhammad Husayn

1942 *Arab Geographers' Knowledge of Southern India.* Madras: University of Madras.

Na-Nakhonphanom, Somchai

1982 Ban Chiang Painted Pottery. *Arts of Asia* 12 (6): 92–94.

Narain, A. K., and Purushottam Singh

1977 *Excavations at Rajghat (1957–58; 1960–65). Part III. Small Finds.* Varanasi: Banaras Hindu University.

Narayan Rao, D.

1929 *Preliminary Report of the Survey of Cottage Industries—Chitoor.* Cited in Dikshit (1969).

Needham, Joseph

1959 *Science and Civilisation in China.* Vol. 3. Cambridge: Cambridge University Press.

Needham, Joseph [with Wang Ling and Kenneth Girdwood Robinson]

1962 *Science and Civilisation in China.* Vol. 4. *Physics and Physical Technology, Part 1: Physics.* Cambridge: Cambridge University Press.

Needham, Joseph, and Lu Gwei-Djen

1974 *Science and Civilisation in China.* Vol. 5. *Part II.* Cambridge: Cambridge University Press.

Nesbitt, Alexander

1879a *Glass.* South Kensington Museum of Art Handbooks. New York: Scribner & Welford.

1879b *Encyclopaedia Britannica: A Dictionary of Arts, Sciences, and General Literature,* 9th ed., s.v. "glass history."

New York Times

1989 Topics of the Times: Good News for Elephants. *New York Times,* 12 June, 18A.

Newbold, Captain

1846 Summary of the Geology of Southern India: Part X: Newer or Overlapping Trap. *Journal of the Royal Asiatic Society* 9:20–42.

Newsome, J.

1964 *Pliny's Natural History: A Selection from Philemon Holland's Translation.* Oxford: Clarendon Press.

Nguyen Thi Kim Dung

1996 The Trang Kenh Jewellery Workshop Site: An Experimental and Microwear Study. *BIPPA* 14:161–165.

Nicholas, C. W.

1990a The North-West Passage between Ceylon and India. In *Sri Lanka and the Silk Road of the Sea,* ed. Senake Bandaranayake, Lorna Dewaraja, Roland Silva, and K. D. G. Wimalaratne, 271–275. Colombo: The Sri Lanka National Commission for UNESCO and the Central Cultural Fund.

1990b Sinhalese Naval Power. In *Sri Lanka and the Silk Road of the Sea,* ed. Senake Bandaranayake, Lorna Dewaraja, Roland Silva, and K. D. G. Wimalaratne, 281–288. Colombo: The Sri Lanka National Commission for UNESCO and the Central Cultural Fund.

Niebuhr, Carsten

1774 *Description de l'Arabie.* Amsterdam / Utrecht: S. J. Baalde / J. van Schoonhover.

Nieuwenhuis, A. W.

1904 Kunstperlen und Ihre Kulturelle Bedeutung. *Internationales Archiv für Ethnographie* 16:136–154.

Nik Hassan Shuhaimi bin Nik Abdul Rahman

1991 Recent Research at Kuala Selinsing, Perak. *BIPPA* 11:141–152.

Nik Hassan Shuhaimi bin Nik Abdul Rahman and Kamaruddin bin Zakaria

1993 Recent Archaeological Discoveries in Sungai Mas, Kuala Muda, Kedah. *JMBRAS* 66 (2): 73–80.

Nikon, Suthiragsa

1979 The Ban Chiang Culture. In *Early South East Asia: Essays in Archaeology, History, and Historical Geography,* ed. R. B. Smith and W. Watson, 42–52. New York: Oxford University Press.

Nilakanta Sastri, K. A.
1932 A Tamil Merchant-Guild in Sumatra. *Tijdschrift voor Indische Taal-, Land- en Volkenkunde* 72 (3): 314–327.
1935 *The Cōḷas. Vol. 1. To the Succession of Kulōttunga I.* Madras: University of Madras.
1949 Takuapa and Its Tamil Inscription. *JMBRAS* 22 (1): 25–30.
1975 *The Cōḷas.* 2d ed. Madras: University of Madras.
1978 *South India and South-East Asia: Studies in Their History and Culture.* Mysore: Geetha Book House.

Nyandoh, R., and Lucas Chin
1969 A Progress Report on Archaeological Work at Gedong (1967–69). *Sarawak Museum Journal* 17:80–88.

O'Connor, Stanley J., and Tom Harrisson
1971 Gold-foil Burial Amulets in Bali, Philippines and Borneo. *JMBRAS* 44 (1): 71–79 + 5 plates.

Okada, Barbra
1976 Japanese Netsuke and Ojime from the Herman and Paul Jaehne Collection of the Newark Museum. *Newark Museum Quarterly* 27 (1/2): 1–71.

Oppenheim, A. Leo
1970 The Cuneiform Texts. In A. Leo Oppenheim, Robert H. Brill, Dan Barag, and Axel von Saldern, *Glass and Glassmaking in Ancient Mesopotamia: An Edition of the Cuneiform Texts Which Contain Instructions for Glassmakers with a Catalogue of Surviving Objects,* 2–104. Corning, N.Y.: Corning Museum of Glass.

Osborne, Douglas
1958 The Palau Islands: Stepping Stones into the Pacific. *Archaeology* 11 (3): 162–171.

Oxford Annotated Bible
1962 *The Holy Bible: Revised Standard Version Containing the Old and New Testaments,* ed. Herbert G. May and Bruce M. Metzger. New York: Oxford University Press.

Palau Community Action Agency
1976 *A History of Palau. Vol. 1. Traditional Palau; The First Europeans.* Palau Community Action Agency.

Paranavitana, S.
1970 *Inscriptions of Ceylon. Vol. 1. Containing Cave Inscriptions from 3rd Century B.C. to 1st Century A.C. and other Inscriptions in the Early Brāmī Script.* Archaeological Survey of Ceylon. Colombo: Department of Archaeology, Ceylon.
1983 *Inscriptions of Ceylon.* Vol. II. *Part I: Containing Rock and Other Inscriptions from the Reign of Kutakaṇṇa Abhaya (41 B.C.–19 B.C.) to Bhātiya II (140–164 A.D.).* Archaeological Survey of Ceylon, Department of Archaeology, Ceylon. Moratuwa: University Press.

Pascoe, Edwin H.
1973 *A Manual of the Geology of India and Burma.* Vol. 3. 3d ed. Delhi: Government of India.

Pattabiramin, P. Z.
1946 *Les fouilles d'Arikamedu (Podouké).* Pondichéry/Paris: Bibliothèque Coloniale/Presses Universitaires des France.

Paxton, John
1977 *The Statesman's Yearbook: Statistical and Historical Annual of the States of the World for the Year 1977–1978.* New York: St. Martin's Press.

Peacock, B. A. V.
1979 The Later Prehistory of the Malay Peninsula. In *Early South East Asia: Essays in Archaeology, History, and Historical Geography,* ed. R. B. Smith and W. Watson, 199–214. New York: Oxford University Press.

Peck, Harry Thurston, ed.
1962 *Harper's Dictionary of Classical Literature and Antiquities.* New York: Cooper Square Publishers.

Pelliot, Paul
1903 Le Fou-Nan. *BEFEO* 3:248–303.

Peralta, Jesus T.
1983 Prehistoric Gold Ornaments from the Central Bank of the Philippines. *Arts of Asia* 13 (4): 51–55.

Perera, B. J.
1951 The Foreign Trade and Commerce of Ancient Ceylon I—The Ports of Ancient Ceylon. *The Ceylon Historical Journal* 1 (2): 109–119.

Petrie, W. M. Flinders
1911 Stones, Precious. In *A Dictionary of the Bible,*

Vol. 4, ed. James Hastings, 619–621. New York: Charles Scribner's Sons.

Pettijohn, F. J.

1977 *Sedimentary Rocks.* New Delhi: Oxford and IBH Publishing Co. (3d Indian reprint of 2d ed. by Harper & Brothers).

Pieris, P. E.

1921 Nágadípa and Buddhist Remains in Jaffna. *Journal of the Ceylon Branch of the Royal Asiatic Society 1919* 28 (72, parts 1, 2, 3, 4): 40–67.

Pigafetta, Antonio

1905 Of Fernandus Magalianes: the Occasion of His Voyage, and the Particulars of the Same, with the Compassing of the World by the Ship Called San Victoria: Gathered Out of Antonio Pigafetta, an Italian of Vicenza, Who Was One in the Said Circum-Navigation, as Also from Divers Other Authors. In *Purchas.* Vol. 2, 84–199.

Pilditch, Jacqueline S.

1992 The Glass Beads of Ban Bon Neon, Central Thailand. *Asian Perspectives* 31:171–181.

Pimenta, Nicholas, and Others

1905 Indian Observations Gathered Out of the Letters of Nicolas Pimenta, Visiter of the Jesuites in India, and of Many Others of that Societie, Written from Divers Indian Regions; Principally Relating the Countries and Accidents of the Coast of Coromandel, and of Pegu. In *Purchas.* Vol. 10, 205–222.

Pinder-Wilson, Ralph

1970 Glass in Asia during the T'ang Period. *Colloquies on Art and Archaeology in Asia* 1:62–70.

Pirazzoli-t'Serstevens, Michèle

1974 *La Civilisation du Royaume de Dian a l'Époque Han d'après le matériel exhumé à Shizhai shan (Yunnan).* Publications de l'École Française d'Extrême-orient 94. Paris: École Française d'Extrême-orient.

Pokorny, Julius

1927 *Aloiswalde Vergleichendes Wörterbuch der Indogermanischen Sprachen: Herausgegeben und bearbeitet.* Band 2. Berlin: Walter de Gruyter & Co.

Posnansky, Merrick

1971 Ghana and the Origin of West African Trade. *Africa Quarterly* 9 (2): 110–125.

1973 Aspects of Early West African Trade. *World Archaeology* 5 (2): 149–162.

Post, G. E.

1911 Peacocks. In *A Dictionary of the Bible,* Vol. 3, ed. James Hastings, 733. New York: Charles Scribner's Sons.

Prasad, Prakash Charan

1977 *Foreign Trade and Commerce in Ancient India.* New Delhi: Abhinav.

Pretty, Francis

1905 The Third Circum-Navigation of the Globe: Or the Admirable and Prosperous Voyage of Master Thomas Candish of Trimley in the Countie of Suffolke Esquire, into the South Sea, and from Thence Round about the Circumference of the Whole Earth, Begun in the Yeere of Our Lord 1586, and Finished 1588. Written by Master Francis Pretty Lately of Ey in Suffolke, a Gentleman Employed in the Same Action, Published by Master Hakluyt, and Now Corrected and Abbreviated. In *Purchas.* Volume 2, 149–187.

Price, Ira M.

1911 Ophir. In *A Dictionary of the Bible,* Vol. 3, ed. James Hastings, 626–628. New York: Charles Scribner's Sons.

Prickett-Fernando, Martha

1990 Mantai-Mahatittha: The Great Port and Entrepot in the Indian Trade. In *Sri Lanka and the Silk Road of the Sea,* ed. Senake Bandaranayake, Lorna Dewaraja, Roland Silva, and K. D. G. Wimalaratne, 115–121. Colombo: The Sri Lanka National Commission for UNESCO and the Central Cultural Fund.

Ptak, Roderich

1998 From Quanzhou to the Sulu Zone and Beyond: Questions Related to the Early Fourteenth Century. *Journal of Southeast Asian Studies* 29 (2): 269–294 [page numbers cited in text refer to pagination in WilsonSelect Internet printout, 27 pp.].

Purchas, Samuel

1905 Of the Popes Bull Made to Castile, Touching the New World. In *Purchas,* Vol. 2, 32–64.

Raats, J.

1958 Römisch-ägyptisch Glasperlen im Ngada-Gebiet auf Flores. *Anthropos* 53:1023–1024.

Rackham, H.

1942 *Pliny Natural History.* Vol. 2, Libri 3–7. Loeb Classical Library. Cambridge, Mass./London: Harvard University Press/William Heinemann.

Rajan, K

1990 New Light on the Megalithic Culture of the Kongu Region, Tamil Nadu. *Man and Environment* 15 (1): 93–102.

1997–1998 Traditional Bead Making Industry in Tamil Nadu. *Purātattva* 28:59–63.

1998 Archaeology of the South Arcot Region with Special Reference to Megalithic Burial Complexes. *Man and Environment* 23 (1): 93–105.

Ram, Sadhu

1962 Grant of Maharajakula Jaitrasimhadeva, VS 1347. *Epigraphia Indica* 32:220–228.

Ramachandran, K. S.

1996 Yavanas and the Ancient Tamils. In *Spectrum of Indian Culture: Professor S. R. Deo Felicitation,* Vol. 1, ed. C. Margabandhu and K. S. Ramachandran, 244–249. Delhi: Agam Kala Prakashan.

1996–1997 Alagankulam an Indo-Roman Port: A Critique. *Purātattva* 27:19–24.

Raman, K. V.

1975 Karaikadu. *Indian Archaeology 1966–67—A Review:* 21.

1991 Further Evidence of Roman Trade from Coastal Sites in Tamil Nadu. In *Rome and India: The Ancient Sea Trade,* ed. Vimala Begley and Richard Daniel De Puma, 125–133. Madison: University of Wisconsin Press.

Rangacharya, V.

1985 *A Topographical List of the Inscriptions of the Madras Presidency (Collected Till 1915) with Notes and References.* Vol. 1. New Delhi: Asian Educational Services. (Orig. published 1919.)

Rao, S. R.

1969 Kaviripaṭṭnam Excavations. In *Archaeological Society of South India, 7th Transactions (1962–65),* 161–165.

1973 *Lothal and the Indus Civilization.* New York: Asia Publishing House.

Ratnagar, Shereen

1990 Dealings with Strangers. *BDC(P)RI* 49:347–356.

Ray, Himanshu Prabha

1996 Early Trans-Oceanic Contacts between South and Southeast Asia. In *Ancient Trades and Cultural Contacts in Southeast Asia,* ed. Amara Srisuchat, 43–53. Bangkok: Office of the National Cultural Commission.

Read, Herbert

1942 *Encyclopaedia Britannica,* 14th ed., s.v. "stained glass."

Reade, Julian

1979 *Early Etched Beads and the Indus-Mesopotamian Trade.* Occasional Paper No. 2. London: British Museum.

Reinecke, Andreas

1996 Bi-cephalous Animal-Shaped Ear Pendants in Vietnam. *BSTN* 28:5–8.

Rihani, Ameen

1930 *Arabian Peak and Desert.* Boston: Houghton Mifflin.

Ritcher, Gisela M. A.

1971 *Engraved Gems of the Romans: A Supplement to the History of Roman Art, Part II: The Engraved Gems of the Greeks, Etruscans, and Romans.* New York: Phaidon.

Ritchie, Patrick D.

1937 Spectrographic Studies on Ancient Glass: Chinese Glass from Pre-Han to T'ang Times. *Technical Studies in the Field of Fine Arts* 5 (4): 209–220.

Rjabinin, Evgenij A., and Valentin A. Galibin

1995 New Data Concerning Early Glass Beadmaking in Ladoga (in the 8th to 10th Centuries A.D.). In *Glass Beads: Cultural History, Technology, Experi-*

ment, and Analogy, ed. Marianne Rasmussen, Ulla Lund Hansen, and Ulf Näsman, 109–112. Studies in Technology and Culture. Vol. 2. Lejre, Denmark: Historical-Archaeological Experimental Centre.

Robert, Paul

1966 *Dictionnaire alphabétique et analogique de la Langue Française.* Tome 5. Paris: Société de Nouveau Littré Le Robert.

Robinson, K. R.

1961a Zimbabwe Beads. In Zimbabwe Excavations 1958, Vol. 3. *Occasional Papers of the National Museum of Southern Rhodesia* 23A: 227–235.

1961b An Early Iron-Age Site from the Chibi District, Southern Rhodesia. *South African Archaeological Bulletin* 16:75–102.

1963 Further Excavations in the Iron Age Deposits at the Tunnel Site, Gokomere Hill, Southern Rhodesia. *South African Archaeological Bulletin* 18:155–171.

Rockhill, W. W.

1915 Notes on the Relations and Trade of China with the Eastern Archipelago and the Coast of the Indian Ocean during the Fourteenth Century, Part II. *T'oung Pao* 16:61–159, 234–271, 374–392, 435–467, 604–626.

Rodziewicz, Mieczyslaw

1984 *Alexandrie III: Les Habitations Romains Tardives D'Alexandrie à la lumière des fouilles polonaises à Kôm el-Dikka.* Varsovie: Editions Scientifiques de Pologne.

Roe, Thomas

1905 Observations Collected Out of the Journall of Sir Thomas Roe, Knight, Lord Embassadour from His Majestie of Great Britaine, to the Great Mogol: Of Matters Occurring Worthy Memory in the Way, and in the Mogols Court. His Customes, Cities, Countryes, Subjects, and other Indian Affairs. In *Purchas.* Vol. 4, 310–468.

Rösch, Cordelia, Rainer Hock, Ulrich Schüssler, Paul Yule, and Anne Hannibal

1997 Electron Microprobe Analysis and X-Ray Diffraction Methods in Archaeology: Investigations on Ancient Beads from the Sultanate of Oman and from Sri Lanka. *European Journal of Mineralogy* 9:763–783.

Rosen, Lissie von

1988 *Lapis Lazuli in Geological Contexts and in Ancient Written Sources.* Studies in Mediterranean Archaeology and Literature, Pocket-book 65. Partille, Sweden: Paul Cströms.

Rostovtzeff, M.

1957 *The Social and Economic History of the Roman Empire.* 2d ed. Rev. P. M. Fraser. Oxford: Clarendon Press.

Roth, Henry Ling

1968 *The Natives of Sarawak and British North Borneo.* Vol. 2. Kuala Lumpur: University of Malaya Press. (Orig. published 1896.)

Rouffaer, G. P.

1899 Waar Kwamen de Raadselachtige Moetisalah's (Aggri-Kralen) in de Timor-Groep Oorspronkelijk van Daan? *Bijdragen tot de Taal-, Land- en Volkenkunde van Nederlandsch-Indië* 50:409–675.

Roux, Valentine, and Jacques Pelegrin

1988–1989 Knapping Techniques and Craft Specialization: An Ethnoarchaeological Investigation in Gujarat. *Purātattva* 19:50–59.

Rowlands, Michael, Mogans Larsen, and Kristian Kristiansen, eds.

1987 *Centre and Periphery in the Ancient World.* Cambridge: Cambridge University Press.

Rowlett, Ralph M., Margaret D. Mandeville, and Edward J. Zeller

1974 The Interpretation and Dating of Humanly Worked Siliceous Materials by Thermoluminescent Analysis. *Proceedings of the Prehistoric Society,* n.s., 40:37–44.

Russell, Fr.

1793 *A Short History of the East India Company.* London: John Sewell & John Debrett.

Rutnin, Somsuda, and Pthomrerk Ketudhat

1983 The 1983 Test Excavation at Khlong Thom: An Interim Report. Privately circulated. (Copy available at the Center for Bead Research, Lake Placid, N.Y.)

Sainsbury, Ethel Bruce

1907 *A Calendar of the Court Minutes etc. of the East India Company 1635–1639.* Oxford: Clarendon Press.

1909 *Minutes 1640–1643.* Oxford: Clarendon Press.

1912 *Minutes 1644–1649.* Oxford: Clarendon Press.

1913 *Minutes 1650–1654.* Oxford: Clarendon Press.

1932 *Minutes 1671–1673.* Oxford: Clarendon Press.

Saitowitz, Sharma Jeanette

1994 The Archaeometry of Glass Beads and Trade between Southern Africa, Egypt and India A.D. 900–1220: A Pilot Study. Paper read at World Archaeology 3 Conference, Delhi. (Copy available at Center for Bead Research, Lake Placid, N.Y.)

Saitowitz, Sharma J., David L. Reid, and N. J. van der Merwe

1996 Glass Bead Trade from Islamic Egypt to South Africa c. AD 900–1250. *South African Journal of Science* 92:101–103.

Salisbury, Amy, and Ian Glover

1997 New Analyses of Early Glass from Thailand and Vietnam. *BSTN* 30:7–14.

Sankalia, Hasmukh Dhirajlal

1945 A Brief Summary of "Studies in Historical Geography and Cultural Ethnology of Gujarat." *Journal of the Gujarat Research Society* 7 (4): 145–163.

1974 *The Prehistory and Protohistory of India and Pakistan.* 2d ed. Poona: Deccan College.

Sankalia, Hasmukh Dhirajlal, and Moreshwar Gangadhar Dikshit

1952 *Excavations at Brahmapuri (Kolhapur) 1945–46.* Deccan College Monograph Series 5. Poona: Deccan College.

Saris, John

1905 The Voyage of Captaine Saris in the Cloave, to the Ile of Japan, What Befell in the Way: Observations of the Dutch and Spaniards in the Molocca's. In *Purchas.* Volume 3, 408–519.

Sauzay, A.

1868 *La verrerie depuis les temps les plus reculés jusqu'à nos jours.* Bibliothèque des Merveilles. Paris: Librairie de L. Hachette et Cie.

Sax, Margaret

1996 Recognition and Nomenclature of Quartz Materials with Specific Reference to Engraved Gemstones. *Jewellery Studies* 7:63–72.

Sax, M., and A. P. Middleton

1992 A System of Nomenclature for Quartz and Its Application to the Material of Cylinder Seals. *Archaeometry* 34 (1): 11–20.

Sayre, Edward V., and Ray W. Smith

1967 Some Materials of Glass Manufacturing in Antiquity. In *Archaeological Chemistry: A Symposium,* ed. Martin Levey, 279–311. Philadelphia: University of Pennsylvania Press.

Schafer, Edward H.

1952 The Pearl Fisheries of Ho-p'u. *JAOS* 72:155–168.

1957 Rosewood, Dragon's Blood, and Lac. *JAOS* 77:129–136.

1963 *The Golden Peaches of Samarkand: A Study of T'ang Exotics.* Berkeley: University of California Press.

Schefer, Charles

1970 *Sefer Nameh: Relation du Voyage de Nassiri Khosrau.* Amsterdam: Philo Press.

Scholes, Samuel R., and Charles H. Greene

1975 *Modern Glass Practice.* Taipei: Central Book Co.

Schurz, William Lytle

1939 *The Manila Galleon.* New York: E. P. Dutton & Co. (Reprint).

Seidel, Brigitte

2000 Some Remarks on Polychrome Chinese Glass of the Fourteenth Century in Southeast China. *BSTN* 35:3–5.

Seligman, C. G., and H. C. Beck

1938 Far Eastern Glass: Some Western Origins. *The Museum of Far Eastern Antiquities (Östasiatiska Samlingarna) Stockholm Bulletin* 10:1–64 + 16 plates.

Sen, Surendranath

1949 *Indian Travels of Thevenot and Careri.* New Delhi: National Archives of India.

Seneviratne, Sudharshan

1984 The Archaeology of the Megalithic—Black and Red Ware Complex in Sri Lanka. *Ancient Ceylon* 5:237–307.

Shamasastri, R.
1915 *Kautilya's Arthasastra.* Bangalore: Government Press.

Shastri, Manmatha Nath Dutt
1968 *The Garuda-Purāṇa*. Varanasi: Chowkhamba Sanskrit Series Office.

Shende, N. J.
1949 The Foundations of the Atharvaṇic Religion. *BDCRI* 9 (3/4): 197–414.

Shi Meiguang, Qu Changzhi, Zhang Riqing, Li Minsheng, and An Jiayao
1987 A Report on the Examination of Early Chinese Glass. Transl. Matthew Henderson. *Oriental Ceramic Society Translations* (Hong Kong) 12:40–46.

Sibree, James, and Frank Richardson Cana
1942 *Encyclopaedia Britannica,* 14th ed., s.v. "Madagascar, history."

Sidebotham, Steven E.
1991 Ports of the Red Sea and the Arabia-India Trade. In *Rome and India: The Ancient Sea Trade,* ed. Vimala Begley and Richard Daniel De Puma, 12–38. Madison: University of Wisconsin Press.

Silva, Roland, and Jan Bouzek
1990 Mantai—A Second Arikamedu: A Note on Roman Finds. In *Sri Lanka and the Silk Road of the Sea,* ed. Senake Bandaranayake, Lorna Dewaraja, Roland Silva, and K. D. G. Wimalaratne, 123–124. Colombo: The Sri Lanka National Commission for UNESCO and the Central Cultural Fund.

Simkin, C. G. F.
1968 *The Traditional Trade of Asia.* London: Oxford University Press.

Singh, Ravindra N.
1980–1981 The Antiquity of Gold-Glasses in India. *Purātattva* 12:157–159.

Sinkankas, John
1969 *Mineralogy: A First Course.* New York/New Delhi: Van Nostrand Reinhold/East-West.

Siriweera, W. I.
1990 Precolonial Sri Lanka's Maritime Commerce with Special Reference to Its Ports. In *Sri Lanka and the Silk Road of the Sea,* ed. Senake Bandaranayake, Lorna Dewaraja, Roland Silva, and K. D. G. Wimalaratne, 125–133. Colombo: The Sri Lanka National Commission for UNESCO and the Central Cultural Fund.

Sleen, W. G. N. van der
1956a Trade Wind Beads. *Man* 56:27–29.
1956b Description of a Lot of Beads Known as the Garner Collection from Johore Lama Malaya. (Typescript, Museum of Anthropology and Archaeology, Cambridge University, Cambridge, U.K.)
1958 Ancient Glass Beads with Special Reference to the Beads of East and Central Africa and the Indian Ocean. *Journal of the Royal Anthropological Institute of Great Britain and Ireland* 88:203–216 + 1 plate.
1966 Trade Wind Beads. *Man,* n.s., 1:244.
1967 *A Handbook on Beads.* Liège: L'Association Internationale pour l'Histoire du Verre, Musée du Verre.
1973 *A Handbook on Beads.* Liège: Librairie Halbart.
n.d. *A Handbook on Beads.* York, Pa.: Liberty Cap Books.

Smith, DeVerne Reed
1983 *Palauan Social Structure.* New Brunswick, N.J.: Rutgers University Press.

Smith, J. D. Main
1942 *Encyclopaedia Britannica,* 14th ed., s.v. "cobalt."

Smith, Marvin T.
1983 Chronology from Glass Beads: The Spanish Period in the Southeast, 1513–1670. In *Proceedings of the 1982 Glass Trade Bead Conference,* ed. Charles F. Hayes III, 147–158. Rochester, N.Y.: Rochester Museum and Science Center.

Smith, Marvin T., and Mary Elizabeth Good
1982 *Early Sixteenth Century Glass Beads in the Spanish Colonial Trade.* Greenwood, Miss.: Cottonlandia Museum.

Solheim, Wilhelm G., II
1959 Sa-Huynh Related Pottery in Southeast Asia. *Asian Perspectives* 3:177–188.
1981 Philippine Prehistory. In Gabriel Casal, Regalado Trota Jose Jr., Eric S. Casino, George R. Ellis, and Wilhelm G. Solheim II, *The People and Art of the*

Philippines, 17–83. Los Angeles: Museum of Cultural History, University of California.

1983 Archaeological Research in Sarawak, Past and Present. *Sarawak Museum Journal* 32:35–58.

Solovev, Sergei

1998 Archaic Berezan: Historical-Archaeological Essay. In *The Greek Colonisation of the Black Sea Area: Historical Interpretation of Archaeology,* ed. Gocha R. Tsetskhladze, 205–225. Historia Einzelschriften 121. Stuttgart: Franz Steiner.

Soundara Rajan, K. V.

1996 Identifying the Megalith-Builders in India—Some Factors. In *Spectrum of Indian Culture: Professor S. R. Deo Felicitation,* Vol. 1, ed. C. Margabandhu and K. S. Ramachandran, 131–135. Delhi: Agam Kala Prakashan.

Sørensen, Per

1957 *Archaeological Excavations in Thailand.* Vol. 2. *Ban-Kao.* Copenhagen: Munksgaard.

SPAFA

1979 *SPAFA Final Report: Consultative Workshop on Archaeological and Environmental Studies on Srivijaya—Bangkok.* Bangkok: SEAMEO Project in Archaeology and Fine Arts (SPAFA).

1982 *SPAFA Final Report: Consultative Workshop on Archaeological and Environmental Studies on Srivijaya—Bangkok.* Bangkok: SEAMEO Project in Archaeology and Fine Arts (SPAFA).

1983 *SPAFA Final Report: Consultative Workshop on Archaeological and Environmental Studies on Srivijaya (T-W3), Bangkok, and South Thailand, March 29–April 11, 1983.* Bangkok: SEAMEO Project in Archaeology and Fine Arts (SPAFA).

1985 *SPAFA Final Report: Consultative Workshop on Archaeological and Environmental Studies on Srivijaya (I-W2b), Jakarta, Padang, Prapet, and Medan, Indonesia, September 16–30, 1985.* Bangkok: SEAMEO Project in Archaeology and Fine Arts (SPAFA).

Sprague, Roderick

1992 The Chinese Bead Trade. Paper read at The Bead Trade in the Americas Conference, Santa Fe, N.Mex.

Sprague, Roderick, and An Jiayao

1990 Observations and Problems in Researching the Contemporary Glass-Bead Industry of Northern China. *Beads* 2:5–13.

Srisuchat, Amara

1987 Archaeology of the Andaman Sea: Old and New Data. *Silpakorn Journal* 31 (3): 15–27 (in Thai).

1989 Talking with the Experts, Bennet Bronson and Pisit Charoenwongsa: "The Silk Road of the Sea" Questions and Answers about the 1989 Excavations at Koh Kho Khao and Laem Pho. *Silpakorn Journal* 33 (1): 34–37.

1996a *Ancient Trades and Cultural Contacts in Southeast Asia* (editor). Bangkok: Office of the National Cultural Commission.

1996b Merchants, Merchandise, Markets: Archaeological Evidence in Thailand Concerning Maritime Trade Interaction Between Thailand and Other Countries Before the 16th Century A.D. In *Ancient Trades and Cultural Contacts in Southeast Asia,* ed. Amara Srisuchat, 237–266. Bangkok: Office of the National Cultural Commission.

Srisuchat, Tarapong

1989 Beads Reflecting Foreign Influence from Archaeological Sites in Thailand. *Silpakorn Journal* 33 (1): 4–19.

Stanley, Henry E. J.

1866 *A Description of the Coasts of East Africa and Malabar by Duarte Barbosa.* Vol. 35. London: Hakluyt Society.

Stern, E. Marianne

1987 The secret of Papanaidupet. *Glastechnische Berichte* 60:346–351.

1991 Early Roman Export Glass in India. In *Rome and India: The Ancient Sea Trade,* ed. Vimala Begley and Richard Daniel De Puma, 113–124. Madison: University of Wisconsin Press.

Sternbach, Ludwick

1955 Gujarat as Known to Medieval Europe [Part II]. *Bharatiya Vidya* 15 (2): 41–152.

Stevens, William K.

1990 Britain Exempts Hong Kong From Ivory Ban. *New York Times,* 23 January, 5C.

Stevenson, Edward Luther
1991 *Claudius Ptolemy: The Geography.* New York: Dover. (Orig. published 1932, New York Public Library.)
Streeter, Patrick
1996 Edwin Streeter's Pearling Expeditions. *Jewellery Studies* 7:41–46.
Stuart, P.
1991 *De Tabula Peutingeriana: De Kaart.* Nijmegen: Museumstukken II, Museum Kam.
Subbarayappa, B.V.
1981 Cultural contours of iron in ancient India. *Science Today* (September): 8–10.
Subramanian, R.
1950 Analysis of Ancient Glass Beads. *Current Science* 19:19–20.
Subramoniam, V. I.
1961 Dravidian Words in Sanskrit. *Tamil Culture* 9 (3): 291–300.
Suchitta, Pornchai
1984 Evidence of Early Contact Between Thailand and Neighboring Countries. In *SPAFA Consultative Workshop on Research on Maritime Shipping and Trade Networks in Southeast Asia (I-W7),* 151–159. Cisarua, Indonesia.
Summers, Augustus
1851 An Account of the Agate and Carnelian Trade of Cambay. *JBBRAS* 3:318–327.
Sun E-Tu Zen and Sun Shiou-Chuan
1966 *T'ien-Kung K'ai-Wu: Chinese Technology in the Seventeenth Century by Sung Ying-Hsing.* University Park, Pa.: Pennsylvania State University Press.
Surleau, Raymond
1943 Rapport sur le Fouctionnement du Service des Travaux Publics pendant l'Année 1942. Establissements Français dans L'Inde, Service des Travaux Publics, Pondichéry. (Typescript in Pondicherry Museum; copy available at the Center for Bead Research, Lake Placid, N.Y.)
1946 Rapport sur le Fouctionnement du Service des Travaux Publics pendant l'Année 1943. Establissements Français dans L'Inde, Service des Travaux Publics, Pondichéry. (Typescript in Pondicherry Museum; copy available at the Center for Bead Research, Lake Placid, N.Y.)

Tagore, Sourindeo Mohun
1879 *Mani-Mala or a Treatise on Gems.* Vol. 2. Calcutta: I. C. Bose.
Taha, Adi bin Haji
1987 Recent Archaeological Discoveries in Peninsular Malaysia (1983–1985). *JMBRAS* 60 (1): 27–44.
Takakusu, J.
1929–1930 Le Voyage De Kanshin en Orient (742–754) par Aomi-no Mabito Genkai (779), part 2. *BEFEO* 27:441–472 (3 parts).
1966 *A Record of the Buddhist Religion as Practiced in India and the Maya Archipelago (A.D. 671–695) by I-Tsing.* Delhi: Munshriam Manoharlal.
Tampoe, Moira
1990 Tracing the Silk Road of the Sea: Ceramic and Other Evidence from the Partner Ports of the Western Indian Ocean (8th–10th c. A.D.). In *Sri Lanka and the Silk Road of the Sea,* ed. Senake Bandaranayake, Lorna Dewaraja, Roland Silva, and K. D. G. Wimalaratne, 85–104. Colombo: The Sri Lanka National Commission for UNESCO and the Central Cultural Fund.
Tan Teong Hing and Abdul Rahim Hj. Samsudin
1990 Gem and Rock Artifacts at Pulau Kelumpang, Perak. *Jurnal Arkeologi Malaysia* 3:15–24.
Team for Technical Research at the Beijing Jade Factory
1985 Some Preliminary Remarks on the Jade Carving Techniques of the Shang Dynasty. In *Chinese Archaeological Abstracts,* Vol. 2, ed. Albert E. Dien, Jeffrey K. Riegel, and Nancy T. Price, 413–417. Monumenta Archaeologica 9. Los Angeles: Institute of Archaeology, University of California. (Orig. published 1976, *Kaogu.*)
Temple, Robert
1986 *The Genius of China: 3,000 Years of Science, Discovery, and Invention.* New York: Simon & Schuster.

Terry, Edward
1905 A Relation of a Voyage to the Easterne India. Observed by Edward Terry, Master of Arts and Student of Christ-Church in Oxford. In *Purchas*. Vol. 9, 1–54.

Theal, George McCall
1898 *Records of South-Eastern Africa*. Cape Town: Government of the Cape Colony. (Reprinted 1964, C. Struik, Cape Town, 9 vols.)

Theunissen, Robert
1997 Agate and Carnelian Ornaments from Noen U-Loke, an Iron-Age Settlement in Northeast Thailand. *BSTN* 30:4–7.

Theunissen, Robert, and Peter Grave
1998 Elemental Characterisation of Agate and Carnelian Ornaments from Iron-Age Southeast Asia: A Preliminary Investigation of Their Assumed Indian Origin. Paper read at the 16th Congress of the Indo-Pacific Prehistory Association, Melaka, Malaysia. (Copy available at Center for Bead Research, Lake Placid, N.Y.)

Theunissen, Robert, Peter Grave, and Grahame Bailey
2000 Doubts on Diffusion: Challenging the Assumed Indian Origin of Iron Age Agate and Carnelian Beads in Southeast Asia. *World Archaeology* 32 (1): 84–105.

Thiel, Barbara
1986–1987 Excavations at Arku Cave, Northeast Luzon, Philippines. *Asian Perspectives* 27:229–264.

Thierry, Solange
1961 Inventaire des Perles de Fouilles à Madagascar. *Bulletin de L'Académie Malgache*, n.s., 37:101–141.

Thijssen-Etpison, Mandy
n.d. *Palau: Portrait of Paradise*. Koror, Palau: NECO Marine.

Thomassey, P., and R. Mauny
1951 Campagne de fouilles à Koumbi Saleh. *Bulletin IFAN* 13 (2): 438–462.
1956 Campagne de fouilles de 1950 à Koumbi Saleh (Ghana?). *Bulletin IFAN* 18 (1–2): 117–140.

Thorpe, W. A.
1935 *English Glass*. London: A. & C. Black.

Tibbetts, G. R.
1979 *A Study of the Arabic Texts Containing Material on South-East Asia*. Oriental Translation Fund, n.s., 44. Leiden: E. J. Brill.

Tiele, P. A.
1885 *The Voyage of John Huyghen Van Linschoten to the East Indies*. Vol. 2. Ser. i, No. 71. London: Hakluyt Society.

Tobler, Arthur J.
1950 *Excavations at Tepe Gawra*. Vol. 2. Philadelphia: University Museum, University of Pennsylvania.

Tod, James
1971 *Travels in Western India*. Delhi: Oriental Publications. (Reprint).

Todd, J. M.
1993 The Continuity of Amber Artifacts in Ancient Palestine: From the Bronze Age to the Byzantine. In *Amber in Archaeology: Proceedings of the Second International Conference on Amber in Archaeology, Liblice 1990*, ed. Curt W. Beck and Jan Bouzek, 236–248. Prague: Institute of Archaeology.

Tokyo National Museum
1978 *Tōyō kodai garasu: Ancient Glass from Orient February 7–March 12, 1978* [catalog]. Tokyo: Tokyo National Museum.

Tornati, M., and W. G. N. van der Sleen
1960 L'analisi chimica aiuta l'archeologia. *Vetro e Silicati* 4 (23): 14–24.

Tosi, Maurizio
1999 Turning to the Sea: The Beginnings of Ocean Exploitation in Eastern Arabia. Paper read at the Fifteenth International Conference on South Asian Archaeology, Leiden.

Trivedi, R. K.
1964 *Agate Industry of Gujarat. The Census of India 1961, V, pt. VII A (2)*. Delhi: Manager of Publications.

Trowbridge, Mary L.
1930 *Philological Studies in Ancient Glass*. University of Illinois Studies in Language and Literature 13 (3/4). Urbana: University of Illinois.

Turner, W. E. S.
1956a Studies in Ancient Glasses and Glassmaking Processes. Part III. The Chronology of the Glass-making Constituents. *JSGT* 40:39T–52T.
1956b Studies in Ancient Glasses and Glassmaking Processes. Part IV. The Chemical Composition of Ancient Glasses. *JSGT* 40:162T–186T.
1959 Studies in Ancient Glasses and Glassmaking Processes. Part VI. The Composition and Physical Characteristics of the Glasses of the Portland Vase. *JSGT* 43:262T–284T.

Urban, Stanislav
n.d. *Jablonec Costume Jewelry: An Historical Outline.* Prague: Orbis.

Vanacker, Claudette
1984 Perles de Verre Découvertes sur le site de Tegdaoust (Mauritanie orientale). *Journal des Africanistes* 54 (2): 31–52.
Vandiver, Pamela
1983 Glass Technology at the Mid-Second-Millennium B.C. Hurrian Site of Nuzi. *Journal of Glass Studies* 25:239–247.
Vávra, Jaroslav R.
1954 *5000 Years of Glass-making: The History of Glass.* Prague: Artia.
Veeraprajak, Kongkaew
1985 Inscriptions from South Thailand. Appendix 5c. In *SPAFA Final Report: Consultative Workshop on Archaeological and Environmental Studies on Srivijaya (I-W2b), Jakarta, Padang, Prapet, and Medan, Indonesia, September 16–30, 1985,* 13–143. Bangkok: SEAMEO Project in Archaeology and Fine Arts (SPAFA).
Venclová, Natalie
1983 Prehistoric Eye Beads in Central Europe. *Journal of Glass Studies* 25:11–17.
1990 *Prehistoric glass in Bohemia.* Prague: Archaeological Institute of the Czechoslovak Academy of Sciences.
Veraprasert, M.
1985 Khlong Thom: An Ancient Bead-Manufacturing Location and an Ancient Entrepôt. In *Proceedings of the Research Conference on Early Southeast Asia, Bangkok and Nakhon Pathom, 8 to 13 April,* 168.9 (abstract), 168.1–168.10 (paper). Bangkok: British Institute in South-East Asia/Silpakorn University.
Verma, O. P.
1972 Organisation and Functions of Some South Indian Guilds. In *Early Indian Trade and Industry,* ed. D. C. Sircar, 76–82. Calcutta: University of Calcutta.
Vernier, Elie, and Jacques Millot
1971 *Archéologie Malgache: Comptoirs musulmans.* Catalogues du Museé de l'Homme, Serie F, Madagascar I. Paris: Museé de l'Hommes.
Villareal, F. William L.
1988 Notes on Philippine Prehistoric Jewelry and Related Items. *Philippine Numismatic Monograph* 24:6–25.
1991 Notes on Philippine Prehistoric Jewelry and Related Items (Part II). *Philippine Numismatic Monograph* 25:22–51.
Villegas, Ramon N.
1983 *Kayamanan: The Philippine Jewelry Tradition.* Manila: Central Bank of the Philippines.
Vu Cong Quy
1991 The Sa Huynh Culture: Recent Archaeological Findings and Relations with Other Ancient Cultures in South East Asia. Paper read at Deuxième Symposium Franco-Thai: Récentes Recherches en Archéologie en Thailande, Bangkok. (Copy available at Center for Bead Research, Lake Placid, N.Y.)

Wadia, D. N.
1990 *Geology of India.* 4th ed. Delhi: Tata McGraw-Hill.
Wales, H. G. Quatrich
1940 Archaeological Researches on Ancient Indian Colonization in Malaya. *JMBRAS* 18 (2): 1–85.
Waley, Arthur
1930–1932 Notes on Chinese Alchemy. *Bulletin of the School of Oriental Studies, London Institute* 6:1–24.
1931 *The Travels of an Alchemist: The Journey of the Taoist Ch'ang-Ch'un from China to the Hindukush*

at the Summons of Chingiz Khan, Recorded by his Disciple Li Chich-Ch'ang. The Broadway Travellers. London: George Routledge & Sons.

Walker, Michael J., and S. Santoso

1977 Romano-Indian Rouletted Pottery in Indonesia. *Mankind* 11 (1): 39–45.

Wang Fuquan

1979 Precious Stones Found in China. *Lapidary Journal* 33 (3): 694–696.

Wang Gungwu

1958 The Nanhai Trade: A Study of the Early History of Chinese Trade in the South China Sea. *JMBRAS* 31 (2): 1–127.

1991 *China and the Chinese Overseas.* Singapore: Times Academic Press.

Warmington, E. H.

1928 *The Commerce between the Roman Empire and India.* Cambridge: Cambridge University Press.

1974 *The Commerce between the Roman Empire and India.* 2d rev. enl. ed. London/New York: Curzon Press/Octagon Books.

Warren, Phelps

1977 Later Chinese Glass 1650–1900. *Journal of Glass Studies* 19:84–126.

Watson, Burton

1961 *Records of the Grand Historian of China Translated from the Shih chi of Ssu-ma Ch'ien.* Vol. 2. *The Age of Emperor Wu 140 to circa 100 B.C.* New York: Columbia University Press.

Watt, George

1889 *A Dictionary of the Economic Products of India.* Vol. 1. Calcutta: Superintendent of Government Printing.

1908 *The Commercial Products of India.* London: John Murry.

Weerakkody, D. P. M.

1997 *Taprobanê: Ancient Sri Lanka as Known to Greeks and Romans.* Indicopleustoi: Archaeologies of the Indian Ocean. Turnhout: Brepols.

Weisshaar, H. J., and W. Wijeyapala

1993 Ancient Ruhuna (Sri Lanka) The Tissamaharama Project: Excavations at Akurugoda 1992–1993. *Beiträge zur Allgemeinen und Vergleichenden Archäologie* 13:127–166 + 3 maps.

Werake, Mahindra

1990 Sino–Sri Lankan Relations during the Precolonial Times. In *Sri Lanka and the Silk Road of the Sea,* ed. Senake Bandaranayake, Lorna Dewaraja, Roland Silva, and K. D. G. Wimalaratne, 221–231. Colombo: The Sri Lanka National Commission for UNESCO and the Central Cultural Fund.

Weyl, Woldemar A.

1959 *Coloured Glasses.* London: Dawson's. (Orig. published 1951, Society of Glass Technology.)

Wheatley, Paul

1959 Geographical Notes on Some Commodities Involved in Sung Maritime Trade. *JMBRAS* 32 (2): 1–137.

1961 *The Golden Khersonese: Studies in the Historical Geography of the Malay Peninsula before A.D. 1500.* Kuala Lumpur: University of Malaya Press.

Wheeler, Mortimer

1954 *Rome Beyond the Imperial Frontier.* London: G. Bell & Sons.

1955 *Still Digging: Interleaves from an Antiquarian's Notebook.* London: Michael Joseph.

1969 Archaeology in India. In *Archaeology,* ed. Samuel Rapport and Helen Wright, 264–274. New York: Washington Square Press.

Wheeler, R. E. M., A. Ghosh, and Krishna Deva

1946 Arikamedu: An Indo-Roman Trading-station on the East Coat of India. *Ancient India* 2:17–124.

Whiston, William

n.d. *The Works of Flavius Josephus, the Learned an Authentic Jewish Historian.* Auburn: John E. Beardsley. (orig. published 1737.)

Whitcomb, Donald S., and Janet H. Johnson

1979 *Quseir al-Qadim 1978: Preliminary Report.* Cairo: American Research Center in Egypt.

1980 *Quseir al-Qadim 1980.* American Research Center in Egypt. Vol. 7. Malibu: Undea.

1981 Egypt and the Spice Trade. *Archaeology* 34 (2): 16–23.

White, Joyce C.
1982 *Ban Chiang: Discovery of a Lost Bronze Age.* Philadelphia/Washington: University Museum, University of Pennsylvania/Smithsonian Institution.
1983 Ban Chiang: Discovery of a Lost Bronze Age. *Archaeology* 36 (1): 52–55.
1990 The Ban Chiang Chronology Revised. In *Southeast Asian Archaeology* 1986, ed. Ian and Emily Glover, 121–128. BAR International Series 561. Cambridge.
1997 A Brief Note on New Dates for the Ban Chiang Cultural Tradition *BIPPA* 16:103–106.

White, William Charles
1934 *Tombs of Old Lo-Yang.* Shanghai: Kelly & Walsh.

Wicks, Robert S.
1992 *Money, Markets, and Trade in Early Southeast Asia: The Development of Indigenous Monetary Systems to AD 1400.* Studies on Southeast Asia. Ithaca: Cornell University.

Wilkinson, Charles E.
1986 *Nishapur: Some Early Islamic Buildings and Their Decoration.* New York: Metropolitan Museum of Art.

Will, Elizabeth Lyding
1991 The Mediterranean Shipping Amphoras from Arikamedu. In *Rome and India: The Ancient Sea Trade,* ed. Vimala Begley and Richard Daniel De Puma, 151–156. Madison: University of Wisconsin Press.

Williams, Bruce Beyer
1991 *Excavations between Abu Simbal and the Sudan Frontier, Keith C. Seele, Director, Part 8: Meroitic Remains from Qustul Cemetery Q, Ballana Cemetery B, and A Ballana Settlement, Part 1: Text and Figures.* The University of Chicago Oriental Institute Nubian Expedition Vol. VIII. Chicago: Oriental Institute of the University of Chicago.

Williams, S[amuel] Wells
1885 *The Middle Kingdom: A Survey of the Geography, Government, Literature, Social Life, Arts, and History of the Chinese Empire and Its Inhabitants.* Vol. 2. New York: Charles Scribner's Sons. (Reprinted 1966, Paragon Book Reprint Corporation, New York.)
1966 *The Chinese Commercial Guide; Treaties, Tariffs, Regulations, Tables, etc., Useful in the Trade to China & Eastern Asia.* 5th ed. Taipei: Ch'eng-Wen Publishing Co. (Reprint; orig. published 1863, Hong Kong.)

Wilson, Horace
1835 *Select Specimens of the Theatre of the Hindus.* London: Parbury, Allen & Co.

Wit, F.
1979 Clove, *Eugenia caryophyllus* (Myrtaceae). In Evolution of Crop Plants, ed. N. W. Simmonds, 216–218. London: Longman.

Woestijne, Paul van de
1953 *La Pérégèse de Priscien, édition critique.* Brugge: De Tempel (in Latin).

Wolters, O. W.
1967 *Early Indonesian Commerce: A Study of the Origins of Śrīvijaya.* Ithaca: Cornell University Press.
1970 *The Fall of Śrīvijaya in Malay History.* Ithaca: Cornell University Press.

Woodhead, H. G. W.
1922 *The China Year Book 1921–2.* Tientsin: Tientsin Press.
1927 *The China Year Book 1926–7.* Tientsin: Tientsin Press.

Woolley, Leonard
1934 *Ur Excavations.* Vol. 2. The Royal Cemetery. London/Philadelphia: British Museum/University of Pennsylvania Museum.

Yamasaki, Kazuo
1987 A Chemical Study of Red Glass Beads of Arikamedu. In *Archaeometry of Glass: Proceedings of the Archaeometry Session of the 14th International Congress on Glass, 1986, New Delhi,* ed. H. C. Bhardwaj. Calcutta: Indian Ceramic Society/Care; Central Glass and Ceramic Research Institute.

Yang Boda
1985 Several Questions Concerning the History of Glass in China. In *Chinese Archaeological Abstracts,* Vol. 2, ed. Albert E. Dien, Jeffrey K. Riegel, and Nancy T. Price, 26–28. Monumenta Archaeologica 9. Los Angeles: Institute of Archaeology, University of California. (Orig. published 1979, *Wenwu* [5] 76–78.)

Yi Jialiang and Tu Shujin
1991 Chinese Glass Technology in Boshan around the 14th Century. In *Scientific Research in Early Chinese Glass,* ed. Robert H. Brill and John H. Martin, 99–101. Corning: Corning Museum of Glass.

Yoshimizu, Tsuneo
1980 *Tombo-Dama.* Tokyo: Heibonsha Ltd. (in Japanese).

Yü Ying-shih
1967 *Trade and Expansion in Han China: A Study in the Structure of Sino-Barbarian Economic Relations.* Berkeley: University of California Press.

Yue Jin and Liao Zhihao
1985 A Cache of Five Dynasties and Northern Song Objects Discovered in the Pagoda of Ruiguangsi in Suzhou. In *Chinese Archaeological Abstracts,* Vol. 4, ed. Albert E. Dien, Jeffrey K. Riegel, and Nancy T. Price, 1813–1816. Monumenta Archaeologica 11. Los Angeles: Institute of Archaeology, University of California. (Orig. published 1979, *Wenwu.*)

Yule, Henry, and A. C. Burnell
1989 *Hobson-Jobson: A Glossary of Colloquial Anglo-Indian Words and Phrases, and of Kindred Terms, Etymological, Historical, Geographical and Discursive.* Calcutta: Rupa & Co. (Reprint; orig. published 1886.)

Zhang Jun-yan
1983 Relations Between China and the Arabs in Early Times. *Journal of Oman Studies* 6 (1): 91–109.

Zvelebil, Kamil
1973 *The Smile of Murugan: On Tamil Literature of South India.* Leiden: E. J. Brill.

Index

About the Author

Peter Francis, Jr., has devoted most of his adult life to the study of beads. He is the director of the Center for Bead Research, which he founded in 1979, and the webmaster of TheBeadSite.com, the most popular internet site of its kind. He is the author of *Beads of the World,* one of the standard books on beads, and has published hundreds of articles. He has worked with librarians, historians, archaeologists, and ethnographers—combining the methods and data of many fields—to uncover the story of beads and how they relate to people.